FOURTH EDITION

GENDER
Psychological Perspectives

LINDA BRANNON
McNeese State University

PEARSON

Boston • New York • San Francisco
Mexico City • Montreal • Toronto • London • Madrid • Munich • Paris
Hong Kong • Singapore • Tokyo • Cape Town • Sydney

Tasopoulos

Series Editor: *Kelly May*
Editorial Assistant: *Adam Whitehurst*
Marketing Manager: *Taryn Wahlquist*
Editorial-Production Service: *Omegatype Typography, Inc.*
Manufacturing Buyer: *JoAnne Sweeney*
Composition Buyer: *Linda Cox*
Cover Administrator: *Linda Knowles*
Electronic Composition: *Omegatype Typography, Inc.*

For related titles and support materials, visit our online catalog at www.ablongman.com.

Library of Congress Cataloging-in-Publication Data

Brannon, Linda
    Gender : psychological perspectives / Linda Brannon.—4th ed.
        p. cm.
    Includes bibliographical references and index.
    ISBN 0-205-40457-X (alk. paper)
        1. Sex differences (Psychology)—Textbooks.   2. Gender identity—Textbooks.   I. Title.
BF692.2.B73 2005
155.3—dc22

                                                                                        2004044258

Printed in the United States of America

10   9   8   7   6   5   4   09   08   07   06

Contents

iii

3 HORMONES AND CHROMOSOMES   47

4 INTELLIGENCE AND COGNITIVE ABILITIES   79

vi   Contents

7   GENDER STEREOTYPES: MASCULINITY AND FEMININITY   159

8   EMOTION   186

5   THEORIES OF GENDER DEVELOPMENT   106

6   DEVELOPING GENDER IDENTITY   134

11   SCHOOL   295

12   CAREERS AND WORK   323

13   HEALTH AND FITNESS   353

14   STRESS, COPING, AND PSYCHOPATHOLOGY   387

PREFACE

This book examines the topic of gender—the behaviors and attitudes that relate to (but are not entirely congruent with) biological sex. A large and growing body of research on sex, gender, and gender-related behaviors has come from psychology, sociology, biology, biochemistry, neurology, and anthropology. This research and scholarship form the basis for this book, providing the material for a critical review and an attempt to generate an overall picture of gender from a psychological perspective.

THE TOPIC OF GENDER

A critical review of gender research is important for several reasons. First, gender is currently a "hot topic," and almost everyone has an opinion. These opinions are not usually based on research. Most people are not familiar with research findings; they simply know their own opinions. People's opinions are strongly influenced by their own experience and also by what they have seen in the movies, on television, and in other media. Whether these programs are news reports or fiction, both types of presentations make an impact. Based on these portrayals, people create images about how they believe women and men should be and attempt to re-create these images in their own lives. This personal reproduction of gender portrayals in the media is another example of what Candace West and Don Zimmerman (1987) described as "doing gender."

In *Gender: Psychological Perspectives,* I present what gender researchers have found, although the picture is neither simple nor complete. Research findings are complex and sometimes contradictory, but I believe that it is important to understand this research rather than draw conclusions based on only personal opinions and popular media portrayals.

Second, research is a valuable way to understand gender, despite the bias and controversy that have surrounded the research process. Although scientific research is supposed to be objective and free of personal bias, this idealistic notion often varies from the actual research process. Gender research in particular has been plagued with personal bias. Despite the bias that can enter into the research process, I believe that research is the most productive way to approach the evaluation of a topic. Others disagree with this view, including some who are interested in gender-related topics. A number of scholars, cspccially fcminist scholars, have rejected scientific research as the best way to learn about gender.

Although I agree that science has not treated women equitably, either as researchers or as participants in research, I still believe that science offers the best chance for a fuller understanding of gender (as well as of many other topics). Some scholars disagree with this view, but I believe that science can further the goal of equity. I agree with Janet Hyde and Kristen Kling (2001, p. 369), who said, "An important task of feminist psychology is to challenge stereotypic ideas about gender and test the stereotypes against data." My goals are consistent with that view—to examine what gender researchers have found and how they have interpreted their findings.

The book's emphasis on gender is similar to another approach to studying gender—through examining the psychology of women. The psychology-of-women approach concentrates on women and issues unique to women, whereas the gender approach focuses on the issue of gender as a factor in behavior and in the social context in which behavior occurs. Gender research and theory draw heavily from research on the psychology of women, but the emphasis differs.

By emphasizing women and their experience, the psychology-of-women approach often excludes men, but gender research cannot. Studying both women and men is essential to an understanding of gender. Researchers who are interested in gender issues may concentrate on women or men, but they must consider both, or their research reveals nothing about gender. Therefore, this fourth edition of *Gender: Psychological Perspectives* examines the research and theory from psychology and related fields in order to evaluate the behavior, biology, and social context in which both women *and* men function.

The gender approach also reflects my personal preferences: I want a psychology of women and men. When I was completing the first edition of this book, I attended a conference session on creating a course in psychology of women. Several instructors who had created such courses led a discussion about obtaining institutional approval and the problems they had encountered, including resistance from administrators (who were mostly men) concerning a course in which the enrollment would be mostly women. One of the group advised trying for approval of a course on gender if obtaining approval for a psychology of women course was not successful. The implication was that the topic of gender included men and would be more acceptable but less desirable. I disagreed. I wanted men to be included—in the research, in my book, and in my classes. This preference comes from the belief that women and men are required in order to consider and discuss gender issues. I prefer the gender approach, and I wanted this book to reflect that attitude.

My interest in gender comes from two sources—my research and my experience as a female psychologist. The research that prompted me to examine gender issues more carefully was on risk perception related to health problems. I was interested in investigating people's perceptions of the health risks they created as a result of their behavior, such as the perceptions of health risks in smokers versus nonsmokers. In this research, I found that women and men saw their behaviors and risks in similar ways, even when the actual level of health risks differed quite a bit for men and women. My research showed gender similarities rather than gender differences.

In examining the volume of research on gender-related attitudes and behaviors, I discovered that many other researchers' findings were similar to mine. Among psychologists, exploration of gender seemed to show more similarities than differences, and when differences appeared, many were small. I came to doubt the widespread belief that men and women are opposites, and to consider that this view is, at the very least, overstated—women and men are more similar than different. Gender-related differences exist, but the tendency to concentrate on these differences has obscured the similarities.

As a female psychologist, I was forced to attend to gender issues from the outset of my career. Sexism and discrimination were part of the context in which I received my professional training and in which I have pursued my career as a psychologist. Women were a small minority in the field during my early years in psychology, but the numbers have since increased so that now women receive over half the doctoral degrees granted each year in psychology. This increase and several antidiscrimination laws have produced some improvements in equitable treatment for women in psychology (as well as in other professions and in society in general).

The psychology-of-women approach came from the women in psychology during the feminist movement of the 1960s. Most of the women in psychology have not been directly involved in the psychology of women and some are not feminists, but the presence of a growing proportion of women has changed psychology, making a psychology of gender not only possible but also, I think, inevitable.

GENDERED VOICES

Although I believe that research is a good way to understand behavior, including gender-related behavior, I accept the value of other approaches, including personal accounts. Louise Kidder (1994) contended that one of the drawbacks of personal accounts is the vividness of the data generated by reports of personal experience. In traditional quantitative research, the data consist of numbers, and each participant's experience is lost in the transformation to numerical data and the statistical compilations of these data. Personal accounts and interviews do not lead to a comfortable blurring of the results. Rather, each person's account is sharply depicted, with no averaging to blunt the edges of the story. I thought that such accounts could be an advantage.

The text of *Gender: Psychological Perspectives* consists of an evaluation of research findings—exactly the sort of information that people may find difficult to relate to their lives. I decided that I also wanted to include some personal, narrative accounts of gender-relevant aspects of people's lives, and I wanted these accounts to connect to the research studies. The perils of vividness seemed small compared to the advantages. I believe that people's personal experiences are distilled in statistical research, but I also know that a lot of the interesting details are lost in the process.

These "Gendered Voices" narratives are my attempt to restore some of the details lost in statistical summaries, allowing men and women to tell about their personal experiences. Telling these stories, separated from the text, was an alternative approach to presenting information about gender and highlighting the relevance of research findings with vivid detail. Some of the stories are funny, showing a lighthearted approach to dealing with the frustrations and annoyances of discrimination and gender bias. Some of the stories are sad, revealing experiences of sexual harassment, violence, and abuse. All of the stories are real accounts, not fictional tales constructed as good examples. When the stories are based on published sources, I name the people who are presenting their experience. For other stories, I have chosen not to name those involved, to protect their privacy. I listened to my friends and students talk about gender issues and wrote down what they told me, trying to report what they said in their own words. I hope that these stories give a different perspective and add a sense of the reality of gender in personal experience to the volume of research reported here.

HEADLINES

Long before I thought of writing a book about gender, I noticed the popularity of the topic in the media. Not only are the sexes the topic of many private and public debates, but gender differences are also the topic of many newspaper, magazine, and television stories, ranging from sitcoms to scientific reporting. I had read warnings about the media's tendencies to oversimplify research findings and to "punch up" the findings to make the stories grab people's attention. I wanted to examine the research on gender to try to understand what the research says, with all of its complexities, and to present the media version along with an analysis of the research findings.

Of particular concern to me was the tendency of the media and of people who hear reports of gender research to want to find a biological basis for the behavioral differences between the sexes, as though evidence of biologically based differences would be more "real" than any other type of evidence. The division of the biological realm from the behavioral realm is a false dichotomy. Even genes can be altered by environment, and experiences can produce changes in behavior as permanent as any produced by physiology. The view that biological differences are real and permanent, whereas experience and culture produce only transient and changeable effects, is a popular myth.

Unlike some other books about gender, this book spends several chapters examining this biological evidence. As Naomi Weisstein (1982) said, "biology has always been used as a curse against women" (p. 41). I want to present and evaluate this research because it is the basis of popular assumptions and media reports about differences between the sexes and also because people accept these findings without question. I want readers to question the extent to which the biological "curse" should apply.

To further highlight the popular conceptualizations of gender, I decided to use headlines from newspapers and popular magazines as a way to show how the media represent gender. Some of the headline stories are examples of responsible journalism that seeks to present research in a way that is easy to understand, whereas other headline stories are more sensational or simplified.

The media tend to portray findings in sensational ways because such stories get attention. Such sensationalism distorts research findings and perpetuates stereotypical thinking about the sexes. I believe that Beryl Lieff Benderly (1989), a science reporter, was correct when she warned about media sensationalism of gender research by writing the headline, "Don't believe everything you read . . ." (p. 67).

ACCORDING TO THE MEDIA AND ACCORDING TO THE RESEARCH

In addition to gender in the headlines, I have included two boxed features called "According to the Media" and "According to the Research" that concentrate on gender portrayals in the mainstream media. "According to the Media" boxes examine how gender is portrayed in the various media—magazines, television, movies, video games, cartoons, and fiction. The corresponding "According to the Research" boxes provide research findings related to the media topics that present a more systematic and unbiased view. The contrast of these two presentations provides an opportunity to examine gender bias and stereotyping in the media. I hope these features lead students to question and think critically about the accuracy and fairness of the thousands of gendered images that they experience through the media.

CONSIDERING DIVERSITY

The history of psychology is not filled with a concern for diversity or an emphasis on diversity issues, but these topics represent an area of increasing interest and concern within psychology. Indeed, gender research is one of the major fields that represents the growing diversity in psychology. In addition, cross-cultural research has begun to provide a more comprehensive picture of psychological issues in the context of different ethnic groups within the United States as well as comparisons to other countries.

To highlight this developing research and tie it to gender issues, this edition of *Gender: Psychological Perspectives* includes a section in most chapters called "Considering Diversity" that discusses the diversity research. Although diversity issues enter the text at other points in the book, the creation of a section to examine diversity ensures the inclusion of these important issues. In some chapters, the research is sufficiently developed to present a cross-cultural review of the topic, but for other topics, cross-cultural research remains sparse, so those diversity sections present a specialized topic that relates to the chapter.

ACKNOWLEDGMENTS

At the completion of any book, authors have many people to thank, and I am no exception. Without the assistance, support, and encouragement of many people, I never could have written this book or completed the fourth edition. I thank all of them, but several people deserve special mention. My colleagues in the psychology department at McNeese State University were supportive and helpful. Jess Feist, my coauthor on the fifth edition of *Health Psychology: An Introduction to Behavior and Health,* provided advice and improved my writing on this book. Patrick Moreno acted as librarian to help me obtain material, and he and Christi Hite also surfed the Net on my behalf. Their assistance was very important in completing this edition.

Husbands often deserve special thanks, and mine is no exception. My husband, Barry Humphus, did a great deal to hold my life together while I was researching and writing—he kept the computer working and offered me his praise, support, and enthusiasm. I would not have attempted (much less completed) this book without him.

I would like to thank all the people who told me their personal stories for the "Gendered Voices" feature of the book. To respect their privacy I will not name them, with one exception. Melinda Schaefer deserves special thanks because her story was so good that hearing it made me realize that others had stories to tell. Without her story, and Louise Kidder's (1994) presentation, I would not have realized how important these accounts are.

The people at Allyn and Bacon have been helpful and supportive. Carolyn Merrill, my editor when I began this edition, helped me do things I didn't know I could do, and Kelly May, my editor as I finished this edition, has supported and helped me complete the manuscript.

I would also like to thank reviewers who read parts of the manuscript and offered helpful suggestions, including Valerie J. Eastman, Drury University; Sarah Estow, Colby College; and Vicki Ritts, St. Louis Community College–Meramec. Thanks also for the suggestions from Luciane A. Berg, Southern Utah University; Christina Byme, Western Washington University; Linda Heath, Loyola University–Chicago; Marcela Raffaelli, University of Nebraska; and Stephanie Riger, University of Illinois–Chicago.

1 THE STUDY OF GENDER

■ HEADLINE   The New Gender Wars
Psychology Today, November/December 2000

The latest skirmish in the war between the sexes has flared up between psychologists study-ing the origins of gender differences. Research has shown that despite feminist advance-ments, gender differences persist. The question no longer is whether there are differences between the sexes but what to make of them.

On one side are those who claim that it is evolution and biology that make us signif-icantly different, and that no amount of feminist agitation will change that. Men will con-tinue to be philandering, non-nurturing and sex-focused, and women will continue to be mothering keepers-of-the-hearth. On the other side are those who claim there's a lot more variation to our gender roles. Society, they say, and not our genes, determines how we react to our biological course. Change, this latter group says, is possible and evident.

How willingly does our biology respond to our environment? And even if biology plays a role, how much of the male–female split is nonetheless reinforced by the culture we live in? . . . Where do these differences come from and where might they go? (Blustain, 2000, p. 43)

Sarah Blustain's (2000) article presented the two sides of one current version of the "bat-tle between the sexes." This conflict lies within psychology, and, as the title of Blustain's article suggests, this "war" is a new one, dating back to only the mid-1990s. At that time evolutionary psychology began to capture headlines proclaiming that differences between men's and women's behavior could be traced to evolutionary history, and recent changes in society would make little difference in women's and men's basic natures.

Evolutionary psychology holds the **essentialist view** that differences between the sexes stem from biological differences. According to most people's views of the relation-ship between biology and behavior, biological differences determine behavior. Therefore, if the differences between women and men are biological, those differences are perceived as fixed and invariant.

The other side of the battle includes psychologists who believe that social roles cre-ate most behavioral differences between women and men. This view holds that strength and reproductive capacity differences between men and women prompt societies to en-courage women and men to adopt different gender roles. The existence of such differences creates the need for socialization pressure to ensure that girls and boys learn and adopt the roles associated with their sex. In this biosocial view, biology is an important factor in the creation and maintenance of differences between women and men, but it is not the main determinant of these differences (Wood & Eagly, 2002).

Perhaps not by coincidence, many evolutionary psychologists are men, whereas many of the psychologists who believe in the preeminence of social gender roles are women. Thus, this new battle is a conflict not only in theoretical, but also in personal terms. This battle is not the first for psychology. Since the early years of psychology, women in this field have struggled for acceptance and equitable treatment in a profession dominated by men.

The struggles in psychology mirror those in the larger culture, in which women have striven to change laws and attitudes concerning social, professional, and personal opportunities. Questioning the "common knowledge" that women were not capable of making rational choices about political candidates, benefiting from education, or occupying a profession, women in the 1800s pressed for the right to vote, get an education, and pursue a professional career. Those successes led to additional questioning of the capabilities and limitations of men as well as women.

Therefore, the new gender war in psychology is the latest incarnation of conflicts and questions that have also permeated the wider culture: Which is more important, nature (biology) or nurture (culture and society)? What is the extent of these differences? What types of differences exist? What is the basis for these differences? Consistent with the position of evolutionary psychology, many people see the answers to these questions as simple and obvious: Women and men are born with biological differences that dictate the basis for different traits and behaviors. Indeed, they are so different that women are the "opposite sex," suggesting that whatever men are, women are at the other end of the spectrum. Those who hold this view find the differences obvious and important. Those who hold the biosocial view see the answers as more complex. Drawing from research in psychology, sociology, biology, and anthropology, the differences between women and men seem to be a complex puzzle with many pieces.

Thus, the psychologists on the two battle lines look to volumes of research, and both sides see evidence to support their respective views. Some people at some times have believed that differences between males and females are few, whereas others have believed that the two are virtually different species. These two positions can be described as the **minimalist** and the **maximalist views** (Epstein, 1988). The minimalists perceive few important differences between women and men, whereas the maximalists believe that the two have large, fundamental differences. Many maximalists also hold an essentialist view, believing that the large differences between women and men are part of their essential biological makeup. Although these views have varied over time, today both the maximalist and the minimalist views have vocal supporters.

This lack of agreement coupled with commitment to a position suggests controversy, which is almost too polite a term for these disagreements. Few topics are as filled with emotion as discussions of the sexes and their capabilities. These arguments occur in places as diverse as playgrounds and scientific laboratories. The questions are similar, regardless of the setting: Who is smarter, faster, healthier, sexier, more capable, more emotional? Who makes better physicians, engineers, typists, managers, politicians, artists, teachers, parents, friends? Who is more likely to go crazy, go to jail, commit suicide, have a traffic accident, tell lies, gossip, commit murder? The full range of human possibilities seems to be grounds for discussion, but the issues are unquestionably important. No matter what the conclusions, at least half the human population (and most probably all of it) will be affected. Therefore, not only are questions about the sexes interesting, but also the answers are important to individuals and to society. Later chapters explore the research concerning abilities and behaviors, and an examination of this research allows an evaluation of these questions.

Answers to these important questions about differences between women and men are not lacking. Almost everyone has answers, but not the same answers. It is easy to see how people might hold varying opinions about a controversial issue, but some consistency should exist among findings from researchers who have studied men and women. Scientists should be able to investigate the sexes and provide evidence concerning these important questions. Researchers have pursued these questions, obtained results, and published thousands of papers. There is no shortage of investigations—or publicity—about the sexes. Unfortunately, researchers are subject to the same problems as everyone else: They do not all agree on what the results are and what the results mean.

In addition, many research findings on men and women are not consistent with popular opinion, suggesting that popular opinion may be an exaggeration or distortion, most likely based on people's personal experience rather than on research. Both the past and the present are filled with examples of exaggerations of differences between women and men.

People have a tendency to think in terms of opposites when considering only two examples, as with the sexes (Fausto-Sterling, 2000; Tavris, 1992). If three sexes existed, people might not have the tendency to draw a comparison of such extremes; they might be able to see the similarities as well as the differences in men and women; they might be able to approach the questions with more flexibility in their thinking. The sexual world may not actually be polarized into only two categories (as Chapter 3 explores in more detail), but people do tend to see it that way. This perception of only two sexes influences people to think of the two sexes as polar opposites. To maintain these oppositional categories, people must exaggerate the differences between women and men, which results in stereotypes that do not correspond to real people (Bem, 1993b). Although these stereotypes are not realistic, they are powerful because they affect how women and men think about themselves and how they think about the "opposite" sex.

HISTORY OF THE STUDY OF SEX DIFFERENCES IN PSYCHOLOGY

Speculations about the differences between men and women probably predate history, but these issues were not part of the investigations of early psychology. Wilhelm Wundt is credited with founding modern psychology in 1879 (although there is some debate over the accuracy of this date) at the University of Leipzig (Schultz & Schultz, 2004). Wundt wanted to establish a natural science of the mind to investigate the nature of human thought processes through experimentation. Others joined Wundt, and using chemistry as the model, they devised a psychology based on an analytical understanding of the structure of the conscious mind. This approach to psychology became known as the **structuralist** school of psychology. The structure of interest was based on adult human cognition, and Wundt and his followers believed that psychology could not be applied to children, the feebleminded, or species of nonhuman animals.

Structuralist psychology was concerned with the workings of the mind as unaffected by individual differences among adult humans. The structuralists were interested in investigating the "generalized adult mind" (Shields, 1975a), and therefore any individual differences, including differences between the minds of women and men, were of no concern to these early psychologists.

This inattention to sex differences did not mean equal treatment of women and men by these early psychologists. They used a method of investigation called *introspection,* a type of self-observation of one's mental processes (Schultz & Schultz, 2004). Students underwent training to become participants in the experiments, and these students (and thus the participants in this early psychology research) were men. The generalized adult mind on which the findings were based was a generalization drawn from data collected from and by men. Indeed, women were expressly prohibited from one of the early groups of experimental psychologists in the United States (Schultz & Schultz, 2004).

The focus of Wundt's psychology changed in the United States. Although virtually all U.S. psychologists received their training in Germany, many found the views of structuralism too limiting and impractical. As psychology grew in the United States, it developed a more practical nature. This change is usually described as an evolution to **functionalism,** a school of psychology that emphasized how the mind functions rather than its structure (Schultz & Schultz, 2004). As these psychologists with a functionalist orientation started to research and theorize, they drew a wider variety of subjects into psychological research and theories, including children, women, and nonhuman animals.

The Study of Individual Differences

Among the areas of interest in functionalist psychology were the issues of adaptability and intelligence. These interests prompted the development of intelligence testing and the comparison of individual differences in mental abilities and personality traits, including sex differences. The functionalists, influenced by Darwin and the theory of evolution, tended to look for biologically determined differences, including a biological basis for sex differences. As Stephanie Shields (1975a) pointed out, these psychologists were hesitant to acknowledge any possibility of social influence in the sex differences they found, and their findings usually supported the prevailing cultural roles for women and men.

The studies and writings of functionalists of this era tended to demonstrate that women were less intelligent than men, benefited less from education, had strong maternal instincts, and were unlikely to produce examples of success or eminence. Women were not the only group deemed inferior: Nonwhite races were also considered less intelligent and less capable.

These findings of the intellectual deficiencies of women did not go uncriticized. As early as 1910, Helen Thompson Woolley contended that the research on sex differences was full of the researchers' personal bias, prejudice, and sentiment (in Shields, 1975a), and Leta Stetter Hollingworth took a stand against the functionalist view of women (Shields, 1975b). These female psychologists argued against the prevailing view. Hollingworth contended that women's potential would never be known until women had the opportunity to choose the lives they would like—career, maternity, or both.

The functionalist view began to wane in the 1920s, and a new school of psychology, **behaviorism,** gained prominence. The behaviorists emphasized observable behavior rather than thought processes or instincts as the subject matter of psychology. With the change from a functionalist to a behaviorist paradigm in U.S. psychology, the interest in research on sex differences sharply decreased. "The functionalists, because of their emphasis on 'nature,' were predictably indifferent to the study of social sex roles and cultural concepts of masculine and feminine. The behaviorists, despite their emphasis on 'nurture,' were slow to recognize those same social forces" (Shields, 1975a, p. 751). Rather, behaviorists were interested in the areas of learning and memory. Research on these topics ignored social factors, including sex roles and sex differences. In ignoring gender, psychologists created "womanless" psychology (Crawford & Marecek, 1989), an approach that either failed to include women as participants or failed to examine gender-related factors when both men and women participated in psychological research. During the time when behaviorism dominated psychology, the only theorists who unquestionably had an interest in sex differences were those with a psychodynamic orientation—the Freudians.

Psychoanalysis

Both Freud's psychodynamic theory of personality development and his psychoanalytic approach to treatment appear in more detail in Chapter 5. However, the history of psychology's involvement in issues of sex and gender necessitates a brief description of Freud's personality theory and his approach to treatment.

Although Sigmund Freud's work did not originate within academic psychology, the two are popularly associated. And unquestionably, Freud's work and Freudian theory concerning personality differences between women and men, have influenced both psychology and society in general. These influences have made the work of Freud very important for understanding conceptualizations of sex and gender.

In the United States, Freud's work began to gain popular attention in 1909, when Freud came to the United States to give a series of invited lectures at Clark University (Schultz & Schultz, 2004). Immediately after his visit, newspapers started carrying features about Freud and his theory. By 1920, interest in Freudian theory and analysis was evident both in books and in articles in popular magazines. Psychoanalysis gained popular interest, becoming almost a fad. Indeed, popular acceptance of Freud's work preceded its acceptance by academicians.

Freud emphasized the role of instinct and physiology in personality formation, hypothesizing that instincts provide the basic energy for personality and that the child's perception of anatomical differences between boys and girls is a pivotal event in personality formation. Rather than relying on genetic or hormonal explanations for sex differences in personality, Freud looked to early childhood experiences within the family to explain how physiology interacts with experience to influence personality development.

For Freud (1925/1989), the perception of anatomical differences between boys and girls was critical. According to Freud, the knowledge that boys and men have penises and girls and women do not forms the basis for personality differences between boys and girls. The results of this perception lead to conflict in the family, including sexual attraction to the other-sex parent and hostility for the same-sex parent. These incestuous desires cannot persist, and Freud hypothesized that the resolution of these conflicts comes through identification with the same-sex parent. However, Freud believed that boys experience more conflict and trauma during this early development, leading to a more complete rejection of their mother and a more complete identification with their father than girls experience. This difference in strength of identification produces enduring differences in personality between men and women. Consequently, Freud (1925/1989) hypothesized that men typically form a stronger conscience and sense of social values than do women.

Did Freud mean that girls and women were deficient in moral standards compared to men? Did he view women as incomplete (and less admirable) people? It is probably impossible to know what Freud thought and felt, and his writings are sufficiently varied to lead to contradictory interpretations. Thus the question of Freud's view of women has been hotly debated. Some authors have criticized Freud for supporting a male-oriented society and the enslavement of women, whereas others have defended Freud and his work as applied to women. In defense of Freud (Tavris & Wade, 1984), his view of women was not sufficiently negative to prevent him from accepting them as colleagues. Freud accepted a number of women into psychoanalytic training during a time when women were not welcome in many academic settings. In addition, he encouraged his daughter, Anna, to pursue a career in psychoanalysis. Freud's writings, however, reveal that he held many negative views about women and seemed to feel that they were inferior to men, both intellectually and morally.

Regardless of Freud's personal beliefs, the popular interpretation of his theory represented women as inferior to men, as being less ethical, more concerned with personal appearance, more self-contemptuous, and jealous of men's accomplishments (and also, literally, of their penises). Accepting the feminine role would always mean settling for inferior status and opportunities, and women who were not able to reconcile themselves to this status were candidates for therapy because they had not accepted their femininity.

Freud's theory also held stringent and inflexible standards for the development of masculinity. For boys to develop normally, they must experience severe anxiety during early childhood and develop hatred for their father. This trauma should lead a boy to identify with his father out of fear and to experience the advantages of the male role through becoming like him. Boys who do not make a sufficiently complete break with their mothers are not likely to become fully masculine but to remain somewhat feminine, and thus experience the problems that society accords to nonmasculine men.

The psychoanalytic view of femininity and masculinity has been enormously influential in Western society. Although not immediately accepted in academic departments, the psychoanalytic view of personality and psychopathology was gradually integrated into the research and training of psychologists. Although the theory has prompted continuing controversy, interest continues, in the form of both attacks and defenses. This continuing stream of books and articles speaks to the power of Freud's theory to capture attention and imagination. Despite limited research support, Freudian theory has been and remains a force in conceptions of sex and gender. Table 1.1 summarizes psychological theories and their approaches to gender. In contrast to these male-dominated theories, some investigators have begun to emphasize the study of women.

TABLE 1.1 *Role of Gender in Psychological Theories throughout the History of Psychology*

Theory	Emphasis of Theory	Role of Gender
Structuralism	Understanding the structure of the human mind	Minimal—all minds are equivalent
Functionalism	Understanding the function of the mind	Sex differences are one type of individual difference
Behaviorism	Studying behavior in a scientific way	Minimal—behavior varies with individual experience
Psychoanalysis	Studying normal and abnormal personality development and functioning	Biological sex differences and their recognition is a motivating force

The Development of Women's Studies

The development of the study of women came as a result of the feminist movement of the 1960s (Freedman, 2002). This movement was not the first to push for changes in women's roles and legal status. Earlier versions of feminism had pressed for the vote for women, the availability of birth control, and other legal changes to improve women's social and economic status. The feminist movement of the 1960s grew out of the civil rights movement and brought about some of the changes that earlier feminist movements had sought.

As feminism grew, several variations emerged. Many of the women who became involved in the feminist movement during the 1960s and 1970s fit the definition of *liberal feminists,* people who want to end discrimination based on sex and to extend to women the rights that men had (Freedman, 2002). Others fit the definition of *radical feminists,* people who believe that women are oppressed by men and that this oppression has served as a model for racial and class oppression. Both varieties of feminism call for political activism designed to bring about changes in laws and in society. *Cultural feminists* may not be as politically active, yet they too believe that society needs to change. This version of feminism holds that society should move toward an acceptance and appreciation of traditionally feminine values. Cultural feminists believe that, were women in charge, many of the world's problems would disappear.

Beginning in the 1960s, women entered the workforce in record numbers, and this trend was connected to the rise of feminism. Although most of these jobs were in clerical or retail sales work, women also entered the professions in increasing numbers. Both professional women and working-class women experienced situations of discrimination that led many to work toward changes for women, not only at work but also at home. Women in colleges and universities pursued their interest in topics related to women, which resulted in the development of courses and curricula devoted to women's studies as an academic discipline. Part of this scholarship has been an examination of the media images of women and men and how the media perpetuate stereotyping (see "According to the Media" and "According to the Research").

ACCORDING TO THE MEDIA . . .

Women Are Dangerous

Depictions of women and men are common in newspapers, radio, television, and movies, and gender-related topics frequently make the headlines and form the central focus for entertainment programming. By reading newspapers, listening to radio or television news reports, watching television entertainment programming, or going to the movies, a person might get the impression that women and men were about equally likely to commit murder, stalking, or sexual harassment (Ruby, 2000). For example, the movie *Fatal Attraction* (1987) portrayed a jilted girlfriend who stalked her ex-lover and his family. The NBC drama *Law & Order* presented an episode about a female Navy officer who killed her lover and then claimed self-defense because of sexual harassment. An episode of the CBS drama *CSI* depicted a mother killed by a daughter who was sexually jealous of her mother's relationship with her father. A front-page story in the *Washington Post* reported on a group of women that planned and carried out the knifing death of another woman (in Ruby, 2000). In all of these depictions, women were the instigators of violence, and millions of people saw or read these stories.

Where are the stories about male violence toward women? In news reports, stories about male violence appear every day, and some of those stories are headlines. However, stories of a group of men knifing another man would not make a front-page headline in most cities. Spectacular acts of violence do make headlines, but these stories rarely highlight the gender of the perpetrator; gender disappears in the assumption that the perpetrators of such violence will be male.

On television, stories of male violence tend to appear on the Lifetime network, a cable channel oriented toward women's programming (Ruby, 2000). On the Lifetime network, men abandon their families, beat their wives, and commit incest with their stepdaughters. By depicting situations of male violence, these programs become "women's viewing" and lose their general interest. The audience for such programming is not only smaller, but so is the advertising revenue. Therefore, media depictions of violence are fairly gender balanced, creating the impression that such behavior is, too.

The dramatic increase of women in psychology and the new area of women's studies changed psychology. Influenced by feminist scholars and their own research priorities, women expanded the earlier area of gender-related behaviors and individual differences to a new psychology of women and gender (Walsh, 1985). Blustain's (2000) headline article referred to this new gender war in psychology. The women's movement in the 1960s and the influx of women into academic psychology laid the groundwork for the current conflict.

In 1968, psychologist Naomi Weisstein presented an influential paper, "'Kinde, Küche, Kirche' as Scientific Law: Psychology Constructs the Female." This paper influenced a generation of psychologists. Weisstein (1970) argued that psychological research had revealed almost nothing about women because the research had been contaminated by the biases, wishes, and fantasies of the male psychologists who conducted the research. Although the criticism was aimed mostly at clinical psychology and the Freudian approach to therapy, Weisstein also charged research psychologists with finding only what they wanted and expected to find about women rather than researching women as they were. She wrote, "Present psychology is less than worthless in contributing to a vision which could truly liberate—men as well as women" (p. 231).

ACCORDING TO THE RESEARCH . . .

The Media Sensationalize Gender Issues

In news reporting, when a dog bites a man, the story is not worth reporting. Dogs bite people all the time. When a man bites a dog, this event is worthy of a report because it occurs infrequently. According to Jennie Ruby (2000), most of the depictions of female violence in the media are cases of "man bites dog." That is, reports of violent actions by women are interesting or newsworthy because they are infrequent and thus contrary to expectation. When men abuse, stalk, or murder women, those incidents may or may not receive publicity, depending on how dramatic the incidents are. When women are the perpetrators, the incidents are much more likely to become headlines, news reports, or scripts. Female victims of male violence tend to become statistics; male victims of female violence tend to become headlines.

"The sexism that is so obvious in everyday life plays differently in the media" (Ruby, 2000, p. 12). Violence is not the only distorted topic; the media play many other topics differently. The media tend to sensationalize all topics as a way to grab people's attention. A news report must seem like news or people will not be interested enough to listen. Entertainment must be absorbing or it is not all that entertaining. Thus, findings that highlight gender differences are more likely to be featured in newspapers and news programming because reports of similarities are not so newsworthy. Researchers who investigate gender and find that women and men behave similarly have produced a "dog bites man" type of result that is less likely to be published and very unlikely to be covered in a media report. This tendency leads to overreporting of findings about gender differences and underreporting of gender similarities.

Television entertainment programming and movies tend to present exaggerated behaviors in order to be dramatic or comic, and gender stereotypes offer many possibilities for exaggeration. The small number of women who are reporters, writers, directors, producers, or programmers makes it more difficult for gender issues to get equitable coverage except on "women's" networks or on specialized programming (Lauzen & Dozier, 2002).

Weisstein's accusations came at a time when the feminist movement in society and a growing number of women in psychology wanted a more prominent place for women in the field and sought to create feminist-oriented research. One of Weisstein's points was that psychological research had neglected to take into account the context of behavior, without which psychologists could understand neither women nor people in general. This criticism seems to have contained a great deal of foresight (Bem, 1993a); psychological research on women began to change in the ways that Weisstein advocated.

Psychologists held no monopoly on this new orientation to the study of women. Sociologists, anthropologists, ethnologists, and biologists also became involved in questions about biological and behavioral differences and similarities between the sexes (Schiebinger, 1999). Motivated by the feminist movement, women began to assert their view about the inequity of stereotypes of the abilities and roles of men and women.

Although the history of studying gender in psychology is lengthy, psychologists' involvement in feminist research is relatively new; the formation of a division of the American Psychological Association (APA) devoted to women's issues and studies did not occur until 1973. Women were admitted as students in doctoral programs from the early years of psychology, but they had to struggle for professional acceptance and had a difficult time finding positions as psychologists. In 1941, a group of women who were psychologists formed the National Council of Women Psychologists to further the work of female psychologists in the war effort (Walsh, 1985). This group became the International Council of Women Psychologists in 1944 and attempted to become a division of the APA but experienced repeated rejections.

Another group succeeded in gaining APA division status in 1973. Division 35, Society for the Psychology of Women, can be directly traced to the Association for Women in Psychology, a group that demonstrated against sex discrimination and advocated for an increase in feminist psychological research at the 1969 and 1970 APA national conventions (Walsh, 1985). Unlike the earlier International Council, Division 35 goals included not only the promotion of women in psychology, but also the advancement of research on women and issues related to gender. The great volume of psychological research on sex and gender that has appeared in the past 30 years is consistent with the Division 35 goal of expanding the study of women and encouraging the integration of that research with current psychological thinking. Indeed, Division 35 members have conducted much of that research, but other disciplines have also contributed substantially. Therefore, not only have psychologists participated in the current plethora of research on sex and gender, but the topic is actively investigated in biology, medicine, sociology, communication, and anthropology.

In summary, psychological research that includes women dates back to the early part of the 20th century and the functionalist school of psychology, but this approach emphasized sex differences and searched for the factors that distinguished men and women. When the behaviorist school dominated academic psychology, its lack of interest in sex differences created a virtually "womanless" psychology. During that same time, Freudian psychoanalysts held strong views on the sexes, but this theory proposed that women are physically and morally inferior to men. This belief in the innate inferiority of women influenced research on women. With the feminist movement of the 1960s, a different type of research arose, producing results that questioned the stereotypes and assumptions about innate differences between the sexes. Not only did this research begin to examine sex differences and similarities, but these researchers also expanded ways to study women and men. This more recent orientation has led to voluminous research in the field of psychology, as well as in sociology, anthropology, and biology.

The feminist movement questioned the roles and stereotypes for women, and soon the questioning spread to men, who began to examine how the inflexibility of gender stereotypes might harm them, too.

The Appearance of the Men's Movement

The men's movement mirrors the women's movement, beginning during the 19th-century women's suffrage movement. During that time, the women's suffrage movement was not the only challenge to men's roles. Men felt increasingly constrained in their masculinity by the change from agricultural to industrial society. An early form of the men's movement was the Boy Scouts, with its emphasis on men and boys involved in outdoor activities (Hantover, 1992).

The contemporary women's movement has also questioned and challenged men concerning the status quo of legal, social, and personal roles and relationships. Some men have failed to see the problem, but other men have begun to consider how the questions pertain to their lives, too. R. W. Connell (2001, p. 44) explained this view:

> Gender is also about relationships of desire and power, and these must be examined from both sides. In understanding gender inequalities it is essential to research the more privileged group as well as the less privileged. This requires more than simply an examination of men as a statistical category (though it is useful to do that, too). We must examine men's gender practices, and the ways the gender order defines, positions, empowers and constrains men. The gender positions that society constructs for men may not correspond exactly with what men actually are, or desire to be, or what they actually do. It is therefore necessary to study masculinity as well as men.

During the 1970s, concerned men sometimes became feminists interested in ending the inequalities in power and privilege accorded to men, because they also saw toxic elements connected to the male sex role. Robert Brannon summarized this view by saying, "I have gradually come to realize that I, with every other man I know, have been limited and diverted from whatever our real potential might have been by the prefabricated mold of the male sex role" (1976, pp. 4–5).

Feminist men formed groups equivalent to the consciousness-raising groups common in the women's movement (Baumli & Williamson, 1997). Although these group members discussed their common problems and sought support from each other, their activities usually did not progress to the larger organizations that sought political power, as the women's groups had done. Many of these groups tended to remain small, local-level organizations, but a few became national organizations.

During the 1970s, men who were interested in furthering feminist goals joined the National Organization for Women and proclaimed themselves to be feminists. During the 1980s, masculinity and the problems of men began to be a focus, and other profeminist men's organizations arose. The National Organization for Men Against Sexism (NOMAS) is a profeminist men's organization that also works to obliterate racism and prejudice against gay men. This type of concern with masculinity and exploring positive options has spread to countries around the world, including Australia, Sweden, Japan, Latin America, and the Caribbean (Connell, 2001).

Within psychology, the Society for the Psychological Study of Men and Masculinity succeeded in gaining divisional status in 1995, becoming Division 51 of the American Psychological Association. The goals of this division include (1) promoting the study of how gender roles shape and constrict men's lives, (2) helping men to experience their full human potential, and (3) eroding the definition of masculinity that has inhibited men's development and has contributed to the oppression of others.

But other national groups within the men's movement are not interested in feminist goals; indeed, some of these men are interested in restoring the traditional gender roles that they believe have been destroyed by the women's movement, whereas others argue that men—not women—are the oppressed sex. One such group is the National Coalition of Free Men (NCFM), a group that opposes sexism but sees feminist groups as sexist. The men in NCFM (Baumli & Williamson, 1997) have argued that sexism oppresses men more than women.

Many men's rights groups are organized around specific issues, such as changing divorce laws or promoting joint child custody, which were the impetus for men's right groups in the United States (Baumli & Williamson, 1997). Many of these men see women's right groups as their enemies because women's groups tend to oppose joint custody and no-fault divorce laws. Only a few of the men in the men's movement actively promote a return of "the good old days" and a reversal of the changes brought about by the women's movement. Many participants in men's groups would like to see a less sharply gendered society, in which both women and men have choices not bound by their biological sex. What would count as fulfilling these goals differs among men, and both antifeminist and profeminist men consider themselves part of the men's movement.

Yet another variation of the men's movement comes from men trying to find a masculine identity. Authors such as Robert Bly (1990) and Sam Keen (1991) contend that modern society has left men with no easy way to form a masculine identity. The culture provides inappropriate models, and fathers are often absent, providing no model at all. This deficit produces men who are inappropriately aggressive and poorly fitted to live in society, to form relationships with women, and to be adequate fathers. Bly proposed explorations of masculinity and ceremonial initiation into manhood as a means of over-

■ GENDERED VOICES

When You Look in the Mirror

"When you wake up in the morning and look in the mirror, what do you see?" a Black woman asked a White woman (Kimmel & Messner, 1992, p. 2). "I see a woman," was the White woman's reply.

"That's precisely the issue," the Black woman replied. "I see a Black woman. For me, race is visible every day, because it is how I am not privileged in this culture. Race is invisible to you, which is why our alliance will always seem somewhat false to me" (p. 2).

As Michael Kimmel witnessed this exchange, he was surprised. He examined his own thoughts and realized that when he looked into the mirror, he "saw a human being: universally generalizable. The generic person" (p. 2).

Just as the White woman did not see her ethnicity, the White man saw neither his gender nor his ethnic background. His privileged status as White and

male had made him blind to these factors. Rather than thinking of himself as White or male, he considered himself a generic human. The White woman saw femaleness because she was aware of the discrimination she experienced as a woman. The Black woman saw both her skin color and her gender when she looked into the mirror due to her experiences of those factors in her life.

Michael Kimmel and Michael Messner (1992, pp. 2–3) summarized these experiences: "The mechanisms that afford us privilege are very often invisible to us. . . . Men often think of themselves as genderless, as if gender did not matter in the daily experiences of our lives. Certainly, we can see the biological sex of individuals, but we rarely understand the ways in which gender—that complex of social meanings that is attached to biological sex—is enacted in our daily lives."

coming the failure to establish the missing masculine role. These initiation ceremonies have been the subject of much ridicule (Pittman, 1992). In many ways, these groups echo the scouting movement, with the emphasis on male bonding in an outdoor setting. The need to find and affirm a masculine identity is a need that many men feel. Unfortunately, Bly's recommendations for achieving masculinity can be characterized as antifeminist, relying on devaluing women and forcefully rejecting feminine values to help men achieve masculinity.

The Promise Keepers do not share Bly's vision of how to reclaim masculinity, but reasserting masculinity is an important goal for these men (Messner, 1997; Silverstein, Auerbach, Grieco, & Dunk, 1999). This organization arose during the 1990s as a phenomenon, filling football stadiums with men who shared the vision of godly manhood (Bartkowski, 2000). This movement was part of neoconservative, evangelical Christianity, and it urged men to reclaim their position as head of the family, living up to their roles and keeping their commitments to their wives and children. The Promise Keepers doctrine rejects the racism that is often associated with the evangelical movement, but it does not accept homosexuality or equal partnerships with women. A study of men who have participated in Promise Keepers (Silverstein et al., 1999) revealed that this movement provides men with support for their attempts to become more nurturant, involved fathers. Table 1.2 lists some important events in both movements and when each event occurred.

A recent area of men's activism has been directed toward the health field (Courtenay, 2000b). For many years, women have claimed the research and delivery of health care has discriminated against them, perpetuating a lack of knowledge about women's health. Recently, men have complained that they, too, have been neglected by health care researchers. Male bodies are often the standard for medical research, but much of that research has neglected men and their special circumstances and needs. For example, funding for prostate cancer research is far less than for breast cancer research, even though these two diseases affect comparable numbers of people. Thus, men have begun to advocate increased funding and inclusion in health research.

The men's movement exists in many versions with diverse views and goals. This diversity has resulted not only in a variety of men becoming involved, but also in a lack of cohesion for the movement. As R. W. Connell (2001, p. 50) noted: "Masculinities, it appears, are far from settled. From bodybuilders in the gym, to managers in the boardroom, to boys in the elementary school playground, a great deal of effort goes into the making of conventional masculinities." Although some men are actively exploring this process, none of the versions of the men's movement has yet exerted the impact of the women's movement in influencing public opinion and changing social policy.

ISSUES IN THE STUDY OF GENDER

With the growing interest in women's and men's issues has come a number of questions and concerns about how to approach this research. Two questions speak to very basic issues: What vocabulary should be used to describe this research, and should researchers pursue this area of study?

TABLE 1.2   *Important Events in the Women's and Men's Movements*

Women's Movement			Men's Movement
First women's rights convention, Seneca Falls, New York	1848		
		1870	15th Amendment to U.S. Constitution gives African American men the right to vote
19th Amendment to U.S. Constitution gives women the right to vote	1920		
National Council of Women Psychologists	1941		
Simon de Beauvoir's *The Second Sex* published	1952		
Betty Friedan's *The Feminine Mystique* published	1963		
The Civil Rights Act prohibits discrimination on the basis of sex	1964	1964	The Civil Rights Act prohibits discrimination on the basis of sex
National Organization for Women formed	1966		
Association for Women in Psychology demonstrates against sexism at APA convention	1969		
APA Division 35 formed	1973		
		1983	National Organization for Changing Men founded
		1990	Robert Bly's *Iron John* published
		1995	APA Division 51 formed
		1995	Million Man March, Washington, DC
		1997	Promise Keepers rally, Washington, DC

Sex or Gender?

Those researchers who have concentrated on the differences between men and women historically have used the term **sex differences** to describe their work. In some investigations, these differences were the main emphasis of the study, but for many more studies, such comparisons were of secondary importance (Unger, 1979). By measuring and analyzing differences between male and female participants, researchers have produced a huge body of information on these differences and similarities, but this information was not of primary importance to most of these researchers. When the analyses revealed statistically significant differences, the researchers provided a brief discussion; when no significant differences appeared, researchers dismissed their lack of findings with little or no discussion. Thus, the differences between male and female participants' responses have appeared in many studies, but not necessarily as the focus of these studies.

What have researchers meant by *sex differences*? One objection to the term is that it carries implications of a biological basis for these differences (McHugh, Koeske, & Frieze, 1986). Another objection is that the term has been used too extensively and with too many meanings, including chromosomal configuration, reproductive physiology, secondary sex characteristics, as well as behaviors or characteristics associated with women or men (Unger, 1979). Rhoda Unger proposed an alternative— the term **gender.** She explained that this term describes the traits and behaviors that are regarded by the culture as appropriate to women and men. *Gender* is thus a social label and not a description of biology. This label includes the characteristics that the culture ascribes to each sex and the sex-related characteristics that individuals assign to themselves. Carolyn Sherif (1982) proposed a similar definition of gender as "a scheme for social categorization of individuals" (p. 376). Both Unger and Sherif recognized the socially created differentiations that have arisen from the biological differences associated with sex, and both have proposed that use of the term *gender* should provide a useful distinction.

Unger suggested that use of the term *gender* might reduce the assumed parallels between biological and psychological sex, or at least make those assumptions explicit. If researchers had accepted and used the term consistently, then its use might serve the function Unger proposed. However, no such consistent usage has yet appeared, and confusion remains. Some researchers use the two terms interchangeably, whereas others have substituted the term *gender* for the term *sex* but still fail to make any distinction. To remedy this situation, other terms have been proposed (Gentile, 1993), including *biologically sex-linked, gender-linked,* and *sex-correlated* to distinguish between biological and social differences, and between differences that are causally linked to sex and those for which a causal link has not been established. Objections to this proposal (Deaux, 1993; Unger & Crawford, 1993) pointed out that the knowledge to make these distinctions does not exist. As Rhoda Unger and Mary Crawford (1993, p. 124) wrote, "The problem of distinctions between sex and gender is due to unresolved conflicts within psychology about the causality of various sex-linked phenomena rather than to the terms used." A more extreme version of this argument (Maccoby, 1988) holds that distinguishing between the biological and social aspects of sex is not possible.

Therefore, psychologists have attempted to draw distinctions between the concepts of sex and gender to distinguish between those differences that are social and those that are biological. Such distinctions have been elusive, but those who use the term *gender* often intend to emphasize the social nature of differences between women and men, whereas those who use the term *sex* mean to imply biological differences. Indeed, the terminology that researchers use can indicate their points of view, with those researchers who are biological essentialists using the term *sex* to refer to *all* differences between men and women, whereas those who use the term *gender* want to emphasize the social nature of such differences.

Should Psychologists Study Gender?

Does the controversy and confusion associated with past research merit further research in the area of gender? Should psychologists continue to study gender? Psychologists have taken both positions, with some advocating that psychologists should do a more objective job of gender research, and some challenging the worth and wisdom of additional research.

On one side of this argument are psychologists Alice Eagly (1987a, 1997) and Diane Halpern (1994), who advocate that all psychological research should report on gender if such comparisons were part of the design. Rather than restricting reporting to theoretically meaningful or replicable results, this view holds that gender should be a routine part of psychological research. Furthermore, both have professed a belief that the methods used by psychologists are sufficiently sophisticated to yield credible results.

On the other side of the argument, psychologists Roy Baumeister (1988) and Bernice Lott (1997) have raised questions about the wisdom of continuing gender research. Baumeister contended that Eagly's strategy would result in virtually all research in psychology becoming gender research. He argued that psychology should go in the opposite direction—away from reporting on gender comparisons. Both Baumeister and Lott pointed out that by reporting and discussing gender *differences,* psychological research serves to focus on differences, which perpetuates the perception of (and even exaggerates) differences. When people believe in large gender differences, they find it easier to categorize and treat women and men differently. The psychologists who take this position would like to see a gender-neutral psychology of people, which would serve society and science better than exaggerating gender differences. Lott advocates a more complex treatment of gender, going beyond the simple comparisons of men and women to find similarities and differences to explore the complexities of human behavior.

Although these suggestions about how to proceed with gender research are in opposition, the concerns are similar—gender research may be misunderstood and inappropriately used to perpetuate stereotypes and discrimination. This concern was also voiced by female psychologists in Blustain's (2000) headline article. Despite these concerns, the suggestion that gender research should be abandoned is not likely to be implemented. The area has gained a momentum that is not likely to stop. Although dangers exist in connection with gender research, it will continue.

Another area of concern for gender research involves the way that researchers make comparisons. In making gender comparisons, there is a tendency to use men as the standard (Bem, 1993b; Yoder & Kahn, 1993). If men are the standard, then women will always appear deficient when they differ from that standard, placing women at an automatic disadvantage in such research findings. Sandra Bem (1993b) referred to this as an *androcentric bias,* contending that this bias has permeated not only psychology and its research, but also society in general. Whenever research finds a gender difference, that finding is interpreted as a disadvantage for women.

Janice Yoder and Arnold Kahn (1993) voiced a concern about a similar process that may occur when research focuses on women from various ethnic groups. White, privileged women have become the standard for research with women, and when women from other ethnic groups are included, they are compared to White, usually middle-class, college-educated women. In such a comparison, the dominant group tends to consider its own experience as the standard, and differences can be interpreted as deficiencies (Unger, 1995). Diversity in psychological research is a desirable goal, but Yoder and Kahn (1993) warned that "just as there is no singular male experience, there is no one experience or characterization that can be applied indiscriminately to all women" (p. 847).

Therefore, the study of gender will certainly continue in psychology, but several concerns exist for this research. Some psychologists have contended that gender research poses dangers by exploring differences, whereas others have argued that such research can be valuable and even essential. Others have pointed out that examining differences has perpetuated discrimination by placing men as the standard in gender comparisons, and yet others have warned against extending this disadvantaged comparison to women from ethnic minorities.

CONSIDERING DIVERSITY

Lack of diversity was the problem that sparked women to protest their exclusion in psychology and in society. Ironically, the diversity that they brought was limited. The women who entered psychology in large numbers and joined women's groups were mostly White, middle-class, college-educated professionals who protested sex discrimination in education and work. Women of color have a long history of discrimination, but many African American women focused their efforts on racial rather than sexual discrimination (Cole & Guy-Sheftall, 2003). Some African American women saw the need for addressing issues of sexism within their communities, but these women were often considered disloyal to the struggle against racism by bringing up gender issues. These criticisms did not stop African American women from opposing sexism and founding several feminist organizations during the 1960s and 1970s, including the Black Women's Liberation Caucus, the Third World Women's Alliance, and the National Black Feminist Organization.

During the 1980s, many feminists came to see their organizations and research as excluding working-class and poor women as well as women of color and sought to include more diversity in their organizations, theories, and research (Weber, 1998). Recognizing that multiple dimensions of inequality exist, more scholars began to explore the connection of not only gender and ethnicity, but also social class and sexual orientation. Scholars sought ways to include these dimensions in their work, recognizing that diversity is essential to feminism.

The field of psychology is guilty of exclusion based on race and social class, but diversity also became a goal within psychology (Reid, 1993; Yoder & Kahn, 1993). Scholars used the same critical thinking that had led them to analyze the male bias in psychology to examine the biases within the psychology of women. As Nancy Felipe Russo (1998, p. ii) explained, "Feminist psychology is now beyond simply critiquing yesterday's findings. The challenge now is to build a knowledge base of theories, concepts, and methods to examine women's lives in all of their diversity." With the recognition that cross-cultural comparisons add to the study of women and gender, feminist psychologists value an inclusive psychology. Thus, diversity was not something that came quickly to the women's movement or to psychology, but it is now a major focus for both.

The history of the men's movement is shorter than that of the women's movement (see Table 1.2), and the timing of that movement influenced its composition. Early men's groups tended to include White, privileged men, but the Million Man March drew African American men together, and gay men have been active in pressing for changes in laws and social attitudes.

The men's movement is less united than the women's movement, encompassing more divergent perspectives. For example, the men's movement is composed of both men who are antifeminist and those who are profeminist. Among antifeminist, conservative men's groups, diversity may not be a goal. Those groups that promote a return to traditional masculinity do not strive to include diverse ethnicities, social class, and sexual orientations among their members. Groups that aim to redefine masculinity often seek to promote changes in society to make it more inclusive. Therefore, the men's movement has a history that reflects more diversity than the women's movement, but some factions of the men's movement reject these goals.

■ SUMMARY

Typically, the first thing that parents learn about their child is the child's sex. This highlights the importance of sex and gender. Beliefs about gender differences are common, but opinions vary, with some people believing in minimal differences and others holding that the differences are maximal and part of essential biological differences.

Within psychology, gender research can be traced to the functionalist school that was influential during the late 1800s. This school held that men and women differ in ability and personality (a view that received criticism at that time). Interest in gender (and other individual differences) faded when the behaviorist school dominated psychology, but that interest persisted in psychoanalysis. Psychoanalysts held that differences in anatomy produce personality differences in women and men, with women being inferior in a number of important ways. The feminist movement of the 1960s produced a resurgence of interest among psychologists concerning questions about gender, and research tended to question stereotypes about the sexes.

The traditional terminology—namely, the use of the term *sex differences*—has been criticized. By proposing the use of the term *gender,* psychologists have tried to clarify the difference between socially determined and biologically determined differences. However, both terms continue in use, and the proposed distinction between sex differences, meaning biological differences, and gender differences, meaning socially determined differences, has not yet come into consistent use. Controversy also exists over the emphasis on gender in research. Some psychologists have argued that gender research should decrease to avoid promoting bias, but others have proposed that such research should become even more common to reflect more complete information about gender.

Ethnic and economic diversity did not appear during the early years of the women's movement, but inclusion is now a goal for feminist scholars. The men's movement has always been diverse, but some factions of the men's movement object to gays, profeminists, and various ethnic groups. Therefore, diversity remains an issue in both women's and men's movements.

GLOSSARY

behaviorism   the school of psychology that emphasizes the importance of observable behavior as the subject matter of psychology and discounts the utility of unobservable mental events.

essentialist view   the view that gender differences are biologically determined.

functionalism   a school of psychology arising in the United States in the late 1800s that attempted to understand how the mind functions. Functionalists held a practical, applied orientation, including an interest in mental abilities and in gender differences in those abilities.

gender   the term used by some researchers to describe the traits and behaviors that are regarded by the culture as appropriate to men and women.

maximalist view   the view that many important differences exist between the sexes.

minimalist view   the view that few important differences exist between the sexes.

sex differences   the term used by some researchers (and considered to be inclusive by others) to describe the differences between male and female research participants.

structuralist   a school of psychology arising in Europe in the 1880s that attempted to understand the workings of the conscious mind by dividing the mind into component parts and analyzing the structure of the mind.

SUGGESTED READINGS

Bem, Sandra Lipsitz. (1993). *The lenses of gender*. New Haven, CT: Yale University Press.

Bem contends that gender provides a lens, and people view the world through the distortion of this lens. She discusses three lenses of gender: androcentrism, gender polarization, and biological essentialism. Bem argues that viewing the world through these lenses provides the basis (and biases) for organizing gender knowledge.

Eagly, Alice H. (1997). Comparing women and men: Methods, findings, and politics. In Mary Roth Walsh (Ed.), *Women, men, and gender: Ongoing debates* (pp. 24–31). New Haven, CT: Yale University Press.

Eagly takes the position that research concerning the study of gender differences is important for creating a more complete picture of gender.

Lott, Bernice. (1997). Cataloging gender differences: Science or politics? In Mary Roth Walsh (Ed.), *Women, men, and gender: Ongoing debates* (pp. 19–23). New Haven, CT: Yale University Press.

Lott takes the position that research concerning the study of gender differences is dangerous. Compare the two discrepant views presented by Eagly and Lott

reflecting the debate concerning the study of gender differences.

Shields, Stephanie A. (1975). Functionalism, Darwinism, and the psychology of women: A study in social myth. *American Psychologist, 30,* 739–754.

This lively article details the history of early psychologists' research on gender differences, with all the biases showing.

Weisstein, Naomi. (1970). "Kinde, küche, kirche" as scientific law: Psychology constructs the female. In Robin Morgan (Ed.), *Sisterhood is powerful: An anthology of writings from the women's liberation movement* (pp. 228–245). New York: Vintage Books. Also reprinted in 1993 in *Feminism & Psychology, 3,* 195–210.

Weisstein's article has been reprinted many times and appears in many anthologies, a testimony to its influence. Originally a presentation, this angry criticism details psychologists' tendency to distort the view of women and describes the failure to study women in an unbiased way. Psychological research is no longer as inadequate as Weisstein charged, partly because of changes made in response to her criticism.

2 RESEARCHING SEX AND GENDER

■ HEADLINE   The Science Wars
                   Newsweek, April 21, 1997

Scientists worship at the shrine of objectivity, but even the pious occasionally lapse. A century ago archaeologists who discovered the great stone ruins of Zimbabwe went through all sorts of contortions to prove that the magnificent oval palace and other structures were built by the Phoenicians of King Solomon's time—or by anyone other than the ancestors of the Bantus. In the 1960s biologists studying conception described the "whiplashlike motion and strong lurches" of sperm "delivering" genes required to "activate the developmental program of the egg," which "drifted" along passively. The model portrayed sperm as macho adventurers, eggs as coy damsels. And throughout the 1970s and later, ornithologists gathered sheafs of data proving that, in birds, a female's success laying eggs and rearing hatchlings was always enhanced by the presence of a male. These acolytes of scientific objectivity were spectacularly wrong. The Bantus' ancestors did build the great stone complex. The human egg does play an active role in conception. And in some bird species, particularly the eastern bluebird, the father's presence makes little or no difference to the survival of hatchlings. But why did scientists get it wrong in all three cases, and many others? (Begley, 1997, p. 54)

According to Sharon Begley (1997), this question is the basis of a major battle in contemporary science. The heart of the battle is the question of objectivity in science. The defenders of traditional science see science as a process of discovering the natural principles that govern the functioning of the world. Although objectivity is not easy to attain, this position holds that through careful research design, it is possible to conduct objective scientific research.

The critics claim that science, like all other human activities, is a reflection of the values of the society in which it functions, and these values include biases that scientists bring with them to their research. These critics argue that science is a process of constructing a view of the world. These **constructionists** believe that "we do not discover reality, we invent it" (Hare-Mustin & Marecek, 1988, p. 455). That is, science does not lead researchers to map a realistic picture of the world, but to construct views of the world in ways that reflect social and personal perceptions and biases. In this view, science is a process of invention rather than one of discovery. Bias is inevitable, the constructionists argue, because all humans are tied to their perceptions and actively try to organize and interpret all information. To disconnect perception to the point of objectivity is impossible, so science must always contain the influence of subjective perceptions: "Knowledge bears the mark of its makers" (Schiebinger, 1999, p. 143).

Although the constructionist position may sound like a minor concession to the limitations of human perception, it is a more fundamental criticism of science because it challenges the philosophies that underlie science (Gergen, 1985). According to science, the only way to legitimately gather information is through observing objective facts and rejecting information gathered from other sources (Anderson, 2002). Constructionists argue that objective facts do not exist, and anything presented as fact is personal and subjective perception. Therefore, science cannot be free of values, nor can it be socially or politically neutral (Schiebinger, 1999).

Feminist scholars are part of the "science wars" because gender issues are among the most controversial in science and society. In addition, scientists have a long history, to paraphrase Judith Lorber (1997), of seeing because they believe, rather than believing because they have seen. Thus, the criticism of bias in science applies to the various disciplines that have explored gender issues, including psychology, sociology, medicine, biochemistry, biology, and anthropology. Researchers in these disciplines may vary in their viewpoints and approaches, but their methods of investigation usually do not—most researchers adhere to a set of methods that are part of traditional science. However, some feminist scholars have proposed alternatives to traditional science for gender (and other) research. However, an understanding of the traditional approach to research is necessary before we examine the alternatives.

HOW SCIENCE DEVELOPED

Modern science arose in the 16th and 17th centuries and came to prominence during the 19th century, bringing about radical changes in ways of knowing and understanding the world (Caplan & Caplan, 1994; Riger, 1992). Instead of looking to religion and the Bible for knowledge and wisdom, the new science looked to knowledge gathered through observation. This view represented a radical departure from ancient and religious thought. This new scientific view assumed that the world works by a set of natural laws and that these laws can be discovered by careful, objective investigation.

Those methods depended on **empirical observation,** gathering information through evidence from the senses. This view rejected information based on authority or the presumption of supernatural powers. Instead, careful human observation furnished the material for the new science. Scientists can understand the laws of nature if they use the correct methods of investigation, but they must be careful to be objective and not allow their personal feelings and biases to affect research. Critics of science argue against these assumptions that underlie science, contending that the required level of objectivity is not possible.

During the 18th and 19th centuries, science proliferated in Europe and spread throughout the Western world. Research in chemistry, physics, biology, and medicine produced findings that changed the world and the lives of most people. New products, medicines, and industries came into existence because of the research of scientists. The success of science created an enthusiasm that fostered the development of more sciences, including the social sciences of psychology, sociology, and anthropology. These social sciences held to the same assumptions and methods as the natural sciences.

What steps do proponents and critics believe to be necessary to conduct scientific research? What makes scientific investigation different from other ways of gaining knowledge? What techniques do scientists use to accomplish these goals, and what are the limitations for each? The following sections explore these questions.

APPROACHES TO RESEARCH

Traditional science remains the dominant approach to research. This approach follows the empiricist tradition, which includes observation and data collection. This research usually follows the procedure of **quantification,** turning observations into numbers, so it is referred to as **quantitative research.** Numbers are the **data** for quantitative research. Data are not the same as the observed phenomenon, but rather are representations of some facet of the phenomenon the researcher considered important. Quantitative researchers usually analyze their studies by performing statistical analyses of their quantitative data.

Some scholars have raised objections to quantitative research, claiming that quantification fails to capture important aspects of the situations under study; that is, something is lost in the process of turning observations into numbers. An alternative to the quantitative approach is **qualitative research,** which focuses on understanding the complexity of the situation rather than trying to reduce the situation to numbers. In addition to a different philosophy of research, qualitative studies include a different set of methods.

Thus, both quantitative and qualitative researchers have a variety of methods available to them. Any particular research question may be approached using a number of different methods, and each has advantages and disadvantages (Hyde & Durik, 2001). Thus, researchers must examine their research question and decide which method is appropriate.

Quantitative Research Methods

Traditional science relies on criteria that guide the collection of information, and the process is critically important. By following the rules, researchers collect information that meets the requirements of science. The requirements demand that scientific information must be observable not only to the person doing the observing, but also to others; that is, it must be publicly observable. This strategy is intended to minimize bias and lead to some level of objectivity.

Another rule of gathering information in science is that scientific observation must be systematic: Scientists must follow some plan or system to gather information. Everyone makes observations, but most people in most circumstances do so in a nonsystematic, personal way rather than according to a systematic plan. This lack of systematicity can lead people to notice certain things while ignoring others—a selection process that can result in distortion and bias. Scientists strive to be systematic in their observations in order to gather information that more accurately reflects the situations they have observed. This procedure does not mean that scientists are free of personal biases; as humans, they are subject to the same perceptual distortions (and even biases) as other humans. Although they cannot avoid personal opinions, scientists strive to treat information fairly (Gould, 1996). Both working with observable information and adopting a systematic plan to gather data are strategies to help researchers minimize bias.

The use of numbers in quantitative research has led to an erroneous impression about science—namely, that science is precise. People tend to believe that numbers lend precision, when actually numbers are only one way to summarize certain characteristics of a situation. The process of quantification does not make science precise; it does the opposite, omitting some aspect of the situation and concentrating on only one.

For example, a researcher who is interested in investigating campus attitudes toward gay, lesbian, and bisexual students might choose to study how such students rate their college campus. The researcher might ask students to rate their progress toward a degree, how their instructors interact with them, how they are treated in the dorms, if they have ever been threatened by other students, and other such questions. The data might consist of having these gay, lesbian, and bisexual students rate each question on a scale ranging from 1 to 7, and these ratings would be the data. The researcher can analyze these numbers to determine the results of the study, but the process of turning people's attitudes and experiences into numbers loses many details of their feelings and experiences.

An additional narrowing of the observations in science comes from the specification of a **variable** or several variables in research studies. A variable is the factor of interest in a research study. The term comes from the notion that the factor varies, or potentially has more than one value (as opposed to a constant, which has only one value). Most things vary, so finding a variable of interest is not nearly as difficult as restricting a study to only a few variables. For example, variables include time of day, family income, level of anxiety, number of hours of practice, gender of participants, and so forth. Thousands of variables are of interest to researchers, yet studies typically include only a few.

Quantitative research can be divided into two types: experimental and descriptive. Each approach has limitations and advantages that the other does not. Experimental research is highly prized because a carefully conducted experiment allows researchers to draw conclusions about cause-and-effect relationships. This type of information is difficult to obtain through any other method, and psychology researchers conduct experimental studies if they can do so. However, this method has requirements that make it unsuited to all research situations.

Descriptive research methods help investigators answer "what" questions. That is, descriptive research can tell what types of things exist, including great detail about those things and even the extent of relationships among various things. Descriptive research methods include surveys and correlational studies as well as methods that overlap with qualitative research.

Experimental Designs.   To obtain information about cause and effect, researchers must do **experiments.** This type of design allows researchers to answer "why" questions—questions with answers that involve explanations rather than descriptions. An experiment is a method that involves the manipulation of one factor, called the **independent variable;**

the measurement of another factor, called the **dependent variable;** plus the requirement of holding all other factors constant. By manipulating the independent variable, the experimenter tries to create a change. Detecting change requires some basis for comparison, so the simplest version of an experiment requires two conditions to provide this comparison. These two conditions consist of two different levels of the independent variable, with all other factors held constant. The manipulation may be more elaborate, consisting of three, four, or more levels of the independent variable, and experiments may include more than one independent variable.

The dependent variable is the one that the experimenter measures. Choosing and quantifying dependent variables can also be complex. In psychological research, dependent variables are always some type of behavior or response. By using such dependent variables, psychology is placed among the sciences that require empirical subject matter—behavior and responses that can be observed and measured.

The logic of experimental design holds that the manipulation of the independent variable should produce a change in the value of the dependent variable if the two are causally related. When the experimenter also holds other factors constant, the only source of change in the dependent variable should be the manipulated change in the independent variable. Thus, in a well-designed experiment, the changes in the value of the dependent variable can be entirely attributed to the manipulation of the independent variable. That is, the changes in the independent variable caused the changes in the dependent variable.

Although the logic of experimental design is simple, creating conditions to effectively manipulate one factor while holding all other factors constant is far from simple. Such a situation would be almost impossible in a naturalistic setting, because any one change would result in many others. Therefore, almost all experiments take place in laboratories. These settings offer the possibility of the necessary control, but they open experiments to the criticism of artificiality. Despite the validity of that criticism, scientists highly value experiments because of their potential to reveal cause-and-effect relationships, a type of information that other methods cannot show.

An example of an experiment on the topic of sexual orientation is difficult to devise. Sexual orientation is not available as an independent variable—researchers cannot change participants' sexual orientation for the purposes of an experiment. However, Laura Madson (2000) conducted an experiment about people's tendency to infer sexual orientation based on physical appearance. She reasoned that people tend to make inferences about behaviors and characteristics based on appearance. Her research included pretesting to find photographs of people whose gender was unclear (physically androgynous), and she matched these photographs to those of equally attractive people who were clearly male or female. She asked college students to rate the people pictured in the photos on a variety of measures, including traits, behaviors, and sexual orientation. Thus in this study, sexual orientation was a dependent variable that the researcher measured. The results were consistent with Madson's predictions: Participants were more likely to rate the people in the physically androgynous photos as homosexual than the people whose physical appearance in the photos was more typically feminine or masculine.

Gender research such as Madson's defines sexual orientation as a social category. Researchers who use this approach investigate how sexual orientation is one piece of information in a complex system of beliefs and expectations about behavior. Gender is another variable that can be used this way in experimental studies. Rather than manipulating information about physical appearance, researchers may provide information about the gender of the target to determine the reaction of participants to this information. This approach allows gender to become an independent variable because researchers can manipulate the gender of a character in a description or photo and yet hold all other factors in the description constant. According to Kay Deaux's (1984) review of this approach, the results indicated that gender is an important piece of information that people use in forming impressions and interacting with people: "The focus is not on how men and women actually differ, but how people *think* that they differ" (p. 110). This approach is especially well suited to investigating stereotypes, attitudes, and conceptions of gender and issues related to gender, such as sexual orientation.

Experiments are prized because, carefully designed and conducted, this method allows conclusions concerning causality. If the experiment is not done carefully, however, interpretation of causality can be in error. The participants in the Madson study saw photographs of people whom they rated based on their appearance. These participants may have behaved differently in a more naturalistic situation—evaluating photos or descriptions differs from evaluating actual people. In addition, the laboratory situation may prompt different behavior than would occur in a more realistic context. Because participants in a laboratory setting are always aware that their behavior is of interest to researchers, they may behave differently than they would in a natural setting. This possibility limits the extent to which researchers can generalize their results to other situations. The artificiality of the situation and its limitations in generalizing results to other situations are drawbacks of the experimental method. Despite some disadvantages, researchers have a prejudice in favor of experiments, which leads them to prize experiments above other methods (perhaps inappropriately), and scientists do experiments whenever they can.

Ex Post Facto Studies.   Researchers cannot always do experiments. Some variables of interest are beyond possible manipulation, for either practical or ethical reasons. For example, researchers might want to know about the effect of brain damage on memory. To do an experiment, researchers would be required to select a group of people and perform the surgery that would cause brain damage in half of them while leaving the other half with undamaged brains. Obviously, this research is unethical, but the question that prompted it—Does brain damage influence memory?—is still of interest. Sexual orientation is similar; it is a variable of interest, but researchers cannot manipulate sexual orientation by assigning people to groups and changing their sexual orientation.

Researchers interested in the question about brain damage and memory have at least two choices. They might choose to do the experiment with nonhuman subjects (although some would object to the ethics of this research, too), but the problems of generalizing the findings to humans would be a severe limitation. Another choice would be the **ex post facto study.** In this type of study, researchers might select people who have sustained brain damage in the area of interest and enlist these individuals as research participants, contrasting them with a group of people who have not experienced brain damage of any sort, or with those who have damage in some other area of the brain. Both groups would participate in the assessment of memory. Therefore, the presence of brain damage would be the **subject variable**—the characteristic of interest in the participants—and the scores on the memory test would be the dependent variable.

Such an ex post facto study would not be an experiment, because the researchers did not produce the brain damage while holding all other factors constant. Instead, the researchers entered the picture *after* the manipulation had occurred through accidents. With no opportunity for precision in creating the values of the independent variable or in holding other factors constant, the ex post facto study lacks the controls of an experiment that would allow researchers to draw conclusions about cause-and-effect relationships (Christensen, 2004).

Ex post facto research is one type of quasi-experimental research, meaning that it shares some characteristics with experimental research but is not really an experiment. The missing elements are manipulation of an independent variable, control of other variables, and random assignment of participants to groups. The similarities include a contrast of two or more groups and measurement of a dependent variable. These similarities can lead to misinterpretations of these studies and incorrect attributions of causality. Researchers are usually careful to use the correct language to interpret their findings from ex post facto studies, but people who read the research may not be appropriately cautious, leading to misunderstandings of research findings.

Gender of participants and sexual orientation of participants are both subject variables, characteristics of the participants that exist prior to their taking part in a study. These characteristics can be the basis for division of participants into contrasting groups. This type of research has a long history in psychology and has constituted the traditional approach to gender research. In 1974, two psychologists, Eleanor Maccoby and Carol Jacklin, published *The Psychology of Sex Differences,* a comprehensive review of research-based psychological findings about gender-related differences. These authors collected over 2,000 studies in which gender was a subject variable, and they organized the findings around different topics, such as aggression and verbal ability. Maccoby and Jacklin then evaluated the findings for each topic, determining how many studies failed to find a difference, how many studies supported a difference, and the direction of the differences for those comparisons that showed differences. Maccoby and Jacklin's book was soon accepted as a classic in this type of research review.

Studies with gender as a subject variable remain a common choice in psychology gender research and have also been applied to the study of sexual orientation. Nathan Berg and Donald Lien (2002) conducted such a study, comparing heterosexual and nonheterosexual individuals (subject variable) in terms of income (dependent variable). These researchers wanted to know if being gay, lesbian, or bisexual was related to differences in earnings. They asked over 4,000 participants the number and gender of their sexual partners within the past five years, which allowed Berg and Lien to construct categories of heterosexual and nonheterosexual. They also asked about income and performed an analysis comparing the incomes of individuals in these two categories. Their results indicated that sexual orientation is related to income, but in a complex way that interacts with gender. Heterosexual men earned more than gay and bisexual men, but heterosexual women earned less than lesbian and bisexual women. These researchers were restricted from interpreting their results in terms of cause and effect because their use of the ex post facto method did not allow such conclusions, and some other uncontrolled variables (such as discrimination against gay men, marital status, or career choice) may have been important in these results. However, Berg and Lien were able to conclude that sexual orientation is a factor in income level.

The studies that approach gender as a subject variable are also ex post facto studies, with all of the limitations of this method. That is, these studies do not and cannot reveal that gender *causes* differences in any behavior. This caution is difficult for many people to keep in mind, and those who are not familiar with research methods have a tendency to believe that gender-related differences in behavior have biological sex as the underlying cause. This reasoning contains two errors: (1) incorrectly attributing causality to a research method that cannot demonstrate cause-and-effect relationships and (2) reducing the many variables that coexist with biological sex to the subject variable gender. Therefore, an erroneous interpretation of such studies can lead people to conclusions for which there is no research evidence.

Figure 2.1 illustrates some of the differences between experimental and ex post facto designs, using sexual orientation as an example. In the experimental design, researchers often randomly divide the participants into groups in order to keep individual differences equal among the groups. Therefore, the groups in an experimental design would not consist of one group of heterosexuals and another group of gays, lesbians, and bisexuals, because random assignment would be very unlikely to yield such a configuration. The ex post facto design, on the other hand, assigns participants to groups on the basis of some factor that the participants already possess, such as sexual orientation or gender. In this type of design, the researcher might have one group consisting of women and another of men. Indeed, thousands of studies use this design to study gender-related differences and similarities.

Experimental Design—Sexual Orientation as a Social Category

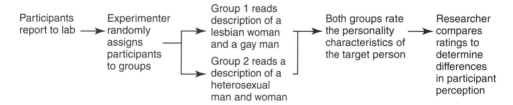

Ex Post Facto Design—Sexual Orientation as a Subject Variable

FIGURE 2.1 *Two Designs with Sexual Orientation as a Variable*

An experimental design can use gender as a variable if the researcher manipulates the gender of some target person whom the participants rate, evaluate, or react to. This approach makes gender a social category, not a subject variable. Further, the subject variable of gender can be included in a study that manipulates an independent variable to study each variable as well as the variables in combination. Therefore, ex post facto designs can examine gender as a subject variable, experimental designs can study gender as a social category to which participants react, and studies can use gender as a subject variable combined with additional, manipulated independent variables. These approaches are not equivalent, and each yields information that requires careful interpretation of findings.

Other types of quantitative research do not concentrate on comparisons and differences, which experimental and ex post facto studies do. Instead, these methods focus on describing characteristics or attitudes of participants, determining the relationship between variables, and other descriptions of variables. These variables may include gender, sexual orientation, or many others, and these methods fit within the category of *descriptive research*. Surveys and correlational studies are examples of such descriptive methods.

Surveys. In **surveys,** researchers construct questionnaires, choose a group of people to respond to the questionnaire, collect the data, and analyze the data to yield results. This method sounds deceptively simple—almost anyone can think of questions to ask. However, the method is filled with choices and pitfalls. For example, researchers using this method must decide about the wording of questions (e.g., "Do you agree . . ." versus "Do you disagree . . ."), the answer format (respondents reply versus respondents choose from a set of answers), the appearance of the questionnaire (number of pages, size of type, page layout), the choice of people responding (representative of the entire population versus a select group, such as registered voters or first-time parents), the number of people needed (what number will give a good estimate for accuracy), and the method of administration (face-to-face interview, telephone interview, mailed questionnaire). Unwise choices on any of these decisions may result in a survey that does not allow the researcher to answer the question that prompted the research or, worse, may give the researcher an answer that is misleading.

The main limitation of the survey method is inherent: Surveys pose questions rather than make direct measurements. That is, surveys typically rely on self-reports rather than direct observations of behavior. Researchers ask people to respond to a series of questions either in person or through a mailed questionnaire or telephone survey. In many surveys, participants are asked to share their opinions and attitudes, but in some surveys participants try to report on past behavior. The responses that people give may not accurately reflect their beliefs or behaviors. Even if people are honest about their beliefs, they may not always behave in a way that is consistent with reported attitudes. Indeed, people may lie, withhold the truth, or simply do not know or remember the information.

Replies to survey questions are open to bias due to participants' beliefs about social standards and their tendency to present themselves in a favorable way. This bias can invalidate a question or even an entire survey, and information obtained through self-reports is generally not considered as strong as information obtained by direct observation. Despite the wide variety of information that can be obtained through the survey method, that information is limited not only by its descriptive nature but also by its potential inaccuracy.

Despite the disadvantages, surveys offer the advantages of allowing researchers to ask people about things that the researchers could not easily (or possibly ethically) observe directly. Thus, the method is flexible and useful in a variety of situations. Surveys are a very common method for measuring people's attitudes. Psychologists, sociologists, market researchers, and political pollsters all use this method to help decide how people feel about a wide variety of issues.

For example, Craig Waldo (1998) surveyed gay, lesbian, and bisexual university students concerning the campus climate and sexual orientation. Gay, lesbian, and bisexual students are more likely to "come out," that is, to reveal their sexual orientation, in college rather than in high school because college is typically a less hostile climate than high school. Nevertheless, colleges often fail to be supportive for students with nonheterosexual sexual orientations. Waldo wanted to assess many aspects of the campus climate for gay, lesbian, and bisexual students and chose the survey method to study this research topic. Waldo was careful to choose a sample that yielded representative data from heterosexual and nonheterosexual students. He also included questions about a variety of factors to try to examine the general campus climate, acceptance by various social groups, progress in academic programs, and acceptance by faculty.

Waldo's results indicated that gay, lesbian, and bisexual students found the campus climate less accepting of their sexual orientation than heterosexual students did. In addition, heterosexual students rated the campus climate for nonheterosexuals as more accepting than gay, lesbian, and bisexual students did. That is, students who were not heterosexual found less acceptance than heterosexual students believed they would. This difference in point of view is not surprising but does highlight how discrimination may be less visible to those who are doing the discriminating than to those who are the targets of such discrimination. This result is only one of the many from this survey. Like many surveys, Waldo's research yielded many results based on the varied responses from participants.

Correlational Studies.   If researchers want to know about the relationship between two specific variables rather than information about several variables, they will do a **correlational study,** another type of descriptive method. Correlational studies allow researchers to determine both the strength and types of relationships between the variables under study.

To do a correlational study, researchers must choose two variables for study, operationalize (create an operational definition of), measure these variables, and then analyze the relationship between them. An **operational definition** is a definition of a variable in terms of the operations used to obtain data on that variable, rather than in terms of the concepts underlying the variable. Operational definitions are one way that researchers use to be more specific about the variables they study. An operational definition provides instructions about how to measure the two variables in a correlational study.

To perform the analysis of the data, researchers calculate a correlation coefficient, the results of a statistical test that reveals the strength or magnitude of the relationship between two variables. The correlation coefficient is described by a formula, and researchers must apply the formula to their data. A number of variations on the correlation coefficient exist, but the most common is the *Pearson product–moment correlation coefficient,* symbolized by the letter *r*. The results of the analysis yield a number that varies between

$r = +1.00$ and $r = -1.00$. Correlations that are close to $r = +1.00$ indicate a strong, positive relationship, which means that as scores on one variable increase, those on the other also increase. Correlations that are close to $r = -1.00$ indicate a strong, negative relationship, which means that as one measurement increases, the other decreases. Correlations that are close to $r = 0.00$ indicate little or no relationship between the two variables.

For example, William Byne (1997) examined the correlation between biology and sexual orientation. He questioned the relationship, considering the possibilities that biology provides hardwiring for sexual orientation and the alternative that biology provides only the background for experiences that determine sexual orientation. Byne cautioned that even if a biological marker demonstrated a high correlation with sexual orientation, that relationship would not demonstrate that biological factors cause sexual orientation. His observation highlighted one of the important limitations of correlational studies: Correlation does not demonstrate causation.

Like other descriptive methods, correlational studies do not reveal why the relationship exists. However, such a deduction may be very tempting. Indeed, a causal relationship may exist between two variables that have a high correlation, but the method does not allow that conclusion. Even a high correlation would not allow a researcher to know the source of the relationship: Did changes in one variable produce changes in the other, or vice versa? Another possibility is that both variables may be causally related to a third variable that was not part of the study, as Byne (1997) suggests for sexual orientation. In any case, a conclusion of causality is not legitimate on the basis of the evidence from a correlational study. Thus, the information that researchers obtain and the conclusions that they may draw from correlational studies exclude causality but include information on the existence and strength of relationships.

In summary, different quantitative research methods yield different types of information. Experimental research allows researchers to explain *why* a relationship exists between independent variables and dependent variables because this method yields information about cause-and-effect relationships. A quasi-experimental method, the ex post facto study, is similar to an experiment in the designation of variables (called subject or participant variables) and dependent variables, but these designs differ from true experiments in that they use the existing values of the subject variable rather than create the values of the independent variable through manipulation. Descriptive research methods include surveys and correlational studies. Such studies help to answer questions about *what* occurs; that is, they describe what exists but reveal no information about causality.

Qualitative Research Methods

Researchers who use qualitative methods often believe that the quantification process removes important information from research. This belief leads qualitative researchers to collect different data and to resist reducing their data to numbers. Such researchers may collect extensive reports, which they transcribe and attempt to organize and understand. This strategy makes statistical analysis difficult or impossible.

Qualitative researchers also reject the notion that they should be detached and impartial; instead, they accept the subjectivity of the research process and attempt to form cooperative relationships with those whom they study. By interacting with research participants as equals, they try to understand the meaning and context of the phenomena they study.

The methods of qualitative research are not necessarily different from those of quantitative research. That is, the methods themselves do not create qualitative or quantitative research; the key to the difference is the type of data collected. However, qualitative researchers tend to use a different selection of methods than quantitative researchers, including case studies, interviews, ethnography, and focus groups.

Case Studies. **Case studies** are an intensive study of a case—that is, a single person (or a small sample of people). Several different factors determine which case might be a good candidate for study. The person may be typical and thus reflective of many other people, or unusual and thus of interest. The unusual cases are more typical choices. Researchers conducting case studies often spend days or months interviewing or observing the person in order to write a case study.

Miguel, a gay Mexican American man, was the subject of such a case study conducted by Joseph Carrier (1997), who studied Miguel over a span of 16 years. The report told of Miguel's sexual life history, contrasting the sexual behaviors and cultural attitudes of Mexican American and European American gay men. In addition, the case study described Miguel's relationships with women, his career, and his problems with alcoholism.

The case study of Miguel offered extensive details of his life that related to his sexual orientation and behavior. This approach allowed Carrier to explore individual and cultural factors that relate to issues such as "coming out," employment discrimination, and the pressure to be heterosexual. Although there are many Mexican American gay men, Miguel's case is an individual story that represents others in some ways and not in others, which reflects the strengths and weaknesses of the case study method.

Interviews. **Interviews** can take many forms, but qualitative interviews differ from interviews conducted as part of survey research in both format and goals. Survey interviews are quantitative, including a specified and uniform set of questions to which all respondents reply. The uniformity of responses allows statistical analysis, but such analysis is not the goal of qualitative interviews. These interviews can take the form of oral or life histories, or the interview may be oriented around a narrower topic.

Deborah Jon and Tharinger Lasser (2003) used the interview method to study gay, lesbian, and bisexual adolescents' ways of dealing with their sexual orientation at school. They conducted extensive interviews with 20 young people who were gay, lesbian, or bisexual to explore the strategies these adolescents use to negotiate school and manage to be safe in a hostile environment. These researchers analyzed the data and concluded that the main strategy could be termed "visibility management," a series of careful decisions that these adolescents made concerning the disclosure and presentation of their sexual orientation. For their safety at school, gay, lesbian, and bisexual adolescents had to be selective to whom and under what circumstances they disclosed their sexual orientation; if they looked or acted "too gay," they faced danger.

Ethnography.   Ethnography, one of the most common qualitative methods, has a long tradition in anthropology, in which qualitative research has been more common than in psychology. However, this method is growing in popularity among psychologists (Crawford & Kimmel, 1999). Researchers using this method spend time becoming immersed in the situation they are studying. For anthropologists, this situation is typically another culture; for psychologists and sociologists, the situation may be a school, company, or hospital. By becoming part of the situation, the researcher can gather and interpret information situated in the context in which it occurs.

George Smith and Dorothy Smith (1998) reported on an ethnography that investigated the high school experience of gay men. This ethnography relied on interviews but also used journals that the students had kept in high school and information about their appearance and behavior. George Smith conducted the extensive interviews, trying to build a rapport with these young men, which included his identification as a gay man. With several sources of data and 19 participants, Smith and Smith were able to analyze their data to build a representation of how school students, staff, and administration largely ignore gay students unless faced with unambiguous declarations of sexual orientation. Such declarations were likely to provoke homophobia and hostility (being called "fag" was a pervasive experience). Thus, this institutional ethnography indicated that high school is a difficult place for gay students and enhances the quantitative research that shows a high percentage of dropouts among gay adolescents.

Focus Groups.   The focus group is another qualitative method that psychologists have borrowed; this method is more common in communications and marketing research than in psychology. A **focus group** is a discussion centered on a specific topic. The individuals in the group can consist either of people brought together for the purpose of the discussion or of people who belong to some existing group, such as a family or sorority. Groups usually consist of 6 to 8 people, and rarely more than 12. Focus groups are similar to interviews in terms of the questions and topics that can be explored. However, this method allows group members to interact with each other as well as with the researcher, making the focus group more similar to naturally occurring situations than the interview method is (Wilkinson, 1999).

Camille Lee (2002) also investigated sexual orientation issues in high school, but she used the focus group approach, studying a group of seven students who were members of the Gay/Straight Alliance at their high school. This group included gay, lesbian, bisexual, and straight students questioned over a 2-year period. Lee was interested not only in the opinions of gay, lesbian, and bisexual students but also in how the heterosexual students changed in reaction to their participation in the Alliance. She found positive changes for all students, including an increased sense of safety for the gay, lesbian, and bisexual students and diminishing of the assumption of heterosexuality among the straight students. The analysis also indicated an improvement in school, which suggests the value of positive action by schools concerning sexual orientation issues.

Table 2.1 presents both quantitative and qualitative research methods, along with advantages and limitations of each approach.

TABLE 2.1 *Advantages and Limitations of Quantitative and Qualitative Research Methods*

Method	Advantage	Limitation
Quantitative Methods		
Survey	Examines a variety of topics without being intrusive	Relies on self-reports rather than direct observation of behavior
Correlational study	Allows determination of strength and direction of relationship between two variables	Cannot reveal any information about causality
Experiment	Allows determination of cause-and-effect relationships	Conducted in laboratory situations that are artificial; can investigate only a few variables at a time
Qualitative Methods		
Case study	Reveals extensive information about one case	Cannot be generalized to other cases
Interview	Allows researchers to question participants extensively about a topic	Does not yield a standard set of answers; may include only a few participants
Ethnography	Allows researchers to become immersed in a situation and to understand the contexts in which behavior occurs	Data collection is not systematic, which may lead to focusing on some and overlooking other information
Focus group	Allows extensive exploration of a topic as well as observation of the interaction among group members	Does not yield a standard set of data, making the information difficult to analyze

Researchers' Choices

Qualitative research methods are growing in acceptance and frequency but still constitute a minority of the research, even in the area of gender (Crawford & Kimmel, 1999). An analysis of two leading journals, *Feminism & Psychology* and *Psychology of Women Quarterly,* revealed that the interview method was the most common of the qualitative approaches (Wilkinson, 1999). That method accounted for over half of the research articles in *Feminism & Psychology* but only 17% of research articles in *Psychology of Women Quarterly.* Other qualitative methods accounted for much lower percentages, and no other qualitative method represented more than 2% of the research studies in these journals. Therefore, the majority of psychology research is quantitative research, even those studies published in journals featuring feminist scholarship.

TABLE 2.2   *Comparison of Quantitative and Qualitative Research*

Quantitative Researchers	Qualitative Researchers
Often work in laboratories	Rarely work in laboratories
Strive to detach themselves from the situation to attain objectivity	Immerse themselves in the situation and accept subjectivity as part of the process
Attempt to study a representative group of individuals to be able to generalize	May seek unusual individuals because they are interesting cases
Create a distinction between researchers and participants	Treat participants as equals
Collect data in the form of numbers	Collect information that is not reduced to numbers
Attempt to control the influence of variables other than the independent variable(s)	Attempt to understand the complexity of the situation as it exists
Use statistics to analyze their data	Do not use statistics to analyze their information

Qualitative research offers alternatives to traditional quantitative research methods. A comparison of the two approaches appears in Table 2.2. The philosophy and practice of qualitative research differ from quantitative studies. Qualitative researchers emphasize context and acknowledge that subjectivity is part of the research process; they become involved in the research situation, interacting with participants in order to understand the patterns of their behavior. Researchers who use these methods believe that this approach offers advantages over the traditional quantitative approach.

A demonstration of the value of widening research methods came from a study that approached the same problem with two methodologies: one quantitative and behavioral, and the other qualitative and based on personal perceptions (Landrine, Klonoff, & Brown-Collins, 1992). The study focused on self-perceptions of African American, Hispanic American, Asian American, and European American women concerning several gender-stereotypical behaviors. The quantitative analysis showed no differences among these groups of women, but the qualitative evaluation revealed ethnic differences by allowing participants to express feelings that the more traditional approach failed to show. This study demonstrated that more diverse methods of investigation have the potential to enrich traditional science.

GENDER BIAS IN RESEARCH

Despite the long history and success of science, some modern scholars have questioned its assumptions and procedures. One criticism is that science grew not only from the activities of men but also from a gendered, masculine bias that is inherently part of science. According to this view, this masculine bias affects our modern conception of science, including the thinking of the men and women who do scientific work. Another criticism of science has come from the constructionists, who contend that science is incapable of revealing an objective picture of the natural world. According to constructionists, objective reality does not exist because all reality is subjective. Thus, researchers cannot escape their personal and societal prejudices. Scholars who take this view have used the study of gender as a particularly good example of the distortions and misrepresentations of science.

Sources of Bias

Bias can enter research at many levels, beginning with the very framework of science. The philosophers whose work spurred the founding of science were all men, and Evelyn Fox Keller (1985) has argued that these philosophers introjected a masculine bias into the very conceptual foundation of science. She has interpreted the emphasis on rationality and objectivity in science as masculine values, and she has contrasted those masculine elements of science with the feminine elements of nature—feeling and subjectivity. Thus, Keller discussed what she interpreted as the gendering of science and nature: masculine for science and feminine for nature. Thus, even at its inception, science carried connotations of maleness, rationality, and dominance. According to Keller, not only have women been discouraged from the pursuit of science as a profession, but also the activity of science itself suggests masculinity (see "According to the Media" and "According to the Research"). The culture of science was and remains masculine (Morawski, 1997).

Theories are another potential source of bias in science. The study of gender is full of examples of situations in which speculations and theories have attained a status in which they are mistaken for results. Freud's theory is probably the most prominent example, with its emphasis on the importance of biological sex differences in building personality. Research has not supported this theory (see Chapter 5 for more on Freud), and supporters of the theory speak with unearned authority.

Additional bias in research on gender (and many other topics) comes from the procedures involved in planning studies and evaluating results. Researchers' values enter the research process as early as the planning stage of studies, influencing the choice of problem to investigate and the choice of questions to ask (MacCoun, 1998; Wallston, 1981). Publications place too much emphasis on results and too little emphasis on the conceptualization of the questions underlying the research process, often ignoring the social and political aspects and implications of research (Harding, 2001). The answers that researchers find depend on the questions they ask, so the planning and questioning aspects of the process are critically important and often neglected.

When researchers formulate their studies, they ask questions and choose methods of gathering information that will allow them to answer their questions. Most researchers know what they expect to find when they ask a question, so research is not free of the values and expectations of the scientists, even at this stage of the research. These expectations lead to the formulation of a **hypothesis,** a statement about the expected outcome of the study. Researchers test hypotheses by gathering data and analyzing them to obtain results. The researchers can then decide whether the results support or fail to support their hypothesis.

To evaluate the data collected from studies, quantitative researchers usually use statistical tests. Many different statistical tests exist, but all of those used to evaluate research

ACCORDING TO THE MEDIA . . .

Scientists Are Men, and Usually Either Mad or Bad

In the movies, scientists are most often male and more often mad or bad than good. If they are good, they are generally bumbling incompetents. These depictions go back to the era of silent film and continue to the present in movies and on television. "The movies have always been full of insane chemists, demonic doctors and obsessive inventors who, whether purposely or inadvertently, unleash malevolent forces that neither they nor anyone else can control" (Ribalow, 1998, p. 26). In addition, being a scientist is dangerous on TV; more scientists are killed than any other profession portrayed (Evans, 1996). About 10% of scientists in entertainment programming die, and about 5% kill someone. On TV, scientists die at a higher rate than police officers do.

Some scientists in the movies want to do evil, but even with noble motivations, movie scientists often cause serious problems when they fail to understand the implications of their actions. Both evil and well-meaning scientists are portrayed as obsessive, self-centered, personally cold, and removed from society. Movie scientists work in isolated laboratories without the support of the scientific community. Their brilliance is ignored or disdained by the rest of the world, and their innovations are revolutionary. Or alternatively, they are not brilliant but misguided in following science; the problem that they conceptualized as part of science was really supernatural (all those *X-Files* episodes), and being a scientist prevented them from seeing the supernatural truth (Evans, 1996).

Women have been background more often than leading characters in media science. In children's science programming, about 80% of the women were in secondary or supporting roles, and the proportion of male to female scientists was 2 to 1 (Steinke & Long, 1996). However, during the 1990s, a new movie scientist appeared: the "brainy babe" (Ribalow, 1998). This female version of the scientist is usually similar to the male versions—either evil or oblivious, obsessive, and also flawed—but she was also more vulnerable. Two examples were Ellie Arroway, Jodie Foster's character in *Contact* (1997), and Emma Russell, Elisabeth Shue's character in *The Saint* (1997). Both were brilliant, obsessive, shy, and personally unsure of themselves. Ellie's vulnerability was the memory of her dead father. Emma's was her heart condition. This combination of brilliance and vulnerability is echoed in TV's *CSI: Crime Scene Investigation,* which depicts two competent female scientists. One is the stereotypical socially incompetent science nerd, and the other experiences repeated traumas with her ex-husband. These brainy babes are outcasts because of their role as scientist, just as the male scientists are, but their vulnerability is a departure from the portrayals of mad or bad male scientists.

data have a common goal—to allow the researcher to decide whether the results are statistically significant. A **statistically significant result** is one due to events other than chance alone. If researchers are careful in the design of their studies, then they can attribute significant results to the factors they have identified in their studies. The procedure for determining the statistical significance of a result involves choosing the appropriate statistical test and analyzing the data using that statistic. If the analysis indicates significant effects, then the researchers can conclude that their results were not due to chance alone; that is, the study worked as hypothesized. If the analysis does not indicate a significant effect, then the researchers cannot claim that their results are due to anything but chance or that their study worked as hypothesized. Researcher bias may enter both at the stage of

ACCORDING TO THE RESEARCH . . .

Science Doesn't Play Well on the Screen

According to author and director Michael Crichton (1999), the problem with science in the movies is not that the media misunderstand science, but that scientists misunderstand the media. The scientific process does not produce the material for exciting entertainment; the situations in which most scientists do research do not contain enough drama to hold the attention of movie audiences. Thus, science is portrayed in the movies in exaggerated ways or with added plot elements for the purpose of entertainment. The media do not single out scientists for negative portrayals; all professions look bad because the point of presenting a profession is to further the plot, not to present accurate career information.

The daily work of scientists includes too little action and too much thought for good entertainment (except to the scientists, who find it fascinating). Unlike the screen presentations, most scientists work in university or hospital laboratories with a research group rather than alone in some isolated, secret lab. The majority of scientific research is funded by government grants obtained through a peer review process, not by some malevolent company intent on taking over the world. This funding process creates research that extends current knowledge in small ways and makes it unlikely that large breakthroughs will occur or that any scientist working outside the system would be able to make a substantial contribution. Thus, the process of scientific research allows for too few heroic acts, too few explosions, and too much time and patience for good plots. Real science is not going to be a really interesting movie.

Scientists disagree with this pessimistic view, in terms of both scientists' image and its dramatic interest (A. Pollack, 1998). At a meeting between scientists and media moguls, scientists voiced their opinion that stories from science hold the promise of a "goldmine" of characters and plots. Funded by a grant by the Alfred P. Sloan Foundation, a $2 million program is aimed at encouraging a more thoughtful treatment of science in the media. However, the problems became clear in the meeting between writers and concept developers from the media and prominent scientists. The scientists saw little reason to develop characters, believing that nature was, in itself, fascinating enough, with no need for character or plot development. The media people found it difficult to construct a dramatic plot relying on good scientists and lamented the absence of villains. The initial results of funding from the Sloan grant seemed to confirm Crichton's (1999) pronouncement; two scripts portrayed stereotypical loner scientists, and the third script removed the science content because it was not interesting enough to develop the plot (A. Pollack, 1998).

planning and at the point of data analysis. For example, an analysis of many studies on the topic of gender development (Tennenbaum & Leaper, 2002) revealed that studies with male first authors showed larger gender differences than studies with female first authors.

Researchers are constrained from making claims about factors that do not produce significant results, because these results are not considered "real," and researchers have no confidence in the validity of nonsignificant results. When researchers obtain statistically significant results, they have confidence that their research has revealed effects that probably are not due to chance. However, the term *significant* may be misleading, because people who are not sophisticated in the logic of statistical evaluation may believe that statistically significant means *important* or *large*.

A large or important result is not only statistically significant but also practically significant. The concepts of statistical significance and practical significance are not the same. A result is statistically significant when it is unlikely to have occurred solely on the basis of chance. A result has **practical significance** when it is important to everyday life. For example, a low correlation ($r = 0.20$) can indicate a statistically significant relationship if the number of people participating in the study was sufficiently large (what constitutes a large sample varies with the design and statistic), but this magnitude of correlation does not reveal a strong relationship between the two variables in the correlation. That is, this correlation would have little practical significance. People who hear about significant results may believe that the results have practical significance when the researchers have reported statistical significance. Confusion between these two concepts can result: "Reasonable people who are repeatedly exposed to findings reported as significant mean differences or nonchance factors . . . sometimes begin to think and talk as if those differences were actually true in most individual cases" (Bernstein, 1999, p. x). Such misunderstandings can lead people to believe that results mean more than they actually do and apply to everyone when they actually do not.

The gender difference in mathematics performance is one such well-publicized difference (Maccoby & Jacklin, 1974). How much better are boys at math? Do all boys do better than all girls? How much do math scores of boys and girls overlap? Figure 2.2 shows some possibilities for the distributions of math scores for boys and girls. Group A of this figure shows two distributions with no overlap. If this figure represented the mathematics performance of boys and girls, then all boys would do better than all girls. Group B shows the performance of boys and girls overlapping slightly. If this figure represented the performance of boys and girls, then most boys would do better than most girls. A few girls would do better than a few boys, but no girls would do better than boys with the highest performance. Group C shows a lot of overlap between the performance of the two. If this figure represented performance, many girls would do better at math than many boys.

Hyde (1981, 1986, 1994) contended that the upper range of difference between men and women is no more than 1% in mathematical ability. Only a small percent of the distribution of math scores for boys and girls fails to overlap, and most of the scores for the two are in the same range. Figure 2.2C comes closer to this distribution of math ability than the other parts of Figure 2.2. These gender-related differences in math performance are sufficiently large to show a statistically significant difference, but not large enough to have any practical significance when applied to the performance of most boys and most girls. This magnitude of difference would not lead educators to create different math classes for boys and girls because their abilities were so dissimilar, nor would counselors advise girls to avoid math courses because of their lack of ability.

Studies that do not find hypothesized differences in outcomes are less likely to be published than studies that offer support for the hypotheses. Thus, a strong prejudice exists in favor of findings that show differences rather than findings that do not succeed in showing differences; that is, there is a prejudice against findings that suggest similarities (Greenwald, 1975). This tendency prompts researchers to highlight the differences they find and to dismiss other, nonsignificant results. Indeed, researchers may omit any mention of failure to find a difference, such as a gender-related difference, but researchers who

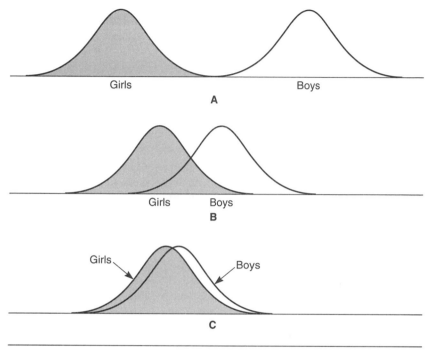

FIGURE 2.2 *Distributions with Varying Degrees of Overlap*

find statistically significant differences will always mention the differences and the level of statistical significance. Researchers cannot discuss an effect they have failed to find, and they must discuss effects that they have found. However, the omission of some information and the mention of other information can lead to a distorted view of overall findings by magnifying differences and obscuring similarities.

Table 2.3 shows the stages of research and how bias can enter at various points in the process. The possibilities for gender bias listed in the table are only a few examples; the history of gender research is filled with too many other examples.

Ways to Deal with Bias in Science

Begley's headline article (1997), which opened this chapter, pointed out that critics have questioned the notion of objectivity and the view that science shows an orderly progression toward "truth." "Ever since the scientific method became a way of learning about nature, including ourselves, some people have hailed science as the only way to comprehend natural phenomena, while others have questioned whether it is an appropriate road to knowledge" (Hubbard, 1990, p. 9).

Those who criticize the bias in science have proposed two very different strategies for dealing with this problem. The constructionists deny the possibility of objectivity and

TABLE 2.3   *Stages of Research and Potential for Bias*

Stage	Ways Bias Can Enter	Gender-Related Example
Finding a problem to investigate	Allowing personal and societal values to influence choice of topic	Studying heart disease rather than breast cancer in middle-aged populations
Selecting variables	Using inaccurate, incomplete, or misleading definitions	Defining rape as vaginal penetration accompanied by force or threat of force (excludes other forced sexual acts and excludes men as victims)
Choosing a design	Choosing a design that does not allow for the evaluation of context	Testing participants in a situation that is anxiety-provoking for women but not for men
Formulating a hypothesis	Failing to consider the validity of the null hypothesis	Always hypothesizing gender differences rather than similarities
	Following a theory that is biased	Following Freudian theory to hypothesize that women have weak superegos
Collecting data	Permitting personal bias to influence measurement; using a definition of the behavior that is too narrow	Defining battering as the number of police reports of domestic violence
Analyzing results	Allowing personal values and expectation to guide the choice of which factors to evaluate	Failing to make a comparison of female and male participants
Interpreting results	Failing to report effect sizes	Interpreting a gender difference in a way that makes it seem large when it is not
	Interpreting gender differences as due to biological factors when no biological data exist	Claiming that boys' advantage in math is biological when no biological data have been collected
Publication bias	Publication of findings showing significant gender differences	Publication and media attention for findings of gender differences, but no attention for findings of similarities

thus reject the basic tenets of science. The extreme of this position calls for abandoning science as a way to deal with its inevitable bias. That position is unlikely to prevail—science has been too successful and is too widely accepted. Nevertheless, a growing number of scholars advocate radical transformation in collecting and analyzing information. Other researchers argue that scientists must try harder to do good science.

Advocating Transformation.   Several scholars have argued that feminist research has the power to transform research with women and even the discipline of psychology. Historian Londa Schiebinger (1999) asked a broader question about the influence of feminism on all of science. She evaluated the possibility that feminism and its criticisms of traditional science have changed modern science. Her conclusions were both positive and negative. On the one hand, Schiebinger contended that feminism (and the presence of women) has brought about some changes in science. On the other hand, nothing has changed in science's basic assumptions or approach. The criticisms concerning masculinist bias in science may be founded, and the women who enter the profession of scientific research must play by the rules of science. In that sense, feminism has not changed science. Women have changed science in terms of what questions researchers ask and possibly how those results are interpreted. Research on issues important to women—such as incest and sexual abuse of children, rape and sexual assault, sexual harassment, spouse abuse, and achievements by women—has increased dramatically within the past 25 years, parallel to the increase in women in psychology (Worell, 1996). In addition, extending research to understudied populations has been a force in expanding psychology research beyond White, middle-class college students (Worell & Etaugh, 1994). Women in psychology have managed to change psychology but not to transform science itself.

Scholars who claim that research should center on women advocate a more radical transformation. This view is *feminist standpoint epistemologies* (Campbell & Wasco, 2000; Riger, 1992), and scholars who take this view claim that women have a unique point of view and different cognitive processes that have been ignored. These researchers believe that the analytical categories that are appropriate for men may not be appropriate for women, and that research should remedy these shortcomings by devising methods to study the unique experience of womanhood. Rather than pushing women's issues to the margins, feminist standpoint scholars make those issues the center (Anderson, 2002; Morawski, 1997).

As a way of gaining additional information about women and their experience, the feminist standpoint epistemologies have considerable value and appeal. Some feminist scholars have rejected traditional quantitative research as impoverished in capturing the female experience and have opted for more qualitative approaches. Such methods allow researchers to be subjective and interpretive, which qualitative researchers believe is critical in studying behavior.

The feminist standpoint epistemologies have the disadvantage of departing radically from accepted methodology, and such departures are difficult for mainstream science to accept (Riger, 1992; Whelan, 2001). The growing interest in qualitative research and its increasing frequency in psychology journals speak to the possibility of including these changes in research. Less radical changes, however, are easier to accept and enact. Thus, decreasing bias in gender research is a more feasible goal.

Decreasing Bias.   Those scholars who advocate a more objective study of gender can be termed *feminist empiricists* (Campbell & Wasco, 2000; Riger, 1992). These feminist researchers have argued that the development of a feminist methodology will not benefit research on women and gender-related behaviors. "A distinctive set of feminist methods for psychological research are not only futile but dangerous," and "any method can be misused in sexist ways" (Peplau & Conrad, 1989, p. 380). This view rejects the notion that methodology is gendered or that feminist research must be conducted by women or exclusively on women. Instead, some feminist psychologists (Hyde & Durik, 2001; Peplau & Conrad, 1989) argue that the use of diverse and appropriate methods is best for the study of women and gender-related behaviors.

To adequately study gender contrasts, research must include men (or boys) as well as women (or girls). Such comparisons are the subject matter of gender similarities and differences, and this research cannot include only one sex or the other. However, the necessary research must differ from much prior research, because so much of the existing research concerning gender is filled with serious bias.

Several groups of feminist empiricist researchers have alerted researchers to the potential for inadvertently introducing sexist bias into research and have presented some suggestions for conducting nonsexist psychological research. Maureen McHugh and her colleagues (McHugh, Koeske, & Frieze, 1986) acknowledged that psychology research has included biases, some of them unintentional. An unwarranted confidence in traditional research methods is one source of bias. In addition, bias can come from the theories and explanations researchers use as well as from inappropriate labeling and definitions.

Unwarranted confidence in traditional research methods occurs, for example, when psychologists accept that observations of behavior are objective. Observations are not necessarily free of sexist (or other) biases, because the observer may be biased and the *context* of the observation is rarely included in the analysis of the situation. The process of measurement itself fails to capture critical aspects of experience. For example, various measurements may fail to capture the experience of women who are battered (Smith, Smith, & Earp, 1999), and these failures influence the design and implementation of effective programs for battered women. More comprehensive definitions and conceptualization can help to solve these problems.

Gender may be part of the context of research and yet go unmentioned in the study. For example, the gender of the participants may be a subject variable in the study, but the gender of the experimenter usually is not. The gender of the experimenter may affect the behavior of participants, yet researchers rarely consider this factor.

Bias in an explanatory system occurs when researchers use broad terms (such as *hormones* or *modeling*) to explain specific behaviors. Appropriate explanations should take many factors into account, including social, cultural, biological, and situational factors. Inappropriate labeling and definitions occur in gender research when differences exist and one variation is labeled in a derogatory way. For example, women's attention to the context of behavior has been labeled as "dependence," a term that carries negative connotations. Researchers should avoid placing value-laden labels on behaviors before they have evidence of the value, consider the context of the behavior, include both women and men in research on gender-related behaviors, or give appropriate emphasis to topics of interest to both men and women (McHugh et al., 1986). It may not be possible to eliminate gender bias in research, but such bias can be decreased. Critical thinking can lead to an appropriate skepticism and a reformulation for gender research that includes a step-by-step consideration of how bias can enter the study of gender at any point (Caplan & Caplan, 1994).

Specific analysis techniques can reduce the bias in evaluating research, depending on the technique chosen. The development and use of a statistical technique called **meta-**

analysis allows researchers to evaluate results from several experimental studies and thereby determine the overall size of various effects. This information is related to practical significance because it can reveal which results are small and which are large. Janet Hyde (1986) explained that meta-analysis allows "the synthesis or integration of numerous studies on a single topic and a quantitative or statistical approach to that synthesis" (p. 3). She contended that meta-analysis is preferred over evaluations that count the outcomes or combine probabilities from various studies because meta-analysis allows similar studies to be combined and statistically evaluated. Researchers have performed hundreds of meta-analyses related to gender, which have contributed to the understanding of the magnitude of these gender-related differences.

Analysis and reporting results also require changes (Hyde, 1994). Researchers should conduct all appropriate significance tests and report all (even nonsignificant) findings and sizes of effects, exercising caution in interpreting results so as to make appropriate conclusions, and applying appropriate scientific standards to assure that findings are not misused. All of these suggestions are intended to make the research on sex and gender more scientifically rigorous and thus eliminate the biases that have been so common in this area, creating a feminist empiricism.

CONSIDERING DIVERSITY

The activities identified as science arose in 16th- and 17th-century western Europe, and science is filled with the assumptions and biases of that cultural climate. However, the urge to understand the world is common for all cultures over the world and throughout history, and all have developed some understanding of physical, biological, and social existence. Some of these conceptualizations have been similar to the views of modern science, yet many have differed substantially. One view holds that the philosophy of the culture was important in its development of how the world works. The cultures that did not develop this type of science took an alternative path due to their view of the world and how it operates. An alternative view is that science is Eurocentric, and its proponents believe that this view of science is more original and unique than it is.

For example, one view of Indian science explains that the theme of the unity of nature and humanity dominated the religions of India (Hinduism and Buddhism), and thus the intellectual climate in India was not conducive to the development of science (Ronan, 1982). An alternative view ("Pages," 2003) holds that a strong rationalist orientation dominated Indian philosophy between 1000 B.C. and A.D. 400, creating the climate for many scientific and medical discoveries. These developments were influential on Greek philosophy and science and are compatible with 18th- and 19th-century European philosophies of science.

Opinions of African contributions to science also vary. One view holds that the African conception of nature is one of connection rather than the opposition, objectivity, rationalism, and dominance that characterize western science (Harding, 1986). This concentration on connection leads to a reluctance to divide the world into nonoverlapping categories, including a split between self and nature. Such a split is essential to the type of objectivity for which science strives, but African philosophy found such divisions impossible. A different view of African science (Emeagwali, 1989/2003) holds that major engineering accomplishments occurred in ancient northern and central Africa. Indeed, one of these accomplishments was mentioned in the headline article: the great stone ruins of Zimbabwe that Europeans had such a difficult time accepting as an African construction.

Divisions of opinion also exist for the scientific contributions from the Middle East and China. One view (Ronan, 1982) proposed that the Chinese outlook regarded the entire universe as a vast unified organism, with humans and the physical world as part of this unity, and this philosophy hindered the development of science. Another view (Ajram, 1992) held that inventions and discoveries from China have been overlooked by western scientists, and many discoveries by Europeans were actually rediscoveries made by Chinese and Middle Eastern scholars hundreds of years earlier.

Native Americans also developed a complex, sophisticated worldview, but that view differs from the western one. The Native American worldview sees nature as intertwined with humanity rather than as describing the two in dynamic opposition (Fee, 1986; Faye, 2001). The earth is a living whole, filled with spirits. This view can be seen as compatible with modern quantum physics (Faye, 2001), but Native Americans did not develop science and technology as Europeans did.

Thus, differing opinions exist concerning science and the assumptions that are necessary for the development of scientific thought. Some opinions hold that science is uniquely western, but other views propose that scientific contributions have developed in many cultures.

■ SUMMARY

A "science war" is currently under way, with critics maintaining that traditional science is not (and cannot be) objective. This criticism has prompted scientists to examine the extent to which societal values are included in the process of research, producing biased and inaccurate results. The history of gender research is filled with examples of scientists' bias in studying gender issues.

Science as a method of gathering information can be traced back to the 16th century and rests on philosophical traditions that assert the advantages of an objective, observation-based understanding of the world. By using descriptive methods such as correlational studies and surveys, researchers gather and evaluate information that leads them to understand the world. By using the experimental method, researchers can develop an understanding of the cause-and-effect relationship between an independent variable and a dependent variable. Although the ex post facto method resembles experimentation, it differs in procedure and in the type of information it yields: Ex post facto studies do not involve the manipulation of independent variables and do not allow the determination of causality.

All studies with gender as a subject variable are ex post facto designs, and none have the ability to reveal the cause of any differences they might show. Gender can be an independent variable in experimental studies when, for example, the researcher manipulates the description of targets, identifying some as male and some as female. This type of approach treats gender as a social category and, like all laboratory research, suffers from artificiality.

Dissatisfaction with traditional quantitative research has led to a growing interest in qualitative research methods among psychologists. These methods include case studies, interviews, ethnography, and focus groups. Researchers using these approaches acknowledge that they are part of the research process, try to treat their participants as equals, and attempt to preserve the complexity of the situations they study.

Bias can enter the research process at any point, and the history of gender studies is filled with examples of bias. Some have argued that science has a masculinist bias, and theories such as Freud's psychodynamic theory have a clear bias against women. Any of the steps in conducting research can be contaminated by personal bias. In addition, studies that reveal gender-related differences may show a difference that is statistically significant—that is, not due to chance. Yet the difference may not have any practical significance; for instance, it may not reveal important differences between women and men.

Solutions to the bias in science include an abandonment of science, which is unlikely. Less drastic measures include recommendations for making researchers more careful. Those researchers who advise taking care to avoid sexist bias in research can be described as feminist empiricists. On the other hand, some researchers advocate abandoning the traditional scientific method and adopting alternatives that center on

women and that use different methods of gaining information, especially qualitative research methods such as ethnography and interview studies. The term *feminist standpoint epistemologies* applies to those who want to create a woman-centered approach to researching the female experience. In psychological research, feminist empiricists are more numerous than feminist standpoint epistemologists, and some psychologists have considered the problems and proposed solutions for carrying out nonsexist research. Feminist standpoint epistemologies can add new dimensions to the study of both women and men, but abandonment of traditional scientific methods is unlikely. Some feminist scholars argue against excluding any method and propose a more objective feminist empiricism.

Science arose in Europe in the 16th century and has spread around the world. All cultures developed a knowledge of the natural world, but many did not develop western-style science because those cultures held a worldview that was incompatible with science. Cultures such as those of ancient China and those of many Native American societies held the view that nature is an integrated whole that cannot be analyzed. Nonetheless, those cultures developed technology and an understanding of how the world works.

▨ GLOSSARY

case study   a qualitative method that focuses on gathering extensive information about a single person or a small group.

constructionists   a group of critics of science who argue that reality is constructed through perception and is inevitably subject to bias. Included in this bias is all scientific observation, thus excluding science from its claim of objectivity.

correlational study   a descriptive research method that requires researchers to measure two factors known to occur within a group of people to determine the degree of relationship between the two factors.

data   representations, usually in numerical form, of some facet of the phenomenon that the researcher observes.

dependent variable   the factor in an experiment that the experimenter measures to determine whether the manipulation of the independent variable has an effect.

descriptive research methods   a group of research methods, including naturalistic observation, surveys, and correlational studies, that yield descriptions of the observed phenomena.

empirical observation   collecting information through direct observation.

ethnography a type of qualitative research in which the researcher becomes immersed in a situation in order to make observations and interpretations of that situation.

experiment a type of study in which a researcher manipulates an independent variable and observes the changes in a dependent variable; only through experiments can researchers learn about cause-and-effect relationships.

ex post facto study a type of nonexperimental research design that involves the comparison of subjects, who are placed in contrast groups, on the basis of some preexisting characteristic of the subjects.

focus group a qualitative research method consisting of a discussion involving a group of people centered around a specific topic.

hypothesis a statement about the expected outcome of a study.

independent variable the factor in an experiment that the experimenter manipulates to create a difference that did not previously exist in the participants.

interview a type of qualitative study in which respondents are interviewed in order to determine patterns or commonalities among their responses.

meta-analysis a statistical analysis that allows the evaluation of many studies simultaneously.

operational definition a definition of a variable in terms of operations used to obtain information on that variable, rather than in terms of concepts underlying that variable.

practical significance an important result with practical implications; different from statistical significance.

qualitative research research that focuses on understanding complexity and context rather than distilling situations to sets of numbers.

quantification the process of turning observations into numerical data.

quantitative research research that uses numerical data and statistical analysis.

statistically significant result a result obtained by analysis with statistical tests and found unlikely to have been obtained on the basis of chance alone.

subject variable a characteristic of the subjects, such as gender, that allows researchers to form contrast groups in quasi-experimental studies.

survey a descriptive research method involving the measurement of attitudes through the administration and interpretation of questionnaires.

variable a factor of interest to researchers; something that can have more than one value, as opposed to a constant, which has only one constant value.

▪ SUGGESTED READINGS

Hyde, Janet Shibley; & Durik, Amanda M. (2001). Psychology of women and gender in the 21st century. In Jane S. Halonen & Stephen F. Davis (Eds.), *The many faces of psychological research in the 21st century.* Retrieved December 12, 2001, from http://teachpsych. lemoyne.edu/teachpsych/faces/facesindex.html
In this online volume sponsored by the Society for the Teaching of Psychology, Hyde and Durik review the methods of psychology as they have been used to research women and gender.

Peplau, Letitia Anne; & Conrad, Eva. (1989). Beyond non-sexist research: The perils of feminist methods in psychology. *Psychology of Women Quarterly, 13,* 379–400. Peplau and Conrad criticize the concept that a feminist methodology is necessary for feminist research in psychology, contending that any method can be sexist or feminist. They instead argue for the use of a variety of methods. Despite its age, this article remains relevant to the discourse on nonsexist research methods.

Riger, Stephanie. (1992). Epistemological debates, feminist voices: Science, social values, and the study of women. *American Psychologist, 47,* 730–740.
Many subsequent articles discuss this topic, but this excellent article clearly outlines the different positions and ongoing debates about the scientific method. Although the article is not easy reading, Riger does a fine job of summarizing these complex issues.

Schiebinger, Londa. (1999). *Has feminism changed science?* Cambridge, MA: Harvard University Press.
Schiebinger's book does not concentrate on psychology but covers diverse fields of science. Her book presents not only feminist scholarship and its influence, but also women who are scientists and the influence that these female scientists have exerted on their specific fields. She also offers a sharp critique of the biases that female students encounter in pursuing science careers.

3 HORMONES AND CHROMOSOMES

 **HEADLINE** Mood for Thought: Is the New Drug Sarafem a Miracle Treatment for Severe PMS or Just Prozac in Disguise?
Harper's Bazaar, September 2001

 **HEADLINE** Testosterone Rules: It Takes More Than Just a Hormone to Make a Fellow's Trigger Finger Itch
Discover, March 1997

> A frazzled grocery shopper nears the point of breakdown as she struggles to wrestle a cart loose from the rack. A harried wife berates her innocent husband because she can't locate her keys. A pained woman clutches her stomach as the words bloating and irritability drift across the TV screen. According to the commercials' voice-over, these women suffer from premenstrual dysphoric disorder (PMDD), the evil cousin of PMS, and finally, there's treatment for it, in the form of Sarafem. (Naversen, 2001, p. 252)

The appearance of the drug Sarafem provoked controversy, such as that featured in Laurel Naversen's (2001) headline story. This story took a skeptical approach to the use of Sarafem for the treatment of premenstrual syndrome (PMS) and unlike most popular reports, even questioned the validity of the diagnoses of PMS and premenstrual dysphoric disorder (PMDD).

In the article "Testosterone Rules," endocrinologist Robert Sapolsky (1997) works toward refuting the role of testosterone in violent behavior. Unlike most of the media coverage and the dominant popular belief, Sapolsky presented the case that the relationship between testosterone and aggression is complex, rather than a simple, straightforward cause and effect.

Both these popular articles considered the role of hormones in a variety of behaviors, and both included some skepticism about the simple view that hormones rule behavior. That skepticism is inconsistent with many people's view, which holds that hormones are not only the basis of femininity and masculinity but also the basis of many behavior problems.

Is the role of hormones in behavior simple or complex? What role do hormones play in physical development and ongoing behavior? Are hormones the key to the differences between males and females? Or are chromosomes the key? To answer these questions, this chapter explores the contribution of chromosomes and the effect of hormones on human development from conception throughout prenatal development and again during puberty. When hormonal or chromosomal abnormalities occur, individuals may vary from the pattern of developing into women or men. Instead, these individuals develop both male and female characteristics, providing revealing examples of the roles of chromosomes and hormones in the development of sex and gender. Finally, this chapter examines the role of hormones in adult behavior, including the relationships mentioned in the headlines between hormone levels and the behaviors associated with premenstrual syndrome and with aggression.

THE ENDOCRINE SYSTEM AND STEROID HORMONES

Hormones are substances released from **endocrine glands** to circulate throughout the body in the bloodstream. Receptors on various organs are sensitive to specific hormones, which produce many different actions at various sites. Although the body contains many endocrine glands that secrete many different hormones, **steroid hormones** relate to differences between the sexes and reproduction. The reproductive organs, the ovaries and testes, are the **gonads.** These organs are obviously among the physical characteristics differentiating the sexes and are also essential to reproduction, but the ovaries and testes are not the only endocrine glands that are important for sexual development and functioning.

Two brain structures, the hypothalamus and the pituitary gland, are essential to regulate the production of sex hormones. The complex action of the hypothalamus results in the production of a class of hormones called **releasing hormones,** including gonadotropin-releasing hormone. This hormone acts on the **pituitary gland,** prompting it to release other hormones. **Tropic hormones** are among those products, including gonadotropins. These hormones circulate through the bloodstream and stimulate the ovaries and testes to release their hormones. Thus, the release of hormones by the gonads is the result of a cascade of events, beginning with the hypothalamus and then the pituitary. Figure 3.1 summarizes the action of these glands and hormones.

Gonadal hormones are of the steroid type; that is, all gonadal hormones are derived from cholesterol and consist of a structure that includes four carbon rings. The two main classes of gonadal hormones are **androgens** and **estrogens.** Although people tend to think of androgens as male hormones and estrogens as female hormones, that belief is inaccurate—each sex produces both types of hormones. The most common of the androgens is **testosterone,** and the most common of the estrogens is **estradiol.** Men typically produce a greater proportion of androgens than estrogens, and women typically produce a greater portion of estrogens than androgens.

The gonads also secrete a third type of hormone, the **progestins.** The most common progestin is progesterone, which plays a role in preparing a woman's body for pregnancy.

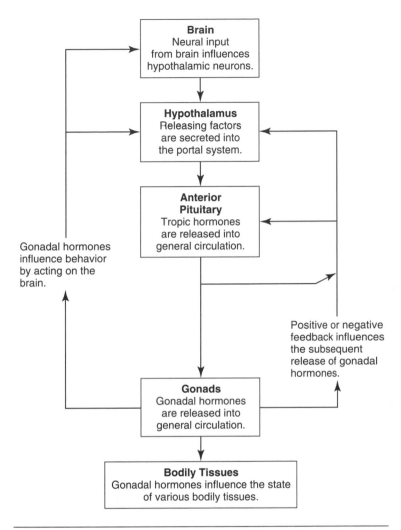

FIGURE 3.1 *A Summary Model of the Regulation of Gonadal Hormones*

Source: From *Biopsychology* (2nd ed.), by John P. J. Pinel, 1993, Boston: Allyn and Bacon. Copyright © 1993 by Allyn and Bacon. Reprinted by permission.

Men also secrete progesterone, but its function for the male body is unknown (Pinel, 2003). The chemical structure is similar for the androgens, estrogens, and progestins.

The gonads are not the only glands that produce steroid hormones; the adrenal glands also produce small amounts of both hormones. These hormones are one factor involved in differentiating male and female.

STAGES OF DIFFERENCES BETWEEN THE SEXES

Humans (and most other animals) are sexually dimorphic; that is, they come in two different physical versions—female and male. This **sexual dimorphism** is the result of development that begins with conception and ends at puberty, resulting in men and women who are capable of sexual reproduction. One way to conceptualize sexual dimorphism is to consider it the product of five stages: genetic, gonadal, hormonal, internal genitalia, and external genitalia (Kaplan, 1980). The *genetic stage* refers to the inheritance of the chromosomes related to sex. The *gonadal stage* includes the development of the gonads. The *hormonal stage* begins prenatally, with the secretion of androgens and estrogens. Hormonal development also occurs at puberty, producing mature, functional gonads. The stage at which *internal genitalia,* the internal reproductive organs, develop occurs prenatally and affects not only the ovaries and testes but also other internal structures relating to reproductive functioning. Therefore, the **internal genitalia** consist of the internal structures related to reproduction: ovaries, Fallopian tubes, uterus, and upper vagina in women; testes, prostate gland, seminal vesicles, and vas deferens in men. The **external genitalia** are reproductive structures that can be seen without internal examination: clitoris, labia, and vaginal opening in women; and penis and scrotum in men. These developments result in differences that are apparent at birth. The stage of developing *external genitalia* occurs later during the prenatal period than the development of internal genitalia.

In the development of sex characteristics, prenatal development is critically important. For a clear pronouncement of "It's a boy" or "It's a girl," a great many prenatal events must occur in a coordinated sequence. These prenatal events occur within a complex set of stages that usually results in a girl or a boy, but sometimes things go wrong. When things go wrong, the result is a baby who has some abnormalities as a result of a combination of female and male patterns of development. These mistakes are rather rare, but these cases are revealing because they provide a means of understanding the necessary elements of normal development.

SEXUAL DIFFERENTIATION

The development of sexual differences is a complex process. Physical differences between men and women start at conception—the fertilization of an ovum by a sperm cell. Most cells in the human body contain 23 pairs of chromosomes, but ova and sperm carry half that amount of chromosomal material. In the fertilized ovum, the full amount of genetic material is present, with half coming from the mother's ovum and half from the father's sperm.

Of the 23 pairs of human chromosomes, pair number 23 is the one that is critical in determining chromosomal sex. Although most chromosomes are X shaped, only those in pair 23 are called **X chromosomes.** An individual who inherits two of these X chromosomes (one X from the mother and the other X from the father) will have the genetic patterns to develop according to the female pattern. Individuals who inherit one X and one **Y chromosome** (the X from the mother and the Y from the father) will have the genetic information to develop according to the male pattern. Therefore, normal girls and women have the XX pattern of chromosome pair 23, and normal boys and men have the XY pattern.

The presence of the XY chromosome constellation is only the first factor that produces male physiology, and its presence is not sufficient to produce a normal male. Other configurations are possible for pair 23, but those patterns are abnormalities, discussed later in the section titled "When Things Go Wrong."

Development of Male and Female Physiology

After conception, the fertilized ovum starts to grow, first by dividing into two cells, then four, and so on. The ball of cells becomes larger and starts to differentiate; that is, they begin to form the basis for different structures and organs. Within the first 6 weeks of prenatal development, no difference exists between male and female embryos, even in their gonads. Both the embryos with the XX pattern and those with the XY pattern have the same structures, and this replication signifies that both types of embryos have the potential to develop into individuals who look like and have the internal reproductive organs of either boys or girls.

The Reproductive Organs.   Both male and female embryos have a **Wolffian system,** which has the capacity to develop into the male internal reproductive system, and a **Müllerian system,** which has the capacity to develop into the female internal reproductive system. During the third month of prenatal development, two processes typically begin to occur to fetuses with the XY chromosome pattern to further the developing male pattern.

The first involves the production of androgens. Information on the Y chromosome prompts the development of fetal testes, which produce androgens. The presence of androgens stimulates the development of the Wolffian system. The growth of the testes further increases production of testosterone, which stimulates development of the male pattern. The second process that prompts male development is the production of Müllerian-inhibiting substance, which causes the Müllerian system to degenerate.

Therefore, one type of secretion prompts the Wolffian system to develop into the male internal reproductive organs, and the other causes the female Müllerian system to degenerate. One action produces a masculinization and the other a defemininization of the developing fetus, resulting in male internal reproductive organs in the fetus.

Figure 3.2 shows how the male reproductive system develops from the Wolffian system, creating testes, vas deferens, and seminal vesicles. This figure also illustrates how both male and female reproductive structures originate from the same prenatal structures.

The fetal ovaries produce few estrogens, but the development of the female reproductive system requires no surge of fetal hormones. In female embryos, the Wolffian system degenerates and the Müllerian system develops, resulting in ovaries, uterus, Fallopian tubes, and the upper part of the vagina. Figure 3.2 also shows how the female reproductive system develops from the Müllerian system.

At 6 weeks, all human fetuses have the antecedents of both male (Wolffian) and female (Müllerian) reproductive ducts.

Male   Wolffian System   **Female**

Developing testis   Developing ovary

Müllerian System

Under the influence of testicular testosterone, the Wolffian system develops, and Müllerian-inhibiting substance causes the Müllerian system to degenerate.

In the absence of testosterone, the Müllerian system develops into female reproductive ducts, and the Wolffian system fails to develop.

Seminal vesicle   Fallopian tube

Vas deferens   Ovary

                                             Uterus

Testis   Upper part of vagina

Scrotum

FIGURE 3.2 *Development of Internal Reproductive Systems*

Source: From *Biopsychology* (2nd ed.), by John P. J. Pinel, 1993, Boston: Allyn and Bacon. Copyright © 1993 by Allyn and Bacon. Reprinted by permission.

Six weeks after conception, the external genitalia of male and female fetuses are also identical. The structures that will become the penis and scrotum in males and the clitoris, outer and inner labia, and vaginal opening in females have not yet differentiated. The fetal structures that exist at this point have the potential to develop into either male or female external genitalia, depending on the presence of androgens, especially testosterone.

Figure 3.3 shows the development of the external genitalia for both the male and female patterns. Notice that the structures are identical at 6 weeks after conception but start to differentiate into the two different patterns after the 7th week of gestation.

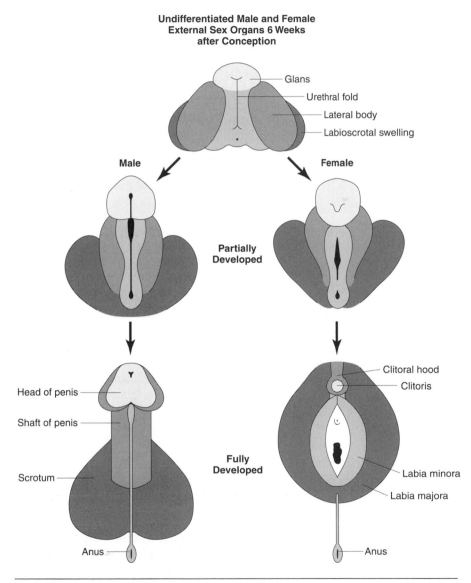

FIGURE 3.3   *Development of Male and Female External Genitalia*

Source: From *Biopsychology* (2nd ed.), by John P. J. Pinel, 1993, Boston: Allyn and Bacon. Copyright © 1993 by Allyn and Bacon. Reprinted by permission.

Prenatal production of androgens produces the male pattern, and the absence of androgens results in an incomplete version of the female pattern. If few or no hormones of either type are present, a fetus will develop external genitals that appear more like the female than the male structures, suggesting that the basic pattern for development is female (Pinel, 2003). These prenatal hormone effects organize developing fetuses around the female or male pattern, resulting in permanent changes in the ability to produce hormones and also in the existence and function of reproductive organs.

The Nervous System.   During prenatal development, the hormones that produce sexual dimorphism in the body also affect the brain, making it possible for the brain structure and function to vary by sex. However, sexual dimorphism of the brain is not as obvious as the differences between female and male reproductive systems.

Investigations of structural differences between the brains of women and men have concentrated on several specific structures, but a gender difference exists concerning the entire brain: The brains of men are larger than those of women. Unlike many of the gender differences, this one is present at birth (Breedlove, 1994). The meaning of this difference, however, is unclear, but most (and perhaps all) of the difference can be explained by differing body size. That is, the ratio of brain weight to body size is very similar for women and men.

Except for the difference in brain size, the other structural differences do not exist at birth. Thus, any differences might be influenced by experience rather than the result of biological development. The identified structural differences are small, but some researchers have interpreted these differences as very meaningful. Figure 3.4 shows two views of the brain, one view as seen from the top, and another view as seen cut down the middle (a cross section). The view of the brain from the top shows that the cerebral cortex is divided down the middle into two halves, or hemispheres. This division forms a left cerebral hemisphere and a right cerebral hemisphere. The view through the midsection shows some of the structures in the brain beneath the cerebral cortex. These structures—the anterior commissure, the massa intermedia, and the corpus callosum—are all structures that, according to some researchers, are sexually dimorphic. In addition, the left and right cerebral hemispheres may also differ in men and women.

Beginning in the 1800s, research indicated that, despite appearances, the cerebral hemispheres are not mirror images of each other (Springer & Deutsch, 1998). Rather, the two hemispheres appeared to direct different mental abilities: The left hemisphere is specialized for language and speech, and the right hemisphere for spatial abilities. The concept of **lateralization** holds that the left and right hemispheres are each specialized for different functions. A great deal of research and theory has explored gender differences in the lateralization of the cerebral hemispheres, and most research is consistent in showing that women have less lateralized cerebral functions than men. That is, women tend to have both the language and spatial functions more equally represented in both hemispheres, whereas men tend to have language represented in the left hemisphere and spatial abilities represented in the right. An evaluation of this research (Hiscock, Inch, Jacek, Hiscock-Kalil, & Kalil, 1994; Hiscock, Israelian, Inch, Jacek, & Hiscock-Kalil, 1995) showed that the gender differences in laterality are small, accounting for 1% to 2% of the variation in

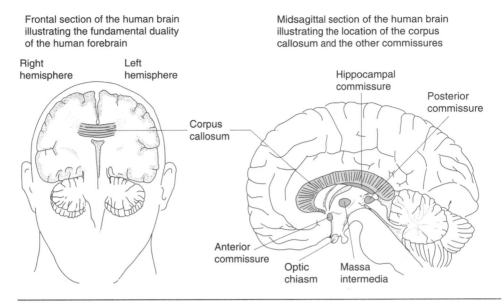

FIGURE 3.4   *Cerebral Commissures and the Hemispheres of the Human Brain*

Source: From *Biopsychology* (2nd ed.), by John P. J. Pinel, 1993, Boston: Allyn and Bacon. Copyright © 1993 by Allyn and Bacon. Reprinted by permission.

GENDERED VOICES

Will I Be Smarter?

Male brains are larger than female brains, and this situation has lead to much debate regarding the relative intelligence of women and men. The relationship between brain weight and intelligence is not entirely clear and has been the topic of research and debate for over a century. The initial belief that larger brains make for greater intelligence has been abandoned—under that metric, elephants would be smarter than humans. The measurement of the ratio of brain weight to body size puts humans at the top of the scale, and thus it has been accepted (by humans, at least) as the standard.

Although the ratio of brain weight to body size among species is an index of intelligence, the variations within species are difficult to interpret. The difference in brain weight between men and women falls into this debate. When considering the ratio of brain weight to body size, the interpretation of gender difference varies; some authorities argue that this gender difference is reduced, others contend that it is eliminated, and some even claim that it is reversed (see Breedlove, 1994, for a brief summary of this argument). The division of opinion may reflect a controversy regarding what measurement to use to define body size. Should the measurement be body weight, height, or skin surface? Each of these measurements has both advocates and opponents.

When I explained these arguments and problems to one of my classes, a student listening to this lecture posed a question that frames the problem: "If I lose weight, does that mean that I will be smarter?" She wasn't serious, but her question highlights the obvious absurdity of using individual body weight in the calculation of intelligence.

lateralization. This magnitude of difference means that other individual factors are much more important than gender in understanding variations in lateralization. Chapter 4 includes an exploration of mental abilities that relate to brain lateralization and an evaluation of this gender difference.

Several of the structures in the brain that connect the left and right sides of the brain show gender differences. The anterior commissure, massa intermedia of the thalamus, and corpus callosum all provide such connections, but clear evidence for their sexual dimorphism is sketchy (Breedlove, 1994).

The evidence for sexual dimorphism in the brain is strongest for a small section of the hypothalamus called the **sexually dimorphic nucleus (SDN).** This structure is larger in male rats and in men than in female rats and in women (Gorski, 1987; Swaab & Fliers, 1985). Although not understood, its function may be related to sexual behavior or gender identity. This nucleus is very sensitive to testosterone and estrogen, so the presence or absence of these hormones influences its development. In humans, gender differences in this structure do not exist at birth. Between birth and ages 2 to 4 years, the number of cells in this structure increases rapidly (Swaab, Gooren, & Hofman, 1995). The number of cells begins to decrease in girls but not in boys, creating a sexual dimorphism that peaks in young adulthood to middle age (Breedlove, 1994). Otherwise, the differences in structure between female and male brains are small. Table 3.1 summarizes the results of studies on structural differences between women's and men's brains.

In addition to brain differences, other nervous system structures show gender differences. For example, one of the nervous system sex differences is in the **spinal nucleus of the bulbocavernosus** (Breedlove, 1994). The spinal nucleus of the bulbocavernosus is 25% larger in men than in women. These neurons aid in the ejaculation of sperm in men and constrict the opening of the vagina in women. These spinal neurons are present in both male and female rats at birth, but the neurons die in female rats. In male rats, the presence of androgens allows these neurons to survive. Therefore, there is a larger difference between the nervous systems of male and female rats than male and female humans, and a simple generalization from rats to humans would be invalid.

TABLE 3.1 *Summary of Brain Differences between Men and Women*

Structure	Difference
Cerebral hemispheres	Men may be more lateralized than women for language and spatial functions
Sexually dimorphic nucleus (SDN) of hypothalamus	SDN in men is 2.5 times larger than in women
Splenium of corpus callosum	Early studies indicated larger and more bulbous splenium in women; later studies found an interaction with age and gender
Anterior commissure	Evidence for sexual dimorphism is sketchy
Massa intermedia of the thalamus	Evidence for sexual dimorphism is sketchy

Another caution is related to interpretations for sex and gender differences in understanding hormonal versus social factors. The tendency exists to see a one-way chain of causality in which genetic and hormonal influences produce physiology, which in turn, produces behavior. As S. Marc Breedlove (1994) pointed out, this reasoning is false because it is impossible to separate biological from social influences and because the causality goes both ways. He contended that it is possible to concentrate on either biological or psychological measurements, but because biologists and psychologists are studying the same phenomena, any distinctions they make are illusory. In addition, social influences can affect behavior, which can alter the brain. For example, any change in the number, size, or connection of neurons in the structure of the brain constitutes a biological measurement, but such alterations will have psychological implications in terms of behavioral changes. Conversely, behavior can affect brain chemistry, which can alter brain structure, resulting in biological changes. Breedlove warned against confusing biological measures and biological influences, claiming that psychological and biological influences are impossible to separate.

Gonadal, hormonal, genital, and brain organization are not sufficient to produce sexually interested and sexually active people capable of reproduction. Such changes depend on the activating effects of hormones during puberty.

Changes during Puberty

The levels of circulating hormones are low during infancy and childhood, but these levels increase during puberty, the onset of sexual maturity. The changes that occur during this period include not only fertility but also the characteristic adolescent growth spurt and the development of secondary sex characteristics. These characteristics constitute the differences between male and female bodies other than reproductive ones (see Figure 3.5). Both sexes experience the growth of body and pubic hair and the appearance of acne. Young men experience the growth of facial hair, larynx enlargement, hairline recession, and muscle development, whereas young women experience breast development, rounding of body contours, and menarche—the beginning of menstruation. All of these changes are prompted by changes in the release of hormones.

The adolescent growth spurt is the result of muscle and bone growth in response to increased release of growth hormone by the pituitary. Increased production of tropic hormones by the pituitary act on the adrenal glands and the gonads to increase their production of gonadal and adrenal hormones. As puberty begins, the pituitary starts to release two gonadotropic hormones into the bloodstream—**follicle-stimulating hormone (FSH)** and **luteinizing hormone (LH).** These hormones stimulate the gonads to increase their production of estrogens and androgens. Increased circulation of these gonadal hormones results in maturation of the genitals, that is, the development of fertility as well as the development of secondary sex characteristics.

In adolescent boys and adult men, the production of androgens is proportionately higher than their production of estrogens; in adolescent girls and in women, the production of estrogens is proportionately higher than their production of androgens. Again, it would be inaccurate to think of androgens as "male" hormones and estrogens as "female"

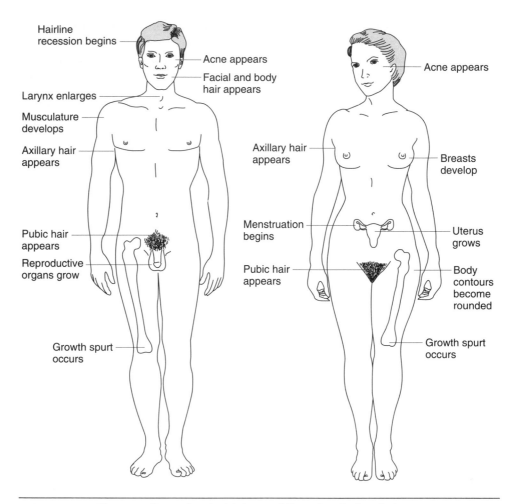

FIGURE 3.5   *Changes Occurring in Males and Females during Puberty*

Source: From *Biopsychology* (2nd ed.), by John P. J. Pinel, 1993, Boston: Allyn and Bacon. Copyright ©
1993 by Allyn and Bacon. Reprinted by permission.

hormones. An example of the influence of one hormone on both sexes is the growth of
pubic and underarm hair: The androgen produced by both boys and girls results in the
growth of pubic and underarm hair in both.

LH and FSH, the hormones that initiate puberty, are also important for reproduction.
In girls and women, the production of these two hormones varies cyclically, whereas in
boys and men, their production is not cyclic (but neither is it entirely steady). The cyclic
variation of LH and FSH produces the menstrual cycle, beginning with an increase in the
production of luteinizing hormone releasing factor and follicle-stimulating hormone re-

leasing factor by the hypothalamus. As with other releasing factors, these two cause the pituitary to produce LH and FSH. Follicle-stimulating hormone stimulates follicles, a group of cells within the ovaries, to mature an ovum. Luteinizing hormone causes the follicle to rupture and release the ovum, which begins to travel down the Fallopian tube toward the uterus. The remainder of the follicle starts to produce the hormone progesterone, which prepares the uterus to receive and implant the ovum, if it happens to be fertilized. Then all of these hormone levels begin to decline. If the ovum is fertilized, pregnancy will produce an increase in estradiol and progesterone, but if the ovum is not fertilized, the prepared lining of the uterus is shed in menstruation, and the cycle starts again. In addition to its biological effects, menstruation also carries a great deal of cultural meaning (see "According to the Media" and "According to the Research").

In boys, puberty causes the maturation of internal and external genitalia, including growth of the penis, seminal vesicles, and prostate. The maturation of seminal vesicles and prostate is necessary for ejaculation of seminal fluid, and sperm production is necessary for fertility. FSH is involved in the production of sperm. LH contributes to the maturation of sperm, but its main function is to stimulate the production of testosterone. Testosterone is controlled by feedback to the hypothalamus, which can inhibit or prompt the production of LH and FSH, which in turn can affect the production of sperm.

The role of hormones is essential in the regulation of fertility, and the role of hormones for sexual activity is very clear in some animals. In rats, for example, the cyclic production of hormones by the females relates to sexual receptivity or level of interest in sexual activity. Female rats are receptive during the time in their cycle that they are fertile, and male rats respond to that receptivity. Hormone levels are also important for the development and maintenance of sexual interest. Rats that have their gonads removed before puberty fail to develop any interest in sexual activity. If their gonads are removed after puberty, their sexual interest fades. In humans, the relationship between hormonal levels and sexual interest is less clear-cut, but some activating effects exist for hormones on sexual interest.

Hormones are also important for the development of sexual interest in humans (Bancroft, 2002). However, sexual interest usually precedes puberty (Hyde & Jaffee, 2000). Around age 10, many children begin to show great curiosity (and perhaps even feelings) concerning sex. One possible mechanism for this development is the maturation of the adrenal glands, which occurs at this time. These glands produce both androgens and estrogens and may be important in the development of sexual interest. Nevertheless, people who do not undergo puberty generally fail to develop much interest in sexual activity (Meyer-Bahlburg, 1980), so hormonal events during preadolescence and puberty may form a cascade of circumstances crucial for the development of sexual interest.

The story is even more complex concerning the maintenance of sexual activity in humans who experience a decline of hormone levels. Such declines can occur for a number of reasons, including removal of the gonads or decreased hormone production associated with aging. For men, removal of the testes tends to produce a decrease in sexual activity, but the extent and rate of decrease varies enormously from person to person (Bancroft, 2002). Some men experience the significant and rapid loss of either ability to get erections or ability to ejaculate or both. Other men experience a slowly decreasing interest in sexual

◪ ACCORDING TO THE MEDIA . . .

Menarche Is a Positive Event, but Menstruation Is Not

Menarche is the first menstrual period, and this event has been depicted in both movies and on television (Kissling, 2002). In both media, girls' first menstrual period appears as an important event, but menstruation is still portrayed as something embarrassing to be concealed or hidden.

In *My Girl* (1991), the character Vada lived with her father, who had not prepared her for her first period (Kissling, 2002). Thus, she was frightened by the sight of the blood. Her father's girlfriend explained menstruation and its meaning, to which Vada replied, "It's not fair! Nothing happens to boys." Vada also interpreted this event as a demarcation between childhood and adulthood, which separated her from her friend Thomas and the activities she had enjoyed as a child.

A similar attitude appeared in the television show *Roseanne,* in an episode in which her younger daughter Darlene has her first menstrual period (Kissling, 2002). This event led Darlene to reject her tomboy childhood and the sports and outdoor activities she had enjoyed in the company of her father. He assumed little had changed, but he felt awkward and embarrassed, an attitude typical of male movie and television characters. Darlene was shown throwing away her sporting equipment because she no longer saw these activities as part of her feminine future, but Roseanne convinced her that her future could be whatever she wanted.

To the characters in the animated television show *King of the Hill,* the menarche of a girl left in the care of Peggy and Hank was a crisis because Hank was in charge. He did not know how to handle the situation and took the young woman to the hospital emergency room. His ineptitude was played for comedy, but the crisis was resolved only when Peggy arrived and took over the task of caring for the girl.

More positive (but still comic) portrayals of menarche appeared in the movie *A Walk on the Moon* (1999) and in the television show *7th Heaven.* The young woman who experienced menarche in *A Walk on the Moon* received support and congratulations from everyone in her family, but her father's knowledge of the event and his remarks embarrassed her. In an episode of *7th Heaven,* the character Lucy was eagerly awaiting her first menstrual period, and the whole family knew about the situation, including a very rare portrayal: a father who was encouraging and supportive. However, his support became an embarrassment to his daughter, and when the awaited event occurred, the father detached himself from the situation, leaving the "women of the house" to arrange a celebration. These media messages are clear in portraying menstruation as an experience into which men should not intrude.

These media portrayals of menarche are relatively recent. Older television shows failed to depict anything related to menarche or menstruation. For example, despite the examination of many facets of the teenage characters' lives in *The Brady Bunch,* menarche and menstruation were never part of any episode (Kissling, 2002). Therefore, the willingness to depict menarche and to show its positive meaning may be a sign that menstruation is losing some of its taboo. On the other hand, the widespread embarrassment and efforts to conceal any signs of menstruation reflect a continuing attitude that it is shameful.

activity, followed by difficulty in ejaculating, and then by loss of ability to achieve erections. Few men remain unaffected by loss of androgens, though replacement testosterone can reverse the decline in sexual interest and possibly in sexual performance. Testosterone replacement therapy has increased with the creation of the testosterone patch and testos-

▣ ACCORDING TO THE RESEARCH . . .

Women Are Ambivalent about Both Their First Menstrual Period and Menstruation

Menarche is a cause for ceremony and celebration in about half of the world's cultures (Beausang & Razor, 2000). However, societies in North America and western Europe are not among those that celebrate menarche. Indeed, the most common attitudes are almost the opposite: shame and embarrassment. Although cultural beliefs hold that the first menstrual period is an important event that signifies the girl is becoming a woman, menstruation is a taboo topic about which many women have ambivalent or negative attitudes. Prepubertal girls receive messages that when they begin to menstruate, they will probably experience discomfort, and they should attempt to conceal their status as a menstruating woman. This combination of information sends the mixed message of celebration and shame that may parallel the portrayals of menarche in the media.

Unlike the media portrayals, most girls receive preparation for their first menstrual period (Koff & Rierdan, 1995). For most girls, this information comes from their mothers, although female friends and school personnel may also be sources of information. When asked to give advice about how younger girls should be prepared for their first period, a group of 6th-grade girls advised more information from mothers and greater willingness on the part of mothers to talk about menstruation while not intruding on girls' privacy. This balance seems difficult for mothers to achieve, but girls expressed a desire to receive information and support from mothers rather than from written material, films, or school instruction.

Like the media portrayals, mothers are the preferred source of information, and college women expressed the value of receiving adequate preparation from mothers (Beausang & Razor, 2000). Over 90% of the women who recalled menarche as a positive event in their lives said that they received information about menstruation from their mothers rather than other sources. However, completely positive feelings about menarche and menstruation were rare among this group, and many believed that they were not adequately prepared for the experience of first menstruation. A similar split of attitudes appeared in a study of Canadian women (Lee, 2002). Some women reported that the experience of menstruating reminded them of being a woman and made them feel renewed. The average rating of the experience of menstruation was positive, but some women reported mixed or very negative feelings associated with the experience, including reports of embarrassment, inconvenience, and discomfort.

Drawing on the negative associations with menstruation, studies have explored how menstrual status affects attitudes toward women. One study (Roberts, Goldenberg, Power, & Pyszczynski, 2002) placed male and female participants in a situation in which they saw evidence that the female confederate with whom they interacted was menstruating (a dropped tampon) or not (a dropped hair clip). Those who saw an item associated with menstruation subsequently expressed less liking for this woman and a tendency to avoid her. Similar negative opinions of menstruating women appeared in a study (Forbes, Adams-Curtis, White, & Holmgren, 2003) that asked female and male participants to rate a menstruating woman and an average woman. Ratings indicated that menstruating women were more irritable, sad, angry, spacey, and annoying but less reasonable, energized, and sexy. The female participants associated menstruation with being maternal, strong, and trustworthy, but the male participants did not. These overwhelmingly negative impressions of menstruation suggest that the menstrual taboo remains strong.

terone gel, and its short-term effects are clear (Sullivan, 2003). However, its long-term safety remains unestablished.

On the other hand, women's sexual interest seems less affected by the removal of ovaries. Indeed, some women report increased sexual motivation after such surgery. One possibility is that the hormones that are important for the maintenance of sexual interest in women are androgens, and so a decrease in estrogen is not critical. Adrenal androgens may be sufficient to maintain sexual interest. Another possibility is that humans are so little controlled by their hormones that drastic physical changes in sexually mature adults are mediated by experience and expectation. Additionally, some combination of hormones and expectancy may account for the variations of sexual motivation in men and women without gonadal hormones.

In summary, LH and FSH produce the changes in reproductive and secondary sex characteristics associated with puberty. In girls, these changes produce cyclic variations in hormone levels that are associated with the maturation and release of an ovum approximately every month. If this ovum is fertilized by a sperm, the fertilized ovum will implant in the uterus and pregnancy will occur. If no fertilization occurs, the lining of the uterus is shed in menstruation, and the process will reoccur. In boys, the changes during puberty produce growth of the penis and maturation of the internal reproductive system, which will allow them to produce and ejaculate sperm. In addition to the physical changes associated with boys' bodies and reproductive systems, raised levels of gonadal hormones seem to be related to the development of sexual interest. Individuals who do not undergo puberty do not develop motivation to participate in sexual activity. However, the maintenance of sexual interest in humans is not directly related to the levels of hormones but instead depends on experience and expectancy.

When Things Go Wrong

A number of events relating to the development of the reproductive system can, but usually do not, go wrong during prenatal development. Problems can originate at several points, beginning before conception with the formation of the mother's ovum or the father's sperm. Yet other problems can arise when the prenatal hormones are not consistent with the genetic configuration of the developing fetus. These mistakes provide contrasts to normal development and highlight the complexities of defining male and female.

Beginning with the single cell consisting of a fertilized ovum, males differ from females in their chromosomes, but the presence of the normal sex chromosome pattern does not guarantee the development of a normal boy or girl. Abnormalities sometimes occur in the assortment of chromosomes carried by the sperm and ova. Instead of the normal 23, sometimes missing or extra chromosomes appear. Several types of chromosomal abnormalities have direct effects on the development of the internal reproductive system, the external genitalia, or both, with resulting hormonal problems.

Abnormalities in Number of Sex Chromosomes.   Several disorders involve the number of sex chromosomes, and studying these disorders allows for an understanding of the role of sex chromosomes in development. All of these disorders result in some problems, often affecting reproductive organs, genitalia, hormone production, fertility, growth, intelligence, and other aspects of development. **Turner syndrome** (or *Turner's syndrome*) occurs when the fertilized ovum has only one chromosome of pair 23—that is, one X. This syndrome is usually described as X0, where the zero stands for the missing chromosome

(Ranke & Saenger, 2001). Individuals with Turner syndrome appear female at birth, because their external genitals develop according to the female pattern. Their prenatal development begins normally, but their Müllerian systems degenerate, producing individuals with no functioning ovaries. At birth the appearance of the external genitalia prompts identification as females, but without ovaries, they produce no estrogens, so they do not undergo puberty or produce ova. With hormone supplements, they appear female but are not fertile.

Another mistake in chromosome number is the presence of an extra X chromosome—the XXX pattern (Harmon, Bender, Linden, & Robinson, 1998). Individuals with the XXX pattern develop prenatally as female, but their development may not be entirely normal. Women with the XXX pattern may have normal intelligence but may have developmental disabilities that affect cognitive ability. They also may have problems that affect their reproductive ability, including menstrual irregularities or amenorrhea (absence of menstrual periods) that results in sterility, but they may not. Women with this chromosomal pattern have been known to have children. Individuals with the XXXX pattern and XXXXX pattern have also been identified (Linden, Bender, & Robinson, 1995). These individuals tend to have more severe developmental problems and are very likely to be seriously developmentally disabled as well as sterile.

Klinefelter syndrome is characterized by the XXY configuration, and this problem is the most common of the sex chromosome abnormalities occurring in 1 case per 600 male births (Visootsak, Aylstock, & Graham, 2001). Individuals with Klinefelter syndrome have male internal and external genitalia, but their testes are small and usually cannot produce sperm, resulting in sterility. They may also develop breasts and a feminized body shape during puberty. Like other people with extra chromosomal material, individuals with Klinefelter syndrome have an increased chance of developmental disabilities. Other configurations of chromosomes are similar to Klinefelter syndrome, including XXXY and XXXXY, which produce more severe problems in the skeletal and reproductive systems as well as severe developmental disabilities.

The XYY chromosome pattern has been the subject of a great deal of publicity. In the early 1960s, articles appeared linking the XYY gene pattern to "aggressive tendencies" and "criminality" (Hubbard & Wald, 1993). These studies were based on the estimate of this gene pattern among men in the general population compared to men in prison, who were more likely to have the XYY pattern than the estimates for men from the general population.

These sensational reports, however, were largely unfounded. When measurements were taken from the general population, the results showed that the large majority of XYY men are not aggressive or criminal. Individuals with the XYY pattern of chromosomes are men who tend to be very tall, and some research (Witkin et al., 1976) indicated that these men were more likely than normal men to be in prison. This further examination of XYY men in prison showed that the XYY inmates were no more likely to be imprisoned for violent crimes than other inmates. They are significantly taller than other men, and like other individuals with extra chromosomal material, XYY individuals are more likely to have lower intelligence test scores. Thus, their height and their lower intelligence, or a combination of the two, may be the reason why a disproportionate number of XYY men are in prison: They are not very adept criminals, and witnesses may find a very tall man easy to identify, making their apprehension more likely than other offenders.

In summary, missing or extra sex chromosomes often affect the development of the sexual organs but more often affect other areas of development, especially intelligence. Both missing chromosomes (Turner syndrome) and extra chromosomes (Klinefelter syndrome) result in sterility, but individuals with the XXX pattern and the XYY pattern may be fertile. This extra chromosomal material does not make individuals "hypermasculine" or "superfeminine." Indeed, extra chromosomes produce developmental problems rather than adding anything useful.

Abnormalities in Prenatal Hormones.   The presence of the XY chromosome pattern is not necessary (or sufficient) for the development of male internal or external genitalia; the hormone testosterone is the key to these developments. Therefore, a fetus that is genetically female (XX pattern) can be masculinized by the addition of testosterone during the period of the third and fourth months of prenatal development. Normally, female fetuses do not produce testosterone during this important period of developing the genitalia, but prenatal exposure to androgens may occur, either through the action of tumors in the adrenal gland or through the pregnant woman's inadvertent or intentional exposure to androgens.

The **adrenogenital syndrome** occurs when the adrenal gland decreases its production of the hormone cortisol, which produces an increase in production of adrenal androgens. For a male fetus or for a boy, increased androgen production is not a very serious problem, except that it accelerates the onset of puberty. For a developing female fetus, however, the presence of excessive androgens produces masculinization of the external genitalia. Although their internal genitals are usually normal because the excess androgens are produced too late to affect this stage of development, these girls are born with a clitoris that may look very much like a small penis. If their genitals appear abnormal at birth, their physicians often recommend to their parents that surgical correction should be done so that their genitals will have a more normal female appearance. This procedure has become very controversial (Fausto-Sterling, 2000) because the surgery often damages nerves to the clitoris, producing permanent sexual responsiveness problems.

These girls have been of interest because their brains were exposed to androgens prenatally, leading researchers to study their behavior and sexual orientation. The early medical and parental attention focused on their genitals makes these girls different from others, so hormone exposure is not their only difference. Early research suggested that adrenogenital syndrome is associated with play activities more typical of boys than girls; that is, these girls are more likely to be "tomboys" (Berenbaum & Snyder, 1995). Later evaluation (Fausto-Sterling, 2000) questioned this interpretation, pointing out the many different criteria that researchers have used to define masculine orientation and the varying results from these studies. As adults, almost all women who had adrenogenital syndrome are heterosexual, like most women.

A more serious problem is **androgen insensitivity syndrome.** This disorder occurs in normal XY male fetuses whose body cells are insensitive to androgens; that is, the androgens produced by their fetal testes will not induce masculinization because the androgen receptors in their bodies do not function normally (Simpson, 2001). These fetuses will develop as though no androgens were present, and at birth the XY baby will appear to be a girl. The internal genitalia are not female, however, because the production of Müllerian-inhibiting substance caused the normal degeneration of the Müllerian system and the presence of the Y chromosome prompted the development of testes (that remain within the abdominal cavity). Thus, these individuals have undescended testes, but their external genitalia appear female.

Individuals with androgen insensitivity syndrome (and their families) can be completely unaware of the disorder until they reach the age at which puberty should occur. Complicating the diagnosis further, their testes produce sufficient estrogen to prompt breast development, increasing their feminine appearance. They have no ovaries, Fallopian tubes, or uterus, so they will not reach **menarche,** the beginning of menstruation. Nor will they grow pubic hair, a characteristic under the control of the androgens, to which they are insensitive. No amount of added androgens will reverse this problem, because their body cells are insensitive to it. Indeed, the levels of androgens circulating in their bloodstream are within the normal range for men, but their bodies are "deaf" to these hormones.

Individuals with androgen insensitivity syndrome are identified as girls at birth, raised as girls, and have no reason to doubt their gender identification for years. At puberty they grow breasts and begin to look like young women, giving them no reason to imagine they are anything but women. Typically, few suspicions arise concerning any abnormality until they fail to grow pubic hair and fail to reach menarche. Even then these symptoms may be discounted for several years due to the variability of sexual development.

When gynecological examination reveals the abnormality of their internal genitalia, these individuals and their families learn that they are, in some sense, men. This information contradicts years of gender role development, and some of these individuals have difficulty adjusting to this information. No treatments exist to masculinize these individuals, so no attempt is made to change their gender identification. However, their gender identity is female, and a longitudinal study of individuals with androgen insensitivity syndrome (Hines, Ahmed, & Hughes, 2003) indicated that they are similar to other women in gender identity, esteem, and well-being. Despite their male chromosomes, these individuals are women in terms of gender identification, physical appearance, and behavior.

All of these examples of when things go wrong illustrate individuals born with characteristics of both sexes. The modern term for these condition is **intersexuality.** The traditional diagnosis for these individuals was **hermaphroditism,** which was restricted to individuals who have both ovarian and testicular tissue—either an ovary on one side of the body and a testicle on the other side, or both types of tissue combined into a structure called an ovotestis. This condition is extremely rare, with no more than 60 cases being identified in Europe and North America within the last century (Money, 1986).

Another provocative example of intersexuality comes from individuals with a genetic enzyme (5-alpha-reductase) deficiency that prevents chromosomal males from developing male external genitalia during the prenatal period. Like individuals with androgen insensitivity syndrome, these babies appear more female than male at birth and are often identified as girls. The appearance of their external genitals is ambiguous, not truly female but definitely not male. Unlike people with androgen insensitivity syndrome, these individuals respond to androgens during puberty and develop masculine characteristics. That is, their voice deepens, their muscles develop, their testes descend into the scrotum, and they grow a penis (Herdt, 1990). If these children had been identified as girls, they no longer fit into that category. However, most of these individuals do not clearly fit into the category of male, either.

Studies of these intersex individuals have reported varying success in their gender identity and sexual functioning. One early study (Imperato-McGinley, Guerrero, Gautier, & Peterson, 1974) reported that the majority of the intersex individuals had made at least fairly successful transitions to the male role. A later study (Rubin, Reinisch, & Haskett, 1981) reported that none did so. A more recent study (Mendonca et al., 1996) reported that some of these individuals choose to be female in their gender identity, whereas most choose to be male. Of those who choose the male role, some are satisfied with their social and sexual identity, whereas some are not. Thus, these individuals may never fit comfortably into either category. Indeed, the New Guinea culture in which this form of intersexuality is relatively common acknowledges the existence of these individuals by devising a third category of sex to describe them (Herdt, 1981).

A third sex or some continuum for sex seems a better choice than the two categories of male and female (Fausto-Sterling, 2000). The intersex individuals represent cases in which chromosomal, hormonal, gonadal, and genital sex are not consistent and show that the determination of sex does not necessarily require complete consistency. These individuals may identify themselves unambiguously as male or female. On the other hand, they may not. For example, individuals with androgen insensitivity syndrome have a male chromosome configuration and normal levels of androgens, but they may look and feel female—they are female in their own opinion and in the opinion of society. Those individuals with 5-alpha-reductase deficiency may have trouble identifying as either male or female. Thus, a dichotomy is not the best conceptualization for the many possibilities of sex.

HORMONES AND BEHAVIOR INSTABILITY

In addition to their role in sexual development and activity, hormones are widely considered to affect other behaviors. The concept of premenstrual syndrome (PMS) has received wide publicity, and with the approval of the drug Sarafem, so has premenstrual dysphoric disorder (PMDD), its "evil cousin," (Naversen, 2001, p. 252). Another of the possible influences of hormones is the effect of testosterone on aggression; the other headline story for this chapter questioned the validity of the belief that this hormone is the basis for aggression: "Raging hormones" might be one cause of unstable, problem behaviors in both men and women, but popular belief may be mistaken about the role of these hormones in problem behavior.

Premenstrual Syndrome

When the advertisements for Sarafem appeared in July 2000, premenstrual syndrome was a very familiar concept, but premenstrual dysphoric disorder was not. "The news of PMDD raised more than a few eyebrows. Women wondered, What is this disorder, and why haven't I heard of it?" (Naversen, 2001, p. 252). The television ads suggested that women who have PMS may have PMDD and need treatment. Millions of women believe that they have PMS, which opened the possibility for those women to consider that they may have PMDD and to ask their physicians for prescriptions of Sarafem. This advertising campaign was quite successful: During the 7 months after its approval, physicians wrote over 200,000 prescriptions for Sarafem (Daw, 2002).

Naversen (2001) reported the case of one woman who was influenced by the advertising and, after a bad day at work and the suggestion by her supervisor that it was "that time of the month," she sought a prescription. Unlike many physicians, this one took the time to ask careful questions about the woman's life and decided that she did not have PMDD, and possibly not even PMS. How, then, did this woman come to see herself as a candidate for a psychoactive drug? What is PMDD and how does it differ from PMS? Is either a legitimate diagnosis? Are these problems produced by hormones or are they the result of advertising and publicity?

Recall that the cyclic variation of LH and FSH produces the menstrual cycle by affecting the release of estrogens and progesterone. In the middle of the cycle, the follicles produce larger amounts of one of the estrogens (estradiol) than during other times of the cycle, and this increase produces a surge of LH and FSH. This surge causes the release of the matured ovum, and the remainder of the follicle then starts to produce progesterone. Therefore, during the ovulatory phase of the cycle, estrogen levels are higher than progesterone levels. During the premenstrual phase of the cycle, both estradiol and progesterone are falling, and progesterone is at a higher level than estradiol. During the menstrual phase, the levels of both hormones are relatively low. Figure 3.6 shows the levels of hormones during the different phases of the cycle.

The notion that women's reproductive systems affect their lives is ancient (Fausto-Sterling, 1992), but the concept of the premenstrual syndrome is quite modern—it can be traced to the 1960s. During this time, Katharina Dalton published research (reviewed by Parlee, 1973) suggesting that women experience a wide variety of negative emotional, cognitive, and physical effects due to the hormonal changes that precede menstruation. These effects became known as a *syndrome,* although the list of symptoms extended to over 150, and some of the symptoms were mutually exclusive (such as *elevated mood* and *depression*).

The symptoms associated with the premenstrual phase of the cycle include headache; backache; abdominal bloating and discomfort; breast tenderness; tension or irritability; depression; increased analgesic, alcohol, or sedative use; decreased energy; and disruption in eating, sleeping, sexual behavior, work, and interpersonal relationships (Dickerson, Mazyck, & Hunter, 2003). The most common among these symptoms are tension and irritability.

All of the hormonal changes that occur during the menstrual cycle have been candidates for the underlying cause of premenstrual syndrome (Dickerson et al., 2003). The possibilities include an excess of estrogens, falling progesterone levels, and the ratio of estrogens to progesterone. However, research has failed to show that hormonal differences vary according to the experience of PMS. This failure to tie any pattern of hormonal changes to the experience of PMS is a major problem for the concept of PMS.

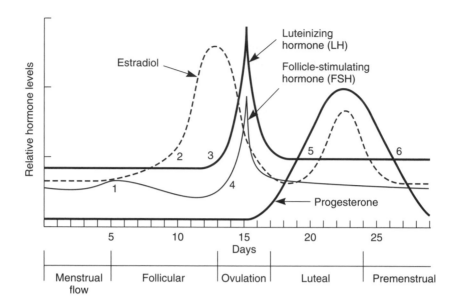

Phases of the Human Menstrual Cycle

1. In response to an increase in FSH, small spheres of cells called ovarian follicles begin to grow around individual egg cells (ova).

2. The follicles begin to release estrogens such as estradiol.

3. The estrogens stimulate the hypothalamus to increase the release of LH and FSH from the anterior pituitary.

4. In response to the LH surge, one of the follicles ruptures and releases its ovum.

5. The ruptured follicle under the influence of LH develops into a corpus luteum (yellow body) and begins to release progesterone, which prepares the lining of the uterus for the implantation of a fertilized ovum.

6. Meanwhile, the ovum is moved into the Fallopian tube by the rowing action of ciliated cells. If the ovum is not fertilized, progesterone and estradiol levels fall and the walls of the uterus are sloughed off as menstrual flow and the cycle begins once again.

FIGURE 3.6   *Hormones during the Menstrual Cycle*

Source: From *Biopsychology* (2nd ed.), by John P. J. Pinel, 1993, Boston: Allyn and Bacon. Copyright © 1993 by Allyn and Bacon. Reprinted by permission.

Other problems come from the changing pattern of research findings on PMS. Inconsistency is one problem (McFarlane, Martin, & Williams, 1988). Until the mid-1970s, researchers tended to find that mood is highest during the ovulatory phase of the cycle and lowest during the premenstrual and menstrual phases. Beginning in the late 1970s, researchers no longer found this pattern. This change may have been attributable to methodological problems in earlier menstrual cycle research. Such problems include the bias that expectation can introduce into studies in which the participants know that the research is about the menstrual cycle, a reliance on participants' memories of symptoms, and the failure to use appropriate comparison groups. Indeed, a random survey of women (Deuster, Adera, & South-Paul, 1999) indicated that only 8.3% experienced PMS.

Jessica McFarlane and her colleagues (McFarlane et al., 1988; McFarlane & Williams, 1994) have conducted two longitudinal studies that avoided the methodological problems from other studies. Both studies involved instructing women (and men) to keep records of their daily moods without knowing that the menstrual cycle was the focus of the study. Both studies included women who were cycling normally, women who were taking oral contraceptives and thus not cycling normally, and men.

The main result of the study by McFarlane and her colleagues (1988) was that no differences in mood stability appeared when comparing the young men and the young women who participated in the study. All participants experienced similar mood changes within a day as well as from day to day. Also, the men and women reported similar variability in mood during the 70 days of the study.

A second study (McFarlane & Williams, 1994) recruited participants who were older than the typical college student participants and lasted at least 12 weeks to cover more menstrual cycles. The analysis for this study included an evaluation of each participant's cyclic mood variation over time. This study also revealed that people experienced cyclic mood variations, but that these changes did not conform to the PMS pattern.

In comparing women who were cycling normally to women taking oral contraceptives and to the men, the women who were cycling normally reported *more pleasant moods* during and immediately after their periods than in the ovulatory or premenstrual periods (McFarlane et al., 1988). The male and female participants experienced cyclicity as the norm, but few reported emotional symptoms consistent with PMS (McFarlane & Williams, 1994). Neither of these studies found evidence to support the concept of PMS, but both studies showed that cyclic variations in mood occur for both men and women.

Several PMS studies have included a component that may provide an explanation for the belief in PMS. These studies (Marván & Cortés-Iniestra, 2001; McFarlane et al., 1988) asked participants to rate their PMS symptoms during the month and then to recall their symptoms at the end of the study. This approach allows an evaluation of the influence of recall bias in memory, which appears as a larger PMS effect in recall than in the daily experience of symptoms. Both of these studies found significant effects for recall: When participants remembered their moods, they reported more symptoms of PMS than when they recorded their moods. These findings strongly suggest that some of the mood changes associated with PMS may be a product of expectation and labeling rather than of hormones. This effect appeared among women in Mexico (Marván & Cortés-Iniestra, 2001) as well as among women in the United States (McFarlane et al., 1988).

In the studies by McFarlane and her colleagues, about half the women who met and about half who failed to meet diagnostic criteria consistent with PMS reported that they had it. Another study (Hardie, 1997) also asked women to self-diagnose, and the results showed that 40% of women reported that they had PMS. However, none of them exhibited the pattern of cyclic emotional changes that are part of the diagnostic criteria. That is, regardless of symptoms, some women believe that they have PMS.

Why do so many women believe that they have PMS? One reason is the appearance of signals that predict the onset of menstruation; as many as 80% of women experience such signals and know when their periods are going to start (Miller, 2002). Some PMS researchers (Daw, 2002) warn that signals should not be confused with symptoms of a disorder, but the publicity about PMS leads to labeling and classification of these signals as PMS. A demonstration of this effect appeared in a study of Mexican women (Marván & Escobedo, 1999), some of whom saw a video about PMS and its negative consequences and others of whom saw a video about menstruation. Those women who learned about the negative aspects of PMS reported significantly more such symptoms after their next period than did the other women in the study. Thus, the widespread publicity about PMS may help create the syndrome.

As the woman in Naversen's (2001) headline story showed, women who experience problems, stresses, and irritations to which they respond emotionally may explain their reactions by their phase of the menstrual cycle and believe that they have PMS or even PMDD. Both women and men are willing to attribute moody behavior to PMS (Koeske & Koeske, 1975). When furnished with information about a woman's cycle, both men and women tended to use this information to partly explain the woman's emotional behavior, just as the woman and her supervisor in the headline story did. If people believe that these symptoms are associated with the premenstrual period as well as menstruation, they can apply this explanation about half the time—the week before and the week during menstruation. When they experience the same situations and reactions at other phases of their cycle, they seek other explanations. In this way, premenstrual syndrome can become a self-perpetuating myth for the women who react to problems, stresses, and irritations in their lives as well as for the people who observe the reactions.

The diagnosis of PMDD is also subject to widespread publicity; this diagnosis increased dramatically when the advertising campaign for Sarafem began (Daw, 2002). Some researchers and clinicians are reluctant to diagnose PMDD without considering other factors in women' lives, such as unhappy marriages, poor working environments, and depression. Sarafem and other prescription drug treatments for PMDD are antidepressants, so women who respond favorably to these drugs may actually have depression that is exacerbated by hormonal variations (Miller & Miller, 2001). As some researchers contend, PMDD may be a created disorder with little validity as a separate diagnosis (Flora & Sellers, 2003).

In summary, PMS has received wide publicity and wide acceptance, but much of the research supporting this concept suffers from flaws in methodology. The results from more careful studies have indicated that premenstrual syndrome is difficult to define on a biological level, and emotional symptoms are subject to expectation and attribution. The moods of both women and men vary cyclically, but not according to the pattern consistent with PMS.

Testosterone and Aggression

The subtitle for Robert Sapolsky's (1997) headline article suggested that "it takes more than just a hormone to make a fellow's trigger finger itch." Sapolsky acknowledged the association between being male and being violent: "We males account for less than 50 percent of the population, yet we generate a huge proportion of the violence" (p. 44). He also admitted that testosterone has behavioral effects, but he argued against the widely accepted belief that testosterone causes aggression. What, then, is the relationship, and how are both women and men affected?

According to research by James Dabbs and his colleagues (Dabbs, 2000), hormone levels play a role in aggression in men and in women, but the research indicates that the role is not a simple one. One of these early studies (Dabbs, de la Rue, & Williams, 1990) investigated differences in testosterone levels for men in various occupations, including physicians, football players, salesmen, actors, ministers, professors, and firemen as well as unemployed men. Their analysis showed that the only significant difference occurred in a comparison of the actors and the football players, who both had higher testosterone levels than the ministers. Another study (Dabbs, Hopper, & Jurkovic, 1990) confirmed the differences between actors and ministers and explored possible reasons for this difference in testosterone levels that might relate to personality differences. Dabbs and his colleagues reasoned that the factors of competition and antisocial tendencies might differentiate the two groups. Ministers' lives have little competition compared to actors' lives; actors also tend to be more selfish and self-absorbed than ministers. Therefore, competition and selfishness, not aggression, showed a relationship to testosterone in this group of men.

Research on the relationship between testosterone level and occupational achievement (Dabbs, 1992, 2000) showed a complex relationship: Men with high levels of testosterone tended to have lower-status occupations. Dabbs interpreted this finding to indicate that high testosterone levels are related to impulsiveness and antisocial behavior, and such behaviors make success in white-collar occupations less likely. An additional study (Heusel & Dabbs, 1996) confirmed this interpretation: For engineers working in the same company, those with high testosterone levels were more likely to quit or be fired than those with lower testosterone levels.

The interpretation that impulsive and antisocial (what Dabbs calls "rambunctious") behaviors are positively related to testosterone level is consistent with other research by Dabbs and his colleagues. Within the normal range of testosterone (which varies by a great deal), testosterone may not be a major factor in behavior. However, for men with the highest levels of testosterone, problems appear (Dabbs, 2000). For example, veterans showed a positive relationship between testosterone level and drug and alcohol abuse, antisocial behavior, and affective disorders (Dabbs, Hopper, & Jurkovic, 1990). Among U.S. military veterans, men whose testosterone levels fell within the upper 10% of testosterone had a history of trouble with parents, teachers, and classmates as well as a history of drug use and more instances of going AWOL (absent without leave) while in the military (Dabbs & Morris, 1990).

A comparison of college students and young men who were delinquents showed higher testosterone levels in the delinquents (Banks & Dabbs, 1996). An assessment of the testosterone levels in two college fraternities showed that men in the "rowdy" fraternity had higher testosterone levels than did the men in the fraternity with a reputation for academic success and social responsibility (Dabbs, Hargrove, & Heusel, 1996). These behaviors can create problems, but they are not necessarily examples of aggression or violence.

A more specific example of the relationship between testosterone and violence appeared in a study of male prisoners (Dabbs, Carr, Frady, & Riad, 1995). Those prisoners who had committed crimes against individuals involving sex and violence had higher testosterone levels than did prisoners who had committed property crimes. The prisoners with higher levels of testosterone also were more likely to be involved with rule violations and personal confrontations while in prison. Table 3.2 summarizes the complex findings from research by Dabbs and his colleagues.

Women also produce testosterone, and some research has focused on the relationship between this hormone and women's behavior. Dabbs and his colleagues (Dabbs, Ruback, Frady, Hopper, & Sgoutas, 1988) also studied the relationship between testosterone level and antisocial behavior in women by measuring the testosterone levels of inmates in a women's prison and contrasting them with testosterone levels of female college students. Within the prison group, they found some indication that testosterone levels were related to violence: Women with the highest levels of testosterone had the highest incidence of un-

TABLE 3.2 *Relationship of Testosterone to Various Behaviors in Men and Women*

Behaviors Associated with Higher Testosterone Levels	
In Men	*In Women*
Occupations of actor and football player	Professional, managerial, and technical occupations
Lower-status occupations	Unprovoked violence among prisoners
Job loss	
Drug and alcohol abuse among veterans	
Antisocial disorders among veterans	
Affective disorders among veterans	
Trouble getting along with parents, teachers, and classmates among veterans	
Delinquent behaviors while young	
Membership in a "rowdy" fraternity	
Incarceration for crimes involving sex or violence	
Rule violations and personal confrontations among prisoners	

Behaviors Not Associated with Higher Testosterone Levels	
In Men	*In Women*
Occupations of salesmen, firemen, professors, physicians, or the unemployed	Violent criminal acts
Personality traits among students	Prisoner versus student
	"Butch" role in lesbian relationships

provoked violence. These researchers found that testosterone levels differed among inmates convicted of unprovoked violence, defensive violence, theft, drugs, and other crimes. The inmates who had committed acts of unprovoked violence had the highest testosterone levels. For these female inmates, testosterone was related to the number of prior charges and to prior parole board decisions about length of time they should serve before being granted parole. Women who had committed violence in protecting themselves, such as those who had murdered an abusive spouse, had the lowest levels of testosterone in the prison group.

Interestingly, the mean levels of testosterone were similar for the inmates and the college students, and both averages fell within the normal range for women. These results provide some support for the notion that testosterone is related to aggression, as the inmates who had committed the most violent crimes—those involving unprovoked violence—also had the highest testosterone levels. However, the failure to find differences between women convicted of crimes and female students indicates that aggression and violence are influenced by factors other than testosterone level, including SES, which moderated the relationship between testosterone and problem behavior in men. For women as for men, testosterone may be more closely related to rambunctious behavior rather than violence (Dabbs, 2000).

The studies by Dabbs and his colleagues show a relationship between high testosterone levels and a variety of problem behaviors, but the behaviors do not always fit within the definition of aggression. Additional complications are highlighted by a finding that testosterone levels do not vary in aggressive versus nonaggressive boys (Constantino et al., 1993). In addition, boys and girls with high testosterone levels showed problem behaviors in bad family environments but not when their relationships with parents were positive (Booth, Johnson, Granger, Crouter, & McHale, 2003). Responses to anabolic steroids (a synthetic analog of androgens) demonstrated that men's responses were variable—most (84%) showed no increase in activity level or aggression, a few (12%) showed mild increases, and very few (2%) experienced substantial increases (Pope, Kouri, & Hudson, 2000).

All of this research shows that the relationship between testosterone and aggression is not a simple cause-and-effect one. In his headline story, Sapolsky (1997) argued that there is a cause-and-effect relationship between testosterone and aggression, but in the other direction—aggression causes increases in testosterone. One line of research supports his contention for a reciprocal relationship between aggression and testosterone.

Allan Mazur and his colleagues (Booth, Shelley, Mazur, Tharp, & Kittok, 1989) examined the relationship between testosterone levels and winning versus losing in athletic competition. Participants were the six members of the University of Nebraska varsity tennis team who agreed to provide saliva samples throughout the season so that the researchers could analyze testosterone levels. These players were measured four times in relation to each of the season's six matches—the day before a match, about 15 minutes before each match, immediately after they had finished playing, and 1 or 2 days after each match. The researchers predicted that winning players would experience increased testosterone levels compared to losing players. The carryover effects of winning on testosterone level were also a topic of the study.

This study was a test of a biosocial theory of status (Mazur, 1985; Mazur & Booth, 1998), which hypothesizes that testosterone level is part of a feedback loop in which testosterone and assertiveness are interrelated. When an individual's testosterone level rises, that person is more willing to compete in contests for higher status. Winning such competitions produces a rise in testosterone or helps to maintain a high level of testosterone, which will sustain the willingness to compete. Conversely, losing produces a drop in testosterone, which deters the willingness to compete. Thus, "losing streaks" and "winning streaks" in competitions are sustained by the feedback loop's relationship with testosterone level. This theory also holds that testosterone level and behavior influence each other rather than a unidirectional cause-and-effect relationship between the hormone level and behavior.

In the study with tennis players (Booth et al., 1989), the researchers compared the changes in testosterone level before and after matches. They expected winners to have higher testosterone levels than losers, but their findings were more complex. Players showed increases of testosterone on days when they played, but their hormone levels were highest before the game. Winners showed rises in testosterone across the matches and losers showed declines, but no significant differences appeared in the average levels of testosterone when comparing winners and losers before and after the matches.

The tennis players also rated their feelings about their overall performance. The players who felt positively about their performance tended to have higher testosterone levels. Therefore, winning and losing did not appear to be simply related to testosterone levels, but rather, some emotional or mood factors might have mediated the hormonal effects. That is, winning might produce positive moods that in turn might heighten testosterone levels. This research was consistent with the biosocial theory (Mazur, 1985), which would highlight the finding that testosterone levels affected *and* were affected by competition. However, the study suggested that the effects of testosterone on performance and responses of players to high levels of testosterone follow complex, rather than simple, patterns related to competition.

As Sapolsky (1997) contended, the influence of androgens on behavior turns out to be complex, bidirectional, and influenced by a multitude of factors. Rather than testosterone simply producing aggression, competition and aggression can also increase testosterone. There is some evidence that men *and* women with high testosterone levels are more likely to commit violent crimes than are people whose testosterone levels are lower, but that correlational evidence does not rule out the possibility of a bidirectional action. People with high testosterone levels are also more likely to commit crimes that do not include violence and to exhibit antisocial but legal behaviors, such as heavy drinking. Conceptualizing all of these behaviors as aggression would be inaccurate. Therefore, hormone levels probably play some role in aggression, but that role is relatively small, and a higher testosterone level is possibly a result, rather than a cause, of aggression. Testosterone is a factor, but probably not the main factor, that accounts for the violence that is associated with men's behavior.

CONSIDERING DIVERSITY

The possibilities for cultural variations in sexual development seem limited: Biological sex is a matter of chromosomes and hormones. Most people develop unambiguously according to the male pattern or the female pattern, and those patterns do not seem subject to cultural variations. The factor that can vary is the way that cultures divide those categories and how the languages of those cultures name the sexes. Although English includes many words to describe variations in sexual interest and behavior, we have no word for people who do not fit either the male or female patterns of sexual development. However, anthropologist Gilbert Herdt (1990) contended that some cultures do; that is, some cultures name a category for a third sex.

These cultures tend to have a factor in common—the relative frequency of the hereditary enzyme disorder that produces one type of intersexuality. This disorder is the result of a deficiency in the enzyme 5-alpha-reductase, which prevents prenatal testosterone from producing a boy with normal external genitals. These individuals are chromosomally normal males with normal internal genitalia, but they are born with external genitals that more closely resemble a girl's than a boy's—a clitoris-like penis, an unfused scrotum that resembles labia, and undescended testes. At birth, these babies are sometimes identified as boys but are more often identified and reared as girls. At puberty they produce testosterone and become "masculinized": Their penis grows, their testes descend, they grow facial hair, and their musculature increases. That is, they change from individuals who look more like girls to ones who look more like boys.

This disorder is very rare but is more common in the Dominican Republic and New Guinea than in most other parts of the world. Herdt contended that these two cultures have a term for a third sex, one that is neither male nor female but that starts out as female and becomes male. In his evaluation of both cultures, Herdt concluded that individuals with this disorder fit into neither the male nor female category and that their cultures acknowledge and respond to these differences. Acknowledgment is not the same as acceptance, however, and neither culture accepts these individuals as normal. Even after these individuals had developed masculine characteristics, the Sambia culture of New Guinea did not grant them full male status.

Several Native American cultures not only designated a category for a third sex but also honored the individuals in this category. More than 130 Native American societies accepted *berdaches*—men or women who adopted the gender-related behaviors of the other gender (Wieringa, 1994). Berdaches were not intersex individuals, but instead individuals who chose to blend masculine and feminine roles. The male berdache tradition was the more common, and male berdaches were not only well accepted but also achieved high spiritual status in their societies. Lakota, Navajo, Crow, and Zuni societies all included berdaches who were not thought of as homosexual but as a merging of feminine and masculine spirits, which they attained through a blessing from the spirits. These departures from the ordinary gender roles, therefore, were not viewed as deviations because they were chosen as special, and there was no connotation of deficiency or pathology. Their behaviors represented a blending of male and female that, to the Zuni and others, constituted a third gender rather than an adoption of the "opposite" gender. Thus, some cultures have a category for a third sex, providing for individuals whose biology has not clearly designated male or female and for those who choose to blend roles.

▆ SUMMARY

Several steroid hormones are important to sexual development and behavior, including the androgens, the estrogens, and the progestins. All normal individuals produce all of these hormones, but women produce proportionately more estrogens and progestins, whereas men produce more androgens. The prenatal production of these hormones prompts the bodies and brains of fetuses to organize in either the male or the female pattern. During puberty, these hormones activate the internal genitalia to develop fertility and prompt the production of secondary sex characteristics, such as facial hair for men and breasts for women. The role of hormones in the activation and maintenance of sexual interest and activity is less clear in humans than in other species, but humans who do not experience the pubertal surge of hormones tend not to develop much interest in sex. Testosterone, one of the androgens, plays a role in maintaining sexual activity in men and possibly in women as well.

Sexual development may be conceptualized as consisting of five stages—genetic, gonadal, hormonal, internal genitalia, and external genitalia—all of which usually proceed according to either the male or the female pattern. The first stage in sexual development is genetic, the inheritance of either XX or XY chromosomes of pair 23. Although the inheritance of chromosomes is the beginning of the pattern, embryos are not sexually dimorphic until around 6 weeks into gestation. Those with the XY pattern start to produce androgens and Müllerian-inhibiting substance during the 3rd month of gestation, which masculinize the fetus. Shortly thereafter, external male genitalia develop, and this development also depends on androgens.

The female pattern is not as dependent on the presence of estrogens as the male pattern is on androgens. During the 3rd month of pregnancy, those individuals with the XX pattern of chromosomes start to develop the Müllerian structures, which become the ovaries, Fallopian tubes, uterus, and upper vagina. In addition, their Wolffian structures start to degenerate. An absence of all steroid hormones will allow the feminization of external genitalia, but the internal reproductive organs do not develop normally.

Prenatal hormones also affect brain development, producing differences in the brains of males versus females. Several brain structures are affected, but the sexually dimorphic nucleus of the hypothalamus shows the biggest difference. Its function is not known. The cerebral hemispheres differ in function between the left and right hemispheres, and this lateralization of function is also hypothesized as a gender difference. Some research indicates that men are more lateralized than women, but this gender-related difference is small.

Things can go wrong at any stage of sexual development, beginning with the inheritance of the chromosomes that determine sex—the X and Y chromosomes. A number of disorders exist that create individuals with too few or too many sex chromosomes, and some of these configurations produce problems with the development of internal or external genitalia. In addition, several of these disorders produce individuals with developmental disorders, especially lowered intelligence. Individuals with Turner syndrome (X0) appear to be female but lack ovaries; individuals with Klinefelter syndrome (XXY) appear to be male, often with feminized body contours, but have nonfunctional testes; XXX individuals are female and may be otherwise normal; XYY individuals are tall males who may be reproductively normal but with low intelligence.

Even normal chromosomes do not guarantee normal development in subsequent stages, and several types of intersexuality exist. These cases of individuals who have the physiology of both males and females highlight the complexity of sexual development and suggest that many components contribute to gender identity and functioning.

Media reports tend to indicate a role for hormones in two areas of problem behavior—premenstrual syndrome (PMS) and aggression. Careful research has indicated that the premenstrual phase of the cycle often includes some physical symptoms, but it also suggests that expectation, not hormones, is the major cause of the emotional symptoms associated with PMS. Both women and men may attribute behavioral symptoms to PMS and the more severe PMDD, when those symptoms may actually indicate other problems.

Research on the role of testosterone in aggression has revealed that the relationship is not a simple cause-and-effect one. Indeed, the relationship may occur in the direction opposite to what was previously expected: Aggression may cause increases in testosterone, rather than vice versa. For women as well as for men, testosterone levels differ for people who have committed violent crimes, with higher testosterone levels found in the criminally violent. However, testosterone is not a very accurate predictor of criminal violence, as both male and female inmates do not differ in testosterone levels from male and female college students. Men with higher than average testosterone levels tend to engage in a wide variety of antisocial behaviors that include (but are not restricted to) violence. Studies of competition and testosterone show that competition raises testosterone levels, suggesting that the relationship between the two may be causal but in the opposite direction from what people have imagined.

The role of hormones in sexual development is not subject to cultural variation, but how culture deals with the sexes varies enormously. In addition to male and female, some cultures define a third sex. One basis for this third sex has been the frequency of a developmental problem that produces individuals who are born with ambiguous external genitalia that masculinizes at puberty. That is, these individuals seem to be born female but become male. The other basis for a third sex was a belief common among Native American societies that allowed for a melding of the two spirits, male and female, in an individual. These conceptualizations highlight problems for cultures that allow only two categories.

GLOSSARY

adrenogenital syndrome   a disorder that results in masculinization, producing premature puberty in boys and masculinization of the external genitalia in girls.

androgen insensitivity syndrome   a disorder in which body cells are unable to respond to androgens, resulting in the feminization of chromosomal males.

androgens   a class of hormones that includes testosterone and other steroid hormones. Men typically produce a greater proportion of androgens than estrogens.

endocrine glands   glands that secrete hormones into the circulatory system.

estradiol   the most common of the estrogen hormones.

estrogens   a class of hormones that includes estradiol and other steroid hormones. Women typically produce a greater proportion of estrogens than androgens.

external genitalia   the reproductive structures that can be seen without internal examination: clitoris, labia, and vaginal opening in women; and penis and scrotum in men.

follicle-stimulating hormone (FSH)   the gonadotropic hormone that stimulates development of gonads during puberty and development of ova during the years of women's fertility.

gonads   reproductive organs.

hermaphroditism   a disorder in which individuals have characteristics of both sexes.

hormones   chemical substances released from endocrine glands that circulate throughout the body and affect target organs that have receptors sensitive to the specific hormones.

internal genitalia   the internal reproductive organs, consisting of the ovaries, Fallopian tubes, uterus, and upper vagina in women; and testes, seminal vesicles, vas deferens, and prostate gland in men.

intersexuality   a more modern term for hermaphroditism.

Klinefelter syndrome   the disorder that occurs when a chromosomal male has an extra X chromosome, resulting in the XXY pattern of chromosome pair 23. These individuals have the appearance of males, including external genitalia, but they may also develop breasts and a feminized body shape. Their testes are not capable of producing sperm, so they are sterile.

lateralization the concept that the two cerebral hemispheres are not functionally equal but rather that each hemisphere has different abilities.

luteinizing hormone (LH) the gonadotropic hormone that prompts sexual development during puberty and also causes a maturing ovum to be released.

menarche the first menstruation.

Müllerian system a system of ducts occurring in both male and female embryos that forms the basis for the development of the female internal reproductive system—ovaries, Fallopian tubes, uterus, and upper vagina.

pituitary gland an endocrine gland within the brain that produces tropic hormones that stimulate other glands to produce yet other hormones.

progestins a group of steroid hormones that prepares the female body for pregnancy; their function for the male body is unknown.

releasing hormones hormones produced by the hypothalamus that act on the pituitary to release tropic hormones.

sexual dimorphism the existence of two sexes—male and female—including differences in genetics, gonads, hormones, internal genitalia, and external genitalia.

sexually dimorphic nucleus (SDN) a brain structure in the hypothalamus, near the optic chiasm, that is larger

in male rats than in female rats and larger in men than in women.

spinal nucleus of the bulbocavernosus a collection of neurons in the lower spinal cord that control muscles at the base of the penis.

steroid hormones hormones related to sexual dimorphism and sexual reproduction that are derived from cholesterol and consist of a structure that includes four carbon rings.

testosterone the most common of the androgen hormones.

tropic hormones hormones produced by the pituitary gland that influence the release of other hormones by other glands, such as the gonads.

Turner syndrome the disorder that occurs when an individual has only one chromosome of pair 23, one X chromosome. These individuals appear to be female (have the external genitalia of females) but do not have fully developed internal genitalia. They do not produce estrogens, do not undergo puberty, and are not fertile.

Wolffian system a system of ducts occurring in both male and female embryos that forms the basis for the development of the male internal reproductive system—testes, seminal vesicles, and vas deferens.

X chromosomes one of the possible alternatives for chromosome pair 23. Two X chromosomes make a genetic female, whereas genetic males have only one X chromosome in pair 23.

Y chromosome one of the possible alternatives for chromosome pair 23. One X and one Y chromosome make a genetic male, whereas genetic females have two X chromosomes in pair 23.

SUGGESTED READINGS

Angier, Natalie. (1999). *Woman: An intimate geography.* Boston: Houghton Mifflin.

Angier's readable book delves into female biology. The first three chapters focus on chromosomes and hormones in development, and Chapters 14 and 15 analyze the contribution of testosterone to behavior. Angier's presentation is both readable and provocative.

Breedlove, S. Marc. (1994). Sexual differentiation of the human nervous system. *Annual Review of Psychology, 45,* 389–418.

Breedlove's article is not easy reading, but it is a thorough and careful review of the research. Breedlove is also careful to acknowledge the interaction of biology and experience in the development of gender differences in the nervous system.

Flora, Stephen Ray; & Sellers, Melissa. (2003, May/June). "Premenstrual dysphoric disorder" and "premenstrual syndrome" myths. *Skeptical Inquirer, 27* (3), 37–42.

This article takes a very skeptical view of PMS and PMDD, contending that behaviors associated with these two "disorders" can be explained in terms of reinforcement and expectation rather than hormones and psychological disorder.

Pinel, John P. J. (2003). *Biopsychology* (5th ed.). Boston: Allyn & Bacon.

For more details about the action of the endocrine system, the brain's involvement in endocrine function, sexual development, and some of the things that can go wrong, see Chapter 13 of this biological psychology textbook.

4 INTELLIGENCE AND COGNITIVE ABILITIES

█ HEADLINE   Lost in Space

Vogue, June 2001

> Brain research, the hot science specialty and the bane of a feminist's existence, says that we
> are, on average, profoundly different from men. Researchers who look at everything from the
> size of the brain (theirs is bigger) to the speed at which it ages (theirs deteriorates faster) to
> the effect of sex hormones come to a single, unnerving conclusion: Biology is a good chunk
> of destiny. Recent studies suggest that while women may excel at reading a map, men may
> be quicker at processing that information and putting it into good use on the road. In other
> words, we are hot-wired to get lost more often than the guys are. (Stabiner, 2001, p. 142)

Citing biological differences as the basis, Karen Stabiner's (2001) headline article argued
that women are "Lost in Space." In her trek to find these gender differences, Stabiner and
her husband participated in an orienteering course in which they had to find their way
around in the woods, and she talked to several prominent cognitive researchers about gender and spatial ability. Neither of these strategies supplied a great deal of evidence to back
up her claims that women do more poorly on finding their way or that the ability to get
around in the world is wired into the brain.

The long-held belief that women get lost and men never ask directions is an enduring gender stereotype that relates to cognitive differences in spatial abilities. This gender
difference is one of many that this chapter will explore. Do women and men have different cognitive abilities, do they use different strategies, or both? If such differences exist,
are they expressions of hormonal or brain differences between the sexes, or do these differences represent different learning and experience?

Like Janet Hyde, one of the experts Stabiner consulted, some researchers contend that
gender differences do not exist, whereas Doreen Kimura, another expert, has argued that the
differences exist and that they have a biological basis. The research in the area of cognitive
abilities is filled with complex findings and strongly held (but opposing) views; dozens of
articles have appeared in the popular press and thousands in the research literature.

This level of controversy reflects the strong feelings that this topic has produced. To
what extent do gender differences explain intelligence and cognitive abilities? Are differences sufficiently large to explain the distribution of men and women into different areas

of study and different occupations, or do these findings represent insignificant differences in how women and men think? Do differences apply only to specific cognitive abilities or to overall intelligence?

COGNITIVE ABILITIES

Other than defining intelligence as "how smart a person is" (a trivial and circular definition), an acceptable definition of this concept has been difficult to formulate. Indeed, heated debate over the nature of intelligence has occurred throughout the history of intelligence testing, a controversy not confined to psychology. The prominence of this concern highlights the importance of the issue: Understanding intelligence and the abilities that contribute to intelligence is a basic question for understanding humans.

Psychologists have been concerned with the concept of intelligence since the 1890s (Schultz & Schultz, 2004). However, the current conceptualization of intelligence was most influenced by the creation of the intelligence test in 1905. This test, formulated by Alfred Binet, Victor Henri, and Théodore Simon, measured a variety of mental abilities related to school performance, including memory, attention, comprehension, vocabulary, and imagination. A version of this test—the Stanford–Binet—appeared in the United States in 1916, and the intelligence testing movement became an important part of psychology, especially in the United States.

The prevailing view of intelligence during the 19th and early 20th centuries was that women's intellect was inferior to men's (Lewin, 1984a; Shields, 1975a). Lewis Terman, who adapted the Binet–Simon test into the Stanford–Binet, did not believe in the intellectual inferiority of women. He himself had no trouble accepting the results of this test, which revealed no average differences between the intelligence of men and that of women. Indeed, the scores on the early versions of the Stanford–Binet showed that women scored slightly higher than men, but after some of the items that showed differences were eliminated, the average scores for women and girls were equal to those of men and boys (Terman & Merrill, 1937).

This general gender similarity, however, has not yet gotten through to people on an individual level. Significant differences exist between women and men in their estimates of intelligence (Furnham & Gasson, 1998). Both women and men judge women's intelligence as lower than men's. These differences occur when students estimate their own intelligence, when college students estimate their parents' intelligence, and when parents judge their children's intelligence (Furnham, Reeves, & Budhani, 2002). The prejudice of the 19th century has lasted into the 21st century.

With the development of the intelligence testing movement came increased attention to the different abilities that might be included within these tests. In the test devised by Binet and his colleagues and adapted by Terman into the Stanford–Binet, most test items could be classified as verbal; that is, most questions require the understanding and use of language. Psychologist David Wechsler created an alternative intelligence test that divided abilities into the categories of verbal and performance skills. The verbal subtests require those being tested to provide verbal answers by performing certain tasks: supplying factual knowledge (information), defining vocabulary items (vocabulary), performing basic arithmetic computation (arithmetic), repeating a series of digits (digit span), understanding similarities between objects (similarities), and properly interpreting social conventions (comprehension).

The performance subtests of Wechsler's test require no verbal responses, but instead people respond by performing some action. The performance subtests include arranging pictures into a sensible story (picture arrangement), duplicating designs with blocks (block design), completing pictures that have some missing part (picture completion), assembling cut-up figures of common objects (object assembly), and learning and rapidly applying digit symbol codes (digit symbols) (Gregory, 1987). Figure 4.1 shows samples of the types of items on the Wechsler tests.

Verbal Subtests	**Sample Items**
Information	How many wings does a bird have? Who wrote *Paradise Lost*?
Digit span	Repeat from memory a series of digits, such as 3 1 0 6 7 4 2 5, after hearing it once.
General comprehension	What is the advantage of keeping money in a bank? Why is copper often used in electrical wires?
Arithmetic	Three men divided 18 golf balls equally among themselves. How many golf balls did each man receive? If 2 apples cost 15¢, what will be the cost of a dozen apples?
Similarities	In what way are a lion and a tiger alike? In what way are a saw and a hammer alike?
Vocabulary	This test consists simply of asking, "What is a _____?" or "What does _____ mean?" The words cover a wide range of difficulty or familiarity.

Performance Subtests	**Description of Item**
Picture arrangement	Arrange a series of cartoon panels to make a meaningful story.
Picture completion	What is missing from these pictures?
Block design	Copy designs with blocks (as shown at right).
Object assembly	Put together a jigsaw puzzle.
Digit symbol	

1	2	3	4
X	III	I	O

Fill in the symbols:

3	4	1	3	4	2	1	2

FIGURE 4.1 *Sample Test Items Similar to Items on Wechsler's Tests of Intelligence*

Source: From *The World of Psychology,* by Ellen R. Green Wood and Samuel E. Wood, 1993, Boston: Allyn and Bacon. Copyright © 1993 by Allyn and Bacon. Reprinted by permission.

Unlike the Stanford–Binet, Wechsler's test shows differences between the scores of men and women, with women scoring higher on the verbal subtests and men scoring higher on the performance subtests. Wechsler's test includes no item adjustment to equate average performance of women and men on the subtests. Although the combined scores on the Wechsler tests do not show gender differences, the subtest scores always have.

Nor are the Wechsler tests the only assessments that have revealed different performance between male and female participants. Eleanor Maccoby and Carol Jacklin's (1974) review of gender differences in intellectual performance likewise found differences on verbal, mathematical, and spatial tasks. More recent research, however, has revealed that the patterns of gender differences in these cognitive abilities are smaller and more complex than the early reviews suggested.

Part of the complexity comes from the tests used to assess these various cognitive abilities. The term *abilities* is somewhat inaccurate, because most of the assessments have been tests of performance or achievement, such as the Scholastic Aptitude Test (SAT), a test used for college admissions. Such tests do not measure innate abilities, so findings of gender differences do not necessarily mean that women and men are inherently different in what these tests measure. Rather, differences imply only different levels of current performance, and any generalizations to innate ability are incorrect. Differences in performance might come from different biological endowment, but could also come from social roles, parental encouragement, school courses, leisure activities, or motivation to perform well on the test.

Verbal Performance

The tasks that researchers have used to study verbal ability include not only the verbal subtests of the Wechsler tests but also verbal fluency, anagram tests, reading comprehension tests, synonym and antonym tasks, sentence structure assessments, reading readiness tests, and writing assessments as well as the spelling, punctuation, vocabulary, and reading subtests from various achievement tests. Researchers have defined all of these tasks as verbal despite the wide variation in the tasks themselves (see Table 4.1); this variation may be one reason why research on verbal performance has not yielded entirely consistent results (Sanders, Sjodin, & de Chastelaine, 2002).

Literature reviews (Halpern, 1994, 1997, 2000; Maccoby & Jacklin, 1974) have taken a variety of verbal tasks into account and have come to the conclusion that girls and women have some advantages in verbal performance. These advantages include the rapidity and proficiency with which girls acquire language compared to boys, an advantage that girls maintain throughout elementary school. The National Assessment of Educational Progress is a test that reflects the achievement of a representative sample of students in 4th, 8th, and 12th grades. This test shows an advantage in reading and writing for girls at all of these grade levels (Coley, 2001). The advantage in writing ability is large and persists throughout college (Willingham, Cole, Lewis, & Leung, 1997).

Meta-analysis is a statistical technique that combines the results from many studies to estimate the size of certain effects, and this technique offers advantages over the literature review approach. Janet Hyde (1981) completed such a meta-analysis of the studies

TABLE 4.1   *Examples of Different Measures of Verbal, Quantitative, and Spatial Abilities*

Verbal	Quantitative	Spatial
Vocalizations during infancy	Pointing to a member of a set	Reproducing geometric forms
Visual-motor association	Estimating proportion	Matching geometric shapes
Talking to mother	WISC arithmetic subtest	Reading maps
Verbalization in free play	Digit-processing task	Matching photos for orientation
Parents' reports of speech problems	Digit-symbol subtest of WAIS	Distance perception
Complete sentences	Math achievement	Assembling puzzles
Anagram task	Math reasoning	Rotating shapes
Carrying out simple and complex tasks	Problem solving	Reproducing patterns
	Addition	Disembedding figures
Judgment of grammatical sentences	Subtraction	Angle matching
Verbal imitation	Arithmetic computation	Maze performance
Verbal reproduction of story	Number arrangement	Localization of a spatial target
Reading speed	Math subtests for SAT	Discrimination of triangles and mirror-image reversals
Reading vocabulary	General Aptitude Test Battery	
Reading comprehension	ACT	Distinguishing right from left, east from west, and top from bottom
Errors in similes		Rod-and-frame task
Spelling		Matching pictures to objects
Punctuation		Seguin Form Board
Synonyms and antonyms		Spatial subtests from:
Verbal subtests from:		Differential Aptitude Test
Peabody Picture Vocabulary		General Aptitude Test Battery
Illinois Test of Psycholinguistic Ability		Piaget's water-level task
Expressive Vocabulary Inventory		Making judgments about moving objects
WISC		WISC Block Design

Source: Adapted from *The Psychology of Sex Differences* (pp. 76–97), by Eleanor Maccoby & Carol Jacklin, 1974. Stanford, CA: Stanford University Press.

from Maccoby and Jacklin's (1974) literature review and concluded that the gender-related differences in verbal performance are small. About 1% of the difference in verbal ability relates to gender, leaving the other 99% of difference related to other factors.

A later meta-analysis by Janet Hyde and Marcia Linn (1988) examined additional studies, and this analysis indicated that women have the advantage in some verbal abilities, but men have the advantage in others. In addition, this analysis indicated that earlier studies showed gender-related differences, whereas more recent studies have not, suggesting a decrease in this gender difference over time. Despite the widespread acceptance of a verbal advantage for girls and women, this advantage is small and may be shrinking.

Mathematical and Quantitative Performance

Research on mathematical and quantitative performance presents a complex picture in which changes during adolescence, patterns of course selection, and attitudes toward math make the assessment of underlying ability very difficult. Most studies with children younger than age 13 show either no gender differences, or certain advantages for girls in mathematical performance, defined as proficiency in arithmetic computation (Fennema, 1980; Hyde, Fennema, & Lamon, 1990). Around age 13, gender differences favoring boys begin to appear in many of the assessments of mathematical performance.

Girls who excel at arithmetic computation do not become women who are poor at such tasks. For example, the numerical ability subtest of the Differential Aptitude Test (DAT) shows no gender differences for students in grades 8 through 12 (Feingold, 1988). The basis of this change is an alteration in measurements for what constitutes mathematical and quantitative performance. Rather than consisting of arithmetic computation, the

◼ GENDERED VOICES

I Was Good at Math and Science

A female chemical engineer said, "I was good at math and science, so my high school counselor suggested engineering. I looked into the various kinds of engineering. I didn't really like physics all that much, so I decided that electrical engineering would not be a good choice. I didn't consider myself very mechanical, so I ruled out mechanical engineering. I liked chemistry, so I thought chemical engineering would be a good choice, but I didn't really know what chemical engineers did. My high school had a cooperative arrangement so I could work for an engineer, but that experience didn't really let me know what the work of a chemical engineer was like. In fact, I didn't really understand the work of chemical engineers until I was a junior in college, and I learned that I didn't find the work all that interesting.

"I went to a technical college that specialized in engineering, and it was definitely male dominated; only about 25% of the students were women. But I never felt any favoritism either for or against the women. Everybody was treated fairly. The courses during the first two years were designed to weed out students, so everybody felt that the curriculum was difficult, but the women did as well as the men, and I never felt that the professors or students showed any bias.

"What was missing on campus were ethnic minorities. The campus was very White. There just weren't any Black students, and there was one Hispanic girl. The geographic area had lots of minorities, but they didn't go into engineering at this school. I noticed the absence of minority students more than the small number of women.

"I didn't feel that being a woman was a factor in school, but it sure was on the job. I didn't necessarily feel discriminated against, but the women were very visible. There were few women, and whatever a woman did stood out. If I did a great job, I got noticed more than a man who did a great job. If I screwed up, I got noticed more than a man who made a mistake. Whatever a woman did—good or bad—came to the attention of everyone."

tests of quantitative ability during the middle and high school years begin to include tasks that are more abstract, as Table 4.1 shows.

The disadvantage for women is not as large as people believe. As Hyde's (1981) meta-analysis of quantitative performance showed, only 1% of the difference was related to gender, which indicates a very small overall gender-related difference in mathematical performance. Later analyses showed no gender difference for a representative group of 12th-grade students (Willingham et al., 1997) and a small, nonsignificant advantage for women in the general population (Hyde, Fennema, & Lamon, 1990). Therefore, these results contradict the stereotype of women's lower performance in mathematics.

Analyzing quantitative abilities into different skills and different ages shows a complex pattern of gender differences (Hyde, Fennema, & Lamon, 1990; Willingham et al., 1997). Girls and women have a small advantage in math computation. Girls' advantage in math concepts changes during high school, and by 12th grade, boys have an advantage (Willingham et al., 1997). During elementary and middle school, no gender difference appears in mathematics problem solving, but boys begin to do better at solving math problems during high school. Changes after high school become more difficult to interpret because individuals who take tests tend to be from selected groups rather than representative of the entire population. Examining mathematics performance for the general population yields no significant difference, but selected groups show substantial differences.

A large gender difference in higher-level mathematics appeared in several studies, showing that, in selected groups, males have a large advantage over females (Benbow & Stanley, 1980, 1983; Willingham & Cole, 1997). Some of the studies that have shown big differences (Benbow & Stanley, 1980, 1983) included mathematically gifted students, of which boys outnumber girls by 4 to 1.

The classification of students as mathematically gifted often involves a standardized test, and this type of test has been part of the controversy related to gender differences in math performance. Some standardized tests have consistently revealed gender-related differences in math performance, including the mathematics subtests from the Preliminary Scholastic Aptitude Test (PSAT) and the Scholastic Aptitude Test (SAT), the Graduate Record Examination (GRE) Quantitative section, and the Advanced Placement Program calculus exam (Feingold, 1988; Willingham et al., 1997). The gender-related differences in performance on these tests demonstrate the influence of a progressively selected group of students, more math training for men, characteristics of the test and test format, and greater variability in scores for men. All these factors contribute to the male advantage in math scores in certain groups of students. Table 4.2 summarizes the findings on math performance.

Students who take these tests are a self-selected group taking the test as a part of entrance into college or graduate school. With progressively selected samples, men show distinct advantages over women in quantitative performance. The selection factor is part of the reason for the advantage; men who have taken these tests completed more math courses than the women who took the tests, providing a difference in preparation (Fennema, 1980; Willingham et al., 1997). This situation changed during the 1990s (Bae, Choy, Geddes, Sable, & Snyder, 2000). Now, the average number of math classes and the pattern of courses that girls and boys complete in high school are equal.

TABLE 4.2   *Gender-Related Differences in Mathematics Performance*

Group	Advantage	Mathematics Skill
Elementary school students	Girls	Arithmetic computation
Elementary school students	Girls	Math concepts
Middle school students	No difference	Problem solving
13-year-old gifted students	Boys	SAT Mathematics subtest
High school students	Boys	Math concepts
High school students	Boys	Problem solving
College-bound students	Boys	SAT Mathematics subtest
College-bound students	Boys	Advanced Placement Calculus test
Grades 8–12	No difference	Numerical Ability subtest of DAT
Representative group of 12th-grade students	No difference	Math performance
College students	Men	Mathematics subtest of GRE
Adults in general population	Women	Arithmetic computation
Adults in general population	No difference	Math performance

Test format and bias within the tests are other factors that favor men, who do better than women on multiple-choice format tests and on tests with time limits (Willingham & Cole, 1997). Both characteristics are common to the mathematics tests that show a male advantage. For as long as the Educational Testing Service (ETS) has collected information on gender, the Mathematics section of the SAT has shown substantial differences, even among young women whose math grades are equal to or better than young men's grades (Schiebinger, 1999). In the 1970s, ETS changed the SAT Verbal section in ways that eliminated the female advantage, but it left the Mathematics section with a substantial male advantage. As a response to a lawsuit in the late 1990s, the PSAT changed to eliminate the gender bias, but the gender gap in SAT scores remains (Neil, 1999).

Researchers at ETS (Willingham et al., 1997) have acknowledged that the SAT Mathematics test systematically "underpredicts" women's college math grades; that is, women make better grades in college math courses than their SAT scores predict. The test also "overpredicts" men's scores; they make lower grades in college than their SAT scores predict. The Educational Testing Service maintains the position that colleges should consider the combination of high school grades and SAT test scores rather than rely on SAT scores alone. The bias against women and ethnic minority students has led a growing number of colleges and universities to go a step farther, eliminating the SAT as part of their admissions criteria (Neil, 1999). Some critics (Zittleman & Sadker, 2002) have wondered why men continue to outperform women on high-stakes tests that have an impact of their future when women outperform men on other standardized tests.

Gender differences in attitudes toward math also play a role in women's and men's quantitative experiences. Beginning at age 12, girls start to feel less confident than boys

◉ GENDERED VOICES

Math Class Is Tough

"Math class is tough," according to Teen Talk Barbie, introduced by the Mattel Toy Company in 1992. Teen Talk Barbie was the company's second talking Barbie, but this particular phrase unleashed a furor. Many women and women's groups protested the perpetuation of the idea that women find math more difficult than men do; they feared that this popular toy's proclamation would reinforce and perpetuate the stereotype that math is not for girls. Mattel soon dropped that phrase from Barbie's repertoire (Smith & White, 2002).

about their ability to do mathematics (Eccles, 1989; Vermeer, Boekaerts, & Seegers, 2000). As students age, the gender difference in confidence increases, and this trend continues into adulthood. College women—even those women whose majors involved taking many math courses—failed to identify math as part of their domain (Nosek, Banaji, & Greenwald, 2002).

Girls also begin to believe that math is not important to them, starting at the same age that their confidence in their ability to do math begins to decline. Boys, on the other hand, have greater confidence in their mathematical ability and evaluate math as more important to their future. Thus, different perceptions and confidence levels exist as the result of believing that math is a male domain (Kimball, 1995; Nosek et al., 2002). Both children and parents share this cultural perception, resulting in the differential beliefs concerning boys' and girls' math abilities.

A meta-analysis of attitudes toward mathematics showed surprisingly few gender-related differences (Hyde, Fennema, Ryan, Frost, & Hopp, 1990). Contrary to the stereotype, girls and women do not dislike and fear math, but when differences exist, women have more negative attitudes than men. Similar to the findings concerning math performance, the results concerning math attitudes showed no gender differences during elementary school, but some differences emerged during high school. The only dramatic difference revealed by this meta-analysis was in gender stereotyping of math, with men being most likely to perceive math as a male domain.

Girls' perception that math is a male domain may lead them to believe that they are unlikely to succeed in the subject and to perceive that math is not important or valuable to them (Eccles, 1987). This combined lack of confidence and the belief that math is not important to their future form a powerful disincentive for girls during high school, when they have the option to choose elective math courses. Perhaps not coincidentally, the differences in math standardized test scores begin to appear at this time.

The choice to avoid math courses can have lifelong repercussions (Sells, 1980). The selection of high school mathematics courses can act as a filter, effectively barring female and ethnic minority students from many professions. For example, if a student has only two years of high school math, that student cannot take calculus as a freshman in college, which thereby eliminates some college majors and filters some students out of those majors and out of careers requiring those majors.

Janis Jacobs and Jacquelynne Eccles (1992) proposed and validated a model for the gender-related factors that influence self-perceptions about abilities, including math ability. Figure 4.2 presents that model, and an examination of that figure reveals that gender stereotypes and the ratings and beliefs of mothers and teachers are important for children in forming beliefs about their abilities. Children's biological sex affects their beliefs about their abilities, but this model also includes an effect for gender stereotypes and an interaction of sex with gender stereotyping, such as the stereotyping of math as a male domain (Hyde, Fennema, Ryan, et al., 1990).

Not only children's sex but also the combination of sex and stereotyping affect mothers' perceptions about children's ability. This interaction means that mothers may see their sons as better at math than their daughters. The effects of these stereotypes may begin before a child has any experience with the subject and act in subtle ways, leading mothers to see evidence that confirms their stereotype and overlook disconfirming evidence (Jacobs & Eccles, 1992). These effects provide a mechanism that prejudices mothers' beliefs and shapes children's perceptions.

This model applies not only to mathematics achievement but also to other areas. Jacobs and Eccles (1992) tested this model for mathematics, sports, and social domains, and further research (Jacobs, Lanza, Osgood, Eccles, & Wigfield, 2002) has included factors that influence perceptions of self-competence in language arts.

Chapter 11 discusses the gender bias that occurs in schools and classrooms. Both parents and teachers enact gender stereotypes, which affect girls' and boys' perceptions of

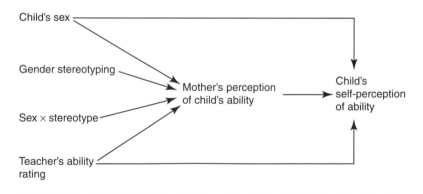

FIGURE 4.2 *Path of Influence for Perception of Abilities*

Source: Adapted from "The Impact of Mothers' Gender-Role Stereotypic Beliefs on Mothers' and Children's Ability Perceptions," by Janis E. Jacobs & Jacquelynne S. Eccles, 1992, *Journal of Personality and Social Psychology, 63,* p. 935. Copyright 1992 by American Psychological Association. Adapted by permission of Janis E. Jacobs and the American Psychological Association.

their competence. These social factors may be more important than ability in shaping school achievement:

> When one considers that females endure remarks from teachers or texts indicating that mathematics is not a female domain, are involved in far fewer interactions with their teachers involving mathematics, are rarely asked high-cognitive-level questions in mathematics, are encouraged to be dependent rather than independent thinkers, spend more time helping their peers and not getting helped in return, and are often not placed in groups that are appropriate to their level, it is amazing that the gap [in mathematics achievement] is not considerably larger. (Koehler, 1990, p. 145)

In summary, gender-related differences in mathematics performance do not exist in the general population, but differences do appear in selected groups. Among students, girls and boys do not differ in mathematics performance until junior high school. At this time, boys begin to show higher average levels of math performance and confidence, and these differences persist throughout adulthood. Studies of gifted children have shown that extraordinary mathematics performance is much more common among boys than girls, although this level of ability is rare even in boys. Differences in mathematics performance and attitudes toward mathematics show small gender differences, despite the stereotype that girls and women dislike math and do poorly in the subject. This stereotype may be the underlying basis for the biased treatment, regarding mathematical ability, that girls and women receive from their peers, parents, and teachers. Differences are disappearing in the number of math courses completed, which may change the current pattern of performance in mathematics.

Spatial Performance

Although the definition of what constitutes spatial ability has varied from study to study (Caplan & Caplan, 1994; Caplan, MacPherson, & Tobin, 1985), this variation has not hindered many people from accepting the notion that men are better at these tasks than women. Variation has existed in the definitions of verbal ability and quantitative ability, but researchers have defined spatial ability in a wider variety of ways. Table 4.1 includes some of these definitions. Any of these tasks represents a reasonable way to measure the concept of spatial abilities, but they vary sufficiently to yield results that may not be consistent from study to study.

Researchers even disagree on the number of spatial abilities that exist. One group (Linn & Petersen, 1986) placed spatial tasks into three groups, but another (Voyer, Voyer, & Bryden, 1995) contended that three categories were too few to capture the complexity of spatial abilities. Another investigator (Stumpf, 1993) argued that there are hundreds of tests of spatial ability that can be classified into 16 groups. This variety of tests illustrates the many ways that researchers have defined and measured spatial ability and substantiates the claim that spatial ability is far from unitary. The complexity of findings relates to this variety of measurement.

The three-category approach (Linn & Petersen, 1986) includes spatial perception, mental rotation, and spatial visualization; a fourth type of spatial task is spatiotemporal or targeting ability. **Spatial perception** includes the ability to identify and locate the horizontal or vertical planes in the presence of distracting information. Examples of measures of spatial perception are the rod-and-frame task and Piaget's water-level task, both shown in Figure 4.3. These tasks usually show gender-related differences, with boys and men outperforming girls and women. The magnitude of this difference is small during childhood and adolescence, but fairly large for adults.

Mental rotation includes the ability to visualize objects as they would appear if rotated in space. An example of a measure of this type of ability also appears in Figure 4.3. The gender-related difference for this spatial ability is large, with boys and men scoring substantially higher than girls and women on speed and accuracy of mentally rotating objects (Halpern, 2000; Voyer et al., 1995).

Spatial visualization refers to the ability to process spatial information so as to understand the relationship between objects in space, such as the ability to see a figure embedded in other figures (also shown in Figure 4.3), find hidden figures in a drawing or picture, or imagine the shape produced when a folded piece of paper is cut and then unfolded. Gender differences do not always appear on measures of these tasks. When such differences appear, they are small, and men have this small advantage.

A fourth category of spatial ability is called **spatiotemporal ability** (Halpern, 2000). This ability involves judgments about moving objects in space, such as predicting when a moving object will arrive at a target. This spatial ability has been less researched than the others. Some research on this ability indicated that men's ability is higher than women's, but other research (Law, Pellegrino, & Hunt, 1993) has shown that prior experience is a factor in performance on this type of task. Feedback concerning performance improved the performance of both men and women. Thus, any advantage that boys or men show might be due to their experience with such tasks.

An additional complication in assessing gender differences in spatial ability comes from the possibility that some tasks labeled "spatial" may include other components. For example, the rod-and-frame task may include situational factors that affect performance (Sherman, 1978). This testing typically occurs in a darkened room, with a male experimenter testing participants. Perhaps the testing situation contributes to the gender differences—female participants may feel uncomfortable in this situation and be less likely to persist in asking the male experimenter to continue to adjust the rod. Thus, lack of assertiveness and uneasiness with the testing situation may contribute to the gender differences that often appear on this measure of spatial ability.

In addition, the presentation of the task may contribute to performance. The male advantage on the rod-and-frame task disappeared when a human figure replaced the rod and the task was presented as a measure of empathy (Naditch, in Caplan et al., 1985). In this situation, women outperformed men. The task still involved the same spatial factors as the original task—namely, judging relative position in space—but the typical gender difference was reversed.

Several research findings provide evidence against a simple conclusion for a male advantage on spatial tasks. A major complication comes from the finding that women show an advantage on some spatial tasks (Halpern, 2000; Montello, Lovelace, Golledge, & Self, 1999). Women tend to do better on tasks of perceptual speed in which people must rapidly

Mental rotation
Which figure on the right is identical to the figure in the box?

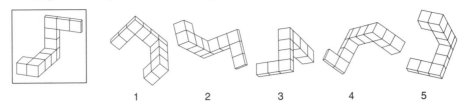

1   2   3   4   5

Piaget's water-level problem
This glass is half filled with water. Draw a line across the glass to indicate the top of the water line.

Rod-and-frame test
Ignore the orientation of the frame and adjust the position of the rod so that it is vertical.

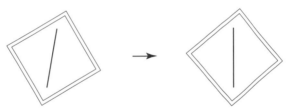

Disembedding
Find the simple figure on the left embedded in one of the four more complex figures on the right.

FIGURE 4.3   *Spatial Tasks Favoring Men*

identify matching items. Women also outperform men on tasks in which people must remember the placement of a series of objects. Examples of these tasks appear in Figure 4.4.
An additional complication comes from the finding that gender differences appear in some

Study the objects in group **A** for one minute and cover it up. Then look at group **B** and put an X through the figures not in the original array. Score one point for each item correctly crossed out, and subtract one point for each item incorrectly crossed out.

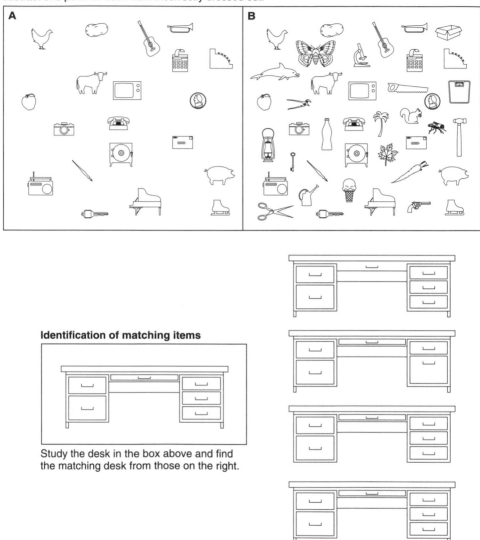

Identification of matching items

Study the desk in the box above and find the matching desk from those on the right.

FIGURE 4.4 *Spatial Tasks Favoring Women*

age groups but not in others, the differences are subject to change with variations in testing procedure, and gender differences in some spatial abilities seem to be decreasing (Voyer et al., 1995). In addition, these differences do not apply to all cultures. Considering studies from nine different nations (Feingold, 1994), men showed a slight advantage overall, but in some cultures, no differences appeared. Another cross-national comparison (Amponsah & Krek-ling, 1997) found a pattern of gender differences that was similar to those in the United States.

These various findings raise the question, Do men really have better spatial abilities than women? The answer is not a simple "yes" or "no." Of the many spatial abilities, men show an advantage in some, and women show an advantage in others. Men in the United States produce reliably better scores than women in spatial perception, such as Piaget's water-level task and in mental rotation, but training and experience decrease this difference (see "According to the Media" and "According to the Research").

The embedded figures task has also yielded complex results for gender and ethnic background, suggesting that men have no clear advantage for this measure of spatial ability. Women's advantage in spatial abilities appears on measures of perceptual speed and on memory for the placement of objects. Therefore, of the gender differences in spatial abilities that exist, a number favor men, a few favor women, and some vary by gender, culture, context, expectation, or some combinations of these factors.

Other Cognitive Abilities

Verbal, mathematical, and spatial abilities are important and have been the subjects of extensive research, but other mental abilities exist. Memory, creativity, musical ability, and nonverbal communication are all abilities that have been the focus of research. Gender has rarely been the emphasis of these studies, and most of the research has failed to show gender-related differences. A consideration of these other cognitive abilities is important for putting comparisons concerning gender-related cognitive abilities in perspective because the gender differences in verbal, mathematics, and spatial performance have been given so much attention.

As the headline story for this chapter explored, one of the persistent stereotypes about men's and women's cognitive abilities is the male advantage in following directions and wayfinding. As the experience of Karen Stabiner (2001) and her husband reflected, both men and women have developed strategies that allow them to find their way, but those strategies tend to differ by gender. Men are more likely than women to use a strategy that involves orienting to directions and forming an abstract map of the area, whereas women are more likely to use landmarks to find their way. Which of these strategies is best? It depends on the situation. In laboratory situations, such as abstract mazes and virtual reality situations, the directional strategy leads to fewer errors and more rapid wayfinding (Malinowski, 2001; Saucier et al., 2002). When allowed to use their preferred strategy in a real-world situation, the differences disappear. That is, women are worse at directions only when they are forced to use the strategy that men typically prefer. A combination of the two strategies is actually the most effective (Schmitz, 1999).

Memory can reflect either verbal or spatial abilities, depending on the type of material. The majority of tasks that psychologists have studied fall into the category of verbal learning and memory. According to Maccoby and Jacklin's (1974) review of research in this area, few gender-related differences exist. However, more recent studies have found a female advantage for both abstract and concrete verbal material (Kimura & Clarke, 2002) but not for visual or spatial material (Lewin, Wolgers, & Herlitz, 2001).

◼ ACCORDING TO THE MEDIA . . .

Video Games Are for Boys

Popular video games are oriented to boys. Both arcade games and home video games contain primarily male characters, lots of action and violence, and games involving plots attractive to boys and even to men (St. John, 2002). Indeed, the video market has been dominated by games for boys, and video games oriented to girls are a more recent development (Goodale, 1999).

The most common portrayal of women in video games consists of nothing—literally. Over 40% of popular video games have no female characters, including 30% of videos that contained human characters (Dietz, 1998). When women appear in video games, sometimes they are helpless and in need of rescuing; sometimes they are evil and in need of conquering. Female characters also appear in the background as supporters of male characters. Occasionally female characters get to be heroes. Regardless of their role, they are often large breasted and provocatively dressed.

The amount of violence in video games is an area of concern (Colwell & Payne, 2000; Dietz, 1998). Early video games tended to depict spaceships and aliens, but human or humanlike characters are now more common. Thus, players have repeated exposure to chasing and doing violence to both male and female characters. In addition, 21% of the games include violence directed specifically toward women. These games give players the opportunity to act within a situation in which women are the designated targets of video violence.

The combination of themes for boys, few female characters, and fewer attractive, powerful female characters makes video games more appealing to boys than to girls. The portrayals of women as victims, targets, or sex objects puts girls in the position of seeing unflattering depictions of female characters, choosing from the limited range of games for girls, or avoiding video games altogether.

Some of the gender-related differences in memory seem strongly related to the gender-stereotypical nature of the task and to the match between that stereotyping and the gender of the learner. For example, when women and men were asked to memorize a shopping list and directions to a particular place, the differences were in a predictable direction (Herrmann, Crawford, & Holdsworth, 1992). Women were better than men at memorizing the shopping list, and men were better than women at memorizing the directions. Furthermore, the labeling of the task influenced women's and men's memories. When people heard that the shopping list pertained to groceries, women showed an advantage, but when the same list was described as pertaining to hardware, men's memories were better. An extension of this study (Colley, Ball, Kirby, Harvey, & Vingelen, 2001) demonstrated again that memory performance depended on a combination of the labeling of the task and the gender of the learner rather than the skill of either women or men as learners. Thus, memory may depend on factors other than ability, with men and women performing according to their attention, interests, and stereotypes.

Creativity is a term that researchers have defined in a variety of ways, leading to a great diversity of findings. Studies of kindergarten and children in 1st grade (Lewis & Houtz, 1986), children in grades 4 through 8 (Rejskind, Rapagna, & Gold, 1992), 5th- and 7th-grade students in China and Germany (Shi, Xu, Zhou, & Zha, 1999), and col-

ACCORDING TO THE RESEARCH . . .

Video Games Can Improve Spatial Skills

Video games may be oriented toward and played mostly by boys, but several research studies indicate that both girls and boys can improve their performance on spatial tasks by playing video games. In a study with 10- and 11-year-olds (Subrahmanyam & Greenfield, 1994), boys had more experience in video games and showed better performance on a spatial task, but children who played a video game improved on the spatial task more than children who played a vocabulary game. A study of 3rd-grade children (De Lisi & Wolford, 2002) allowed some boys and girls to play a computer game that provided practice with mental rotation while others played an alternative game. After spatial practice, the gender difference that had existed at the beginning of the study disappeared. College students also improved performance on mental rotation and spatial visualization after experience with a video game (Okagaki & Frensch, 1994). These results suggest that playing video games improves spatial skills.

The notion that practice can improve performance on spatial tasks is not new. A meta-analysis (Baenninger & Newcombe, 1989) and research on training procedures (Liben & Golbeck, 1984; Vasta, Knott, & Gaze, 1996) confirmed that experience erased the gender differences in performance on Piaget's water-level task. The notion that video games, which have been considered potentially damaging (Colwell & Payne, 2000), might be beneficial is recent.

However, the design and marketing of video games for boys puts girls at a double disadvantage. By appealing to boys, these games are unattractive to many girls, keeping them away from this type of activity. Boys have a greater incentive to participate in activities that boost skills on which they already have higher performance, whereas girls have lower motivation to play video games that could improve their spatial skills.

lege students (Goldsmith & Matherly, 1988) have failed to show gender-related differences in creative thinking. In addition, a musical expert rated the compositions of female and male composers equal in possessing musical creativity (Hassler, Nieschlag, & de la Motte, 1990).

When researchers define creativity in terms of achievement, men have showed higher levels of creativity. This advantage, however, may not be due to greater creative ability but rather to access to training, parental and societal encouragement, and limited acceptance of women in creative fields. A study of women who have become successful musicians (Stremikis, 2002) showed that these women focused on professional success, often from young ages, and conformed less to gender stereotypes than did women who have not pursued such careers.

The discrepancy between the numbers of male and female visual artists and musicians may be due to encouragement rather than talent (Piirto, 1991). Creatively gifted boys and girls are very similar in personality but differ in level of commitment to their field. The differences in creative accomplishments come from lesser commitment on the part of girls and women, and commitment comes from encouragement. If gifted girls were encouraged to devote themselves to their talents in the same ways that boys are encouraged, the gender differences would be smaller.

▣ GENDERED VOICES

It's Not Something on the Y Chromosome

"I don't think that it's something on the Y chromosome," a 13-year-old girl said, referring to the ability to play percussion. "But some boys act like it is. The boys in the school band are used to me because I've played percussion all through junior high school with them, but when I go to competitions, the boys act like I shouldn't be playing percussion. Almost like it's an insult that a girl should be playing."

She explained that lots of girls play in the school band. There is generally no prejudice against girls who are musicians, but the band is gender segregated by musical instrument. The instruments toward the front of the band are more "feminine," such as violins, clarinets, and cellos. The instruments toward the back are more "masculine," such as tubas and the percussion instruments: "There are lots more girls toward the front of the band, and the boys dominate the back.

"At the all-city band competition, it was especially bad. The boys who played percussion were especially obnoxious, acting like I shouldn't be trying. They acted like it was their right as boys to be able to play drums or other percussion—like there was something on the Y chromosome that gave them the gift. Well, I guess they were really surprised when I won."

Nonverbal communication includes a variety of behaviors related to conveying and receiving information through gestures, body position, and facial expressions, and some gender differences exist in both expressing and interpreting nonverbal behaviors (LaFrance & Henley, 1997). Women are more likely than men to make and keep eye contact and touch themselves. In addition, their facial expressions are more revealing of their emotions (Thunberg & Dimberg, 2000). One large difference is women's tendency to smile; women smile more often than men do (LaFrance & Hecht, 1999). This tendency may not reveal more pleasant moods for women. Rather, smiling may reflect their subordinate status.

Indeed, gender differences in nonverbal behavior may relate to power and status. Early research by Sara Snodgrass (1985, 1992) showed that no gender differences existed in the ability to read cues about people's motives, feelings, and wishes. Instead, she found that people in subordinate positions were better at reading the nonverbal behaviors of those in dominant positions. This finding presented the possibility that women's better ability to decode nonverbal cues—often described as "women's intuition"—is really the intuition that develops for those of subordinate status. For such individuals, advantage rests in understanding small nuances in the behavior of those in charge. This interpretation remains controversial (Hall & Halberstadt, 1997; LaFrance & Henley, 1997) but offers a way to understand why women show an advantage in interpreting nonverbal behaviors without any advantage in the ability to do so.

Although the gender differences are small in verbal, mathematical, and spatial abilities, differences are even smaller or nonexistent in other cognitive abilities such as memory, creativity, musical ability, and nonverbal communication. The studies that have revealed gender-related differences in performance in these areas have shown that the differences come from social stereotypes and expectations rather than from ability.

SOURCE OF THE DIFFERENCES

If social stereotypes and expectations shape performance on aptitude and achievement tests, then are these factors the source of differences between men and women? Does biology play no role in the gender differences in cognitive performance? The possibility that cognitive gender differences can be traced to biology appeals to many people, possibly because it offers a simple answer to many complex questions. The tendency to resort to biological essentialism is strong, both in the media and among the general population. This appeal has prompted theories and research.

Biological Evidence for Gender Differences in Cognitive Abilities

Several theories have proposed a biological basis for gender differences in cognitive abilities. These theories concentrate on chromosomes, hormones, or structural differences in the brain that create functional differences in cognition. One biologically based view emphasizes the role of evolution in gender differences in lateralization of the brain, placing this theory in the category of explanations that look for gender differences in brain structure (Kimura, 1999; Levy, 1969).

Following this explanation, different role demands of men and women in the hunter–gatherer societies of prehistory posed different task demands and resulted in different brain organization. Thus, men should be better at spatial tasks because their evolutionary history included traveling to hunt, whereas women stayed home; women should be better at verbal tasks because they talked to their children. Although the logic of these stories may be appealing, these speculations are impossible to confirm or disconfirm—those early societies are gone and can no longer be observed.

Also, alternative stories make as much sense. For example, more remote periods in prehistory when prehumans were tree dwellers would present similar selection pressures for spatial abilities for both females and males (Benderly, 1987). For example, poor spatial abilities would result in falling out of trees, which would not be conducive to survival and reproduction. Humans are the product of evolutionary history, but the strategy of hypothesizing which evolutionary pressures resulted in what types of cognitive abilities has many possible versions, and it is impossible to confirm any of these versions.

Another biologically based theory came from Norman Geschwind and Albert Galaburda (1987). This theory emphasizes the role of prenatal testosterone exposure in cerebral lateralization and the effects on subsequent mental abilities. (Chapter 3 discussed the lateralization of mental abilities.) This theory hypothesizes that boys and men will have better spatial abilities than girls and women because of the pattern of prenatal growth of the right hemisphere. The theory also predicts that this pattern of prenatal development will result in better verbal abilities for girls and women than for boys and men. Geschwind and

Galaburda's theory is complex and difficult to test (McManus & Bryden, 1991), but some evidence supports and other evidence fails to support this theory. However, this theory emphasizes the effect of prenatal hormones on brain development, and this component of the theory has a good deal of supporting evidence.

Recall from Chapter 3 that, beginning at about 6 weeks in prenatal development, male fetuses begin to produce androgens. These androgens exert masculinizing effects on the developing fetus, creating the male pattern of internal and external reproductive organs. These androgens have the potential to affect the developing brain, perhaps producing changes in the structure and function of the brain. Gender differences in brain structures exist and change during adolescence (Durston et al., 2001). The production of androgens and estrogens in women and men allow for the continued possibility for hormonal effects on the brain. As Diane Halpern (2000) pointed out, however, drawing conclusion about hormones as the sole cause of any type of difference is practically impossible because almost all individuals who have more testosterone than estrogen also have male genitals, are identified as boys at birth, and have been treated as male throughout their lives. Therefore, hormones become an inseparable part of the process of development.

Nevertheless, researchers have attempted to tease out the effects of hormones on gender differences in cognitive abilities. One line of research has concentrated on the cyclic variations of hormones during women's menstrual cycle and the seasonal variations that men experience in testosterone (Kimura, 1999). These studies have yielded interesting results that suggest that women's task performance is better for verbal and manual dexterity tasks when their estrogen and progesterone levels are high and worse when those hormone levels are low. Their spatial performance is higher with lower estrogen levels. For men, their spatial performance is better when their testosterone levels are lower compared to higher. However, the size of these effects is too small to make a difference in the daily lives of men and women. That is, these hormonal effects may produce differences large enough to be statistically significant, but the differences are not large enough to have any practical significance (Halpern, 2000). However, these studies indicate that brains respond to hormones throughout the life span, not just during prenatal development, and researchers may find other hormone-related cognitive effects.

Another strategy for studying gender differences in cognition involves using brain imaging technology to determine whether women's and men's brains function differently while performing some cognitive task. This strategy makes use of brain imaging technology such as positron emission tomography (PET) and functional magnetic resonance imaging (fMRI), which can detect metabolic changes in the brain that accompany heightened neural activity (Raichle, 1994). Researchers can examine brains while the participants are engaged in various cognitive tasks. This approach allows researchers to determine the similarities and differences in the function of female and male brains.

Several studies using brain imaging have found the expected differences for brain processing during cognitive tasks: The left hemisphere is more active during verbal performance and the right hemisphere is more active during spatial tasks. In addition, these studies have shown some differences in the activation patterns of men's and women's brains. For example, women's brains showed a higher level of metabolic activity than men's brains during a verbal memory task (Ragland, Coleman, Gur, Glahn, & Gur, 2000), and the difference related to better performance. Both men's and women's left hemispheres were more active during a verbal task (Baxter et al., 2003), but women's right hemispheres were also active during this task. In a comparison of brain activation during a verbal and a spatial task (Gur et al., 2000), the expected differences appeared in both women and men, but other areas of the brain were also activated, including left hemisphere activation for women when they performed the spatial task. Yet another study (Jordan, Wuestenberg, Heinze, Peters, & Jaencke, 2002) found different patterns of brain activation for women and men as they performed a mental rotation task.

Do such results suggest that men and women use their brains differently? Possibly, but the studies also tend to show that the patterns of activation are more similar than different and that not all male or female brains react in the pattern that is typical for their sex.

For example, one research project (Shaywitz et al., 1995) studied women and men by using fMRI as the two groups performed three tasks involving language sounds. The results showed that men used their left cerebral hemisphere, whereas women used both hemispheres, in performing a rhyming task. No gender differences appeared in brain activation for the two other tasks, nor were the patterns of activation divided neatly by gender. Over 40% of the women in the study exhibited the activation pattern more typical of the men. Furthermore, the pattern of brain functioning may be of little or no practical significance because the male and female participants performed comparably. That is, the difference in patterns of brain activation made no behavioral difference. As brain researcher Ruben Gur and his colleagues (1995, p. 531) commented, "the brains of men and women are fundamentally more similar than different."

Researchers have concentrated on gender differences to try to understand the intricacies of how brains function. Many of these research projects have become headlines that have sensationalized small differences, leaving people with the impression that hormones or brain structures produce large, important gender differences in cognition. The evidence indicates that, under some circumstances, men's and women's brains (on the average) function differently. The variation from person to person is much larger than the difference between women and men. However, the research indicates that hormonal and functional brain differences influence cognitive performance in men and women.

Evidence for Other Sources of Gender Differences

Although many people have a tendency to think in terms of either biology or social factors, almost all researchers acknowledge that both contribute to cognitive performance. Furthermore, separating biological from environmental factors is virtually impossible. Therefore, the list is extensive for other sources of gender differences in cognitive performance.

Training and experience play a role in cognitive performance. An example of this effect appeared in a study of spatial performance (Voyer, Nolan, & Voyer, 2000). This study asked women and men to complete several spatial performance tasks and to report on their toy and sports preferences. The men showed better performance on the spatial tasks, but people with better spatial performance also reported preferences for spatial activities, which suggest that experience affects spatial performance. A second study with similar findings (Roberts & Bell, 2000) showed that men's advantage on a spatial task disappeared when the women in the study were allowed to familiarize themselves with the computer that was part of the study before they performed the mental rotation task. Another study (Scali, Brownlow, & Hicks, 2000) suggested that the gender difference in spatial task performance could be erased by the directions that researchers give to participants. When these researchers told the participants that accuracy was very important, gender differences occurred, but other instructions failed to produce the expected male advantage. All of these studies suggest that performance on spatial tasks—the type of task on which the largest gender difference appears—can change with experience and with instructions.

Another environmental factor that is capable of affecting cognitive performance is *stereotype threat,* a term originated by Claude Steele (Steele & Aronson, 1995). Stereotype threat describes situations in which the presence of negative stereotypes affects the performance of those to whom the stereotype applies. Many studies have indicated that stereotype threat is a factor in women's lower performance in mathematics, but recent research has indicated that the effect is applicable to a wider variety of situations. For example, the performance of college women was worse on a math test when they heard that men do better on this type of test, but men's performance declined when they heard that Asians outperform Whites (Smith & White, 2002). Stereotype threat also applies to performance on a mental rotation task (Burns, Peterson, Bass, & Pascoe, 2002).

Therefore, in addition to the biological factors that affect performance on cognitive tasks, a variety of experiences, instructions, and expectations also contribute. These factors form a complex interaction with biological factors influencing behavior and behavior influencing biology (Halpern, 1997). In addition, the factors that influence academic choices are critically important. Choices are rooted in a cultural setting influenced by gender roles and stereotypes, parental pressure, and teacher perception. Refer back to Figure 4.2, which illustrates a model that captures the influences on self-perception of abilities. These perceptions affect the choices that may lead to very different paths for girls and boys.

IMPLICATIONS OF GENDER-RELATED DIFFERENCES

As reviewed in previous sections of this chapter, gender-related differences in cognitive performance are small. These small differences should mean equally small differences in scholastic and occupational achievement for which these abilities are required, as well as small differences in confidence in mental abilities. Instead, there are large differences in the choices that men and women make concerning careers and in their confidence in their abilities. These choices and levels of confidence may be mediated through social beliefs about the abilities of men and women. People's behavior may be more closely related to their images of what men and women can do than to what women and men actually do.

Misunderstandings of gender research have contributed to these images. Hyde (1981) has discussed the ways in which research on gender-related cognitive differences has led to erroneous beliefs about these abilities. Her meta-analyses have been important in demonstrating that the magnitude of these differences is small and possibly decreasing. These small differences mean that a factor, such as gender, that accounts for 1% of the variance in an ability leaves 99% of the difference in that ability due to other factors. Figure 4.5 presents

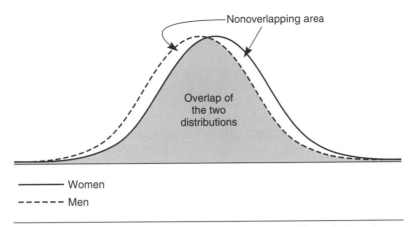

FIGURE 4.5   *An Example of Two Distributions with 99% Overlap*

Note: This distribution represents differences similar to those for verbal ability in men and women.

two distributions of scores that have a 99% overlap and a 1% difference. This figure shows how similar the two distributions are. If 1% of the variance in verbal ability were due to gender, we would not know much about any specific person's verbal ability by knowing that person's gender, because too much variation in verbal ability would be due to other factors.

Assumptions about the person's verbal ability would be unfounded if they were based on the knowledge that the person were a woman, because many men have verbal abilities that equal or exceed most women's verbal abilities. Stereotypes based on gender differences in these cognitive abilities will lead to incorrect conclusions about the abilities of men and women, because women and men vary more from one person to another than from one gender to another. With only a small percentage of the variance attributable to gender, individual differences overwhelm any gender difference.

Hyde (1981) also contended that the term *well-established* should be distinguished from *large*. (At this point, using the term *well-established* to describe cognitive gender differences may be inaccurate, but this usage persists.) Hyde suggested that people tend to consider the two terms as similar, but in this case they are not the same. When researchers conclude that a difference is well-established, that conclusion does not mean that the difference is also large, merely that it has been found in numerous studies. Hyde criticized those psychology textbooks that include information about women's advantage in verbal abilities and men's advantage in quantitative and spatial abilities. Although many studies have found these small differences (making them well-established), most of these differences are by no means large. Describing the differences as well-established in texts and in the media can lead people to misunderstand their own abilities as well as the abilities of others.

Even small differences can have larger implications, as one computer simulation study (Martell, Lane, & Emrich, 1996) showed. Researchers created an organization with eight levels. A computer algorithm then simulated promotion based on ability within this hypothetical organization, with a 5% and a 1% difference in ability (with women having less ability than men). With an initially equal number of women and men in the hypothetical workforce, the simulation resulted in 35% of the top-level jobs going to women (for the 1% deficit). When women were given a 5% deficit in ability, they ended up in 29% of the top-level positions.

Does this simulation mirror workplace situations? Probably not. Few specific abilities show as much as a 5% difference between women and men. Mental rotation ability shows about a 9% difference between men and women, which is enough to make a sizable difference for any occupation that relies entirely on mental rotation. However, none does. Indeed, no occupation relies entirely on one mental ability, and social abilities also contribute to workplace success. The simulation also varied from actual employment situations in another respect: An equal number of men and women were hired, which is true of almost no occupation. The selection factors begin years prior to employment and result in a much greater gender inequality in most occupations than in this simulation. For example, the gender gap in engineering has been much larger than the difference in the simulation analysis (Martell et al., 1996). Until the 1970s, about 1% of students receiving engineering degrees were women, and that percentage rose to around 18% in 2000 (U.S. Bureau of the Census, 2002). This magnitude of difference would not occur on the basis of the gender differences in mental abilities.

The size of the differences in gender-related cognitive ability is sufficiently small to have limited implications for men's and women's lives, yet people's beliefs allow these small differences to have a large impact. When parents, teachers, and children come to accept that boys are better at math than girls, this acceptance of a gender-related difference leads to differential expectations for math achievement. Even when achievement is similar, parents have different beliefs about the underlying reasons. Parents in the United States (Yee & Eccles, 1988) and in Finland (Raety, Vaenskae, Kasanen, & Kaerkkaeinen, 2002) explained the mathematics success of their sons in terms of natural talent and their daughters in terms of hard work. These beliefs and expectations influence the level of encouragement that children receive, thus affecting how girls and boys feel about their own abilities. These feelings affect the choices that girls and boys make concerning their elective math courses, and these choices have lifelong consequences for careers as well as attitudes toward the subject. Although the gender-related differences in cognitive abilities are small, people throughout society largely accept these differences, which creates additional divergence.

In summary, meta-analysis has shown that the magnitude of gender differences is small for verbal, quantitative, and spatial abilities. Gender differences in these three areas account for between 1% and 5% of the differences, too small a difference to explain or predict most variation from person to person. The gender stereotyping of cognitive domains has magnified small differences, thus perpetuating the belief that gender-related differences exist and that there are large differences in the abilities of women and men.

CONSIDERING DIVERSITY

Most of the studies on cognitive abilities have focused on European Americans in the United States, and many imagine that these results apply to other groups. Cross-cultural research indicates otherwise. Studies on various ethnic groups in the United States and research in other countries have indicated that cognition varies with culture.

Anneliese Pontius (1995, 1997a, 1997b) reported on her program of cross-cultural research on gender differences in spatial perception. One result (Pontius, 1997b) from the Auca Indians, a Stone Age culture living in the Amazon basin, revealed a very different pattern of gender differences in spatial performance from testings in the United States. In this culture, the women outperform the men in block design tasks in which U.S. men have an advantage over women. Her analysis of boys and girls in northwestern Pakistan revealed no gender differences in the spatial abilities she measured. A study of children in eastern Ecuador (Pontius, 1997a) failed to find gender differences in a mental rotation task. A study with Norwegian sixth-grade students (Manger & Eikeland, 1998) also failed to reveal gender differences in spatial visualization. Therefore, a variety of cultures fail to show the gender differences typical of the United States.

A cross-cultural analysis of verbal, mathematical, and spatial abilities failed to find in other cultures the pattern of results that appeared in U.S. samples (Feingold, 1994). In some cultures, men score higher in math ability, but in others, women do. The same variability appeared for spatial abilities. In summarizing the meta-analytic studies of mathematical abilities, Janet Hyde (1994) discussed analyses of different ethnic groups in the United States. The gender difference was largest for Whites, showing a small advantage for men. For African Americans, Hispanic Americans, and Asian Americans, no differences appeared. She concluded, "Perhaps the traditional belief of psychologists that men do better at math tests is a result of reliance on mostly White samples in research" (Hyde, 1994, p. 457). Therefore, the patterns discovered by U.S. researchers may be a result based on inadequate comparisons rather than universal advantage.

Richard Nisbett (2003) also questioned the universality of cognitive processes, concentrating on differences between Western and Eastern cognitive styles. Nisbett argued that a long traditional of analytic, individualistic thought in Western cultures and a similarly long traditional of holistic, relational thinking in Eastern cultures has produced very different ways of thinking. He described studies that demonstrated a tendency among people in China, Japan, and Korea to notice and remember a wider variety of things in a picture, to be more influenced by the context of an event, and to have difficulty in separating the situation from the person. This dependence on situation led to poorer performance on the rod-and-frame test, one of the tests for spatial performance, than that by people in the United States (Ji, Peng, & Nisbett, 2000). Additional support for cross-cultural differences in cognitive performance on another spatial task came from a study (Kuehnen et al., 2001) that compared performance of people from two Western countries (United States and Germany) and two non-Western countries (Russia and Malaysia). The results indicated that the people from Russia and Malaysia performed more poorly on the embedded figures test; that is, they had more trouble seeing figures embedded in a drawing. Nisbett (2003) contended that his research has isolated few gender differences that are as large as cultural differences in cognitive processes. He noted a tendency for women in both Asian and European cultures to be more holistic in their thinking than men, but he maintained that men and women within a culture tend to think in similar ways and that the larger differences are cultural.

■ SUMMARY

The assessment of intelligence and cognitive abilities has a long history in psychology, dating from the development of the intelligence test. The Stanford–Binet, an early intelligence test, showed no gender differences, but the Wechsler tests revealed advantages on verbal tasks for women and girls and advantages in performance tasks for men and boys.

Assessing gender differences in various types of cognitive performance is complicated by the definition of what the assessments measure, and verbal, mathematics, and spatial performance have all been defined in various ways. Despite the stereotypical views that women have an advantage in verbal abilities, and men have an advantage in mathematics and spatial performance, the research shows a more complex picture. Women and men have advantages and disadvantages in each of these categories, depending on the skill, and individual factors are much more important than gender in each of these cognitive abilities.

The verbal advantage that was once associated with women is not only small but also disappearing, except for performance on writing tasks. Differences in some types of mathematics performance continue, but these differences are not clearly attributable to differences in innate ability and may be attributable to differences in the number of math courses completed, the selection of people who take the test, test construction factors, and higher male variability in performance. Men show an advantage in performing spatial visualization and mental rotation tasks and an occasional advantage on spatial perception tasks, but women show advantages on tasks of perceptual speed and memory for placement of objects. Therefore, any conclusion about a male advantage in spatial ability is overly simplistic.

Other cognitive abilities show no gender-related differences. These abilities include learning and memory, creativity, musical ability, and the ability to read nonverbal cues. Some studies have shown gender differences in these abilities, but these studies have fallen along gender-stereotypical lines. Studies on wayfinding have revealed differences in strategies, with women preferring landmarks and men preferring position orientation. These strategy differences do not make significant differences in success in finding one's way. The differential achievement for men and women in creative arts and music reflects variance in social support and access to these careers rather than differences in ability.

Both biological and social theories attempt to explain gender differences in cognitive abilities. The biological theories have focused on prenatal hormones and their effects on developing brain structures. A growing body of evidence indicates that hormones play a role in both brain development and functioning, but the magnitude of differences is small and may lack any practical significance.

Theories that emphasize the social aspects of gender-related cognitive differences hypothesize that biological differences become magnified and selected through cultural and experiential processes, producing larger differences in the choices that women and men make than the differences that come from their abilities. The differences in performance on cognitive tasks are small, and individuals vary from each other a great deal, but men's and women's choices differ a great deal. These choices have huge implications for the lives of men and women.

Studies of other cultures and other ethnic groups have revealed that the advantage for men in mathematics and spatial ability tests may be the result of testing a limited group. White college students in the United States show larger gender differences than other groups around the world. However, cross-cultural research on cognition indicates that cultural influences on thought may be large.

◼ GLOSSARY

mental rotation   a subtype of spatial ability that in-cludes the ability to visualize objects as they would appear if rotated in space.

spatial perception   a subtype of spatial ability that in-cludes the ability to identify and locate the horizontal or vertical in the presence of distracting information.

spatial visualization   a subtype of spatial ability that refers to the ability to process spatial information so as to understand the relationship between objects in

space, such as the ability to see a figure embedded in other figures, find hidden figures in a drawing or pic-ture, or imagine the shape produced when a folded piece of paper is cut and then unfolded.

spatiotemporal ability   a subtype of spatial ability that involves judgments about moving objects in space, such as making a judgment about when a moving ob-ject will arrive at a target.

◼ SUGGESTED READINGS

Halpern, Diane F. (2000). *Sex differences in cognitive abilities* (3rd ed.). Mahwah, NJ: Erlbaum.

Halpern examines the complexities of cognitive per-formance, including details about the biological and environmental factors that affect performance on cog-nitive tasks. She believes that biology is an important contributor to cognition and the gender differences in performance, but she is also critical of these views.

Hyde, Janet Shibley. (1996). Where are the gender differ-ences? Where are the gender similarities? In David M.

Buss & Neil M. Malamuth (Eds.), *Sex, power, con-flict: Evolutionary and feminist perspectives* (pp. 107–118). New York: Oxford University Press.

This review by one of the leading researchers in the area of gender comparisons provides a brief summary of the history of gender research, an explanation of the technique of meta-analysis, and a summary of cogni-tive and other gender differences and similarities.

5 THEORIES OF GENDER DEVELOPMENT

■ HEADLINE   Freud Was Way Wrong
New York Times, June 11, 2000

In examining the lives and goals of contemporary women, Maureen Dowd (2000, p. 17) proposed that "Freud believed that men had something that women wanted. But it wasn't what he thought." Dowd referred to Freud's theory of personality and its emphasis on gender differences, but she described Freud as "way wrong" when he contended that women wanted to be like men.

The main thing that Freud believed that women wanted was a penis. Indeed, the concept of *penis envy* was an important element in Freud's conceptualization of female gender development. Dowd (and many others) differ with Freud's view of what women want and also in how women and men develop gender identity. Dowd argued that women want power and the possibility of controlling important factors in their lives. This view is similar to that of some of Freud's critics, who have reformulated psychodynamic theories of personality development.

In addition, other theorists have proposed alternative views of gender development. This chapter explores those theories, beginning with Freud and his psychodynamic theory.

THE PSYCHODYNAMIC APPROACH TO PERSONALITY

Sigmund Freud, a Viennese neurologist, devised a theory that emphasizes the differences between personality development and functioning of men and women. Freud's theory was controversial when he developed it, during the last part of the 19th century, and remains so, partly because he saw women as inferior to men. Countering the sexism in Freud's theory, Karen Horney proposed an alternative psychodynamic theory of personality and gender development, and Nancy Chodorow devised a contemporary version of psychodynamic personality theory.

Freud's Theory of Personality

Freud's theory hypothesizes the existence of the **unconscious,** a region of the mind that functions beyond conscious personal awareness. He described the basic energy for personality development and functioning with a word that is most often translated as "instinct" but might also be translated as "drive" or "impulse" (Feist & Feist, 2002). Freud hypothesized that the life, or sexual, instinct and the death, or aggressive, instinct furnish the dynamic energy for personality development and functioning. That is, these **instincts** are the forces that underlie thought and action.

Freud's View of Gender Identity Development. Freud's medical background led him to consider these instinctive forces to be biologically determined. The role of biology was also important in personality development, which Freud described in terms of **psychosexual stages.** These stages start at birth and continue through adulthood in a sequence named according to the regions of the body that were most important for sexual gratification. The early stages were the most important for personality development, emphasizing the importance of early childhood for personality formation.

By hypothesizing that the first psychosexual stage began at birth, Freud described infants as sexual beings and explained many of their actions as sexually oriented. Freud termed the first psychosexual stage the *oral stage,* during which babies receive sexual gratification from putting things into their mouths. Although this interpretation can be difficult to accept, his description of infants' behavior is easy to verify: Babies have a strong tendency to put things into their mouths.

During the next stage, the *anal stage,* the child receives pleasure from excretory functions. The main frustrations at this stage come from toilet training, and unresolved problems in this psychosexual stage appear in adult behavior as concerns with neatness, stubbornness, and retaining possessions.

The *phallic stage* begins in children around 3 or 4 years of age and is the first of Freud's psychosexual stages that describes a different course of personality development for boys and girls (Freud, 1933/1964). During this stage, sexual pleasure shifts from the anal region to the genitals; children begin to focus on their genitals, and they gain pleasure from masturbation. Parents are often disturbed by their children's masturbation and try to discourage or prevent this activity, furnishing one source of frustrated development during this stage.

Freud believed that the focus on genital activity resulted in a sexual attraction to the parent of the other sex and an increasing desire to have sex with this parent. These dynamics occur on an unconscious level, outside of children's awareness, and set the stage for the **Oedipus complex.** Freud used the Greek tragedy *Oedipus Rex* as an analogy for the interactions that occur within families during the phallic stage. According to the story, the oracle prophesied that Oedipus would kill his father and marry his mother, and this prophecy came true. Freud hypothesized that all boys feel jealousy, hatred, and aggression directed toward their fathers and sexual longing for their mothers. In boys, these family interactions result in competition with their fathers for their mothers' affections and growing hostility of the fathers toward their sons.

Boys in the phallic stage concentrate on their genitals and prize their penises. They notice the anatomical differences between girls and boys, which leads them to realize that everyone does not have a penis (Freud, 1925/1989). The realization that girls lack penises is shocking, disturbing, and threatening because, boys reason, penises must be removable.

Indeed, boys come to fear that their fathers will remove their penises because of the boys' hostility toward their fathers and affection for their mothers. Thus, boys experience the **castration complex,** the belief that castration will be their punishment. Boys believe that girls have suffered this punishment and are thus mutilated, inferior creatures.

These feelings of anxiety, hostility, and sexual longing are all intense and produce great turmoil for boys. All possibilities seem terrible: to lose their penises, to be the recipient of their fathers' hatred, or to be denied sex with their mothers. To resolve these feelings, boys must end the competition with their fathers and deny their sexual wishes for their mothers. Both goals can be met through identification with their fathers. This identification accomplishes several goals. First, boys no longer feel castration anxiety, because they have given up the sexual competition that originated such feelings. Second, boys no longer feel hostility toward their fathers; they now strive to be like their fathers rather than competing with them. Third, boys no longer desire their mothers sexually, but instead, they receive some vicarious sexual gratification from the identification with their fathers, who have a sexual relationship with the mothers. By identifying with their fathers and becoming masculine, boys develop a sexual identity that includes sexual attraction to women. Therefore, identification with fathers is the mechanism through which boys resolve the Oedipus complex and develop a masculine identity.

Freud hypothesized a slightly different resolution to the Oedipus complex in girls. During the phallic stage, girls also notice the anatomical differences between the sexes. Aware that they do not have penises, girls become envious of boys and experience *penis envy* (Freud, 1925/1989). Freud hypothesized that penis envy is the female version of the castration complex and that girls experience feelings of inferiority concerning their genitals. Their clitorises are so much smaller than penises, and they perceive their vaginas as wounds that result from their castration. Furthermore, girls hold their mothers responsible for their lack of penises and develop feelings of hostility toward them. Fathers become the

◼ GENDERED VOICES

Big Guns

"I just joined a gun club," a man told me, "and the men in the club do appear to have a relationship with their guns that seems symbolic to me. Of course, guys who own guns are pretty macho, but I have noticed two distinct styles, one of which seems more Freudian than the other.

"One style concentrates on shooting, and those men seem to like weapons that allow accuracy. Those types of guns tend to be rifles and are pretty light-weight. Maybe that's symbolic, but the other style concentrates on the size of the weapon. With some of these guns, it's just not possible to shoot accurately, but they are big guns with lots of firepower. That's all that some of these guys go for, that's all they talk about—how many guns they have and how big they are. They don't really want to shoot targets, but they want to shoot, and they seem to love their big guns. It's pretty embarrassing, in a symbolic sense."

object of their affection, and girls wish to have sex with their fathers and to have babies. Freud saw both the desire for sex and the wish for a baby as substitutes for penises and as expressions of penis envy. It was this part of Freud's theory that Dowd (2000) considered "way wrong."

The feelings that accompany the male Oedipus complex—hostility and competition— are also present in the female version. Girls, however, cannot experience the castration complex in the same way that boys do, because girls have no penises to lose. Thus, girls do not experience the trauma of the phallic stage as strongly as boys. Girls must still surrender their sexual desires for their fathers and identify with their mothers, but the process is not as quick or as complete as it is for boys (Freud, 1933/1964).

After the resolution of the Oedipus complex, children enter the *latency stage,* during which little overt sexual activity occurs. This stage lasts until puberty, when physiological changes bring about a reawakening of sexuality, and children enter the *genital stage*. During the genital stage, individuals will desire a genital relationship with people of the other sex. The regions of the body that have furnished sexual pleasure during childhood are now secondary to genital pleasure obtained through intercourse.

Table 5.1 shows Freud's psychosexual stages and the types of gender-related differences that he hypothesized for these stages. Development is similar for girls and boys in several stages but differs drastically in the phallic stage. Freud also believed that women have a more difficult time achieving a mature sexual relationship than men do. He described

TABLE 5.1 *Freud's Psychosexual Stages and Gender-Related Differences in Each Stage*

Stage	Gender-Related Difference
Oral	None
Anal	None
Phallic	Boys notice that they have penises and that girls do not
	Girls notice that boys have penises and that they do not
	Oedipus complex
	Boys experience extreme trauma connected with the Oedipus complex, undergo stronger identification with their fathers, and develop a stronger sense of morality
	Girls experience less Oedipal trauma, undergo weaker identification with their mothers, and develop a weaker sense of morality
Latency	None
Genital	Women must transfer their sexual pleasure from their clitorises to their vaginas, making mature sexuality more difficult for them
	Men's penises remain the center of their sexuality, making mature sexuality easier for them

the sexuality of the phallic stage, with its emphasis on masturbation, as immature sexuality that should be replaced in the genital stage with mature, heterosexual intercourse. For men, such activity involves their penises, but women must redirect their sexual impulses away from their clitorises and toward their vaginas.

Freud believed that girls have little awareness of their vaginas until puberty and that the redirection of their sexual energies is another difficult task for women. Freud believed that women who failed to achieve pleasure from vaginal intercourse had not achieved the mature, genital type of sexuality that signaled adequate personality development.

Freud and Women.   Freud knew that his theory was uncomplimentary to women, because his female associates, such as Karen Horney, told him so (Gay, 1988). He gave the matter a great deal of thought and heard many criticisms but never changed his mind about women being, essentially, failed men. Although Freud may have thought women were inferior in some ways, intelligence was not among them. Freud considered that an intelligent, independent woman deserved credit and praise and might be "virtually as good as a man" (Gay, 1988, p. 507).

Freud seemed to have held contradictory attitudes about women (Feist & Feist, 2002). On the one hand, Freud was a proper Victorian gentleman who wanted women to be sweet, pleasant, and subservient. On the other hand, he admired women who were intelligent and "masculine" in their pursuit of intellectual achievement and careers. Freud acted on both beliefs. His wife, Martha, held the role of wife and mother and shared none of his professional life. Feminists were prominent among the intellectual circles of Vienna and Germany where psychoanalysis gained prominence, and many women participated in these discussions (Kurzweil, 1995).

Although Freud contended that the sexes could never be equal and disparaged the efforts of feminists, who argued for the equality of men and women, he also admitted women into the ranks of psychoanalytic training at a time when women were admitted to few professions (Tavris & Wade, 1984). The person who carried on his work was his daughter, Anna, whom he encouraged to become an analyst. However, his most intimate personal friends were all men.

Therefore, Freud's attitudes about women and their personalities showed some inconsistency. Freud undoubtedly held negative attitudes about women, and he expressed his lack of understanding and lack of certainty about women in several of his papers. One of Freud's last statements about women appeared in his 1933 paper, "Femininity." He concluded with a tentative statement about women, acknowledging his awareness of the criticisms and also his own far-from-complete understanding:

> That is all I had to say to you about femininity. It is certainly incomplete and fragmentary and does not always sound friendly. But do not forget that I have only been describing women in so far as their nature is determined by their sexual function. It is true that that influence extends very far; but we do not overlook the fact that an individual woman may be a human being in other respects as well. If you want to know more about femininity, inquire from your own experiences of life, or turn to the poets, or wait until science can give you deeper and more coherent information. (Freud, 1933/1964, p. 135)

Other researchers and theorists have attempted the last alternative rather than the first two. In general, they have sought other information about personality and gender. One of those theorists was Karen Horney, a colleague of Freud.

Horney's Theory of Personality

Horney was one of the first German women to enter medical school, in which she specialized in psychiatry. After completing a training analysis with one of Freud's close associates, she began to attend seminars and to write papers on psychoanalysis (Feist & Feist, 2002). Soon, however, Horney became a vocal critic of Freud's theory of personality, especially concerning gender differences in personality development. Horney reexamined Freud's concepts of penis envy, inferiority feelings in women, and the masculinity complex (the expression of masculine behavior and attitudes in women). In addition, Horney's interpretation of feminine **masochism** (deriving pleasure from pain) differed from the Freudian version.

Her reexamination included pointing out the masculine bias in psychoanalytic theory (Quinn, 1987). Although she argued for a course of personality development that differed from Freud's view, Horney stayed within the framework of psychodynamic theory, as shown by her acceptance of the unconscious as a motivating force in personality, her emphasis on sexual feelings and events in personality development, and her belief in the importance of early childhood experiences for personality formation. She differed from Freud in her interpretation of the significance of the events of early childhood and her growing belief in the importance of social rather than instinctual, biological forces in personality development.

Part of Horney's reinterpretation of psychoanalysis was an alternative view of the notion of penis envy, the feelings of envy that girls have when they discover that boys' penises are larger than their own clitorises. Horney (similar to Dowd's headline story) argued that penis envy was a symbolic longing for the social prestige and position that men experience, rather than a literal physical desire for penises. Indeed, she hypothesized that men envy women's capability to reproduce and proposed the concept of *womb envy*. She interpreted the male strivings for achievement as overcompensation for their lack of ability to create by giving birth.

Horney believed that men fear and attribute evil to women because men feel inadequate when comparing themselves to women. To feel more adequate, men must see women as inferior, which keeps men from contending with their own feelings of inferiority. She explained that men still retain the feelings of inferiority that originated with the perception of the small size of their penises during childhood, when they initially noticed them. Therefore, men go through life needing to prove their masculinity, and they do so by having sexual intercourse. Any failure in erection will be perceived as a lack of masculinity, making men constantly vulnerable to feelings of inferiority. Women have no similar problem and do not suffer feelings of inferiority for reasons related to sexual performance.

This resentment can lead men to attempt to diminish women, and these attempts may succeed, leaving women with feelings of inferiority. Therefore, female inferiority originates with male insecurities rather than, as Freud hypothesized, with the female perception

TABLE 5.2 *Points of Agreement and Disagreement in Horney's and Freud's Psychoanalytic Theories*

Concept	Horney's Theory	Freud's Theory
Existence of unconscious	Yes	Yes
Importance of early childhood experiences	Yes	Yes
Gender differences in personality	Yes	Yes
Source of differences	Social	Biological
Feelings of envy for other gender	Men envy women's ability to give birth	Women envy men's penises
Feelings of inferiority	Constant need to perform sexually leads men to feel inferior	Lack of penises leads women to feel inferior
Masculinity complex	Driven by girls' lack of acceptance of femininity and identification with their fathers	Driven by girls' feeling of inferiority
Masochism	Socially determined part of development that is abnormal for women as well as men	Biologically determined, inevitable part of feminine development; abnormal in men

of inferior genitals. These female feelings of inferiority are perpetuated by men's behavior toward women and by the masculine bias in society.

Table 5.2 shows the points of agreement and disagreement between Horney's and Freud's psychodynamic theories. As this table shows, both theories accept the importance of unconscious forces and early childhood experiences. However, the difference in their interpretations of the importance and causes of other events makes the two theories substantially different.

Contemporary Psychodynamic Theories of Personality Development

Freud's theory of personality appeared during the late 19th and early 20th centuries in a Victorian culture that viewed women as passive, dependent, and intellectually inferior to men. This view of women was easy for Freud to accept, not only because it was the view of his culture but also because his female patients reflected these characteristics. Freud built his theory on the basis of observing his patients, many of whom were upper-class, bored, unhappy, mentally unhealthy women who lived in a repressive society that assumed women's inferiority. The extent to which their experiences reflect that of contemporary women is questionable, but Freud's female patients and the culture in which they lived influenced his view of women.

During the time that Freud formulated his theory, a feminist movement was active in Europe and the United States (Kurzweil, 1995), and Freud's theory was never popular among those women and men who believed in and worked for fair treatment for women, both by society and in personal relationships. That discontent also emerged during the 1970s, when feminist scholars turned their attention to gender development. Some created psychodynamic theories of personality development that not only removed the objectionable elements of Freud's theory but also created revisions of his theory that are compatible with a positive view of women. Sociologist Nancy Chodorow (1978, 1979, 1994) and psychologist Ellyn Kaschak (1992) have formulated psychodynamic theories that are significant departures from Freud's view. Chodorow's theory proposes a progression of development that gives women advantages, and Kaschak's theory replaces the emphasis on male psychological development with a woman-centered view of personality. Both theories are examples of feminist psychoanalytic theory.

Chodorow's Emphasis on Mothering.   Like Freud, Chodorow (1979) expressed pessimism about any potential equality between men and women. Unlike Freud (who concentrated on the perception of anatomical differences), Chodorow's reasons for believing in the continuation of inequality focused on the early experiences of children in relation to their mother. Chodorow described a psychodynamic theory of development that concentrates on the **pre-Oedipal period** during early childhood, before the Oedipus complex, and centers on the process of being mothered by a woman.

Although Chodorow (1978) acknowledged that women are not unique in their capacity to care for infants, she also granted that mothers (or other women) provide most nurturing, and fathers (or other men) do little caregiving. Thus, Chodorow explained how this early relationship between mother and infant makes a permanent imprint on personality development—an imprint that differs for boys and girls.

Chodorow (1978) described early infant development in terms similar to traditional psychodynamic theory. Babies have no sense of self versus other people or the world; infants are one with the world, and most of their world is their mother. The early mother–daughter relationship is closer than the mother–son relationship, because mothers and daughters are of the same sex. Infants have no initial perception of their sex or gender, but mothers always know about the sex of their infants and treat girls and boys differently.

Chodorow (1978) hypothesized that when children start to develop a sense of self and to separate from their mothers, events differ for girls and boys. Girls have an easier task in developing a sense of self because they have already identified with their mothers. This identification gives them an advantage in developing a separate identity, because this identity will likely be feminine and much like their mothers. Boys, on the other hand, have a more difficult time in developing separate identities because they have already identified with their mothers. To become masculine, boys must reject the femininity of their mothers and develop an identity that is different as well as separate. Thus, boys have a more difficult task than girls in accomplishing these developmental goals of separation and identity.

But according to Chodorow, girls never separate from their mothers as completely as boys do. The gender similarity is something that both mothers and daughters know, and this similarity between the two influences each. One study (Benenson, Morash, & Petrakos, 1998) confirmed the difference in emotional closeness between daughters and sons, as Chodorow's theory hypothesizes. Boys must work to accomplish their separation, even with the aid of their mothers. This effort extracts a price. Chodorow (1978) described the aftermath of boys' separation in terms of their rejection of all femininity and the development of fear and mistrust of the feminine. Chodorow thus explained the almost worldwide denigration of women by men as a by-product of boys' efforts to distinguish and separate themselves from their mothers. On the other hand, girls have no such need, and they accept their mothers and the feminine role without the turbulence that boys experience. Girls grow into women and reproduce their early relationships with their mothers in their own mothering.

Table 5.3 shows the differences between Chodorow's feminist psychoanalytic theory and traditional psychoanalytic theory. Notice that the differences lie not only in the outcomes but also in the stage of development that each theory hypothesizes to be important in personality development and in gender-related differences.

Thus, Chodorow's psychodynamic theory represents an alternative to Freud's theory. Although she retained the emphasis on early childhood, Chodorow concentrated on the pre-Oedipal period and on the early infant–mother relationship. She also hypothesized a different course of personality development for boys than for girls, but in Chodorow's theory girls have an easier time in developing gender. Their similarity to their mothers makes femininity an easier identity to develop than boys, who must find ways to separate themselves from their mothers and find masculine gender identity.

Kaschak's Antigone Phase.   Ellyn Kaschak's (1992) psychodynamic theory makes an analogy in personality development to Antigone who, like Oedipus, is a character from Greek plays by Sophocles. Kaschak argued that the Oedipus legend was useful in Freud's theory of male personality development, but that the minor changes Freud made to accommodate women in his female Oedipus complex were inadequate. Instead, Kaschak casts female personality development in terms of Antigone, Oedipus's daughter (and half-sister).

In Sophocles' plays, Antigone was the daughter of Oedipus and Jocasta (who was Oedipus's mother). After Oedipus learned of his incest with Jocasta, he destroyed his eyes,

TABLE 5.3   *Differences between Chodorow's Feminist Psychoanalytic Theory and Traditional Freudian Theory*

	Stages	*Gender-Related Outcome*
Chodorow's Theory	Pre-Oedipal stages	Boys work toward separation from mother, rejecting femininity. Girls retain connectedness with mother, becoming feminine.
	Oedipus conflict	Gender differences have already emerged.
Freud's Theory	Pre-Oedipal stages	No gender-related differences emerge.
	Oedipus conflict	Family dynamics and perception of differences in genitals prompt personality differences.

and Antigone then became her blind father's guide and caretaker. Antigone sacrificed an independent life to care for her blind father, and he considered it his right to have this level of devotion. Kaschak (1992) interpreted personality development of men and women in similar terms: "As Oedipus' dilemma became a symbol for the dilemma of the son, so might that of Antigone be considered representative of the inevitable fate of the good daughter in the patriarchal family" (p. 60).

Men grow and develop in societies that allow them power in those societies and in their families, and in taking this power, men come to consider women their possessions. Women grow and develop in situations of subservience in which they are men's possessions, and women's lives and personalities reflect this status. Kaschak (1992) hypothesized that many men and women never resolve these complexes because the social structure perpetuates differential power for women and men, encouraging both to adhere to these different roles.

For men, an unresolved Oedipus complex results in treating women as extensions of themselves rather than as independent people. With this sense of entitlement, men tend to seek power and sex in self-centered ways that may be destructive to others, such as family violence, incest, and rape. Consistent with Kaschak's formulation, Michael Johnson (1995) researched family violence and proposed that some men engage in systematic violence within their families because they feel that they have the right to do so. He called this form of family violence *patriarchal terrorism.*

When women fail to resolve the Antigone phase, they allow themselves to be extensions of others rather than striving for independence. Girls learn that men are important and their own wishes are less so, thus limiting their lives with this knowledge. Among those limits are restrictions on what women may do in the world and conforming to a limited sexuality, all defined and controlled by men. In addition, women learn to deny their physicality and try to make their bodies invisible, and this denial can be expressed in terms of eating disorders. These limits can lead to feelings of self-hatred and shame and the need to form relationships with others to feel self-worth.

Men who resolve their Oedipus complex relinquish their grandiosity and drive for power, see women as whole persons rather than possessions, and come to see themselves as individuals who act within boundaries and limits, rather than as kings.

Women who successfully resolve the Antigone phase achieve separation from their fathers and other men to become independent people. This independence allows them to form relationships with women, which Kaschak believes to be a problem for women who have not resolved the Antigone phase. In their relationships with men, women who have resolved these issues are able to stop making men central to their lives and can form interdependent, flexible relationships. Table 5.4 shows the four possibilities in Kaschak's view of personality development—men and women who have and have not resolved major developmental issues.

Is feminist psychodynamic theory an improvement over traditional psychoanalytic theory? All versions of psychoanalytic theory have the shortcoming of relying heavily on unconscious mental processes to explain important events in personality development, which poses problems for scientific testability. Therefore, any psychoanalytic theory shares the problem of providing adequately observable research evidence.

TABLE 5.4   *Possible Outcomes of Personality Development According to Kaschak*

	Not Resolved	*Resolved*
Men *(Oedipal phase)*	Patriarchical	Nonpatriarchical
	Gaining power a major goal	Gaining power not a major issue
	See women as extensions of self—they have the right to have women serve them	See women as independent
	Sexually self-centered	Sexually unselfish
Women *(Antigone phase)*	Accept subservience	Reject subservient role
	Passive and dependent	Assertive and independent
	Accept male-defined sexuality	Define their own sexuality
	Deny their own needs, including physical needs	Accept and express their own needs
	Cannot form friendships with other women	Form friendships with other women

Both traditional and modern psychoanalytic theory emphasize the importance and inevitability of gender differences, but other theories of gender development do not share this view. Several theories concentrate on the social factors in children's lives to explain how gender develops. Like Dowd (2000) in the headline story for this chapter, they contend that "Freud was way wrong," but in different ways than Dowd proposed. The influence of social factors forms the foundation for social learning theory, cognitive developmental theory, gender schema theory, and gender script theory.

SOCIAL LEARNING THEORY

Social learning theory explains gender development in the same way that it explains other types of learned behaviors, by placing gender development with behaviors that are learned. The process of gender development is learning a **gender role,** which consists of socially significant activities that men and women engage in with different frequencies. Robert Brannon (1976) discussed the origin of the concept of *role,* tracing its adoption in the field of social science back to the terminology of the theater. The word *role* was French for "roll," referring to the roll of paper on which an actor's part was printed. This usage is particularly meaningful, if we consider that the role, or the part a person plays, differs from the person. Therefore, the male gender role or the female gender role is like a script that men and women follow to fulfill their appropriate masculine or feminine parts. Social scientists use the term *role* to mean expected, socially encouraged patterns of behavior exhibited by individuals in specific situations. Thus, a person acts to fulfill a role by behaving in the expected way in the appropriate situation.

Social learning theory emphasizes the influence of the social environment. Biological sex differences are the basis for gender roles, but social learning theorists contend that a great many other characteristics and behaviors that have no relation to sex have been tied to gender roles. In this view, gender role development is the result of social factors (Bandura, 1986; Bussey & Bandura, 1999).

The social learning approach is a variation of traditional learning theory, which includes the principles of operant conditioning developed by B. F. Skinner. **Operant conditioning,** is a form of learning based on applying **reinforcement** and **punishment.** To understand the relationship between social learning theory and traditional learning theory, a consideration of traditional learning theory and the concept of operant conditioning is in order.

In this traditional view, learning is defined as a change in behavior that is the result of experience or practice. Operant conditioning is one type of learning. In operant conditioning, a person (or other animal) changes behavior after receiving either reinforcement or punishment. The behavior is more likely to be repeated in the future if that person (or animal) has received a reinforcer after performing the behavior in the past. That is, a reinforcer is any stimulus that increases the probability that a behavior will recur. On the other hand, a person is less likely to repeat a behavior in the future if that person has been punished after performing the behavior. Punishment is any stimulus that decreases the probability that a behavior will recur. The previous consequences of a behavior thus influence the resulting behavior, with reinforcers making the behavior more likely and punishments making it less likely. Patterns of reinforcement or punishment produce change in behavior, which is the definition of learning. Table 5.5 gives an example of how reinforcements and punishments can work to mold gender-related behaviors.

Traditional learning theorists attempted to avoid mentalistic concepts and terminology in their explanations of behavior. They rejected all concepts of internal mental processes

TABLE 5.5 *Results of Reinforcement and Punishment for Gender-Related Behaviors*

Behavior	Consequences	Result
Little girl plays with doll	*Reinforcement:* Her mother praises her toy choice	Girl plays with doll again
Little girl plays with truck	*Punishment:* Her mother scolds her for choosing a truck	Girl does not play with truck again
Little boy plays with doll	*Punishment:* His mother scolds him for choosing a doll	Boy does not play with doll again
Little boy plays with truck	*Reinforcement:* His mother praises his toy choice	Boy plays with truck again

that might underlie learning and concentrated instead on objectively observable behaviors. This approach emphasized the importance of the conditions under which learning occurs and the factors that affect performance, especially reinforcements and punishments received, rather than the cognitive factors within the learner.

The experiences of reinforcement and punishment furnish each individual with a unique learning history: No other person has exactly the same experiences. The reinforcements and punishments in each individual's history contribute to present and future behavior. Thus, future behavior can be predicted from past experience.

Social learning theory also includes the concepts of reinforcement and punishment, but it extends learning theory to include cognitive processes. This addition changes the emphasis of learning by increasing the importance of observation. Social learning theorists consider observation more important to the process of learning than reinforcement. To these theorists, learning is cognitive, whereas performance is behavioral. The social learning approach thus separates learning from performing learned behaviors, and it investigates factors that affect both.

According to social learning theory, learning is produced by observation rather than by directly experiencing reinforcement or punishment (Mischel, 1966, 1993). Observation provides many opportunities for learning, including the learning of gender-related behaviors among children. The social environment provides children with examples of male and female models who perform different behaviors, including gender-related ones. The models who influence children include mothers and fathers, but also many others, both real people and media images of boys, girls, men, women, and cartoon characters. In observing these many male and female models, children have abundant opportunities to learn. However, not all models have the same influence for all children, and not all behaviors are equally likely to be imitated.

The differential influence of models relates to their power or prestige as well as to the observer's attention and perception of the similarity between model and observer. Children tend to be more influenced by powerful models than by models with less power (Bussey & Bandura, 1984), but children are also more influenced by models who are similar to them. This similarity extends to gender, with children more likely to imitate same-sex models than other-sex models.

Another important factor in performing a learned behavior is observing the consequences of that behavior. If people observe a behavior being rewarded, then they are more likely to perform that behavior than if they see the same behavior punished or unrewarded. Social learning theorists believe that reinforcement and punishment are not essential for learning, which occurs through observation. Instead, reinforcement and punishment are more important to performance, affecting the likelihood that a learned behavior will be performed in circumstances similar to those observed.

Children develop in an atmosphere in which they are exposed to models of gender-stereotypic behaviors "in the home, in schools, on playgrounds, in readers and storybooks, and in representations of society on the television screens of every household" (Bandura, 1986, p. 93). These presentations do two things. First, all children are exposed to both female and male models, so all children learn the gender-related behaviors associated with *both* genders. Second, children learn which behaviors are gender-appropriate for them.

Children learn that certain behaviors are rewarded for girls but not for boys; for other behaviors, the rewards come to boys and not to girls.

For example, children see girls rewarded for playing with dolls, whereas they see boys discouraged and ridiculed for this same behavior. Children see boys rewarded for playing with toy trucks, but they may see girls discouraged from that behavior. Both boys and girls learn how to play with dolls and trucks, but they are not equally likely to do so due to the differential rewards they have seen others receive. Their learning is not based on observation of merely a few models; the world is filled with examples of men and women who are rewarded and punished for gender-related behaviors. The portrayals of gender-related behavior are especially stereotypical in the media (Lont, 1995) and offer a multitude of sexist examples for children to model (see "According to the Media" and "According to the Research"). Therefore, children may behave in ways different from their parents, including expressing sexist views that their parents do not endorse.

Not all observed consequences are consistent with each other; some people are rewarded and others punished for the same behavior. Consistency is not necessary for children to learn gender-related behaviors (Bandura, 1986). Children observe many models; they notice the consistencies among the behaviors of some models and start to overlook the exceptions. As more same-sex models exhibit a behavior, the more likely children are to connect that behavior with one or the other sex. Through this process, behaviors come to be gender related, although these behaviors may have no direct relationship to sex. Children learn to pay attention to sex and the activities associated with each, and thus they become selective in their modeling.

Children experience many sources of modeling and reinforcement, and these sources influence the development of gender-related behaviors (Bussey & Bandura, 1999). Beginning before birth, parents often have some preference for a boy or a girl—more often for a boy. When their children are infants, parents interact differently with their sons and daughters. For example, young children do not show strong preferences for gender-typical toys, but when parents choose toys for play, they tend to pick masculine toys for boys and feminine or neutral toys for girls (Wood, Desmarais, & Gugula, 2002). Parents are not alone in these preferences; in one study (Campenni, 1999), adults who were not parents showed even more stereotypical toy choices than parents did.

Studies that observe parental interactions with children have confirmed gender differences in treatment, but earlier studies tended to find greater differences than more recent studies. One early study (Fagot & Hagan, 1991) found that fathers gave fewer positive responses to their 18-month-old sons who chose to play with "girls' toys" and that mothers spent more time communicating with their daughters. A more recent study (Wood et al., 2002) showed fewer differences in how mothers and fathers play with their young children, but the tendency to choose "masculine" toys when playing with boys was still evident. For girls, these parents chose "feminine" or gender-neutral toys but not masculine ones. Thus, children receive differential reinforcement and encouragement for their toy choices. During the preschool years, boys come to believe that their fathers disapprove of cross-gender toy choices and behave accordingly, rejecting these toys (Raag & Rackliff, 1998). Thus, parents encourage some and discourage other gender-related behaviors.

ACCORDING TO THE MEDIA . . .

Girls Are in the Background in Cartoons

Children's television programming has always been oriented toward boys. The programming executives believe that boys are more numerous in the Saturday morning audience, and that boys will not watch programs with female lead characters (Thompson & Zerbinos, 1995). The early analyses of cartoon programming indicated few female characters; male characters outnumbered female characters by more than 3 to 1. A later analysis (Leaper, Breed, Hoffman, & Perlman, 2002) found that boys were more numerous in traditional action cartoons (such as *Spiderman*) but not in nontraditional adventure (such as *Reboot*) or in comedy cartoons. In both analyses, female characters were less visible, important, and active, but more polite, romantic, and supportive. These characteristics are stereotypically feminine and cast girls and women in traditional roles.

Between the 1970s and 1990s, gender portrayals in cartoons changed (Thompson & Zerbinos, 1995). Gender stereotyping persisted but at lower levels, and the presentation of female characters changed more than that of male characters. One of the factors in these changes was the nature of cartoon programming. Many of the cartoons in the earlier decades involved chases and pratfalls, and the main and secondary characters in such cartoons tended to be male. Such cartoons have declined in popularity, and thus the typical characters in cartoons have changed.

Continuing adventures have become the most common format for cartoons (Thompson & Zerbinos, 1995). Female characters are now more independent, assertive, intelligent, competent, and responsible and less emotional, sensitive, and tentative. The male characters in continuing adventures still behave in stereotypical ways for men, giving orders and being brave and aggressive. However, female characters are most independent and least domestic in this cartoon format.

The changes in the ways male and female characters are portrayed do not imply that gender stereotyping has disappeared from cartoons; it has not. Traditional action cartoons are very popular, especially among boys, and these cartoons still contain a high degree of gender-stereotypical portrayals (Leaper et al., 2002). Male characters still appear more often, talk more often, and are more active and assertive than female characters. Female characters still ask for and need more help, care for others, and show more affection than male characters. That is, male and female gender role traits and behaviors remain prominent in children's cartoons.

Social learning theory hypothesizes that these forces affect gender-related thinking, and children come to develop gender knowledge and gender standards for their own behavior. In children age 2 to 4 years, behavior typical of the same sex was more common than behavior typical of the other sex for all ages of children (Bussey & Bandura, 1992). The younger children in the study reacted to their peers in gender-stereotypical ways but did not regulate their own behavior by these same standards, whereas the older children did both. These results indicate that these 4-year-olds had begun to develop a coherent set of standards that they applied to their gender-related behaviors.

When children start interacting with peers outside the home, these other children become a major source of both modeling and approval. Children's play groups tend to be gender segregated, especially in school settings. Children often put a great deal of effort into maintaining this segregation and even begin to use insults and severe prohibitions aimed at those who attempt to join an other-sex group (Thorne, 1993). The formation of

ACCORDING TO THE RESEARCH . . .

Gender Depictions of Cartoon Characters Convey a Message

Children must notice and be influenced by the disparity in presentations of female and male cartoon characters for this stereotyping to be a factor in children's behavior, and they do. According to Kay Bussey and Albert Bandura (1999), the media offer many more opportunities for children to observe stereotypical gender behaviors than actual experience does. The extent of the influence depends on a number of factors, including how similar the media characters are to the children's perceptions of themselves. Thus, gender is one of the salient characteristics that influence whether a child will model a particular behavior.

Children who identify with television characters tend to choose gender-stereotypical characteristics as the basis for their identification (Hoffner, 1996). When asked to identify their favorite television characters, nearly all the boys and about half of girls chose a same-gender character. For the children who identified with male characters, intelligence was the most important characteristic, regardless of the gender of the child, but for boys, strength was also important. For the children who identified with female characters (all of whom were girls), attractiveness was the only significant factor. These choices reflect stereotypical criteria used by the 7- to 12-year-olds in the study.

Children not only notice but are also influenced by gender portrayals in cartoons. Interviews with children between ages 4 and 9 years (Thompson & Zerbinos, 1997) showed that 78% noticed that cartoons contained more male than female characters, and 68% noticed that boys talked more in cartoons. When asked what cartoon characters did, the children named behaviors stereotypically associated with men (being violent) and women (being considerate). In addition, the children who noticed the gender differences in the cartoon characters tended to be more likely to envision themselves in a gender-stereotypical job than did children who were less aware of the gender portrayals in cartoons. This tendency was stronger for boys than for girls. In contrast, the children who noticed characters behaving in nonstereotypical ways were the ones who were more likely to see themselves in nontraditional jobs. This tendency applied to both girls and boys.

Therefore, the gendered presentation of characters in cartoons has the power to do harm. Children notice and are influenced by these stereotypical presentations, and young children take this information into account when they imagine themselves in an occupation.

relationships, including the gender composition of play groups, is a topic explored in Chapter 9.

The differential treatment of boys and girls is enhanced by parents' and teachers' expectations and encouragement during the school years. Both parents and teachers are more likely to urge boys to persist in solving problems than they are to urge girls. By the time children reach adolescence, their models and reinforcements tend to encourage boys toward careers and sexual expression and girls toward domesticity and physical attractiveness (Peters, 1994). Therefore, children develop in environments that contain many sources of social learning that will lead to differences in the gender-related behaviors of boys and girls.

In summary, social learning theory views the development of gender-related behaviors as part of the overall development of many behaviors that children learn through observation and modeling. This theory emphasizes the contribution of the social environment

GENDERED VOICES

I Wouldn't Know How to Be a Man

"I never thought of myself as very feminine, but I wouldn't begin to know how to be a man," said a woman in her 30s. "There are thousands of things about being a man or being a woman that the other doesn't know. It takes years to learn all those things. I have been struck several times by the differences in women's and men's experience, by small things.

"During college one of my roommate's boyfriends decided to paint one of his fingernails. It was an odd thing to do, but he said that it was an experience he hadn't had, and he just wanted to try it. What was interesting was that he didn't know how to go about it—didn't know how to hold the brush, which direction to

apply the polish. It was interesting to watch him. That was the first time that I really thought, 'Men and women have some unique experiences that the other does not know.' I've had that thought several times since then, usually about small experiences or skills that women have and men don't.

"I'm sure that it works the other way, too. There's a world of little experiences that are part of men's lives that women don't have a clue about. For example, I wouldn't know how to go about shaving my face. In some sense, these experiences are trivial, but they made me think about the differences between the worlds of women and men."

to learning and behavior. Social learning theory sees learning, which occurs through observation, as cognitive and separate from performance, which is behavioral. Whether a learned behavior is performed depends on the observed consequences of the behavior and the observers' beliefs about the appropriateness of the behavior. Thus, children have many opportunities to observe gender-related behaviors from a wide variety of models, to develop beliefs about the consequences of those behaviors, and to exhibit appropriate gender-related behaviors as a result of their observation of these models.

Sandra Bem (1985) criticized social learning theory, arguing that the theory portrays children as too passive. Bem pointed out that children's behavior shows signs of more active involvement than social learning theory hypothesizes. Children do not exhibit a gradual increase in gender-related behaviors, but rather seem to form cognitive categories for gender and then acquire gender-related knowledge around these categories. In addition, research evidence suggests that children may develop stronger gender stereotypes than their parents convey, which implies that children actively organize information about gender. Other social theories of gender development place a stronger emphasis on cognitive organization than does social learning theory.

COGNITIVE DEVELOPMENTAL THEORY

The cognitive developmental theorist Lawrence Kohlberg (1966) described this theory by saying, "Our approach to the problems of sexual development starts directly with neither biology nor culture, but with cognition" (p. 82). Cognitive developmental theory views the acquisition of gender-related behaviors as part of children's general cognitive development. This development occurs as children mature and interact with the environment, forming an increasingly complex and accurate understanding of their bodies and the world around them.

This approach follows Jean Piaget's theory of cognitive development, which places the development of gender-related concepts into the category of growth of cognitive abilities, and which emphasizes children's active role in organizing their own thoughts (see Ginsburg & Opper, 1969). Piaget described four stages of cognitive development, beginning at birth and ending during preadolescence, throughout which children achieve cognitive maturity. During childhood, limitations in cognitive abilities lead children to have problems in classifying objects according to any given physical characteristic such as size or color. During their elementary school years, children gain in cognitive abilities but may still have difficulty in dealing with abstractions, such as the ability to imagine hypothetical situations—"what if." Piaget believed that once children reach cognitive maturity, at around age 11 or 12 years, they no longer have any cognitive limitations on their understanding. (Although lack of information may be a limitation at this or any age, this problem is different from the limits on cognitive ability that appear during childhood.) Thus, Piaget explained cognitive development as a series of stages leading to an increasing ability to understand physical reality and deal with abstract, complex problems. Infants are capable of almost no abstract thought, but by preadolescence, children have fewer limitations on their cognitive abilities.

Cognitive developmental theorists see the development of gender-related behaviors as part of the larger task of cognitive development. Very young children, lacking a concept of self, can have no concept of their gender. Most 2-year-olds are unable to apply the word *boy* or *girl* consistently to self or others; thus they fail at **gender labeling.** Kohlberg (1966) hypothesized that children acquire some preliminary category information about gender during early childhood. Gender labeling does not signal development of **gender identity,** the process of identifying oneself as female or male. Young children do not see gender as a permanent feature; they believe that a boy can become a girl if he wishes or that a girl might become a boy if she dressed in boys' clothing (Kohlberg, 1966). **Gender constancy** is the belief that gender will remain the same throughout life. This concept is a cognitively more complex and rarely appears before age 4. Children then begin to develop a gender identity based on a classification of self and others as irreversibly belonging to one gender or the other. This gender constancy is part of children's growing ability to classify objects based on physical criteria.

These cognitive developments in conceptualizing gender parallel other cognitive changes in children. Below age 5 or 6 years, children have an incomplete understanding of the qualities of physical objects, and their misunderstanding of gender is part of this limitation. By around age 6 years, children have developed a correct, if concrete, understanding of physical reality, including gender identity. Cognitive developmental theory sees changes that occur in gender identity as part of this process, and the mistakes that children make concerning gender identity are seen as part of their general cognitive limitations during the course of development.

The cognitive developmental approach is similar to the social learning approach in its emphasis on the role of cognition. However, the two approaches differ in several ways.

Cognitive developmental theory hypothesizes that development moves through a series of stages, whereas social learning theory does not rely on the concept of stages in development. That is, cognitive developmental theory sees gender role development as proceeding through discrete stages. Each stage has internal consistency and a set of differences that delineate it from successive stages. Social learning theory sees development as more continuous and not bounded by stages. Figure 5.1 illustrates the difference between development as a continuous process and as a series of stages.

Cognitive developmental theory views the acquisition of gender-related behaviors as a by-product of the cognitive development of gender identity. Children begin to adopt and exhibit gender-related behaviors because they adopt a gender identity and strive to be consistent with this identity. On the other hand, social learning theory hypothesizes that children come to have a gender identity because they model gender-related behaviors. Through the performance of these behaviors, children conform to either the masculine or the feminine social roles of their culture. Thus, social learning theory sees gender identity as coming from performance of gender-related behaviors, whereas cognitive developmental theory sees gender-related behaviors as coming from the cognitive adoption of a gender identity.

When children develop an understanding of categories, including gender categories, they tend to concentrate on the classification rules and show a great reluctance to make exceptions. Applied to gender, this strategy leads to classifying all women and all men by invariant physical or behavioral characteristics. Therefore, cognitive developmental theory

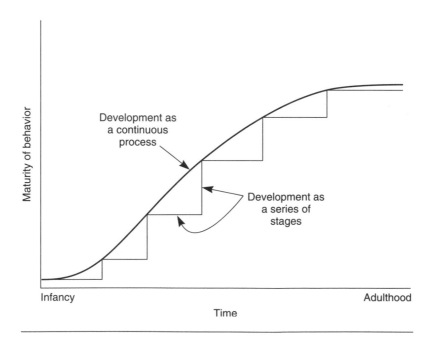

FIGURE 5.1 *Two Views of Development*

predicts that children will develop gender stereotypes as part of their process of developing gender identity. A great deal of research evidence substantiates the notion that children form stereotypical gender concepts beginning early in their lives. Children as young as 2 years old exhibit stereotypical gender-related knowledge, and this level of knowledge relates to their comprehension of gender identity and gender constancy (Poulin-Dubois, Serbin, Eichstedt, Sen, & Beissel, 2002; Kuhn, Nash, & Brucken, 1978). The process of acquiring gender stereotypes is related to the development of gender constancy (Warin, 2000). Stereotype development and maintenance are complex, and Chapter 7 explores this process more fully.

One problem with cognitive developmental theory comes from its emphasis on gender constancy as the primary force underlying the development of gender identity. Although Kohlberg's predictions are not completely clear on this point (Stangor & Ruble, 1987), he hypothesized that gender constancy is the most important component of cognitive developmental theory, and that all other facets of gender identity stem from establishing gender constancy. Research has failed to substantiate this contention (Martin & Little, 1990), leaving a major component of this theory in doubt.

Another problem with cognitive developmental theory comes from the need to treat gender the same as any other cognitive category. As Sandra Bem (1985) put it, "The theory fails to explicate why sex has primacy over other potential categories of the self such as race, religion, or even eye color" (p. 184). This theory fails to explain why children choose gender as a primary domain around which to organize information. This problem has been addressed in gender schema theory, which extends the concepts in cognitive developmental theory.

GENDER SCHEMA THEORY

Gender schema theory is an extension of the cognitive developmental theory. A **schema** is "a cognitive structure, a network of associations that organizes and guides an individual's perceptions" (Bem, 1981a, p. 355). Piaget used the term *schema* (plural, *schemata* or *schemas*) to describe how cognitions are internalized around various topics; gender schema theory hypothesizes that children develop gender-related behaviors because they develop schemata that guide them to adopt such behaviors. In this view, gender-related behaviors appear not only as a result of general cognitive development, but also because children develop special schemata related to gender.

According to gender schema theory, the culture also plays a role in gender development, providing the reference for the formation of gender schemata. Not only are children ready to encode and organize information about gender, but they also do so in a social environment that defines maleness and femaleness (Bem, 1985). As children develop, they acquire schemata that guide their cognitions related to gender. These schemata influence information processing and problem solving in memory and also regulate behavior (Martin & Halverson, 1981; Martin, Ruble, & Szkrybalo, 2002). Gender schema theorists believe that children use these schemata to develop a concept of self versus others, and each child's gender schema is included in that child's self-schema, or self-concept. In addition, gender schemata can provide a guide for concepts of personal masculinity and femininity, including personal judgments about how people personally fit, or fail to fit, these schemata (Janoff-Bulman & Frieze, 1987). Thus, gender schema theory provides an explanation for the concepts of masculinity and femininity and how people apply these concepts to themselves.

Bem (1985) emphasized the process rather than the content of gender schemata. The information in the schemata is not as important as the process of forming schemata and acting in ways that are consistent with them. Gender schema theory predicts that the cognitive changes that accompany schema formation lead to the ways that children process gender-related information, which changes the ways in which they behave. Research (Levy, Barth, & Zimmerman, 1998) confirmed these predictions, showing that gender-schematic preschoolers behaved in more gender-typical ways than less schematic children.

Gender schema theory also predicts that developing gender schemata increases accuracy and memory for gender-consistent information compared to gender-inconsistent information. A number of studies have demonstrated such memory effects in both children and adults. Gender-typed college students tended to remember words in clusters related to gender—for example, the women's proper names in one cluster and the men's names in another (Bem, 1981a). This schematicity did not affect the number of words remembered, but the organization of memory differed according to participants' gender schemata. In addition, participants with strong gender schemata were faster at making gender-related judgments that were consistent with their gender schemata than they were at making judgments inconsistent with their schemata. A longitudinal study with children in Hong Kong (Lobel, Bar-David, Gruber, Lau, & Bar Tal, 2000) demonstrated that the process of developing gender schemata is similar for these Asian children and results in similar changes in cognitive processing. Thus, gender schema theory has some validity across cultures.

The types of differences found among gender-schematic college students prompted further research using a similar approach, but with participants of various ages. A review of the research on gender schema and information processing (Stangor & Ruble, 1987) indicated that children with well-defined gender schemata tend to remember gender-consistent information better than gender-inconsistent information. For example, when children see drawings, photos, or videotapes in which men and women perform activities such as cooking and sewing or driving a truck and repairing appliances, gender-schematic children remember the gender-typical pairings (women cooking and sewing and men driving trucks and repairing appliances) better than the gender-atypical pairings (women driving trucks and repairing appliances and men cooking and sewing). In addition, children tend to change their memories to fit the gender-typical activities, such as remembering a man driving a truck when he was pictured as cooking. This tendency to distort memory in ways consistent with gender schemata suggests that the development of gender schemata influences the way that people interpret information.

In developing gender schemata, children become increasingly ready to interpret information in terms of gender. A tendency to interpret information in gender-schematic terms may lead to gender stereotyping—exaggerated and narrow concepts of what is appropriate and acceptable for each gender. The formation of gender stereotypes can be understood as a natural reflection of the use of gender schemata (Martin & Halverson, 1981;

Martin et al., 2002). Some of the effects of gender stereotyping are positive, such as increased ease in classifying behaviors and objects, which can give children the feeling that the environment is manageable and predictable. But stereotyping can also have negative effects, leading to inaccurate perceptions and failures to accept information that does not fit the stereotype. Thus, the existence of gender schemata prompts the formation of gender stereotypes, with both positive and negative consequences.

In summary, gender schema theory extends the cognitive developmental theory by hypothesizing the existence of gender schemata, cognitive structures that internally represent gender-related information and guide perception and behavior. Children internalize their schemata for masculinity or femininity to form a self-concept, or self-schema, for gender-related behaviors. Research has indicated that gender schemata can affect the processing of gender-related information and can lead to gender stereotyping.

GENDER SCRIPT THEORY

Gender script theory is an extension of gender schema theory, proposing that the social knowledge that children acquire concerning gender is organized in sequential form. Schemata are representations of knowledge, whereas scripts depict events as an organized sequence. That is, the concept of a script enlarges on the notion of schema by adding the component of sequential order. The script allows for the understanding of social relations and can be described as "an ordered sequence of actions appropriate to a particular spatial-temporal context, organized around a goal" (Nelson, 1981, p. 101).

Children as young as 3 years of age show evidence of the type of generalized sequential event knowledge that may be considered a script. Children can describe how to get ready to go out, how to eat lunch at day care, and many such sequences. If young children have well-organized knowledge of events, perhaps they use this organization to acquire information about gender.

Applied to gender role acquisition, gender scripts are "temporally organized event sequences. But in addition, gender scripts possess a gender role stereotype component which defines which sex stereotypically performs a given sequence of events" (Levy & Fivush, 1993, p. 113). For scripts such as eating lunch, the gender of the actor is not important, but the script for cooking lunch is likely to be gender specific.

Researchers have investigated the existence of gender scripts in information processing and memory, using tests that are similar to the ones used to test gender schema theory. Children of varying ages were given colored line drawings representing several gender scripts, such as building with tools and cooking dinner, and were asked to arrange the drawings in the order that these events would happen (Boston & Levy, 1991). The results indicated that older children were more accurate than younger children in doing so, but also that children (especially boys) were more accurate in ordering own-gender rather than other-gender sequences.

Gender scripts also influence memory. One study (Levy & Boston, 1994) presented children with two own-gender and two other-gender scripts and asked them to recall as many parts of the scripts as they could. The children were more accurate in recalling own-sex scripts, a similar memory effect to findings from research on gender schema theory. Another similarity in the cognitive difficulty with schemata is the tendency of younger children to be stricter in their adherence to the script than older children are (Levy & Fivush, 1993).

Therefore, the sequencing component of gender script theory seems to broaden the concept of gender schemata. The research on gender script theory is less complete than on the other theories of gender role development, but this theory is a promising addition to the other social theories of gender development.

Social learning theory, cognitive developmental theory, gender schema theory, and gender script theory all attempt to explain how children come to exhibit gender-related behaviors and choose personal concepts of masculinity and femininity. These theories all emphasize children's surroundings in the family and in society, but each theory has a different view of how children come to understand gender. Table 5.6 compares these theories. Each of these theories hypothesizes a course of development of gender-related knowledge and behavior, but what does the research on this topic indicate? How do children come to understand gender and develop gender typing, and how does the research fit with the theories?

WHICH THEORY IS BEST?

Each of these theories of gender development presents an orderly pattern of development, but the research shows a complex pattern with many components that do not necessarily match the theories. That is, none of the theories is able to explain all the data from research on gender development.

Social learning theory predicts a process of learning gender roles that results in a gradual matching of gender-related behaviors to the culturally prescribed pattern through modeling and reinforcement of gender-appropriate behaviors. Although the research shows that children begin learning information consistent with gender stereotypes at an early age, gender knowledge consists of several different concepts that do not appear incrementally. The finding that children learn gender labeling before gender-typical toy and clothing preferences indicates a pattern of gender knowledge development that social learning theory does not predict.

Research has substantiated the influence of parents, siblings, and peers in directing gender-related behaviors. Social learning theory predicts that family, peers, teachers, and media images of men and women affect children in their learning and performance of gender-appropriate behaviors. Modeling can be a powerful force in prompting the performance of gender-related behaviors (Bussey & Bandura, 1984, 1992, 1999), and same-sex siblings, parents, peers, and teachers are all important influences in the child's development of gender flexibility (Katz & Ksansnak, 1994). These findings are consistent with the predictions of social learning theory.

Social learning theory allows that girls and boys might differ not only in their gender-related behaviors but also in their cross-gender behaviors. The male gender role carries more power, and power is one of the factors that affects children's modeling. During childhood, boys are discouraged from performing feminine behaviors, whereas girls may not be discouraged from performing behaviors typical of boys. These differences lead to the

TABLE 5.6   *Comparison of Theories of Gender Development*

	Psychodynamic Theories	*Social Learning Theory*	*Cognitive Developmental Theory*	*Gender Schema Theory*	*Gender Script Theory*
Gender differences develop through . . .	Early childhood interactions with parents	Reinforcement and observation of models	General cognitive developmemt, especially gender constancy	Development of gender-specific schemata	Learning gender scripts
Children's participation involves . . .	Passively moving through stages	Choosing which models to imitate	Organizing information about physical world	Developing schemata specific to gender	Developing scripts through social interaction
Gender development begins . . .	During Oedipal period (Freud); during pre-Oedipal period (Chodorow)	As soon as the culture emphasizes it, usually during infancy	During preschool years	During preschool years	During early preschool years
Gender development proceeds . . .	Through resolution of Oedipus complex (Freud); through identification with or separation from mother (Chodorow)	Gradually becoming more like adult knowledge	Through a series of stages	Through development of schemata	Through learning script components
Gender development finishes . . .	With identification with same-sex parent	During adulthood, if at all	During late childhood or preadolescence	During late childhood	When all scripts are learned
Girls and boys . . .	Develop very different personalities; girls are inferior (Freud); boys have a more difficult time separating from mother (Chodorow)	May develop different gender knowledge as well as different gender-related behaviors	Develop similar cognitive understanding of gender	May develop different structures and schemata, depending on parents and family patterns	Develop different scripts, guided through learning stereotypes

prediction that boys should be more strongly gender-typed than girls, and research supports this difference. Cognitive developmental theory does not allow for a different pattern of development for boys and girls, whereas gender schema theory hypothesizes that parental attitudes and family patterns may produce variations in individual schemata. This theory does not specifically address differences in schemata between girls and boys.

Cognitive developmental theory hypothesizes that gender development comes about through cognitive changes that occur by way of general cognitive development. Research has indicated that gender development produces cognitive changes in accuracy and memory for gender-related information, but gender schema theory also predicts that cognitive changes come with the development of gender schema, making findings that support these cognitive changes applicable to either theory.

The prediction that gender constancy is the basis for developing all other gender knowledge has not been substantiated. Indeed, research has shown that gender constancy develops late, with many other components of gender knowledge appearing earlier. This failure is a serious problem for cognitive developmental theory. Another problem for this theory is that gender development continues during adolescence. According to cognitive developmental theory, children undergo no additional cognitive changes after early adolescence, but research has shown that late adolescence is a time during which individuals gain flexibility of gender beliefs.

Gender schema theory predicts that children develop a cognitive organization for gender, a schema, that forms the basis for their understanding of gender and directs their gender-related behaviors. The types of cognitive changes that this theory predicts have been found in modes of information processing, such as accuracy of judgments and memory effects. In preschool children, gender schematicity was a significant predictor of masculine and feminine gender-typed behaviors, but gender constancy was not related (Levy et al., 1998). In addition, women in traditional versus nontraditional jobs have different conceptualizations of gender-appropriate behavior (Lavallee & Pelletier, 1992), a finding consistent with gender schema theory.

Gender development seems to consist of several different cognitive abilities. One team of researchers (Hort, Leinbach, & Fagot, 1991) proposed that the cognitive components of gender development do not have a great deal of coherence; they postulated that such knowledge varies among individual children of the same age and stage of cognitive development. That is, gender knowledge may not fall into a pattern sufficiently coherent to be called a schema.

Gender script theory makes many of the same predictions as gender schema theory. Differentiating scripts from schemata allows for some additional predictions, and some research has confirmed children's abilities to learn and behave according to sequentially ordered patterns like scripts. Gender script theory has not been the subject of sufficient research to make firm conclusions, but it may offer advantages over gender schema theory.

It is evident from this discussion that all of the social theories of gender development make predictions that research has supported, and all make predictions that research has failed to confirm. The picture drawn from the research shows that gender development presents a more complex process than any of the theories can fully explain. Gender development consists of separate components—gender labeling, preferences for gender-typed activities, gender stereotyping, and gender constancy. These components appear to develop in a pattern, but the pattern does not exactly conform to any of those predicted by the theories. Thus, all of the social theories of personality development have been useful and have been partially confirmed, but none is without weakness.

SUMMARY

Psychoanalytic theory, originated by Freud, is the traditional approach to psychodynamic personality theory and relies on the concepts of unconscious forces and biologically determined instincts to explain personality development and functioning. Freud's theory hypothesized a series of psychosexual stages—oral, anal, phallic, latency, and genital—to account for the influence of childhood experiences on adult personality. Gender differences appear during the phallic stage, with its Oedipus complex in which children are attracted to their other-sex parent and feel fear and hostility toward their same-sex parent. Boys experience a more traumatic and a more complete resolution of the Oedipus complex than girls.

Horney disputed Freud's view that women inevitably experience inferiority by arguing that social, not biological, forces form the basis for personality differences between the sexes. Her analysis of the differences in personality development between men and women showed that men have feelings of inferiority compared to women, especially regarding women's ability to give birth. Horney hypothesized that men try to feel more adequate by disparaging women.

Feminist psychoanalytic theories include those originated by Nancy Chodorow and Ellyn Kaschak. Chodorow's theory emphasizes the primacy of the early relationship with mothers and hypothesizes that boys have a more difficult time separating themselves from the feminine than do girls. Men's success in forming a masculine identity results in a denial of all that is feminine, including a rejection of female values. Kaschak's theory relies on the Oedipus legend,

hypothesizing that Oedipus personifies men's drives for power and feelings of entitlement, whereas Antigone, the faithful daughter, personifies women's self-sacrifice. She maintained that patriarchal culture perpetuates these roles and makes resolving these complexes difficult for men and women.

The social theories of gender development provide alternatives to psychoanalytic theory to explain how infants come to identify themselves as male or female, to understand gender, and to behave in ways that their culture deems gender-appropriate. The social learning approach, a variation on traditional learning theory, relies on the concepts of observational learning and modeling to explain how children learn and perform gender-related behaviors. Initially the family, and later the broader culture, provide models and reinforcements for adopting certain gender-related behaviors while discouraging others. Research has supported the power of children's family and social surroundings to influence the development of gender-related behaviors, but the orderly pattern of gender development that occurs is not consistent with this theory.

Cognitive developmental theory holds that gender identity is a cognitive concept that children learn as part of the process of learning about the physical world and their own bodies. Children younger than 2 years of age have no concept of gender and cannot consistently label themselves or others as male or female. When children learn to classify genders, they have developed gender constancy, the understanding that gender is a permanent personal characteristic that will not change with any other physical transformation.

According to cognitive developmental theory, additional facets of gender development arise from gender constancy; however, research has indicated that gender constancy is among the last types of gender knowledge to be acquired. These findings present a problem for this theory.

Gender schema theory is an extension of cognitive developmental theory that explains gender identity in terms of schemata—cognitive structures that underlie complex concepts. When children acquire a gender schema, they change the way that they deal with information concerning gender and also change their behavior to conform to gender roles. This theory suggests that gender stereotyping is a natural extension of the process of developing gender schemata, and that children become stereotypical in their gender behavior and judgments. Parents who wish to raise nonsexist children can attempt to substitute alternative schemata that are less sexist than the ones predominant in their culture, although completely avoiding the formation of gender schemata is not possible for children.

Gender script theory is an extension of gender schema theory. Rather than holding that children develop gender schemata, this theory says that children learn about gender by acquiring scripts—ordered sequences of behavior with a gender stereotype component. These scripts allow children to organize their knowledge and facilitate social relationships. This theory shares many predictions with gender schema theory, but the body of research testing this theory is smaller than that for other theories. Thus, assessment of this theory is difficult at this point.

Psychodynamic theories have little research support, and gathering such evidence is difficult for these theories because they draw on unconscious factors. Evaluating the social theories of gender development leads to the conclusion that although each has supporting research, this research fails to confirm any one theory to the exclusion of the others.

GLOSSARY

castration complex in Freudian theory, the unconscious fear that the father will castrate his son as a punishment for the son's sexual longings for his mother.

gender constancy the knowledge that gender is a permanent characteristic and will not change with superficial alterations.

gender identity individual identification of self as female or male.

gender labeling the ability to label self and others as male or female.

gender role a set of socially significant activities associated with being male or female.

instincts in Freudian theory, the drives or impulses that underlie action, thought, and other aspects of personality functioning, which include the life, or sexual, instinct and the death, or aggressive, instinct.

masochism feelings of pleasure as a result of painful or humiliating experiences.

Oedipus complex in Freudian theory, the situation that exists during the phallic stage in which the child feels unconscious hostility toward the same-sex parent and unconscious sexual feelings for the opposite-sex parent. Freud used the story of Oedipus as an analogy for the family dynamics that occur during the phallic stage of personality development.

operant conditioning a type of learning based on the administration of reinforcement or punishment. Receiving reinforcement links the reinforcement with the behavior that preceded it, making the behavior more likely to be repeated.

pre-Oedipal period time during early childhood, before the phallic stage and the Oedipus complex. Some feminist psychoanalytic theorists, including Chodorow, have emphasized the importance of this period for personality development.

psychosexual stages in Freudian theory, the series of stages ranging from birth to maturity through which the individual's personality develops. These stages are the oral, anal, phallic, latency, and genital stages.

punishment any stimulus that decreases the probability that a behavior will be repeated.

reinforcement   any stimulus that increases the probability that a behavior will be repeated.

schema   (plural, **schemata** or **schemas**) an internal cognitive structure that organizes information and guides perception.

unconscious   in Freudian theory, a region of the mind functioning beyond a person's conscious awareness.

▪ SUGGESTED READINGS

Bussey, Kay; & Bandura, Albert (1999). Social-cognitive theory of gender development and differentiation. *Psychological Review, 106,* 676–713.
This lengthy article presents information in support of social learning theory and makes an argument that this theory is sufficient to explain gender development.

Chodorow, Nancy. (1978). *The reproduction of mothering: Psychoanalysis and the sociology of gender.* Berkeley, CA: University of California Press.
Chodorow's book is difficult reading, with its psychoanalytic terminology, but it offers a compelling alternative to Freud's theory and has influenced many of the scholars who take the feminist standpoint on personality development.

Kaschak, Ellyn. (1992). *Engendered lives.* New York: Basic Books.
Kaschak's book is not easy reading, but she offers an interesting, radical alternative to traditional psychoanalytic theory. Chapter 3, "Oedipus and Antigone Revisited: The Family Drama," presents her revision of Freudian theory, but the entire book is worth reading for its different view of gender and the impact of gender on all facets of psychology and culture.

Martin, Carol Lynn; Ruble, Diane N.; & Szkrybalo, Joel. (2002). Cognitive theories of early gender development. *Psychological Bulletin, 128,* 903–933.
This massive review of cognitive theories of gender development includes both cognitive developmental and cognitive schema theory as well as a defense of their research support and their importance to understanding gender development.

6 DEVELOPING GENDER IDENTITY

HEADLINE My Son Doesn't Act Like a Boy
Family Life, April 1, 2001

> When he was 4, he loved to wear red, sparkly shoes at school; he still [at age 8] enjoys playing with dolls. . . . What does this type of behavior really mean—if anything? . . . Today, few adults would question a girl who would rather play with a soccer ball than with Barbie. But the issue isn't as simple for boys. (Kalish, 2001, p. 60)

Nancy Kalish's (2001) article carried the subtitle "What It's Like to Have a Child Who Challenges Gender Stereotypes," which reported on boys who behave in ways that are typically associated with girls. Some of these boys wear girls' clothing, and others prefer playing with dolls over playing sports. These gender-atypical behaviors prompt concern among parents and even the children themselves. Like the mother in Kalish's article, parents of such children know that their sons' behavior is different, but feminism and the burgeoning men's movement have made parents hesitant to apply restrictions to their sons that they would not impose on their daughters. However, many of the parents do not know what this difference means. Most fear that these behaviors signal that their sons will be gay.

Experts such as William Pollack (1998) offer reassurance about boys who fail to fit the narrow restrictions of gender role and call for the type of expansion for the male gender role that has occurred for girls and women. As one mother in Kalish's story said, she had no trouble buying a baseball bat for her daughter, so why should she feel differently about getting her son a Barbie? As both Pollock and this mother had realized, the development of gender role behaviors is more rigidly fixed for boys than for girls, yet each goes through similar processes and stages in developing a self-concept of gender.

This chapter first traces the development of gender, then examines several sources of influence in the process of gender development, and finally considers those individuals for whom the process diverges.

GENDER IDENTITY DEVELOPMENT

Traditionally, a child's sex was announced at birth, but now many parents know their child's sex prenatally; this knowledge allows for gender differentiation even *before* a child is born. In either event, the pinks and blues appear early in children's lives. All social theories of gender development rate this type of differential treatment as important in causing children to attend to and adopt particular behaviors. But to what extent do typical gender behaviors signal the adoption of gender identity? Is it possible to behave in ways that are not typical for one gender or the other and yet have a firm notion of one's gender identity? Does the behavior of the boys in Kalish's (2001) headline story signal confusion over male gender identity or indicate only gender role behaviors that are not typical for boys?

Most people think of gender identity and gender role as the same thing, but many researchers have found it necessary to separate these concepts. The concept of **gender identity** has been defined in many ways, but the definitions include identifying and accepting the self as male or female. Gender role behaviors are those behaviors that are typically associated with males or females. Thus, children may behave in ways that are not typical for their gender and still have a clear gender identity, but exhibiting gender-atypical behaviors may also signal some problem in the development of gender identity.

For gender identity to develop, an individual must understand the categories of male and female and the characteristics that distinguish the two, what labels apply to each gender, what activities are associated with each category, and how she or he fits into one or the other category. Research indicates that these elements of gender identity are separable and that they develop at different times during childhood. This process might start early in infancy.

Development during Childhood

Some research indicates that infants possess gender-related knowledge, including the ability to tell the difference between male and female faces. Although infants' thoughts are difficult to study, one approach involves showing an infant objects such as photos of faces and measuring how long these objects hold the infant's attention. When infants see something new, they tend to gaze at the novel object; when they grow bored, they begin looking around rather than at the object. The process of becoming accustomed to an object is called *habituation.* By noting when infants attend to an object and when they grow bored (habituate), researchers can deduce which stimuli infants can distinguish and which they cannot. This technique also allows researchers to determine which objects infants find interesting and which are less so.

Results using such a procedure showed that infants had the ability to distinguish between women and men (Fagot & Leinbach, 1994; Leinbach & Fagot, 1993). Infants 7, 9, and 12 months old could distinguish male from female faces, mainly by using hair length as the distinguishing cue. This ability gives infants some basis to begin to make gender distinctions.

By age 24 months, infants showed some knowledge of gender-typical activities (Serbin, Poulin-Dubois, & Eichstedt, 2002). When presented with photographs of women and men performing gender-typical or gender-atypical activities, these young children attended longer to those performing gender-atypical activities. This attention reflected their knowledge of what activities were and were not typical of men and women. Another study of children between 12 and 24 months old (Serbin, Poulin-Dubois, Colburne, Sen, & Eichstedt, 2001) showed that girls (but not boys) demonstrated some knowledge of gender-typical toys.

These results suggest that gender knowledge begins to develop early, but the ability to make a distinction between the categories of men and women is far from possessing a gender concept or identity. Infants may be able to distinguish between men and women, but they use hair length to signal gender, thus missing the true basis of the distinction.

The Sequence of Childhood Gender Role Development.   When children begin to talk, they soon start to use words that denote gender. That is, they use gender labels to refer to women (or girls) and men (or boys). However, children's use of gender words may not be correct; they may use gender words incorrectly or apply them inconsistently. For example, a child may label all people she likes or all members of her family as "girls" and all others as "boys."

In one study (Fagot & Leinbach, 1989), none of the toddlers passed the gender-labeling task before age 18 months. In another study (Levy, 1999), few of the 20-month-olds were successful with the gender-labeling task. Children begin to be more successful at this task by age 2 years. By age 27 months, half of the children in one study (Fagot & Leinbach, 1989) could apply gender labels correctly, in another study (Campbell, Shirley, & Caygill, 2002) 67% of 24-month-olds were correct in their gender labeling, and in a third study (Levy, 1999) all the 28-month-olds were successful. Therefore, before age 2, few children show behaviors that indicate a concept of gender, but between ages 2 and 3 years, the ability develops to use gender words accurately.

Labeling is a necessary step in the sequence of gender development, but success in this task does not ensure correct performance on other types of gender knowledge (Levy, 1999). When children can consistently apply gender labels, they often do so on the basis of some external and irrelevant physical characteristic, such as clothing or hairstyle. Knowledge of gender-related behaviors and the traits and behaviors associated with each gender develop after gender labeling. Children between ages 20 and 28 months showed some indication of understanding for the categories of male and female (Levy, 1999), including objects associated with each category. Evidence (Martin & Little, 1990; Ruble & Martin, 1998) indicates that 3-year-old participants were able to label the sexes, form groupings based on gender, and exhibit some knowledge of the behaviors typically associated with women and men.

At age 3, most children lack **gender constancy;** they do not understand that being female or male is a permanent, unchangeable feature. Young children may believe that they can change their sex if they want to or that changes in clothing or hair length will change their sex. The concept of gender constancy is very important in cognitive developmental theory. Kohlberg (1966) contended that developing gender constancy is the basis for other gender development. Research has suggested that this concept develops later than others, casting doubt on that theory. Reformulations of cognitive developmental theory place less emphasis on gender constancy, acknowledging that this concept may be multifaceted, complex, and not the sole criterion for gender development (Martin, Ruble, & Szkrybalo, 2002).

Gender constancy may consist of two separable components: *gender stability,* the knowledge that gender is a stable personal characteristic, and *gender consistency,* the belief that people retain their gender even when they adopt behaviors or superficial physical features associated with the other gender. For example, a child who shows gender stability will say that she was a girl when she was a baby and will be a woman when she grows up. A child who shows gender consistency will say that a boy will remain a boy even if he grows long hair or puts on a dress. Some children showed gender stability without gender consistency, but never the other way around (Martin & Little, 1990). Thus, gender constancy might consist of these two separable cognitive components, which would explain why researchers have found age variation in this aspect of development.

Around age 4, the majority of children succeed on tests of gender discrimination and gender stability, and their understanding of gender-typical clothes and toys is closer to the stereotypes (Martin & Little, 1990; Ruble & Martin, 1998). However, preschoolers and even some children in early elementary school may not have attained gender stability and gender consistency (Warin, 2000). Changes in appearance and name of a character may produce confusion about the character's gender in elementary school children (Beal & Lockhart, 1989). For example, changing the appearance of a target child to make the target look more like the other sex, or changing the name and pronoun used to refer to this target child may lead children to make mistakes if their concept of gender consistency is not firmly established.

For children who have developed both aspects of gender constancy, gender becomes a more salient aspect of their lives: They are more concerned about gender-appropriate behavior and making same-gender friends (Warin, 2000). Children who develop gender constancy become motivated to adopt gender role behaviors, causing them to avoid some activities and engage in others (Newman, Cooper, & Ruble, 1995). Children who are gender constant, therefore, have the motivation to adopt gender-typical behaviors.

In summary, children begin to acquire knowledge concerning gender at an early age. Although infants show some signs of being able to differentiate between women and men, this ability does not constitute cognitive knowledge about gender. Between ages 2 and 3

▣ GENDERED VOICES

You Could Be a Boy One Day and a Girl the Next

"When my daughter was 2 or 3 years old, she clearly had no concept of gender or the permanence of gender," a man told me. "She would say that she was a girl or a boy pretty much randomly, as far as I could tell. One day, she would say one, and maybe even later the same day, the other—for both herself and others. You could be a boy one day and a girl the next. This lack of permanence also extended to skin color. She would say that your skin was the color of your clothes, so that changed from day to day, too. One day, you were blue, the next day, your skin was red. I thought that was very odd, even more odd than being a boy one day and being a girl the next.

"She's 5 years old now, and gender is a very salient characteristic for her. She seems to realize that she is a girl, and I think that she knows that she will always be a girl, but she is very concerned with gender and gender-related things—as though she is working on sorting out all this information and making sense of it."

TABLE 6.1   *Stages of Developing Gender-Related Knowledge*

	Gender Labeling	*Gender Preferences or Knowledge*	*Gender Constancy*
Stage 1	No	No	No
Stage 2	Yes	No	No
Stage 3	Yes	Yes	Possibly
Stage 4	Yes	Yes	Yes

Source: Based on "The Relation of Gender Understanding to Children's Sex-Typed Preferences and Gender Stereotypes," by C. L. Martin & J. Little, 1990, *Child Development, 61*, pp. 1434–1435.

years of age, children succeed at gender labeling but have usually not developed other aspects of gender knowledge, such as gender preferences, gender stability, gender consistency, or knowledge of gender stereotypes. These aspects of gender knowledge develop between the ages of 3 and 6 for most children and do so in a regular pattern: first gender labeling, then gender stereotype knowledge and gender preferences, and then the two components of gender constancy—gender stability and gender consistency. Table 6.1 shows these four stages of development of gender knowledge. An analysis of the children's responses showed that 98% of them fell into one of these categories (Martin, Wood, & Little, 1990).

Differences between Girls and Boys.   The course of gender development shows some differences between boys and girls. Such a difference is reasonable, given the greater pressure placed on boys to adopt the typical and approved gender role (Sandnabba & Ahlberg, 1999). As the parents in Kalish's (2001) headline story reported, boys experience a more severe version of gender socialization. Girls are allowed greater leeway in behaving in ways typical of boys than boys are allowed in acting like girls (Martin, 1995; O'Brien et al., 2000). That is, being a "tomboy" is more acceptable than being a "sissy." Indeed, many women reported positive attitudes toward tomboys (Morgan, 1998), and tomboys are judged to be as attractive as their nontomboy sisters (Bailey, Bechtold, & Berenbaum, 2002).

Feminine boys are not so fortunate. College men and women (Martin, 1995), elementary school boys (Zucker, Wilson-Smith, Kurita, & Stern, 1995), and parents of young children (Sandnabba & Ahlberg, 1999) all expressed negative opinions. Thus it is not surprising that, beginning around age 3, boys tend to show greater knowledge of the male gender role than of the female gender role (O'Brien et al., 2000) and greater stability of gender-typed preferences (Powlishta, Serbin, & Moller, 1993). However, girls develop gender knowledge faster than boys (Poulin-Dubois, Serbin, Eichstedt, Sen, & Beissel, 2002), and they tend to be more knowledgeable about both male and female gender roles than boys are (O'Brien et al., 2000).

Both gender schema and gender script theory predict that children attend to and master information about their own gender more rapidly than about the other gender

◼ GENDERED VOICES

Raising a Sissy

"Being twins, my brother and I were closer than most brothers and sisters. We didn't look alike, but we were together a lot," a college student told me. "We had different interests. I was the one who went outside and helped my dad, while my brother stayed inside with my mother. Everybody always said I should have been the boy and he should have been the girl.

"He didn't want to play alone, so he played with me and my friends—dolls, or whatever we played. He never got to choose. And when we played dolls, he got the one that was left after me and my friend chose the ones we wanted. My mom said, 'Let him play with the Ken doll—you have two Ken dolls—don't make him play with a Barbie,' but we didn't. So he got the Barbie with one arm missing or something.

"I always liked the outdoor activities, and my brother didn't. I was so upset that I couldn't join the Cub Scouts. My dad was a troop leader, and I just couldn't understand why I couldn't join; I had always done outdoor things with my dad. Besides, the Brownies did wimpy things, and the Cub Scouts did neat stuff. I was so ticked off.

"When we were in about the 7th grade, I told my mother, 'Mom, you're raising a sissy,' and I told her that my brother should stop hanging around with her and start doing things more typical of boys. She was really angry with me for saying so.

"Did we change as we grew up? I don't consider myself very feminine—I don't take anything off anybody. My mom can't believe that her daughter acts like I do. I still like outdoor activities—camping, hiking, bicycling. I don't think I've changed as much as my brother has. I wouldn't consider him a sissy now. In high school he played football, and he started being more in line with what everyone would consider masculine. As an adult, he's not a sissy at all, but I'm still kind of an adult tomboy."

(Levy & Fivush, 1993). Research has confirmed these predictions: Young children have better-organized knowledge of events and behaviors stereotypically associated with their own rather than the other gender (Levy, 1999; Martin, Wood, & Little, 1990). In addition, children evaluate their own gender more positively than the other gender, with girls saying that "girls are better" and boys contending that "boys are better." In elementary school-aged children, these positive evaluations were not based on the value of the traits but rather on the children's association of positive characteristics with their own group (Powlishta, 1995).

Later Development

The emphasis on the sequence of gender development during early childhood has led to the widespread belief that gender development is complete by about age 6 years. This belief has resulted in relatively little research conducted with older children, adolescents, or adults. Some researchers have explored the many dimensions of gender identity, but the majority of the research on continuing gender development has concentrated on the development of gender stereotypes and role flexibility.

One study that explored the dimensions of gender identity (Egan & Perry, 2001) concentrated on middle childhood and investigated how comfortable 4th- through 8th-grade children were with their gender identity, how pressured they felt to conform to gender-typical behavior, how free they felt to explore cross-gender behaviors, and how highly they valued their own gender. In addition, this research related each of the dimensions to adjustment. The results indicated that these dimensions were not highly related to each other, but each had a relationship to adjustment. Perceived pressure to conform showed a negative relationship, but the other dimensions were positively related to adjustment. Another study of gender development during middle childhood (McHale, Updegraff, Helms-Erikson, & Crouter, 2001) confirmed the multidimensional nature of gender identity.

Some early research on continuing gender development (Urberg, 1979) indicated that gender stereotyping was highest among 12th-grade students, lowest among adults, and intermediate among 7th-grade students. Thus, this research indicated that stereotyping did not show a linear relationship with gender-related knowledge and suggested the operation of some process other than knowledge acquisition.

Another study (Alfieri, Ruble, & Higgins, 1996) attempted to pinpoint the timing of this fluctuation by examining children during important life transitions. These researchers drew on findings that indicated an increase in gender flexibility during junior high school, which seemed at odds with the inflexible gender roles that early adolescents exhibit. Their longitudinal study showed that the transition to junior high school is an event that prompted an increase of gender flexibility. This flexibility did not continue, however, and gender stereotyping became more rigid during the years of junior high school and persisted through high school. These researchers speculated that the transition from elementary to junior high school prompts some reexamination and reorganization of gender-related cognitions and beliefs that produce temporary gender flexibility.

Other studies have found a linear relationship between gender flexibility and age—that is, as age increases, so does gender flexibility (Katz & Ksansnak, 1994; Welch-Ross & Schmidt, 1996). When children acquire gender role knowledge, they tend to apply it inflexibly, but with an increasing comfort with gender role comes an increasing willingness to make exceptions, especially when the standard is applied to self rather than others.

Some of the apparent discrepancies among the studies of gender role flexibility may be due to the different research methods used and variations in the measurement of flexibility (Bigler, 1997; Signorella, Bigler, & Liben, 1993). For example, when forced to choose whether a behavior is performed by or is an occupation held by women or men, children are likely to show increasing evidence of gender stereotyping as they get older. On the other hand, if allowed the option to indicate that both perform the behavior or either can have that occupation, even middle school children show signs of gender flexibility. This difference highlights the importance of the format and wording of questions, especially in research with children. Children and adolescents also tend to be stricter in applying inflexible standards for gender-related behavior to others than to themselves. Therefore, researchers who ask only about others or about cases that are typical may overlook the exceptions that children and adolescents are willing to make for themselves.

Nevertheless, children, adolescents, and even adults vary in their gender role flexibility, and several researchers have explored factors that relate to flexibility versus inflexibility. In one study (Katz & Ksansnak, 1994), a complex pattern of gender role flexibility appeared: Both family and peer social environment influenced gender-related behavior, but participants showed a general increase in tolerance for gender-atypical activities for self and others with increasing age. Another study (Welch-Ross & Schmidt, 1996) found that increases in gender role knowledge preceded increases in gender role flexibility, with flexibility beginning to develop during middle childhood. Figure 6.1 shows the course of development for gender knowledge and for application of gender-related rules over the life span: The knowledge component and application of gender-related rules increase throughout childhood, indicating decreases in flexibility. During adolescence, application of gender-related rules declines, signaling increased flexibility.

Gender role flexibility may increase during adolescence, but young women and men apply different standards to their own gender than to the other. Male and female participants reported similar self-perceptions for characteristics such as affiliation, personal effectiveness, control, and impulsivity, but they tended to perceive the other gender in more stereotypical ways (Urberg, 1979). Therefore, male and female participants described the other gender in more stereotypical terms than they described themselves.

In addition, girls are more likely than boys to endorse gender flexibility throughout adolescence (Jackson & Tein, 1998; Signorella et al., 1993). Girls show more flexibility in their own activity preferences and greater tolerance for gender-atypical behaviors in others. Research has shown that both adolescent girls (Burt & Scott, 2002) and women (Kulik, 2002) were more likely to endorse egalitarian gender roles than were boys and men. These attitudes apply not only to the United States but also to European countries (Frieze et al., 2003).

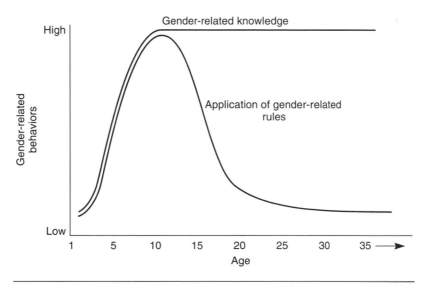

FIGURE 6.1   *Course of Knowledge and Application of Gender-Related Rules for Behavior throughout the Life Span*

Some research has traced the correlates of both gender flexibility and inflexibility in men. Men who were stereotypically masculine tended to see women as stereotypically feminine; that is, men who show little gender flexibility in their own roles also show little toward women (Hudak, 1993). In adolescents, inflexibility increases as traditional young men approach high school graduation and begin to contemplate marriage and careers (Jackson & Tein, 1998).

Some men have very different attitudes, however, and tend to reject stereotypically masculine and feminine roles (Christian, 1994). Those who did were demographically diverse but showed several commonalities. Their early life experiences differed from those of more typical men in the study, with many of them having nurturing fathers and mothers in the workforce. In addition, most of these gender-flexible men had had at least one adult relationship with a feminist woman. These two themes echo the findings on the development of gender flexibility, which demonstrate that both parenting and social environment are related to gender flexibility.

It is apparent that gender identity continues to develop during adolescence and even into adulthood. When children have developed the cognitive and motivational components of gender identity, they tend to be inflexible in applying their understanding of these rules; they are intolerant of gender-atypical behavior in themselves and even more so in others. Young children appear to be tolerant of gender flexibility, but this apparent tolerance is due to a lack of understanding of gender-typed behaviors. Children are "sexist piglets" who apply rigid rules of gender-related behavior to themselves and to others, but this inflexibility begins to dissipate as early as middle childhood. Adolescents and adults tend to be more flexible in their application of gender-related rules of behavior.

INFLUENCES ON GENDER IDENTITY DEVELOPMENT

The process of developing gender identity begins early in childhood and continues into adulthood. Although this process can be divided into stages, individuals vary in how rapidly they proceed through the stages and in the outcome of their gender identity development. The most obvious difference is which gender constitutes the outcome of the gender identity process—whether a person develops a male or female gender identity. Another consideration is the factors that influence the process. Not only biology but also family, peers, and media exert influences on gender identity development.

Biological Factors and Gender Development

The most obvious biological influence for gender identity is the configuration of the external genitalia, which lead to labeling an individual as male or female. This pronouncement, traditionally rendered at birth, has now been moved backward for parents in industrialized societies, who often know whether "it's a boy" or it's a girl" several months before birth. This identification rests on the appearance of the external genitalia, and health care professionals rarely carry out further examination that might reveal complications. These biological structures prompt a host of social factors to swing into action, but do the hormones that underlie the development of external genitalia also play a role in the development of gender-typed behavior? Beyond creating the basic equipment, how influential are biological factors in the development of gender identity?

As Chapter 3 discussed, the presence of prenatal testosterone prompts development of internal and external reproductive organs consistent with the male pattern and affects brain development, but some researchers believe that the influence of prenatal testosterone includes gender-typed behaviors and even gender identity. The evidence for hormonal influences on gender development comes from two lines of research, one on girls with a disorder called congenital adrenal hyperplasia and another on the gender development of boys who have experienced sexual reassignment during early childhood.

Congenital adrenal hyperplasia (CAH) is a disorder resulting in female fetuses that are exposed to high levels of androgens. These girls usually are born with "masculinized" genitalia, identified as intersex individuals, and treated medically and surgically to make their genitalia appear more female. Studies have examined their childhood behavior, and some studies have identified behavioral differences between these girls and those who do not have this disorder. For example, one study (Berenbaum & Hines, 1992) found that CAH girls spent more time playing with boys' toys than did other girls, but another study (Hines & Kaufman, 1994) showed that CAH girls were no more likely than other girls to engage in "rough and tumble" play, a play pattern typical of boys. When they are children, girls with CAH may be more oriented toward activities typical of boys and more likely to be dissatisfied with being a girl (Zucker, 2001). Nonetheless, the vast majority of girls with CAH accept themselves as women and develop female gender identity. Thus, prenatal exposure to testosterone seems to be more strongly related to gender-related behaviors than to gender identity. A recent study (Berenbaum & Bailey, 2003) confirmed this view: Girls with CAH were similar in terms of gender identity to girls with no prenatal exposure to testosterone.

Another recent study (Hines, Golombok, Rust, Johnston, & Golding, 2002) explored the effects of prenatal testosterone in children with normal amounts of testosterone exposure. These researchers were able to study a large group of children whose mothers had agreed to be involved in a longitudinal study of pregnancy and childhood behavior. They asked the children's caregivers about gender-typical behaviors such as favorite toys and chose girls and boys whose scores indicated extremes of masculinity and femininity. Then, these researchers checked the blood samples that the children's mothers furnished during pregnancy. The results indicated that girls who were high in masculine activities had mothers whose testosterone level was higher during pregnancy compared to girls with more feminine toy and activity choices. For the boys in the study, no relationship existed between maternal testosterone and childhood behavior. If further research is capable of pinpointing the timing of exposure and the brain structures affected, this line of research may develop into evidence of biological mechanisms involved in gender-typed behaviors.

One type of girl is very high in masculine interests and activities—tomboys. These girls like boys' games, prefer boys as playmates, and often shun activities that girls usually prefer. A study of tomboys (Bailey et al., 2002) examined how different tomboys were from their sisters and brothers. The results indicated that tomboys were more masculine than their sisters and even more masculine than CAH girls in terms of toy and playmate preferences. Their gender identities varied, with some tomboys showing poor identification with the female gender role, but others showed the extremes of female gender identity. No evidence exists that these girls experienced any abnormal hormone exposure during gestation, and thus they provide no evidence of a biological basis for their behavior. However, their gender-atypical behavior remains an area of interest to researchers for what it can reveal about gender identity and gender role behaviors.

A second line of evidence for a biological basis for gender identity comes from boys who have experienced sex reassignment during childhood. Such boys are rare, and the drama surrounding one case made headlines. The case involved a boy (known as John) who lost his penis when he was 7 months old in a mishap during circumcision (Colapinto, 2000). His parents received medical advice to have sex reassignment surgery performed to change him into a girl. When he was 2 years old, they did so (creating Joan), and the case was followed by researchers to determine the difficulties of such a transition. Although reports of the reassignment indicated that Joan developed a female gender identity, those reports were untrue. Throughout childhood, Joan's behavior was not typical for a girl, and she refused to conform to many behaviors typical of girls. When she was an adolescent, Joan found out her history and sought sex reassignment surgery to become male again. Joan is now John, who has made a successful adjustment to a male gender identity. John's case made headlines and has been the subject of television reports, all of which suggested that gender identity is a biological phenomenon determined before birth.

The John/Joan case contrasts with a similar situation but a different outcome—a boy whose penis was destroyed at age 2 months and who underwent sex reassignment at age 7 months (Bradley, Oliver, Chernick, & Zucker, 1998). This child, however, identified herself as a girl. Despite some behaviors that were more typically associated with boys and some sexual attraction to women, at age 26, this individual had no question about her female gender identity.

What does this research convey about the biological basis of gender identity? The evidence is too inconsistent to conclude that gender identity is decided before birth on the basis of testosterone exposure, but those prenatal events exert some influence. Babies may arrive primed (but not determined) to identify as male or female. Of course, the appearance of the external genitals is also the main signal for a cascade of social influences, making a distinction between the biological and other influences virtually impossible to disentangle.

Family Environment and Gender Development

Despite claims that parents have little influence in children's development (Harris, 1998), the family context is critically important, including its role in gender development. Susan Witt (1997, p. 253) summarized the influences that shape gender attitudes: "These attitudes and behaviors are generally learned first in the home and are then reinforced by the child's peers, school experience, and television viewing. However, the strongest influence on gender role development seems to occur within the family setting, with parents passing on, both overtly and covertly, their own beliefs about gender." Families, however, consist of more than parents (and sometimes fewer than two parents); siblings are also part of the family environment that influences gender development.

A majority of the research investigating family influences on gender development has concentrated on parents and how their gender-related attitudes and behaviors may influence their children. This influence may take place through two processes, one consistent with social learning theory and the other consistent with cognitive developmental and gender schema theories. That is, parents may provide models for their children, who imitate these gendered behaviors, or parents may convey their attitudes and beliefs through behaviors that change the way children think about gender. Research has indicated both of the processes occur with gender socialization in families.

Parents' gender ideologies are influential on children's gender development in both overt and subtle ways. The dimension that has received the most study is how traditional or nontraditional parents are in terms of their gender beliefs and attitudes. The expectation that nontraditional parents will have children with less traditional gender attitudes and behaviors is consistent with research findings (Tennenbaum & Leaper, 2002). However, parents tend to differ from each other in terms of traditionalism, with fathers being more traditional than mothers (Kulik, 2002; Sidanius & Pena, 2003) and spending less time with children (Tennenbaum & Leaper, 2002). Despite the decreased contact, evidence suggests that fathers' and mothers' influence is not equal. Fathers exert more influence, which means that fathers tend to influence their children toward adopting traditional gender roles (Sidanius & Pena, 2003), especially their sons (Peters, 1994). This effect is not restricted to families in the United States but occurs in Canada, Sweden, and Australia as well. African American fathers, however, tend to be more egalitarian than fathers in other ethnic groups in the United States (Hill, 2002).

Evidence from families with only one parent (Slavkin & Stright, 2000) confirms the influence of fathers in developing traditional gender roles. Without fathers, children, especially girls, develop less traditional gender roles. Single-parent families headed by mothers produced children who were higher in traits considered masculine (more independent, assertive, and self-reliant) than two-parent families, in which girls reported more of a mixture of masculine and feminine traits. Women who work outside the home provide nontraditional models and have daughters who showed more gender role flexibility than other girls (Levy, 1989). Thus, mothers are more likely to encourage gender egalitarianism than are fathers.

Parents may differ in their gender-related attitudes, but even parents with a commitment to gender equality fail in some ways. Most parents create very different environments for boys and girls (Witt, 1997). The examples and opportunities that parents provide are important in producing traditional or nontraditional gender attitudes in their children. For example, most parents make different choices for clothing, room decorations, and toys for girls versus boys. Parents talk differently to daughters than to sons (Leaper, Anderson, & Sanders, 1998); the stories that they tell differ according to children's gender (Fiese & Skillman, 2000).

Although many parents endorse gender equality, they provide a variety of examples of gendered behavior and tend to encourage such behavior in their children. For example, one study (Peters, 1994) found that adolescent sons got to use the family car more than adolescent daughters, who were more restricted in their curfews than the sons. Another big difference in gender socialization within families lies in the area of household chores, which tend to be sharply gendered. This gendering applies both to parents who perform household work and to the chores assigned to daughters versus sons (Antill, Goodnow, Russell, & Cotton, 1996). This division affects skills as well as attitudes.

The presence and the gender of siblings also influence gender socialization within families. One study (Levy, 1989) showed that children who interacted more with their parents showed *less* gender role flexibility than children who spent less time with their parents, and children with fewer siblings showed *more* gender role flexibility than those with more brothers and sisters. These results suggest that siblings are an important factor in gender development. Indeed, siblings may be more important than parents in developing gender role flexibility (Katz & Ksansnak, 1994). Same-sex siblings showed an especially important effect in the development of gender flexibility—either increasing or decreasing flexibility, depending on siblings' attitudes.

A longitudinal study (McHale et al., 2001) demonstrated the influence of siblings by measuring first-born and second-born children over a span of 3 years. The results indicated that the qualities of first-born children during the first-year assessment appeared in second-born children three years later. Thus, later-born children were influenced by their older siblings, but not the other way around. Indeed, the first-born children seemed to experience a de-identification process in terms of gender-related behaviors in which they became less like siblings. Therefore, sibling influences are not a simple matter of modeling, and birth order may be important in the process.

The gender composition of siblings may also interact in ways that are important for gender socialization. In a study that measured several aspects of attitudes and behaviors (McHale, Crouter, & Tucker, 1999), families with a girl and a boy tended to show stronger gender typing than did families with single-gender siblings. This constellation seemed to be related to traditional gender roles, and once again, fathers were influential in creating traditionality. However, the presence of a son and a daughter provides a situation that is conducive to the application of traditional gendering—one child of each gender is available to do the activities stereotypically associated with each (Crouter, Manke, & McHale, 1995). When the children are all boys, someone still has to do the dishes—a situation that may prompt flexibility.

Therefore, families are important for gender socialization in many ways, including parents' attitudes and behavior, the gendered environment of the home, and the complex influence of siblings. Gender socialization also occurs outside the family environment, and as children get older, they encounter a wide variety of others who send messages about gender and gender-related behaviors.

Peers and Gender Development

Interaction with age-mates also influences children and adolescents to adopt gender-typical behaviors. Beginning in their third year, girls develop a preference for other girls as playmates, and boys begin to prefer playing with other boys a bit later (Maccoby, 1998). These preferences become stronger over the next few years, making gender segregation one of the most prominent features of elementary school children's peer interactions, who spend between 50% and 60% of their time with same-gender peers (Martin & Fabes, 2001). Adults often urge children toward same-gender peers, but even when adults try to get children to play in mixed-gender groups, the tendency toward gender segregation usually prevails.

The types of relationships and activities that occur in groups of girls typically differ from those in groups of boys (Maccoby, 1998). Boys tend to be rougher, more competitive, more likely to form a hierarchy, and less likely to play near adults. Girls often (but not always) find boys' activities and interaction style unappealing; so, many girls do not want to play with boys. Those girls who do are rarely allowed to join boys' playgroups; only the hardiest of tomboys succeed in breaking this childhood gender barrier. That success may come at a price, making these girls less accepted by other girls.

Boys who do not maintain gender segregation face harsher sanctions, as the boys in Kalish's (2001) headline story demonstrated. Both girls and boys devalued children who violated gender norms for appearance and, to a lesser extent, for behaviors (Blakemore, 2003). Boys, however, received harsher judgments than girls. During the school years, children and adolescents tend to have inflexible gender roles, so peer pressure acts to maintain traditional gender-related behaviors. Therefore, peers often operate as the "gender police," acting to maintain inflexible gender roles for children and adolescents.

Peers can also promote gender flexibility, which often occurs during the college years. Research with college students (Bryant, 2003) demonstrated that both men and women became less traditional in their gender attitudes during four years of college. Consistent with other research, women were less traditional than men, but both changed during college. One important influence was their peers. Therefore, peers may act to promote or to curtail gender flexibility and do each at different times during development.

The Media and Gender Development

Print, broadcast, film, and electronic media are an integral part of daily life for most people in developed countries, and gender portrayals are daily events for those who are exposed to these media. Children, adolescents, and adults learn about gender from entertainment programming, advertisements, and news reports. These media begin to influence children as early as parents do. Entertainment programs show men, women, boys, and girls in a wide variety of situations, and these programs transmit messages about what is desirable and attractive in each gender. Advertising sends signals about gender as well as sells products. News reports cover gender research, and examining the style of the news report as well as the content reveals the attitude behind the story.

Media portrayals can be so powerful and persuasive that these portrayals become the standard on which people judge what is normal and desirable for their own lives. Indeed, the media can be more important than personal experience in shaping attitudes and behavior, and this view is compatible with the cultivation theory of media effects (Gerbner, Gross, Morgan, & Signorielli, 1994). This theory holds that depictions in the media cultivate beliefs and attitudes about the real world, leading people to imagine that their lives should match the media depictions.

One reason that the media have become so persuasive is the tendency toward what Gregg Easterbrook (1996) called **synthesized realism,** a mixture of actual information with phony details blended into a realistic portrayal that is really fiction. When this mixture is done with sufficient skill, people cannot tell the difference. Thus, people absorb information that is a toxic blend of reality and fiction and use this information as a basis by which to judge their own (and others') behavior. Children are especially vulnerable because their cognitive limitations make them unable to distinguish the accurate from the inaccurate portrayals, leaving them even more vulnerable to media misinformation.

Gender Bias in the Media.   A number of analyses have revealed how the media provide inaccurate and systematically biased information about gender. One of the prime assumptions is that women and men are different. As Janet Bing (1999, p. 5) said, "The media continue to seek new ways to ask 'How are men and women different?'" By assuming difference, drawing women and men into stereotypical categories, and then presenting these stereotypical depictions as attractive, the media perpetuate restrictive roles for both men and women. These depictions appear in television entertainment programming, television commercials, movies, magazines, music videos, and video games.

Television is almost unavoidable for people in the United States. Most homes have at least one (and many have more than one) television, and the average viewing is over 3 hours per day (Signorielli, 1998). Thus, television depictions of women and men have many opportunities to influence all who view them. Women's roles have changed a great deal over the past 30 years, but television's portrayals of women have not made such drastic changes. Although the number of female characters and their roles have altered since the early 1970s, these alterations are not proportional to the actual changes in women's employment and responsibilities. Women are underrepresented on television, which shows fewer female than male characters (Glascock, 2001; Signorielli & Bacue, 1999). Nor are the depictions equal in other ways: Female characters are younger, less likely to be employed, and more likely to appear in secondary and comedy roles than are male characters. Thus, women on television are less visible and less significant than men.

Male characters on television are older and occupy more prestigious positions than female characters (Glascock, 2001; Signorielli & Bacue, 1999). Men also are more often the leading characters in drama and adventure programs, activities that take them away from home and family relationships. These characteristics devalue women by making them less visible and credible on television, and limit men by restricting them to aggressive, competitive roles. Indeed, men are disproportionately depicted as police officers and criminals in television dramas (Scharrer, 2001).

Advertising on television also conveys stereotypical gender messages similar to those on entertainment programming. Commercial messages on television include more men than women, and the women are younger than the men (Furnham & Mak, 1999). Men are more likely to be the authoritative central figures, whereas women are shown as secondary and often decorative. Men appear as professionals; women are shown at home. The gender of the people in advertising tends to be consistent with the gender stereotyping of the product—women appear in commercials for personal products and men in commercials selling automobiles and sports-related products. These differences apply not only to the United States, but also to television advertising in 14 countries in North and South America, Europe, Asia, and Africa (Furnham & Mak, 1999).

The underrepresentation of women also occurs in movies. In top-grossing movies from the 1940s through the 1980s, women appeared less frequently than men (Bazzini, McIntosh, Smith, Cook, & Harris, 1997). This underrepresentation was true for women in both primary and secondary roles, and it applied more strongly to older than younger women. In addition, older women were portrayed in less favorable ways than older men. Thus, the lower visibility for women on television extends to movies.

Some people (including network programmers and studio executives) argue that television and movies furnish entertainment, and people know that the depictions are not accurate. Despite the knowledge that entertainment programming is fictional, the gender messages on those programs have the power to influence people when they experience similar characters in real life (Murphy, 1998). Knowing that a character is fictional does not decrease that character's appeal and may not diminish the character's credibility. Therefore, media portrayals have the power to influence, and this process occurs for people of all ages.

Children and Media.   For children, television is probably the most influential of the media because it is such a part of most children's lives (Witt, 2000). Preschool children average about 30 hours a week of TV viewing, including about 20,000 commercial advertisements a year. Television has the power to teach positive attitudes and behaviors, but researchers, critics, and parents worry about the negative messages that children receive. Many of those concerns have centered on the topics of violence and encouragement for smoking and drinking, but perpetuating gender stereotypes has also been a concern.

The types of gender bias in television directed toward adults also appear in children's television (Witt, 2000). Boys are portrayed as more powerful, smart, ambitious, competitive, and violent, whereas girls appear as more timid, warm, sensitive, peaceful, and attractive.

These gender biases in children's entertainment programming also appear in advertisements on children's television. Commercials are of great interest for children's television viewing because children attend to the commercials more than to the regular programming (Larson, 2003). According to one analysis (Larson, 2001), when commercials depict girls and boys together, the gender stereotyping is minimal. However, when either gender appears alone in a commercial, gender stereotypes abound, and children see girls in kitchen settings and boys being violent. Similar stereotyping appeared in a study that examined the voice-overs for children's commercials (Johnson & Young, 2002). A study that investigated the form and style (such as editing, transitions, and voices-overs) of toy commercials (Chandler & Griffiths, 2000) also found significant differences in the commercials for girls versus boys. That is, not only did the advertised product differ but also the appearance and sound of toy commercials varied with the gender of the target audience.

The U.S. Federal Communications Commission established a ruling that, beginning in 1997, mandates television stations to broadcast at least three hours of educational and informational programming per week for children. People who know about this rule favor it and believe that this type of programming is a way to present television that has less objectionable content than regular programs. One analysis (Barner, 1999) indicated that such programs might contain less violence but no less gender stereotyping. Just as in other types of programming, male characters outnumbered female characters, and both acted in gender-stereotypical ways.

Adolescents watch less television than children or adults, but they too receive messages from the programming they see (Signorielli, 1998). For adolescent girls as for women, television, magazines, movies, and music videos send the message that looks count, often more than anything else. The dimension of looks that is most important is body image and weight. Most of the attractive girls and women on television are very thin, and this message comes across to adolescent girls. Television and movies also send messages about the importance of getting and keeping a boyfriend as well as unrealistic images of career possibilities.

Despite being more plentiful and powerful in media portrayals, adolescent boys also are subject to unflattering and unrealistic television and movie depictions (Greven, 2002). The prominence of violence is the most dramatic feature associated with boys in the media, and the recent emphasis on bullying has led to various depictions of such situations successfully resolved by violence. In addition, adolescent boys often appear as inept with girls and obsessed with sex. This combination furnishes the material for many teen comedies in which boys appear as stereotypes.

Even if children do not watch television, videos, or movies, they will be exposed to biased media gender portrayals in the form of children's books. An examination of the contents of children's stories before the 1980s (Hoffman, 1982) revealed that male characters appeared more often in children's stories and were more likely than female characters to be brave, curious, creative, and achieving. With increasing sensitivity to gender equity, male and female characters became more evenly distributed (Evans & Davies, 2000; Turner-Bowker, 1996), but the portrayals did not change as much as the proportions. Female characters are more likely to behave in nonstereotypical ways in contemporary books, and both male and female characters are more likely to cross gender barriers (Gooden & Gooden, 2001). However, gender stereotyping remains prominent in children's literature.

The widespread gender stereotyping that appears in the media, combined with the power of the media to shape attitudes and behavior, has led several groups to formulate guidelines for helping parents to teach their children to be media literate. Children Now (1997) is an advocacy organization for children that collects information about media influence and bias and also strives to counteract some of the negative effects that media can convey, including gender stereotyping. Media Matters is a national public education campaign of the American Academy of Pediatrics begun in 1997 (American Academy of Pediatrics, 2003). In addition to advocating for media education, Media Matters includes materials to help parents teach their children how to analyze media messages in critical ways. Thus, the power of media portrayals are well recognized, and individuals as well as organizations are attempting to counter these powerful messages that include gender stereotyping.

Is It Possible to Avoid Traditional Gender Roles?

Is it possible to avoid or counteract the development of traditional gender roles and stereo-types in children, or do stereotypes inevitably accompany gender socialization? Gender stereotyping may be a typical outcome, but Sandra Bem (1985, 1987) argued that it is avoidable. Parents, however, must take measures to raise "gender-aschematic children in a gender-schematic world" (Bem, 1985, p. 213). Those measures do not include ignoring gender, because peers, schools, the media, and society do not. Rather, parents can attempt to eliminate gender differentiation that has nothing to do with gender, they can concentrate on the biological rather than social correlates of sex, and they can substitute some alternative way of thinking about gender.

Bem advised parents to eliminate the multitude of cultural messages concerning gender that have no relation to sex except by association. For example, occupations, household chores, leisure activities, and even color preferences are gender-typed by their association with either men or women, and none of these need to be so. Bem advised parents to eliminate gender-related differences from their own activities and to teach their children about the media's biased messages about gender. She also recommended that parents emphasize the biological rather than the social correlates of sex. By teaching children about anatomy and reproduction, Bem argued that parents could limit gender-related associations to biological sex, thus minimizing the pervasive associations of gender with so many aspects of life. Bem also suggested that parents substitute alternative ways of organizing information about gender, such as emphasizing individual differences, for traditional gender stereotyping.

Do Bem's suggestions help to alter the development of gender schemata and lessen the strength of gender stereotyping? Several lines of evidence suggest that they do. One study of a group of parents who sought to establish egalitarian child-care routines showed that these efforts were successful (Fagot & Leinbach, 1995), not only in involving both parents in their children's lives, but also in altering the development of their children's gender knowledge. Another study (Fulcher, Sutfin, & Patterson, 2001) focused on lesbian parents, contrasting them with mixed-sex couples to determine differences in gender roles and the impact on the children in these two types of families. The results showed that the division of labor in the household (and not the gender composition of the couple) made a difference in children's stereotyping of future occupational choices. That is, what children see influences how they see themselves in the future.

The study with lesbian parents is but one study that has explored the types of family patterns that influence gender traditionality. Traditional families, of course, are likely to have children with strong gender typing, but some nonconventional families also produce children with strong gender stereotypes (Weisner & Wilson-Mitchell, 1990). The families that followed Bem's suggestions—by using egalitarian behavior patterns combined with questioning of societal norms—produced children with less gender-typed knowledge than did other family patterns. Table 6.2 summarizes the factors that relate to children with and without strong gender stereotyping and shows the combination of factors that tends to make children sexist. Regardless of family attitudes and behavior, all children displayed

TABLE 6.2   *Factors in the Development of Gender-Related Attitudes in Children*

Children Who Exhibit Inflexible Attitudes about Gender	Children Who Exhibit More Flexible Attitudes about Gender
Are male	Are female
(Kulik, 2002)	
Have parents who exhibit traditional attitudes concerning gender-related behaviors	Have parents who question traditional attitudes concerning gender-related behaviors
(Tennenbaum & Leaper, 2002; Weisner & Wilson-Mitchell, 1990)	
Have parents who concentrate on the social correlates of gender	Have parents who concentrate on the physical determinants of sex
(Bem, 1989)	
Interact more with parents	Interact less with parents
(Levy, 1989)	
Have same-gender siblings who are gender-inflexible	Have same-gender siblings who are gender-flexible
(Katz & Ksansnak, 1994)	
Have same-gender peers who are gender-inflexible	Have same-gender peers who are gender-flexible
(Katz & Ksansnak, 1994)	
Are more likely to have mother who are homemakers	Are more likely to have mothers who work outside the home
(Levy, 1989)	
Live in two-parent homes with fathers	Live in single-parent families dominated by mothers
(Sidanius & Pena, 2003; Slavkin & Stright, 2000)	
Live in families with both boys and girls	Live in families with children all the same gender
(McHale, Crouter, & Tucker, 1999)	
Are high school boys who are seniors and who are contemplating careers and marriage	Are high school girls who have mothers who work outside the home
(Jackson & Tein, 1998)	

gender-related information that went far beyond the knowledge that genitals determine a person's sex. That is, no family attitudes or behavior can completely counteract the influence of society's pervasive gender associations.

CONSIDERING DIVERSITY

Most children adopt the gender-related behaviors typical for their biological sex, but the boys described in Kalish's (2001) headline story had not. Those who do not readily adopt typical gender-related behaviors experience increasing pressure to do so, as these boys did. For example, one study (Raag & Rackliff, 1998) showed that most 4- and 5-year-old boys believed that their fathers would think it was "good" if they played with boys' toys and "bad" if they played with girls' toys. None of the boys who imagined their fathers would disapprove actually played with girls' toys in an observed play situation. Thus, children feel pressure to adopt gender-typical behaviors, and boys experience more pressure than girls.

As William Pollack (1998) emphasized, most children show behaviors that represent a combination of the typical masculine and feminine, which does not indicate any type of gender confusion. For example, one 5-year-old boy wanted a pink bicycle because pink was his favorite color (Rosenfeld, 1998). His parents knew that the color would be a problem, but they accepted his choice; the salesman did not and tried to convince him that a "boy's" color would be much better. His peers, including the girls, also teased him for having a pink bicycle. Boys who make many such cross-gender choices face a great deal of social censure.

What behaviors signal variation in gender-typical behaviors and what behaviors indicate some problem in developing gender identity? As the parents in Kalish's story (2001) had learned, the answer to this question is difficult, even for the experts. Some parents and psychologists are willing to allow children a good deal of freedom in their choice of activities, but peers are less acceptant. Thus, children who exhibit cross-gender behaviors usually experience some censure, yet their behaviors may persist, which brings the possibility of gender identity disorder.

Gender Identity Disorder and Transsexuals

Gender identity disorder is among the classifications of behavior disorders in the American Psychiatric Association's *Diagnostic and Statistical Manual of Mental Disorders* (DSM) (American Psychiatric Association, 2000), making it an official psychiatric diagnosis. According to the fourth edition of the DSM (DSM-IV-TR), exhibiting interests and behaviors typical of the other gender is not sufficient to result in this diagnosis. Children must exhibit four of five of the following symptoms: (1) cross-sex behaviors, (2) cross-sex toy and activity preferences, (3) cross-sex peer affiliation, (4) cross-dressing, and (5) a stated desire to be the other sex.

Richard Green (1987) conducted a longitudinal study of boys who showed signs of gender identity disorder to discover differences between these boys and others who had more typical gender role development. His study indicated that some of these "sissies" had received reinforcement for their cross-gender behaviors, whereas others were ignored by parents or other adults for such behavior. The majority of these boys continued to have gender identity problems into adulthood; some attempted to change their biological sex through transsexual surgery. Around 60% to 70% did not develop a completely heterosexual sexual orientation but experienced sexual attraction to men or to both women and men (Green, 1987; Zucker & Bradley, 1995).

Do these statistics mean that the parents in Kalish's article have realistic fears concerning their sons' sexual orientation? For most of the cases described, the boys' behaviors did not fit clearly into the diagnosis of gender identity disorder. One key criterion is the expressed lack of acceptance, even hatred, of one's own sex (Zucker, 2002). A large majority of children with gender identity disorder insist that they want to be the other gender. This component of gender identity disorder is called *gender dysphoria,* and its persistence is a strong indication of gender identity problems.

Green chose not to include girls in his study because too few girls showed symptoms of gender identity disorder. In a clinical study of gender identity disorder, boys were more than six times more likely than girls to receive a referral (Zucker, Bradley, & Sanikhani, 1997). Girls showed more cross-gender behaviors than boys but were less prevalent in the clinic referrals, reflecting the greater social tolerance for such behavior from girls. Indeed, girls tend to see advantages in being boys (Baumgartner, in Tavris & Wade, 1984). When asked what would happen if they changed sex, elementary school girls imagined advantages, whereas boys imagined disaster. Adults make similar judgments, believing that being male offers advantages and being female presents disadvantages (Cann & Vann, 1995). Nevertheless, more boys than girls reject their gender and receive a diagnosis of gender identity disorder.

The individuals who experience these symptoms also encounter many negative consequences of their cross-gender behaviors from parents and peers, and the lack of acceptance and failure to fit in with peers may constitute a situation that produces the most distress for children with gender identity disorder (Bartlett, Vasey, & Bukowski, 2000). As they grow into adolescents, individuals with gender identity disorder often express increasing dissatisfaction with their bodies and continue efforts to have a body of the other sex. That is, these adolescents and adults may say they feel "trapped in the wrong body." Such feelings may prompt them to seek hormonal treatment and surgical sexual reassignment. The term **transsexual** describes these individuals, and those who are in the process of acquiring a new sex sometimes refer to themselves as *transgendered individuals.*

Many people find this terminology confusing and assume that all conditions go together, but all are separable. Feeling "trapped in the wrong body" (gender dysphoria) does not mean that the person is homosexual (has feelings of sexual attraction for people of one's own gender). *Transvestism* (dressing in clothing appropriate to the other gender) is associated with gender identity disorder but may also occur as a sexual fetish (receiving sexual pleasure from the behavior) rather than an expression of gender dissatisfaction. Thus, these phenomena may overlap, but they are separable. For example, a large majority of gay men and lesbians have no gender dysphoria. Only 17% of male transvestites reported feeling trapped in a man's body (Docter & Prince, 1997). Therefore, dissatisfaction with one's gender may be associated with other cross-gender behaviors, but most individuals who exhibit these behaviors do not do so as part of gender identity disorder (see "According to the Media" and "According to the Research").

Gender identity disorder is a rare and controversial disorder. Indeed, controversy exists over its classification as a disorder (Bartlett et al., 2000; Zucker & Bradley, 1995). As children, individuals who exhibit gender dysphoria and cross-gender behaviors are subject to diagnosis and treatment to make them accept their biological sex as their gender identity. If they develop sexual attraction to people of the same gender (homosexual sexual orientation), they are not subject to treatment; the American Psychiatric Association has not considered homosexuality a disorder for over 25 years. If they experience persistent gender dysphoria as adolescents and adults, they are free to seek sexual reassignment surgery. Although transsexuals may have some problems in being accepted by society, research (Cohen-Kettenis & van Goozen, 1997; Rehman, Lazer, Benet, Schaefer, & Melman, 1999; Smith, van Goozen, & Cohen-Kettenis, 2001) has indicated that their gender dysphoria disappears and their overall functioning improves. Therefore, gender identity disorder presents a number of unresolved issues for those who study it as well as for children and parents faced with this diagnosis.

Cross-Cultural Views of Cross-Gender Identities

Cross-gender behavior is not unique to western society nor even to modern times. Anthropologists have studied the behaviors of many cultures and found individuals who adopt the behaviors and even identities of the other gender. In some cultures, these individuals are rejected, but in others, they are accepted and even revered, constituting a "third sex."

When Europeans arrived in North America, they found many Native American tribes in which gender roles were less fixed than in European societies (Wieringa, 1994). More than 130 Native American societies accepted *berdaches*—men or women who adopted the gender-related behaviors of the other gender. Male berdaches were more common than female berdaches, but both versions existed. For example, the Zuni saw gender roles as learned rather than fixed by biology. Each gender had a specific role, but individuals were not necessarily tied to that role by their biological sex. Boys who wanted to dress like women, perform work typical of women, and marry a man were well accepted rather than discouraged. Richard Trexler (2002) argued that some boys were encouraged or perhaps even required to become berdaches. Some Latin American native cultures had the belief that parents should choose a child's gender, regardless of the child's biological sex. These transformed individuals were accepted members of their societies. Indeed, the category of berdache carried a special spiritual status (Roscoe, 1993).

Indian society also has a "third sex," the *hijras*. These men take the gender role of women and may undergo castration, the removal of their gonads (Nanda, 2000). They see their conversion as part of the worship of Bahuchara Mata, one of the many versions of the Mother Goddess. They may renounce all sexuality, but many have sex with other men, even becoming "wives." Throughout Indian society, hijras are seen as having special powers to convey fertility to newborn babies, but they have also experienced rejection and persecution. Members of the hijras see themselves as chosen to be special rulers. Recently, hijras have begun to seek and gain political power, capitalizing on their marginalized social status and proclaiming that "You don't need genitals for politics; you need brains and integrity" (Reddy, 2003, p. 163). Their success reflects a different categorization for gender than the conceptualization that underlies the diagnosis of gender identity disorder and highlights the possibilities for other ways to think about gender identity.

ACCORDING TO THE MEDIA . . .

Boys Don't Cry

The movie *Boys Don't Cry* (Peirce & Kolodner, 1997) is a fictionalized story, and *The Brandon Teena Story* (Muska & Olafsdittir, 1998) is a film documentary. Both told the story of Teena Brandon, a young women who felt as though she should have been a man and who tried to transform herself into one, Brandon Teena. This transformation had tragic consequences, resulting in multiple murders.

Teena became Brandon during high school and moved to a small town after leaving Lincoln, Nebraska, to avoid legal trouble over thefts and forged checks. In this small town, he begins to enact his fantasy of hanging out with the guys, fighting, and dating women. He fell in love with a woman who returned his feelings, and he became friends with her friends. This group included young adults on the margins of society, many of whom had criminal records and money problems. When two of these men discovered that Brandon was a woman rather than the man whom they had befriended, they became enraged and raped her. When she reported the rape, local law enforcement was more interested in her gender identity disorder than the crime (Ramsland, 2003). The sheriff took no action to protect Brandon from these men, who planned murder, hunted down Brandon, and killed him and two other people on New Year's Eve, 1993.

Filmmaker Kimberly Peirce was drawn to Brandon's story while she was in film school, and she spent

five years doing research and getting *Boys Don't Cry* made into a major film that won critical praise and awards (Morris, 2000). The movie showed Brandon as a charming, romantic person who wanted to fulfill a fantasy version of being a boy (Ramsland, 2003). Brandon described himself as being attracted to women but not a lesbian; he saw his attraction as male heterosexuality that his body did not match. He had a string of girlfriends, all of whom liked him and found him more attractive than other men whom they dated. To those who knew he was really female, Brandon sometimes described himself as a hermaphrodite and sometimes said he was saving up for a sex change operation. He never had doubts about his gender identity, which was male.

Susan Muska and Greta Olafsdittir's documentary, *The Brandon Teena Story,* paralleled Peirce's fictionalized account quite closely. This view of Brandon reflected charm and romanticism but was more forthcoming about the legal problems and less adamant about a strong male gender identity.

In both media versions, Brandon was an individual on the margins of society who had a difficult life of longing for a body and a life that were unattainable. To support his romances, he turned to theft, and to enact his view of maleness, he turned to violence.

SUMMARY

The process of gender development may begin during infancy, but between ages 2 and 3, most children learn to apply gender labels and to understand some behaviors and features as stereotypically associated with gender. Their understanding of gender is far from complete, however, and children may be 6 or 7 years old before they have a complete understanding of all the components of gender, including gender constancy, gender consistency, and gender stability.

When children develop an understanding of gender, they tend to be rigid and inflexible in their application of gender rules to themselves and others. Gender stereotyping is not as strong during adolescence and adulthood, indicating that additional gender development occurs after childhood.

ACCORDING TO THE RESEARCH . . .

People with Gender Identity Disorder Are at Risk

As portrayed in the movies, Brandon Teena was not typical of individuals with gender identity disorder in many ways; some of his experiences were all too common, but other difficulties are even more likely.

The real story of Teena Brandon included the hint that Teena wanted to become male as a result of sexual abuse during childhood (Ramsland, 2003), which varies from the typical case in terms of both background and age of onset for gender dysphoria (Zucker & Bradley, 1995). Most children with gender identity disorder have no history of sexual abuse and express their gender discontent during early childhood rather than adolescence.

Most individuals with gender identity disorder do not have the experience of legal problems that Brandon encountered (Burr, 2002). Indeed, these individuals may have ordinary occupations, but their personal lives are far from ordinary. Like Brandon, individuals with gender identity disorder struggle to sort out their gender identity, and those with strong convictions often seek hormone treatments and sexual reassignment surgery. Brandon talked of but never actively sought these treatments.

Also like Brandon, the lives of transgendered and transsexual individuals reflect difficulties in forming and maintaining personal and sexual relationships. Indeed, research indicates that being accepted is a problem for these individuals beginning in early childhood (Cohen-Kettenis, Owen, Kaijser, Bradley, & Zucker, 2003).

Research has revealed another similarity between Brandon and other individuals with gender identity disorder: a vulnerability to violence. Since his murder, two other transgendered adolescents were killed (DuLong, 2002). Fred Martinez was 16 and Eddie/Gwen Araujo was 17; both lived as girls, and both were beaten to death by men who had learned that their sex did not match their gender.

Violence is a risk for transgendered individuals as well as those who are gay and lesbian while they are still in school as well as when they are in the community (Lee, 2000). In addition to the danger of violence from others, individuals with gender identity problems also face violence in the form of suicide (Lee, 2000). Failure to conform to gender roles is a risk for suicide, placing those with gender identity disorder at increased risk. As many as 40% of lesbian, gay, and transgendered youth have seriously thought about or attempted suicide. This risk does not diminish as these individuals become adults unless their gender dysphoria is resolved. In addition, these individuals are at increased risk for a variety of health problems such as depression and substance abuse. Unfortunately, lesbian, gay, and transgendered people experience bias within the health care system, and they receive poorer care. Thus, the short and tragic life of Brandon Teena captures some, but not the full extent, of problems associated with gender identity disorder.

Biology influences gender development, but its effects are difficult to separate from social influences because the identification of a child's genitals as male or female prompts a cascade of social events related to gender development. The influence of prenatal hormones on gender-typed behaviors is a provocative but not well-established possibility.

Families exert an important influence on the gender socialization of children. Traditional families tend to have children with more traditional gender attitudes, but fathers tend to be more traditional than mothers, and fathers' influence promotes traditional gender identities. Even parents who attempt to avoid gender stereotyping have difficulties; the tendency to assign girls and boys gender-typical chores is strong, and both parents and siblings often create a gendered environment for children. Peers also tend to push children and adolescents toward inflexible gender role behaviors.

The media influence all members of society, and that influence includes gender stereotyping in television entertainment programming and commercials, movies, music videos, video games, and magazines. Girls and boys are subject to similar gender stereotyping in programming oriented toward children, even educational television and children's books. Thus, media exposure is a strong force in establishing and perpetuating traditional gender roles. All of the forces that create gender role traditionalism are difficult to counteract, but parents can raise children who are more flexible in their gender roles.

The large majority of children develop gender identities that are consistent with their biological sex, but some do not. Those children who identify with and want to be the other gender may be diagnosed as having gender identity disorder. As adults, these individuals may seek sexual reassignment surgery and fulfill their wish to be the other gender. This choice is poorly accepted in modern North America, but over 130 Native American cultures included berdaches, who represented cross-gender roles and behaviors and were accepted, respected members of their societies. Indian hijras also constitute a "third sex" that is becoming politically powerful in that society.

▓ GLOSSARY

gender constancy   the knowledge that gender is a permanent characteristic and will not change with superficial alterations.

gender identity   individual identification of self as female or male.

gender identity disorder   a disorder that occurs when a child rejects the gender role that corresponds to biological sex and adopts cross-gender behaviors and possibly a cross-gender identity.

synthesized realism   a mixture of actual information with phony details into a realistic portrayal that is really fiction.

transsexual   an individual who receives hormonal and surgical treatment to be changed to the other sex.

▓ SUGGESTED READINGS

Bem, Sandra Lipsitz. (1985). Androgyny and gender schema theory: A conceptual and empirical integration. In Theo B. Sonderegger (Ed.), *Nebraska Symposium on Motivation, 1984: Psychology and gender* (pp. 179–226). Lincoln, NE: University of Nebraska Press.
Bem evaluates the other theories of gender development and presents gender schema theory, the research supporting her theory, along with advice about raising nonsexist children.

Keller, Teresa. (1999). Lessons in equality: What television teaches us about women. In Carie Forden, Anne E. Hunter, & Beverly Birns (Eds.), *Readings in the psychology of women: Dimensions of the female experience* (pp. 27–35). Boston: Allyn and Bacon.
This short article provides a good introduction to the treatment of women in various media, the stereotypical portrayal of media images, and the effects of this stereotyping.

Pollack, William. (1998). *Real boys.* New York: Holt.
The first two chapters of Pollock's book about boys explore the rigid gender role socialization that boys undergo and the damage that this socialization can do to boys.

Ruble, Diane N.; & Martin, Carol Lynn. (1998). Gender development. In Nancy Eisenberg (Ed.), *Handbook of child psychology, Vol. 3: Social, emotional, and personality development* (5th ed., pp. 933–1016). New York: Wiley.
Ruble and Martin's massive review of gender development, presented in Chapter 14 of the handbook, may be a bit overwhelming in length, but their discussion of the research is clear and well-organized. The article includes other material in addition to a review of social factors in gender development. The first half of Chapter 14 is more pertinent to this topic than the last.

7 GENDER STEREOTYPES: MASCULINITY AND FEMININITY

From "white men can't jump" to "girls can't do math," negative images that are pervasive in the culture can make us choke during tests of ability. . . . The power of stereotypes, scientists had long figured, lay in their ability to change the behavior of the person holding the stereotype. . . . But five years ago, Stanford University psychologist Claude Steele showed something else: It is the targets of a stereotype whose behavior is most powerfully affected by it. A stereotype that pervades the culture the way "ditzy blondes" and "forgetful seniors" do makes people painfully aware of how society views them—so painfully aware, in fact, that knowledge of the stereotype can affect how well they do on intellectual and other tasks." (Begley, 2000, pp. 66–67)

According to Sharon Begley (2000), stereotypes present a trap into which many people can fall. In 1995, Claude Steele and Joshua Aronson reported on a study that showed how the existence of negative stereotypes affects those who are part of the stereotyped groups. They proposed that people feel threatened in situations in which they believe that their performance will identify them as examples of their group's negative stereotype. Steele and Aronson labeled this situation **stereotype threat** because the presence of these negative stereotypes threatens performance and self-concept. Even if the person does not believe the stereotype or accept that it applies, the threat of being identified with a negative stereotype can be an ever-present factor that puts a person in the spotlight and creates tension and anxiety about performance.

By setting up a situation that manipulated expectations of the implications of taking a test, Steele and Aronson showed that those expectations affected participants' performance. For example, African Americans who believed that the test they were taking was a test of basic scholastic ability performed worse than African Americans who thought the test was just another test. Women who believed that the mathematics test would reveal their underlying ability performed more poorly than women who had different beliefs about the test's diagnostic ability (Steele, 1997). In addition, African Americans and women performed more poorly than White men, who are not threatened by negative stereotypes of their abilities in math. However, White men can be threatened by stereotypes of math ability. A study (Smith & White, 2002) that reminded White men that Asians are superior at math provoked poorer performance on a math test. Some people get a double dose of stereotype threat, such as Latino women, who were affected by stereotype threat on a test of mathematical and spatial ability (Gonzales, Blanton, & Williams, 2002).

Begley's (2000) article included examples of how widespread stereotype threat may be, how easily stereotype threat can be summoned, and how powerful stereotypes are in affecting performance. Reminding people of their membership in a stereotyped group, such as asking them to mark a question about their gender just before starting the test, was enough of a cue to affect performance negatively. However, when reminded of their affiliation with a positively stereotyped group, Asian American women's math performance improved. Additional research (Smith & White, 2002) suggests that nullifying stereotype threats may not be too difficult. Just the suggestion that men and women perform equally well on this test was enough to avert the effects of stereotype threat on a math test.

Stereotypes thus can be a positive influence, but much more evidence indicates that they can do damage and require additional steps to nullify. This powerful process affects both those who impose the stereotypes and those who are the targets of stereotyping.

FROM GENDER ROLES TO GENDER STEREOTYPES

As Chapters 5 and 6 explored, a gender role consists of activities that men and women engage in with different frequencies. For example, in the United States, repairing cars and repairing clothing are associated predominantly with men and women, respectively. These gender-related behaviors thus become part of a pattern accepted as masculine or feminine, not because of any innate reason for these differences, but because of the association with women and men.

A **gender stereotype** consists of beliefs about the psychological traits and characteristics of, as well as the activities appropriate to, men or women. Gender roles are defined by behaviors, but gender stereotypes are beliefs and attitudes about masculinity and femininity. The concepts of gender role and gender stereotype tend to be related. When people associate a pattern of behavior with either women or men, they may overlook individual variations and exceptions and come to believe that the behavior is inevitably associated with one gender but not the other. Therefore, gender roles furnish the material for gender stereotypes.

Gender stereotypes are very influential; they affect conceptualizations of women and men and establish social categories for gender. These categories represent what people think, and even when beliefs vary from reality, the beliefs can be very powerful forces in judgments of self and others, as the headline story for this chapter showed. Therefore, the history, structure, and function of stereotypes are important topics in understanding the impact of gender on people's lives.

Stereotypes of Women and Men

Chapter 6 discussed children's acceptance of the rigid formulation of what is acceptable for women and men, but gender stereotyping is not unique to children or even to contemporary society. The current gender stereotypes, especially those about women, reflect beliefs that appeared during the 19th century, the Victorian era (Lewin, 1984c). Before the 19th century, most people lived and worked on farms where men and women worked together. The Industrial Revolution changed the lives of a majority of people in Europe and North America by moving men outside the home to earn money and leaving women at home to manage households and children. This separation was unprecedented in history, forcing men and women to adapt to different environments and roles. As men coped with the harsh business and industrial world, women were left in the relatively unvarying and sheltered environments of their homes. These changes produced two beliefs: the Doctrine of Two Spheres and the Cult of True Womanhood.

The Doctrine of Two Spheres is the belief that women's and men's interests diverge—women and men have their separate areas of influence (Lewin, 1984a). For women, the areas of influence are home and children, whereas men's sphere includes work and the outside world. These two spheres are different, with little overlap, forming opposite ends of one dimension. This conceptualization of opposition forms the basis not only for social views of gender, but also for psychology's formulation of the measurement of masculinity and femininity.

The Cult of True Womanhood.   The Cult of True Womanhood arose between 1820 and 1860. "The attributes of True Womanhood, by which a woman judged herself and was judged by her husband, her neighbors, and society could be divided into four cardinal virtues—piety, purity, submissiveness, and domesticity" (Welter, 1978, p. 313). Women's magazines and religious literature of the 19th century furnished evidence of society's emphasis on these four areas. The Cult of True Womanhood held that the combination of these characteristics provided the promise of happiness and power to the Victorian woman, and without these no woman's life could have real meaning.

The first virtue was piety, which originated with society's view of women as more naturally pious than men. Women's natural superiority also appeared in their refinement, delicacy, and tender sensibilities. Religious studies were seen as compatible with femininity and deemed appropriate for women, whereas other types of education were thought to detract from women's femininity. These other types of education included studying through formal means and even reading romantic novels—either of which might lead women to ignore religion, become overly romantic, and lose their virtue or purity (that is, their virginity).

Although women were seen as uninterested in sex, they were vulnerable to seduction. The loss of the second virtue, purity, was a "fate worse than death." Having lost her purity, a woman was without value or hope: "Purity was as essential as piety to a young woman, its absence as unnatural and unfeminine. Without it she was, in fact no woman at all, but a member of some lower order" (Welter, 1978, p. 315).

Men, on the other hand, were not naturally as religious and thus not naturally as virtuous as women. According to this view of True Womanhood, men were, at best, prone to sin and seduction, and at worst, brutes. True Women would withstand the advances of men, dazzling and shaming them with their virtue. Men were supposed to be both religious and pure, although not to the same extent as women, and through association with True Women, men could increase their own virtue. True Women could elevate men.

The third virtue of the Cult of True Womanhood was submissiveness, a characteristic not true of and not desirable in men (Welter, 1978). Women were expected to be weak, dependent, and timid, whereas men were supposed to be strong, wise, and forceful. Dependent women wanted strong men, not sensitive ones. These couples formed families in which the husband was unquestionably superior and the wife would not consider questioning his authority.

The last of the four virtues, domesticity, was connected to both submissiveness and to the Doctrine of the Two Spheres. True Women were wives whose concern was with domestic affairs—making a home and having children: "The true woman's place was unquestionably by her own fireside—as daughter, sister, but most of all as wife and mother" (Welter, 1978, p. 320). These domestic duties included cooking and nursing the sick, especially a sick husband or child. Table 7.1 summarizes the elements of the Cult of True Womanhood.

Women who personified these virtues passed the test of True Womanhood. Of course, the test was so demanding that few, if any, women met the criteria. However, beginning in the early 1800s, women's magazines as well as teachings from social and religious leaders held these virtues as attainable and urged women to match these ideals. Although the Cult of True Womanhood was dominant during the 19th century, remnants linger in our present-day culture and influence current views of femininity.

Masculinities.   The 19th-century idealization of women also had implications for men, who were seen as the opposite of women in a number of ways. Women were passive, dependent, pure, refined, and delicate; men were active, independent, coarse, and strong. These divisions between male and female domains, the Doctrine of the Two Spheres, formed the basis for the polarization of male and female interests and activities. The Cult of True Womanhood reached its height in the late Victorian period, toward the end of the 19th century. The Victorian ideal of manhood was the basis for what Joseph Pleck (1981,

TABLE 7.1   *Elements of Stereotyping of Women and Men*

The Cult of True Womanhood	Male Sex Role Identity
Piety: True Women were naturally religious.	*No Sissy Stuff:* A stigma is attached to feminine characteristics.
Purity: True Women were sexually uninterested.	*The Big Wheel:* Men need success and status.
Submissiveness: True Women were weak, dependent, and timid.	*The Sturdy Oak:* Men should have toughness, confidence, and self-reliance.
Domesticity: True Women's domain was in the home.	*Give 'Em Hell:* Men should have an aura of aggression, daring, and violence.

Sources: Based on "The Male Sex Role: Our Culture's Blueprint of Manhood and What It's Done for Us Lately," (p. 12), by Robert Brannon, in Deborah S. David & Robert Brannon (Eds.), *The Forty-Nine Percent Majority,* 1976, Reading, MA: Addison-Wesley; and "The Cult of True Womanhood: 1820–1860," by Barbara Welter, in Michael Gordon (Ed.), *The American Family in Social-Historical Perspective* (2nd ed.). New York: St. Martin's Press.

1995) referred to as the Male Sex Role Identity (now called the Male Gender Role Identity). Pleck discussed the Male Gender Role Identity as the dominant conceptualization of masculinity in our society and as a source of problems, both for society and for individual men.

R. W. Connell (1995) explored the historical origins of attitudes toward masculinity. Connell looked back into 16th-century Europe and the changing social and religious climate to trace the development of individualism. He contended that industrialization, world exploration, and civil wars became activities associated with men and formed the basis for modern masculinity. Pleck (1984) also reviewed the social climate of the late 19th century, citing examples from the late 1800s of the increasing perception that men were not as manly as they once had been. Growing industrialization pressured men to seek employment in order to be good providers for their families, roles that became increasingly difficult for men to fulfill (Bernard, 1981; Faludi, 1999), thus endangering their masculinity. In addition, education became a factor in employment, and men often held better jobs (and were thus better providers) when they were educated. Pleck discussed how the occupation of early-childhood educator became the province of women, and how these female elementary school teachers tried to make boys into well-behaved pupils—in other words, "sissies." This issue remains part of a debate over boys in the classroom (Kimmel, 2000; Sommers, 2000).

The prohibition against being a sissy and the rejection of the feminine are strong components of modern masculinity. According to Robert Brannon (1976), No Sissy Stuff is one of the four themes of the Male Sex Role. The other three themes include The Big Wheel, which describes men's quest for success and status as well as their need to be looked up to. The Sturdy Oak component describes men's air of toughness, confidence, and self-reliance, especially in a crisis. Finally, the Give 'Em Hell aspect of the Male Sex Role reflects the acceptability of violence, aggression, and daring in men's behavior. Table 7.1 summarizes these elements.

The more closely that a man conforms to these characteristics, the closer he is to being a "real man." As Brannon pointed out, the pressure is strong to live up to this idealization of masculinity, which is equally as ideal and unrealistic as the "true woman" of the Cult of True Womanhood. However, even men who are fairly successful in adopting the Male Gender Role Identity may be poorly adjusted, unhappy people—this role prohibits close personal relationships, even with wives or children, and requires persistent competition and striving for achievement. These difficulties lead men to make significant departures from the role's requirements.

Pleck (1981, 1995) proposed a new model, which he called Sex Role Strain (now Gender Role Strain), which departs in many ways from the Male Gender Role Identity. Pleck argued that during the 1960s and 1970s, both men and women started to make significant departures from their traditional roles as men began to behave in ways that violated the Male Gender Role. He also suggested that the features of the Male Gender Role Identity have retained a powerful influence over what both men and women believe men should be. Many men deviate from the role, and some even believe that the role is harmful to them personally and to society, making adherence to the role a strain. Even men who succeed feel the strain in doing so, and the toxic components of the role present problems even for the successful. Confirming research (Mahalik, Locke, Theodore, Cournoyer, & Lloyd, 2001; Robertson et al., 2002) supports this view.

Connell (1987, 1992, 1995) argued that gender has been constructed as part of each society throughout history, a view that is consistent with the belief that gender is something that people do rather than part of what people are (West & Zimmerman, 1987). This construction of masculinity includes both sanctioned and less accepted behaviors. Thus, masculinity varies with both time and place, creating a multitude of masculinities. For each society, Connell contended that one version of masculinity is sanctioned as the one to which men should adhere, which he termed *hegemonic masculinity*. This version of masculinity attempts to subordinate femininity as well as less accepted versions of masculinity, such as male homosexuality. Like Pleck, Connell recognized many disadvantages to this narrow, dominant form of masculinity and saw many problems for society and for individual men who adhere to it.

Despite the notion that masculinity has undergone drastic changes in the past two decades, evidence indicates little change in hegemonic masculinity and strong representation of the four themes of the Male Sex Role (Bereska, 2003). Boys and men are still supposed to be stoic, aggressive, dependable, and not feminine.

Development of Stereotypes

In examining the research on social theories of gender development, Chapter 6 reviewed the process of developing gender knowledge and identity, including some information about forming gender stereotypes. Along with the process of developing gender knowledge comes gender stereotyping. Thus, children as young as 3 years old start to show signs of gender stereotyping (Martin & Little, 1990). This development is not uniform or simple, and 6-year-old children showed a pattern of selective stereotyping in which they made gender-stereotypical judgments about children whose toy interests were similar to their own but failed to make stereotypical judgments for children whose interests were different from their own. This behavior probably reflected a more complete development of knowledge about self and others like self, which extended to gender. Children do even more gender stereotyping as they get older (Martin, Wood, & Little, 1990), and 8- to 10-year-olds made stereotypical judgments for both genders.

This pattern of stereotype development appears in Table 7.2. Children in the first stage have learned characteristics and behaviors associated directly with each gender, such as the toy preferences of each. In this stage, they have not learned the many indirect associations with gender, associations that are essential for stereotypes to form. In the second stage, children have begun to develop the indirect associations for behaviors associated with their own gender, but not yet for the other gender. In the third stage, children have learned these indirect associations for the other gender as well as their own, giving them the capability of making stereotypical judgments of both women and men.

A specific cognitive process allows children (and adults) to maintain stereotypes once they have formed (Meehan & Janik, 1990). This process is called **illusory correlation:** "the erroneous perception of covariation between two events when no correlation exists, or the perception of a correlation as stronger than it actually is" (Meehan & Janik,

TABLE 7.2 *Stages of Gender Stereotype Development*

Stage	Gender Knowledge	Status of Gender Stereotypes
1	Behaviors and characteristics directly associated with gender	Undeveloped
2	Beginnings of indirect associations with gender for own sex but not other sex	Self-stereotype but none for other sex
3	Complex, indirect gender-related associations for same and other sex	Stereotypes for self and other sex

Source: Based on "The Development of Gender Stereotype Components," by C. L. Martin, C. H. Wood, & J. K. Little, 1990, *Child Development, 61,* pp. 1891–1904.

1990, p. 84). These researchers maintained that people perceive that relationships exist between gender and various behaviors when no relationship exists, or when the relationship is not as strong as their perception indicates.

Studies (Meehan & Janik, 1990; Susskind, 2003) have demonstrated that illusory correlation operates in 2nd- and 4th-grade children in a way that is consistent with developing gender stereotypes. Furthermore, these studies indicated that children's tendency to gender stereotype creates distortions in their memory for gender-related information. The perception of correlations can be an important factor in maintaining stereotypes for both children and adults; when people believe that activities are related to one or the other gender, then they feel comfortable in thinking in terms of these categorizations. This perceptual bias acts to maintain stereotypes. However, one study (Susskind, 2003) indicated that children do not ignore counterstereotypical information, and the presentation of such information may be a way to diminish gender stereotyping. Thus, when children see fathers cooking and mothers performing home repairs, these observations may act to decrease stereotyping by breaking down illusory correlations.

Gender stereotyping follows age-related trends similar to the development of other gender knowledge. That is, younger children show less gender stereotyping than older children (Durkin & Nugent, 1998), men are subject to harsher stereotyping than women, and girls stereotype less strongly than boys. Studying gender stereotyping in individuals ranging from kindergarten children to college students showed that the flexible application of gender stereotypes increases with age (Biernat, 1991). Younger children relied more on gender information than on information about individuals when making judgments about people, whereas older individuals took into account information about deviations from gender stereotypes. This pattern of development indicates that the acquisition of full information concerning gender stereotypes is accompanied by greater flexibility in the use of stereotypes. The tendency to rely on the stereotype is always present, and both children and adults showed a tendency to attribute gender-stereotypical traits to women, men, and children, including a reluctance to attribute feminine characteristics to males and a tendency to associate femininity with being childlike (Powlishta, 2000).

Although stereotype flexibility increases with age, the knowledge that underlies this development also has negative implications. Between the ages of 6 and 10 years old, children become aware of the stereotyping that others do (McKown & Weinstein, 2003). In addition, children from stigmatized groups (such as African American and Latino children) become aware of others' stereotyping before children from more privileged groups did so. This knowledge builds the basis for stereotype threat, and children with knowledge of the stereotyping process from stigmatized groups were more likely to exhibit the negative performance effects of stereotype threat than were other children. Hence, this negative effect of stereotyping occurs along with increased knowledge.

Therefore, the development of gender stereotypes begins early, with 3-year-olds knowing about gender-related differences in behavior. As children acquire information about gender, they become capable of forming and maintaining elaborate stereotypes for men and women, but they also become more willing to make exceptions to the gender rules they have learned. Nevertheless, gender stereotypes provide a system for classifying people that operates throughout people's lives; these influence their expectations for self and others, as well as the judgments they form about people based on their gender-related characteristics and behaviors.

The Process and Implications of Stereotyping

The term *stereotyping* has negative connotations, but some theorists do not emphasize the negative aspects of the process. Some (Macrae & Bodenhausen, 2000) have concentrated on the convenience of this type of categorical cognitive processing, and others (Jussim, McCauley, & Lee, 1995) have contended that stereotypes have positive as well as negative effects. Yet other theorists have argued that stereotyping produces such a magnitude of distortions and incorrect generalizations that its disadvantages are overwhelming (Allen, 1995; Bobo, 1999; Glick & Fiske, 2001). The negative effects of stereotyping are apparent in stereotype threat, the subject of the headline article for this chapter.

Those who study stereotyping as a cognitive process (Macrae & Bodenhausen, 2000) emphasize people's need to streamline the way they interact with a complex world; forming simplified categories is a way to do so. The limits on children's cognitive abilities make this need even more pressing during childhood. Taking this view, gender stereotyping is a normal cognitive process that allows children to form categories based on gender and to understand this important attribute, if in a simplified and distorted way (Martin & Halverson, 1981). The simplification and distortion inherent in stereotyping can have negative effects, but the positive benefits to children of forming gender stereotypes outweigh the negative effects of making some mistakes and thinking too narrowly about gender-related behaviors. Therefore, the function of gender stereotyping can be understood in developmental terms as a useful way to approach the complexities of gender.

A knowledge of gender stereotyping in children does not necessarily lead to an understanding of the factors that maintain stereotypical behavior in adults (Eagly, 1987b). The advantages of gender stereotyping during childhood do not necessitate that adults maintain gender stereotypes. Research has indicated that older children, adolescents, and adults become more flexible in their application of stereotypes; they are willing to make exceptions to the dictates of their gender stereotypes, both for themselves and for others. However, gender stereotypes persist throughout life. Stereotypes provide not only descriptions of how people think about women and men but also prescriptions about what women and men should be, which means that gender stereotyping places limits on what traits and behaviors are allowed (Prentice & Carranza, 2002). Thus, theorists and researchers have explored the formation, function, and effects of holding gender stereotypes.

One issue relevant to stereotyping is its accuracy. The "kernel of truth" position holds that stereotypes have some valid as well as some inaccurate points (Martin, 1987). Gender roles, the set of behaviors performed more often by men or women, form the basis for gender stereotypes. That is, the social roles that women and men fulfill allow people to perceive differences between men and women and to extend these differences to areas where none exists. The issue of accuracy has provoked a great deal of controversy but no resolution. A meta-analysis of studies on the accuracy of gender stereotyping (Swim, 1994) confirmed that overestimation and underestimation occur. Perceptions of gender differences may be accurate when measuring average group judgments, but individuals differ a great deal, and some individuals exhibit substantial inaccuracies (Hall & Carter, 1999). Such inaccuracies should create problems, and prejudice and discrimination are among the effects that arise from stereotyping.

Prejudice is a negative evaluation of an entire group, which allows prejudiced people to react to members of the group without any personal contact or without knowing anything about people in the group as individuals. *Discrimination* is behavior that holds people or groups apart from others and results in different treatments for those people. Thus, prejudice is an attitude but discrimination is behavior. People may be prejudiced yet not actively discriminate, but the two often go together.

Psychology's traditional view of prejudice holds that people within a group (the in-group) form negative feelings about those in another group (the out-group) (Allport, 1954). The identification of the out-group may include stereotyping that sharpens the difference between the two groups and erases the individual differences of those people in the out-group. The results of prejudice include an increased feeling of worth for people in the in-group and a devaluation of those in the out-group. For example, one study (Nielsen, 2002) explored the types and frequency of derogatory public remarks based on ethnicity and gender and found that women and people of color were frequent targets of this type of discrimination. Every one of the African Americans in this study reported that he or she had been the targets of offensive racist remarks made by a stranger in public. Does gender fit into this model? Are men and women in-groups and out-groups to each other?

Listening to the conversations of groups of women or men saying terrible things about the other may seem to confirm this view, but research results are not consistent with such a conceptualization. Although women are the targets of various types of discrimination in terms of economic, political, educational, and professional achievement, attitudes about women are not uniformly negative. Indeed, one line of research from Alice Eagly and her colleagues (Eagly, Mladinic, & Otto, 1991) showed that women as a category receive more *favorable* evaluations than men. Results from a meta-analysis (Feingold, 1998) indicated that women received slightly more favorable ratings than men. Thus, people in general have positive feelings about the characteristics stereotypically associated with women; people believe that these characteristics provide fine examples of human qualities. These findings are not consistent with an overall prejudice against women.

Peter Glick, Susan Fiske, and their colleagues (Fiske, Cuddy, Glick, & Xu, 2002; Glick & Fiske, 2001; Glick et al., 2000) have researched this puzzle in gender stereotyping and formulated interesting answers. The focus of their research is their conceptualization of sexism, that is, prejudice based on sex or gender. Their view separates positive from negative aspects of sexism. They call the negative aspects *hostile sexism,* and this concept includes negative attitudes toward women. They also consider *benevolent sexism,* which they conceptualize as positive attitudes that nonetheless serve to belittle women and keep them subservient. Benevolent sexism is reflected in the attitudes that women deserve special treatment, deserve to be set on a pedestal, and should be revered. Despite the positive nature of these beliefs, people who hold such attitudes tend to see women as weaker, more in need of protection, and less competent than men (Fiske et al., 2002).

Ironically, it may be the favorable traits stereotypically associated with women that serve to perpetuate their lower status (Glick & Fiske, 2001). When people see women as warm and caring but less competent than men, they may give women positive evaluations but still feel that women need men to protect and take care of them. Thus, women's subservience is justified. Men are not exempt from this type of ambivalent sexism; the stereotypic characteristics of men can also be analyzed into hostile and benevolent components that are analogous to those that apply to women, but women's hostile attitudes toward men do not erase men's dominance (Glick & Fiske, 1999). This type of benevolent prejudice may rationalize racism as well as sexism, casting the dominant group as benevolent protectors rather than oppressors.

Research on the contents of stereotypes (Eckes, 2002; Fiske et al., 2002) has shown that combinations of two dimensions—competence and warmth—capture many beliefs about stereotyped groups. The mixed values of low competence–high warmth and high competence–low warmth have been of most interest to researchers, but the two other combinations of high warmth–high competence and low warmth–low competence also occur. Figure 7.1 shows these combinations, the feelings associated with each, and examples. Research on this stereotype content model (Eckes, 2002; Fiske et al., 2002) confirmed that people evaluated a number of lower-status groups (women, ethnic minority groups, older people, disabled people) as less competent but warm and thus rated them positively. People from some high-status groups were not so well-liked; they were respected and judged as competent but not warm. Therefore, this view promotes a complex analysis of the components of stereotypes as well as a broad view of the effects of such stereotyping as it applies to gender and other stereotyped categories.

Thus, several lines of research highlight the negative aspects of stereotyping and point out that stereotyping has wider implications than ease of cognitive processing. For children, such simplification may be a necessary part of dealing with a complex world, but adolescents and adults are able to deal with individual information, yet tend not to do so. Rather, adults stereotype on a variety of dimensions, including gender. Stereotypes form the basis for prejudice and discrimination, and both men and women are subject to these negative processes.

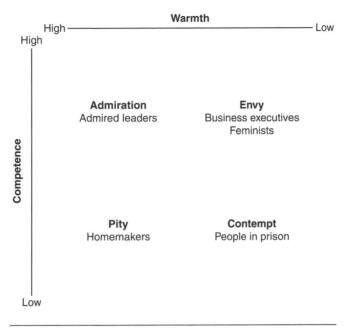

FIGURE 7.1 *Combinations of the Two Dimensions of the Stereotype Content Model and Examples of Each Combination*

Perceptions of Women and Men

The stereotype of women as warm and caring but incompetent and men as competent but not warm (Fiske et al., 2002) is consistent with the Victorian notion of the Cult of True Womanhood and with the Male Gender Role Identity. Are women and men still measured by these standards, or have the changes in women's and men's behaviors produced changes in the stereotypes and broadened the boundaries of acceptable behaviors for men and women?

The content of gender stereotypes may be analyzed into four separate components that people use to differentiate male from female—traits, behaviors, physical characteristics, and occupations (Deaux & Lewis, 1984). All these components are relatively independent, but people associate one set of features from each of these with women and another set with men. On the basis of knowledge of one dimension, people extend judgments to the other three. Figure 7.2 shows the components of this model; the arrows indicate the associations people make among components. Given a gender label for a target person, people will make inferences concerning the person's appearance, traits, gender role behaviors, and occupation. Information about one component can affect inferences made about the others, and people will attempt to maintain consistency among the components.

Physical features seem to be central; people viewed men and women as differing more in physical features than in psychological characteristics (Deaux & Lewis, 1984).

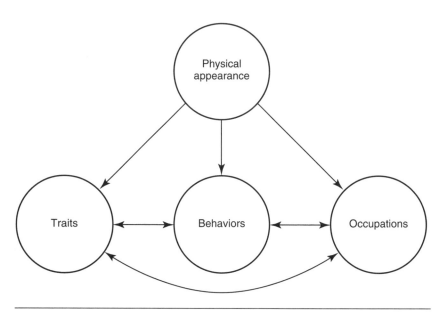

FIGURE 7.2   *Components of Deaux and Lewis's Model of Gender Stereotyping*

As Figure 7.2 shows, when people have information about behaviors, they make inferences about traits, and information about occupations can affect judgments about behaviors. However, physical appearance affected judgments about the other components more strongly than information about traits, behaviors, or occupations influenced judgments about appearance. In addition, specific personal information can outweigh gender as a factor in subsequent judgments about a person. For example, men who were described as managing the house or taking care of children were also judged as likely to be emotional and gentle. Such counterstereotypical information about men also increased the likelihood that such men would be judged to be nontypical in other ways, such as likely to be homosexual.

Although the participants in this stereotyping study saw differences in the physical characteristics, traits, behaviors, and occupations of women and men, their ratings of the two categories reflected the possibility that women may have some characteristics more typical of men, or men may have some characteristics more typical of women. That is, people do not view the stereotypes for women and men as separate and dichotomous categories, but as probabilistic and overlapping. Participants judged the probability of a man and woman having certain characteristics on a scale of 0 (no chance) to 1.00 (certainty). The participants judged the probability that a man would be strong as .66, a high probability but not a certainty. However, they also judged the chances that a woman would be strong as .44, a lower probability but far from unlikely. Although these judgments reflected stereotypical views of the relative strength of men and women, being male was

◼ GENDERED VOICES

Just Another Walking Stereotype

Michelle Fisher (2003, p. 40) explained her dilemma: "So what if I drive a four-wheel-drive vehicle? 'It's not a lesbian car,' I hear myself whine to people who give me that knowing look when they see me get out of my vehicle for the first time." Her dilemma was not that people might identify her as lesbian by her choice of vehicles. Michelle was not trying to hide her sexual orientation.

She described her participation in Gay Pride events, including threats to her safety that resulted from her ac-

tivism. Those threats did not faze her, but the thought that she fit the stereotype of lesbian did. "As I sit here today, I have to face the fact that being perceived as a stereotype is worse than folks chucking bottles at me" (p. 40).

"Nobody likes to be figured out in a split second. I don't care if people know I am gay. . . . But I don't want them to think that because I'm gay, they already know everything about me" (p. 41).

not perfectly associated with strength, nor was being female associated with complete lack of strength.

Therefore, people use several dimensions to categorize men and women, drawing inferences on one dimension based on information from another. What traits are stereotypically associated with these categories? Studies in the 1960s and 1970s often found evidence for beliefs that matched elements of the Male Gender Role Identity or the Cult of True Womanhood, and recent studies have also found remnants of these beliefs (Lueptow, Garovich-Szabo, & Lueptow, 2001). (See "According to the Media" and "According to the Research" for examples of stereotyping in the media and its potential effects.) However, some recent research has reflected changes in attitudes.

Beliefs held by college students in the 1960s showed strong acceptance of gender stereotypes by both college men and women (Rosenkrantz, Vogel, Bee, Broverman, & Broverman, 1968). Table 7.3 (p. 174) shows how some of the items that differentiated women and men match the components in the Cult of True Womanhood and Male Gender Role Identity. Not all of the traits these college students named match these categories; for example, one of the characteristics of women was "talkative," which does not fit into traits for the Cult of True Womanhood, and college students in the 1960s did not mention sexual purity as a defining trait of women. They did, however, mention several characteristics of men that relate to sex, including "worldly" and "talks freely with men about sex," which matches the suggestion (Good & Sherrod, 2001) for an additional component of the Male Gender Role, Be a Stud. Both the women and men in the study by Rosenkrantz and colleagues (1968) and a later study (Broverman, Vogel, Broverman, Clarkson, & Rosenkrantz, 1972) gave more positive ratings to the characteristics associated with men than with women. Thus, these stereotypes reflected gender bias.

The social roles of men and women began to change during the 1960s, and according to several studies, attitudes toward women reflect those changes. Administering the Attitudes toward Women Scale (AWS) to students at the same university over a 20-year

ACCORDING TO THE MEDIA . . .

White Men Are in Charge

In both television commercials and entertainment programming, White men are more common, more prominent, and more dominant than others. According to a content analysis of commercials, White male characters were more prominent than any other group (Coltrane & Messineo, 2000). Male prominence extended to those who appeared in voice only—male voices narrated commercials more than 10 times more often than female voices. The patterns of men in positions of authority and men as the voice of authority exist in the United Kingdom, Europe, Australia, and Asia as well as in the United States (Furnham & Mak, 1999).

In the United States on entertainment programming, women have a history of underrepresentation. Despite increases in female characters during the 1980s and 1990s, women are not only portrayed less often than men, but women's roles also tend to be less significant and less serious (Harwood & Anderson, 2002). Women have been more likely to be shown as dependent, and around the world, women appear more often at home than in other settings (Furnham & Mak, 1999).

Women are not the only group that appears on television as stereotypes. In the United States, African Americans appeared in the background more often than as main characters in commercials, and they were often subordinate to Whites (Coltrane & Messineo, 2000). Additional stereotyping appeared in the portrayal of African American men, who tended to be shown as aggressive but less likely to be shown in home settings or with women. African Americans were less visible, failing to get the attention that White women received. The proportion of African Americans in television commercials (Coltrane & Messineo, 2000) and entertainment programming (Harwood & Anderson, 2002) was not substantially different from their proportion in the actual population—about 11%. However, African Americans were concentrated in a small number of entertainment programs, which tended to "ghettoize" these characters.

Hispanics were drastically underrepresented in both television commercials (Coltrane & Messineo, 2000) and entertainment programming (Harwood & Anderson, 2002). In addition, entertainment television depicted Hispanics in less positive ways than any other ethnic group. Therefore, television's depiction of the world is disproportionately White and dominated by White men.

period showed that students became more egalitarian between the 1970s and the 1990s (Spence & Hahn, 1997). Using the same assessment over the same time period, a study with Canadian university students (Loo & Thorpe, 1998) revealed parallel changes. A meta-analysis of studies that used the AWS revealed a positive relationship between feminist attitudes and the year of administration (Twenge, 1997). For women, the relationship was strong, and for men, the relationship was still positive but not as strong. Another study (Prentice & Carranza, 2002) showed changes in the stereotypes for women but not for men; women were seen as having both the traits associated with their traditional gender roles as well as the traits necessary for achievement in nontraditional occupations. Another study (Diekman & Eagly, 2000) indicated that people perceive that gender differences are decreasing, but with faster changes for women's than for men's roles. Therefore, these studies show that attitudes toward women have become more feminist/egalitarian over the past 25 years, which signals some changes in the traditional stereotypes of women, but attitudes toward men have not shown equivalent changes.

ACCORDING TO THE RESEARCH . . .

Biased Media Portrayals Perpetuate Stereotyping

When people see women and ethnic minorities portrayed in stereotypical ways, those presentations influence the way they think about and judge individuals from those groups. That is, biased portrayals perpetuate stereotyping. The effect of biased portrayals on individuals' thoughts appeared in a study (Murphy, 1998) in which participants read a fake autobiography about an African American man who was aggressive, lazy, unintelligent, and criminal—the most prominent of the negative characteristics associated with this ethnic group. By presenting this stereotypical information, the participants were "primed" to believe negative things about African Americans, and this priming exerted an effect. In a later survey, the same participants judged that the events that happened to Rodney King (receiving a beating from police) and Magic Johnson (being infected with HIV) were situations that they had "brought on themselves." Participants who read neutral or counterstereotypical stories made significantly different judgments. Therefore, negative stereotypes in the media influenced judgments in subtle ways.

Another view of the power of television (and other media) stereotyping is through its representation of various groups (Harwood & Anderson, 2002). This position holds that the way ethnic groups, women, children, and older people appear in the media reflects their power and vitality in society. Groups that are minimized, distorted, or marginalized are at risk because these portrayals make the groups seem less significant than they really are. Thus, media content is important not only for the power that it exerts on individuals' views but also for how it reflects and shapes cultural values.

Concerning gender stereotypes on television, there is bad news and good news. The bad news is that stereotypical portrayals of women and ethnic minorities abound on television, and these presentations have the power to do harm. Regardless of people's knowledge that "it's only on television," these messages are persuasive and powerful (Murphy, 1998). The good news is that the media can also work to counteract stereotyping. Commercials and programming that present counterstereotypical information can counteract stereotypes. These presentations can offer models who behave in ways contrary to stereotypes and open behavioral possibilities (Browne, 1998). Therefore, the media tend to perpetuate negative stereotypes, but changes in portrayals could exert a very different, positive influence.

The stereotype for men seems to be more stable, and men may be the victims of more stringent stereotyping than women. College students who described their views of women and men applied more stereotypical terms to men than to women (Hort, Fagot, & Leinbach, 1990). For both physical and social characteristics, the masculine stereotype was more extreme than the feminine. In addition, men are the targets of some negative attitudes. Assessments of women's attitudes toward men have revealed that women hold ambivalent (Glick & Fiske, 1999) and negative (Stephan, Stephan, Demitrakis, Yamada, & Clason, 2000) attitudes toward men. The ambivalence includes feelings of hostility toward men and their gender role combined with admiration and attraction. The disapproving attitudes originate with women's negative contacts with men more than with the influence of negative stereotypes of men. Indeed, the results of a study (Edmonds & Cahoon, 1993) of evaluations of same- and other-gender individuals showed that women tended to believe that men held higher degrees of bias concerning women than the men expressed. That is, women showed negative stereotyping of men.

TABLE 7.3 *Stereotypical Traits of Men and Women Matched to Descriptions from Rosenkrantz et al. (1968)*

Men		Women	
Male Gender Role Identity Component	*Stereotypic Traits in Study*	*Cult of True Womanhood Component*	*Stereotypic Traits in Study*
Give 'Em Hell	Aggressive Not uncomfortable about being aggressive Adventurous Competitive	Pious	Religious
Sturdy Oak	Unemotional Hides emotions Not excitable in a minor crisis Able to separate feelings from ideas	Submissive	Aware of feelings of others Gentle Tactful Quiet
Big Wheel	Dominant Skilled in business Knows the ways of the world Acts as a leader Self-confident Ambitious Worldly	Domestic	Neat in habits Strong need for security
No Sissy Stuff	Never cries Not dependent Direct Thinks men are superior to women Not conceited about appearance	Purity	Does not use harsh language

Source: Based on material from: "Sex-Role Stereotypes and Self-Concepts in College Students" by P. Rosenkrantz, S. Vogel, H. Bee, I. Broverman, and D. M. Broverman, 1968, *Journal of Consulting and Clinical Psychology, 32,* p. 291.

Some evidence suggests that a process moderates the application of gender stereotypes: Men and women may not apply stereotypes to themselves as strictly as they apply these stereotypes to others. U.S. college students hold stereotypical beliefs about gender, but they have also shown that they are willing to exempt themselves from these stereotypes (Williams & Best, 1990). That is, these students rated themselves as varying from the

⬛ GENDERED VOICES

The Problem Disappeared

"Our car was having some problem, and my wife took it to be repaired," a man said. "She called me from the auto repair place, furious with the treatment she had received. The men there were stonewalling her—failing to listen to what she was telling them and treating her as though she couldn't possibly be capable of relating problems concerning an automobile. She was steamed.

"I went down there, and the problem disappeared. I was a man and apparently privy to the innermost secrets of automobiles. They treated me as though I would understand everything perfectly. Both my wife and I thought it was really absurd."

"One of my friends was upset that it cost $3.20 to get her shirt dry-cleaned," a woman told me. "She asked them why it was so much—the shirt was a tailored, plain shirt. They told her that women's blouses cost more than men's shirts, regardless of the style, because women's clothes don't fit on the standard machine for pressing and must be hand-pressed. She wondered if that was really true, and she gave the shirt to a male friend to take to the same dry cleaners. The problem apparently disappeared, because they charged him $1.25 for the very same garment. Isn't that beyond stereotyping?"

stereotype. Although people hold stereotypical views of men and women, they may make exceptions for themselves, allowing themselves a wider variety of behaviors than the stereotype would permit. By allowing such personal exceptions as routine, people decrease the power of stereotypes to control and restrict their lives.

Therefore, some of the positive attitudes about men and negative attitudes about women found in earlier studies seem to show some changes. More recent studies have shown a shift toward greater acceptance of gender role flexibility for women and an increase in positive attitudes toward women. Some studies have indicated that men have now become the object of more severe stereotyping and some negative opinions from women.

MASCULINITY, FEMININITY, AND ANDROGYNY

The concepts of *male* and *female* are relatively easy for people to understand because these words relate to biological differences understood by everyone except young children. But the concepts of masculine and feminine are much less closely related to biology and thus much more difficult to separate into two nonoverlapping categories: "One can be more or less feminine. One cannot be more or less female" (Maccoby, 1988, p. 762). Nonetheless, these dimensions seem important—perhaps critically important—and psychologists have attempted to conceptualize and measure masculinity and femininity along with other important personality traits. After many years of difficulty with such measurements, the concept of **androgyny**—having both masculine and feminine characteristics—appeared as an addition to the conceptual framework. Several techniques now exist for measuring this attribute.

Psychologists' attempts to understand and measure masculinity and femininity have a long history but not a great deal of success (Constantinople, 1973; Lewin, 1984a, 1984b). The problems began with the first measures developed, and no measurement technique used since has escaped serious criticism.

Lewis Terman (who adapted the Binet intelligence test into the Stanford–Binet test) and Catherine Cox Miles constructed the Attitude Interest Analysis Survey, a 456-item test that appeared in 1936 (Lewin, 1984a). This test yielded masculinity–femininity (MF) scores that were increasingly positive in the masculine direction and increasingly negative in the feminine direction. Therefore, this early test conceptualized masculinity and femininity as a single dimension, with strong masculinity lying at one extreme and strong femininity at the other. The test was not valid in any way other than distinguishing men from women, and critics (Lewin, 1984a) thus argued that the test actually measured Victorian concepts of masculinity and femininity rather than the masculinity and femininity of individuals. This test is no longer used, but its existence influenced others to develop measurements of masculinity and femininity.

When the Mf scale of the Minnesota Multiphasic Personality Inventory (MMPI) appeared in 1940, it soon became the most common measure of masculinity and femininity, largely because of its inclusion in this personality test developed to measure psychological disorders (Lewin, 1984b). This scale was also unidimensional and bipolar, with masculinity and femininity at opposite ends of the scale. The psychologists who developed the MMPI were more interested that their Mf scale was able to measure homosexual tendencies in men than masculinity and femininity in heterosexual men and women. As a result of this interest, their **validation** procedure included a comparison of the Mf responses of 13 homosexual men to the responses of 54 heterosexual male soldiers. They used the responses of the 13 homosexual men as a standard for femininity, thus defining femininity as the responses of these men.

The test makers knew that the scale should not be used as a valid measure of femininity, and they were initially tentative in describing its use for a heterosexual population. But the test was soon extended to thousands of people, and the reservations disappeared. "It is rather staggering to realize that *the femininity dimension of this popular test was 'validated' on a criterion group of 13 male homosexuals!*" (Lewin, 1984b, p. 181; emphasis in original). The scale was not even very successful in diagnosing homosexuality in men, and this confusion of masculinity—femininity and sexual orientation posed a problem for understanding both concepts.

An alternative means of conceptualizing masculinity and femininity used the terms *instrumental* and *expressive,* with men's behaviors considered instrumental and women's behaviors as expressive (Lewin, 1984b). This distinction was based on an analysis of families around the world, with the conclusion that men occupy the role of autonomous- and achievement-oriented leaders, whereas women provide nurturance and support. This terminology has become important to those who have attempted to reconceptualize and measure psychological masculinity and femininity. Despite the problems with a unidimensional measure of masculinity–femininity and the limited success with identifying homosexuals with these scales, this approach to the measure of masculinity and femininity was the most common until the 1970s. When theorists realized that the dimensions of masculinity and femininity were separate from sexual orientation, the measurements of both changed, helping to clarify both areas.

In 1974, Sandra Bem published a different approach to the measurement of masculinity and femininity by adding the concept of androgyny. She proposed that some people have characteristics associated with both masculinity and femininity; that is, some people are androgynous. The androgyny concept requires both masculinity and femininity in combination, so it is incompatible with a unidimensional view of masculinity–femininity. Instead, Bem constructed two scales to capture her concept of androgyny. Her test, the Bem Sex Role Inventory (BSRI), included one scale to measure masculinity and another to assess femininity. Figure 7.3 illustrates the difference between the traditional unidimensional approach to personality measurement and Bem's two-dimensional approach.

People who take the BSRI respond to 60 characteristics by rating how well each of these characteristics applies to them on a 7-point scale ranging from *Always or almost always true* to *Never or almost never true.* Of the 60 items, 20 represent cultural stereotypes of masculinity (ambitious, independent, competitive), 20 represent femininity (gentle, warm, understanding), and 20 are filler items. Scores on the masculinity and femininity scales yield four different possibilities: masculine, feminine, androgynous, and undifferentiated. People who score high on the masculinity scale and low on the femininity scale would be classified *masculine,* whereas people who score high on the femininity scale and low on the masculinity scale would be considered *feminine.* These people not only accept cultural stereotypes of masculinity or femininity, but they also reject the other role. Thus, such individuals fit the stereotypical notions of masculinity or femininity, classifications similar to those obtained on other masculinity/femininity tests.

Bem labeled those people who score high on both scales *androgynous* and those who score low on both scales *undifferentiated,* classifications that do not appear in traditional tests of masculinity–femininity. Androgynous people evaluate themselves as having many

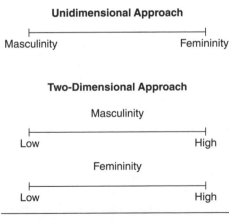

FIGURE 7.3 *Two Approaches to the Measurement of Femity and Masculinity*

of the characteristics that our culture associates with men and women, whereas those people who are undifferentiated report few traits of either gender.

The concept of androgyny experienced a rapid growth in popularity. Another test, the Personal Attributes Questionnaire (PAQ) (Spence, Helmreich, & Stapp, 1974), soon appeared to overcome problems with the BSRI (see Spence & Helmreich, 1978). The PAQ also identified people as masculine, feminine, androgynous, and undifferentiated; both tests have undergone revisions and continued in use. Researchers interested in measuring masculinity or femininity usually choose the BSRI or the PAQ.

Not all researchers accept that the concept of androgyny offers improvements. Critics contend that tests that include measures of androgyny have provided no revolutionary reconceptualization of the measurement of masculinity and femininity (Lewin, 1984b). Indeed, many researchers now refer to scores on these two scales in terms of instrumentality and expressiveness, rather than masculinity and femininity. Janet Spence (1985; Spence & Buckner, 2000), one of the developers of the PAQ, has acknowledged the weaknesses of this conceptualization of masculinity and femininity and now uses the terms *instrumental* and *expressive* to describe the traits that such tests measure. Some researchers have adopted David Bakan's (1966) terminology of *agentic* to refer to the assertive, controlling tendencies that are associated with men, and the term *communal* to refer to the concern with the welfare of others associated with women. Any change in terminology fails to solve the underlying problem of assessment of masculinity and femininity. Spence discussed the conceptual inadequacies of psychology's measurements of masculinity and femininity and proposed that gender identity is multifactorial and complex (Spence & Buckner, 2000). Thus, none of the existent tests provide adequate assessments of these constructs.

Other research (Ricciardelli & Williams, 1995; Woodhill & Samuels, 2003) has tested an alternative conceptualization that involves positive and negative dimensions for masculinity, femininity, and androgyny. The PAQ contains only positive aspects of masculinity and femininity, and the BSRI includes mostly positive aspects of both but has some examples of negative femininity. Table 7.4 gives examples of the four categories of positive and negative masculinity and femininity. Positive and negative androgyny consist of combinations of the positive and negative traits from both.

Research that has shown positive effects associated with androgyny may be biased by the consideration of only those positive aspects. Research into the concept of negative and positive androgyny (Woodhill & Samuels, 2003) indicated that the separation of positive and negative aspects of masculinity, femininity, and androgyny was a useful addition. This study measured positive and negative aspects of all three orientations and found that people with positive androgyny showed better mental health and well-being than all other groups, but those with positive masculinity and positive femininity were only slightly less so. The presence of negative masculinity, femininity, or androgyny was less conducive to health and well-being, especially negative masculinity.

Although the terms *masculinity* and *femininity* are meaningful to most people, psychologists have not yet managed to measure them in theoretically meaningful and valid ways. Problems exist both in the measurement of masculinity and femininity as well as in the concept of androgyny (Constantinople, 1973; Lewin, 1984b; Woodhill & Samuels, 2003). In answering the question, "Are MF tests satisfactory? [The answer is] No. There is no evidence that the MF tests of the last sixty years provide a valid measure of the rel-

TABLE 7.4 *Examples of Positive and Negative Femininity and Masculinity*

Femininity		Masculinity	
Positive	*Negative*	*Positive*	*Negative*
Patient	Timid	Strong	Aggressive
Sensitive	Weak	Confident	Bossy
Devoted	Needs approval	Firm	Sarcastic
Responsible	Dependent	Forceful	Rude
Appreciative	Nervous	Carefree	Feels superior

Source: From "Desirable and Undesirable Gender Traits in Three Behavioral Domains," by Lina A. Ricciardelli & Robert J. Williams, 1995, *Sex Roles, 33,* pp. 637–655.

ative femininity of women or the relative masculinity of men" (Lewin, 1984b, p. 198). Instead, these tests measure our society's conceptualization of what women and men should be by using values that date from the Victorian era, although research indicates that society and self-concepts of masculinity and femininity are changing. The MF tests purport to measure masculinity and femininity, but actually measure gender stereotypes rather than personality characteristics. The tests that include the concept of androgyny offer some improvement but do not solve the problem.

CONSIDERING DIVERSITY

Gender stereotypes affect how women and men think of themselves and how they evaluate their own behaviors as well as the behaviors of others. "Although every individual belongs to at least one sexual, racial, and social class category simultaneously, such categories do not have an equal social meaning" (Unger, 1995, p. 427). How do these factors interact to form the basis for stereotypical categories? Do cultures around the world make similar distinctions between what is considered masculine and feminine? Do other cultures stereotype gender-related behaviors, and are these stereotypes similar to those in North America? Research aimed at answering these questions can be divided into attempts to compare masculinity and femininity in various ethnic and cultural groups in North America and studies that explore gender stereotypes around the world.

Cross-Cultural Assessments of Masculinity and Femininity

Results from studies using the Bem Sex Role Inventory (BSRI) have suggested that the conceptualizations of masculinity and femininity that are the basis for this test are culturally specific to the United States and to White people. As a reflection of stereotypes of femininity and masculinity, the test remains valid for many groups (Harris, 1994; Konrad & Harris, 2002), but for other groups in the United States and for people in other countries, concepts of masculinity and femininity vary to the extent that the BSRI is not applicable.

Research with Hispanic Americans (Harris, 1994; Sugihara & Warner, 1999), African Americans (Harris, 1994; Konrad & Harris, 2002), and Native American women (Portman, 2001) indicated that women, men, or both failed to match the norms for scoring the BSRI that were derived from Stanford students in 1978. These studies did not indicate that any ethnic group lacked gender-related identity or stereotypes but that the traits associated with masculinity and femininity varied among cultures. In general, studies with the BSRI indicate fewer diversions from the norm sample when testing White participants, but various ethnic groups within the United States have somewhat different gender stereotypes than Whites do. Indeed, the current version of the BSRI includes norms for interpreting the results for Hispanic Americans and African Americans (Bem, 1981b).

The discrepancies for ethnic groups within the United States lead to predictions of even more problems in administering the BSRI to people in other countries. One study comparing Chinese and U.S. college students (Zhang, Norvilitis, & Jin, 2001) encountered validity problems with the Chinese students. The researchers speculated that the Chinese concepts of masculinity and femininity are more polarized in the United States than in China, leading to difficulties in placing Chinese students in the same categories of femininity and masculinity with Americans students. Thus, the BSRI may measure a reflection of gender stereotypes for some groups in the United States, but conceptualizations of masculinity and femininity vary with ethnicity and geography.

Gender Stereotypes across Cultures

An attempt to understand the development of gender differences across many cultures has led to several large cross-cultural studies of the development of social and gender-related behaviors. One such study (Whiting & Edwards, 1988) included children from 12 different communities in Kenya, Liberia, India, the Philippines, Okinawa, Mexico, and the United States who were studied to better understand the development of gender in various regions of the world. Some differences appeared in the treatment and subsequent behavior of boys and girls, but many similarities also emerged in the types of interactions children experienced. The analysis showed that age was more important than gender in predicting the experiences of children in these various cultures, but the definition of chores and the freedom to roam and be independent tended to show large gender differences that were common to many cultures.

Another cross-cultural investigation of gender stereotypes (Williams & Best, 1990) took place in 30 different countries in North America, South America, Europe, Asia, Africa, and Oceania. College students in these countries rated a list of 300 adjectives according to the extent to which each was more frequently associated with men or women. The goal was to study the associations that people in different cultures make about women and men and to look for female and male stereotypes.

Some Things Are Different There

"I think of femininity more in terms of what a woman wears than anything else," a young man told me. He had grown up on an island in the Mediterranean, lived in Paris for two years, and now lives in the United States. He sees some differences in what is considered feminine and masculine in the three cultures he has known. "Where I grew up, there was very little sexual activity among teenagers; it was a very conservative culture, and adolescent sexuality was strictly discouraged. The girls didn't dress in any way that was sexual, so they didn't seem very feminine to me. I guess I would consider some of them more feminine than others, probably in the same way that a person in the U.S. would: Small and dainty girls were more feminine. So I don't see any differences there.

"In Paris, nothing was hidden—things were openly sexual. The U.S. is a very sexualized culture, but there are differences. For example, kinds of clothing that people wore in Paris were different from in the U.S., and those differences related to femininity. Wearing jeans and tennis shoes would be considered very unfeminine rather than just another way to dress. I remember one girl in my student group who often wore tennis shoes, jeans, and a big sweater, and she was considered very unfeminine. Not that her way of dressing kept her from being pretty or attractive, but she didn't seem feminine. I guess I would say that Paris was less casual, and the women seemed more feminine than in the U.S. or in the Mediterranean.

"There were also some differences in what was considered masculine. At home, men tend to be small, so masculinity is not determined by size but more by behavior. Even men who are 5'4" or 5'6" can be macho, depending on what they do. Gangsters are very masculine, and so are those who are involved in politics, especially radical politics. The communists are considered the most masculine—lots of testosterone there. Men can demonstrate their masculinity by drinking—it has to be liquor and straight, without ice—and by smoking unfiltered cigarettes. Also, women who drink or smoke are considered masculine. So masculinity is a matter of what you do in the Mediterranean, not how you look—except the gangsters always have a three-day growth of beard.

"One of the differences in what is considered masculine involves bodybuilding and weight lifting. Men in the Mediterranean and in Paris just didn't do anything like that. They wouldn't consider bodybuilding masculine; it would be considered odd rather than a way to demonstrate masculinity. If they exercise, it's oriented more toward fitness than bodybuilding, so that seems very American to me.

"Political activism is masculine where I come from, whether men or women are involved. As I said, the communist radicals are considered very macho, and women who become involved in politics or become lawyers are considered masculine. As career opportunities increase for women, this may change, but now, women lose their femininity when they gain power through legal or political careers—even more than in the U.S.

"Also, on the island where I grew up, there was a status for women that I haven't seen anywhere else. Postmenopausal women lose their sexuality but they gain power and can become very influential in the community. They are considered almost neuter in terms of sexuality, so they are not feminine at all, but these women can have a lot of power, whereas younger women do not. As long as a woman is young and unmarried or married, she has almost no voice in the community, but these older women can make a transition to a position of respect and power.

"The only men who lose their sexuality in a similar way are artists, who are not considered feminine but almost neutral. Being an artist is well accepted and doesn't really carry any connotations of femininity, unlike homosexuality, which is strongly prohibited. It is a conservative culture, and homosexual activity is not tolerated at all—unlike Paris, where gay men and lesbians are very open about their sexuality. The U.S. seems to be the worst of both cultures in that respect; homosexuality is fairly open but poorly tolerated. That seems like a bad combination to me. As far as masculinity and femininity and homosexuality are concerned, I can't see any relationship. I know I can't tell who is homosexual by how masculine the men seem or how feminine the women seem. So sexual orientation does not seem to coincide with these characteristics to me."

The results revealed more similarities than differences in these gender stereotypes. Six adjectives were associated with males in all of the cultures—*adventurous, dominant, forceful, independent, masculine,* and *strong*—and three adjectives were identified with females in all cultures—*sentimental, submissive,* and *superstitious.* In addition, a wide list of adjectives appeared as male-associated or female-associated in a large majority of the cultures, and only a few adjectives were male-associated in one culture and female-associated in another. These findings furnish evidence for similarities in gender stereotypes across cultures, but the similarities were far short of being universal.

A reanalysis of some of these data (Williams, Satterwhite, & Best, 1999) in terms of the Five Factor Model of personality revealed even more similarities across cultures than the original analysis. Using averages for the 25 countries, differences in gender stereotypes appeared in all five factors. Participants scored the male stereotype higher in Extraversion, Conscientiousness, Emotional Stability, and Openness to Experience and placed the female stereotype higher on Agreeableness. Not all countries adhered to this pattern, and individuals within the countries did not necessarily believe they fit the stereotypes. However, the beliefs about the characteristics of men and women showed many similarities across a variety of cultures.

Despite similarities in many aspects of gender stereotypes, not all cultures hold the same views of what traits, characteristics, and patterns of behavior men and women should exhibit. One cross-cultural review (Gibbons, Hamby, & Dennis, 1997) found that no one gender distinction applied to all cultures.

Japan was one of the cultures that showed a different pattern of gender stereotypes than many others (Williams & Best, 1990; Williams et al., 1999). Research on gender roles in Japan (Sugihara & Katsurada, 2002) showed that the characteristics that differentiate women and men in the United States, such as independent, assertive, and self-reliant, do not do so in Japan. Indeed, these characteristics are not considered desirable for either Japanese women or men. As Richard Nisbett (2003) discussed, Asian culture promotes the development of strong family ties and obligations, making conformity and obedience valued traits for everyone. In the United States and Europe, these characteristics would be considered feminine, but in Japan, they are not tied to either gender. In China, the ideal man is a warrior but also a cook, teacher, artist, and musician (Chia, Moore, Lam, Chuang, & Cheng, 1994). In the United States, some of these roles are associated more with women than with men. People in both Japan (Sugihara & Katsurada, 2002) and China (Hong, Veach, & Lawrenz, 2003) exhibit gender stereotyping, but the contents of the gender stereotypes show some variations among cultures because different societies hold varying views of what women and men should be.

Going beyond variation in specific gender-related characteristics, some scholars have asked questions concerning how gender stereotyping creates gender-related attitudes that are common over many cultures. The prevalence of male dominance has prompted a broader question: Are men dominant and women subordinate in all cultures? Is this pattern universal and thus the basis for much of gender stereotyping?

The answer from anthropology to the question of universal male dominance is "no" (Bonvillain, 1998; Salzman, 1999). Some societies have included equal access to resources and power for both women and men. Egalitarian cultures tend to be simple, pastoral societies rather than complex, industrialized cultures. Many more societies have placed men than women in positions of power and control; few have enacted egalitarian arrangements. The reasons for this dominance are debatable, but some speculations involve men's tendency to a social dominance orientation versus women's greater emphasis on forming relationships (Sidanius, Pratto, & Bobo, 1994).

Another view is based on the conflicts that come from women and men living in male-dominated societies that depend on and value women. This situation sets up attitudes that are sexist yet still include positive components. Peter Glick, Susan Fiske, and their colleagues (2000) have delineated the concepts of benevolent and hostile sexism, which relate to the stereotypically positive (warm, nurturing) and negative (incompetent, need to be cared for) characteristics of women. These researchers demonstrated the implications of these two components of gender stereotypes by testing over 15,000 people in 19 countries around the world to determine the relationship between hostile and benevolent sexism. They found that, in every one of the 19 nations, a positive relationship appeared between these two dimensions. That is, higher hostile sexism scores were related to higher benevolent sexism scores. They explained the connection as a result of the relationships between men and women in male-dominated cultures, which create both women's subordination and their value as sexual and domestic companions and caregivers. For such systems to remain stable, both women and men must hold attitudes that support the system, and these ideologies form a complementary system that perpetuates societies in which men dominate. Their results confirmed the prediction that both men and women hold these attitudes. Although women were more likely than men to reject hostile sexism, both women and men endorsed both beliefs. Furthermore, the degree of men's hostile sexism predicted the level of gender inequality in these societies.

As the Glick et al. (2000) results showed, women often hold more egalitarian views of women and women's roles than men endorse, but even this difference is not universal. No differences in attitudes toward women appeared in a study (Gibbons et al., 1997) of people in Malaysia or Pakistan, and men in Brazil expressed more liberal views of women than women did. The distinction between traditional beliefs and beliefs concerning equal opportunity and equal power might apply to all cultures, but the specifics of what constitutes traditionality vary. The division of activities and behaviors into male and female domains is universal, without worldwide agreement about what those activities and characteristics are. Such divisions of activities, however, form the basis for gender roles and furnish the potential for gender stereotyping.

■ SUMMARY

The term *gender role* refers to the activities or behaviors typically associated with women or men, whereas *gender stereotype* refers to the beliefs associated with the characteristics and personalities appropriate to men and women. Current stereotypes of women and men have been influenced by historical views of women and men. The Cult of True Womanhood that arose during Victorian times held that women should be pious, pure, submissive, and domestic. For men, several models of masculinity show gender role stereotypes. One of these is the Male Gender Role

Identity, which holds that to be successful as men, males must identify with the elements of that role, including the need to avoid all feminine activities and interests, have an achievement orientation, suppress emotions, and be aggressive and assertive.

Gender stereotyping begins early in development and results in children holding rigid rules for gender-related behavior. Stereotyping is maintained by the illusion that more activities and characteristics are associated with gender than actually are. Children become flexible in applying gender rules as they approach adolescence, allowing themselves more exceptions for individual variation. The tendency to make exceptions increases with development toward adulthood.

During childhood, stereotyping may serve to simplify cognitive processing and allow children to make easier decisions and judgments, but adults do not require such simplification. Nevertheless, stereotyping continues, and prejudice and discrimination are frequent consequences.

Gender stereotypes have four different aspects—physical characteristics, traits, behaviors, and occupations. Each aspect may vary independently, but people make judgments about one based on information about another, to form an interdependent network of associations. People use this network of information in making deductions about gender-related characteristics.

The concepts of masculinity and femininity have a long history in the field of psychology as personality traits measured by various psychological tests. The first such test was the Attitude Interest Analysis Survey, which conceptualized masculinity and femininity as opposite poles of one continuum. The Minnesota Multiphasic Personality Inventory still uses this unidimensional approach. A more recent approach to the measurement of masculinity and femininity includes the concept of androgyny. Several tests have adopted this strategy, including the Bem Sex Role Inventory and the Personal Attributes Questionnaire. These tests include separate scales for masculinity and femininity, allowing classification of people as not only masculine or feminine but also as androgynous. However, some critics have argued that none of the personality tests that purport to measure masculinity and femininity do so. At present, the underlying concepts of masculinity and femininity remain elusive.

Cross-cultural research on gender roles and gender stereotyping indicates that all cultures delegate different roles to men and women, but what traits are associated with each show some cultural variation. Gender stereotypes have more similarities than differences across cultures, with the male stereotype fitting the instrumental, or agentic, model and the female stereotype fitting the expressive, or communal, model.

▓ GLOSSARY

androgyny   a blending of masculinity and femininity, in which the desirable characteristics associated with both men and women are combined within individuals.

gender stereotype   the beliefs about the characteristics associated with, and the activities appropriate to, men or women.

illusory correlation   the incorrect belief that two events vary together, or the perception that the relationship is strong when little or no actual relationship exists.

stereotype threat   a phenomenon that occurs in situations in which the presence of negative stereotypes affect the performance of those to whom the stereotype applies.

validation   the process of demonstrating that a psychological test measures what it claims to measure; the procedure that demonstrates the accuracy of a test.

■ SUGGESTED READINGS

Good, Glenn E.; & Sherrod, Nancy B. (2001). The psychology of men and masculinity: Research status and future directions. In Rhoda Unger (Ed.), *Handbook of the psychology of women and gender* (pp. 201–214). New York: Wiley.

Good and Sherrod examine the models of masculinity and discuss its components, along with research that supports the existence of each. In addition, they consider the implications of masculinity in this and other cultures.

Kite, Mary E. (2001). Changing times, changing gender roles: Who do we want women and men to be? In Rhoda Unger (Ed.), *Handbook of the psychology of women and gender* (pp. 215–227). New York: Wiley.

Kite reviews gender belief systems, gender stereotypes and their measurement, and what men and women think of men and women. In addition, she carefully considers the cost of violating these gender stereotypes.

Lewin, Miriam. (1984). "Rather worse than folly?" Psychology measures femininity and masculinity: 1. From Terman and Miles to the Guilfords (pp. 155–178); and Psychology measures femininity and masculinity: 2. From "13 gay men" to the instrumental–expressive distinction (pp. 179–204). In Miriam Lewin (Ed.), *In the shadow of the past: Psychology portrays the sexes.* New York: Columbia University Press.

Although Lewin's two articles are not recent, they furnish a critical review of attempts in the field of psychology to measure masculinity and femininity. She points out the difficulties and the mistakes, including conceptualizing femininity as the responses of 13 gay men.

8 EMOTION

HEADLINE   Are Girls Really As Mean As Books Say They Are?
Chronicle of Higher Education, July 5, 2002

In July, 2002 psychologist Carol Tavris wrote about the recent books and stories in which "Journalists, academics, and psychologists alike have all been offering their observations on the 'discovery' of female aggression and meanness" (p. 7). She continued to say,

> . . . old news about female inequality won't do, such as those pesky world problems of discrimination, poverty, illiteracy, genital mutilation, rape, and lack of birth control. Old news about female superiority won't do, either. The feel-good genre of the 1980s and 1990s—with its notion that women are kinder, better at friendship, and more moral, compassionate, earth-loving, and nurturant than men—is toast. And so the time and economy were just right for the "new," not-new news that girls aren't sweeter than boys, but just as bad, sexual, and aggressive—maybe even meaner. . . . (Tavris, 2002, p. 7)

The "news" about girls' meanness came after the publicity about boys' aggression and violence that followed the rash of school shootings in the late 1990s. Those stories focused on bullying and the violence that boys do. What seemed to be news was that girls are not exempt, but as Tavris (p. 8) noted, "Unquestionably, many aspects of our culture foster aggression, competition, and selfishness, and girls and women are hardly immune from those influences." Why, then, should female aggression be so shocking?

The answer probably lies in the divergence of female aggression from the stereotype of female emotionality, which centers on caring and nurturing. Although the "tender" emotions were part of Victorian stereotypes of womanhood, that notion received a modern boost when Carol Gilligan published *In a Different Voice* in 1982. This book was part of the 1980s and 1990s notion that women are kinder and more moral than men. Gilligan presented the view that men are oriented toward "separateness" and develop a moral sense based on abstract principles of justice, whereas women are oriented toward "connectedness" and "care" and use these principles as the basis for their morality. This concept of care and the value of relationships form the basis for their "different voice" and for women's arguably superior moral sense. This view appealed to many women and captured

186

media attention, despite subsequent research (Crandall, Tsang, Goldman, & Pennington, 1999; Johnson, 1988; Lyons, 1988) that demonstrated that this different voice was not unique to women and thus not so different after all. However, this view is a sharp contrast with the current books that emphasize female aggression.

Tavris (2002) argued that women and men show some differences in their expression of aggression but that there are more similarities than differences. Neither gender has the exclusive on physical fights or on name-calling and spite. This chapter explores the experience and expression of emotion for women and men, and then examines two emotional reactions that these recent books have examined: maternal instinct and aggression

PHYSIOLOGICAL, COGNITIVE, AND BEHAVIORAL ASPECTS OF EMOTION

Emotion has been a subject of interest in the field of psychology since its early years as a discipline. Even before psychologists began experimental investigations of behavior, emotion was a topic of interest to philosophers. From the start, western philosophers tended to conceptualize emotions as irrational and to place emotion opposite the rational thought processes (Averill, 1982). This attitude shaped the rational–emotive dichotomy that persists today.

Psychologists have devised several theories to explain the various components of emotion and their relative contribution to the experience. Early theories (McDougall, 1923) emphasized the physiology of emotional reactions and proposed their instinctual nature. Other theories attempted to integrate the contribution of cognition to explain the physiological reactions that accompany emotion (Cannon, 1927; James, 1890). All approaches held that both the physiology and the cognitive components were important to experiencing emotion.

An experiment by Stanley Schachter and Jerome Singer (1962) demonstrated that similar levels of physical arousal could result in different emotions, depending on the setting and the expectation of the participants. This study showed that both physiological arousal and cognitive labeling are important components in the individual's experience of emotion. Despite the results from Schachter and Singer's study, the relative contributions of physiology and cognition have been the source of continued controversy in psychology. Some theorists have asserted that the physiological component is more important (Zajonc, 1984), and others have argued that cognitions are more critical to the experience of emotion (Lazarus, 1984).

The primacy of either physiology or cognition has important implications for understanding emotion. If cognition were the primary factor in emotion, then an emotional experience should be dependent on the setting and expectation, and the physiology of the underlying emotion should be the same, regardless of the emotion evoked. If physiology were the primary factor, then the emotional experience should vary with bodily states, and each emotion would have a characteristic pattern of physical responses.

Both theories may be correct: one for men and the other for women (Pennebaker & Roberts, 1992). In this view, women rely more on cognitive information, whereas men use physical cues, to identify their experiences. Several types of evidence support this view. In laboratory studies, men are better than women at gauging their internal physical states, such as heart rate, blood pressure, and blood glucose levels. These gender differences do not appear in studies done in more naturalistic settings, where women and men are equally adept in judging their internal physical responses. Outside the laboratory, women are better than men in gauging the emotions of others. They cannot know others' physiological responses, so this expertise must come from reading the situation. Women's reliance on situational and contextual cues in interpreting emotion may be the result of socialization that teaches them not to listen to their bodies. Women, therefore, may become skilled in interpreting cues from the environment, whereas men do not undergo this social pressure and continue to use internal bodily cues to understand their emotion. This intriguing hypothesis of a "his and hers theory of emotion" allows that two competing theories of emotion may both be true and that both describe some gender-related differences in perception of emotion.

Paul Ekman and his colleagues (Ekman, 1984; Ekman, Levenson, & Friesen, 1983) have concentrated on similarities between genders in emotional experience. Indeed, their emphasis has been on the universals of emotional experience. This evolutionary view can be traced to Charles Darwin (1872), who believed that both humans and animals innately experience emotions. Ekman and his colleagues studied the different facial movements that accompany the experience of emotion and found that certain facial expressions are characteristic of emotional states across societies. That is, people experience a standard set of emotions regardless of the culture of origin. Ekman argued that this consistency exists because emotions have evolved to help people deal with life tasks.

Regardless of the consistency of emotional *experience,* people do not show similar consistency in emotional *expression*. That is, the behaviors associated with emotion show some cultural and individual variation. Some associations are known to exist between emotion and expression in terms of behavior, for example, between anger and aggression. However, the experience of emotion requires no behavioral manifestation: People do not have to *do* anything when they feel an emotion. The emotional experience is internal, and behavior is not an inevitable consequence of that experience.

The lack of correspondence between emotion and behavior results in the ability to disguise or conceal emotion. People can experience an emotion and yet manifest no overt behavior that signals their inner experience. Ekman (1984) defined the concept of **display rules** as "overlearned habits about who can show what emotion to whom and when they can show it" (p. 320). These display rules make it possible to experience one emotion and display another, or to display no emotional reaction at all despite the internal experience of strong emotion. In addition, the learning of display rules provides an explanation for the variability of emotion from person to person and from culture to culture.

How does learning provide an explanation for the gender differences in emotion? Do men and women learn different display rules and show different emotions, or do they experience differing types and intensities of emotions?

GENDER AND THE EXPERIENCE OF EMOTION

"From the 19th century onwards, rationality and emotionality have largely become associated with the supposedly different natures of men and women, the former fitted for productive labor and the latter for household and emotional labor" (Fischer, 1993, p. 303). This emotional double standard holds that women are more emotional than men, but only for a restricted range of emotions—happiness, sadness, disgust, fear, and surprise. Anger is notably absent from the list of emotions stereotypically associated with women. Men are also subject to a parallel stereotype—one of restricted emotionality for most emotions except anger (Heesacker et al., 1999). However, the process of recalling and reporting emotional experience may introduce gender bias. Indeed, when women and men gave immediate reports of their current emotions in everyday situations (Larson & Pleck, 1999), the results showed very few differences.

The stereotypes of overemotional women and restrained men do not apply to all emotions or all situations, but college students revealed similar gender stereotyping of emotions in two studies. In one study (Kelly & Hutson-Comeaux, 1999), college students rated how characteristic underreactions and overreactions were in relationship and achievement situations. The results showed a stereotypical view of emotionality, dependent on context. For women in personal relationships—a domain associated with women—people rated women's overreactions as more characteristic than men's. For men in achievement situations—a domain associated with men—participants expected men to overreact. The exception to this general finding was anger, which was rated as characteristic of men regardless of the situation. An extension of this study (Hutson-Comeaux & Kelly, 2002) showed that when men or women exhibited a strong emotion not stereotypical of their gender, people perceived their reaction to be more genuine than when they showed a typical emotion.

Another study on stereotyping of emotion (Plant, Hyde, Keltner, & Devine, 2000) also showed a bias in associating anger with men and not women. Participants tended to interpret women's reactions as sadness rather than anger and had trouble seeing women as angry, even when women's expressions were clearly angry. These studies demonstrate that gender stereotypes for emotionality are very strong.

Rather than detailing the gender differences and similarities in a list of emotions, this chapter concentrates on two types of emotional experience that have figured prominently in the stereotypes of emotion: the concept of maternal instinct (a "feminine" expression of emotion), and the concept of aggression (a "masculine" expression of emotion). In addition, the concept of instinct, connected with biological determinism, is often associated with both maternal behaviors in women and aggression in men. These two concepts provide a good contrast for considerations of gender and emotion. Psychologists have considered both as primary instincts basic to humans and animals (Hilgard, 1987). Those who consider these two instincts as primary believe that large gender differences exist, with nurturing and caregiving behaviors being the province of the female of many species, and anger and aggression being a male specialization.

The Myth of Maternal Instinct

The concept of maternal instinct holds that nurturing behaviors of mothers toward their children are determined by biological factors and are largely insensitive to environmental or situational conditions. Charles Darwin and the late-19th-century scientists who accepted maternal instinct have shaped subsequent research on the topic (Shields, 2002). Notions of instinctive nurturing can be traced to assumptions from the 19th century, which accepted both women's intellectual inferiority and their emotional reactions to infants and children. Scientific thought of that time held that women could not be as intellectually developed as men because their energies were required to go toward reproduction and caregiving. Nature had suited them to focus on immediate situations rather than abstract ones (hence their intellectual inferiority) and to be more perceptive and emotional (hence their attraction to small and helpless beings).

Instinct as an explanation of behavior fell into disfavor among psychologists with the rise of behaviorism and its emphasis on learning and certain environmental factors known to shape behavior (Hilgard, 1987). Despite the decline of instinct as a general explanation for behavior, the concept of maternal instinct did not fade from psychological explanations of behavior. Fields as disparate as primate biology and social policy have shown the influence of assuming that biology determines motherhood and fatherhood (Hrdy, 1999). Scientists and social policy makers have accepted the views of early primatologists, who linked manhood with male aggression and sexuality, and feminine pursuits with female passivity and nurturance. Despite this acceptance, research evidence from studies of human parenting (Silverstein & Auerbach, 1999) as well as cross-species work (Hrdy, 1999) failed to support this view.

According to primatologist Sarah Blaffer Hrdy (1981, 1999), observations of various primate species have changed academic opinions of mothers, fathers, and infants. Evolutionary biology places primary emphasis on producing offspring and the factors related to this success, making sexual selection a prominent topic. However, success in evolutionary terms includes not only having offspring but also having offspring that live long enough to have offspring themselves, so the processes of motherhood and nurturing young are of paramount importance. The study of nonhuman primates brings a wider perspective to the topic of mothering and parental care. Rather than aggression or a lack of male involvement, these studies have shown that male primates' involvement with infants varies from being the primary caretaker to showing benign disinterest. This research (Hrdy, 1999) reveals little dangerous aggression toward infants from adult males within the social group (although males from other social groups can be very dangerous). Differences for paternal involvement vary enormously across species; some males formed numerous relationships with infants and young primates, even those they had not fathered, whereas other males of the same species were less involved with the young (Silverstein, 1993). The evidence from studies of other primate species shows the behavioral flexibility of caregiving and does not support the concept of maternal instinct (and paternal disinterest). The behavior of primates offers no evidence for biological invariance of nurturing among females and lack of nurturing among males.

The view that maternal behaviors are instinctive lingered longer than belief in other instincts. As Judith Lorber (1997, p. 13) quipped, "Believing is seeing," so researchers tended to avoid research in this area and then had trouble accepting their own observations. One of these hard-to-convince scientists was psychologist Harry Harlow, whose research ironically provided evidence *against* the validity of the concept of maternal instinct.

Maternal Deprivation and Its Consequences for Nurturing.   During the 1950s, Harry Harlow and his colleagues (including his wife, Margaret) conducted a series of experiments concerning affection and attachment. Harlow (1971) was concerned about the nature of attachment—of mothers for their babies, of babies for their mothers, of fathers for their babies, of children for each other, and so forth. One of Harlow's questions concerned the effects of maternal deprivation on children, but ethics prevented him from using humans as participants. Therefore, he chose to experiment on monkeys.

Harlow's research on maternal deprivation originated from his desire to raise infant monkeys in a controlled environment, but he noticed that the infant monkeys raised in isolation behaved abnormally. They stared into space for hours, circled their cages or rocked repetitively for long periods of time, and repeatedly injured themselves, especially when humans approached (Harlow & Harlow, 1962). Not only did these young monkeys behave oddly when alone, but they also exhibited abnormal behavior when placed in a social group of other monkeys. They failed to fit into the social group; they fought more and interacted less than monkeys raised normally. They were also sexually abnormal; they appeared interested in sex but unable to mate. Thus, Harlow noticed that the experience of maternal deprivation seemed to have permanent effects on the social and sexual behavior of these monkeys.

Isolation also affected the monkeys' maternal behavior. When the isolated female monkeys became mothers themselves, they made spectacularly poor ones. These monkey mothers were negligent and abusive, refusing to allow their infants to nurse and sometimes beating them for trying to establish physical contact. Such negligent and abusive behavior did not support the concept of maternal instinct, but rather suggested that the experience of isolation from their mothers affected their nurturing behavior. This research suggests that caregiving is dependent on experience and not on any inherent biological factors.

Harlow (1959) initially believed that being mothered was the critical experience that would allow a monkey to become an adequate mother, but subsequently, a series of studies revealed that other social experiences could substitute for being mothered. Harlow and his associates discovered that physical contact was an important factor in learning "mothering." They constructed two types of surrogate mothers, one a wire "mother" and the other a cloth-covered wire "mother." Neither type of surrogate was very much like a real mother monkey; neither moved, held the infants, or responded to them in any way. In some of Harlow's studies, both types of surrogates offered milk for nursing, whereas in some conditions, only the wire surrogate offered milk. Although the surrogate mothers were unresponsive, the infants were not. The infants strongly preferred the cloth-covered surrogates to the wire surrogates, even if the wire surrogate was the sole source of food. Infants nursed from the wire "mother" but clung to the cloth-covered surrogate for hours and ran to it when frightened. Harlow concluded that the cloth-covered surrogates provided some comfort that the wire surrogates could not, and he called this factor *contact comfort,* the security provided by physical contact with a soft, caring, or comforting object. However, even these monkeys did not become socially, sexually, or maternally normal, indicating that the cloth surrogate had failed to provide all the experiences that are necessary for normal monkey development.

Additional research showed that the experiences that promote normal nurturing and caregiving in monkeys involve contact with other monkeys. Despite the logic of modeling and imitation, such contact does not have to include the experience of being mothered. That is, being a good mother does not require being adequately mothered. Harlow and Harlow (1962) reported on studies that indicated that age-mates can provide the social experiences necessary for normal development. The study involved separating infant monkeys from their mothers and raising them together as a group. Although these monkeys showed some abnormal behavior as infants—they clung together practically all the time they were together in their cage—these infants developed into normal adolescent monkeys. In addition, another study in which infants were raised with their mothers but without peer contact showed that mothering alone would not be adequate for normal development; some contact with peers appeared to be essential.

Therefore, the studies by Harlow and his colleagues demonstrated (at least in monkeys) that maternal behavior is not the product of instinct. As Table 8.1 shows, nurturing and caregiving are not behaviors that appear in all females. Instead, Harlow's research showed that specific social experiences are necessary for the development of adequate maternal (and other social) behavior. Without these experiences, adequate maternal behaviors fail to appear.

Attachment.   Although research has demonstrated no innate, fixed pattern of caregiving, the contention that nurturing behavior has innate components has not disappeared from psychological theory. Instead, that notion has been transformed into the concept of attachment, or **bonding,** an emotional attachment that develops between infant and caregiver within a few days after birth (Hrdy, 1999). Bonding, however, is not restricted to mother–infant attachment, but can also occur between fathers and infants, or with any others who happen to be present during the critical time period.

The concept of bonding is a variation on **critical periods,** a term that comes from ethnology, which is the study of animal behavior in natural settings. Konrad Lorenz discovered one type of attachment in geese that isolated a critical time after goslings hatch and during which they form an attachment to their mothers (Eyer, 1992). During this critical period, goslings learn to follow their mother after only one exposure to her walking past, showing that critical-period learning is not like typical learning, which requires repetition or practice. If the timing and the mother's behavior coordinate, the goslings im-

TABLE 8.1   *Types of Deprivation and Effects on Nurturing in Monkeys*

Type of Deprivation	*Adequacy of Nurturing*
No deprivation—contact with mother and peers	Normal
Complete isolation	Inadequate and abusive
Wire or cloth "mother"	Inadequate
Contact with mother only	Inadequate
Contact with peers, but not with mother	Normal

print on their mother and follow her, which helps them to avoid danger and to learn behaviors important to their survival. If the critical period passes without the mother walking past, then the goslings do not imprint on her, leaving them without making an attachment to a caretaker and increasing their risk for the many dangers that may befall small fowl.

Although Lorenz's research concentrated on how young attach to their mothers rather than mothers' feelings and behavior toward their offspring, the popular concept of bonding is similar to imprinting. Bonding, however, is a reciprocal process; it applies to mother–infant as well as infant–mother attachments. This concept is a variation on the idea of maternal instinct because bonding also depends on innate components that are known to occur in the early interaction between infant and caregiver. However, bonding is not restricted to mothers, so the concept definitely varies from that of maternal instinct.

The concept of bonding was popularized with published research (Klaus & Kennell, 1976) contending that in the first few hours after children's birth, their attachment to mothers is critically important. Other researchers have failed to confirm these results, and the concept has been subject to critical review (Chess & Thomas, 1982; Eyer, 1992). As a result, the concept of bonding remains more favored by the popular press than by developmental researchers. The notion of attachment remains part of psychology research, and understanding the mutual interaction of caregiver and infant is an important factor in children's survival and well-being (Hrdy, 1999). The concept of attachment is more complex than bonding; attachment may have components that begin during pregnancy and extend for months or years.

Gender and Caring for Children.   Recent research has explored hormonal involvement in mothers' preparation to nurture. During late pregnancy, delivery, and especially nursing, hormonal changes occur that may "prime" mothers to tend their babies (Hrdy, 1999). These hormonal events are not sufficient to prompt maternal behavior, even in rats, so the existence of biological circumstances related to mothering is not the same as maternal instinct. Indeed, the investigation of attachment need not be limited to mothers and infants but might extend to a variety of relationships. However through circumstance as well as physiology, women remain the primary caregivers for children in the great majority of cultures; fathers' involvement varies. In some species and in some human cultures, fathers have virtually no contact with their children, whereas in some species and some human cultures, fathers are primary caregivers (Silverstein & Auerbach, 1999).

The circumstances of childbearing and nursing place many women in continued contact with children. This association with caregiving is the basis for the classification of women as more nurturant than men. Two possible explanations for gender-related differences in nurturing behavior exist: responsiveness to children and pleasure in taking care of children. That is, perhaps girls and women respond more quickly and strongly to children or derive greater satisfaction from caring for children than men do, or both.

Gender differences in responsiveness to babies appear by age 3 years (Blakemore, 1998) and increase throughout childhood (Melson, 2001). Many of the studies that have shown gender differences in responsiveness to babies used self-report measures that are subject to biases from expectation (Berman, 1980), but some studies have measured behavioral reactions. One study (Melson & Fogel, 1988) found that preschoolers' interest in babies was similar before age 4, but with age, involvement with an infant in a play situation increased for girls and decreased for boys. In a naturalistic situation, girls showed more interest and nurturance toward babies than boys did, even at age 3 years (Blakemore, 1998). This pattern was stronger for boys whose parents held traditional gender roles compared to boys with more egalitarian parents. Therefore, parental and social encouragement are clearly factors in responsiveness to infants.

Girls' responsiveness to babies may not reflect a complete picture of nurturance. Boys tended to care for and nurture pets as they became less interested in babies (Melson, 2001). This behavior may represent the tendency for boys to become aware of the gender role they should follow, which does not include caring for babies. Boys still have the capacity to be nurturant caregivers, which they express by their feelings for and behavior toward pets. Boys may be as nurturant as girls, although this nurturance may be expressed in different ways.

▣ GENDERED VOICES

If Men Mothered

"I think that men could do as good as women at taking care of children," two college students told me. Both the young man and the young woman said that they believed that women have no instinctive advantage in nurturing children. Both of them said that the differences were due to experience rather than inherent biological factors. Indeed, both said that they believed there were few differences in ability to care for children.

"Well, men can't breast-feed," the young man said, "but I think that is about the only advantage women have except for experience. They have a lot more experience in caring for children. Girls babysit, and boys don't." He knew how difficult it was for men to get experience caring for young children because he had attempted to obtain such experience. He had volunteered to care for the young children in his church while their parents attended the service and had answered advertisements for babysitters. Neither of these efforts had met with enthusiasm from others; he had gotten the impression that wanting to care for children was considered odd for a man. He considered the possibility that people might think he was a pedophile, when all he really wanted was to learn to be more nurturant.

"I think if men were responsible for caring for children, there would be more changes in men than in children. If men had to learn to care for children, then they would. It wouldn't be automatic, because they don't have the experience, but they could learn. I don't believe in maternal instinct—that women have some innate advantage over men in caring. But women do have more experience, and men would have to learn the skills they lack.

"Men would learn to care for children if they had to, and they would become more nurturant in other aspects of their lives, maybe even in their careers. They might not care so much about competition and high-status careers.

The young woman had a slightly different view: "I think that the children would be different. This opinion is based on my own family and the differences between my mother and my father. My father was more willing to let us be on our own, but my mother was more involved. My mother took care of us, but my father let us make our own decisions. Maybe that wouldn't be good for young children, but I think I would have learned to be more self-reliant with my father's style of caretaking. But maybe if he had been the one who had to look out for us, he would have been as protective as my mother was."

The differences in patterns of child care—namely, that women perform the vast majority of child care—complicate comparisons of the pleasure that women and men derive from these activities. Although some fathers are involved in all aspects of child care, the accepted role for fathers is helper, whereas the role for mothers is primary caregiver. Despite the changes in patterns of women's employment and fathers' family involvement, this division remains (Renk et al., 2003). Even fathers and mothers who spend comparable amounts of time with their children tend to hold traditional roles in which mothers provide primary care and fathers were present for play and outings (Laflamme, Pomerleau, & Malcuit, 2002). Thus, contrasts of the pleasure of nurturing experienced by mothers and fathers are not based on a direct comparison of the satisfaction each derives from specific caregiving activities, but rather on a comparison of their roles as mothers or fathers and the types of caregiving each provides. Within the context of these differences, men rate their emotional experience within the family setting more positively than in their work setting experiences (Larson & Pleck, 1999). That is, men experience more positive and less negative emotion at home than at work. However, men feel the strain of trying to construct a fathering role in which they become the type of fathers they want to be, which often is at odds with their role as breadwinner and societal expectations for masculinity (Silverstein, Auerbach, & Levant, 2002).

The time and effort mothers spend in child care lead to feelings of both satisfaction and dissatisfaction (Renk et al., 2003). The experience of involvement in parenting, coupled with their feelings of the social value of nurturing children, produce satisfaction, but the loss of freedom and the irritation of attending to the demands of small children can lead mothers to feel dissatisfaction. In addition, many mothers held expectations that their partners would participate more fully in child care than they did, which led to feelings of being burdened.

Traditional gender roles are often enacted in the child-care situation, but gay fathers experience a situation that removes the gender factor. The majority of gay fathers are men who have fathered children in heterosexual relationships. These men do not often get custody of their children, but an increasing number of gay couples are adopting or choosing surrogacy in order to become fathers (Patterson & Chan, 1997; Silverstein et al., 2002). These men are highly motivated to become fathers, and they place a high value on relationships with their children. Without an automatic division of gender roles, gay fathers struggle with devising a "degendered" system of child care. They tend to divide child care more evenly than do heterosexual couples and to be more satisfied with this division of labor. Contrary to general beliefs, gay fathers are as able as heterosexual fathers to parent and to help their children develop (Armesto, 2002).

Heterosexual fathers who participated in the care of their children experienced feelings and behavior toward their young children that were similar to those of women who provided similar levels of care (Risman, 1989). Those fathers who were very involved in child care expressed high feelings of satisfaction with their choice, even though they made career sacrifices to be involved fathers (Duindam & Spruijt, 1997). Therefore, the greater pleasure that women derive from caring for children seems to be a function of their greater involvement with their children, and men who have similar levels of involvement experience similar feelings.

If no instinctive force compels women toward and men away from nurturing, why, then, have men been involved so little in caring for children? Powerful social forces operate to prevent fathers from becoming more intimately involved with their children. In industrialized societies, fathers hold the role of breadwinner, which usually takes them outside the home and away from their children's lives. Social pressures toward achievement and monetary success have convinced men that they can best contribute to their families by devoting themselves to their jobs, and this devotion results in many hours at work, which also takes them away from their families.

The traditional pattern of the male breadwinner who is a distant, uninvolved father has undergone changes over the past 40 years (Pleck & Pleck, 1997), but the well-publicized image of the "new" father who is involved with children's upbringing may be an overstatement (Silverstein, 1996; Renk et al., 2003). Nevertheless, fathers are more involved with their children than in past decades, and an increasing number of fathers feel motivated to be more intimately involved in their children's lives (Pleck, 1997; Sanderson & Sanders Thompson, 2002). Few institutional supports exist for increased paternal nurturance. Their childhood socialization tends to push them away from learning how to care for children, which leaves men feeling less capable of child-care tasks (Sanderson & Sanders Thompson, 2002). The fathers who are involved in the care of their children diverge from traditional expectations, which can make them targets of disapproval when they decrease their income in efforts to make additional time to spend with their children (Riggs, 1997). The limited research on these fathers indicates that the children, mothers, and fathers all can benefit from positive involvement by fathers in their children's lives (Pleck, 1997).

The Prominence of Male Aggression

Aggression has also been the primary focus of gender role studies of instinct, again with explanations of men's evolutionary advantage (Dabbs, 2000). The standard version says that during human prehistory, while the women were at home caring for the children, the men were out hunting and defending the group against various threats. In both the hunting and the defending, aggressive actions could be adaptive and even essential. Thus, women became passive homebodies and men became aggressive conquerors.

This view of human prehistory may be fictionalized, based more on the theorists' personal views than on prehistoric human behavior. There have been questions about both the idea of female passivity and the notion of the adaptive advantage of aggression (Hrdy, 1981, 1999; Weisstein, 1982). Women in the hunter–gatherer societies of prehistory probably not only gathered plants for food but also participated in small-game (and perhaps even large-game) hunting, thus making them essential contributors to their groups' food supply and far from passive. As for aggression, it can offer advantages if directed at the proper targets outside the group, but it can also be disruptive and dangerous within a group (de Waal, 2000). The men in these societies must have needed to become selectively rather than pervasively aggressive; therefore, natural selection would not favor those who were aggressive in all situations.

A definition of aggression turns out to be difficult to formulate in completely behavioral terms. The notion that human aggression is behavior directed toward another person intended to cause harm (Anderson & Bushman, 2002) relies on the intention of the aggressor and thus is not entirely behavioral. This difficulty in definition is not confined to theorists and researchers; not all people agree on which behaviors should be included and which consequences of these behaviors constitute harm. Actions such as hitting, kicking, and biting obviously fit into the definition of aggression, but aggression can cause not only physical but also psychological harm. Relational and indirect aggression are additional categories that also fit into the definition. *Relational aggression* involves behaviors that harm others through damage to personal relationships, such as sulking or the "silent treatment" (Crick et al., 1999), and *indirect aggression* causes harm through indirect means, such as arranging for someone to be blamed for a serious mistake at work or mocking someone's actions (Bjorkqvist, 1994). These versions of aggression are highlighted in the books that Tavris (2002) featured in her headline article, which focused on how painful and damaging this type of aggression can be.

Anger and Aggression.   Anger and aggression seem intimately related—anger is the internal emotion and aggression is its behavioral reaction. However, the two are not inevitably connected: A person can experience anger and take no action, aggressive or otherwise, but a person can also act aggressively without feeling anger, such as the careful planning of harm to another for personal benefit (Anderson & Bushman, 2002).

Psychological and popular explanations of aggression have accepted that aggression is the outcome of some prior circumstance, either in the emotions or in the environment. Psychologist William McDougall and psychoanalyst Sigmund Freud believed that aggression was the result of instinctive expressions of frustrated wishes. This contention gave rise to the frustration–aggression hypothesis (Dollard, Doob, Miller, Mowrer, & Sears, 1939), which holds that aggression is the inevitable result of frustration, and frustration is the inevitable consequence of aggression. In this formulation, anger is not an important concept (Averill, 1982). The volume of research testing the frustration–aggression hypothesis has been conducted primarily in laboratory settings with a limited set of frustrating stimuli and measures of aggression. These experiments have yielded information about one facet of aggression but have failed to explore aggression prompted by everyday events in more natural settings.

Several types of investigations have explored people's experience of anger and the connection to aggression using methods other than laboratory experiments. Interviews and surveys have the advantage of tapping into personal experiences in ways that laboratory experiments cannot, but both have the disadvantage of relying on self-reports and lacking direct measurements of either anger or aggression. Several such studies have concentrated on children and their experience of anger. One study (Peterson & Biggs, 2001) asked 3-, 5-, and 8-year-olds about emotional situations, including anger. Five-year-old boys were most likely to label anger, but few other gender differences appeared. An assessment of self-reports of anger (Hubbard et al., 2002) found no gender differences in anger for 2nd-grade girls and boys. Among 4th- and 5th-grade rural, urban, and suburban students (Buntaine & Costenbader, 1997), no gender differences appeared in levels of reported anger, but boys said they expressed their anger as aggression more often than girls did.

Two surveys of anger in adults also showed very limited gender differences. In a survey of university students in eight European countries, Klaus Scherer and his associates (Scherer, Wallbott, & Summerfield, 1986) found that anger occurred more often than other emotions, with about 75% of participants reporting anger within the four weeks prior to the survey. A survey of community residents and college students in the United States (Averill, 1982) also found that anger was very common—85% of the respondents reported at least one experience of anger within the week prior to the survey. However, this survey revealed little connection between anger and aggression; respondents had few experiences of physical aggression and little inclination toward that type of expression for their anger. Gender differences appeared in the targets of anger, with men being somewhat more frequent targets of anger than women. However, the relationship between the two people was also an important factor. Among people who were not well-known to each other, men were more likely than women to be the targets of anger. Among loved ones, men and women were equal targets. Among friends, anger toward same-gender friends was the most common pattern. This survey also found that women reported more intense experiences of anger than did men, and women's responses were more varied, especially in their tendency to cry when they were angry.

The tendency for women to cry when they feel angry became clear in an investigation by June Crawford and her colleagues (Crawford, Kippax, Onxy, Gault, & Benton, 1992). Crawford and her research group conducted their study by exploring their own memories of emotional experiences, including those involving anger. They found a common experience of crying in response to anger. They explained this experience as an acceptable means for girls and women to express anger, whereas physical aggression is less acceptable. However, crying is often misinterpreted as sadness or grief, especially by men. Crying is discouraged among boys, and men are much less likely to cry than women (Lombardo, Cretser, & Roesch, 2001). This tendency for women to cry in situations in which men would not may be a major reason that women receive the label of overemotional.

Gender role rather than gender may have a stronger relationship with anger and the expression of anger (Kopper & Epperson, 1991, 1996). In one study (Kopper & Epperson, 1996), masculinity (rather than being male) was related to the expression of anger and aggression, and femininity (rather than being female) was related to the suppression of anger. These studies show that the stereotypical association of men and anger is incorrect, although men are more likely than women to respond to anger with physical aggression.

In summary, the relationship between anger and aggression is far from automatic, with feelings of anger occurring far more often than acts of aggression. Of the studies that have explored gender differences in the experience of anger, few have found the expected differences between men and women. Instead, these studies have shown that men and women both experience anger from being similarly provoked. Other studies have indicated that gender role—not gender—shows a relationship between the expression of anger as physical aggression.

Developmental Gender Differences in Aggression.   Observing gender differences in aggression during the early months and even early years of life is very difficult, because what counts as aggression in an infant is virtually impossible to define. Rather than attempting to assess aggression in young children, researchers have used other behaviors, beginning with children's activity level during infancy. Some studies have failed to find a gender difference in activity level, but Maccoby and Jacklin's (1974) review concluded that boys showed higher activity levels than girls.

The existence of gender differences in aggression among preschool children is controversial, but using the definition of aggression as physical action, boys are more aggressive than girls. One meta-analysis (Hyde, 1984) evaluated the developmental nature of these differences and their magnitude. This analysis indicated that gender differences decrease with age; that is, boys and girls show greater differences in aggression during elementary school than during college. In addition, a decrease in the magnitude of aggression occurs over the course of development, with both boys and girls becoming less aggressive as they develop into adults.

Another way to approach the question of the stability of aggression over the course of development is through longitudinal research—in studies that test the same group of people over many years. Leonard Eron, Rowell Huesmann, and their colleagues (Dubow, Huesmann, & Boxer, 2003; Eron, 1987; Huesmann, Eron, Lefkowitz, & Walder, 1984; Lefkowitz, Eron, Walder, & Huesmann, 1977) have been involved in a longitudinal study of aggression that has spanned three generations. In the first phase, 600 children were followed from 3rd grade (approximately 8 years old) until young adulthood. The researchers assessed the children's opinions about who acts aggressively with questions such as "Who in the class pushes other children?" This measure provided an assessment of peer-defined aggression.

The researchers compared this aggression score to parenting styles and found that parents who were less nurturant and acceptant at home tended to have children who behaved more aggressively at school than the children brought up by more nurturant and acceptant parents. Both the girls and boys rated as aggressive at age 8 received similar peer ratings 10 years later. These children saw themselves as aggressive, rated others as such, and saw the world as an aggressive place.

In the third phase of this 22-year longitudinal study (Eron, 1987; Huesmann et al., 1984), participants were around age 30, and aggression during childhood predicted a number of aggressive behaviors during adulthood, including criminal behavior, traffic violations, convictions for driving while intoxicated, aggressiveness toward spouses, and severity of punishment of children. Table 8.2 shows the stability of aggression among the participants in these studies.

The results of this longitudinal study demonstrated that adult aggression can be predicted to some degree from childhood aggression, indicating that the two are related on a conceptual level. The continuation of this project has shown several important factors to be related to the persistence of aggression, both within a person's life and across generations. Individuals who experience harsh and inconsistent parenting, see the world as a violent place, and see violence as a good choice for resolving conflicts. They are not only violent themselves, but also tend to raise aggressive children.

A component of this longitudinal study (Eron, Huesmann, Brice, Fischer, & Mermelstein, 1983) investigated the influence of watching violent television programs; the researchers found that the violence on television acted as an effective model for aggressive

TABLE 8.2 *Aggression over the Life Span*

Children Identified at 8 Years of Age by Their Peers as Aggressive toward Other Children		
At Age 8	*At Age 18*	*At Age 30*
Had less nurturant and acceptant parents	Were still rated by peers as aggressive	Were more likely to have a criminal record
also	*also*	*also*
Preferred violent TV programs	Rated themselves as aggressive	Were more likely to abuse spouse
	also	*also*
	Rated others as aggressive	Were more likely to have DWI (DUI) conviction
	also	*also*
	Saw the world as a dangerous place	Were more likely to have traffic violations
		also
		Were more likely to use severe punishment with children

children. Indeed, the preference for violent television programs at age 8 was a good predictor of how aggressive the male adolescents would be at age 19. An additional longitudinal study (Huesmann, Moise-Titus, Podolski, & Eron, 2003) demonstrated a relationship between watching violent television programs during childhood and aggression in young adulthood, 15 years later. Those children who were most strongly influenced saw the TV violence as more realistic and also tended to identify with the aggressive television characters. Both boys and girls were subject to this influence.

Another longitudinal study (Cairns, Cairns, Neckerman, Ferguson, & Gariépy, 1989) explored the developmental differences in aggression between boys and girls from 4th through 10th grade. The researchers found that 4th-grade boys were much more likely to have confrontations that involved physical aggression with other boys than with girls, and this pattern became stronger over the 6-year time span. As adolescents, boys were much more likely to engage in physical confrontations but little cross-gender aggression. Expressions of aggression among girls in this age group tended to be indirect and relational, involving attempts to alienate or ostracize another girl from the social group or to defame her character. This type of social aggression has become the topic of media attention, as Tavris's (2002) headline story highlighted. Although girls are less likely to engage in physical confrontations, they find ways to be mean to each other. Girls exhibit opposition and defiance of parents as often as boys do (Lahey et al., 2000), but they are less likely to fight.

Both boys and girls are discouraged from being physically aggressive, but they are not held to the same standards; boys are allowed to be more aggressive than girls—"boys will be boys." By middle childhood, both boys and girls have developed different expectations about expressing aggression (Perry, Perry, & Weiss, 1989). Boys expected less parental disapproval for their aggression, and both expected less parental disapproval for aggression against a boy than against a girl. Even with general parental disapproval for aggression, children learn about circumstances under which their aggression is more acceptable and more effective, and boys learn different rules for displaying aggression than girls learn. By adolescence, the gender differences in physical aggression are even larger, and again, parental behavior is important. Parents monitored girls' behavior more strictly than boy's behavior (Carlo, Raffaelli, Laible, & Meyer, 1999), and this difference was a significant mediating factor in the higher levels of aggression exhibited by boys.

Boys tend to enact the most serious types of aggression more often than girls do (Cairns et al., 1989). Some girls appear in the same range of violence as the most aggressive boys, but a study of girls in gangs (Campbell, 1993) showed that high levels of male and female violence served different purposes. Men used aggression to exert control over others, whereas women's aggression usually represented a loss of emotional self-control. The violence in male gangs is consistent with this interpretation: Boys in gangs use aggression and violence to gain social recognition and to get money. Girls in gangs also use violence to create recognition, but unlike boys, they do not seek money as much as they seek to avoid becoming victims by creating a reputation for being tough. As other research has indicated (Keltikangas-Jarvinen, 2002), some groups allow and even encourage violence, and under some circumstances, aggression can have high benefits and low costs. These gang girls represent an extreme, but their use of and benefit from violence are similar to those of their male counterparts, even though their goals differ from those of boys.

Therefore, a developmental trend occurs toward a decrease in aggression from middle childhood to young adulthood, and gender-related differences appear in the use of aggression. Boys and girls tend to use different strategies and behaviors in their displays of aggression, with boys using more confrontational, physical aggression and girls using indirect and relational aggression. Despite its lower frequency, aggression during adolescence and adulthood is more dangerous than childhood aggression. With their size, strength, and greater likelihood of owning a weapon, adolescent boys become more likely to use aggression that causes serious damage and violations of the law than are adolescent girls.

Gender Differences in Aggression during Adulthood. If gender-related differences in aggression decrease during development as children age, then few differences should exist between adult men and women, although differences might exist in the styles of expression. Reviews of the experimental research on aggression have confirmed these conclusions, finding that the differences between aggression in men and women are not large, but that significant differences exist in circumstances and styles.

Both literature reviews and meta-analyses have been used to explore gender differences in aggression. One such review (Frodi, Macaulay, & Thome, 1977) evaluated experimental studies in psychology, omitting surveys and crime statistics and concentrating on laboratory studies. These situations are artificial but controlled. Several meta-analyses have evaluated research on gender differences in aggression (Bettencourt & Miller, 1996; Eagly & Steffen, 1986; Knight, Guthrie, Page, & Fabes, 2002).

The earlier analyses (Eagly & Steffen, 1986; Frodi et al., 1977) found that men were more aggressive than women under neutral and unprovoked situations. When women were provoked or felt justified, however, they became as aggressive as men. The factor of provocation was the topic of one meta-analysis (Bettencourt & Miller, 1996). This analysis showed that gender differences decreased or disappeared with some types of provocation. For example, women do not as readily respond aggressively to insults to their intelligence as men do, but both respond similarly to the frustration of someone blocking their path through an intersection. This analysis showed that some of the gender differences found in experimental research are due to the various provocations researchers have used. Table 8.3 summarizes some gender-related differences in tendencies to respond with anger and aggression for both children and adults.

Aggression can be a very effective way of exerting power and forcing others to behave according to one's wishes (Campbell, 1993; Hawley & Vaughn, 2003). When considering aggression as a method of exerting power, women may be reasonably concerned about the potential for reprisal; the size and strength differential between men and women makes women more vulnerable to the effects of aggression. Women's reluctance to use aggression may relate to their fear of retaliation. Even when women and men hear the same description of a situation, women's fear of retaliation is greater than men's, and this factor decreases their likelihood of responding with physical aggression (Bettencourt & Miller, 1996).

Men's control of their emotional arousal may be important to their higher levels of aggression. In a recent meta-analysis (Knight et al., 2002), the results showed that gender differences in aggression varied in relation to how emotionally arousing the situations were. When emotional arousal was low, gender differences in aggressive responses were minimal, but those differences became larger when the arousal was higher, with men responding more aggressively. This meta-analysis indicated that men have more trouble regulating emotion-arousing states, so they are prompted toward aggression more easily than women.

When the definition of aggression includes the infliction of psychological or social harm, women are as likely to become aggressive as men. These situations are more common among adults than those involving physical aggression (Bjorkqvist, 1994), so this type of aggression is important. Although not without the danger of retaliation, relational and indirect aggression are less risky than physical confrontation, and women are more likely to use this strategy than men. This difference is the major reason that research has shown men to be more aggressive than women: Laboratory studies offer a limited range of choices in carefully controlled (and contrived) situations that focus on physical aggression. With more comprehensive definitions of aggression and in more naturalistic situations, women are as aggressive as men.

The experiences of aggression tend to be quite different for women and men (Graham & Wells, 2001). A random sample of Canadian women and men reported their last experience of physical aggression, and results revealed that men were more likely than women to report involvement in some sort of violence. For women, the most common re-

TABLE 8.3 *Gender Differences in Situations that Provoke Anger and Aggression*

For Children*	
Type of Provocation	*Tendency toward Anger*
Being hit accidentally	Boys report more anger
Not being invited to a party	Girls report more anger

For Adults**	
Type of Provocation	*Tendency toward Aggression*
No provocation	Men respond with much more aggression in everyday contacts
Physical attack	Men respond with slightly more aggression
	Men consider attacks more serious

Insults:
   Insensitive behavior
   Condescending behavior
   Impolite treatment
   Rude comments
	Women consider insults more serious
	Women respond with more aggression

Frustrations:
   Not able to succeed
   Not able to finish task
   Recognize own inability
   Traffic congestion
	Men respond with more aggression

Negative feedback concerning intelligence	Men respond with much more aggression Women are much less angered by this type of provocation

Sources: *From "Self-Reported Differences in the Experience and Expression of Anger between Boys and Girls," by Roberta L. Buntaine & Virginia K. Costenbader, 1997, *Sex Roles, 36,* pp. 625–637. **From "Gender Differences in Aggression as a Function of Provocation: A Meta-Analysis," by Ann Bettencourt & Norman Miller, 1996, *Psychological Bulletin, 119,* pp. 422–447.

port was a conflict with a male partner or friend, many of which fit the description of intimate partner violence. For men, the most common response was a fight with another man, usually in a public place such as a bar. These results are consistent with research on the gendered nature of violence. Men are the more common perpetrators and victims. Women are capable of violence, but the context is often in private settings and directed toward partners or children (Archer, 2000; U.S. Department of Health and Human Services, Administration on Children, Youth, and Families, 2003). In these settings, women can be as violent as or more violent than men.

The dynamics of partner conflicts and the escalation to violence are complex (Eisikovits, Winstok, Gelles, 2002; Winstok, Eisikovits, & Gelles, 2002), but the outcome is not: Women are much more likely to sustain serious injuries or to be killed in such encounters. The context of violence makes a great deal of difference to crime statistics. Domestic violence is less likely than public violence to result in arrest, so women and men do not have similar levels of involvement with the criminal justice system.

Gender and Crime.   Despite minimal gender difference in aggression, the statistics on societal aggression reveal large gender differences. Men commit many more criminal acts than women do, and their arrest and incarceration rates are much higher. According to the statistics for the United States (Federal Bureau or Investigation [FBI], 2002), men are about 3.5 times more likely than women to be arrested for various types of offenses, such as murder, robbery, vandalism, fraud, drunkenness, and so forth. Although not all of these viola-

■ GENDERED VOICES

Intimate Partner Violence: He Said/She Said

Two studies (Eisikovits, Winstok, & Gelles, 2002; Winstok, Eisikovits, & Gelles, 2002) reported on men who had beaten their partners and women who had stayed with their abusive partners. The men's stories reflected their beliefs that they were provoked into violence and reflected how they felt justified in hitting their partners.

He said:

> She starts making those faces and talking ugly, and this is expressed in a million ways. "You make yourself coffee, I won't do it for you." So after I hit her, she becomes a real disciplined child, just like I used to like her. After a month or two, slowly, slowly, she becomes self-confident again and gets out of line. (Winstok et al., 2002, p. 136)
>
> I am unable to beat her to death. I give her a slap and that's all, no more than that. Just to deter her. Stop it and that's it. She's getting just what she deserves, no more, sometimes less, but never more. (Winstok et al., 2002, p. 135)

These abusive men told stories about trying to silence their partners' voices.

The women's stories reflect a different view of these violent situations. Some abused women told stories about how uncontrollable and unpredictable their partners' violence was.

She said:

> Most of the time everything is OK. But sometimes we're sitting talking about something and the argument starts. From the argument . . . he . . . erupts just like a volcano, he raises his voice, and then I say something, and then he raises his voice some more and then I do too. . . . And we're screaming and arguing and not listening to each other. And it goes wherever it goes . . . (Eisikovits et al., 2002, p. 142)

Other women told about how they recognized and managed their partners' escalation of violence.

She said:

> I prefer not to answer him at all, because I know that if I answer back it'll only get worse. Slowly I understood that if I shut up his anger would be less than if I answer him back. (Eisikovits et al., 2002, p. 142)

These abused women told stories about how their voices were silenced.

tions involve violence, many do; as Table 8.4 shows, such offenses are more likely to be committed by men than by women. However, increases in violent crimes committed by girls and women have occurred in more categories of crime over the past 10 years than for boys and men (FBI, 2002). Those increases have been slight, leaving the disproportionate levels of arrest shown in Table 8.4.

Not all crimes result in arrest, and the possibility exists that the ratio of crimes committed by men and women is closer to equal than the arrest rates suggest. Surveys have indicated that although the reported rates of crime exceed the arrest rates, men still outnumber women in committing crimes (Steffensmeier & Allan, 1996). Crime was so strongly associated with men before the 1970s that most criminologists and officials in the criminal justice system assumed that crime was an almost exclusively male problem.

During the 1970s, research interests turned to female offenders, prompted by the increase of criminal activity among women. Although one hypothesis about this increase was that it resulted from the women's movement—equal opportunity applied to crime—research indicated that female offenders tended to be traditional rather than feminist in their beliefs. Even considering the increase in crime rates among female offenders, the rate

TABLE 8.4 *Percent of Male and Female Offenders Arrested for Various Offenses*

Offense	Men	Women
All arrests	77.5%	22.5%
Murder	87.5	12.5
Rape	98.8	1.2
Robbery	89.9	10.1
Aggravated assault	79.9	20.1
Burglary	86.4	13.6
Larceny/theft	63.5	36.5
Motor vehicle theft	83.6	16.4
Arson	84.1	15.9
Forgery	59.8	40.2
Fraud	54.6	45.4
Embezzlement	50.4	49.6
Vandalism	83.8	16.2
Prostitution	33.4	66.6
Drug abuse violations	82.2	17.8
Domestic violence	76.9	23.1
Drunkenness	86.3	13.7
Disorderly conduct	76.1	23.9
Curfew violation/loitering	69.0	31.0
Runaway	40.6	59.4

Source: Based on information from *Uniform Crime Report, 2001,* Federal Bureau of Investigation, Table 42. Retrieved Nov. 24, 2003, www.fbi.gov/ucr/01cius.htm.

of offenses remained lower, and the offenses committed by women were less serious than those committed by men (Small, 2000). That is, the increase in crimes committed by women has been due more to nonviolent rather than violent crimes. Therefore, the gender difference in violent crime persists, but the role of gender in criminal behavior remains poorly understood (Burton, Cullen, Evans, Alarid, & Dunaway, 1998).

Men are not only more likely to commit acts of violence, but they are also more likely than women to be the victims of crime (see "According to the Media" and "According to the Research"). This pattern of male-against-male violence substantiates research on aggression during childhood and adolescence (Cairns et al., 1989). Those findings showed that boys were much more likely than girls to use confrontation and aggression as a strategy for managing conflict, and that physical aggression between boys and girls decreased during adolescence. Despite decreases in physical violence among male adolescents, their size, strength, and likelihood of owning weapons made young men more likely than young women to become both perpetrators and victims of physical aggression.

Despite their lower rate of victimization in crime statistics, women are more likely than men to fear being the victims of crime. Early research indicated large differences, but later research (Pain, 2001) has revealed than men also fear crime victimization but, adhering to male gender role stereotypes, fail to mention or act on this fear. For some crimes,

ACCORDING TO THE MEDIA . . .

Women Are Stalked by Crazed Killers but May Fight Back

Since the 1970s, the "slasher" film has captured large audiences, especially among adolescents (Nolan & Ryan, 2000). *The Texas Chainsaw Massacre* was one of the early films of this genre and exemplified many of the common elements of slasher movies, including a maniac killer stalking young women with frightening weapons. These young women (often dressed very scantily) ran screaming with fear, only to be pursued, menaced, caught, and killed. The slasher posed a threat to women, and some of the films showed the action of stalking through the eyes of the slasher, who was always a man. Thus in slasher movies, the victims are young women, and the killers are men.

As intended by the filmmakers, men and women react differently to slasher films (Nolan & Ryan, 2000; Oliver, Sargent, & Weaver, 1998). In general, men find these movies more exciting and enjoyable than do women, who find the films more frightening and disturbing. These reactions are not surprising, if viewers identify with the characters: Female victims are the targets of graphic violence, whereas men are the perpetrators who menace sexy young women.

But recently in the media, women have gotten to do some of the menacing (Corliss, 2002), or at least successfully defended themselves against killers. Rather than the helpless victim, women are beginning to be depicted as capable of defeating crazed killers by escaping or by outwitting them. In movies such as *Panic Room* and *Murder by Numbers* and television programs such as *Dark Angel,* women were strong, resourceful, and capable. These women were not the female counterparts of crazed killers but rather active enforcers of justice who successfully avoided being victims.

women's higher fear is completely realistic because they are at greater risk, and sexual violence is the most prominent example.

Sexual Violence. Women's fears of sexual violence are not misplaced—rape is a common crime. But their fears are not entirely realistic; women fear stranger rape when sexual violence from acquaintances and intimates is a more common experience (U.S. Department of Justice, 2003). Based on reported cases, only about 32% of rapes and attempted rapes are by strangers. In addition, rape often goes unreported, making the official estimates lower than actual occurrences.

A study of U.S. college students (Koss, Gidycz, & Wisniewski, 1987) clarified the rate of sexual violence. Asking both men and women about their sexual behaviors revealed that 15.4% of the women reported being raped since the age of 14 years, and another 12.1% reported experiences that met the legal criteria for attempted rape. Yet only 7.7% of the men reported behaviors that met the legal definition of rape or attempted rape. These rates yielded estimates for rape that were 10 to 15 times greater than the arrest rates for this crime, as well as perpetration rates that were 2 to 3 times higher than official estimates for the risk of rape. These results suggest that many rapes go unreported. The findings from this study provoked controversy, but subsequent research has confirmed these figures. Sexual coercion and violence are common experiences, and most incidents go unreported.

ACCORDING TO THE RESEARCH . . .

Men Are More Often the Victims of Violent Crime, and Women Are Most Often Killed by Intimate Partners

Men are more likely than women to be the perpetrators of violent crimes such as assault and murder, but they are also more likely to be the victims of such crimes (FBI, 2002). Men are more involved in all types of crime than women are, but men are much more likely than women to be involved in violent crime, which makes the movie image of the maniac killer stalking beautiful young women inaccurate in several ways.

First, most people who commit murder kill people whom they know well, rather than people whom they do not know or know only slightly. Second, most people with psychological problems are not violent. Of those people who are violent and have psychological problems, most commit crimes that lead to their prompt arrest, giving them no opportunity to continue with a series of killings. Indeed, serial and mass murder are much more common in the media than in real life. Third, young women are not the most typical victims—young African American men are disproportionately the victims of violence in the United States (U.S. Bureau of the Census, 2002).

When women are the victims of violence, crazed killers are rarely the perpetrators. Instead, husbands and boyfriends are more likely to be the ones who harm women. Women are more likely to be assaulted or killed by men whom they love than by strangers (Heise, Ellsberg, & Gottemoeller, 1999). Therefore, the portrayal of deranged, menacing stalkers with female victims is not how most real-world violence occurs, nor is the image of the female hero who prevails over menacing criminals accurate. For most female and male victims, violence has a familiar, male face.

Not only does rape go unreported to legal authorities, but also many women are reluctant to tell anyone about being raped. Although this reluctance is common, women from some ethnic backgrounds are more reluctant than others. Despite a similarity in the numbers of attempted and completed rapes for African American and European American women, African American women are significantly less likely to tell anyone about being raped (Donovan & Williams, 2002). Women from both ethnic groups had difficulty in identifying attacks by their acquaintances as "real" rape, and other research (Pino & Meier, 1999) confirmed the reluctance to discuss rapes.

Asian Americans hold more negative attitudes toward women as rape victims than European Americans do (Mori, Selle, Zarate, & Bernat, 1994). Both Asian American men and women were more likely than European Americans to endorse rape myths, such as the myth that rape is the woman's fault or that women secretly enjoy rape. Asian American men had more negative attitudes about women than any other group, so Asian American women's acceptance of blame for rape may make them particularly unlikely to report this crime.

The stigma of rape involves the sexual nature of the crime and the tendency to blame the victim. Blaming and stigmatization are particularly common in rape cases, but the stigma is even more severe when men are the victims (Dreyfus, 1994). Male victims of rape or other types of sexual coercion have been accorded much less attention than have female victims, partly because they are not victimized nearly as often, and partly because of the difficulty of accepting that men can be raped (Struckman-Johnson & Struckman-Johnson, 1994). Men are even less likely than women to report rape, and a major reason for their reluctance is that rape violates their masculine self-identity (Pino & Meier, 1999).

Despite these obstacles, a growing body of research indicates that men are sexually coerced and victimized by women as well as by men in ways similar to women's experience of coercion: through bribery, threats of withdrawal of affection, intoxication, physical intimidation, physical restraint, and physical harm (Krahe, Scheinberger-Olwig, & Bieneck, 2003). Both men and women are victims of sexual coercion, and both are censured for being victimized. The problem of female victimization is much more urgent because of its frequency and because women are more traumatized by coercive sexual experiences than men are (Rickert, Vaughan, & Wiemann, 2003). Therefore, a great deal of research has concentrated on understanding the characteristics of men who rape and coerce women into sex.

Diana Scully (1990) studied convicted rapists by conducting extensive interviews that revealed some of their motivations and attitudes. Her results revealed that the rapists had not experienced an unusually high level of treatment for psychopathology or an unusually high rate of childhood physical or sexual abuse. Their family histories were filled with instability and violence, but so were the backgrounds of other felons in the study. The rapists were able to form relationships with women, but their attitudes toward women showed a combination of beliefs: that women belong "on a pedestal," and that men have the right to treat women with violence. Many of these rapists told Scully that they planned their actions because they were angry with their wives or girlfriends and wanted to do violence to some woman. These men reported that the common characteristic of their victims was their vulnerability: They were in the right place at the wrong time—usually alone somewhere at night. Their physical appearance made no difference—many of the rapists had trouble describing their victims. This disregard for appearance highlights the violence of the act and argues against a sexual motive for this type of rape.

Scully's sample underrepresented rapists who were acquainted with their victims; acquaintance rape is less likely to result in complaint, prosecution, or conviction than stranger rape. Yet the violent attack by a stranger is the vision of rape that women fear, even though the most common experience of rape is an attack by an acquaintance, termed *date rape* or *acquaintance rape*. One survey (Koss et al., 1987) of rape and attempted rape included questions that allowed participants to estimate their involvement in various types of sexual coercion. A total of 54% of the women in the survey reported some type of forced or coerced sexual activity, but only 25% of the men in the survey admitted to some level of sexual aggression. The discrepancy in the rates for men and women is not due to a few sexually predatory men, but rather to some degree of denial or failure by many men to recognize their own sexual aggression. This failure to recognize sexual aggression also occurred among the convicted rapists in Scully's study and in a study with a representative sample of U.S. residents (Laumann, Gagnon, Michael, & Michaels, 1994). All of these researchers have found that men may have trouble recognizing their own behavior as sexually coercive.

Neil Malamuth and his colleagues (in Malamuth, 1996) have worked toward developing a model to predict sexual aggression. Drawing from the fields of evolutionary psychology and feminist scholarship, Malamuth proposed that the convergence of two factors relate to rape: (1) high levels of uncommitted, impersonal sex, and (2) hostile masculinity—hostility toward and desire to dominate women. When combined, these two factors relate to men's use of sexual coercion. Figure 8.1 presents this model and the paths leading toward coercive sexuality. Malamuth's research team has conducted several studies that support the model and its ability to predict coercive tactics to obtain sex.

A meta-analysis of studies on attitudes toward rape (Murnen, Wright, & Kaluzny, 2002) also confirmed elements of Malamuth's model. The combination of hostility toward women, male dominance, and an acceptance of violence showed a moderately strong relationship to sexual aggression. Additional research (Hill & Fischer, 2001) has identified a sense of entitlement as an important component in sexual aggression. That is, men who feel that they are entitled to have sex, even if women refuse, are more likely to be sexually aggressive.

In summary, male aggression is not a myth, but the notion that men are aggressive and women are passive is not true. Both genders experience similar levels of anger, but men are more likely to express their anger as physical aggression. This likelihood can be traced to different social expectations and reinforcements for aggression experienced by boys and girls. As adults, men are more likely to be violent in public, to use aggression to gain power over others, and to experience legal problems associated with their aggression. Women are more likely to be violent in private, to use indirect or social aggression, and to respond violently if they feel justified in doing so and protected from retaliation. These patterns of aggression show gender-related differences, but they do not suggest that aggression is a male instinct or even a male domain.

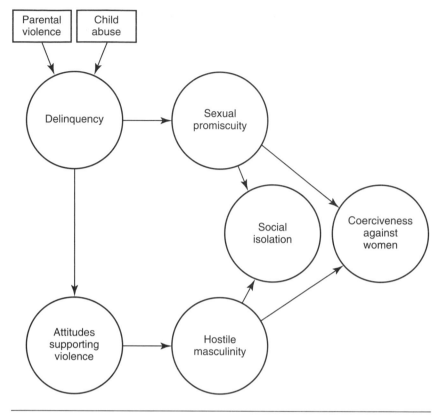

FIGURE 8.1   *Model of Characteristics of Men Who Are Coercive against Women*

Source: Adapted from "The Characteristics of Aggression Against Women: Testing a Model Using a National Sample of College Students," by N. Malamuth, R. Sockloskie, M. P. Koss, & J. Tanaka, 1991, *Journal of Consulting and Clinical Psychology, 52,* p. 676. Adapted by permission of Neil Malamuth and the American Psychological Association.

EXPRESSIVITY AND EMOTION

The similarities in the feelings that men and women experience and the differences in their behavior suggest that the gender differences in emotion may occur in the way emotions are expressed. Indeed, women have been described as the expressive gender, whereas men are described as failing to express their emotions (Fischer, 1993). This interpretation is possible only by using a selective definition of what counts as emotion (Shields, 2002). Only by concentrating on the emotions of fear and sadness in women and by overlooking aggression in men could women be considered more expressive than men. This difference in expressivity can be explained by differences in display rules: Men and women are supposed to restrain displays of certain emotions, yet are free to show others.

In his discussion of compliance with the Male Gender Role Identity model, Robert Brannon (1976) listed four criteria, two of which relate to these gender differences in emotionality: (1) No Sissy Stuff, meaning men must avoid anything vaguely feminine, such as crying or fear, and (2) Give 'Em Hell, meaning men are proud to display anger and aggression. (See Chapter 7 for a discussion of all four components.) The stereotype holds that men must avoid all things feminine and women are emotional, thus the display of most emotion is prohibited. Anger is acceptable, however, because it is the essence of "giving 'em hell." These two components are essential elements of the display rules for men, which allow women to express more of what they feel, with the penalty of being stereotyped for their display (Shields, 2002).

The discrepancies among the three types of measures of emotionality (self-reports, observed behavior, and physical arousal) support these gender differences in display rules. When researchers have used participants' self-reports to measure emotion, they often find that women are more emotional than men. For example, one review of self-reports of emotionality (Maccoby & Jacklin, 1974) showed that girls and women were more likely than boys and men to admit to feelings of fear and anxiety. When researchers have used observations of participants' behavior in public, they have measured the enactment of display rules and the potential bias of observers, who may be influenced by the stereotypes governing emotion. Such studies tend to find gender differences (Eagly & Steffen, 1986), although the differences are not large, on the average. When researchers unobtrusively measure behavior in private, participants are more likely to display their emotions, and such studies often fail to find gender differences (Eisenberg & Lennon, 1983).

Women learn a slightly different set of display rules for emotion than men do, and the behavior of both men and women tends to conform to the display rules they have learned. According to these display rules, women should be more nurturant than men, and in self-reports and in public behavior, they are. Boys and men should not be interested in

GENDERED VOICES

They Put a Lot of Effort into Showing Nothing

I talked to a psychologist who had been employed as a therapist in a prison, and he told me that the prisoners exhibited what he considered to be an inappropriate level of emotion—none. He said, "I thought they put a lot of effort into showing no emotion. Their goal seemed to be to show no sign of any emotion. For example, even if they were hurt, their faces didn't change expression. Every once in a while, I would see a slip, and a prisoner would show some sign of pain when he got hurt. I assume that they had feelings that were similar to anyone's, but their expression of emotion was very abnormal.

"Showing no emotion didn't mean that they let things go. They would retaliate against another prisoner who had hurt them, even if it was mostly an accident and he hadn't meant to hurt anyone. But they didn't show any emotion when they were hurt or when they hurt the other guy. It was part of the prison society to keep their faces like masks, showing nothing about what they felt, closing themselves off from the others."

babies or responsive to them, and under some circumstances, they are not. However, boys tend to nurture pets, and men who care for children are as nurturant and responsive as women who perform these tasks. According to these display rules, men should be more physically aggressive than women, and in self-reports and in public behavior (including criminal violence), they are. However, women experience anger as strongly as men do, and when they feel justified (and anonymous), women are as likely to show as much physical aggression as men. Women also use indirect aggression, which involves doing harm indirectly. Therefore, the gender differences in emotion are more a function of circumstances and social learning of display rules than biologically determined differences due to instinct.

CONSIDERING DIVERSITY

Some of the research on diversity and emotion has focused on universality rather than cross-cultural differences. The quest to understand the basics of human emotions and the commonalities across cultures has focused on facial expressions as a reflection of emotional experience. Paul Ekman (1992, 1994), who is the leading proponent of this position, has traced his view back to Darwin and the notion that facial expressions reflect basic emotional experience for humans and nonhuman animals. Ekman's research led him to propose that at least six basic human emotions exist—happiness, surprise, fear, sadness, anger, and disgust combined with contempt. His approach typically involves showing photographs or drawings of a human face and asking participants to identify the emotion that the person is experiencing. Results from a variety of cultures indicate that people in industrialized and preliterate cultures are able to identify these facial expressions of emotions at higher than chance levels.

Ekman (1992, 1994) argued that the widespread recognition of these different emotions suggests universality, but he also acknowledged that many aspects of emotional experience and expression are culture-specific. Consistent with this view, the search for universals in human emotions has revealed both consistency and diversity across cultures (Elfenbein & Ambady, 2002). Research confirms that people in many cultures are able to identify the six basic emotions that Ekman identified, but cross-cultural studies also show many variations in the experience and expression of emotion within and across countries.

Cross-cultural studies often include countries that emphasize individuality (such as the United States and Australia) compared to countries that value collectivist goals (such as China and Taiwan). One such study (Eid & Deiner, 2001) confirmed both universal and country-specific emotionality. Many of the differences were consistent with expectations, such as people in individualist countries would feel more pride and those in collectivist cultures would feel more guilt. However, people in individualist cultures varied less in their experience of emotion, especially positive emotions, which may reflect a cultural bias that pushes people toward feeling good, even when they do not.

Other cross-cultural research (Scherer, Walbott, & Summerfield, 1986) found more similarities than differences in the experience of emotion, but some unexpected results appeared. For example, this survey revealed the expected stereotypical gender differences— women reported more expressions of emotion than men—but the differences were small.

This survey also revealed some evidence against the emotional stereotypes associated with various countries: The English were very talkative rather than reticent; the Italians were very concerned with achievement rather than personal relationships; and the Swiss were very emotional rather than very reserved.

Another cross-cultural study (Mesquita & Frijda, 1992) analyzed the evidence on emotion by examining the components of emotion rather than only their categorization. By doing this type of analysis, similarities and differences appeared across cultures. The similarities included the experience of anger, disgust, joy, fear, sadness, and surprise. For example, loss of a loved one was associated with sadness in all cultures. Interaction with strangers was a source of anger in many cultures. However, within these broad similarities in emotion, specific differences appeared. For example, interactions with strangers were a source of anger for 52% of Japanese, compared with 15% of Americans and 20% of Europeans—a substantial cultural difference.

Despite the universality of anger, its experience differs substantially across cultures. For the Utku Eskimos, anger brings shame; it is considered dangerous, and its display is completely unacceptable for adults. The Vanatinai also believe that anger and aggression are unacceptable (Lepowsky, 1994). The inhabitants of this small island society in the south Pacific near New Guinea value independence and assertiveness but find physical aggression shameful; adults who commit such acts are thought to be out of control and embarrassing to their families. Fighting is rare, even among children. This society is notable for its egalitarian values as well as for its lack of aggression, and women are somewhat more likely than men to be physically aggressive. This culture is not passive, nor are the gender roles reversed. The men are fierce warriors, and women are not allowed to participate in warfare or use spears. However, this society holds different display rules than western societies, placing women rather than men in the role of displaying aggression.

Therefore, at an abstract level of analysis, emotions show many similarities across cultures—the types, the antecedent situations, the labels used, and the physical reactions and facial responses people exhibit (Elfenbein & Ambady, 2002). However, cultural differences exist in the specifics of each component. Cultures vary both in restricting and in prescribing the display of emotion—who should express what emotion under what circumstances. "Although there are universal patterns of expressive behavior, there also are culture-specific behavior modes, deriving from culture-specific models and from culturally based expectations regarding behavior that is appropriate under particular circumstances" (Mesquita & Frijda, 1992, p. 199). People may all feel the same emotions, but they do not express them in the same ways or under the same circumstances.

SUMMARY

The stereotype of gender and emotion presents women as emotional and men as rational, but research on the different components of emotion has revealed that there may be few gender differences in the inner experience of emotion. Gender differences appear in how and when emotion is displayed. Included in the components of emotion are the physiological dimension and the cognitive dimension. Both expectation and social setting exert significant effects on the experience of emotion, and psychologists continue to debate the relative contributions of physiology and cognition to the experience of emotion.

The notion that some emotions are the result of instincts can be traced to Charles Darwin's theory of evolution. In psychology, the explanation that emotion is instinctive has faded, with the exception of beliefs about a maternal instinct and an instinct toward aggression. Belief in a maternal instinct has continued, although research by Harlow and his colleagues demonstrated that monkeys deprived of contact with other monkeys during the first 6 months of their lives failed to show adequate nurturing and caregiving. Another version of maternal instinct supports the concept of bonding—the attachment formed between adult and infant during the first hours of the infant's life—although this concept has not found as much research support.

Research on gender differences in responsiveness to babies has shown differences in self-reports, but not in physiological measures, of responses to babies. These findings indicate that girls and women show more responsiveness to babies because they believe they should, and that boys and men show less responsiveness for the same reason. Women still have a great deal more involvement in child care than men. Self-reports indicate that the greater pleasure of women in caring for children is coupled with their greater irritation in caring for them; however, men who are very involved in child care tend to report similar feelings. Although fathering has not included the type of intimate caregiving that mothering has, research indicates that fathers have increased their involvement with their children, demonstrating their interest and ability in nurturing. Therefore, the concept of maternal instinct has no support as a biologically based explanation for caregiving, and both men and women have similar emotions related to nurturing.

Aggression has also been nominated as an instinct, with the belief that men have more innate tendencies toward showing aggressive be-

havior than women. When considering the link between anger and aggression—that is, between emotion and behavior—few gender differences appear. Women and men experience anger similarly, but there are gender differences in emotional expression. Boys and men tend to be more likely to use direct, physical confrontation when they are angry, whereas girls and women are more likely to use more indirect and relational aggression. There is no difference in the use of verbal aggression; however, girls and women are more likely to cry when angry, an expression that men often misunderstand.

Developmental gender differences in aggression exist, with boys more likely than girls to use physical aggression at all ages. Longitudinal studies have revealed that aggression is moderately stable over time and even over generations; aggressive children are more likely than less aggressive children to become violent adults and to have children who are more aggressive. However, both boys and girls tend to become less aggressive as they develop, and by adulthood, the gender difference in aggression has diminished.

Despite small gender differences in aggression in laboratory studies, very large gender differences exist in crime rates—men are about 3.5 times more likely than women to be arrested for committing a violent crime. The victims of these violent crimes are likely to be other men. However, women fear crime victimization more than men, especially sexual violence. Their fear has some basis: Official reports underestimate the incidence of rape, and more representative surveys show that at least 20% of women are the targets or rape or attempted rape. Attitudes of hostility toward women, an acceptance of violence, and a sense of entitlement to sex make men more likely to be sexually violent.

Although men have more experience with violence and less experience with nurturance than women, these differences may relate to how emotion is expressed rather than to women's or men's subjective experiences of emotion. The cultural display rules that govern the behaviors associated with emotion differ for men and women, and these allow women more expression and restrain men from expressing emotions except anger, which men are more free to show than are women.

The search for universals in emotion has yielded evidence of both consistency and diversity across cultures. Research indicates that people across the world experience the same range of emotions, including the six basic emotions of happiness, surprise, fear, sadness, anger, and disgust combined with contempt. However, the situations that evoke these emotions and the rules that govern their display differ enormously across cultures and apply differently to women and men.

GLOSSARY

bonding an emotional attachment that develops between primary caregiver and infant within a few days after birth.

critical period a time early in development during which baby animals are capable of rapid learning when presented with the necessary stimulus. Once the critical period has passed, no amount of exposure will produce the learning.

display rules the learned social rules that govern who may display which emotion to whom, and in what situation each emotion may be displayed.

SUGGESTED READINGS

Hrdy, Sarah Blaffer. (1999). *Mother nature: A history of mothers, infants, and natural selection.* New York: Pantheon Books.
Primatologist Hrdy examines mothering from an evolutionary point of view, considering mothers, fathers, and offspring. She uses nonhuman species to provide contrasts and to draw similarities to the complexities of bearing and raising children.

Larson, Reed; & Pleck, Joseph. (1999). Hidden feelings: Emotionality in boys and men. In Dan Bernstein (Ed.), *Nebraska Symposium on Motivation, 1999: Gender and motivation* (pp. 25–74). Lincoln, NE: University of Nebraska Press.
Larson and Pleck review theories of emotion and present results from several studies that compare emotional responses of girls, boys, women, and men in a variety of situations. Their gender-as-process approach and innovative methodology provide an interesting presentation of gender and emotionality.

Shields, Stephanie A. (2002). *Speaking from the heart: Gender and the social meaning of emotion.* Cambridge, UK: Cambridge University Press.
Shields reviews research related to how emotion fits into social conceptualizations of gender and how emotional meaning is often sharply gendered.

Silverstein, Louise B.; & Auerbach, Carl F. (1999). Deconstructing the essential father. *American Psychologist, 54,* 397–407.
Silverstein and Auerbach analyze the changes in views of fathering, considering research and social policy.

9 RELATIONSHIPS

The scientist behind "The Science of a Good Marriage" (Kantrowitz & Wingert, 1999) is psychologist John Gottman, and his science includes a variety of techniques to measure reactions of partners in the "Love Lab," the Family Research Laboratory on the Seattle campus of the University of Washington. Most researchers who have studied marriage used surveys and self-reports, but Gottman (1991, 1998) chose to gather direct behavioral observations and to make physiological measurements of partners as they interacted. Gottman prefers to collect information on partners as they experience conflict, and his approach has revealed some surprising findings.

One surprising finding was that anger is not the problem in bad marriages. Indeed, anger was common to both good and bad marriages. Thus, angry couples do not necessarily have relationships that are in trouble. The danger signs for a marriage come from what Gottman calls the Four Horsemen of the Apocalypse—criticism, contempt, defensiveness, and stonewalling. These reactions to conflict situations signal troubled relationships.

Several relationship patterns characterize couples whose relationships are in trouble, and those patterns differ from what many people assume. For example, Gottman's research also contradicts the Mars–Venus school of relationships promoted by John Gray (1992), which holds that men and women come from two very different emotional worlds. According to Gottman's studies, "gender differences may contribute to marital problems, but they don't cause them" (Kantrowitz & Wingert, 1999, p. 54).

According to Gottman's research, one problem in marital relationships is an unequal balance of power. Husbands tend to have more power than wives, and when they do not share the power, the relationship suffers. Gender differences also occur in connection with other problems. For example, wives are more likely to engage in criticism, but husbands are more likely to stonewall, that is, to disengage during conflict. Both behaviors are typical of couples with unstable relationships. In addition, a clear signal of problems is a facial expression reflecting contempt. These behaviors all relate to a pattern of negative reaction with few attempts to reinstate any positive interaction. That is, couples headed toward splitting up tend to interact differently than couples who will stay together. Gottman's observation and physiological measurements allowed him to know which aspects of marital interaction were important in predicting divorce, and Gottman claims that he can predict divorce with 90% accuracy.

The gender differences in patterns of behavior in problem marriages may relate in part to women's and men's different styles in relationships, which have implications for friendships as well as love relationships, both with same-sex and other-sex individuals. Robert Sternberg (1986) proposed a model for understanding all relationships, including friendship and romantic love. He called this model the triangular theory of love because it hypothesizes love's three points: intimacy, passion, and commitment. His conception of intimacy encompasses feelings of closeness, passion includes romantic and sexual attraction, and commitment involves the decision that love exists and the relationship should continue. Figure 9.1 shows Sternberg's model and the different types of relationships that result from the combinations of these elements.

Sternberg argued that if none of these components exists, there is no relationship. His model distinguishes between two types of friendships—liking and companionate love. Liking occurs when people share intimacy, but not passion or commitment. Sternberg (1987) included both sharing feelings and sharing activities as intimacy. The combination of intimacy and commitment without passion results in **companionate love,** a definition that would come close to what most people regard as close but platonic friendship.

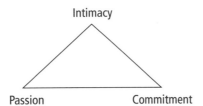

Intimacy

Passion   Commitment

Liking =	Intimacy without Passion or Commitment
Companionate love =	Intimacy + Commitment without Passion
Romantic love =	Intimacy + Passion without Commitment
Empty love =	Commitment without Passion or Intimacy
Fatuous love =	Passion + Commitment without Intimacy
Infatuated love =	Passion without Commitment or Intimacy
Consummate love =	Passion + Commitment + Intimacy

FIGURE 9.1 *Sternberg's Triangular Theory of Love*

Source: Adapted from "A Triangular Theory of Love," by R. J. Sternberg, 1986, *Psychological Review, 93,* pp. 123, 128. Adapted by permission of Robert Sternberg and the American Psychological Association.

FRIENDSHIPS

Although Sternberg's triangular theory of love makes no distinction between intimacy developed through sharing feelings or through sharing activities, these two styles tend to be associated with women and men, respectively. These gender differences in relationship styles have been the source of friction and contention, with men being accused of deficiencies in intimacy because their friendships do not take the same style as women's friendships. The view that men are deficient at friendship has not always existed, nor do all cultures discourage intimate, emotional friendships between men (Nardi, 1992a). The Greeks believed that true friendships could exist only between free and equal individuals, which restricted true friendship to a limited number and omitted all women, slaves, and men of lesser social standing.

During the 19th century, intimate friendships were common for both men and women (Crain, 2001; Nardi, 1992a). Courage and loyalty were seen as the basis for a special type of friendship that men could share. Men were considered capable of experiencing closeness and feelings for other men that women could not feel for other women and that women and men could not feel for each other. Those beliefs have changed, and currently, women are seen as more capable of intimate friendship. Women's style of friendship is viewed as more intimate than men's relationships.

Development of Styles

Children tend to segregate themselves according to gender starting at preschool age and continuing throughout elementary and middle school (Maccoby, 1998). This segregation is noticeable during preschool, becomes much more pronounced during the elementary school years, and may be imposed by parents or teachers. When girls and boys are put into situations in which they must interact, they do, but the tendency to group into same-gender associations is a persistent pattern for children (Strough, Swenson, & Cheng, 2001). Furthermore, the interaction patterns of boys and girls differ, beginning very early in development.

Children show gender differences in interactions as early as 33 months (Jacklin & Maccoby, 1978). Researchers studied pairs of children who interacted in all possible combinations—boys with boys, girls with girls, and boys with girls. The results showed that children interacted more with those of the same than with the other gender, in both positive and negative ways. Children in same-gender pairs were more likely to offer toys to their partners or try to take toys from their partners than the children in mixed-gender pairs. The girls in mixed-gender pairs tended to be passive and the boys unresponsive. Girls in such pairs tended to stand by and watch the boys play or to withdraw and seek their mothers. The boys in such pairs tended to ignore what the girls said to them. In contrast, girls and boys behaved similarly when they interacted with children of the same gender: The girls were active in their exchanges, and the boys were responsive to their partners' messages. The reactions of children partnered with an other-sex child may relate to the gender segregation that is typical of children's play and friendships: Playing would not be that much fun if your partner failed to react and did not listen. These interactions may make each gender more eager to seek the company of others of the same gender.

During the preschool years, children show signs of a concept of friendship and the mutuality that is involved (Lindsey, 2002). Between ages 3 and 6 years, children begin to be able to name a person as a friend and even to say who is a "best" friend. As they develop, children enlarge their notion of friendship so that personal characteristics such as loyalty become important. The process of developing and maintaining friendships seems to be involved in forming adequate social relationships with children other than friends. During elementary and middle school, children begin to become more involved in friendships, relying on friends for companionship and intimacy (Hartup & Stevens, 1999). During preadolescence, children form a more complex concept of friendship, becoming increasingly able to integrate the notion that conflict is an acceptable part of friendship.

During elementary school, children begin to rely on peers for companionship and intimacy rather than on siblings and parents (Cleary, Ray, LoBello, & Zachar, 2002). These relationships reflect the closeness or intimacy component of Sternberg's triangular model of relationships. The research on elementary school children has demonstrated that friends were important sources of companionship for these 2nd, 3rd, 5th, and 6th graders. Gender differences in the development of intimate friendship also appeared, with girls both seeking and valuing intimacy more than boys did. Friendship begins to be very important during this time, becoming an influence that can be either positive or negative in social development (Berndt, 2002).

One possible basis for the gender differences in friendships during middle childhood comes from the different activities that girls and boys enjoy during these years. For example, boys are more fond of rough-and-tumble play than girls are. Such play involves play-fighting and chasing and is very common among preschool children, especially boys (Rose & Asher, 2000). The persistence of rough-and-tumble play throughout middle childhood and into preadolescence might seem to escalate into aggression, but such play is actually done in a spirit of fun. Boys also tend to play in somewhat larger groups, to spend more time outside, and to be more fond of activities that involve **gross motor skills,** such as running, jumping, and throwing a ball.

These gender differences in activity preferences seem to be a reasonable basis for gender segregation during childhood. According to one study (Bukowski, Gauze, Hoza, & Newcomb, 1993), boys who preferred high levels of motor activity preferred the company of other boys, and girls who disliked such activities preferred the company of other girls. However, a later study (Hoffman & Powlishta, 2001) found that preferred activities showed no relationship to patterns of gender segregation. The children in this study exhibited gender segregation, but an analysis of the patterns of play preferences did not reveal activity preferences as the basis for this choice.

Gender is not the only basis for self-segregation during the early school years. Ethnic and racial background are also characteristics that children notice and use as a basis for forming groups, but ethnic background showed less of an effect than gender as a basis for groupings in one study (DuBois & Hirsch, 1990). When put into a position to choose, children crossed ethnic lines before gender lines. Interracial friendships form at school, but tend to be less common as children get older (Aboud, Mendelson, & Purdy, 2003). However, the patterns of crossing ethnic lines to form friends may persist into adulthood (Joyner & Kao, 2000), and cross-ethnic friendships are similar to other friendships in terms of loyalty and intimacy. Attending an integrated school increases the chances of making friends with someone from another ethnic group, but ethnicity remains a basis for grouping.

Gender segregation is a strong force during elementary school, with few children voluntarily crossing the boundary (Thorne, 1993). Children impose this division on themselves, even when adults do not. The segregation is so strong, that the boundary crossings are of interest. Animosity often accompanies such interactions, taking the form of name-calling, invading another's space, pollution games and rituals ("cooties"), and occasional fights. Some of the hostile interactions contained the hint of heterosexual awareness and future romantic relationships, but sexuality was more commonly used as a way to taunt. Situations of comfortable interaction appear only rarely between girls and boys. These situations tended to be either very absorbing activities, such as group projects or interesting games, or activities organized by an adult so as to include both girls and boys, such as games involving assigned rather than chosen teams. Few children traveled easily between the social worlds of both girls and boys.

Preadolescents must avoid members of the other gender except under certain sanctioned circumstances, yet each gender must have sufficient contact to learn about the other. One reason for interaction is the formation of future relationships, and research has suggested that friendships are important in the development of romantic relationships. One study (Furman, Simon, Shaffer, & Bouchey, 2002) analyzed friendship and parental relationships to understand formation of romantic relationships and found that characteristics of friendship were a better predictor than parental relationships. Considering that both friendships and romantic relationships are peer relationships of relative equality, this similarity makes sense. Thus, same-gender friendships during childhood may serve the function of allowing individuals to learn how to form relationships without the pressure of sexual contact. Referring back to Sternberg's model of relationships, these relationships allow the development of intimacy and commitment without passion. Childhood friendships, then, might be regarded as a type of practice for adolescent and adult romantic relationships. The active avoidance that children practice for the other sex changes to active interest during adolescence; contact between girls and boys becomes more common, but friendships between girls and boys remain uncommon.

Friendships over the Life Span

Friendships during adolescence are similar to those of preadolescence, but adolescents intensify the intimacy in their relationships with a greater degree of personal sharing and self-disclosure than those of younger children. The gender differences in the value and attainment of intimacy persist, with girls more likely to be interested in forming emotionally intimate friendships with a smaller set of girls, and boys more likely to form activity-based friendships with a more extensive set of boys. This pattern results in boys being alone less often than girls, but girls talking with each other more often than boys do (Smith, 1997).

Adolescent girls use talk as a way to develop intimacy, to reveal and learn intimate knowledge about each other, which includes a greater involvement with problems and life transitions than boys' friendships do (Roy, Benenson, & Lilly, 2000). A meta-analytic review (Collins & Miller, 1994) showed that self-disclosure is an important factor in friendship, increasing liking in those who hear disclosures. Self-disclosure is not as characteristic of boys' as of girls' friendships, and this difference may relate to different conceptualizations of friendship for boys and girls. Alternatively, disclosure may be something that boys feel they cannot do. An interview study with poor, urban, adolescent boys (Way, 1997) revealed that the boys wanted intimacy but did not trust their peers sufficiently to disclose important thoughts to them. These boys expressed regret over that situation and longed for the closeness of a "best" friend to whom they could really talk.

This attitude of aloofness and withdrawal from intimacy is a set of behaviors that Richard Majors and his colleagues (Majors & Billson, 1992; Majors, Tyler, Peden, & Hall, 1994) labeled *cool pose*. Cool pose is a way that African American men present themselves, used as a compensation and coping strategy. The poses, postures, humor, readiness to use violence, and suppression of emotional displays are intended to create visibility for those who have been made invisible by a society that fails to grant African American men the status of European American men. The violence and suppression of emotion are elements of the masculine gender role, and cool pose uses an exaggeration of this role. This exaggeration allows African American men to feel a sense of masculinity. Cool pose magnifies some of the destructive elements of the masculine gender role, creating problems for those who take this pose. In addition to the violence associated with interpersonal conflicts, the emotional remoteness that is essential to the cool pose also inhibits the development of intimacy, both with women and with other men.

Fear of homosexuality is another factor that discourages boys from forming the same type of intimate friendships that girls experience (Morman & Floyd, 1998; Way, 1997). The current prohibitions against same-gender sexual activity make men hesitant about emotional closeness in friendships, and the activity-based relationships of adolescent boys and adult men illustrate one strategy for avoiding the emotional intimacy that could suggest homosexuality (Nardi, 1992a). Gay men do not have this obstacle, and their friendships with both gay and straight men show similarities and differences to heterosexual men's friendships (Fee, 2000). Gay men are often more willing than straight men to discuss personal relationships and problems; thus their friendships with both differ from the activity-based relationships typical of men. Their friendships with straight men are often tinged with caution over potential sexual attraction.

Studies of friendship among college students (Caldwell & Peplau, 1982; Roy et al., 2000) confirmed the gender differences in the bases for friendships in men and women. These studies failed to find differences in the number or importance of friendships or in the time spent with friends. Men were more likely than women to choose an activity to do with a friend rather than "just talk" and to choose their friends on the basis of shared activities rather than shared attitudes. Women were more likely to talk about personal problems and celebrate personal accomplishments with female friends. These differences did not lead to differential evaluations of intimacy; women and men were equally likely to consider their friendships intimate.

With the formation of committed love relationships, birth of children, and transition to the workforce, changes occur in existing friendships and the opportunities to form new friendships. Workplace settings become important in friendship formation, presenting people with similar interests with whom colleagues spend time. Research on young professionals' work-based friendships (Gibbons & Olk, 2003) indicated that young professionals readily crossed gender but not ethnic boundaries in making friends at work.

During the early years of marriage, both spouses may relinquish other relationships to develop their marriage, seeking emotional intimacy and support from each other rather than from friends. In addition, when couples have children, the children take up time that might have been devoted to friends (or even to spouses). Young couples, especially those with children, tend to devote less time to other friendships than people who are unmarried or childless. Thus, several circumstances can alter friendships (Fehr, 2000). If people lose proximity and fail to put effort into maintaining friendships, they tend to dissolve. Women are more likely than men to work at maintaining a network of social relationships, and the social support derived from these networks is important for happiness and even for health.

When children become adults, their family members may become their friends. Due to the wide difference in power and authority between parents and children, this possibility is not likely during childhood or adolescence, but adult children and their parents can form relationships that have the emotional sharing and self-disclosure that characterize other friendships. These relationships also show gender differences consistent with other findings: Daughters and mothers are closer than other combinations of family members (Lye, 1996). Indeed, the closeness of families with adult children often depends on mothers' efforts to maintain contact. In addition to parent–adult child relationships, siblings are often close after they become adults, maintaining relationships that are as close as friends (Floyd, 1995).

Aging produces changes in friendships, with the elderly needing more practical support while their number of friends decreases due to death. Children often become the source of this caregiving and practical support, but the older people attempt to maintain social networks (Akiyama, Elliott, & Antonucci, 1996). Older people receive different types of support from family and friends, and both are important to healthy aging (Blieszner, 2000). Women become more numerous in the social networks of the elderly because men die at younger ages, leaving more women. Thus, men's same-gender friendships tend to be replaced with relationships with women. Therefore, friendship becomes more female-based among the elderly.

Flexibility of Styles

Men may find emotional intimacy easier with women than with other men. As Francesca Cancian (1987) proposed, love has come to be "feminized," that is, defined in feminine terms, as the expression of feelings and as self-disclosure. These characteristics are commonly associated with women and are actually more common in women's than men's friendships. Some evidence exists that men can also use this style of relationship and tend to do so when they relate to women, either as friends or as romantic partners.

When people think of friends, they imagine people of the same gender, so cross-gender friendships break this "rule" (Werking, 1997). The model for cross-gender relationships is romantic partners, so cross-gender friendships also break this rule. Cross-gender friendships are a recent development that did not exist 100 years ago when Western societies were strongly gender segregated, and women governed the home and men occupied the world of work, politics, and business (Swain, 1992). Although gender segregation still exists in many situations, school and work offer opportunities for cross-gender relationships, and women and men have formed such friendships.

Because these friendships deviate from people's stereotypes of what friendship should be, cross-gender friendships face challenges and constraints. The friends frequently must explain, "we're just good friends," to others, especially romantic partners. Some research has found that cross-gender friendships face barriers (Werking, 1997), but other research (Monsour, Harris, Kurzweil, & Beard, 1994) found that these problems affect only a small percentage of cross-gender friendships. For most cross-gender friends, these special challenges and problems were "much ado about nothing" (Monsour et al., 1994, p. 55).

Both men and women may be able to use different styles of relating in different relationships. This flexibility appeared in a study of college students' relationships (DeLucia-Waack, Gerrity, Taub, & Baldo, 2001). Rather than a stereotypical association of relationship styles for women and men, this study revealed a great deal of flexibility; women could take charge and be assertive but tended to do so in their relationships with other women rather than in romantic relationships. Men showed less overall flexibility of styles in different types of relationships, but men whose Bem Sex Role Inventory scores indicated androgyny showed a great deal of flexibility in their styles across types of relationship and gender of partner.

The ability to adapt to the situation by using a more "feminine" or "masculine" style of interaction indicates that styles of friendship are indeed roles that men and women learn. Although not all men may learn the intimate sharing and self-disclosure that are typical of women's friendships, most do, and these men use this style when they form friendships with women (Werking, 1997). Men may feel uncomfortable in enacting this friendship style for several reasons. As several researchers have pointed out, **homophobia**—the unreasonable fear and hatred of homosexuality—restrains men from seeking emotional intimacy with other men. Even when men know the style, they may be reluctant to use it. When they use it, they may feel more comfortable in this type of relationship with women rather than with other men.

The constraints on women's behavior are not as strong; their typical style of emotional intimacy with other women carries no homosexual connotations. However, emotional intimacy between women and men often has an element of a sexual relationship, so women who seek friendships with men also often feel that they must be vigilant in maintaining these as nonsexual friendships. Women who adopt an activity-based style of relationship with men, being "one of the boys," can participate in the same activities that men enjoy with each other—playing baseball, poker, or other recreational activities. This choice creates a style of relationship typical of men and not necessarily one infused with emotional intimacy. Some men and women have chosen to break the boundaries established during preschool and form friendships with members of the other gender. The research indicates that men and women know about both friendship styles, suggesting that any limitations in creating cross-gender friendships come from reluctance to apply these styles.

LOVE RELATIONSHIPS

As the headline story on John Gottman (Kantrowitz & Wingert, 1999) described, maintaining love relationships proves difficult. Women's greater ease in emotional sharing can make men uneasy, and men's tendency to emotionally withdraw from a discussion is one of the warning signs that a marriage is in trouble. Currently in the United States, divorce is common, but problems in relationships are not new. The changes have come from what is expected of marriage and the ease of divorce, not with relationship problems. Elaine Hatfield and Richard Rapson (1996) contended that romantic, passionate love is universal, but this type of love has not been the basis for permanent relationships until recently in industrialized Western countries.

Historically, passionate, romantic love has posed a threat to the existing social structure and has rarely been the basis for permanent relationships (Hatfield & Rapson, 1996). Many cultures have literature or legends about lovers who have died tragically as the result of their passion and the unsuitability of any permanent relationship. The story of Romeo and Juliet is an example familiar to English-speaking cultures, but Hatfield and Rapson have described similar stories from ancient and modern societies around the world. Passionate love has been seen as madness rather than a good basis for marriage. The more common pattern for forming permanent relationships has been (and in many cultures remains) arranged marriages in which families choose mates for children. In such arranged marriages, financial considerations rather than love or passion have been the motivations for the match.

Several different patterns of love relationships have existed over the past several centuries in Western cultures (Cancian, 1987). Before the 1800s, agriculture was the basis for most people's livelihood, and both men and women worked together on family farms, making the family the center of both men's and women's lives. Although men were the heads of households, both men and women believed that marriage gave them the duty to love and help one another. Despite sharply divided gender roles in the home and community, love was not differentiated according to gender.

In Sternberg's (1986) triangular model of love, this Family Duty blueprint ensured an equal relationship between the partners. Such marriages were formed around commitment, and the sharing of home life made intimacy very likely, but the component of passion might have been missing from such duty-bound relationships. In arranged marriages, this component might never be part of the relationship of a married couple.

By the end of the 1700s, the Industrial Revolution had changed the pattern of many people's lives, including marriage and family. Work and family were separated, with men working in jobs in factories and offices rather than around the home. Women, too, might work in factories, but the ideal pattern was for men to fulfill the Good Provider role (Bernard, 1981) and for women to be mothers and wives. This division led to the Doctrine of the Two Spheres (Welter, 1978), the division that resulted in women's preeminence in family life and men's dominance in the outside world.

Women became responsible for the maintenance of the home and family, a sanctuary from the hostility of the outside world of business and factory. This responsibility made women the experts in love: They were the ones who had the tender feelings and experienced the emotions; they were the ones who needed love and depended on men and children for it; they were the ones most capable of providing love to others.

Through this family arrangement, women became dependent on men for financial security, so maintaining the love of a husband became essential to women's financial security. During the 1920s, however, women started to invade the male world of work, taking paid jobs outside the home. With increasing economic power, women were less dependent on men for financial security, which changed the blueprint for marriage to the Companionship model (Cancian, 1987). Cancian credited the Companionship blueprint for love relationships with the feminization of love. This model focused on affection and support for each other, but women were still the experts on love and held the responsibility for the relationship: "Marriage was to be all of a woman's life but only part of a man's" (Cancian, 1987, p. 34).

The Companionship model for marriage emphasized the similarity of the partners, and personal characteristics in the selection of marriage partners became important as this model of marriage became the standard. Spouses were supposed to love each other before they married and to choose their partners rather than relying on partners chosen by family. Using Sternberg's model to analyze these relationships, consummate love was the ideal, with an equal mixture of intimacy, passion, and commitment. However, romantic love was also a possibility, with its combination of passion and intimacy but lack of commitment. As evidence for the rising lack of commitment under the Companionship blueprint, the divorce rate increased (Cancian, 1987).

The emphasis on personal compatibility and romance in marriage prompted a different method of selecting marriage partners. Rather than relying on the family to choose their partners or making decisions on an economic basis, individuals started to choose their own mates. Dating arose as a way of finding suitable marriage partners for Companionship-style marriages.

Dating

Dating began during the 1920s as a form of courtship but has expanded to fulfill a variety of other functions, including recreation, status, companionship, sexual exploration, and the ability to form intimate relationships (Quatman, Sampson, Robinson, & Watson, 2001). Along with this form of courtship came a format for dating, which can be analyzed in terms of a script that guides young men's and women's behavior on dates (Rose & Frieze, 1993). College students adhered to this script in describing an actual and a hypothetical first heterosexual date, with a great deal of agreement between the two scripts but a big difference in the scripted roles for women and men. Following the script leads men to act and women to react. The man's active role includes initiating the date, controlling the activities, and initiating sexual activity. The woman's reactive role includes being concerned about her appearance, participating in the activities her partner planned, and reacting to his sexual advances. Both the hypothetical and actual dates reflected this script, which follows traditional gender stereotypes. Although they do not have traditional gender stereotypes to follow on first dates, one study (Klinkenberg & Rose, 1994) indicated that gay men's and lesbians' first dates also follow a script that is very similar to that of heterosexual couples.

Greater variety in dating began to appear after the 1940s, with girls initiating, planning, and paying for dates and the evolution of a pattern of mixed-gender group dating (Miller & Gordon, 1986). Despite the existence of variations on the pattern of male-initiated dates, the traditional script for heterosexual dating has changed little, and most dates adhere to this scripted pattern (Laner & Ventrone, 2000).

Dating has become an important part of adolescent life, and 57% of young people in the United States between 12 and 17 years old go out on dates regularly; about a third have a steady boyfriend or girlfriend (Fetto, 2003). Older adolescents are more likely to be involved in a romantic relationship than younger adolescents (Shulman & Scharf, 2000). Younger adolescents reported that excitement was more important to their dating choices than did older adolescents, but companionship and emotional involvement were important for all ages of adolescents involved in dating.

Although dating is a highly desired activity for most adolescents, dating presents disadvantages as well as advantages. Advantages include an increase in prestige and self-esteem, but disadvantages include stress, an increased chance of depression, and a decrease in academic motivation and achievement (Quatman et al., 2001). Both the advantages and disadvantages intensified with more frequent dating and applied to boys and girls. In ad-

▣ GENDERED VOICES

I Was Terrible at Being a Girl

"I was fairly bad at being a girl when I was a child," a middle-aged woman told me. "I did tomboy-type things. But I was really terrible at it when I was a teenager and trying to date and attract boys. Dating seemed like a game, and the rules were so silly. And I was bad at the game. Flirting was a disaster—I felt so silly and incompetent.

"My mother practically despaired of my ever behaving in ways that would lead to dates. She would give me advice, such as 'Hide how smart you are, because boys don't like to date girls who are smarter than they are,' and 'Wait for him to open the door for you.' I thought both those things were pretty pointless. Why should I hide how smart I was? I had gone to school with most of the guys in my high school since we were all in elementary school, so they knew how smart I was. Besides, if I could have fooled one, I didn't think that I could have kept up the charade. I wasn't smart enough

to play dumb for all that long. Also, why would I want to date a guy who wanted a dumb girl? Sounded like a poor prospect to me.

"I know that opening doors became an issue in the 1970s feminist movement, but my objections were about 10 years earlier. It just seemed silly to me that a perfectly capable person, me, should inconvenience a guy to open a door. I was more than capable of doing so, and I never saw why I shouldn't—still don't for that matter. I now see having doors opened as a courtesy, which is O.K. I open doors for both men and women. There's probably too much made of that particular issue, but when I was a teenager, it was something my mother warned me about on numerous occasions. I just had a hard time getting the rules of the game—I was terrible at the girl stuff. I am much better at being a woman than I was at being a girl."

dition, having a boyfriend/girlfriend does not compensate for being unpopular among same-sex peers. Early adolescents who were unpopular with peers and had a boyfriend or girlfriend were more poorly adjusted and showed more behavioral problems than unpopular adolescents who did not (Brendgen, Vitaro, Doyle, Markiewicz, & Bukowski, 2002). Therefore for adolescents, dating and romantic relationships are important and desirable but not entirely positive experiences.

A poll of single adults (*People,* 2003) indicated that over half of single women and men were not dating anyone, and about one fourth had not been on a date for 6 months or more. Women and men gave very similar answers to most of the questions about dating; a high percentage of men (59%) and women (68%) said that companionship was their reason for dating, which outnumbered men (12%) and women (14%) who said they were looking for a spouse. A similar number (12% versus 14%) said that the online world had affected their dating; they had used the Internet or an online dating service to get dates.

The advent of the ability to meet people online has affected relationships for both adolescents and adults. A nationwide survey of adolescents (Wolak, Mitchell, & Finkelhor, 2002) revealed that 14% had formed a close relationship with someone online within the year. Only 2% described their online relationship as a romance, but 71% were cross-gender relationships. Despite widespread publicity about teenagers victimized by adult predators online, most of the relationships reported by these adolescents were with age peers (70%). Many led to face-to-face meetings (41%), but adolescents reported that they told parents or friends about the meeting (89%) and had someone accompany them to the meeting (77%). For adults who date, 12% of women and 16% of men said they had used an online dating service, and 6% said that they had gone out on a date with someone they met online (*People,* 2003). However, the rise of electronic introductions has not revolutionized dating; most people (65% to 75%) met through introductions by friends or coworkers.

What people want in casual dating partners may differ from what they seek for long-term relationships (Sprecher & Regan, 2002). The qualities of warmth and kindness, expressivity and openness, and a good sense of humor were common across all types of relationships, but an emphasis on physical attractiveness and social status was high for

GENDERED VOICES

Dating Strategies

Two women in their 30s were talking about their lives, and one told the other that she had gone on a date with a man but didn't see the point of continuing to do so because it didn't show much promise of turning into a serious relationship. The other woman tried to convince her friend that all dates were not prospective mates, so dating does not necessarily lead to a serious relationship.

These two attitudes reflect the research about dating, with some adults concentrating on finding lifelong partners and others dating as part of an active social life. The reluctant woman remained difficult to convince, but her friend told her, "Just think of it as your own catch-and-release program."

dating relationships, especially long-term ones. In the study of dating adults (*People,* 2003), very little difference appeared in women's and men's emphasis on physical attractiveness. This result stands in contrast to stereotypes about men's emphasis on physical attractiveness, which is a prominent feature of evolutionary psychology's conceptualization of mate selection.

Evolutionary psychology is an area of psychology that examines how adaptation pressures have shaped contemporary behavior. "Evolutionary psychologists believe that females and males faced different pressures in primeval environments and that the sexes' differing reproductive status was the key feature of ancestral life that framed sex-typed adaptive problems" (Eagly & Wood, 1999, p. 408). According to this concept, remote prehuman history left gender-related differences that appear today in people's selection of mates. This view hypothesizes that men's best strategy was to reproduce as often as possible, whereas women are limited in their reproductive abilities because they can bear a limited number of children. Thus they must select mates who will help them raise their children (Buss, 1994). Preference for physical attractiveness is one of the factors that evolutionary psychology sees as a gender difference, with men valuing attractive partners because attractiveness is a sign of health and reproductive fitness. According to this view, women are less concerned with looks; women value mates who can provide resources to support them and their children.

Men do emphasize the attractiveness of their partner more than women do, but a study spanning almost 60 years (Buss, Shackelford, Kirkpatrick, & Larsen, 2001) indicated that men are not alone—attractiveness has become more valued by both women and men. Thus, the value of attractiveness is closer now than in the past. In addition, the adaptive advantage of attractiveness is questionable; attractiveness is not closely related to health and reproductive ability. Many women considered beautiful have fertility problems. A more reliable sign of reproductive capability is having borne children; however, the evolutionary psychologists do not hypothesize that women with young children are the most attractive potential mates, despite their demonstrated reproductive success.

Evolutionary psychology also predicts that attractiveness should be more important in heterosexual attraction than for gay or lesbian couples. A test of this hypothesis failed: Few differences in partner preference appeared in the descriptions of desirable partner characteristics in male–male, female–female, as well as male–female couples (Howard, Blumstein, & Schwartz, 1987). All said they wanted romantic partners who were kind, considerate, and physically attractive. The partners in same-gender couples expressed a preference for partners who were more athletic and expressive about their feelings than the mates described by partners in male–female couples, but these differences were small. Regardless of sexual orientation, people seek similar qualities in romantic partners (Peplau & Spalding, 2000). Thus, key points in evolutionary psychology's conceptualization of mate selection have failed to gain research support.

Other characteristics that attract people to romantic partners include similarities of personal values. Mate selection is more a matter of "birds of a feather flock together" than "opposites attract" (Antill, 1983). That is, people are romantically attracted to others who are more like them than different from them. These similarities include not only personal values, but also ethnicity, social class, and religion (Martin, Bradford, Drzewiecka, & Chitgopekar, 2003; *People,* 2003). In addition, the reasons for selecting a partner have converged for women and men over the past 60 years (Buss et al., 2001). Love and mutual attraction rank as the most important reason, but intelligence, education, and a pleasing personality were valued highly. In addition to initial similarity of values, partners tend to become more similar as their relationship continues (Davis & Rusbult, 2001).

Despite the opinion of adolescents that their dating is not oriented toward mate selection, dating is the process through which most men and women find partners. The patterns of relating to each other established during dating carry over into marriage, but marriage is a major life transition. When people marry, they assume the new roles of husband and wife.

Marriage and Committed Relationships

Marriage is not the only form of committed romantic relationship. Gay and lesbian couples cannot legally marry in most places, and heterosexual couples sometimes choose to live together without marrying. The number of cohabiting heterosexual couples has dramatically increased since the 1960s. In the United States in 1960, less than half a million heterosexual couples were cohabiting, but in 2000, almost 5 million were, representing an increase of more than 1,000% (U.S. Bureau of the Census, 2002). As shown in Figure 9.2, this change is the most dramatic trend in committed relationships. For some couples,

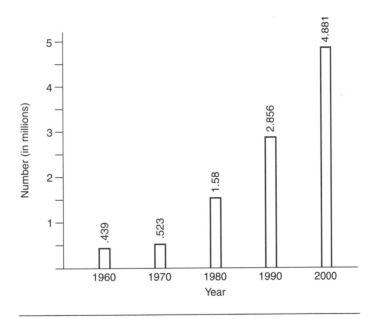

FIGURE 9.2 *Increases in Number of Unmarried Couple Households, 1960–2000*

Sources: Data from *Statistical Abstracts of the United States, 1999* (119th ed.) (p. 75), U.S. Bureau of the Census, 1999, Washington, DC: U.S. Government Printing Office; and *Statistical Abstracts of the United States, 2002* (122nd ed.) (p. 48), U.S. Bureau of the Census, 2002. Washington, DC: U.S. Government Printing Office.

cohabitation has replaced marriage, and members of these couples see more costs than benefits to marrying (McGinnis, 2003). For many cohabiting couples, cohabitation pre-cedes marriage, and its increased social acceptance has made cohabitation a factor in in-timate relationships.

Marriage and divorce have also changed over the past 50 years. The rate of marriages declined between 1980 and 2000. Divorce rates doubled between 1960 and the 1980s, but now have begun to decrease slightly. Figure 9.3 shows these trends.

Despite the increased prevalence of cohabitation, the majority of research on gender and committed relationships has focused on marriage. Several styles of marriage now exist, following the patterns Cancian (1987) called the Companionship, Independence, and In-terdependence blueprints. The Companionship blueprint discussed earlier was the model for most marriages in the United States from the 1920s until the 1960s. Partners who fol-low this pattern tend to have well-defined and separate gender roles, with women respon-

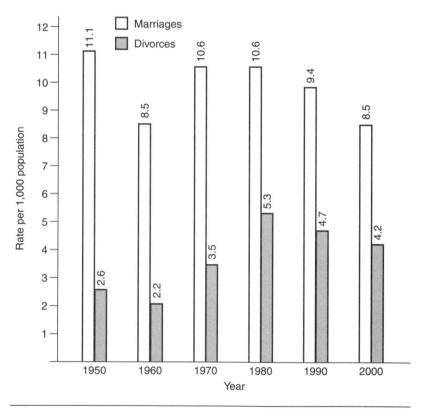

FIGURE 9.3   *Trends in Marriage and Divorce in the United States, 1950–2000*

Source: Data from *Statistical Abstracts of the United States, 2002* (122nd ed.) (p. 59), U.S. Bureau of the Census, 2002, Washington, DC: U.S. Government Printing Office.

sible for maintaining the love relationship. This type of marriage is now considered traditional, because its adherents oppose self-development for women, a major tenet of the Independence blueprint.

The Independence blueprint arose during the 1960s, a period that emphasized personal freedom and change. Increases in paid employment for women and the women's movement led to an examination of the ground rules for relationships, and both men and women started to believe that marriage should be a partnership of equals. This model emphasizes self-development over commitment and obligations, holding that relationships are the meeting of two independent individuals. The emphasis on self-development resulted in less well-defined gender roles, and the concept of androgynous marriage arose. Cancian criticized this blueprint for encouraging empty relationships without sufficient commitment.

Interdependence is an alternative to the Independence blueprint. The Interdependence model also includes flexible gender roles, but calls for commitment based on mutual dependence. Cancian argued that self-development and interdependence were compatible goals for relationships, and that partners are always dependent on each other in marriage. Both the Companionship and Independence blueprints ignore this inevitable interdependence. Table 9.1 shows the three blueprints and the important characteristics of each.

Sternberg's (1986) triangular model of love explains these different blueprints for marriage as differing in the three components of intimacy, passion, and commitment. Companionship-style marriages would have all three components but not in equal proportion for men and women. Under this blueprint, women seek more intimacy than men, producing an unequal balance between such partners. As Cancian contended, the Independence blueprint lacks the component of commitment, but Interdependent marriages should fit what Sternberg called consummate love, the equal balance of all three components.

Marriages and other committed relationships may follow any of the blueprints, and contemporary couples may build any of these various types of relationships. However, a longitudinal study of expectations for marriage (Botkin, Weeks, & Morris, 2000) revealed that changes have occurred in women's conceptualizations of marriage. Between the 1960s and the 1970s, a large shift occurred toward beliefs in egalitarian marriages. After the 1970s, those beliefs have persisted, and the percentage of college women who believe in

TABLE 9.1   *Cancian's Blueprints for Love Relationships*

	Companionship (devotion to each other)	Independence (self-development)	Interdependence (mutual dependence)
Are traditional gender roles maintained?	Yes	No	No
Is the relationship stable?	Yes	No	Yes
Who is responsible for maintaining the relationship?	Women	Neither partner	Both partners
Who develops personal interests?	Men	Both partners	Both partners

egalitarian marriage relationships is over 90%. This percentage has implications for several facets of committed relationships, including men's and women's concepts of romantic love and marriage, communication between partners, division of labor in households, power and conflict in marriage, and the stability of love relationships.

Concepts of Love and Marriage.   Contrary to popular expectation (see "According to the Media" and "According to the Research"), men have more traditional concepts of love and marriage and are more romantic than women. Although men and women tend to choose partners who have similarly traditional or nontraditional beliefs about gender roles, the man of any given couple is likely to be more traditional than the woman and more likely than women to endorse statements such as "Women's activities should be confined to the home" (Glick & Fiske, 2001). This tendency for men to be more traditional concerning gender roles appears in many cultures (Hatfield & Rapson, 1996), but some research (Mirowsky & Ross, 1987) has indicated that these discrepancies become smaller through the years of marriage. The continued association of marriage partners does not produce identical beliefs, however, and the majority of the differences remain. Thus, even after years of marriage, husbands are more likely than wives to hold traditional, conservative beliefs about gender roles.

Men's idealized romantic beliefs extend across ethnic groups in the United States and exist in China (Sprecher & Toto-Mourn, 2002). For example, men are more likely to have romantic beliefs such as "Love lasts forever" and "There is one perfect love in the world for everyone." Women, however, are more likely to report physical symptoms of being in

▨ ACCORDING TO THE MEDIA . . .

Bad Men Can Be Transformed by Women's Love

Movies are filled with images of selfish, roguish scoundrels transformed into heroes by women's love (Aronson & Kimmel, 1997). Self-absorbed scoundrel Rick Blaine (played by Humphrey Bogart) becomes a hero in the film *Casablanca* out of love for Elsa (Ingrid Bergman). Indeed, his love was so great that he gave up that love for the Allied cause—a true hero. Charlie Allnut (again, Humphrey Bogart) is transformed from a drunk into a hero by the love of Rose (Katharine Hepburn) in *The African Queen*. Humphrey Bogart was not the only actor who played this transformation repeatedly; the image of a scoundrel who becomes a hero is a movie staple.

Women have been affected by these portrayals, coming to believe that their love has the power to transform a bad man into a good one. *New York Times* columnist Anna Quindlen (reported in Aronson & Kimmel, 1997) asked female readers to choose a mate—either a kind, faithful, careful man or a roguish, self-interested scoundrel, and the vote was overwhelmingly for the nice guy. When she identified one as Ashley Wilkes and the other as Rhett Butler, however, some women felt differently. One woman said, "Well, that's different. . . . Rhett Butler's never been loved by me. When I love him, he'll change" (Aronson & Kimmel, 1997, p. 32). This quotation demonstrates the idealization of love and the extent to which some women believe in the media-based romantic fantasy of the transformational power of their love.

love, such as feeling like they are "floating on a cloud." In other ways, men and women are similar in idealizing love, believing that love and mutual attraction are the most important factors for marriage

Romanticism does not necessarily make men feel more favorably toward marriage (Whitehead & Popenoe, 2002). Men are supposed to elude marriage, considering it a "trap," whereas women are perceived as planning and scheming to "land a husband." Despite men's lack of enthusiasm for marriage, married men are physically and mentally healthier than single men (de Vaus, 2002). Married women may experience more satisfaction from marriage than men do (Kiecolt-Glaser & Newton, 2001), but they also find more stresses in their marriages and do not show the same level of health benefits (Sachs-Ericsson & Ciarlo, 2000). Both women and men tend to find marriage a more satisfying experience than cohabitation (Moore, McCabe, & Brink, 2001).

Most of the studies of marital satisfaction have questioned only European American participants, however, and this choice has limited the conclusions about attitudes toward marriage (Ball & Robbins, 1986). Investigating marital satisfaction among African Americans showed that married African American women were more satisfied with their lives than single women were, but this difference disappeared when these researchers controlled for demographic factors such as age and health. Thus, the positive attitudes about marriage may be attributable to factors associated with marriage, such as having a stable life and financial security, rather than to positive feelings about marriage itself. The life satisfaction of African American men, on the other hand, was lower among married than single men, and these differences did not disappear when controlling for demographic factors. These

◼ ACCORDING TO THE RESEARCH . . .

Bad Men Are Dangerous to the Women Who Love Them

When women hope to change bad men through love, they put themselves in danger of being victimized by these men. Perhaps some scoundrels change through love, but many remain scoundrels who harm the women who love them. Some abused women are in positions that offer them limited options to leave their situations, but others choose to stay with abusive men (Heise, Ellsberg, & Gottemoeller, 1999). Women may be reluctant to leave their abusive partners, partly for the reasons that attracted them to their partners. In addition, the notions that "he will change" and "this time will be the last time he will hit/be unfaithful to/humiliate me" allow women to believe that their abusive partners will change (as they often promise) to become the men these women fantasized.

Women who do leave their abusive partners do not necessarily escape the danger they have experienced. Indeed, women who leave their abusive partners are at increased risk for harm (Tjaden & Thoennes, 2000a). Angry, resentful, or jealous former partners may stalk and do violence to the women who have left them. Indeed, women are more likely to be killed by an intimate partner during a separation than when living with these violent men. Staying with them is also dangerous—women experience over 1.3 million physical assaults from male partners each year. Therefore, the romantic notion that the love of a woman can transform a bad man into a good one appears more often in movies than in daily life.

results suggest that African American men may differ from African American women and European American couples in their feelings of satisfaction in marriage.

Communication between Partners.   The issue of couples' communication in marriage has received an enormous amount of publicity. Indeed, it has become an industry; John Gray's (1992) *Men Are from Mars, Women Are from Venus* topped the best-seller list for years, prompting sequels, and allowing Gray to hold seminars, train other counselors, and present a Broadway show based on the concept. His concept of men and women from different planets originated from his advice to women to communicate with their husbands as if they were beings from another planet. Gray's characterization of men and women from different planets is an overstatement of gender differences in communication, but differences do exist.

The same gender differences that researchers have found in friendship styles also influence communication in marriage: Women create emotional intimacy through talk and self-disclosure, whereas men do so through activity. In marriage, sex is often the activity that men use to create intimacy. Cancian (1987) argued that in most contemporary couples, wives do not count sex as communication or as a method for establishing intimacy. This difference can produce a discrepancy in what each thinks is the level of communication in their relationship. Her survey of couples revealed that wives value talking about feelings more than husbands do, but husbands may feel threatened when their wives want to talk. "Talking about the relationship as she wants to do will feel to him like taking a test that she has made up and he will fail" (Cancian, 1987, p. 93).

Communication is a major task for couples, and research confirms that people hold stereotypical views of women's and men's styles of communication. For example, the belief that women's speech is more emotional than men's remains an influential stereotype, although it has decreased over the past 25 years (Popp, Donovan, Crawford, Marsh, & Peele, 2003). People also believe that women will be more likely to show sympathy and communicate their support in problem situations (Basow & Rubenfeld, 2003). However, this research showed that gender role was more important than gender in willingness to provide help.

The differences between men's and women's typical styles of communication provide one potential source of conflict in marriage. Deborah Tannen (1990) examined the barriers to communication for men and women, citing different strategies for men and women even when the goals are similar. Tannen argued that men and women see communication as "a continual balancing act, juggling the conflicting needs for intimacy and independence" (p. 27). She contended that women's communication is oriented toward intimacy, focusing on forming communal connections with others, whereas men's communication is oriented toward hierarchy, focusing on attaining and demonstrating status.

The differences in communication styles make it difficult for women and men to talk to each other. Both interpret the underlying messages as well as the words, and the differences in styles may lead men and women to understand messages that their partners did not intend to send. For example, Tannen cited an example of a husband who had failed to tell his wife about a pain he had been feeling in his arm. When his wife found out, she was very upset with him for withholding information that was important to her. She felt excluded from his life. He had not intended to exclude her from anything important, but instead had wanted to protect her from worrying about his health. Tannen contended that such miscommunication is common for women and men and constitutes a persistent problem for couples.

According to Tannen, learning the conversational style of the other is not the answer to all communication problems. She described sensitivity training as an attempt to teach the conversational style of women to men, and assertiveness training as a method to teach the conversational style of men to women. Although flexibility of styles has benefits, Tannen expressed pessimism concerning changes in communication that would blend these divergent styles—both women and men like their ways of communicating.

Thus, men and women tend to differ in style of intimate communication and in verbal styles. Women's reliance on self-disclosure and communal, empathic communication varies from men's reliance on sex and their competitive, hierarchical communication style. These differences can cause misunderstanding rather than foster communication, and women's subordinate role has an impact on many facets of the relationship.

Division of Household Labor. The division of household labor has become an area of interest to gender researchers, and their results have revealed another potential source of conflict for couples—an unequal division of this labor. Traditional gender roles include a division of labor in households, with men working outside the home for wages, and women working in the home providing housekeeping and child care. This division arose during the Industrial Revolution, when men started working for wages rather than working in agricultural or home-based trades, and domesticity became associated with women. Throughout the 20th century, however, an increasing number of women joined the paid workforce. Now, a majority of women, even those with young children, work for wages outside the home.

The changes in paid labor for women should have prompted a concomitant change in the division of housework, but those changes have been slow in coming. Researchers who examined division of household labor during the 1970s and 1980s found that employed women still performed the large majority of household labor (Coltrane, 2000). Sociologist Arlie Hochschild (1989) called this arrangement the Second Shift, an arrangement in which women work for wages outside the home plus perform the majority of housework and child-care chores at home. This arrangement can result in a situation in which women work the equivalent number of hours of two full-time jobs. According to an extensive review completed during the 1980s (Thompson & Walker, 1989), wives did about three times more housework and child care than husbands. A more recent review (Coltrane, 2000) noted some changes, with women doing less and men doing somewhat more household work. However, women still perform about twice as much household work as men do.

Many factors contribute to the inequity. A very important factor is the belief that household work is gendered—some chores are "women's work" and others are "men's jobs" (Coltrane, 2000). The five most time-consuming chores (meal preparation, housecleaning, shopping for groceries, washing dishes, and doing laundry) are all work associated with women. Men's chores tend to be less time-consuming and less frequently required (household repairs, taking out the trash, mowing the lawn). When couples adhere to this gendered division of labor, women do far more work than men.

Women's employment is another important factor in household division of labor. When women are employed, they do less household work (Coltrane, 2000). Wives who have high-status, highly paid employment (such as professional or managerial jobs) also experience increased power in their marriages, and this increased power may give these wives the freedom to do less housework (Deutsch, Roksa, & Meeske, 2003). High income does not always equate to high power for women, but earning a high salary is an advantage for women in their marriages.

Several demographic variables are also factors, including marital status, education, and presence of children (Coltrane, 2000). Being married increases the amount of household work that women do and decreases the amount men do. Education also shows different patterns of influence for women and men. Women with higher levels of education tend to do less household work than women with lower levels of education, but men with higher levels of education are likely to do more household work than men with lower levels of education. The presence of children increases women's work and decreases men's household work, probably because women tend to decrease and men tend to increase their employment when children are born.

Gender role attitudes are also important in who does the dishes. Men are unlikely to do much household work unless both they and their wives hold egalitarian attitudes (Greenstein, 1996). That is, the interaction of husbands' and wives' attitudes determined whether husbands performed housework. When husbands or wives held traditional gender role attitudes, men did little work around the house. Even when men held egalitarian beliefs but their wives did not, men still avoided chores. That situation may not persist. A recent study (Donaghue & Fallon, 2003) showed that women who do not conform to gender stereotypes (as an increasing number do not) were most dissatisfied with the prospect of being the underbenefitted partner in a relationship. Men who did conform to gender stereotypes were upset at the thought of giving up their privileged status. Table 9.2 summarizes some of the factors that relate to sharing of household work.

These attitudes seem to forecast trouble for some people in their relationships, and signs of that trouble have appeared. Marital satisfaction has decreased over the past 20 years for both men and women (Rogers & Amato, 2000). An analysis of the factors that relate to this decrease pinpointed dissatisfaction with relationship inequities, including conflicts between work and family and an unfair sharing of household work. Indeed, this analysis indicated that if men had not increased the amount of household work they do, the dissatisfaction would be higher.

Household labor may also be divided according to the demands of the family's situation. For example, women who work the evening shift may have to go to work immediately after an early dinner, leaving their husbands and families with the night-time chores. Shift work is more common in working-class than middle-class or upper-middle-class families, making working-class couples somewhat more likely to share equally in housework than more affluent couples (Hochschild, 1997; Coltrane, 2000). Although working-class men do not have more egalitarian attitudes than other men, their family situations may push them toward a greater sharing of household work. Therefore, social class is an important indicator in family patterns of housework.

Ethnicity is not an important factor in attitudes toward family work. In a study of couples from a variety of ethnic groups (Stohs, 2000), conflict over household work was

TABLE 9.2 *Factors Related to Division of Household Work*

Men Do More Household Work When	Men Do Less Household Work When
Wives are employed outside the home	Wives are not employed outside the home
Wives earn money that husbands consider important to household	Chores are "feminine"
Both wives and husbands have high educational levels	Husbands or wives hold traditional gender role beliefs
Wives' shiftwork schedule requires husbands' cooperation	They are married, especially in first marriages
Both husbands and wives hold egalitarian beliefs	A first child is born
Husbands believe that it is fair to share household work	
Chores are "masculine"	
Timing of task is flexible	

common. The Hispanic American women worked fewer hours per week in their jobs outside the home than African American or Asian American women did, which might lead them to feel less burdened by doing more household chores. However, the feeling that husbands were not doing a fair share of household work was shared among all ethnic groups.

The differences in division of household labor by social class and gender role attitudes may relate to the differences of power in these couples. Working-class wives' economic contributions are more essential to their families' subsistence than middle-class wives' salaries. By making essential contributions, these women may gain power in their marriages, and their husbands may respond to the more equal balance of power by sharing housework. For example, middle-class Hispanic American wives whose income made them coproviders were more likely to get their husbands' help than were women who contributed less to family income (Coltrane & Valdez, 1993). However, husbands' assistance was not easy to get; even the husbands who acknowledged the importance of their wives' income were often reluctant to do household chores and child care, using their own job demands as an excuse for not contributing to household work.

The notion of inequity is important within the issue of household work. A large majority of women and most men believe in an equitable distribution of household work (Van Willigen & Drentea, 2001). During the 1970s and 1980s, researchers found that wives perceived that their husbands were not doing a fair share of household work, but they found rationalizations to allow themselves to think of this inequitable contribution as "fair" (Coltrane, 2000). That situation changed during the 1990s, and researchers began to find that women reported increasing dissatisfaction with an inequitable distribution of household work. Men tended to agree. Thus, those who are performing too much and also those who are doing too little household work tend to feel uncomfortable with the inequity. Married couples allot tasks primarily on the basis of gender, but gay and lesbian couples cannot use this strategy and use different methods to determine who does what chores (Kurdek, 1993; Peplau & Spalding, 2000). Both gay and lesbian couples tended to share household work more equitably than heterosexual married couples, but the patterns of sharing differed. Gay couples were more likely to split tasks, with each partner performing a set of chores. Lesbian couples were more likely to alternate in sharing tasks, taking turns in performing the same chores.

Division of chores has become a more prominent topic of research and a more heated issue among couples (Coltrane, 2000; Stohs, 2000; Van Willigen & Drentea, 2001). Between 25% and 33% of wives believe that their husbands are not doing a fair share of housework and want them to do more. Even a mutual desire to share household work may not allow husbands and wives to negotiate this problem to the satisfaction of both. The increasing desire for equity in contributions to household work and the continuation of inequity are a prescription for conflict. Thus, the issue of household work may be related to both power and conflict within marriages.

Power and Conflict.   Most dating couples believe that marriages should be an equal sharing of power and decision making, but the members of these couples acknowledged that their own relationships failed to show an equal balance of power (Felmlee, 1994; Sprecher, 2001; Sprecher & Felmlee, 1997). Although a large majority of both women and men said that they believed each partner should have an equal voice in the relationship, just less than half reported equal power in their relationships. This finding suggests that, even before couples marry, the balance of power tends to be unequal. A longitudinal study (Sprecher & Felmlee, 1997) indicated that the power imbalances are fairly stable over time.

For those couples whose relationships are not equal in power, traditional gender roles dictate that the man will be the leader and head of the household. This division may relate to an overall desire for dominance among men, called social dominance orientation (Sidanius, Pratto, & Bobo, 1994). This view holds that as a group, men endorse the superiority of some groups over others and also believe in a hierarchical structure between social groups. This orientation tends to make men more likely than women to attempt to dominate and to try to oppress those who are not members of their group. Thus men will attempt to maintain a dominance over women.

Current relationships often reflect traditional gender roles, and men are likely to have more power in marriages than women. According to an extensive survey of couples by Philip Blumstein and Pepper Schwartz (1983), almost 64% reported an equal balance of power. The remaining couples reported an unequal balance of power in their marriages— 28% of husbands and 9% of wives said they had more power. Other studies have shown a higher percentage of male dominance in heterosexual couples (Peplau & Campbell, 1989; Sprecher & Felmlee, 1997). One study (Sprecher & Felmlee, 1997) measured the discrepancy between power and decision making in dating couples and found that men's decision-making power was higher than their overall power. In addition, both male and female partners rated men's decision-making power as well as men's overall power as higher than women's decision-making and overall power. Table 9.3 shows the power structure in couples according to three studies.

TABLE 9.3   *Ideal and Actual Power Structure in Couples*

	Peplau and Campbell Study (1989)		Blumstein and Schwartz (1983)	Sprecher and Felmlee Study (1997)	
	Men	*Women*	*Couples*	*Men*	*Women*
Believe in equal power	87%	95%			
Have equal power	42	49	64%	47%	48%
Husband has more power			28	35	29
Wife has more power			9	19	24

One drawback of a majority of research is the educational and ethnic composition of the participants: Couples are often college-educated, and most are White. A consideration of other ethnic groups brings other factors relating to power. The concepts of **matriarchy** and **machismo** have been associated with African American and Hispanic American families, respectively. A review of research on families, however, found that both patterns of unequal power were more myths than descriptions of the actual balance of power in these families (Peplau & Campbell, 1989). African American families are more likely to be headed by women than White families, but Black couples do not have significantly different power relationships in the family than White couples do. An equal sharing of power, the most common pattern in Blumstein and Schwartz's study, was also the most common pattern in African American couples. For couples with an unequal balance of power, male dominance was more common than female dominance. The same patterns appeared in Mexican American families, with the most common pattern being one of shared power. Despite the prominence of the concepts of matriarchy and machismo, a fairly equal balance of power seems to be the rule for most couples in the United States, regardless of ethnic group.

Saying that couples exhibit an equal balance of power does not mean that both partners have an equal say in all decisions. Decision-making power may be divided along traditional lines, with men making financial decisions and women making household decisions. What couples report as an equal balance of power may actually be a division of decision making into husbands' and wives' domains. This division may reflect wives' lack of real power; wives may be put into the position of making decisions that their husbands consider too trivial for their own attention. For example, wives may decide what to have for dinner and what brand of cleaning products to use, and husbands may decide which house to buy and where to live.

Paid employment is a factor in the balance of power in marriage. Women who do not have paid employment tend to have less power in their marriages than women who earn money (Deutsch et al., 2003; Steil, 2000). The amount earned is also a factor: Husbands who earn more money have more power. However, husbands do not receive as much appreciation for earning money as wives do (Deutsch et al., 2003), mostly likely because it is an expected part of their breadwinner role.

Wives' earnings show a complex relationship to power in their marriage. In working-class couples, wives who earn more money tend to have more power, but middle-class wives may not gain power by making money (Tichenor, 1999). These differences may have to do with the necessity of wives' earning income in the two social classes. Working-class wives' salaries are more likely to provide essential incomes, whereas middle-class wives' salaries may not be as necessary to their families. When husbands acknowledge the importance of their wives' salaries, this acknowledgment may give wives more power. In the growing number of families in which wives earn more than their husbands, the balance of power does not necessarily tip in the wives' favor. Wives receive appreciation for their earnings, but husbands may minimize wives' contributions, even when those contributions are greater than their own. Therefore, wives who earn no income have low power, and earning money brings increased power, but achieving marital power through income is difficult for women and easy for men to achieve.

Lesbian and gay male couples also experience power differentials, also related to money (Peplau & Spalding, 2000). In Blumstein and Schwartz's (1983) survey and other investigations, money appeared as an important factor in the power equation for these couples. For gay men and lesbians, both partners typically are employed, but incomes may be unequal.

◼ GENDERED VOICES

When I Got Sober

"The balance of power in my marriage didn't change when I went to work, but when I got sober," a woman in her 40s told me. She had been a homemaker for a number of years before she started a career, and she said that earning money didn't make much of a change in her marriage. By the time she began her job, she had already started drinking heavily, and she continued to do so.

"Everybody took care of me, so I could drink and take drugs and get away with it. So I did. My daughter took care of me for most of her childhood. My husband also let me get away with being drunk most of the time. I was dependent on them, but then I got sober, and things changed.

"When I got sober, I started being able to take care of myself, and my family wasn't used to it. The balance of power changed in my marriage, and we eventually split up. I was sober and involved in AA, and my husband was still drinking, but that wasn't the main problem. I started to become independent, and he couldn't adjust. I realize that it was quite an adjustment: I had never taken care of myself—never in my life—and then I started.

"I remember one incident in particular. I was trying to change the batteries in my small tape recorder, and my husband came over and took the recorder out of my hands and did it for me. I thought, 'I can do that for myself.' I started thinking that about a lot of things. As I started to become more independent, our marriage changed. In fact, our entire family changed, and most of those changes were good. The kids could come to me rather than go to their father for everything. I became a responsible person. With that responsibility came a growing desire to be independent, and now I am. The marriage became an emotional power struggle, with my growing self-reliance and my husband still trying to be in control."

For gay men, the relationship between money and relationship power was clear—those with more money had more power. The relationship between money and power was less clear for lesbians, who tried to maintain an equal monetary contribution in their relationship so as to avoid unequal power. The failure to do so was a source of problems for these women.

How couples resolve conflicts reflects differentials in power. The partner who has more power tends to behave in different ways than the partner whose power is less. Indeed, an examination of conflict resolution strategies can reveal the power dynamics in a relationship (Gottman & Notarius, 2000). Women are more likely to start a marital conflict discussion and to direct that discussion, but women reported that this behavior did not reflect their feelings of power. To the contrary, women said that their strategies were aimed mostly at avoiding upsetting their husbands.

Another study examining conflict resolution (Neff & Harter, 2002) also revealed women's strategy to avoid upsetting men, sometimes at the expense of hiding their own true feelings. This study found few gender differences in the likelihood to use any of three strategies: compromise, place personal needs over partner's needs, or subordinate personal needs to the partner's wishes. Both women and men reported compromise as their most frequent strategy, saying that relationships consist of "give and take." A similar percentage of women and men said that they put their own wishes and desires first and that they subordinated their own preferences to their partner's wishes. However, the reasons that men and women were self-sacrificing differed significantly. When men subordinated their wishes to their partner's, they were more likely to do so out of genuine feelings for their partners. When women were self-sacrificing, they were much more likely to be acting in ways to avoid conflict with their partners. These different reasons reflect discrepant power in relationships and the pressure that women feel to avoid conflict.

Are women justified in taking steps to avoid conflict? Men tend to display more coercive styles of conflict resolution than women (Gottman & Notarius, 2000), which can constitute the first step toward couples violence. Historically, domestic violence has been considered appropriate, with women as targets of marital (and even premarital) violence in many societies and throughout many time periods (Bonvillain, 1998; Jewkes, 2002). Even though physical abuse is not the most common method of resolving conflicts in contemporary relationships, violence is not unusual between married, cohabiting, or even dating partners (Silverman, Raj, Mucci, & Hathaway, 2001). Both men and women use violence toward each other, but women are at a disadvantage in physical conflicts with men (Tjaden & Thoennes, 2000a). The rate of violence may even be close to equal for women and men in relationships (Archer, 2000), but the rate of injury is not: Women are much more likely to sustain serious injury as a result of domestic violence.

One way to understand the types of couples violence is to follow Michael Johnson's (1995) distinction between common couples violence and patriarchical terrorism. Johnson used the term *common couples violence* to describe the situation in which conflicts become physical fights. This type of violence is all too common, and women or men may be the instigators; both may behave violently toward the other. *Patriarchical terrorism,* on the other hand, is a severe form of violence that men use to control their families. Such men consider that they should be the unquestioned head of the family and have the right to enact any measure to maintain their dominance.

Contrary to what people may perceive, several national surveys of couples in the United States have revealed a decreasing amount of violence between partners. A survey in the 1980s (Straus & Gelles, 1986) showed 16% of homes reported some kind of violence between spouses within the previous year, which represented a 27% decrease from a similar survey in 1975. An examination of crime victimization records (Rennnison, 2003) revealed that intimate partner violence decreased by more than 40% between 1993 and 2001. Even with this magnitude of decrease, over 700,000 incidents occur each year. The majority of these incidents were minor, but discounting the acts of minor violence in domestic conflict is not wise; even minor violence is predictive of more serious violence between spouses (Feld & Straus, 1989). Furthermore, women who fight back are likely to escalate rather than halt the violence directed toward them.

Unfortunately, many people find some level of violence between partners acceptable. About 25% of wives and over 30% of husbands found violence toward each other acceptable under some circumstances (Straus, Gelles, & Steinmetz, 1980). With these attitudes, the escalation of minor violence to abuse is not surprising, nor is it likely to change.

Marriages in which the partners have an equal balance of power are less likely to involve physical violence than marriages in which one partner is dominant (Jewkes, 2002). Regardless of which partner has more power, both partners are more likely to be the targets of violence in couples with a dominant and a subordinate partner. Inequalities of power promote violent conflict in couples, putting both partners at increased risk.

Therefore, a connection exists between the issues of power and conflict in committed relationships. The majority of couples endorse equal power within their love relationships, but most also acknowledge that their relationships have not attained an equal balance of power. Men are more likely to be dominant than women, as they traditionally occupy the provider role and typically earn more money. Both gender roles and money affect the balance of power in relationships. Power also affects conflict and conflict management. When conflict results in violence, women are more likely than men to be injured in the confrontation. Many women and men find physical violence acceptable as a conflict resolution strategy under some circumstances, an attitude that perpetuates domestic violence.

Stability of Relationships.   Relationships that involve physical violence are less stable than those with no violence, but some of these violent relationships endure. Many people find it difficult to imagine why a woman would stay with a man who repeatedly abuses her, but some women do (Eisikovits, Winstok, & Gelles, 2002). Abusive men often work to isolate their wives from family and friends, depriving them of social support and alternative residences (Heise, Ellsberg, & Gottemoeller, 1999; Jewkes, 2002). Abused women who are unemployed, with few marketable skills and young children in need of financial support, may feel as though they have no options except to stay in the relationship, no matter how abusive. With the rise of shelters for women to escape abusive homes, abused women have an option, and thousands take this option each year.

Abusive relationships are an extreme case of conflict in love relationships, but all couples experience some level of conflict. These conflicts tend to decrease the stability of a relationship and increase the chances of the relationship ending. Blumstein and Schwartz (1983) found that couples who experienced conflicts over money, wives' employment, power, division of household labor, or sex were more likely to split up than couples who experienced fewer of these conflicts. They found that couples who were married were less likely to break up than cohabiting heterosexual, gay, or lesbian couples, but married couples also tended to have a lower level of conflict except in the early years of marriage. The institution of marriage often holds couples together when they might otherwise dissolve their relationships.

Couples who do not have the support of the institution behind them, such as gay men and lesbians, are thus more likely to part (Kurdek, 1998). However, these couples can stay together; 84% of lesbian couples and 86% of gay male couples were together for at least 5 years. In a study of heterosexual and same-sex couples who had stayed together for an average of 30 years (Mackey, Diemer, & O'Brien, 2000), several factors were related to psychological intimacy and continuation of the relationship, including lack of conflict, method of handling conflict, quality of communication, equity, and expression of affection. Lesbians reported their relationships as closer than did gay men or heterosexuals.

Similarity is not only a factor in attraction, it is also a factor in the stability of relationships. Dating couples are more likely to stay together if their attitudes match rather than conflict (Felmlee, 1994; Hendrick, Hendrick, & Adler, 1988). Similarities diminish the frequency of differences of opinion and other conflicts. Experiencing conflicts is related to decreased satisfaction in relationships (Cramer, 2002). The number of conflicts mattered but the magnitude did not; either minor or major conflicts contributed to lower ratings of satisfaction with the relationship.

As the headline story for this chapter related, conflict, even heated conflict, is not necessarily threatening to the stability of marriages. John Gottman (1991, 1998) and his colleagues (Gottman & Notarius, 2000; Levenson, Carstensen, & Gottman, 1994) have investigated the elements and styles of conflicts that strengthen relationships as well as those that signal problems in relationships over the long run. Surprisingly, their research indicated that marital satisfaction was not a strong predictor of separation, but that the level of physical arousal during conflict was. That is, couples whose heart rates, blood pressure, sweating, and physical movement during an argument were elevated were more likely to separate within the next 3 years than couples with lower levels of arousal. Couples whose physiological reactions were calmer tended to have marriages that improved over a 3-year span.

Behavioral factors also predicted divorce, including wives' tendency to be overly agreeable and compliant, and husbands' tendency to stonewall by withdrawing emotionally, avoiding eye contact, holding the neck rigid, and being unresponsive to their wives during an argument. In their conversations, both members of couples who were likely to separate were more defensive; additionally, the wives complained and criticized more and the husbands disagreed more than did couples who remained together. The couples who were headed toward separation also showed different facial expressions during their conversations, the most important of which was wives' expressions of disgust. Husbands' fear also related to later separation, as did a facial expression Gottman called the "miserable smile," a smile that affected only the mouth, as when people try to "put on a happy face." Gottman concluded that the couples who would later separate were in the process of dissolving their relationship emotionally, and their physiological reactions, conflict tactics, and facial expressions signaled their impending separation. Table 9.4 summarizes these factors.

TABLE 9.4 *Factors Relating to Marital Separation*

Factor	Prediction
Marital satisfaction	No strong relationship to separation
Physical arousal during conflict—heart rate, blood pressure, sweating, moving	Higher levels predict increased likelihood of separation; calmer reactions predict strengthening of relationship
Wives being overly agreeable	Increased likelihood of separation
Husbands participate in housework	Increased satisfaction for husbands and wives; increased health in husbands
Husbands stonewall	Increased likelihood of separation
Wives criticize and complain	Increased likelihood of separation
Husbands disagree with wives	Increased likelihood of separation
Couples are defensive	Increased likelihood of separation
Facial expressions during conflict—"miserable smile," wives' disgust, husbands' fear	Increased likelihood of separation

According to Sternberg's (1986, 1987) triangular theory of love, relationships that have only one of the components should lack stability. Two-component relationships will be less stable than those that have all three. Friendships will be less enduring if only intimacy is present, rather than intimacy plus commitment. Furthermore, love relationships that have two components will be more stable than those with only one. For example, romances that have only the passion component would not last as long as those with both passion and commitment. Indeed, passion alone is the classic "one-night stand," whereas passion plus commitment is a "whirlwind courtship." A combination of all three components in equal proportion would offer the most stability, but maintaining all three components is difficult.

The commitment component of Sternberg's model is the most important for relationship stability. Commitment "can be essential for getting through hard times and for returning to better ones. In ignoring it or separating it from love, one may be missing exactly that component of loving relationships that enables one to get through the hard times as well as the easy ones" (Sternberg, 1986, p. 123).

Dissolving Relationships

Relationships go through phases of attraction, development, and sometimes dissolution. All relationships are subject to these stages, but people expect the dissolution of casual relationships and believe that such breakups pose no problems for the people involved. Unfortunately, even relationships with commitment sometimes fail to endure. When close friendships or love relationships dissolve, the end of such relationships poses problems for both people involved as well as for their social network of friends and family, who must make adjustments in their relationships with the members of the separated couple.

Love relationships without institutional support, such as cohabitation, are more likely to break up than are marriages. Only about 10% of heterosexual cohabiting couples live together long-term without marrying (Brown & Booth, 1996). In two studies of couples (Blumstein & Schwartz, 1983; Kurdek, 1998), married couples were more likely to remain together than gay or lesbian couples. Figure 9.4 shows the separation rates for different types of couples.

The institutional support for marriage is no guarantee of stability for such relationships. Although marriages have never been permanent, divorce increased dramatically over the past 50 years (Hendrick & Hendrick, 1992), hit a high level in the 1980s, decreased slightly, and remains at a high level today (see Figure 9.3). The high divorce rate is not necessarily a condemnation of marriage as much as the failure of women and men to fulfill their vision of what they believe marriage should be. Evidence from studying engaged couples (Bonds-Raacke, Bearden, Carriere, Anderson, & Nicks, 2001) suggests that, compared to dating and married couples, engaged couples have an idealized vision of marriage. This

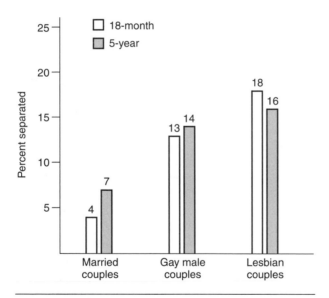

FIGURE 9.4 *Separation Rates for Couples over 18-Month and 5-Year Periods*

Source: The data for 18-month period are from *American Couples,* by Philip Blumstein and Pepper Schwartz, 1983, New York: Pocket Books. The data for 5-year period are from "Relationship Outcomes and Their Predictors: Longitudinal Evidence from Heterosexual Married, Gay Cohabiting, and Lesbian Cohabiting Couples, by Lawrence Kudek, 1998, *Journal of Marriage and Family, 60,* pp. 553–568.

GENDERED VOICES

I Wasn't Any of His Business Anymore

A woman, talking with her friend about her ex-husband, said, "I saw Ed at a country western club last Friday night. He was there with some of his friends, drinking. I went there because I wanted to get out and have some fun. He didn't see me at first, and then he kept looking in my direction, trying to make sure he was seeing right.

"Finally, he came over to me and said, 'What are you doing in a place like this? You shouldn't be here.' I told him that what I did wasn't any of his business anymore. We were divorced, and I could do what I wanted. I didn't need his permission to go to a bar, and he didn't have any right to say anything to me. He said some pretty ugly things, calling me a bitch and a whore, and I just walked away from him. I had enough of his ordering me around when we were married."

idealization may lead couples to unrealistic expectations that build a foundation for conflict. As Gottman's research (1991; Gottman & Notarius, 2000) has indicated, how partners handle conflicts in the early years of marriage is a predictor of divorce.

Two intensive studies tell similar stories about the effects of divorce. One study by Catherine Riessman (1990) was an interview study of divorced men and women, and the other study by Mavis Hetherington (Hetherington & Kelly, 2002), the Virginia Longitudinal Study of Divorce and Remarriage, has lasted over 30 years and followed almost 1,400 families. The studies have revealed similarities in the factors that underlie divorces and the process of recovery. Both studies show that men and women experience similar feelings, but they also show substantial differences in the process of divorce for women and men.

Most people who divorce keep their ideas of marriage and what it should be. That idea often matches what Cancian called the Companionship blueprint for marriage. When they separated and divorced, women and men usually failed to question the blueprint. Rather, they found fault in their own marriages, blaming either their former spouses or themselves for failing to fulfill some component of their marital ideal.

Although divorced men and women both described failures to live up to their ideals, their descriptions showed some variation according to gender. Both women and men saw failures in achieving emotional intimacy, but each attributed the failures to different reasons. Women tended to say that their husbands had not talked and shared feelings with them as they had expected. They claimed their husbands just didn't communicate with them.

Divorced men largely agreed with this assessment, blaming themselves for not communicating with their former wives and maintaining that they had difficulties in talking about their feelings and sharing the important elements of their work. Divorced men also believed that their wives had failed to give them emotional support, which they tended to define as physical affection. The working-class men in one study (Riessman, 1990) repeatedly said that their wives were not waiting "with their arms open and a kiss" when the men came home from work. Such physical manifestations of intimacy were lacking, re-

■ GENDERED VOICES

My Ex-Wife Acts Like We're Still Married

"Although we were divorced three years ago, my ex-wife acts like we're still married," a man in his mid-30s said. "I understand why she calls me when something involves the kids, but she calls me when she needs things done to the house." He considered these requests inap- propriate because he and his ex-wife had both remar- ried. "I can't help it if she married a wuss who can't fix the toilet. I don't think she should be calling me to do the chores. We're not married anymore, and taking care of her house is not part of my job now."

sulting in their feelings that their marriages lacked emotional intimacy. These gender-re- lated differences reflect the talk-based versus action-based styles of showing support that are typical of women and men and highlight the importance of these differences in the dis- solution of relationships.

The relationships of divorced people also failed to meet their expectations in other ways, including a lack of shared interests, feelings that the partner did not come first, al- coholism, physical abuse, and extramarital sexual affairs. The lack of shared interests pulled partners in different directions, and the lack of primacy made partners feel unim- portant. Alcoholism, physical abuse, and extramarital affairs did not necessarily end rela- tionships, but the lack of rewards from the partner combined with these factors pushed couples toward divorce (Hetherington & Kelly, 2002).

The divorced people in both studies mentioned problems with sex in connection with their divorce. The men mentioned dissatisfaction with the frequency of sex and resentment over their wives' refusal to have sex as often as husbands wanted. Sexual affairs were a fac- tor in 34% of the divorced people in Riessman's study, and both women and men believed that affairs had been the impetus for the dissolution of their marriage. The women took their own as well as their husbands' affairs as a sign of emotional betrayal, signaling that their marriage was over. The men did not necessarily share that attitude, but they also ac- knowledged that affairs had been a factor in their divorces. Wives found it difficult to for- give husbands' affairs, and wives who had had affairs tended to leave their husbands for their lovers.

These feelings suggest that women might be the ones to initiate breakups, and find- ings from the Virginia Longitudinal Study confirmed this finding, stating that women ini- tiate about two thirds of the breakups of heterosexual couples. This gender difference may be due to women's tendency to be more vigilant about monitoring their relationships so that they know when something is going wrong more quickly than men do. This finding highlights a substantial asymmetry in love relationships: Women fall out of love more quickly and fall in love more slowly than men do.

Women and men both experience different lives after the dissolution of a love rela- tionship. For couples who have been married or have cohabited, the dissolution of the re- lationship is usually financially as well as emotionally difficult. Women's lower earning power coupled with their custody of children tends to create financial hardship, whereas men's financial position tends to improve after divorce. Women's increasing earning power has moderated the financial impact of divorce (McKeever & Wolfinger, 2001), and women are not as financially disadvantaged following divorce as they were in the 1980s and earlier (Hoffman & Duncan, 1988). However, divorce poses financial difficulties, especially for women and children.

Men and women find positive as well as negative consequences as a result of the divorce experience. Both said they enjoyed the freedom that came with divorce, but their feelings had different sources: Women liked being free from their husbands' dominance, whereas the men liked being free of their wives' expectations. The women in both divorce studies experienced more positive as well as more negative emotions in connection with their divorces than the men experienced. However, women were more likely than men to find something positive about the experience. Men were more likely to "lose" in the divorce, finding nothing positive in the experience and being deprived of their family life. The women experienced more symptoms of depression, but they also discovered heightened self-esteem and feelings of competence through performing activities their husbands had done when they were married.

Dissolution of marriage often deprives men not only of companionship and emotional support from their wives, but also of their children and of their network of friends and family (a network typically maintained by women). Women tend to use these support networks after divorce, but men do not. The men in Riessman's study (1990) were surprised at the difficulties of being alone, but they also described feelings of satisfaction from their developing competencies in domestic chores.

Divorced men and women are likely to feel displeased with their ex-spouses rather than with marriage itself, and most showed their endorsement of marriage by remarrying (Hetherington & Kelly, 2002). Second marriages may differ from first marriages, but these marriages show many more similarities than differences (Allen, Baucom, Burnett, Epstein, & Rankin-Esquer, 2001). People in second marriages endorsed an equal sharing of power and the value of communication but differed in their value for autonomy in financial matters, child-rearing decisions, and friendships outside the marriage. Second marriages are even more likely to end in divorce than first marriages, which Riessman (1990) interpreted as an increased unwillingness to endure an unhappy relationship combined with the knowledge that divorce offered positive as well as negative experiences.

CONSIDERING DIVERSITY

The blueprints for marriage have changed over time in the United States (Cancian, 1987). In the 1800s, the Family Duty blueprint was the rule: Couples often entered arranged marriages for economic reasons, and their feelings revolved around a sense of duty to each other and their children. Looking further back into history and to other cultures, Nancy Bonvillain (1998) analyzed gender and marriage in a variety of settings, contrasting male-dominated and egalitarian societies. Her analysis pointed to economics as an important factor in the power that women have in their marriages and in the society in general.

In societies in which women contribute significantly to household subsistence, the women have power in their personal relationships. For example, the Ju/'hoansi are a society of foraging people who live in Botswana and Namibia. Ju/'hoansi society has differences in gender roles and behaviors, but women's foraging is essential to band survival, and this contribution is reflected in Ju/'hoansi women's full participation in social decisions. Parents typically arrange marriages between an older man who has gained some success as a hunter and a younger woman, which can tip the balance of power in favor of men. However, recently married couples live with the woman's family for the first years of marriage, and this arrangement protects women from male domination and violence.

The Inuit of Arctic North America are also a foraging band society, but they have a male-dominated culture (Bonvillain, 1998). Again, an economic analysis showed that the scarcity of foods to gather results in men's hunting as the main source of the food for these people. In Inuit society, women are forbidden to hunt. Consequently, women's contributions are perceived as less important, and their status is lower. In addition, the Inuit have a preference for couples' living in proximity to the husbands' family, leaving wives with no automatic allies. Wife beating is common and accepted, and husbands practice sexual exchange of wives for husbands' economic benefit.

For larger and more complex societies, the economic analysis still seems to reflect women's status and power within relationships. In tribal societies, both egalitarian and male-dominated societies have existed. When Europeans arrived in North America, the Iroquois allowed women access to economic resources, whereas the Yanomamo of Brazil and Venezuela were a tribal society that did not allow such access. These two societies showed the predicted patterns of egalitarianism and male dominance, respectively. In even larger and more complex groups such as state and industrialized societies, the restriction of economic production to men gives them power and puts women in the position of subordinates in many ways, including in marriages.

Bonvillain contended that when women's contributions are seen as minor, their status is lower, and they have little power in their relationships. Lack of power manifests itself in the inability to leave unhappy marriages or to avoid physical abuse. A cross-cultural analysis of violence against women (Heise et al., 1999) also related domestic violence to societies with strong male dominance. Consistent with Bonvillain's view, this analysis cited financial dependence and restriction of access to resources as contributors to domestic violence.

Examining domestic violence against women across cultures revealed a great deal of variation in the percentage of women who reported abuse (Heise et al., 1999). In cultures that endorse men's right to control women and to "discipline" wives, the rates of abuse were high—over 40% of women in studies conducted in Turkey, New Guinea, Ethiopia, Uganda, India, and Nicaragua reported physical abuse by their intimate partners. In societies that support abuse against women, men (and sometimes women too) find a variety of justifications for abuse, including failure to obey husbands' orders, asking for money, failure to take care of children, suspicion of adultery, or refusing sex. Other societies set stricter limits on domestic violence, and these societies have a lower rate of reported partner violence. Indeed, domestic abuse does not occur in all societies.

Social sanction is not the only factor that relates to domestic violence: Individual, family, and community factors are also important (Heise et al., 1999). These factors are similar around the world. Men who are victims of physical abuse or who observe domestic violence as children are more likely to be abusive as adults. Use of alcohol increases the chances of an individual becoming violent. Within the family context, an imbalance of power promotes violence among couples. At the community level, women's isolation and lack of support increases their chances of being victimized.

Therefore, the cross-cultural analyses of domestic violence have revealed many commonalities among societies and individuals who are abusive to intimate partners. Another commonality is the growing worldwide campaign against this type of abuse. Since 1993, when the United Nations General Assembly passed the Declaration on the Elimination of Violence Against Women, countries around the world have developed initiatives to curb domestic violence. China (Xinhua News Agency, 2000), South Africa (Foster, 2002), Europe (Women's International Network, 2000), and countries throughout the Americas (Hawkins & Humes, 2002) have begun widespread efforts to decrease domestic violence through public health campaigns, government agencies, churches, women's advocacy groups, and legislative efforts. These many efforts aim to change societal attitudes, community standards, and individual behaviors to create a world that is safer for women in their intimate relationships.

■ SUMMARY

Sternberg's triangular model of relationships provides a framework for understanding all relationships, including friendships and love relationships. Gender differences in friendship styles appear early in development; children voluntarily segregate themselves according to gender before age 5 years. Girls are fond of talking and sharing secrets, and boys tend to enjoy active games. Even the girls and boys who do not like their gender-typical activities are not welcome in cross-gender groups.

Adolescents are more concerned with developing emotional intimacy in their relationships, but girls emphasize this aspect of relationships more than boys. Although young men say that they value intimacy in relationships, they often find it difficult to develop such relationships, especially with other men. Some men develop emotionally intimate love relationships with women, and such relationships often decrease the amount of time and emotional energy men have to devote to male friends. Friendships tend to be tied to developmental stages of life, and

marriage and the birth of children tend to restrict friendships.

Cancian has argued that love has become feminized. The current concept of love is emotional intimacy—a pattern closer to the typical relationship for women than for men. This definition slights the styles of intimacy men tend to adopt—the activities of providing help and doing things together. Some research has indicated that both men and women have a flexibility of friendship styles and that they use different styles to relate to male and female friends. Cross-gender nonsexual friendships are a recent phenomenon, and both men and women acknowledge that such relationships require special rules.

Love relationships currently form through dating, an activity that first arose during the 1920s as a response to changing patterns of mate selection. Dating has now become not only a method of courting, but also a forum for recreation, socialization, and sexual exploration. Adolescents tend to choose dates similar to future mates, and men and women prefer partners who are warm and kind, expressive, intelligent, and physically attractive. People with either heterosexual or homosexual orientation describe their preferred partners in similar ways.

Currently, marriage and other committed relationships can follow several different blueprints: Companionship, Independence, and Interdependence. The Companionship blueprint involves separate gender roles and emphasizes the woman's role in maintaining a love relationship. Both the Independence and Interdependence blueprints emphasize self-development for both men and women, but they differ in the importance of commitment.

Gender researchers have explored several issues in love relationships, including beliefs about love, communication, division of household labor, power and conflict, and relationship stability. Men are more romantic in their conceptualization of love than women are, and marriage tends to benefit them more, but they are not necessarily happier with their marriages. Men and women may have trouble communicating in love relationships, partly because their styles and goals of communication differ, with men trying to establish independence and dominance, and women trying to share feelings and make connections.

The division of household labor is usually unequal in marriages: Women perform far more of this work than men, even when women have paid employment outside the home. Women have become increasingly dissatisfied with this inequitable division, and men have begun to do more household work. Although paid employment is a source of power, both partners do not usually have equal power in a marriage. Couples experience conflict from many sources, but some marital conflict results in violence. Over 25% of women and men find violence acceptable in their personal relationships under some circumstances, but women are more likely than men to be injured as a result of relationship violence.

Violence decreases the stability of relationships, but does not necessarily end them. Stable love relationships tend to occur in couples with similar attitudes and values, and the commitment factor in marriage produces greater stability than in other love relationships. But even marriages dissolve, and divorce has increased in the past several decades. People who have divorced tend to see the fault in their ex-spouses rather than in the institution of marriage. Although divorce brings financial and emotional problems, most women and men also find positive factors in divorce. Most remarry, and some evidence suggests that both women and men form more equitable second marriages.

Across time and cultures, many patterns of marriage have existed. Analyzing the economic contributions of women in a variety of societies leads to the conclusion that women experience more egalitarian relationships and roles in societies in which they make significant economic contributions. Male-dominated cultures restrict women's access to resources, tend to establish restrictive marriages, and tend to allow greater intimate-partner violence. A worldwide campaign against domestic violence has sensitized people in many countries to the problems that result from this type of abuse.

GLOSSARY

companionate love a combination of commitment and intimacy without passion.

gross motor skills skills involving use of large muscles of the body, producing large movements, such as throwing, kicking, running, and jumping.

homophobia the unreasonable fear and hatred of homosexuality.

machismo a Spanish word meaning strong and assertive masculinity and implying complete male authority.

matriarchy a family pattern in which women are dominant or a pattern in which women are the head of the household due to the father's absence.

◼ SUGGESTED READINGS

Gottman, John (with Silver, Nan). (1994). *Why marriages succeed or fail.* New York: Simon and Schuster.
Gottman's popular book summarizes his research on factors related to success and failure in marriage. In addition, he includes self-quizzes so that couples can assess their relationships.

Hartup, Willard W.; & Stevens, Nan. (1999). Friendships and adaptation across the life span. *Current Directions in Psychological Science, 8,* 76–79.
This brief article offers a life span approach to friendships, including a discussion of children's behavior with friends and nonfriends, the developmental significance of friendship, and the characteristics of friends.

Hatfield, Elaine; & Rapson, Richard L. (1996). *Love and sex: Cross-cultural perspectives.* Boston: Allyn and Bacon.
Hatfield and Rapson's book examines love and sex across contemporary cultures as well as delving into history for additional examples. They consider attraction, the difficulties of forming relationships, and the problems involved in ending romantic relationships. Their cross-cultural and historical review adds a valuable (and fascinating) point of view to the understanding of passionate love.

Hetherington, E. Mavis; & Kelly, John. (2002). *For better or for worse: Divorce reconsidered.* New York: Norton. Respected researcher Mavis Hetherington teams with writer John Kelly to present the findings from the Virginia Longitudinal Study of Divorce and Remarriage in a format that everyone can understand. This book offers research-based findings and advice about the impact of divorce on women, men, and children.

10 SEXUALITY

We're Not in the Mood
Newsweek, June 30, 2003

> Lately, it seems, we're just not in the mood. We're overworked, anxious about the economy—and we have to drive our kids to way too many T-Ball games. Or maybe it's all those libido-dimming antidepressants we're taking. We resent spouses who never pick up the groceries or their dirty socks. And if we actually find we have 20 minutes at the end of the day—after bath time and story time and juice-box time and e-mail time—who wouldn't rather zone out to Leno than have sex? (Deveny et al., 2003, p. 41)

The answer to that question is that a great many people would rather have sex than watch Leno, but the situation posed in the story by Kathleen Deveny and her colleagues (2003) reflects the sex lives of some couples. An increasing number of people feel time pressure, stress, and annoyance with their partners to the point that sex is not their preferred activity at the end of the day. This situation has become the topic of self-help books, talk shows, and sitcoms.

Most couples experience a decrease in the frequency of sexual activity after the first years of their relationship, but for some couples, the decline is steep. "It's difficult to say exactly how many of the 113 million married Americans are too exhausted—or too grumpy to get it on, but some psychologists estimate that 15 to 20 percent of couples have sex no more than 10 times a year, which is how the experts define sexless marriage" (Deveny et al., 2003, pp. 41–42).

This headline story contrasted this situation with statistics from sex surveys that show that married couples have sex more often than singles and that most married people are happy with their sexual relationships (Laumann et al., 1994). However, there are reasons to doubt studies about sex: ". . . any efforts to quantify our love lives must be taken with a shaker of salt. The problem, not surprisingly, is that people aren't very candid about how often they have sex. Who wants to sound like a loser when he's trying to make a contribution to social science?" (Deveney et al., 2003, p. 44). This uncertainty arises because one of the major methods that researchers have used to investigate sexual behavior is the survey, which asks people to report on their behavior. People may, indeed, be less than truthful when they respond, and the image of what is "normal" affects those self-reports.

Sex researchers have acknowledged that measuring the frequency of sexual activity is biased by respondents' expectations of what they should be doing and failure to be truthful (Christopher & Sprecher, 2000). Therefore, sex research is subject to some problems specific to the topic of sex.

This chapter considers sexuality by first exploring one issue from this headline article—the considerations and methods involved in studying sex. Later sections explore the development of sexuality during childhood and the development of the sexual orientations of heterosexuality, homosexuality, and bisexuality.

THE STUDY OF SEXUALITY

Researchers who want to know about sexual behaviors and attitudes have several options in choosing a method of investigation. They may question people about their sexual behavior, or they may directly observe people's sexual behavior. Both of these approaches present scientific, practical, and ethical problems.

Those researchers who choose to question people about their sexual behaviors or attitudes are using the survey method. As the headline story discussed, this method is limited by people's truthfulness, which may be lacking when they respond to questions about a private, personal issue such as sex. An additional problem occurs when some people refuse to participate in sex surveys; those who decline very likely differ from people who are willing to answer questions about their sexual attitudes and behavior. Potential participants who refuse to cooperate can bias results because their opinions are systematically excluded.

Another possibility for investigating sexual behavior is through direct observation of sexual activity. Most people are even less willing to participate in this type of research than in a survey, but nonhuman animals have (or at least have voiced) no such objections. The problems of generalizing results from these studies to humans are more serious, but a prominent example of this type of research appears in *Patterns of Sexual Behavior* (1951) by anthropologist Clellan Ford and psychologist Frank Beach. These two researchers presented not only a cross-cultural study of human sexual behavior, but cross-species comparisons as well.

Only a small percentage of people have been willing to have sex in a research laboratory. Such participants allowed William Masters and Virginia Johnson (1966) to study human sexual behavior in ways that no other researchers had managed. Not only were Masters and Johnson's participants willing to answer questions about sex, they were willing to have sex in the lab and to have their physical responses measured during the activity. Although the results of Masters and Johnson's research have become widely accepted, their participants were less typical of the general population than those of any of the major surveys, a situation that Masters and Johnson considered unimportant but that others have criticized.

Although sex researchers have several options, most have surveyed people about their attitudes or behavior, or both, by asking questions and recording the responses. The problems with survey research include finding a **representative sample**—a group of people that reflects the characteristics of the population from which the sample was drawn—as well as securing truthful and accurate responses. Despite the problems connected with surveying people about sex, this approach has been the most common one. Sex surveys often suffer from the problem of **self-selection of participants.** When participants rather than researchers choose who is to complete the survey, then the sample is not representative. Such surveys can still reveal interesting and important information, but self-selected participants prohibit researchers from generalizing the results to the general population.

Sex Surveys

Before Alfred Kinsey's groundbreaking survey of men's and women's sexual behavior in the 1930s and 1940s, several other investigators completed reports on sexuality (Brecher, 1969). Henry Havelock Ellis, a British physician, wrote a series of books between 1896 and 1928 in which he detailed the differences in sexual customs of various cultures and collected sexual case studies of women and men. These studies led him to the conclusion that the Victorian social norms of repression and denial of sexuality that he saw around him were not reflected in people's sexual behavior. Ellis came to a conclusion that is applicable today: "Everybody is not like you and your friends and neighbors," and even, "Your friends and neighbors may not be as much like you as you suppose" (in Brecher, 1969, p. 39). Ellis was one of several sex researchers in the 1800s who was important in making sex an acceptable topic for scientific research, and this research helped to end the sexual repression that was the standard of that time.

Clelia Duel Mosher was a physician who began questioning women in the United States about their sexual behavior and enjoyment in 1892 (Degler, 1974). Although Mosher's sample size was small—only 45 women—and far from representative—all were college students—the responses to her survey indicated that sexual repression might not have been as common as Victorian standards held. About half of the women reported that they had no knowledge of sex before their marriages, but 35 of the 45 women reported sexual desires, and 34 of the 45 said they had experienced orgasm. This small, unrepresentative sample might not reveal the average woman's attitudes for that time, but the existence of women who enjoyed sex seems to contradict the prevalent view of the Victorian period.

Several other researchers completed small-scale sex surveys during the early 1900s. The most famous of the surveys on sexual behavior were those completed by Alfred Kinsey and his colleagues.

The Kinsey Surveys.   In 1937, biologist Alfred Kinsey began to teach a newly created course in sex education, which was a controversial topic at that time. Kinsey found that little systematic research existed on sexuality, and this gap prompted him to begin such research. He started collecting data in 1938 with a preliminary interview that he later expanded to include extensive information about nine areas: social and economic background, marital history, sex education, physical characteristics and physiology, nocturnal sex dreams, masturbation, heterosexual history, history of same-gender sexual activity, and sexual contact with animals. Each of these areas included subdivisions, making the interview extensive and time consuming. Amazingly, Kinsey completed more than 7,000 such interviews himself. His associates—Wardell Pomeroy, Clyde Martin, and Paul Gebhard—conducted other interviews, for a total sample of 17,500 (Brecher, 1969).

Although the interviews were extensive and many people participated, Kinsey's sample was drawn primarily from the university and the surrounding community. His final groups of 5,300 men and 5,940 women were White, well educated, mostly from Indiana, and largely Protestant. He did not necessarily strive to obtain a representative sample, but this failure means that his results cannot be generalized to the U.S. population.

Kinsey was skilled at getting a wide variety of people to talk with him candidly about their sexual histories (Brecher, 1969; St. Lawrence & McFarlane, 1999). His technique included asking questions that required participants to deny rather than admit a practice, such as, "At what age did you first experience full intercourse?" This approach assumed that everyone had done everything. Perhaps this strategy helped to make people more comfortable and encouraged them to tell the truth. Reinterviewing some participants 18 months after their first interview revealed mostly minor inconsistencies that came from memory lapses rather than intentional deception, indicating to Kinsey that people were telling the truth. Thus, Kinsey's surveys managed to overcome some problems associated with survey research.

The results from Kinsey's surveys appeared in two parts, *Sexual Behavior in the Human Male* (Kinsey, Pomeroy, & Martin, 1948) and *Sexual Behavior in the Human Female* (Kinsey, Pomeroy, Martin, & Gebhard, 1953). Kinsey's reports appeared during a time when sex was not a topic of polite conversation, when women were supposed to be reluctant to have sex, and when same-gender, premarital, and extramarital sexual activities were illegal in many areas. The results of the surveys surprised (and even shocked) many people, because the participants reported such a wide variety of sexual behaviors, including some that were socially unacceptable and even illegal.

Kinsey's results indicated that women enjoyed sex; that many men had participated in male–male sexual behavior; that children experienced sexual excitement and activity; and that masturbation, premarital sex, and extramarital sex were common for both women and men. Around 90% of the women in the study had experienced orgasm by age 35 years. Of the 10% who had not, another 8% reported experiencing sexual arousal, leaving only 2% of women who had failed to enjoy sexual activity, a figure much lower than most people had imagined.

Some of Kinsey's most controversial findings concerned same-gender sex. People with sexual partners of their own gender have objected to the term *homosexual,* a term that Kinsey used to describe male–male and female–female sexual behavior. The term has become stigmatized because it highlights the sexual aspect of these individuals' lives. A relationship with a same-gender partner is much more than sexual, and other terms have replaced *homosexual.* The term **gay** is an alternative that many find preferable and that may apply to both men and women, but it is more often used to describe men who have sexual relationships with men. The term **lesbian** refers to women who have sexual relationships with other women.

A total of 37% of the men in Kinsey's survey reported at least one sexual experience with another man; that is, an experience with another man that led to orgasm. This figure included men who had had sexual experiences with other men only as young adolescents, and men who had had only one such experience. Some of these men reported that they no longer felt sexual attraction toward other men or had no subsequent sexual experiences with other men. Both the percentage of men who had some type of sexual experience with other men (37%) and the percentage of men who primarily or exclusively had sex with other men (13%) were higher than previous estimates (Brecher, 1969). Kinsey's figures on female sexual activity with other women were similar to the figures for men, but the percentages were smaller. Twenty-eight percent of women had at least some sexual experience with other women, but only 7% reported primarily or exclusively lesbian sexuality. Table 10.1 shows these figures.

These figures for the frequency of same-gender sexual attraction and activity are at the center of a continuing controversy. Kinsey's figures for the number of men who primarily or exclusively have sex with other men are not only higher than previous estimates, but they are also higher than later estimates (Hunt, 1974; Laumann et al., 1994). A biography of Kinsey (Jones, 1998) contended that Kinsey's figures were biased by his personal interest and participation in sexual activity with men and his desire to portray these sexual activities as common. He therefore chose to question a disproportionate number of gay men, inflating the figures for this type of sexual activity.

Another controversial finding related to childhood sexuality. Many participants in the Kinsey survey reported that as children they had sexual feelings and sometimes acted on those feelings. The most common type of childhood sexuality was **masturbation,** manipulation of the genitals to produce sexual pleasure. Infants and young children masturbate, some to orgasm. A total of 14% of the women and 45% of the men in Kinsey's survey said

TABLE 10.1 *Percentage of Participants Reporting Sexual Activities in Three Sex Surveys*

Sexual Activity	Kinsey Surveys (1948, 1953)		Playboy Foundation Survey (Hunt, 1974)		National Opinion Research Center (Laumann et al., 1994)	
	Men	Women	Men	Women	Men	Women
Masturbation to orgasm	92.0%	58.0%	94.0%	63.0%	—	—
Masturbation before age 13	45.0	14.0	63.0	33.0	—	—
Masturbation during marriage	40.0	30.0	72.0	68.0	57.0%	37.0%
At least one homosexual experience	37.0	28.0	—	—	7.1	3.8
Primarily homosexual orientation	13.0	7.0	2.0	1.0	4.1	2.2
Premarital intercourse	71.0	33.0	97.0	67.0	93.0	79.0
Extramarital sex	50.0	26.0	41.0	18.0	<25.0	<10.0
Sexual abuse during childhood	10.0	25.0	—	—	12.0	17.0

that they had masturbated before the age of 13 years. They also remembered other-gender and same-gender exploratory play with peers as well as sexual contact with adults. Men recalled preadolescent intercourse more frequently than women did. Almost one fourth of the women recalled incidents during which adult men had shown their genitals, touched them, or attempted intercourse. Over half of the incidents reported by women involved acquaintances or family members. Adults' recollections of their childhood sexual activities are most likely not completely accurate, but Kinsey's results suggested that children experience sexual curiosity and exploration as well as sexual abuse by adults.

Kinsey's survey revealed that masturbation was a common sexual activity. A small percentage of people reported preadolescent masturbation, but the activity increased during adolescence. By the time they were adults, almost all of the men and about two thirds of the women had reached orgasm by masturbating. Married women and men told Kinsey that they continued to masturbate, although they also had sex with their spouses. Around 30% of married women and 40% of married men reported that they masturbated. These figures contradicted the popular notion that masturbation was primarily a practice of adolescence and that people with a sexual partner no longer masturbated.

Kinsey surveyed people who lived in a society that accepted different sexual standards for men and women. Although both were supposed to be sexually inexperienced before marriage and to have sex only with their spouses, men were not held to this standard but women were. This **double standard for sexual behavior** has a history that stretches back at least a century, and Kinsey found evidence for it in the different rates for both premarital and extramarital sex. By 25 years of age, 83% of unmarried men but only 33% of unmarried women said that they had participated in intercourse. A similar discrepancy occurred in the reports of extramarital affairs—that is, about half the men but only 26% of the women admitted having extramarital affairs.

In summary, Kinsey and his associates interviewed thousands of men and women during the 1930s and 1940s to determine the sexual behavior of people in the United States. They questioned a variety of people, but not a representative sample, so the results have limitations. Kinsey's results suggested that people engage in a wide variety of sexual activities, beginning during childhood. He found that most women experience orgasm, and that masturbation and extramarital sex are common. In addition, Kinsey's results showed that more than one third of men have had some type of sexual experience with another man, but that few were exclusively gay. The reports of female–female sexual activities were less common but with parallel findings: Few women were exclusively lesbian, but more had past or occasional sexual experiences with other women. After the Kinsey reports, many other sex researchers chose the survey method of investigation.

Hunt's Playboy Foundation Survey.   In the 1970s, the Playboy Foundation commissioned a survey of sexual behavior in the United States, and in 1974, Morton Hunt reported the results in his book *Sexual Behavior in the 1970s*. The researchers involved in this survey wanted to update the Kinsey findings. They also attempted to obtain a more representative sample than Kinsey had managed, but they did not succeed because a high rate of people contacted refused to participate. However, the final sample matched characteristics of the U.S. population in terms of ethnic background, education, age, and marital status.

The 2,026 participants filled out a lengthy questionnaire about their backgrounds, including sex education, attitudes toward sex, and sexual histories. A total of 200 also participated in an even more lengthy interview that was similar to the Kinsey interviews.

As Table 10.1 shows, this survey confirmed the prevalence of masturbation, with an even higher rate of preadolescent masturbation than Kinsey had found and a similar rate of masturbation during adulthood. Hunt found a lower percentage and a different pattern of same-gender sexual activity than Kinsey had found. He concluded that most such activity occurs as a form of adolescent experimentation, with most of the women and men who had same-gender sexual experiences discontinuing this form of sexuality by age 16 years. Hunt estimated that 2% of men and 1% of women were exclusively gay or lesbian in their sexual orientation.

Hunt found some evidence for a sexual revolution in the form of increases in certain sexual activities. More unmarried people had engaged in intercourse than the Kinsey surveys reported. A total of 97% of the unmarried men and 67% of the unmarried women reported having intercourse by age 25 years, representing an increase in intercourse and a decrease in the double standard. According to Hunt, by the 1970s, extramarital sex was more common, especially among younger women.

The Playboy Foundation survey also found evidence that more people were engaging in a wider variety of sexual activities than Kinsey reported. For example, a higher percentage of respondents in the Playboy Foundation survey reported oral–genital sexuality than in Kinsey's surveys. **Fellatio** is oral stimulation of the male genitals, and **cunnilingus** is oral stimulation of the female genitals. Kinsey found a difference in popularity of oral–genital sexuality according to educational background: Sixty percent of people with a college education, 20% of those with a high school education, and 10% of those with a grade school education had engaged in oral–genital sexual activity. Hunt reported that 90% of the young married couples in his survey said they had engaged in oral–genital stimulation, revealing a dramatic increase in prevalence and a leveling of social class differences.

In summary, Hunt's Playboy Foundation survey attempted to obtain a representative sample of U.S. residents and interview them so as to furnish updated comparisons for Kinsey's results. The results showed that Kinsey was correct in concluding that people's sexual behaviors are more varied than the social norms suggest, and it confirmed the prevalence of masturbation and childhood sexuality. Hunt's estimates for same-gender sexuality were much lower than Kinsey's figures, but Hunt found evidence for an increase in premarital, extramarital, and oral–genital sexual activity.

The National Opinion Research Center Survey.   Two major U.S. sex surveys appeared during the 1990s, one conducted by Samuel and Cynthia Janus (1993), and the other by a team headed by Edward Laumann, John Gagnon, Robert Michael, and Stuart Michaels (1994) for the National Opinion Research Center (NORC). Although both groups claimed that theirs was the first survey to obtain a representative sample of adults in the United States, the NORC survey relied on a random sampling technique rather than on volunteers. After collecting their information, Laumann and his colleagues compared their sample to information known about U.S. adults, and they concluded their group was representative.

The NORC survey revealed a slightly different picture of sex in the United States than either the Kinsey or Hunt survey had shown. One difference was a continuation of the trend toward more liberal sexual standards, with sex serving either as an important factor in love relationships (regardless of marital status) or as a recreational activity (without any necessity for a committed relationship). Only around 30% of respondents expressed the traditional, conservative view that sex outside marriage is always wrong and that procreation is the main reason for having sex.

The other difference expressed in the NORC survey indicated some degree of conservatism concerning sex. For example, a low percentage of participants reported attraction to and practice of a variety of sexual behaviors. Indeed, the NORC survey found that vaginal intercourse was not only the most frequent form of sexual activity with a partner, but also the most appealing to both men and women. Giving and receiving oral sex and watching a partner undress were at least somewhat appealing to a majority of participants, but group sex, anal intercourse, sex with strangers, and forcing or being forced to do something sexual were not appealing to the majority of participants.

This survey also found gender differences in sexuality, just as the other surveys had done. One large gender difference related to the experience of first intercourse: Twenty-eight percent of women but only 8% of men said that they did not want to have intercourse at the time, but either did so out of affection for their partners or were forced to do so. Men also reported more varied sexual interests and behavior, including more lifetime sex partners and a slightly higher interest in group sex, anal intercourse, watching others do sexual things, visiting sex clubs, viewing sexually explicit books or videos, and giving and receiving oral sex. Men were more likely to masturbate, but women were more likely to report feeling guilty about masturbating. Table 10.1 summarizes information from this survey.

Consistent with the couples in the headline story, the results from the NORC survey showed "The general picture of sex with a partner in America shows that Americans do not have a secret life of abundant sex" (Michael, Gagnon, Laumann, & Kolata, 1994, p. 122). The most common category for frequency of intercourse was *a few times a month,* and only about 7% reported having sex four or more times a week. In addition, about two thirds of both men and women said that they had only one sex partner within the past year, with reports showing only small variations across different ethnic groups, religious affiliations, or educational levels. The NORC survey reflected a less sexually varied United States than the media or people's imaginations often present, but it also showed an acceptance of sex for pleasure and outside the boundaries of marriage.

Gender Differences (and Similarities) in Sexual Attitudes and Behavior.   The three major (and many smaller) sex surveys have shown gender differences in several sexual behaviors and in some attitudes toward sexuality. Although the more recent surveys have indicated a smaller difference in sexuality of men and women, even the NORC report indicated gender differences. A meta-analysis (Oliver & Hyde, 1993) and later summaries (Christopher & Sprecher, 2000; Peplau, 2003) have indicated that gender differences exist in some aspects of sexuality but not in others.

Two large, gender-related differences emerged from the meta-analysis (Oliver & Hyde, 1993) that were confirmed by later reviews: incidence of masturbation and attitudes toward casual premarital sex. Studies have indicated a higher rate of masturbation and a greater acceptance of casual premarital sex for male than for female adolescents and adults. These researchers pointed out that the magnitude of the differences for these comparisons surpasses other gender-related differences, such as those in mathematics or verbal performance. (See Chapter 4 for a discussion of these cognitive differences.) The greater acceptance of casual premarital sex applies to men in a variety of cultures, including Canada, Africa, Hong Kong, Sweden, and all ethnic groups in the United States (Hatfield & Rapson, 1996). The term *casual* also seems to apply to online sex, and about 85% of those who engage in this type of sexual activity are men (Cooper, Scherer, Boies, & Gordon, 1999).

A proposal that may encompass many gender-related differences in sexuality comes from the notion of greater flexibility of female sexuality (Baumeister, 2000) or alternatively, less flexibility of male sexuality (Hyde & Durik, 2000). This view holds that women's sexuality is more influenced by cultural and situational factors, making women more sexually adaptable than men but also more variable in their sexuality. Either an evolutionary (Baumeister, 2000) or a sociocultural (Hyde & Durik, 2000) explanation is possible for this gender difference, but any wide-scale explanation of gender differences in sexuality may explain too much; male and female sexuality shows few large differences.

Gender-related differences in other aspects of sexuality were smaller, and some of the meta-analysis (Oliver & Hyde, 1993) comparisons failed to show gender differences. Of the differences that appeared, men reported being, and actually were, more acceptant of those sexual behaviors than women were. Small differences also appeared in the acceptance of premarital and extramarital intercourse, sexual permissiveness, number of sexual partners, and frequency of intercourse. In addition, men reported feeling less sexual guilt or anxiety than women felt. Analysis of acceptance of the double standard for sexual behavior indicated, ironically, that women believed in the double standard more than men did. No gender differences appeared in attitudes toward same-gender sexuality, rights for gays or lesbians, attitudes toward masturbation, incidence of oral sex, or sexual satisfaction. Table 10.2 shows some of the behaviors and attitudes from this meta-analysis, along with the magnitude of gender-related differences.

Changes over time have also appeared in all reviews of gender differences of sexuality. The existing gender differences show signs of decreasing over time. Thus, analyses of gender differences in sexuality confirm the trends that appeared in the comparison of the three major surveys, as shown in Table 10.1—that is, a decrease of differences between men's and women's sexual attitudes and behavior, along with a few continuing differences.

Masters and Johnson's Approach

As noted earlier, researchers who want to observe sexual behavior directly can conduct their studies on nonhuman animals, or they can enlist the cooperation of people who are willing to engage in sex in a research laboratory. Although such participants are far from average, they might furnish important information about sex. The most famous researchers to take this approach were William Masters and Virginia Johnson.

During the 1950s, Masters became interested in the physiology of the sexual response. After some initial work with prostitutes as participants, he sought volunteers from

TABLE 10.2 *Sexual Attitudes and Behaviors Showing and Failing to Show Gender-Related Differences*

Sexual Behaviors/Attitudes	Direction of Difference
Large Differences	
Incidence of masturbation	Higher for men
Acceptability of casual sex	Higher for men
Moderate to Small Differences	
Acceptability of sexual permissiveness	Higher for men
Incidence of sex in committed relationship	Higher for men
Incidence of intercourse by engaged couples	Higher for men
Acceptability of premarital sex	Higher for men
Age at first intercourse	Lower for men
Frequency of intercourse	Higher for men
Incidence of same-gender sexual experiences	Higher for men
Anxiety, fear, and guilt associated with sex	Higher for women
Acceptability of double standard of sexual behavior	Higher for women
Acceptability of extramarital sex	Higher for men
Number of sexual partners	Higher for men
No Differences	
Incidence of oral sex	
Incidence of kissing	
Incidence of petting	
Acceptability of masturbation	
Acceptability of same-gender sexuality	
Belief that gays and lesbians should be given civil rights	
Sexual satisfaction	

the medical community in St. Louis and found people who were willing to masturbate or have intercourse while being observed in the laboratory (Brecher, 1969). During the time Masters was recruiting participants for the laboratory studies, he also recruited Virginia Johnson to assist him with the interviewing, and she became an essential part of the research.

Masters and Johnson chose 276 married couples and single women and men, all of whom not only had to be willing to have sex in the lab but also had to regularly experience orgasm. All participants received payment for their participation, resulting in an overrepresentation of medical school students who were interested in contributing to scientific research and who also needed the money. These criteria and procedures resulted in a sample that was far from representative. This situation was not of great concern to Masters and Johnson; they believed that the physiological sexual responses varied little from person to person. Others (Kaschak & Tiefer, 2001; Tiefer, 1995) argued that Masters and Johnson's selection of participants biased the interpretation of their results. In addition, these critics have claimed that Masters and Johnson's interpretation was biased by their preconceived notions, forcing the sexual experience into stages that are not necessarily appropriate for everyone.

In these laboratory studies, the married couples had intercourse, masturbated each other, or engaged in oral–genital stimulation. The unmarried participants did not have sex with a partner; the men masturbated and the women either masturbated or were stimulated by an artificial penis designed to measure vaginal responses during sexual arousal and orgasm. In addition to collecting information by measuring genital activity during sex, Masters and Johnson gathered physiological measurements such as heart rate, muscle contraction, and dilation of the blood vessels from both men and women. Their findings (Masters & Johnson, 1966) suggested that four phases of sexual excitement exist—excitement, plateau, orgasm, and resolution. The two researchers contended that these four phases describe the sequence and experience of sexual arousal and orgasm for both women and men. Figures 10.1 and 10.2 show the four phases, the organs that are affected, and the responses for both women and men. An examination of these figures reveals similarities as well as differences throughout these stages.

Not only did Masters and Johnson's research suggest that both women and men are similar in experiencing four stages of sexual response, but it also showed that women experience one type of orgasm through clitoral stimulation. Freud hypothesized that women experience two types—clitoral and vaginal orgasm. He believed that girls experience clitoral orgasm during masturbation, beginning during early childhood, and that women are immature if they continue to require clitoral stimulation for orgasm. Freudian theory described women who experience orgasm through intercourse as healthier and more mature than women who have only clitoral orgasms. Masters and Johnson's results disconfirmed Freud's hypothesis, showing that women experience only one type of orgasm—a clitoral orgasm. Some women have clitoral orgasms during intercourse and some do not; intercourse may not provide sufficient clitoral stimulation to produce orgasm in some women. This important finding has not had the impact it should have. A study on research, teaching, and popular usage of sexual terms (Ogletree & Ginsburg, 2000) revealed that the word *clitoris* is not used as the female counterpart to *penis*. Indeed, the word *clitoris* is not often used, and this omission may have important implications for sexuality.

Masters and Johnson's research has been both controversial and influential. As with other physiological processes, individual variations exist in the experience of these stages, and Masters and Johnson ignored these variations (Tiefer, 1995). Their conceptualization has become so well accepted that people who do not conform to these stages are open to being diagnosed with sexual dysfunctions. The Masters and Johnson research has been valuable in measuring sexual physiology, but their research findings may not be as universal as they have contended.

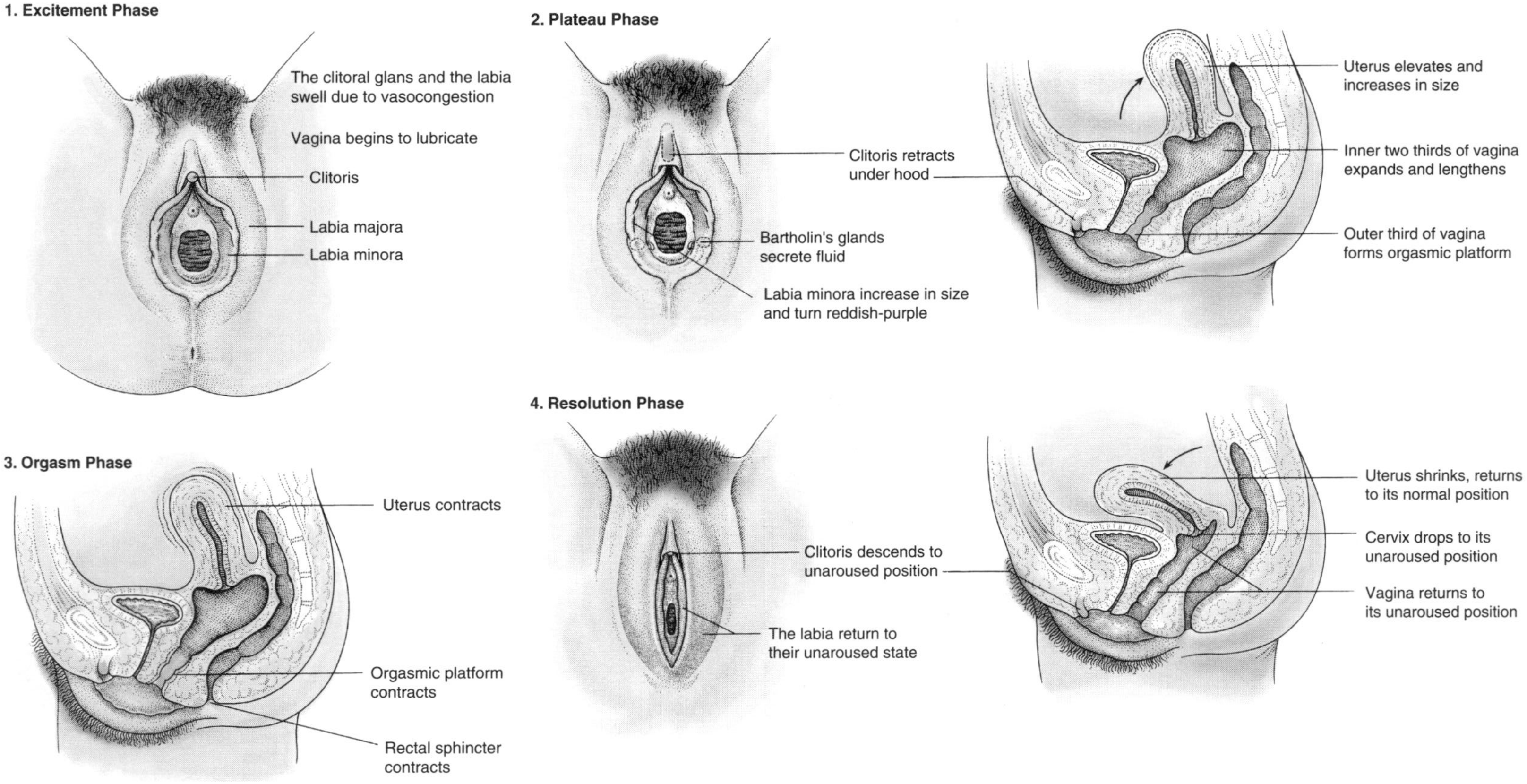

1. Excitement Phase

The clitoral glans and the labia swell due to vasocongestion

Vagina begins to lubricate

Clitoris

Labia majora

Labia minora

2. Plateau Phase

Uterus elevates and increases in size

Inner two thirds of vagina expands and lengthens

Outer third of vagina forms orgasmic platform

Clitoris retracts under hood

Bartholin's glands secrete fluid

Labia minora increase in size and turn reddish-purple

3. Orgasm Phase

Uterus contracts

Orgasmic platform contracts

Rectal sphincter contracts

4. Resolution Phase

Uterus shrinks, returns to its normal position

Cervix drops to its unaroused position

Vagina returns to its unaroused position

Clitoris descends to unaroused position

The labia return to their unaroused state

FIGURE 10.1 *Female Genitals during the Phases of the Sexual Response Cycle*

1. Excitement Phase

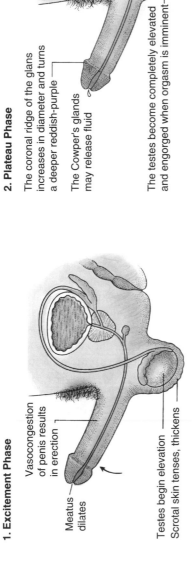

Vasocongestion of penis results in erection

Meatus dilates

Testes begin elevation

Scrotal skin tenses, thickens

2. Plateau Phase

Cowper's gland

The coronal ridge of the glans increases in diameter and turns a deeper reddish-purple

The Cowper's glands may release fluid

The testes become completely elevated and engorged when orgasm is imminent

3. Orgasm Phase

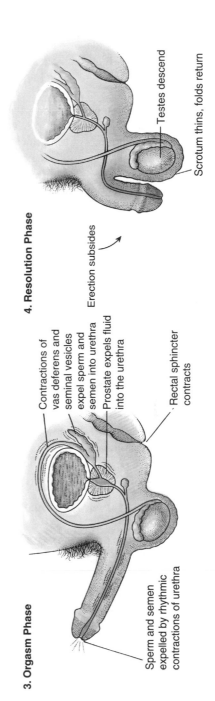

Contractions of vas deferens and seminal vesicles expel sperm and semen into urethra

Prostate expels fluid into the urethra

Rectal sphincter contracts

Sperm and semen expelled by rhythmic contractions of urethra

4. Resolution Phase

Testes descend

Scrotum thins, folds return

Erection subsides

FIGURE 10.2   *Male Genitals during the Phases of the Sexual Response Cycle*

CHILDHOOD SEXUALITY: EXPLORATION AND ABUSE

As the Kinsey, Playboy Foundation, and NORC surveys have shown, sexuality begins before puberty. Even as infants, children take part in sexual exploration, and they are sometimes the victims of sexual abuse. Infant boys have erections, and infant girls experience erections of the clitorises as well as vaginal lubrication (DeLamater & Friedrich, 2002). Infants touch their genitals as they explore their bodies, and this exploration teaches children that their bodies can produce pleasurable sensations. Preschool-aged children masturbate, sometimes several times a day. Sexuality is part of children's lives.

Parents who notice their children's masturbation may accept it, or they may be surprised or shocked. Their attitude and their method of dealing with their children's masturbation can convey positive or negative messages about sexuality, and these messages can have a lasting impact (DeLamater & Friedrich, 2002). Parents who say, "That's not nice," or "Nice boys and girls don't do that," or who move their children's hands away from their genitals send negative messages about sexuality.

Another aspect of childhood sexuality that may make parents uncomfortable revolves around their children's questions about sexuality, pregnancy, and birth as well as their children's sexual exploration with other children. By age 4, most children have a concept of gender and the roles that women and men occupy. They know that women have babies and men do not, and pregnancy and birth are topics that stimulate curiosity and questions. Parents may feel embarrassed about giving straightforward descriptions and resort to analogies such as "Daddy plants a seed inside Mommy." Due to their concrete thought processes, children have the tendency to misinterpret these fanciful descriptions and analogies.

Children's tendency to invent and fill in the details of stories they do not fully understand means that concealing information will not keep children from knowing about sex. But what they "know" may be incorrect. Table 10.3 presents examples of children's descriptions of how babies come into being. As these explanations show, children have trouble understanding sex and birth, and even older children misunderstand some aspects of the process. Therefore, formulating appropriate answers to young children's questions about sex and birth requires a delicate balance of providing the correct amount of information without excessive details. Parents' discomfort with the topic of sex complicates these discussions.

"I would love for him to grow up to be a doctor, but I sure wish he'd wait another twenty years to specialize in gynecology," the mother of a 5-year-old said (Segal & Segal, 1993, p. 131). This mother humorously expressed her concern over her son and the neighbor's daughter, who were exploring each other's genitals. The Segals explained to the mother that her son's explorations were more curiosity than sexuality and that his behavior was normal. They advised this mother to set limits on her son's explorations and urged her not to be concerned about her son's curiosity about female genitals.

Sexual explorations during preschool or elementary school are rarely harmful, but parental punishment can give the impression that something is wrong with such activities (DeLamater & Friedrich, 2002). In addition, the double standard for sexual behavior starts

TABLE 10.3 *Examples of Children's Beliefs about Sex and Birth*

How Do People Get Babies?

According to 3- to 5-year-olds:

"You go to the baby store and buy one."

"Mommy bought me in a shop."

"They grow inside. I don't know how it starts. It just grows."

"The babies are in the stomach. I already have a baby in my stomach. . . . It won't grow 'cause I'm little. When I'm big, then it can grow. . . . You have to be very careful because the baby may get loose in your stomach."

According to 4- to 6-year-olds:

"To get a baby to grow in your tummy, you just make it first. You put some eyes on it. Put the head on, and hair, some hair all curls. You make it with head stuff you find in the store that makes it for you."

"Maybe from people. They just put them in the envelope and fold them up and the mommy puts them in her 'gina and they just stay in there."

"From marrying people. They put seeds in their vaginas. The mommies open up their tummy, but sometimes they open up their vaginas. So the daddies, so they can put their eggs in them, and they can put the seeds in them."

According to 7- to 10-year-olds:

"Well, I first thought, when I was seven that all you have to do is get married. And then all you would have to do is read a book, and then you would have a baby."

"The sperm is like a baby frog. It swims into the penis and makes a little hole. It bites a hole in its little mouth and swims into the vagina."

"I don't know how they get the baby. Maybe some special germs."

"From the daddy. He has something that helps the mommy get the baby. Some sort of medicine. I don't know what it's called, but it's here. [She pointed to her crotch.] Well, it goes in to some sort of part, I think it's the vagina, and just fixes up and helps around there, and makes it have a baby."

"Well, I think, but I'm not sure, that the penis goes into the vagina and, well, I think it does something. I was thinking that it might touch something in a body, and then it starts growing a little sperm. Like it might touch some blood, or a blood vein or a bone, well doubtfully a bone, but something around the clitoris. Maybe the sperm comes out from that little thing, near the clitoris. It comes out and it starts. Then I think it might break off, come loose and break off and it stays in that one place, or goes up the stomach."

"I don't know much about it. Well, I know one thing. The man and the woman get together. And then they put a speck, then the man has his seed and the woman has an egg. They have to come together or else the baby, the egg won't really get hatched very well. The seed makes the egg grow. It's like plants. If you plant a seed, a flower will grow."

According to 11- and 12-year-olds:

"When the egg is fertilized it sort of comes to life. If you want to . . . the chemicals make it come to life. The sperm are injected to where the eggs are, and they just, I guess, coat them. There's some chemical in the sperms that activates another chemical in the egg, which starts the development of the baby."

"Sexual intercourse? Well, it should only be brought on by love, and it helps if you're married. And it's when the man and the woman come together, and the man sticks his penis into the lady's, near the womb, and then the egg that comes down through a little tube, down into the womb, is fertilized, and becomes a child."

Source: The Flight of the Stork, by Anne C. Bernstein, 1978, New York: Delacorte Press.

during this age range; girls are warned about sexual exploration and sex play, and boys are allowed more freedom in their sexuality.

Parents may be unaware that sexual explorations during childhood include same-gender as well as other-gender sexual play, but both are common. In a study that asked high school students to recall their childhood sexual experiences (Larsson & Svedin, 2002), over 80% remembered some sexual activity with an age-mate. In addition, parents are not aware of most sexual contact between siblings. The majority of such contact consists of examining the genitals and touching, and a low percentage of sibling sexual activity includes attempted or successful intercourse. Nonetheless, sexual activity between siblings qualifies as **incest**—sexual activity between family members. David Finkelhor (1980) reported that 15% of college women and 10% of college men recalled sexual experiences with their siblings. The majority of these college students did not believe that the experience had harmed them, but an important factor in this evaluation was the age difference between the two siblings; a large age difference was associated with a greater perception of harm.

Age has been a critical factor in defining sexual exploitation of children (Finkelhor, 1984). When sexual contact occurs between children who are close to the same age, this activity falls into the category of *exploration*. When a child has sexual contact with an adult or an adolescent at least 5 years older than the child, that activity falls into the category of *exploitation* or *sexual abuse*. Also included as abusive are sexual relationships between adolescents and adults whose age exceeds the adolescents' age by at least 10 years.

Incest is one form of sexually abusive relationships, but children can also be sexually abused by nonrelatives, including strangers and adults in positions of authority. The Kinsey et al. (1948, 1953) surveys included questions about childhood sexual experiences with adults, and his results revealed that 25% of girls and 10% of boys reported such contact. Over half the cases involved adults whom the children did not know, but later research has shown that most abusers are known to the children whom they target.

Beginning in the 1970s, several groups of researchers attempted to determine the rate of sexual abuse of children, but obtaining accurate numbers is difficult. The honesty and memory problems that affect all surveys are more serious when adults are asked about sexual abuse during childhood. For example, in U.S.-government-sponsored surveys, only individuals 12 years old or older may respond, so children are never asked about their experiences (Tjaden & Thoennes, 2000b). If abuse is reported, an adult must recall a past event as a victim or report current abuse as the perpetrator; both are difficult admissions. In addition, those who sexually abuse children are capable of convincing themselves that the relationships are "special" and have not harmed the child (Gilgun, 1995), which can lead them to distort their reports of the events.

Assessment of childhood sexual abuse has been conducted with a wide variety of people in different geographic locations using varying definitions of sexual abuse and several different research methods (Tjaden & Thoennes, 2000b). These variations have resulted in differing rates for sexual abuse, ranging from 11% to 40% for women and from 3% to 8.6% for men (Bagley & King, 1990). Due to the sampling techniques in the various studies, these percentages may be underestimates. The reports of sexual abuse of boys are probably more greatly underestimated than the statistics for girls (Spataro, Moss, & Wells, 2001). Considering the difficulties with obtaining accurate statistics, at least 15% of girls and 5% of boys are sexually abused during childhood or adolescence.

Several reviews (Bagley & King, 1990; Greenfield, 1996; Tjaden & Thoennes, 2000b) have shown some commonalties: Girls are sexually abused more often than boys, and men are the instigators of abuse far more frequently than women. Both girls and boys are at risk during their entire childhoods and adolescence from family members, family friends, adult authority figures, and strangers, but the risk is not equal for all ages or from all adults. Table 10.4 shows the range of estimates and the characteristics of sexual abusers and victims.

Girls are not only more likely to be sexually abused, but they are also more likely to be abused at younger ages than boys. The preadolescence years are the riskiest age period for both, with girls between ages 10 and 11 years and boys between ages 11 and 12 years at the highest risk. These ages represent the time during which the first victimization is most likely to occur. For many children, sexual abuse continues for years, often for as long as they remain in contact with their abusers.

Between 94% and 100% of those who abused girls were men, and around 84% of those who abused boys were men. Although abusers are sometimes strangers, more often

TABLE 10.4 *Summary of Offender and Victim Characteristics for Childhood Sexual Abuse*

Characteristic	Range of Estimated Occurrence	
	Lowest	Highest
Girls abused while under age 16 (average age 10.2–10.7 years)	11.0%	40.0%
Girls who rated the experience negatively	66.0	
Girls whose abuser was male	94.0	100
Boys abused while under age 16 (average age 11.2–12 years)	3.0	8.6
Boys who rated the experience negatively	38.0	
Boys whose abuser was male	83.0	84.0
Children whose offender was a stranger	11.0	51.0
Children whose offender was a friend or an acquaintance	33.0	49.0
Children whose offender was a relative	14.0	50.0
Girls whose offender was a sibling	15.0	
Boys whose offender was a sibling	10.0	
Children whose offender was a biological parent	1.0	6.8
Girls whose offender was a stepfather	7.6	17.0
Children who had force or threats used against them	55.0	
Children whose abuse consisted of exhibition	26.0	28.0
Children whose abuse consisted of being fondled	26.0	40.0
Children whose abuse consisted of forced fondling of offender	10.0	14.0
Children whose abuse consisted of intercourse	15.0	18.0

Source: Based on *Child Sexual Abuse: The Search for Healing,* by C. Bagley & K. King, 1990, London: Tavistock.

these men are known to their victims as family members, family acquaintances, or as adult authority figures such as neighbors, day-care workers, teachers, scout leaders, or religious leaders. Ethnicity is a factor in sexual abuse of children; Whites are more likely to be imprisoned for these offenses than African Americans or Hispanic Americans are (Greenfield, 1996). Compared with perpetrators of other types of sexual abuse, those who abuse children are, on the average, about 5 years older.

Both female and male abusers exist, but the emphasis in research and therapy has been on boys and men as perpetrators and girls and women as victims. This emphasis is not entirely inappropriate, but not all abuse follows this pattern. Female–male abuse (female offender) occurs and differs from the male–female (male offender) pattern. For example, male strangers represent approximately one third of the cases of male abusers, but almost all female abusers are acquaintances of those whom they molest (Duncan & Williams, 1998). Girls or women who sexually abuse boys are often caregivers, including mothers and baby-sitters (Rudin, Zalewski, & Bodmer-Turner, 1995). In addition, female perpetrators are very likely to have themselves been the victims of abuse, most commonly by a family member.

The sparse research on female perpetrators and male victims has demonstrated that such abuse occurs, but some women victimize boys in the guise of initiating them into sexuality. Some boys have difficulty identifying this activity as abuse (Larsson & Svendin, 2002). Such cases are rarely reported to authorities (Duncan & Williams, 1998), making the proportion of male abusers seem higher than it actually is. The overwhelming focus on female victims and male perpetrators has left sexually abused men and sexually abusive women neglected in both research and treatment, but this situation is beginning to change.

Incest involving biological fathers and their daughters is not the most common type of sexual abuse; stepfathers or mothers' boyfriends are much more likely to force this type

GENDERED VOICES

My Parents Never Said Anything Until . . .

"My parents never said anything to us about sexual abuse until my brother was molested," a teenager said. "Then our whole family talked sexual abuse. My brother had to tell us what happened, tell us what the person had done very explicitly. Maybe that wasn't a good thing for him to have to do, because he had to talk about it a lot, but we learned about what to be careful about. And they never said anything before he was molested.

"It was tough on the family, because the person who molested him was a cousin. He was about 4 or 5 years older than my brother, and our families don't speak to each other anymore. It was hard to know what to do, because the cousin had been molested when he was younger, so he was just repeating what happened to him. Should he be punished for doing what he had learned? My brother was still hurt, but it was difficult not to feel sorry for my teenage cousin.

"We went for counseling as a family, and I think it helped. I hear that it can be much worse to ignore it, because it won't go away if you don't talk about it. We talked about it afterward, but not before something happened."

of relationship. One estimate (Russell, 1986) was that 17% of stepdaughters were molested by their stepfathers, whereas only 2% of daughters were victims of sexual abuse by their biological fathers. Cases of incest involving a father or father figure are the most serious and may have serious, long-term consequences, including difficulties in school and in personal relationships, sexual dysfunction, as well as alcohol and substance abuse (Heise, Ellsberg, & Gottemoeller, 1999; Paolucci, Genuis, & Violato, 2001). Some evidence exists for both the short-term and long-term effects of sexual abuse (Finkelhor, 1990; Heise et al., 1999; Paolucci et al., 2001). The short-term effects include fear, anxiety, depression, anger, sexually inappropriate behavior, and academic problems. The long-term effects include posttraumatic stress disorder, depression, suicide, sexual adjustment problems, and substance abuse disorders. Few gender differences exist between boys and girls who have been the victims of sexual abuse; both suffer similar negative effects from their victimization (Paolucci et al., 2001).

Despite the impression that news reports have created about pedophiles, the sexual abuse of children may be declining (Jones & Finkelhor, 2001). In the United States, the statistics for both reported and confirmed cases of child abuse of all types rose during the 1970s and 1980s, but during the 1990s, those rates began to decline. The decrease in number of cases for sexual abuse has been larger than for other types of violence against children; the decline represents a 37% decrease. Experts are not certain if the decrease relates to reporting procedures or to an actual decline in child sexual abuse, but these lower numbers may represent some success in the efforts to stop the sexual abuse of children.

In summary, childhood sexuality is more active than most parents imagine; it begins during infancy when children explore and manipulate their own genitals and then progresses to curiosity about and exploration of others' genitals. Although parents may find these signals of sexuality distressing, they are normal. Sexual exploitation also occurs when older adolescents or adults initiate sexual activity with children. Obtaining accurate estimates is difficult, but the results of various surveys indicate that at least 15% of women and 5% of men have been sexually abused as children. Girls are much more likely to be abused than boys, and men are much more likely than women to be abusers. There are few gender differences in short-term and long-term effects of childhood sexual abuse, which include posttraumatic stress disorder, depression, and suicide, as well as adult sexual and substance abuse problems. However, the rate of sexual abuse may be declining.

HETEROSEXUALITY

Most people develop erotic or sexual interests that result in attraction to people of the other sex rather than people of the same sex. That is, most people develop a heterosexual, rather than a same-gender, **sexual orientation.** Signs of heterosexual erotic interest may begin during childhood, but sexual activity during childhood mainly takes the form of masturbation and exploratory play, which can be directed toward same- or other-gender children (Larsson & Svendin, 2002). Thus, children's sexuality often is not clearly heterosexual.

During late childhood and preadolescence, children seek the company of same-gender peers and avoid associating with other-gender peers (see Chapters 6 and 9). This gender segregation restricts the opportunities for heterosexual activity, but does not signal children's lack of heterosexual interest. Indeed, children often tease each other by announcing who "likes" whom and by threatening to kiss others who are unwilling (Thorne, 1993). Such games demonstrate an awareness of heterosexuality and an early knowledge of gender roles in heterosexual interactions.

During Adolescence

Although a distressing number of children are introduced to sexuality through force or coercion, adolescence is the period during which most people explore sexuality. These explorations consist of formal and far more informal education. The traditional view in the United States and many other societies has situated sexuality within marriage, which discourages adolescent sexual activity. These cultures also send many messages about sex and its pleasures, which pose problems for adolescents who see the promised joys of sex, but who are urged not to participate.

These messages are not equal for girls and boys: Girls receive many more messages to beware of sex than boys do (Baldwin & Baldwin, 1997). Although a double standard of sexual behavior is sharply apparent in adolescent sexuality, neither boys nor girls experience adequate sexuality education (Fine, 1988; McCormick, 1994; Whatley, 1990). An evaluation of sexuality education programs (Song, Pruitt, McNamara, & Colwell, 2000) indicated that such programs are effective in increasing knowledge about sex, but most sexuality education programs are oriented toward the dangers rather than the pleasures of sex.

Publicity about teen pregnancy, date rape, and sexual exploitation conveys the impression that sexuality is dangerous, especially for young women, and this danger has been the focus of most sex education. Rather than emphasizing how to develop successful sexual relationships, most sex education for teenagers focuses on abstinence as the best choice and pregnancy, sexually transmitted diseases, and vulnerability to rape as the alternatives. This emphasis appears to be successful in conveying a sense of sexual vulnerability in young women; such feelings develop during adolescence. Deborah Tolman (2002) found confirmation for this sense of vulnerability in extensive interviews with adolescent girls about their sexuality. In these interviews, Tolman heard "dilemmas of desire," problems in reconciling sexual desire with being the "nice" girls that parents, peers, and schools urged them to become. The girls repeatedly mentioned the reluctance of their families to acknowledge their sexuality and the frequent reminders of the dangers that sex could bring, especially in the form of pregnancy. The image of self-centered sexuality was acceptable—even expected—for boys but not for girls. These girls felt that they had to choose either sexual desire or safety.

The different attitudes toward early sexual experiences also appeared in a study that included interviews with adolescent girls asking about their first sexual experiences (Thompson, 1999). These girls' stories fell into two groups. Girls in the first group were unhappy with their first sexual experience and had sex because of pressure. They had not planned or wanted to have sex, and they tended to describe it as something that "just happened," depersonalizing the experience and absolving responsibility. Girls who told stories of wanting sex expressed different views. These girls grew up in homes with positive attitudes about sex, and the girls were knowledgeable and prepared. Having sex was a deci-

▣ GENDERED VOICES

Sex De-Education

"A shiver goes up my spine remembering my 'sex education' experience in the 6th grade. Now, I don't know if the teacher had some problems with sexuality in general, or if perhaps it was part of her job, but I'll never forget the fear of sex and sexual contact she put into about 95%, if not all, of the young girls in that class.

"The majority of the information was in reference to reproduction and sexually transmitted diseases. My teacher brought in this old, old medical book and proceeded to show these pictures of people with severe stage STDs. These pictures showed people with ulcerated sores all over their bodies; parts of their flesh were falling off, and she said, 'This is what happens to people who have sex when they're not married.' It was disgusting, not to mention terrifying.

"As if that wasn't bad enough, when she taught the section on the male genitalia, she brought another visual aid. She brought in a rubber replica of a male penis and testicles, and the thing was HUGE and she represented it as actual size. I've never heard so many young girls gasp in terror at the same time in my life. She was very quick to relay how painful sex with a man was. I never understood her motivation. She was married with three kids. Maybe her husband was that big, but it seems unlikely.

"To this day, I still wonder how many of these young girls were traumatized by their 'sex education' and how that affected their first sexual encounter with a man. I've also wondered what techniques were used to teach the boys in our school."

sion they clearly made, often with anticipation and desire. This trend toward planning first intercourse and using contraception has increased dramatically in the United States during the 1990s (Hogan, Sun, & Cornwell, 2000).

First intercourse has been a developmental milestone that traditionally was associated with marriage. Kinsey's surveys during the 1930s and 1940s revealed that a majority of young men had intercourse before marriage. The substantially smaller percentage of young women who had intercourse before marriage reflected the double standard, but this discrepancy has decreased over the past 60 years (Brooks-Gunn & Furstenberg, 1989). In 1938, approximately 7% of European American girls had intercourse by age 16 years, but by the 1980s, the percentage had risen to 44%. Information does not exist to make comparisons for boys, but estimates suggest that boys were more sexually active than girls from the 1940s to the 1960s, with between one third and two thirds of boys having intercourse as teenagers. The difference diminished during the 1970s and 1980s. By age 18 years, 60% of young men have had intercourse, and by age 19 years, the percentage was similar for young women.

The average age of first intercourse for boys and girls in the United States now varies by only a few months: 16.6 years for boys and 17.2 years for girls (Upchurch, Levy-Storms, Sucoff, & Aneshensel, 1998). Age of first intercourse shows more variation across ethnic backgrounds in the United States, however. A study of an ethnically diverse sample of adolescents from the Los Angeles area (Upchurch et al., 1998) revealed a lower age of first sexual activity for African American adolescents (15.8 years), and a higher age for Asian American (18.1 years) than for White (16.6 years) or Hispanic American (17.0 years) adolescents. A survey of adolescents in Great Britain (Wellings et al., 2001) showed that the average age of first intercourse was comparable to the United States: 16 years.

The reasons for girls' and boys' decisions to have sex often differ. For boys, having sex is a means not only to pleasure but also to social prestige (Baldwin & Baldwin, 1997). "For teenage boys, their first sexual experience may be the primary symbol of manhood—a rite of passage" (Stark, 1989, p. 12). Boys feel pressure from their peers to "score," and their sharing the stories is a way to gain admiration from their peers. The pressure boys experience may be conveyed to the girls they date by demands for sex. Boys may have sex to prove a point. Girls may refuse sex to prove a point, or they may give in to this pressure and have sex.

Women who readily consent to sex are at risk for being considered promiscuous, and that potential consequence may influence the decision to say "no" more than a lack of desire (Tolman, 2002). Openly acknowledging desire may lead to many unkind labels because the double standard for sexual behavior has not disappeared, it has only diminished. The continued existence of a double standard appeared in a study (Kelly & Bazzini, 2001) in which college students judge a woman or a man who furnished a condom in a sexual encounter. The female college students expressed the view that the man in the sexual encounter would judge the women negatively if she (rather than he) furnished the condom. The male college students did not concur; they expressed more positive evaluations of the assertive woman.

Messages about the dangers of sex have some basis—forced sex and pregnancy are all too common in the lives of adolescent girls. **Date rape** or **acquaintance rape** is forced sexual activity between people who are dating or otherwise acquainted. Chapter 8 discussed rape as an aggressive crime disproportionately committed by men. Most people picture rape as an attack by a stranger, but the majority of rapes and other acts involving forced or coerced sex occurs between acquaintances. Mary Koss and her colleagues (1987) surveyed college students about sexual activities and found that 54% of the young women in the survey claimed to have been the victims of some type of coerced or forced sexual activity at some time during their lives, and over 15% had been raped. Questioning a wider age range of women, the NORC survey (Laumann et al., 1994) found that 22% of women said that they had been forced to do something sexually by a man. Of these women, 46% said that they were in love with the man and another 22% said that the man who forced them was someone they knew well. As this study shows, women are less likely to report sexual assaults if they know (and especially if they are in love with) the perpetrator, leading to an underrepresentation in crime statistics of the incidence of rape by acquaintances.

Miscommunication may be a factor in acquaintance rape. The dynamics of sexual negotiation are complex, but the acceptability of forced sex is an important factor in the prevalence of acquaintance rape. Some men consider forced sex acceptable, at least under some conditions (Muehlenhard, Friedman, & Thomas, 1985). Men with more traditional attitudes toward women rated date rape as acceptable under a wider variety of conditions than did men with egalitarian attitudes. If the woman asked the man out, the man paid the expenses of the date, and the woman agreed to go to his apartment, men found rape more justifiable than if the date followed another script. Women, however, may be unaware of these conditions and may not feel that they owe sex to their partners. Thus, dating partners follow complex, often unexpressed, and possibly unshared rules about sexual activities on dates. Their assumptions about the right to have sex may make men more likely to force women into the sex they believe they deserve—that is, to commit date rape.

Concerns over pregnancy are another issue for adolescents who have sex. This anxiety affects girls more than boys. Although some pregnancy education is aimed at teenage boys, most is directed at girls and emphasizes the danger of sex. The concern is not without reason; every year 85 of every 1,000 teenaged girls between 15 and 19 years old living in the United States get pregnant (Henshaw, 2001). Although that rate declined 27% during the 1990s, the United States still has a very high rate of teen pregnancies compared to other industrialized nations.

Pregnancy during adolescence is associated with a number of negative outcomes, including a decrease in life satisfaction (McCabe & Cummins, 1998). Teenage boys are also involved in these pregnancies, but their lives may be less affected. A substantial minority of the men involved in teen pregnancies are at least 5 years older than their female partners (Lindberg, Sonenstein, Ku, & Martinez, 1997). The percentage of older partners was higher for younger girls (ages 11 to 12), and not surprisingly, these partnerships tended to produce more problems for these young girls (Leitenberg & Saltzman, 2000). Therefore, some of these teen pregnancies involve sexual relationships with men that fit into the category of exploitation or even abuse.

In summary, as adolescent sexuality becomes increasingly oriented toward heterosexual encounters, some gender differences appear. Girls receive messages of danger and vulnerability rather than pleasure, and boys receive messages about how pleasurable sex is. Sex education may not meet the needs of either girls or boys. Gender differences in the rate and age of first intercourse have diminished over the past 60 years. Although these changes signal a decline of the double standard, sex may have a different meaning for boys and girls. Although peer pressure is a factor for both, boys use sex as proof of their masculinity, whereas validation of their femininity is not a common reason for girls to have sex. Messages about adolescent sexuality remain negative, especially for young women.

During Adulthood

Traditionally, marriage has been not only a major transition but also the primary context for adult sexuality, often in the form of vaginal intercourse. The more recent studies of college students and surveys with more representative samples have indicated that the standards for sexual behavior have changed. Lower ages of first intercourse, increases in sexual activity among female adolescents, and increases in the acceptability of a variety of sexual activities suggest that more frequent and more varied sexual behaviors are now accepted for both women and men. Sexuality has become an important part of life for young adults, regardless of their marital status (Christopher & Sprecher, 2000; McCabe & Cummins, 1998).

Despite the importance of sexual satisfaction for adults, some are celibate. **Celibacy,** refraining from sexual activity, is sometimes a voluntary choice. For example, some religions require celibacy for clergy and for those who are not married. Inspired by religion or other codes of personal morality, some people choose celibacy, but the number of young adults who have sex before they are married is high—around 88% of men and 81% of women (Christopher & Sprecher, 2000). In studies of those who were celibate (Donnelly,

Burgess, Anderson, Davis, & Dillard, 2001; Netting, 1992), lack of opportunity was a more frequent reason than choosing to abstain for moral or religious reasons. Among college students (Netting, 1992), celibacy was the choice of many young women, who were waiting for love; celibate young men tended to be waiting for a willing partner.

According to the NORC survey (Laumann et al., 1994), celibacy described the sexuality of about 9.8% of men and 13.6% of women in the year prior to the survey. Lifelong celibacy is, however, unusual—only 2.9% said they had never had a sex partner. Those who are ill or whose partners have died are especially likely to be celibate, and both circumstances are associated with increasing age. Thus, celibacy increases sharply after age 60. Older women's longer life expectancy makes them far more likely to be celibate than men of the same age.

Celibacy can even occur in marriage. An Internet survey of celibacy (Donnelly et al., 2001) found that sexless marriages occur. Sexual activity tends to decrease with age, and older married couples have sex less often than younger married couples (Laumann et al., 1994). Most couples believe that sex is an important part of marriage, and like the couples in the headline story (Deveny et al., 2003), partners tend to be dissatisfied with celibacy within marriage.

Monogamy means having only one sexual partner in a committed love relationship. This choice represents the ideal for many people within many cultures (Christopher & Sprecher, 2000; Hatfield & Rapson, 1996), but lifelong monogamy represents the actual lifestyle for a smaller number. Some people who strongly endorse monogamy are not involved in a relationship (Donnelly et al., 2001; Netting, 1992). Some advocate monogamy but practice **serial monogamy,** in which a person has relationships with a series of partners, one at a time. Series of exclusive dating partners and divorce and remarriage are representations of this pattern. Still others say that they believe in monogamy but "cheat" by having sex with other partners. Thus, many several varieties of departures from monogamy allow people to subscribe to the ideal without adhering to the practice of having one sexual partner for life. The percentage of men who had or wanted a monogamous relationship was lower than the percentage of women.

Among a group of college students (Netting, 1992), 61% of the women and 37% of the men described monogamy as their ideal relationship. Another study of college students (Pedersen, Miller, Putcha-Bhagavatula, & Yang, 2002) found that 98.9% of men and 99.2% of women said that they wanted to settle down with one exclusive sexual partner at some point in their lives. For married couples, monogamy is the most common style of sexuality. Indeed, 93.7% of married couples in the NORC survey were monogamous in the year prior to the study (Laumann et al., 1994). Unmarried cohabiting heterosexual partners (76.7%), those who had never been married and were not cohabiting (38%), and those who were divorced or separated (40.5%) were less likely to be monogamous.

For all types of couples, failure to maintain the ideal of monogamy can cause major relationship problems. People become upset when their partners have sex with someone else (Christopher & Sprecher, 2001). One of the hypotheses of evolutionary psychology and its view of mate selection is that men and women experience jealousy, but over different behaviors. In the view, men's jealousy is prompted by sexual infidelities because such behavior would create uncertainty concerning parentage of offspring, whereas women's jealousy is sparked by emotional infidelities because such behavior would threaten continued partner support (Buss, 1994). However, a study that tested reactions to different types of infidelities (Nannini & Meyers, 2000) failed to confirm these predictions. Women were more upset than men by both types of infidelities, but both men and women were more upset of infidelities that involved a sexual component than an emotional one.

Some people choose sexual freedom over monogamy, opting for a sexual style of free experimentation. This choice is more common among young, unmarried people (Laumann et al., 1994; Netting, 1992), but even some married people have many sexual partners. People who choose this style tend to value sexual freedom and want to participate in a variety of sexual relationships. Counting those who had more than one partner during their lives, about half the students in one study (Netting, 1992) were in this category. Some of these young adults were in a committed relationship with one partner at the time of the study, but believed in having different partners on the way to a monogamous relationship. Among adults (Laumann et al., 1994), a small percent of both men and women reported having five or more sex partners in the year prior to the survey. Table 10.5 summarizes the styles of sexuality among the college students and adults.

The sexual attitudes and behaviors of women and men show few differences, but those few differences may have larger implications for heterosexuality, including the choices of monogamy or free experimentation. One way to understand these gender differences is through the framework of script theory (Simon & Gagnon, 1986). This view proposes that sexual behavior follows a sequentially organized set of steps, and that men and women learn and internalize somewhat different scripts. The differences between male and female scripts can throw couples into conflict. One of the large gender differences in sexuality is in the acceptability of casual sex, with men being more acceptant than women (Oliver & Hyde, 1993). The script approach helps in understanding this gender difference and its implications. Women are encouraged to associate sex with love, and they come to believe that sex should occur in the context of a committed relationship, whereas the script for men is not so relationship centered (McCormick, 1994). Thus, sex may have different meanings for women and men.

The implications of this difference can be large, forming areas of conflict for couples. For women, the association between commitment and sex leads them to believe that commitment should exist before having sex, but men may not share these requirements or expectations. These differing beliefs lead to differences in expectations about the timing of intercourse in a relationship (Cohen & Shotland, 1996). As predicted, men expected sex after significantly fewer dates (9 to 11) than women did (15 to 18). A recent survey (*People,* 2003) confirmed the difference: While 55% of men said they expected to have sex within the first five dates, only 24% of women shared these expectations. These differing expectations could be a source of conflict if men begin to pressure women to have sex and the women do not feel ready, or if women refuse sex when men believe that their relationship warrants it.

The difference in acceptability of casual sex can also have an impact on sex outside the primary relationship. With less acceptant attitudes, women are more likely to be monogamous than men, and they are more likely to consider sex outside the relationship as violations of trust or as betrayals by their partners. For example, 15% of dating men said that they had more than one sexual relationship at a time, whereas only 3% of women did

TABLE 10.5 *Styles of Sexuality among College Students and Adults*

	Percentage		
Style Chosen	*Women*	*Men*	*Comments on Choices*
College Students			
Celibacy	36	32	Women were waiting for love; men were waiting for an opportunity
Monogamy	61	37	Considered monogamy the ideal type of sexuality
	48	34	Were currently monogamous
	25	19	Had had only one partner during their lives
Sexually active but not monogamous	5	28	Believed in monogamy but did not live up to the idea
Free expression	14	33	Valued freedom of expression, including expression of sexuality
Never Married Adults			
Celibacy (no sex partners)	24.5	17.4	Waiting for partner; believed in sex only within marriage
Monogamy (one sex partner)	50	38.3	Believed in monogamy but not in waiting for marriage to have sex
Sexually active but not monogamous (2–4 sex partners)	20.9	32.1	May represent a series of partners
Free expression (5 or more partners)	4.6	12.0	Young adults were much more likely than older adults to be in this group
Married Adults			
Celibacy (no sex partners)	2.7	1.7	Partner absent; illness; bad relationship
Monogamy (one sex partner)	94.8	92.2	Commitment to sexual exclusivity
Sexually active but not monogamous (2–4 sex partners)	2.1	4.9	Represents affairs or casual sex
Free expression (5 or more partners)	0.01	1.1	Represents affairs, casual sex, and paid sex

Data for college students based on "Sexuality in Youth Culture: Identity and Change," by Nancy Netting, 1992, *Adolescence, 27*, pp. 961–976. Data for never married adults and married adults based on *The Social Organization of Sexuality*, by Edward O. Laumann et al., 1994, Chicago: University of Chicago Press, and the number of reported sex partners within the past 12 months.

(*People*, 2003). The perception of what constitutes "cheating" also differs for women and men (Sprecher, Regan, & McKinney, 1998). When the man is the cheating partner, people predict that he will not necessarily leave his wife for his lover, but people see women's extramarital sex as more indicative of the end of the relationship. Thus, the gender difference in the acceptability of casual sex affects dating and extramarital sex and people's beliefs about what affairs sexual relationships imply. (See "According to the Media" and "According to the Research.")

The other large gender difference in sexuality is the frequency of masturbation (Oliver & Hyde, 1993); men masturbate more often than women. At first, any relationship between masturbation and partnered sex may not seem apparent, but Janet Hyde (1996) has explained a connection. She proposed that women's lower frequency and greater guilt concerning masturbation results in less familiarity with their bodies and less certain knowledge of how to reach orgasm. Women are less likely to experience orgasm during intercourse than are men, and this difference causes distress for many couples. Hyde pointed out that many sex therapists direct women who are having orgasmic difficulties to masturbate, thus demonstrating to them the importance of masturbation. She hypothesized that women's lower frequency of masturbation may lay the foundation for women to have difficulties in reaching orgasm during heterosexual sex.

Other gender differences may also have some relationship to the problems that heterosexual couples face. One issue is desire for and frequency of intercourse. The double standard proposes that women will be less interested in sex because they are less sexual creatures than men, and evolutionary psychology (Buss, 1994, 1996) holds that women must be more sexually selective than men in order to choose mates who will be able to provide for offspring. These two views agree that women are less sexual but disagree over the reason. Determining a social or biological explanation is very difficult because society influences everyone. And because many societies control women's sexuality, any interpretation of "natural" sexuality is impossible.

Sarah Blaffer Hrdy (1981, 1986, 1999) criticized the view that women are less sexual than men, which she called the Myth of the Coy Female, by reporting on females unaffected by cultural expectations and the double standard—nonhuman primates. She argued that male scientists who have seen female reluctance to engage in sex have been influenced by the double standard and have projected these human differences onto nonhuman primates. Hrdy argued that any tendency to see patterns similar to human sexual behavior in the behavior of other species tells more about the human observer than about the observed species.

According to Hrdy, the sexual behavior of nonhuman animals varies from species to species. The females of some species, such as baboons and chimpanzees, initiate multiple, brief sexual relationships and show no coy reluctance to engage in sex, whereas the females of other species, such as blue monkeys and redtail monkeys, are very selective about their mating habits. Their selectivity might appear coy, but these animals reflect only one version of primate sexuality.

Women's lower interest in sex may be related to accepting of the double standard for themselves. A meta-analysis of attitudes toward sexuality (Oliver & Hyde, 1993) showed that women accepted the double standard more strongly and felt more guilt over sex than men did (Oliver & Hyde, 1993). Script theory suggests that women have internalized the cultural view that their sexuality is weaker. If women believe that they are or should be less sexual, they may behave accordingly and become less sexual. Masters and Johnson (1966)

ACCORDING TO THE MEDIA . . .

Women Have Lots of Sex in the City

The HBO series *Sex and the City* portrayed the romantic and sex lives of four women who had a great deal of sex in New York City. Through six seasons, this series detailed the sexual experiences of Carrie, who wrote a relationship and sex column for a newspaper and looked for Mr. Right; Miranda, who was a staunch feminist and successful attorney; Charlotte, who was a romantic searching for love and a husband; and Samantha, who was a sexually voracious public relations executive. Despite their different attitudes toward love and sexual relationships, all of these characters had multiple sex partners. Even the conservative Charlotte had sex with about as many different men as the promiscuous Samantha (Royal, 2003).

The stories unfolded through Carrie's eyes as she wrote her column (Royal, 2003). Viewers saw not only wealthy, glamorous, trendy single women in their 30s struggling with relationship issues but also the men whom they bedded, and they saw them through the eyes of the women rather than the men. These women saw the men as being in short supply—they often complained about the difficulties of finding single men in Manhattan, and they went to extraordinary lengths to attract these men. In addition, the ones they found had lots of problems. There were the "toxic bachelors" who feared long-term commitment and cheated on their girlfriends and the many losers who were too new-age sensitive, lacking money and power, or lacking sexual competence.

Romance and commitment were continuing issues in this series, but both the men and the women had problems with those issues. In one episode, Carrie wondered if monogamy is too much to expect. That question was a difficult one for many of the characters in this series; in a later episode, Carrie had sex with an old boyfriend while she was engaged to another man. After her many ponderings concerning problems with male commitment, she broke her engagement. Both women and men had sex in the city, and both were portrayed as plagued by problems with sex and relationships.

argued that women could be just as sexual or even more sexual than men if women were free to express their sexuality and to participate in the activities that gave them sexual pleasure. Rather than loosening the constraints on female sexuality, however, Masters and Johnson's research may have added to these restrictions by prescribing that women should be as sexual as men and that the sexuality of the two genders should be similar (Tavris, 1992).

Is sexuality very different for women and men? Gender differences in sexual behavior have decreased, suggesting that both female and male sexuality are subject to change and are influenced by social standards. During the Victorian era, women were presumed to be less sexual than men, and so they became. In our sexualized modern culture, women are portrayed as being more sexual than in the past but still less so than men, and so they have become. Sexuality is created by each culture and shows enormous differences across cultures. Thus, women and men exhibit a wide variety of sexual behaviors depending on their physiologies, cultures, personal backgrounds, and personal expectations. Carol Tavris (1992, p. 245) summarized heterosexuality by saying, "The question is not whether women are more or less sexual than men. (The answer to that is yes, no, both, and sometimes.) The questions are: What are the conditions that allow women and men to enjoy sex in safety, with self-confidence, and in a spirit of delight? And how do we get there?"

ACCORDING TO THE RESEARCH . . .

Sex in the City Is Not Like "Sex and the City"

The portrayal of single sex in New York City in the HBO series *Sex and the City* did not reflect the singles' life, even in Manhattan. The discrepancies appeared at many points, beginning with the demographics. Men in Manhattan are not as scarce as the women from *Sex and the City* lamented. Although the number of single women outnumbered single men in Manhattan (*American Demographics,* 2002), the figures are 2 million women to 1.5 million men, not overwhelmingly bad odds. However, most people in their 30s are married, so the high number of singles portrayed in the show reflected an inaccurate view of singles in the city.

The hesitation for commitment may have some basis in reality, but most men as well as most women want a committed relationship, and both emphasize the importance of love (Buss, Shackelford, Kirkpatrick, & Larsen, 2001). Furthermore, the prevalence of multiple sexual relationships depicted in *Sex and the City* does not reflect typical sexual behavior in the United States. For young adults who were single and dating, only 3%

of women and 15% of men of reported that they had more than one sexual relationship at a time (*People,* 2003). Therefore, monogamy is more common and multiple sex partners less common in Manhattan than in *Sex and the City.*

If there are women like the sexually predatory Samantha, one man (Burton, 2000) reported that he had yet to meet one, and his experiences of sexually aggressive women were more like Mimi on *The Drew Carey Show* than like Kim Cattrall as Samantha. In real life, actress Kim Cattrall is nothing like Samantha, despite being an author of a book about sexual satisfaction. When Cattrall published the book, one of her goals was to discuss how her sex life had not been like Samantha's. Her book emphasized the importance of relationships and intimacy (*People,* 2002), whereas Samantha used sex more as a way to avoid than to achieve intimacy. Therefore, the reality of sex in Manhattan varies from the television version, including the sex lives of the actresses who portrayed these single women.

HOMOSEXUALITY

Some people develop erotic attraction toward people of the same gender and engage in same-gender sexual activities. The number of people with same-gender sexual interests, behavior patterns, and identities constitute a minority, but estimates vary on how small a minority. Most of the variation in estimates can be explained according to the variation in definitions. Is sexual attraction to those of the same gender sufficient? Are persons lesbian or gay if they have engaged in sexual activity with persons of the same gender at any time during their lives? Does having sex primarily or exclusively with members of one's own gender define homosexuality? Or must people identify themselves as gay or lesbian? These varying criteria produce different estimates.

Kinsey and his colleagues (1948) found that 37% of the men said that they had engaged in male–male sexual activity at some time during their lives, and 28% of women reported at least one female–female sexual experience during their lifetimes (Kinsey et al., 1953). Therefore, a substantial number of both men and women who participated in the Kinsey surveys reported sexual experiences with members of their own gender, but most did not engage in such relationships as the primary form of sexuality throughout their lives.

About 13% of the men and about 7% of the women Kinsey's surveys identified themselves as primarily gay or lesbian. This estimate has been controversial (Jones, 1998).

Other surveys have asked different questions and obtained lower estimates. Table 10.6 presents a comparison of the various measures of homosexuality for several studies, one of which questioned people in three countries. As this table reveals, the different measures (and cultures) show variations in the percentage of people who might be classified as gay or lesbian. Thus, same-gender sexual orientation is complex, and estimates depend on

TABLE 10.6 *Differing Estimates of Same-Gender Attraction and Behavior*

Study	Men	Women
Kinsey et al. (1948, 1953)		
At least one same-gender sexual experience	37%	28%
Primarily or exclusively same-gender sex	13	7
Janus and Janus (1993)		
At least one same-gender sexual experience	22	17
Primarily same-gender sex	4	2
Laumann et al. (1994, NORC survey)		
Same-gender desires or experiences	10.1	8.6
Done anything sexual with same-gender partner	9.1	4.3
Same-gender sex partner since puberty	7.1	3.8
Same-gender sex partner in past year	2.7	1.3
Attracted to same-gender individuals	7.7	7.5
Self-identified as gay or lesbian	2.8	1.4
Sell, Wells, and Wypij (1995)		
United States		
Same-gender attraction but no activity	8.7	11.1
Same-gender sexual activity since age 15	6.2	3.6
United Kingdom		
Same-gender attraction but no activity	7.9	8.6
Same-gender sexual activity since age 15	4.5	2.1
France		
Same-gender attraction but no activity	8.5	11.7
Same-gender sexual activity since age 15	10.7	3.3

Column header: Percent (Men, Women)

whether researchers ask about attraction or behaviors as well as the frequency of behavior and the age of respondents.

Understanding homosexual sexual orientation has been a challenge for theorists and researchers. For years, psychologists failed to make a distinction between *gender role,* the social behaviors associated with one or the other gender, and *sexual orientation,* the erotic attraction to members of one or the other gender (or to both). Psychologists confused gender role and sexual orientation, when the two are separate constructs (Constantinople, 1973; Lewin, 1984a, 1984b). This conceptualization of same-gender sexual orientation as an inversion of gender role was usually not productive, and a separation of gender role and sexual orientation has clarified the process of measuring masculinity and femininity and demonstrated that same-gender sexual orientation has a far from perfect relationship to these traits. That is, men who are erotically attracted to other men are not necessarily feminine in appearance or behavior, and women who find other women sexually attractive are not necessarily more masculine than other women.

The issue of sexual orientation is socially controversial and poorly understood scientifically. The concept of sexual orientation has received relatively little attention, except in relation to homosexuality. Recently, Lisa Diamond (2003b) questioned the meaning of sexual orientation and proposed that erotic attraction and romantic attraction were separable components that usually—but not always—go together. These questions about the underlying meaning of sexual orientation have been exceptions; most researchers have accepted the assumption that heterosexuality is the standard and thus needs no explanation, whereas homosexuality requires theory and research. This attitude of compulsory heterosexuality (Hyde & Jaffee, 2000) reflects the lack of acceptance for homosexuality in many societies. This lack of acceptance is a prominent feature of the social controversy, which also questions the underlying basis for sexual attraction to those of the same gender: Is sexual attraction biologically determined (and if so, how)? Or is sexual attraction the result of experiences (and if so, which ones)? The social controversy continues because research has not yielded clear answers concerning the basis for sexual orientation.

The lack of clear answers is not due to a lack of theory or research. The theories fall into approaches that take a biological view versus those that take a social view of sexual orientation. The biologically based approaches have variations that emphasize genetic or hormonal factors. Therefore, many variations of theories of homosexual sexual orientation exist.

Early biological theories of sexual orientation focused on genetics and hormones. No simple relationship exists between sexual orientation and either genetic background or hormonal levels, but both may exert influences in complex ways. The evidence is strong that sexual orientation has a genetic component, but how that genetic component operates remains unclear. One large, representative study of twins (Bailey, Dunne, & Martin, 2000) found a lower rate of genetic influence for sexual orientation than in prior studies. When one of a pair of identical twins was gay, lesbian, or bisexual, about 20% of the other twins also were not heterosexual. This study also showed a higher degree of heritability for male than for female homosexual twins, suggesting the possibility than the genetic mechanisms for sexual orientation differ in men and women.

The mechanisms that may affect sexual orientation through prenatal hormonal exposure also remain poorly understood but the subject of much research. These studies explore how exposure to prenatal androgens might influence the developing brain and brain structures, and thus affect sexual orientation (Breedlove, 1994; Cohen, 2002; Lalumiere, Blanchard, & Zucker, 2000). The reasoning is that too much or too little exposure to androgens produces brain variations that underlie the development of nonheterosexual sexual orientation. Thus, studies have examined physical correlates of atypical prenatal androgen exposure and related these physical differences to sexual orientation. For example, one hypothesis holds that being left-handed is related to prenatal testosterone exposure, so left-handedness might appear more often among gay than heterosexual men. Some studies have found this difference (Lalumiere et al., 2000), but others (Cohen, 2002) have not. Another marker for androgen exposure is the ratio of the length of the second (index) and fourth (ring) fingers, which is typically lower in men than in women. One study (Hall & Love, 2003) found evidence that the finger ratios of lesbians were more like those of men than women; another study (Robinson & Manning, 2000) found that gay men's finger ratios did not match the pattern typical for men. These results are consistent with the hypothesis that prenatal exposure to androgens is a factor in sexual orientation.

To demonstrate the relationship between prenatal hormone exposure and sexual orientation, research must demonstrate not only differences in physical correlates and their relationship to sexual orientation but also what brain structures are affected. Several brain structures are candidates, but the third interstitial nuclei of the anterior hypothalamus have received the most attention. Two studies (Byne et al., 2001; LeVay, 1991) have found that this area of the brain is larger in men than in women and that this area is smaller in gay men than in heterosexual men. Other areas of the brain have failed to show reliable differences based on sexual orientation. Therefore, the hypothesis that sexual orientation can be traced to prenatal hormones that affect brain structures has some support, but the biological pathways for this process are not yet clear.

In addition, some theories have attempted to explain how physiological factors become manifested in sexual orientation through an interaction with experiences. One such theory is Daryl Bem's (1996, 2000) theory, the Exotic-Becomes-Erotic. According to this view, individuals become erotically attracted to the class of people from whom they felt different during childhood. For most people, gender segregation makes the other gender that class of people; through separation from the other gender, those in that class seem different and exotic. When adolescents begin to experience sexual feelings, the objects of those feelings are those who were exotic. Thus, Bem contended that the perception of differences leads to the development of sexual interest and orientation.

For individuals who develop a same-gender sexual orientation, the Exotic-Becomes-Erotic view hypothesizes that these individuals had childhood activity preferences that were more typical of the other gender. Thus, boys who would rather play with dolls and kitchen sets tend to associate with girls, which makes girls more familiar and less exotic. For girls who prefer boys' toys and games, girls would be more exotic. Therefore, this theory predicts that gay men and lesbians will have childhoods in which gender-atypical activities predominated. Many studies confirm this prediction for boys (Bailey et al., 2000; Bem, 2000), but the evidence for girls is much weaker (Garnets & Peplau, 2000). Bem (2000) argued for an interactional view in which some biological predisposition (either genes or hormone exposure) affects personality traits, which pushes individuals toward typical or atypical activities. Thus, this view holds that what is exotic varies, creating homosexual and heterosexual sexual orientations.

During Adolescence

Adolescence is a time of sexual exploration, and adolescent sexual activity has become more common and more accepted over the past 40 years—for heterosexual individuals. Same-gender sexual activity is discouraged but still occurs. Indeed, most of the people who have same-gender sexual experiences do so as part of adolescent experimentation and not as the beginning of a gay or lesbian sexual identity. However, some adolescents who are attracted to persons of the same gender do not act on these desires during adolescence (Savin-Williams & Diamond, 2000). Therefore, sexual orientation and sexual activity during adolescence do not correspond completely to sexual identity or to sexual activity during adulthood.

The process of developing a sexual identity must include the recognition of sexual attraction; labeling self as gay, lesbian, bisexual, or heterosexual; engaging in sex; and acknowledging sexual orientation (Savin-Williams & Diamond, 2000). These milestones do not necessarily occur in that order, and women and men show gender-related as well as individual variations in their trajectories of developing sexual identity. However, the recognition of sexual attraction tends to be the first milestone, which often occurs between ages 8 and 10 years old.

Some gays and lesbians say they knew about their same-gender sexual attraction even before adolescence, but many of them have tried to develop heterosexual interests and fit into this accepted pattern of sexuality (Zera, 1992). Some may succeed; as many as 90% of lesbians have entered sexual relationships with men (Rust, 2000). Also, sexual orientation in women appears to be less fixed than in men; over 25% of young women who had identified themselves as lesbian changed that identity within a 5-year period (Diamond, 2003a). Furthermore, the milestone of identifying oneself as gay or lesbian varied for gay men versus lesbians (Savin-Willaims & Diamond, 2000). Women tended to self-identify before they engaged in same-gender sex, but most gay men had a same-gender sexual experience before they identified themselves as gay.

The acceptance of same-gender attraction is a milestone that presents a major challenge for gay adolescents. They often struggle with feelings that something is wrong with them, and self-esteem may be a problem. Self-acceptance is different (and often comes more easily) than revealing one's same-gender sexual orientation or behavior to family and friends. **Coming out** is the process of personally recognizing and publicly acknowledging one's gay or lesbian orientation to others (Bohan, 1996). The term originated with the phrase "coming out of the closet," referring to the hidden (closeted) nature of sexuality for many gays and lesbians. Thus, coming out is a positive affirmation of sexuality. This process may be part of adolescent development, or it may occur at any time during adulthood. One study (Savin-Williams & Diamond, 2000) indicated that the time between experiencing same-gender attraction and acknowledging gay or lesbian sexual orientation was about 10 years.

Coming out may include a public acknowledgment of sexual orientation, or the revelation may be limited to friends and family. Parents may be acceptant and supportive, or they may be angry and have trouble accommodating the sexual orientation of this child

GENDERED VOICES

In My School

In schools, boys and girls are the targets of name-calling and gender harassment based on sexual orientation. The basis of the name-calling is rarely related to sexual behavior.

"If you use good grammar and good English, the kids in my school call you a faggot. It's crazy." 15-year-old African American boy attending a suburban school

"If you belong to the drama club in my school, everybody thinks you are gay." 15-year-old White boy (in the drama club)

"If you belong to the science fiction club, everybody thinks you are gay because those kids dress all in black and hug each other before they go to class." 14-year old White girl attending a suburban school in a large city

"You don't have to do anything to be called a faggot in my school. The athletes call everybody faggot, just because they are jerks who are trying to intimidate other kids." 14-year-old White boy attending a private school

(Bohan, 1996; Zera, 1992). In addition, friends may react negatively to coming out, and peer verbal or physical attacks are not unusual (Savin-Williams, 1995). Thus, gay and lesbian adolescents may be estranged from family and peers, and they are at increased risk for home- and school-related problems.

For adults, coming out often includes acceptance into the gay community. For adolescents, such acceptance is not as easy, because activities in the gay community are oriented toward adults. Charges of seducing adolescents or of promoting same-gender sexual activities present situations that make gay adults sensitive about including adolescents in the gay community.

Coming out can be a positive statement of sexuality for adolescents as well as for adults, but adolescents face many challenges in establishing a gay or lesbian identity: "Despite the pain and confusion in this process of development, it is important to bear in mind that most gay people do successfully resolve these issues and are able to be happy with themselves and participate in healthy relationships" (Zera, 1992, p. 854).

During Adulthood

Women and men who engage in same-gender sexual activities are often in danger of being arrested if they make their sexual activities public because such activities are often illegal. This lack of legal sanctions reflects the lack of social acceptability for gays and lesbians as well as for same-gender sexual activities (Kite & Whitley, 1996; Whitley, 2001). Men have more negative attitudes than women do toward homosexuality, especially regarding gay men, but both men and women with strong gender role identities tend to be more prejudiced against gays and lesbians than other people are (Whitley, 2001).

This lack of acceptance is one reason for the formation of self-contained gay communities. In many large cities, such communities form the context for the lives of many gay people, who may rarely interact with the outside world of heterosexuals. This life is

■ GENDERED VOICES

Treated Like a Gender Traitor

"When I came out as gay, I got a lot of homophobia re-actions" a college student in his 20s said. "Men were es-pecially bad. Their reactions weren't exactly fear, although they were nervous. And it wasn't hatred. It was more like resentment. I wasn't a real man anymore and like I was some kind of traitor to the male gender."

not typical of gays, however, and the vast majority must deal with disapproval, lack of ac-ceptance from the larger society, and discrimination (Sandfort, de Graaf, & Bijl, 2003). This lack of societal approval means that the need to form friendships and social networks is an essential part of gays' and lesbians' social lives.

The development of friendships and sexual relationships differs in gay men and les-bian women (Nardi, 1992b). Gay men were much more likely than lesbians to have had sex with both casual and close friends. Indeed, among gay men, sexual activity can form the basis for later friendships, which may represent conformity to the traditional mascu-line gender role in which men use sexual activity as a means to establish intimacy.

Women's romantic friendships have a long history, but until recently these rela-tionships have been presumed to be nonsexual (Rust, 2000). Perhaps the passionate friendships that were common among women in the 18th and 19th centuries included no sexual activity, but in other respects, these love relationships were similar to today's les-bian relationships, having an emphasis on feelings of closeness and emotional expression (Savin-Williams & Diamond, 2000).

Lesbians and gay men form love relationships that have the elements of intimacy, passion, and commitment in them, just as in heterosexual couples' relationships. Philip Blumstein and Pepper Schwartz (1983) surveyed gay male and lesbian couples as well as heterosexual couples, and their survey revealed similarities as well as differences among these various configurations of couples. The survey included questions about sexual activ-ities and satisfaction with these activities.

Lesbian couples reported a lower level of sexual activity than any other type of cou-ple and had some reluctance to perform cunnilingus. Blumstein and Schwartz speculated that lesbians' socialization as women might have had an influence on their sexuality, mak-ing both partners hesitant about initiating sex. The result was a lower frequency of sexual activity than in couples formed with men, who are socialized to initiate sex. Lesbians who had frequent oral sex were happier with their sex lives and with their relationships than those who had less oral sex. Nevertheless, only 39% of the lesbian couples in the survey reported having oral sex very frequently, and mutual masturbation was the most common sexual activity among these couples. Lesbians also valued nongenital physical contact, such as hugging and cuddling, activities that promoted intimacy but not orgasm.

The validity of Blumstein and Schwartz's analysis has been questioned (Frye, 1997), with an accusation of a heterosexual bias that did not allow for an understanding of lesbian sex. "Having sex" was defined as genital contact and intercourse, and lesbian sex may not

■ GENDERED VOICES

I Never Imagined the Pain

"Lesbians have been telling me about their problems in coming out," a female graduate student in counseling said. "For some reason, two women have confided in me about the problems with staying in the closet and coming out. They are women I knew and they came to trust me, but I'm not their counselor. I never imagined the pain and the problems. I guess I have led a sheltered life. I have known gays and lesbians, but I had never known or imagined the difficulties in essentially leading two lives—one for the public and the real, private one.

"One woman has been in a relationship for 17 years. During those years she and her lover have had to pretend to be 'just roommates' who share a house. She felt that she could never let the people at work know she was lesbian; she thought she would lose her job.

"She said that she felt pressured and tried to be heterosexual. She was even engaged to be married when she was in her early 20s, but her mother sensed something was wrong and told her that she didn't have to get married if she didn't want to. She broke the engagement and stopped trying to be something she wasn't, but she kept her sexual orientation secret for another 20 years.

"This woman has started to come out selectively to people she trusts. Her family still doesn't know—or at least she hasn't told them. She has found coming out a great relief and would like to be able to be completely out but does not feel comfortable enough to do so.

"The other woman has not yet come out. I guess you would say she is bisexual rather than lesbian; I'm not sure about these classifications. She is married and has a child, but she is attracted to women and has had a number of lesbian affairs, but they upset her. She says that she was 'good' when she went on a shopping trip to a large city and did not pursue a lesbian relationship, but 'bad' when she did. She is very unhappy and troubled over whether she should leave her husband and come out as a lesbian. I am really very concerned for her, because she is suicidal, and I am afraid that she might harm herself. This conflict is really a problem for her.

"In listening to these women, I was struck by their pain in essentially living a charade, pretending to be something they know they are not. That must be so difficult and so stressful. Coming out has been like removing a huge burden for the woman who has, but I see the problems in that choice, too. Talking to these two women has really been an education for me."

conform to these boundaries. What body parts must be touched for sex to occur? Did a couple "have sex" if neither experienced orgasm? "What violence did the lesbians do their experience by answering the same question the heterosexuals answered, as though it had the same meaning for them?" (Frye, 1997, p. 206). Therefore, simple comparisons of heterosexuality and homosexuality may not be valid.

Sex is a very important part of life for gay men, and their relationships typically include a lot of sexual activity, especially early in the relationship (Blumstein & Schwartz, 1983). Fellatio is an important activity for gay men, but their sex lives are varied, and mutual masturbation is also a common activity. Anal intercourse was never as common an activity as either oral sex or manual stimulation, and its dangers for spreading HIV infection have made it less common than before the appearance of AIDS. Gay men engage in a variety of sexual activities, and their frequency of sexual contact is higher than for any other configuration of couples during the early years of their relationships. The frequency of activity with their partners falls sharply after approximately the first 2 years of the relationship, but this decrease in frequency may only be a decrease in sex with their long-time partners, and not in total sexual activity.

Gay men are more acceptant of casual sex than lesbians are, and even gay men who are involved in long-term relationships often have sex with men other than their partners. Affairs can present a problem for any couple, but sex outside the relationship is not as likely to be a factor in the dissolution of gay men's relationships as it is for other couples. However, all types of couples are subject to sexual jealousy (Sheets & Wolfe, 2001).

Many similarities appeared among all configurations of couples. For example, heterosexual, lesbian, and gay couples all reported sex as important (Blumstein & Schwartz, 1983), and couples who had sex less than once a week were not as happy as couples who had sex more often. Sex formed a physical bond for all the types of couples and helped them maintain their relationships, but it was also a common source of problems. Those couples who fought about sex were less stable than those who were happy with their sexual relationships. For all of the couples, their sexual relationships reflected the problems that happened in other aspects of their relationships: Sex went well when the relationships went well, and unhappiness with the sexual activity in the relationships tended to be associated with unhappiness in the quality of affection in the relationships.

BISEXUALITY

In Kinsey's survey of sexual behavior (Kinsey et al., 1948), a relatively high percentage of men and women reported some same-gender experiences but did not have an exclusive same-gender sexual orientation. This situation suggested to Kinsey that sexuality should not be considered in terms of independent categories. He created a continuum for classifying people's sexual experience and attraction to members of their own and the other gender. This 7-point scale ranged from strongly heterosexual to strongly homosexual, with gradations in between representing people who have both types of sexual relationships in varying proportions. These gradations reflected people who are attracted to individuals of both genders, who are referred to as **bisexual.**

The status and even the existence of bisexuality remain controversial (Fox, 1996; Rust, 2000). In psychoanalytic theory, attraction to both sexes was part of sexual development, but it was abandoned in normal gender development. In this view, bisexuality is not an acceptable form of sexuality. Those who find homosexuality unacceptable will object to the same-gender sexual element of bisexuality. For gays and lesbians, bisexuality is seen as an unwillingness to acknowledge a gay or lesbian identity by clinging to heterosexuality. Therefore, bisexuality has been condemned by several discrepant groups.

Although one view of bisexuality holds that this sexual orientation represents conflict, another view sees it as flexible (Zinik, 1985). Both views may be correct. For some individuals, bisexuality represents a developmental step on the way to forming a gay or lesbian sexual orientation. These individuals experience conflict over their sexuality, and bisexuality is a way to postpone accepting their sexual identity. For others, bisexuality is a successful integration of same- and other-gender sexuality and represents flexibility.

The frequency of bisexuality is difficult to assess. With a behavioral criterion, the vast majority of gays and lesbians would be considered bisexual. That is, most gay men and lesbians have had heterosexual experiences at some time during their lives. In addition, some individuals whose primary sexual orientation is heterosexual have had same-gender sexual experiences. A behavioral criterion would count these groups of individuals as bisexual, making a substantial percentage.

Heterosexual activity may represent a type of adolescent sexual exploration among gay and lesbian adolescents (Herdt & Boxer, 1995). Just as many adolescents who go on to have a heterosexual sexual orientation experience some same-gender sex, many adolescents who develop a gay or lesbian sexual orientation experiment with heterosexuality. Indeed, the social approval for heterosexuality pushes many gay and lesbian adolescents toward cross-gender sexual experiences. However, a bisexual identity does not increase acceptance. Indeed, a study of attitudes toward bisexuals (Herek, 2002) indicated that this sexual orientation was less well accepted than any other.

Those who identify themselves as bisexual and who accept the possibility of romantic and sexual relationships with both women and men are much less common than those who identify themselves as gay or lesbian. According to the NORC survey (Laumann et al., 1994), 0.8% of men and 0.5% of women identified themselves as bisexual. So few people are bisexual that no community exists to offer support, and most bisexuals are not integrated into the existing gay and lesbian communities, leaving many bisexuals isolated (Bohan, 1996). This situation is beginning to change, and many gay and lesbian community centers and agencies include services oriented to bisexuals. Despite this increased acceptance, bisexuality remains the least-researched, least-understood, and least-accepted sexual orientation.

CONSIDERING DIVERSITY

Cultures around the world have chosen a variety of sexual activities for acceptance as "normal" and have designated other choices as abnormal, sinful, or repulsive. Cultures shape sexuality by "choosing some sexual acts (by praise, encouragement, or reward) and rejecting others (by scorn, ridicule, or condemnation), as if selecting from a sexual buffet" (Vance, 1984, p. 8). This selection from the array of available choices has resulted in virtually no universally accepted and no universally rejected set of sexual behaviors. What some cultures have found disgusting, others have found essential.

Forced fellatio performed on adult men by adolescent boys would be the basis for criminal prosecution in many cultures, but the Sambia in New Guinea find this practice not only acceptable but also required (Herdt, 1981). According to their beliefs, femininity is natural to girls but masculinity is not natural to boys. Thus, a preadolescent boy attains masculinity by leaving his mother and living with men. Part of the process involves swallowing semen, and the Sambia encourage boys to engage in fellatio with unmarried adolescent and adult men. The men must restrict their same-gender sexual activities to these boys, and fellatio with men their own age is strictly forbidden. When these adolescents and young men marry, they are supposed to make the transition to heterosexuality and to end all same-gender sexual activities.

Children in some societies are allowed and even expected to experiment with sex, whereas other societies restrict sexuality during childhood (Blackwood, 2000; Ford & Beach, 1951). For the societies that allow children to express their sexuality, genital touching and simulated intercourse are more likely to be allowed between peers than between a child and someone older. The Sambia, with their institutionalized adult–adolescent fellatio are an exception, and so are the Lepcha of India, who believe that girls will not mature unless they engage in early intercourse.

The variety of selected and rejected options is not equal across cultures. Some activities (kissing, heterosexual intercourse) are a common choice in many societies; other activities are less common but still appear in many societies (intercourse for unmarried adolescents, oral–genital stimulation); still other activities are very uncommon in the world but standard in one society, such as biting off one's partner's eyebrows during intercourse.

Societies that restrict childhood sexuality tend to do so not only through restricting intercourse but also by limiting information about sex, prohibiting masturbation, and enforcing different standards of sexual behavior for men and women. That is, sexually restrictive societies tend to have a double standard and put more restrictions on the sexuality of girls and women than on that of boys and men.

The double standard is diminishing in some countries but not in others. The most dramatic trend in attitude change has been a greater acceptance of premarital sex, which has occurred in the United States, Canada, and Europe (Scott, 1998). Attitudes in China remain very conservative, with both women and men less accepting of premarital sex and women's sexual expression (Higgins, Zheng, Liu, & Sun, 2002). Chinese women endorse the double standard more strongly than Chinese men do. Those traditional attitudes influence Chinese Americans, who tend to be less sexually active as adolescents, reluctant to report sexual abuse and rape, and less acceptant of gays and lesbians than White Americans (Okazaki, 2002). These conservative attitudes did not apply to all Asian American groups; the behavior and attitudes of Filipinos were less traditional. In addition, as Asian Americans become acculturated to North American society, their attitudes and behavior tend to change.

Many countries have prohibitions against same-gender sexual activity, but others allow, encourage, or even require such activities (Blackwood, 2000; Herdt, 1981). Several nonwestern cultures have traditions that allow women to form love and sexual relationships with other women in addition to their heterosexual couples relationships (Blackwood, 2000). The tradition and social acceptance of these relationships made them well accepted, whereas other societies may exert social sanction against same-gender sexuality. In the United States, Canada, and Europe, attitudes toward homosexuality have become more tolerant over the past 40 years (Scott, 1998). However, same-gender sexual relationships are not as well accepted in the United States as in many European countries.

Extramarital sex is condemned in most western (Laumann et al., 1994; Scott, 1998) as well as many Asian (Okazaki, 2002) societies. However, attitudes and behavior are not the same thing, and people may condemn and yet practice a sexual behavior. Therefore, disapproval of any specific sexual behavior does not mean that people do not engage in that behavior.

![ ] SUMMARY

Gender differences in sexual attitudes and behavior have been the object of speculation and research. Most sex research has used the survey technique—questioning people about their sexual attitudes or behavior. Problems with this method include the possibility of inaccuracy with self-reports and the problem of obtaining a representative sample that allows generalization to the population. Kinsey and his colleagues conducted the most famous sex surveys of male (1948) and female (1953) sexual behavior. The results showed the prevalence of many sexual activities, which differed from social norms; the results shocked many people. Kinsey's results have been disputed, but the importance of his work has not. He made the study of sexuality a legitimate part of scientific research.

The Playboy Foundation survey (Hunt, 1974) and the National Opinion Research Center survey (Laumann et al., 1994) attempted to obtain a representative sample of U.S. residents and succeeded to a greater degree than Kinsey had. These surveys indicated some changes in sexuality over the intervening years—especially a decrease in the double standard of sexual behavior for men and women—but all of the surveys have shown that people engage in a wide variety of sexual behavior.

Masters and Johnson measured sexual responses directly during masturbation and intercourse in an attempt to understand the physiology of sexual response. Their 1966 book detailed four stages of the sexual response—excitation, plateau, orgasm, and resolution. Although the people who were willing to have sex for the sake of science are not representative of the general population, Masters and Johnson believed that sexual response is similar in all people.

Childhood sexuality includes both exploration and the potential for abuse. Exploration begins very early in childhood, and parents may find these explorations disturbing. Condemning these behaviors may convey the impression that sexual feelings and activities are unacceptable. Exploitation may also begin early in childhood. Sex surveys have revealed that at least 15% of women and 5% of men were sexually abused as children. The large majority of the perpetrators of sexual abuse of children are men, often family members or those in positions of authority, but girls and women are also perpetrators of abuse. Abuse has both short-term and long-term negative effects for male and female victims.

Sex education tends to emphasize the dangers rather than the pleasures of sexuality, leaving boys with information about the damage that their male sexuality can do and leaving girls with a sense of vulnerability. Adolescence is a time of increasing sexual interest and exploration. As an average, boys engage in intercourse at a younger age than girls, and this difference appears in many ethnic groups. Gender differences in premarital intercourse as well as in other sexual activities have decreased over the past 50 years.

Marriage is no longer the only acceptable context for sexual activity; a majority of both young men and young women now have intercourse before age 25. Celibacy may be a choice or a lack of opportunity. Monogamy is the ideal sexual relationship for many people, but women rate monogamy more highly than men do. Choosing sexual free expression with many partners is not a common choice, but more men than women have multiple sexual partners at the same time. This difference may relate to men's greater acceptance of casual sex, which is one of the largest gender differences in sexuality. Another large difference is frequency of masturbation, which may lead to women being less likely to experience orgasm during partnered sex.

Another difference that influences sexuality is the existence of a double standard for sexual behavior, which holds that girls and women are less sexual than boys and men. Comparisons of the data from the Kinsey surveys and more recent analyses show that acceptance of the double standard has declined, but its continuation is a factor influencing the sexuality of women and men and contributing to conflicts in couples.

Same-gender sexual activity is not uncommon among children and adolescents, but a minority of people experience erotic attraction to only members of the same gender. Estimates vary according to the definition, but a small percentage of men and an even smaller percentage of women have primarily or exclusively gay or lesbian sexual orientation. The underlying reasons for a gay or lesbian sexual orientation are not understood, but recent research has concentrated on biological factors that may relate to sexual orientation. These biological factors may interact with personality traits and preferences to produce heterosexuality, homosexuality, or bisexuality.

Lesbian and gay sexuality is not well accepted, and adolescents who are attracted to members of their own gender may have trouble accepting themselves and their sexual orientation as well as struggling with coming out—revealing gay or lesbian interests and behavior to friends and family. The sexuality of gay men and lesbian women shows both similarities with and differences from heterosexual couples and from each other. One survey indicated that lesbian couples have sex less often than other couples do, but the definition of what constitutes sex is typically intercourse, which does not fit within lesbian sexuality. Gay men value and have sex often, especially in the first several years of their relationships. For all types of heterosexual, gay, and lesbian couples, sex provides both a bond of pleasure and a potential for conflict in their relationships.

When individuals form romantic and sexual relationships with both men and women, they are bisexual. This sexual orientation is controversial and difficult to define because many individuals experiment with sexuality, having both male and female partners. Few, however, have a true bisexual sexual orientation, so this sexual orientation remains the least-researched and most poorly understood of the sexual orientations.

Across the world, some cultures condemn the sexual behaviors that other cultures require, producing a wide variety of sexuality throughout the world. Some cultures are very restrictive, and those cultures tend to restrict women's sexuality more than men's. In western cultures, attitudes toward sex have become more liberal over the past 30 years, especially in the increased acceptability of premarital sex, but also in same-gender sexuality.

GLOSSARY

bisexual   a person who is sexually attracted to individuals of the same as well as the other gender.

celibacy   refraining from sexual activity.

coming out   the process of recognizing and publicly acknowledging one's gay or lesbian sexual orientation.

cunnilingus   oral stimulation of the female genitals.

date rape or **acquaintance rape** forced sexual activity occurring between people who are acquainted with each other.

double standard for sexual behavior the social standard that allows men greater freedom of sexual expression than women.

fellatio   oral stimulation of the male genitals.

gay   an alternative for the term *homosexual*, emphasizing the entire lifestyle instead of only the sexual aspects of it; sometimes used to refer to both men and women, but more often to men, who feel sexual attraction for and choose sexual activity with people of the same gender.

incest   sexual activity between family members.

lesbian   a woman who feels sexual attraction for and chooses sexual activity with other women.

masturbation   manipulation of the genitals to produce sexual pleasure.

monogamy   having only one sexual partner.

representative sample   a sample (subset) of the population that reflects the characteristics of the population from which the sample was drawn.

self-selection of participants   when participants rather than researchers choose who will take part in the research. This problem biases the results and prevents generalization to a wider population.

serial monogamy   the practice of having a series of monogamous sexual relationships.

sexual orientation   the erotic attraction to members of the same or the other gender (or to both).

■ SUGGESTED READINGS

Blumstein, Philip; & Schwartz, Pepper. (1983). *American couples.* New York: Pocket Books.
Although this book is not new, its interviews with married, cohabiting, gay, and lesbian couples remain fascinating and revealing. The chapter about sex examines what couples do and enjoy as well as what role sex plays in conflict and maintenance of the relationship.

Diamond, Lisa M. (2003b). What does sexual orientation orient? A biobehavioral model distinguishing romantic love and sexual desire. *Psychological Review, 110,* 173–192.
Diamond asks a provocative question concerning the meaning of sexual orientation and offers an answer that shakes the underlying assumptions of love and sex.

Oliver, Mary Beth; & Hyde, Janet Shibley. (1993). Gender differences in sexuality: A meta-analysis. *Psychological Bulletin, 114,* 29–51.

This meta-analysis concentrates on sexual attitudes and reports of sexual behaviors. The authors have determined the size of gender differences, finding large differences for a few aspects of sexuality, smaller differences for some attitudes, and no difference for others. Their interpretation is tied to the various theories of sexuality and makes an interesting summary of gender differences in sexuality.

Tolman, Deborah L. (2002). *Dilemmas of desire: Teenage girls talk about sexuality.* Cambridge, MA: Harvard University Press.
Tolman's extensive interviews with adolescent girls present the difficulties of developing a healthy sexuality within the current cultural context. Although the book focuses on girls, boys receive some attention.

11 SCHOOL

During the 1980s, many stories detailed how schools were inhospitable places for girls, but at the turn of the millennium, boys began to be the center of attention: "Across the country, boys have never been in more trouble: They earn 70 percent of the D's and F's that teachers dole out. They make up two thirds of students labeled "learning disabled." . . . They account for 80 percent of high school dropouts and attention deficit disorder diagnoses. And they are less likely to go to college than ever before. By 2007, universities are projected to enroll 9.2 million women to 6.9 million men" (Mulrine, 2001, p. 42).

Some of these school-related problems are not new; boys have always experienced more discipline problems, and their academic achievement is more variable—sometimes better but sometimes worse than girls. However, the expectation that boys will be leaders and will succeed overpowered the difficulties that many boys always experienced in school. According to experts quoted in Anna Mulrine's (2001) headline story, these expectations allowed parents and educators to ignore the evidence that boys are in trouble at school. The image of male strength and success has prevented the acknowledgment of boys' weaknesses.

School is a setting that brings out boys' vulnerability. Sitting still, paying attention, and being quiet for extended periods of time may be difficult for boys, and when they experience problems, they receive negative attention and possibly even labels of behavior disorder or attention deficit/hyperactive disorder (ADHD). Boys may excel in sports, but one expert observed that he often sees girls who are the combination of excellent student and good athlete but rarely sees that combination in boys. Boys also no longer dominate the school activities they did 25 years ago: "Girls now outnumber boys in student government, honor societies, school newspapers, and debating clubs" (Mulrine, 2001, p. 42).

Some parents and educators have considered a remedy that became popular for girls' school problems during the 1980s—single-gender classes in coed schools or single-gender schools. One set of parents interviewed in Mulrine's story told about how their son experienced attention and behavior problems, was diagnosed as ADHD, and prescribed medication. However, they decided to switch him to a boys' school rather than have the prescription filled. Other boys' parents flock to single-gender classes offered in coed schools, just as girls' parents did when schools offered science and math classes for girls (King, 1999). Gender-equity advocate David Sadker (in Mulrine, 2001) criticized the strategy of separating girls and boys rather than trying to fix the problems with coed classrooms.

What are those problems and inequities? When do they start? And what are the consequences of the school experience for women's and men's lives?

THE SCHOOL EXPERIENCE

Even before children begin school, their parents and the society in which they live treat boys and girls differently. Chapter 7 included examples of the process of gender stereotyping: dolls for girls but trucks for boys, quiet games for girls but noisy games for boys, frilly dresses for girls but grubby jeans for boys, staying close to home for girls but venturing out for boys.

Not all girls or all boys conform to these stereotypes, but by age 4 or 5, children know what behaviors are expected and approved for each. (See Chapter 6 for a more complete discussion of the development of gender identity.) Thus, when children start kindergarten, they already hold beliefs about what clothes, games, and behaviors are appropriate for boys and girls, and they bring these beliefs to the school experience. Schools often reinforce these stereotypical beliefs, producing differences in attitudes and expectations about careers that result in differences in preparation to pursue careers.

Title IX of the Education Amendments of 1972 prohibits gender discrimination in school programs that receive federal funds. Although law now prohibits gender discrimination, a study by the American Association of University Women, the AAUW, (1992) presented a great deal of evidence illustrating a continuing lack of gender equity. Problems included unequal attention and access to education materials, promotion of stereotypical gender roles, unequal expectations concerning careers, and sexual harassment in school by classmates and teachers.

The AAUW report focused attention on girls and how schools may not serve their educational needs. The subsequent attention to gender equity in education prompted a backlash such as the one discussed in the headline story for this chapter (Mulrine, 2001), which details the problems that boys have in school. The publicity about gender equity has gotten the attention of many teachers (Arnot, 2000), who strive to be fair in their interactions with children in the classroom. Even so, they may fail. Teachers who believe that they are treating girls and boys the same may still fail at fairness (Jones, Evans, Byrd, & Campbell, 2000).

The reasons for gender inequity in schools have many roots. Gender equity is not a large part of the curriculum for prospective teachers; neither is it a frequent topic of inservice training for teachers (AAUW, 1992; Sadker & Sadker, 1985; Zittleman & Sadker, 2002). A 1980 examination of textbooks used for teacher training found that these texts devoted very little space to gender equity issues (Sadker & Sadker, 1980). This study concluded that teachers could not be trained to be gender fair when their training minimized these issues. A later study (Zittleman & Sadker, 2002) presented a comparable analysis of teacher education textbooks and found that these recent texts also gave little space to issues of gender equity. The percent of coverage for gender equity issues had increased from less than 1.0% to 3.3%. General education texts included the most coverage (7.3%), but methods books still devoted very little coverage to gender issues (1.3%). Considering the challenges of teaching boys and girls in subjects that are identified as gendered domains, this coverage is probably not adequate.

Early Schooling

The problem of teachers promoting stereotypical gender roles can begin very early in the school experience and may occur even in teachers who do not realize that they are treating girls and boys differently (Garrahy, 2001). Children tend to practice gender segregation, and teachers usually allow and sometimes even encourage this separation (Thorne, 1993). In addition, children have the experience of being taught by an overwhelming majority of female kindergarten and elementary school teachers. The only man in many elementary schools is the custodian. The women who choose elementary teaching differ from men who have made the same choice (Montecinos & Nielsen, 1997). Women reported that they decided to become elementary teachers when they were in elementary school more often than men did, and more women than men expected to teach in elementary school for the duration of their careers. These differences may reflect varying degrees of commitment.

Male elementary school teachers are still rare, but their behavior is similar to female elementary school teachers: Both tend to reward children for being compliant (Cohen, 1992). Benefits of having male elementary teachers include a decrease in students' gender stereotyping: Those with male teachers make significantly fewer stereotypical explanations for the behavior of men and women than do students who have had only female teachers during the elementary grades (Mancus, 1992). This advantage extends to both boys and girls, but there is no clear evidence that girls benefit and boys are damaged by the gender imbalance in elementary school teachers.

The preponderance of female elementary school teachers has led to the "myth that early-education environments meet the needs of girls better than boys" (AAUW, 1992, p. 18). The AAUW report argued that the opposite is true: Early schooling consists of activities in which girls have more proficiency than boys, giving boys more training in the skills they lack, such as reading, while ignoring skills that girls lack, such as science investigation. Girls need practice with gross motor activities, investigatory activities, and experimental activities, but these activities tend to be considered part of "play" rather than part of their education, and thus they have been excluded from the curriculum. Furthermore, these activities are more likely to result from boys' play than the play girls prefer. Thus, the activities of the early elementary classroom may be difficult for boys because these activities concentrate on the skills boys lack. Girls do not have the same problems, but they also do not receive the same benefits.

To benefit from the lessons that school presents, boys must be quiet, pay attention, and concentrate. For some boys, this behavior is out of line with the gender role they are developing; that is, school requires that they act like "sissies." Either rebellion or difficulties in meeting the school requirements may contribute to the situation of boys being much more likely than girls to present behavior problems. Indeed, a great deal of the extra attention that boys receive revolves around controlling boys' misbehavior.

Few gender differences exist in school achievement during the early years of school, but the differences favor girls (Bae, Choy, Geddes, Sable, & Snyder, 2000). Tests have shown that girls outscore boys on reading and writing, and this difference persists throughout schooling. In addition, girls make better grades. Socioeconomic status is a more important predictor of elementary school achievement than gender, with children from lower socioeconomic levels having consistently poorer school records than children from wealthier families. Even controlling for socioeconomic status, girls tend to make better grades in school, beginning during the elementary grades and persisting through college.

Several social factors combine to predict academic success and to explain gender differences during elementary school (Serbin, Zelkowitz, Doyle, Gold, & Wheaton, 1990). Girls' advantage relates to their tendency to respond to social cues and to comply with adults' requests. That is, the training that girls receive in complying with the female gender role is a factor in their early school success. Problems in school occur when students fail to comply with adults' rules and requests, and boys are more likely to behave in these ways, creating problems for themselves in school. Indeed, conformity to gender-typical behaviors relates to both girls' success and boys' problems.

Boys are more likely than girls to receive referrals for special education services, and this gender difference has led to the suspicion that gender discrimination may be operating. In a study of such referrals (Wehmeyer, 2001), results indicated that gender bias was a factor. However, the bias prevented girls from receiving special education services from which they might benefit rather than producing inappropriate referrals for boys.

Academic success is complex; both intellectual and social factors relate to success in school. Figure 11.1 shows a model of factors that one study (Serbin et al., 1990) related

GENDERED VOICES

Treated Like a King

"I'm not sure why I wanted to work with kids," a young male elementary school teacher told me. "I started as a camp counselor, and that job was attractive because of the other counselors—lots of girls. They thought it was cool that I was a counselor and was good with kids. They seemed to think that getting along with children meant I was sensitive. I can get a line of my ex-girlfriends who will testify that I am not any more sensitive than most guys, but I do like working with kids, so I became a teacher.

"The principal and coach are both men, but there is only one other male teacher in my school, so I get a lot of attention from the students and from the female teachers. The kids love me; I'm treated like a king. When I walk down the hall, they want to be near me, and my attention is something special. Some of them live in single-parent families with their mothers, but even the ones who live with fathers seem starved for male attention. I believe that their fathers may not be too emotionally accessible, and I am, so they are drawn to me. I try to have good relationships with them, and it is work that I enjoy, but the administration keeps hinting that I should get a degree so that I can become an administrator. I don't want to; I'm satisfied doing what I'm doing."

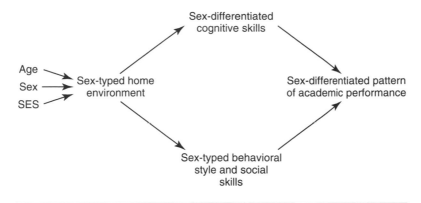

FIGURE 11.1 *Model of Social and Cognitive Abilities Predicting Academic Performance*

Source: "The Socialization of Sex-Differentiated Skills and Academic Performance: A Mediational Model," by L. A. Serbin, P. Zelkowitz, A. Doyle, D. Gold, & B. Wheaton, 1990, *Sex Roles, 23,* p. 616. Reprinted by permission of Plenum Publishing and Lisa Serbin.

to academic success. As previous research had indicated, socioeconomic status (SES) variables predicted academic success, including mothers' occupational and fathers' educational levels. These variables also indirectly influenced the single cognitive factor most strongly related to academic success: visual–spatial ability. This study suggested that children's conformity to gender-typical behaviors plays a role in girls' academic success and in boys' poor performance. Thus, a complex picture emerges to describe academic success during elementary school, with socioeconomic factors, gender role socialization, and cognitive abilities all contributing.

Changes during Middle School

The gender differences that begin to appear during middle and junior high school relate more strongly to attitudes than to achievement and more to interests and preferences than to abilities. Girls show interest in participating in science activities, but boys are more likely to participate in and perform science, such as using microscopes and electricity meters. These different experiences with science activities both in and outside of the classroom are a factor in girls' lower achievement and interest in physical science (Lee & Burkam, 1996). These inequalities are the focus of equity education efforts aimed at providing single-gender classrooms so that girls do not get pushed out of the way and have access to science and technology. Such classes are controversial, and little evidence exists that they provide long-term solutions to this problem (Signorella, Frieze, & Hershey, 1996).

A great deal of attention has focused on the decline in academic confidence that girls experience during middle and junior high school. Older research (Bush & Simmons, 1987) indicated a decrease for girls and an increase for boys in confidence, but a recent longitudinal study (Jacobs, Lanza, Osgood, Eccles, & Wigfield, 2002) found that the differences were not in what people believed and the changes over the school years were not as expected.

Children's beliefs in their competence for language arts (a stereotypically female domain), sports (a stereotypically male domain), and mathematics (another stereotypically male domain) were higher when they entered school than at any other point in their education. That is, this longitudinal study (Jacobs et al., 2002) showed a pattern of decreases in beliefs about self-competence over the 12 years of schooling. Boys' self-ratings were generally higher than girls' ratings initially, but boys' beliefs fell faster than girls', especially in the academic domains of language arts and mathematics. This study also measured how valued these areas were and found a strong relationship between ratings of competence and value placed on the area. Children and adolescents value what they believe they are able to do. Therefore, beliefs concerning declining competence are a signal of school trouble. These findings are consistent with the academic problems that boys experience in school and also with girls' beliefs about their abilities in math.

By junior high school, girls show less interest in mathematics than boys. This interest does not have a large impact on their grades; girls continue to make comparable or better grades in math class, but they come to find mathematics less interesting as a field of study (Davis-Kean, Eccles, & Linver, 2002). One factor in their declining interest may be the perception that math is a male domain. That perception is widely shared by boys, girls, parents, and teachers (Nosek, Banaji, & Greenwald, 2002; Tiedemann, 2000). Some research (Nosek et al., 2002) has shown that this association is stronger for people who more strongly associate themselves with the general category of men or women. In addition, the association of men with math is not a completely conscious process, resulting in a pervasive but subtle version of stereotyping.

Athletic performance is another gendered behavior, and it becomes more gender segregated during late childhood and early adolescence. "That's a game for girls" is an insult to boys, and few girls are competent at boys' sports. The preferred activities of girls and boys continue to differ along paths that appeared during early childhood: Boys more often engage in physical activities requiring gross motor skills that use the large muscles of the body. Games that include running, jumping, throwing, and kicking—namely baseball, football, soccer, and basketball—are preferred by boys more than by girls.

Girls are not necessarily more sedentary than boys, but their leisure activities are less likely to involve gross motor skills. Indeed, both boys and girls are increasingly sedentary; they watch television and play video and computer games, resulting in decreased levels of physical fitness. The intensification of gender roles during junior high school pushes girls away from, and boys toward, athletics. In a longitudinal study (Jacobs et al., 2002), boys' beliefs in their athletic competence remained higher than beliefs about their academic abilities between 1st and 12th grade, and their beliefs about athletic abilities were higher than girls' opinions of their abilities.

Therefore, the middle school years show a continuation of better grades and academic accomplishment for girls but a decline in girls' interest in mathematics and physical sciences. Their decreased participation may be one reason for their decreased interest in science, but the continued lack of encouragement by their teachers and parents may also contribute to girls' declining interest in science and math during middle school. Both boys and girls experience a decline in confidence in their academic abilities during this time, which may affect boys more strongly than girls.

High School

High school represents a significant transition for adolescents, both in educational and social terms. Students become more focused on careers, and high school students may make choices about coursework that younger students are not allowed. The social environment revolves around school activities and heterosexuality, which may also influence the academic choices that students make. Adolescent girls believe that they will combine a family with paid employment, reflecting the current reality of contemporary family life, but they also understand that having children when they are young will affect their educational attainment (Mahaffy & Ward, 2002). Boys do not see how children might affect their educational plans.

Physical appearance and athletic ability are important to high school students because both are ways to gain prestige in the school social structure (Suitor & Reavis, 1995; Suitor & Carter, 1999). Both female and male high school students have other ways to gain social status, but appearance remains important for girls and athletic ability is a plus for boys (Weinberg, 2000). However, some changes have occurred in how boys and girls may gain prestige at school. In comparing students from the late 1970s to those from the late 1980s, physical appearance remained a primary way for girls to attain social prominence in their schools, and athletics continued to be as important for boys (Suitor & Reavis, 1995). The 10-year comparison showed that sports had become more important, and cheerleading less important, ways for girls to gain prestige. For boys, having fast cars became less important. However, having sex remained a way to gain prestige in the high school environment. For both girls and boys, getting good grades, being considered intelligent, sports participation, and physical attractiveness conferred prestige. Sports dominated the avenue to prestige for boys, whereas all the factors contributed to girls' prestige (Suitor & Carter, 1999).

The increased emphasis on sports for young women has resulted in the current acceptance of sports as a way for young women to gain positive recognition, especially at parochial schools (Weinberg, 2000). Their increased sports participation has been dramatic. In 1971, girls constituted only 7.5% of athletic participants in high schools, but in 1996, the percentage had grown to 39.0% (Owens, Smothers, & Love, 2003). Not only has the number of female athletes grown, but the variety of sports in which they participate has also increased. High schools have added women's teams in cross country, gymnastics, soccer, field hockey, softball, swimming, track, volleyball, and other sports. The success of U.S. women's teams in Olympic and world competition for soccer, basketball, and softball has provided exciting role models. Expanded opportunities for high school girls have allowed them to develop their physical abilities and talents in ways that previously were reserved for boys.

The differences in confidence and attitudes toward various subjects become more pronounced during high school. With the greater choice that high school students have about their coursework, these differences have the potential for great impact. For example, students who choose not to take advanced math and science courses will limit their access to certain college majors and careers; the choice to play sports, date, or get a job can detract from study time and affect grades, which can limit career options.

From middle to high school, girls experience more of a decrease than boys in interest and confidence concerning math and science. A meta-analysis (Weinburgh, 1995) indicated that boys had more positive attitudes toward science than girls did, and the relationship between attitudes and achievement was positive. Furthermore, the relationship was stronger for girls than for boys, indicating that their attitudes may have a stronger influence on their performance and choices.

Unfortunately, even high levels of ability do not guarantee that students will have positive attitudes or high achievement. The overall gender differences in mathematics course participation have disappeared, and now girls and boys are equally likely to take advanced math classes (Bae et al., 2000). However, some students who are intellectually gifted and have the ability to succeed at the highest levels fail to develop their abilities. Mathematically talented girls are less likely than comparably talented boys to pursue math or science careers (Ayalon, 2003; Walker, Reis, & Leonard, 1992).

Male and female high school students who pursue science are not equally represented in all types of science courses (AAUW, 1992). The only gender-related difference that remains in academic course enrollment in high school is science courses. Female students are more likely to enroll in advanced biology and social science classes, whereas boys are more likely to take physics and physical sciences (Bae et al., 2000). In addition, students enrolled in the same course may have different views of how the course fits into their career plans. For example, young men who enroll in calculus and advanced science in high school are very likely to take these courses in preparation for careers in science or engineering, whereas fewer young women enrolled in the same courses pursue those careers.

A study completed in Israel explored this puzzling situation (Ayalon, 2003). Israeli students receive bonuses from universities for taking advanced courses in high school, which boosts the number of students enrolling in such courses. Thus, many women complete advanced math and science courses and have the background to pursue science, mathematics, and engineering in college. However, they tend not to do so. The results of this study showed that women were more likely to choose psychology or humanities as majors or to pursue a career in medicine rather than mathematics or engineering. A similar pattern appeared among groups of mathematically talented youth in the United States (Benbow, Lubinski, Shea, & Eftekhari-Sanjani, 2000). Among these math-talented students, men were more likely to go on to earn doctorates in math, engineering, or physical sciences, whereas women were more likely to earn doctorates in biology, medicine, or law. Thus, even with the ability and background, young women do not choose physical science or technology careers at the same rate that young men do.

These different choices have been considered a problem for women because the careers are high in prestige and income. When education experts judge the enrollment of women as low, they are using men and their enrollment statistics as the standard (Noddings, 1991/1992). The implication is that women's enrollment is deficient and something to be remedied. Nel Noddings suggested that educators have given too little consideration both to what women are doing and to the reasons behind their choices. She pointed out that stereotypical thinking has imposed limitations on both young women and young men, restricting both from a full range of choices in coursework and careers. Most of the criticisms and research have centered on girls and how they are diverted from math and science. Fewer considerations have been directed toward boys and how they might be steered toward math and science when those subjects and careers might not be the ones for which they have the highest interest or aptitude. That is, the current situation may reflect both an underrepresentation of women and an overrepresentation of men in math and science.

Counselors' stereotyping of gender-appropriate careers is a factor in the courses that boys and girls take in school as well as in the careers they choose. Gender bias in counseling may be either overt or covert (Hoffman, 1982). Overt bias includes sexist statements, such as telling girls that they are not expected to be good at math or discouraging boys from enrolling in cooking classes. Covert bias includes encouraging girls and boys to behave in stereotypical ways, such as providing information concerning traditional but not nontraditional careers, or failing to take nontraditional career interests seriously.

Although school counselors receive training that directs them to concentrate on the individual's abilities and interests, the process of advising students about careers offers many possibilities for subtle bias. Counselors may steer adolescents toward traditional careers or offer alternatives that differ for girls and boys with similar levels of ability (Hoffman, 1982). Counselors may steer girls toward careers that require education and ability but not to high status and prestige. For example, counselors are more likely to recommend that girls become science teachers than chemists and that boys become chemists rather than science teachers. As girls get older and closer to a career choice, the levels of discrimination become stronger.

Vocational education is another area in which girls and boys have received unequal attention: "Vocational education was originally designed to give work skills to high school boys who were not planning to attend college. But research indicates that it may not serve

GENDERED VOICES

I Might Have Been an Engineer

"I probably would have been an engineer if I had been given the opportunity. Well, maybe *opportunity* isn't exactly the right word, because nothing really prevented me, but nobody encouraged me, either," a high school science teacher in her early 40s said. "I always liked science and did well in it, but none of my counselors mentioned engineering, or being a chemist, or any science career except teaching. I think they mentioned those careers to the boys who were good at science, but not to the girls. They steered us toward teaching. That's just the way it was, and I'm not sure how much it has changed.

"They just didn't expect girls to be good at science and math, and when we were, they didn't consider science careers, so they didn't tell us about being a scientist. Teaching science, yes, but not being a scientist. If a boy was interested in science, they wouldn't have mentioned teaching, even if that was what he would have been best at. I wonder how many women would have been better scientists and engineers than science teachers, and how many men would have been better science teachers."

either males or females very well in the current environment" (AAUW, 1992, p. 42). This pessimistic assessment comes from the finding that men who complete vocational educational courses in high school earned less money than those who did not take these courses.

The situation for young women is much worse; vocational education pushes young women toward low-paying jobs. In 2002, the National Women's Law Center petitioned the U.S. Department of Education to investigate the gender discrimination in vocational education (*School Law News,* 2002). This petition was based on statistics about enrollment in vocational education, which has sharp discrepancies in enrollment according to gender. For example, 87% of those in child-care classes were women, and over 90% of those receiving training to become electricians were men. However, the salaries differ significantly for the two careers—hourly wage of $7.43 for child-care workers versus $20.00 for electricians.

One factor that affects women who choose to pursue nontraditional vocational education is sexual harassment. **Sexual harassment,** unwanted sexual attention from students and teachers, is a situation that happens to both girls and boys at school. Although young men experience sexual harassment, fewer mention being troubled by unwanted sexual attention by their female peers or teachers (AAUW, 1993, 2001). However, same-gender sexual harassment by peers is a common experience, especially for boys.

Harassment involving gender may be sexually oriented or not; it consists of unwanted sexual remarks, statements about the unsuitability of women for various types of

ACCORDING TO THE MEDIA . . .

High School Is Near the Mouth of Hell

During the six years of its broadcasts (1997–2003), *Buffy the Vampire Slayer* sent unorthodox messages about high school and college life, family relationships, friends, and gender. The series featured Buffy Summers, who moved to southern California and enrolled in Sunnydale High School. Buffy was not part of the "in crowd" and felt like an outcast. This experience is not unusual for the new girl in school, but in *Buffy the Vampire Slayer,* Sunnydale High was located on top of one of the mouths of hell and Buffy had superhuman powers. She was the Chosen One, a once-in-a-generation slayer who had the power to save humanity and kill the monsters that escaped from hell. She befriended other outcast students, who helped her in her mission to protect humanity.

The series used monsters as metaphors for the high school world of cliques, coolness, anti-intellectualism, and unreasoning adult authority (Early, 2001). In Buffy's high school, the bullies were literally demons. The vampires and demons were both male and female, but as the Slayer, Buffy occupied a role that is unusual for a woman: She was not only a hero but also a warrior. Female characters have occupied this role in comic books more often than on television or in movies; action heroes are usually men. Buffy was a small, thin, blonde, pretty young woman who happened to be able to "kick some serious demon ass" (in Early, 2001). Buffy struggled with her mission, as heroes do, trying to do what was right. She and her friends patrolled Sunnydale, attempting to keep the demons from destroying humanity, but Buffy tried to avoid violence in many episodes as well as performed martial arts–based slayings.

jobs, or derogatory remarks about women or men and their abilities. As the AAUW reports (1993, 2001) pointed out, harassment is about power and authority, and the vast majority of incidents involve boys harassing girls. Although sexual and other harassment that affects the educational process is prohibited by Title IX of the Education Amendments of 1972, those who harass have been allowed to continue. The attitude was often "boys will be boys," with harassment not considered a serious offense. When legal changes allowed school systems to be sued for monetary damages, school systems began to take sexual harassment more seriously (Fineran, 2002). However, most incidents still go unreported, and fear of harassment may make girls reluctant to enroll in courses with a majority of boys or to enroll in nontraditional vocational courses.

Surveys of junior high and high school students (AAUW, 1993, 2001; Timmerman, 2003) have revealed that three fourths or more of students said they had been the target of unwelcome sexual behavior while at school or a school function. Adult school employees were the perpetrators in about one fourth of cases, so the majority of harassment incidents are perpetrated by other students. Girls were more common targets than boys, but both girls and boys admitted perpetrating sexual harassment. Student perpetrators tended to consider harassment part of school life and "no big deal" (Bryant, 1995, p. 41). The targets felt differently. Harassment made school more difficult; victims were less interested and involved in school, made lower grades, and expressed more doubt about graduating (see "According

ACCORDING TO THE RESEARCH . . .

High School May Be Close to Hell for Some Adolescents

Some adolescents may think of other students at their high schools as demons; high school is a difficult experience for many adolescents who are outcast, marginalized, bullied, and harassed. However, the difficulties experienced by those harassed about their sexual orientation are especially serious and often systematic. Many students who are the targets of harassment fail to conform to gender-stereotypical behaviors but may not be gay, lesbian, or bisexual. Accusations of homosexuality are frequent occurrences, and those who use them often know of their lack of truth (AAUW, 1993). The harassment sometimes goes beyond name-calling and into physical attacks, with young gay men in particular peril:

> "Faggot" is the ultimate insult used by kids and teenagers all over the country to designate those who are different or simply disliked, whether they are gay or not. It was the epithet of choice the students at

Columbine High School hurled at the Trench Coat Mafia, helping to drive two of its nail-painting, Hitler-worshipping techies into their murderous rage. It was the word young gay bashers carved into the flesh of the 17-year-old Marin County lad whom they beat senseless after he founded a Gay-Straight Alliance at the high school in his supposedly liberal and tolerant community. (Ireland, 1999, p. 8)

These incidents of harassment and violence take their toll, making school unpleasant and dangerous. Gay and lesbian students are more likely to drop out of school and attempt suicide than other students (Lock & Steiner, 1999). Some schools approach the problem by beginning counseling programs and by appointing personnel to coordinate services for gay, lesbian, and bisexual students (Livingston, 1994). Some schools do nothing, and those schools can be close to the mouth of hell for gay and lesbian adolescents.

to the Media" and "According to the Research"). Although sexual harassment may be part of high school life, it is a major problem with serious consequences.

In summary, both overt and subtle forces affect adolescents during high school, with both girls and boys tending toward more traditional, stereotypical choices. Enrollment in math and science classes is now comparable for boys and girls, but attitudes about those subjects differ. Those girls who complete advanced math and science courses tend not to view these courses as part of their career preparation as boys do. High school counselors may act as source of gender bias, steering more boys than girls toward prestigious careers. In vocational education, boys are more likely to be guided toward higher-paying skilled craft jobs, and girls into lower-paying business and service jobs. Girls who enroll in non-traditional courses face the possibility of sexual or other harassment, and, although illegal, this behavior is a common experience. Peers are more common harassers than teachers or other school personnel.

College and Professional School

The effects of stereotyping and gender bias influence young women and men before they enter college, creating differences in expectations and choices. Young men receive messages from society, the media, and specific people in their lives that they should prepare for careers that will support a family. Young women get a different message: They need to be able to support themselves until they marry (and possibly after they divorce), but their careers will be less important than their husbands' employment.

These differing expectations are consistent with the history of women's roles, but not necessarily with contemporary life in industrialized countries. College education for women developed gradually during the 19th century, but never approached equal education for men and women, either in numbers or in type of training (Owens et al., 2003). Instead, women went to college to find husbands and to prepare for careers that would last only until they married. Thus, higher education for women prepared them for careers that would be flexible; chances for advancement were unimportant. One of the early careers available to women was teaching, and beginning in the 1800s, women were in demand as teachers in the growing public school system. One of the reasons female teachers were in demand was their willingness to work for low salaries.

Throughout most of the 20th century, men attended college in greater numbers than women, but the number of female college students in the United States and Canada has grown to the point that women now receive more undergraduate degrees than men do (U.S. Bureau of the Census [USBC], 2002). This pattern applies to few other countries. Especially in countries that are less industrialized, women do not participate in higher (or other) education nearly as often as men do. Table 11.1 presents the percentage of students who are women in various countries, but it does not reveal the number of students who are eligible to attend college. In the United States, a higher percentage of high school graduates enroll in college than in most other countries, even compared to other industrialized countries. That high percentage combined with the proportion of female U.S. college students results in U.S. women being better educated than their counterparts in most other countries (USBC, 2002).

TABLE 11.1   *Percentage of All Female College and University Students in Various Countries*

Country	Percentage of Women	Country	Percentage of Women
Argentina	47%	Japan	29%
Australia	53	Kenya	28
Brazil	53	Mexico	45
Canada	55	Nigeria	27
China	20	Peru	34
France	55	Russian Federation	50
Germany	41	Saudi Arabia	42
India	32	South Africa	48
Iran	31	Switzerland	40
Israel	51	United States	53

Source: Adapted from "United Nations International Conference on Population and Development," 1995, New York: United Nations.

Men have historically received the overwhelming majority of advanced degrees (master's and doctoral) and professional degrees (such as medical, dental, law, veterinary), but that pattern also has changed. In the 1960s, women earned only about 3% of professional degrees, but by the 1980s, the percentage had grown to 33%, and in 2000, women received 58% of all master's, and 44% of all doctoral degrees granted in the United States (USBC, 2002). Women have made comparable gains in earning professional degrees, such as medicine and law degrees, as Figure 11.2 shows. This growing number of women in professional fields has changed the composition of most professions, but past differences will take many years to equalize. Like undergraduate and professional degrees, doctoral degrees also show patterns of gender segregation: A greater proportion of doctoral degrees in physical sciences and engineering still go to men, whereas a greater proportion of doctoral degrees in education and psychology go to women.

Table 11.2 shows the percentage of degrees awarded to women in 1971 compared to 2000 for different majors. Most professions now have a larger proportion of women as a result of the changes in degrees awarded during the past 30 years. Some areas have experienced less change, some areas remain dominated by women, and some areas have become dominated by women. In addition, African American and Hispanic American women are more likely to receive degrees than men in these ethnic groups (USBC, 2002). Whites are overrepresented and other ethnic groups underrepresented among those who receive master's and doctoral degrees. For example, in the year 2000 about 5% of doctoral degrees went to African Americans, another 5.3% to Asian Americans, 2.9% to Hispanic Americans, and 0.7% to Native Americans.

Gender disparities continue to exist on college athletic fields, and the attempts to remedy these inequities have become the center of continuing, heated controversy. Title IX of the Educational Amendments of 1972 prohibited discrimination in educational programs that receive federal funding, including college athletic programs. Funding has been far from

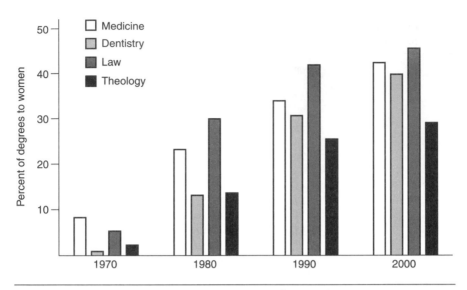

FIGURE 11.2   *Percent of Women Earning Professional Degrees, 1970–2000*

Source: Statistical Abstract of the United States, 2002 (122nd ed., p. 178), by U.S. Bureau of the Census, 2002, Washington, DC: U.S. Government Printing Office.

equal in athletics; men's sports receive far more scholarships, equipment, facilities, staff, and publicity than women's sports do. Colleges have struggled (and sometimes mounted legal challenges) against increased funding for women's athletics (Maimer, Bergeron, Bosetti, & Teed, 2003).

Critics of Title IX argue that women and men do not show the same interest in sports participation, making equal funding unfair to men who want to participate. Supporters contend that female students' low level of interest in college athletics reflects the bias against women in sports that begins even before girls go to school (Hogshead-Makar, 2003). Increased opportunities for women to participate in competitive athletics have increased the number of women who compete. In the 1970s, only 7% of college women participated in organized athletics, but that percentage has grown to about 35%. The increase has not resulted in equal participation, equal funding, or equal acceptance for women in athletics. Enforcement of Title IX has not yet resulted in equal opportunities for training, use of locker rooms, medical services, or scholarships (Maimer et al., 2003; Suggs, 1999).

The growing numbers of women who compete in college athletics receive support in the form of scholarships from their colleges and universities, but they have also received encouragement to develop their athletic abilities before they reach college. Mothers, older siblings, friends, and coaches in high school and junior high were all forms of social support to women who were college athletes (Weiss & Barber, 1995). Furthermore, these sources of support have improved over the past 20 years. Therefore, today's female athletes have benefited not only from the laws that mandate access to sports but also from the changes in attitudes that have made athletic competition more acceptable and admired for women.

TABLE 11.2 *Percentage Degrees Awarded to Women in Various Fields, 1971 versus 2000*

Field	Bachelor's Degree		Master's Degree		Doctoral Degree	
	1971	2000	1971	2000	1971	2000
Agriculture	4.2%	42.9%	5.9%	46.0%	2.9%	31.3%
Architecture	11.9	38.6	13.8	41.2	8.3	34.1
Biology	29.1	58.3	33.6	55.3	16.3	44.1
Business and management	9.1	49.7	3.9	39.8	2.8	31.9
Communications	35.3	61.2	34.6	63.3	13.1	52.9
Computer and information science	13.6	28.1	10.3	33.3	2.3	16.9
Education	74.5	75.8	56.2	76.4	21.0	64.6
Engineering	0.8	18.5	1.1	20.9	0.6	15.5
English/literature	65.6	67.9	60.6	66.9	28.8	58.8
Ethnic studies	52.4	67.7	38.3	59.5	16.7	51.2
Foreign language	74.0	70.8	64.2	69.6	34.6	59.0
Health science	77.1	83.8	55.3	77.3	16.5	61.2
Home economics	97.3	87.9	93.9	83.9	61.0	76.8
Law	5.0	73.0	4.8	41.5	—	33.8
Liberal studies	33.6	66.1	44.6	64.9	31.3	50.6
Library science	92.0	50.0	81.3	79.3	28.2	72.1
Math	37.9	47.1	27.1	44.9	7.6	25.0
Philosophy/religion	25.5	34.0	27.1	39.5	5.8	24.3
Physical science	13.8	40.3	13.3	35.4	5.6	25.5
Protective services	9.2	43.4	10.3	41.2	—	46.2
Psychology	44.4	76.5	40.6	75.4	24.0	67.4
Public administration	68.4	81.1	50.0	73.4	24.1	57.7
Social sciences	36.8	51.2	28.5	50.1	13.9	41.2
Visual/performing arts	59.7	59.2	47.4	57.2	22.2	52.4

Source: Statistical Abstract of the United States, 2002 (122nd ed., pp. 176–177), by U.S. Bureau of the Census, 2002, Washington, DC: U.S. Government Printing Office.

Athletic departments have struggled to provide funding for women's athletics in times of dwindling budgets. Indeed, much of the controversy over women's athletics concerns money rather than a desire to prohibit women from participating in sports. After a 1988 U.S. congressional affirmation that campuses cannot discriminate in funding for sports and athletics, and a 1997 U.S. Supreme Court ruling that left Title IX intact, college athletic departments still continue to attempt legal and political challenges (Hogshead-Makar, 2003).

GENDERED VOICES

I Didn't Get to Play

"When I was a teenager, I was interested in sports, and I was good, especially at baseball," a woman in her 40s told me. "That was before Title IX, and there was no effort at all to allow women access to athletics, so I didn't get to play. It was partly social censure. Girls weren't supposed to be athletic, except for acceptable athletics. Dancing and cheerleading were acceptable for girls, but not baseball, which was the sport I liked.

"My mother didn't like my athletic inclinations and tried to urge me away from baseball and volleyball. I think I could have made the boys' baseball team, but of course, that was out of the question. No more. The

changes are amazing. Girls play on boys' teams in baseball and even football in junior high and high school. Of course I regret not being able to play the sports I liked, but the changes in access to sports for women and even in attitudes toward athletic women are substantial.

"Rather than being discouraged from pursuing sports, my cousin got a volleyball scholarship that paid for her college education. I saw a news story about a girl who played linebacker on her junior high school football team. Those changes have not come easily, but I can remember when things were much different for athletic women. There has definitely been improvement."

In many ways, college amplifies the gender issues that exist in high school, making the college experience different for women and men in the classroom as well as in the locker room. Although both women and men report a generally positive campus climate (Fischer & Good, 1994), women experience more feelings of gender bias than men, and these feelings relate to the number of male instructors and classmates. Men also reported some negative feelings, including indifference and lack of recognition from their instructors. Both men and women agree that women were not as well represented in the curricula as men were.

The choice of coursework results in some majors and classes that are dominated by one gender or the other. Although men are in the minority in many college classrooms, they may still dominate. For example, men interrupt more often in college classroom discussions and take leadership roles in mixed groups (Condravy, Skirboll, & Taylor, 1998). College instructors are more likely to be men, and this factor influences classroom interaction styles. Women and men tend to have different preferences for classroom interactions with teachers and peers (Kramarae & Treichler, 1990). Women feel more comfortable in discussions in which teachers and students collaborate than in situations in which teachers try to impose their views on students. Men feel more comfortable in classrooms with a clear hierarchy and an emphasis on specified goals. That is, women and men carry their conversational preferences (see Chapter 9) into classroom interactions, and the preferences of each gender may make the other uncomfortable.

Women's uneasiness with the campus climate extends to professional and doctoral training, at which point women feel less encouraged and supported than their male colleagues (Bickel, 2001; Kennedy & Parks, 2000). The majority of professors are men, and they tend to support, encourage, and assist their male students more than their female students (Schroeder & Mynatt, 1999). The lower percentage of female faculty contributes to less encouragement and fewer role models for female undergraduates to attain advanced degrees (Rothstein, 1995). Women in male-dominated doctoral programs reported lower career commitment and feeling less supported than male students in these programs and also less supported than female students in more gender-balanced programs (Ulku-Steiner, Kurtz-Costes, & Kinlaw, 2000).

Role models and mentoring relationships can be very important to career advancement, because young professionals benefit from the guidance and aid of older, more experienced professionals. Mentors tend to choose protégés who reflect themselves, so there is a tendency for men to choose men and women to choose women. With fewer women in high positions in academia, young women are at a disadvantage in finding mentors, and cross-gender mentoring does not offer the same benefits as same-gender mentoring, especially for women (Schroeder & Mynatt, 1999).

The close working relationships of mentoring also provide situations that can lead to sexual attraction and action. With the imbalance of power between students and faculty, sexual relationships are almost inevitably exploitative and often meet the definition of sexual harassment. A review of sexual harassment in college (Paludi, 1997) noted the frequency of incidents, with both men and women as the targets. That frequency does not mean that students see themselves as sexually harassed; labeling sexual harassment is a problem for college students, but they report behaviors that meet the definition (Shepela & Levesque, 1998). The problems come from interpreting the behaviors as sexual harassment or even as inappropriate. A study that included hypothetical situations (Olson, 1994) confirmed this problem. College students read scenarios of situations that met the legal definition of sexual harassment, but when they evaluated whether they thought the scenarios constituted harassment, both women and men had difficulty applying the label sexual harassment.

To understand the frequency of sexual harassment, researchers must ask about specific behaviors that meet the criteria of harassment. One study that focused on behaviors (Shepela & Levesque, 1998) found that harassment was very common. Between 50% and 78% of women and from 29% to 74% of men had experienced incidents of peer sexual harassment in school. Behaviors such as sexual comments and pushing, shoving, and sexual

▣ GENDERED VOICES

My Professor Said. . . .

One of my students reported to me: "My engineering professor announced to the class that women should not be engineers. Women just didn't have what it takes; they weren't tough enough."

I told her that such remarks were unacceptable and probably illegal. I urged her to report this incident, but she refused even to name the professor. I reported the incident to the Dean of Engineering, who also agreed that this faculty member's behavior was unacceptable. Our concern did not solve this student's problem. By the end of the semester, she had changed her major to math education.

intimidation were common. Between 20% and 55% of women and from 15% to 44% of men had been the targets of faculty sexual harassment, such as sexist language and inappropriate sexual touching.

Students are reluctant to report distressing behavior, and the most common coping strategy is trying to avoid the harassing faculty member and the situation—evading professors, changing majors, and altering examining committees (Hotelling, 1991). Sexual harassment is not limited to students; both female and male faculty members are subject to harassment from students (DeSouza & Fansler, 2003). Female professors are more likely to be the target of sexual harassment by their male students than other gender combinations.

Therefore, like high school, college is another school situation in which women and men have different experiences, which relate to choices of majors and careers. The range of majors and careers is similar, but the proportion of men and women in the range of majors is not. Women choose majors in education and social science more often than men do, who choose engineering and physical science majors more often than women do. Although women now receive more undergraduate degrees than men, they do not receive equal numbers of professional and doctoral degrees. The number of women in professional programs has increased dramatically in the past 30 years, and these women have had to contend with less attention and support than their male peers receive. Sexual harassment is not an uncommon experience on college campuses, despite legal prohibition, and women are more likely than men to be harassed by those in positions of authority, their male peers, and even their students. The problem is more common for female graduate students than for female undergraduates, providing an additional barrier to women in professional training.

ACHIEVEMENT

Achievement can have many meanings, including success in school. As the previous section showed, girls and women are successful in school, as measured by grades, but men are more successful when the criteria include prominence in prestigious careers and high salaries. How achievement is defined determines the extent to which women and men are high or low achievers.

Achievement Motivation

Traditionally, researchers have defined job success and recognition as achievement and have not considered personal or family relationships as comparable achievements. Therefore, neither women's nor men's roles in homemaking and family care have gained the same type of recognition as business, scientific, and political accomplishments. Indeed, women did not play a prominent part in psychology's early studies on achievement.

David McClelland and his colleagues (McClelland, Atkinson, Clark, & Lowell, 1953) studied the motivation to achieve, formulating the concept of *need for achievement.* These researchers looked at the expression of this need by asking people to interpret ambiguous drawings; that is, to tell a story about a picture that had many possible interpretations. The rationale behind this technique is that people reveal inner wishes and motivations in interpreting ambiguous situations by projecting their personal thoughts and feelings into unclear situations.

McClelland and his colleagues used this type of projective technique, reasoning that people would reveal their need for achievement by including achievement-related imagery in their stories about the pictures. Their results confirmed this prediction, revealing that people varied in the amount of achievement-related imagery in their stories. The need for achievement not only varied among people but also was stronger in people who had chosen achievement-oriented careers and in college students who had chosen careers with high risk and high responsibility.

This definition of achievement ignores forms of achievement other than business careers, which is clearly too restrictive (Hyde & Kling, 2001). In addition, the need-for-achievement construct was formulated by examining only men, even though McClelland et al. (1953) found some overlap in the achievement needs of some men and women. However, another achievement-related concept has been applied specifically to women—fear of success.

Fear of Success

As David McClelland and his colleagues had done, Martina Horner (1969) also investigated the imagery associated with achievement and success. When she presented women and men with a description of a successful medical student, the women sometimes imagined negative consequences for the successful female medical student, but the men usually described the successful male medical student in positive terms.

Horner interpreted the women's descriptions of negative consequences accompanying success as a **fear of success,** or a motive to avoid success. She reasoned that women equate success with loss of femininity and feel anxious about success, especially when it involves competing with men. Her investigations showed that women often do better when working alone or when in competition with other women than when they must compete against men. Men, on the other hand, often perform better when they are in competition than when they work alone. Horner concluded that competition is a negative factor in women's achievement and that women see achievement situations differently than men do.

Although Horner used the terms *fear of success* and *motive to avoid success,* these labels are somewhat misleading, as they imply that women do not wish to succeed. What she called fear of success may have been women's acknowledgment that success in male-dominated professions is not socially well accepted for women, and that success will have negative as well as positive consequences for women. What Horner found was that competition may pose problems for women. She did not demonstrate that women try to avoid success, but that they anticipate and attempt to manage some of the negative consequences they believe will accompany success in male-dominated fields. Rather than finding that women fear success, Horner may have demonstrated that women understand the social consequences of competing with men in school and careers.

The social consequences of success in nontraditional careers may be negative for both men and women. An early study (Cherry & Deaux, 1978) found that men showed fear of success when describing a man in nursing school compared to a man in medical school, and women indicated awareness of negative consequences of success for a woman in medical school but not for a woman in nursing school. That is, perceptions of the negative aspects of success were related to the perceived gender appropriateness of the occupation rather than the gender of the person making the evaluation. Both women and men showed misgivings about violating gender stereotypes related to occupations.

A review during the 1980s (Paludi, 1984) showed that both men and women recognized the negative aspects of success at similar rates. In 64 studies on the topic, a median of 49% of women and 45% of men exhibited the "fear of success." These figures represent a considerable acknowledgment of the negative aspects of success, but show few gender differences.

More recent studies (Krishnan & Sweeney, 1998; Tomkiewicz & Bass, 1999; Yoder & Schleicher, 1996) have indicated changes related to fear of success. One study (Tomkiewicz & Bass, 1999) found that men showed as high a level of fear of success as women did. Other studies have related changing evaluations of women to changes in the gender composition of occupations. When an occupation is no longer dominated by one gender, then it is not "gendered," and neither women nor men in the occupation should receive negative evaluations for pursuing that career. Such a change seems to be occurring in medicine; women no longer receive negative evaluations when they are described as being at the top of their medical school class, and no difference exists between women's and men's fear of success imagery and achievement motivation (Krishnan & Sweeney, 1998). Indeed, both men and women in nontraditional occupations received positive evaluations concerning their competence and success (Yoder & Schliecher, 1996). Women, however, were seen as less socially competent and less attractive when they were successful in nontraditional occupations. Therefore, women are no longer judged to fear success, but their success is seen as having personal costs.

Examining the dilemma of achievement from both a gender and an ethnic point of view (Gonzalez, 1988), achievement for Mexican American women can be a double bind situation. This dilemma occurs as a result of the desire to form relationships with men from the same ethnic background plus the tendency of Mexican American men to feel threatened by women's achievements. The men in the survey reported that they were not threatened by women's accomplishments, but that the women believed otherwise. This situation creates stress in the women from what they see as conflicting demands for achievement and relationships. Wanting to preserve their ethnicity, these Mexican American women may be caught more severely in the dilemma of all women who strive for high achievement because they "experience conflict as their behavior is changing more rapidly than their sex role attitudes and the attitudes of their male counterparts" (Gonzalez, 1988, p. 378).

Self-Esteem and Self-Confidence

Self-esteem is conceptualized as a global evaluation of self that can range from positive to negative (Kling, Hyde, Showers, & Buswell, 1999). Although men and women have comparable concerns about success in nontraditional fields, their self-esteem and confidence in their own abilities show some differences. The AAUW (1992) contended that girls experience a sharp drop in self-esteem during junior high school, which negatively influences their education and careers. Two meta-analyses (Kling et al., 1999; O'Brien et al., 1996) and a longitudinal study (Jacobs et al., 2002) failed to find evidence of a dramatic decrease in self-esteem for girls during adolescence.

The meta-analyses compared women's and men's self-esteem throughout adolescence and in adulthood. The findings from the meta-analyses were similar: Boys and men have higher levels of self-esteem than girls and women have. These differences were small, however, even during adolescence. One meta-analysis (Kling et al., 1999) specifically addressed the changes during adolescence and found that the gender difference was greatest during late, not early, adolescence.

Ethnicity is also a factor in self-esteem. Within the United States, European Americans showed a small advantage for men, but for African Americans, no gender differences appeared in self-esteem (Kling et al., 1999). Table 11.3 summarizes findings from several countries, showing that not all have the pattern that appears in the United States. Furthermore, self-esteem may not be as important for school success as people have believed. Asian American children scored lowest on self-esteem of any ethnic group in the United States but had the highest grade point averages (Bankston & Zhou, 2002). African Americans scored the highest in self-esteem yet had the lowest grades. In addition, children who immigrated rather than were born in the United States showed more self-esteem problems but also made better grades than children of the same ethnicity who were born in the United States. Therefore, overall feelings of self-esteem may not be an important predictor of school achievement.

Self-esteem may be a factor in confidence, but no global concept of confidence applies to all situations. Confidence in one's ability to succeed varies with the task, and the gender typing of the activity is important in this evaluation. Men express more confidence in their abilities than women do when they perceive a task as "masculine," but this

TABLE 11.3 *Differences in Self-Esteem for Males and Females*

Age Group	Sample Population	Size of Effect	Higher In
Children	U.S. residents	Small	Males
Young adolescents	Norwegian	Small	Males
Adolescents	Chinese	Small	Females
Adolescents	Finnish	None	—
Young adults	Japanese	Small	Males
Young adults	Canadian	Small	Males
Adolescents to adults	U.S. European Americans	Small	Males
Adolescents to adults	U.S. African Americans	None	—
Adolescents and adults	Australian	Moderate	Males
Adults	U.S. residents	Small to moderate	Males
Elderly	U.S. residents	Moderate	Males

advantage disappears when the task is perceived as "feminine." Women showed lower expectancy of success on a masculine task than on a feminine or neutral task (Beyer, 1998, 2002), but this bias did not apply to men. An interesting note: Women's low predictions underestimated their performance, indicating that women have inaccurately low confidence in their performance on masculine tasks.

In addition, ability for specific tasks is an individual factor differentiating the self-confidence of men and women. When such information is available, the ability estimates of men and women are similar, but when this information is absent, men estimate their ability more highly than women estimate theirs. The same is true for situations in which people expect their performance to be compared to others; that is, women make lower estimates of their performance than men do, but they make similar estimates when they expect comparisons to be based on social rather than performance factors. Thus, situational factors are important in self-confidence, and women tend to feel less confident than men in performance situations.

Other people's evaluations also influence men's and women's self-assessments of their performance in achievement situations, with women tending to be more responsive to others' evaluations than men are (Roberts, 1991). That is, women are more likely than men to revise estimates of their performance based on the evaluations they receive from others. This responsiveness might be due to women's greater social responsiveness or to lower confidence, but it may also be due to women's tendency to accept the feedback from others as more informative than men do.

Additional studies on the gender difference have confirmed that it occurs in a variety of performance contexts. However, the reason that women accept evaluative feedback is not lack of confidence (Roberts & Nolen-Hoeksema, 1994). Instead, girls' and boys' experiences with evaluative feedback may lead to a difference; girls receive less feedback about their classroom performance, so they take what feedback they get quite seriously. Boys, on the other hand, tend to receive information not only about their performance but also about their (mis)behavior. Indeed, a great deal of the attention that classroom teachers give to boys is oriented toward misbehavior. This situation could lead them to discount evaluative feedback, which sets up a gender difference. Women tend to consider the evaluations of others important, whereas men tend to reject these evaluations. This tendency for women to accept and men to reject evaluations appeared in a study of bank employees' reactions to performance evaluations (Johnson & Helgeson, 2002).

Either ignoring or accepting evaluative feedback has advantages and disadvantages. Women's typical strategy of accepting feedback may make them responsive to evaluations and eager to change, but it may also make them overly sensitive to others' opinions and allow them to rely too little on their own evaluations. Men's typical strategy of ignoring feedback may allow them to feel higher self-esteem but also make them overly resistant to advice from others and reluctant to change their behavior when changes would improve their performance.

The tendency to be very responsive to criticism may also relate to the higher levels of distress that girls experience during school (Pomerantz, Altermatt, & Saxon, 2002). Despite receiving better grades and having fewer disciplinary problems, girls reported a higher degree of distress than boys during elementary and middle school. Girls evaluated their abilities as lower than boys (including the subjects in which they were making higher grades), rated their overall self-worth as lower, and showed a higher degree of anxiety related to school performance. This responsiveness may persist throughout women's lives and present a source of stress and anxiety.

Confidence and ability are not the same; one may be inappropriately confident or inappropriately unsure of one's abilities. Unduly low expectancies are more characteristic of girls and women than of boys and men. For example, women estimate their IQs as lower than men judge their IQs (Furnham & Gasson, 1998), and women predict lower college grade point averages than men do (Beyer, 1999). In some cases, the lower estimates may be underestimates, but these judgments are more accurate in some cases (Furnham, 1999). However, men's predictions are overestimates that represent a tendency toward positive self-presentation (Brown, Uebelacker, & Heatherington, 1998). Therefore, men have a tendency to see themselves as more intelligent and academically capable than women see themselves. This tendency may lead men to be more confident in academic (and perhaps many other) situations, but it may also make them believe that they are more capable than they are.

Attributions for Success and Failure

Research has also indicated that gender differences exist in explanations for success and failure. People can attribute success or failure to either internal factors, such as ability and effort, or external factors, such as luck and the difficulty of the task. Although both ability and effort are factors that come from within each person, ability is a stable factor, whereas effort can vary from situation to situation. Persons who believe that they succeeded because they worked hard have no assurance that they will succeed again without additional, similar effort. On the other hand, those who attribute their successes to intelligence should believe that similar success will continue—that is, they will still be intelligent next week and next year. Likewise, the external reasons for success and failure also differ in their stability. People who believe they failed because of bad luck would believe that their luck could change, leading to success on another attempt at the same task. People who attribute their failure to the difficulty of the task should believe that this task will always be difficult and that they will fail on each attempt. Therefore, people can explain their success or failure in terms of internal or external factors, and they can see each as either stable or unstable. Figure 11.3 shows the possibilities in combining these two dimensions. These explanations, or attributions, for success and failure can affect the amount of effort and time a person is willing to expend in order to succeed.

Early research (Karabenick, Sweeney, & Penrose, 1983; Rosenfield & Stephan, 1978) showed that the gender typing of the activity is a factor in preferences and attributions for success. One study (Karabenick et al., 1983) demonstrated that men preferred tasks with high skill components when the tasks were "masculine," and women showed the same preference pattern on "feminine" tasks. Expectancy of success was influenced by the gender typing of the tasks. Another study (Rosenfield & Stephan, 1978) showed that the task need not actually be gender-typed to show differences; describing the task as gender-typed was sufficient to prompt the effect. Men tended to explain success on a task described

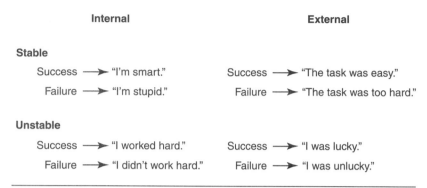

FIGURE 11.3   *Attributions for Success and Failure According to Two Dimensions*

as "masculine" as due to internal factors and failure as due to external factors. That is, if they succeeded, they took personal credit, but if they failed, bad luck was to blame. The women showed a similar pattern for the task described as "feminine." Both men and women tended to use different attributions for their performance on the cross-gender task, explaining success or failure in less personal terms and attributing the outcome, either positive or negative, more to external factors, such as luck or task difficulty.

These attributions apply to grades in college classes. When asked to explain their grades in college classes, gender differences appeared in the attributions (Campbell & Henry, 1999). Female college students were less likely to attribute their success to ability than were male college students. Although effort was the most common explanation for both men and women, women chose this explanation significantly more often than men did. Effort can change, and this study suggests that women tend to believe that they need to continually put forth effort to succeed, but men feel more confident in their abilities. These gender differences echo differences expressed by parents, who tend to see their sons' math performance as an expression of talent and their daughters' math achievement as the result of effort (Raety et al., 2002).

In summary, achievement has been defined as career success, which made women less achievement oriented. However, the concept of fear of success, or the motivation to avoid success, was applied only to women. This concept became a popular explanation for women's lower levels of achievement, but further studies have questioned the validity of this concept and found that men as well as women exhibit misgivings about achievements in gender-inappropriate occupations. Research has failed to confirm the widely publicized drop in self-esteem for adolescent girls, but overall, women show slightly lower levels of self-esteem than men. More specific confidence varies according to situation, and the gender typing of the activity is an important factor in confidence. The gender typing of the task also influences the attributions that women and men use to explain their performance, with women tending to attribute success to effort rather than to ability, which may indicate significant gender differences in explanations for achievement.

CONSIDERING DIVERSITY

Gender equity is a major diversity issue in education, but other diversity concerns are also important. The ethnic diversity and social class composition of the United States present problems to the educational system, and these two factors often combine to produce serious barriers to quality education. During the 1990s, between 35% and 40% of students in elementary and high schools were ethnic minorities, and around 5% of them had trouble speaking and understanding English (U.S. Department of Education [USDE], 2000).

Over the past 40 years, high school graduation rates have increased for all groups, but substantial differences exist among ethnic groups in the United States (USBC, 2002). Asian Americans and Whites have comparable and high graduation rates (around 85.0%), but African Americans and Hispanic Americans finish high school at lower rates—78.5% and 55.0%, respectively. Employment opportunities have decreased for high school dropouts, but increased for those who attend college (*Business Week,* 1999); thus, those who fail to finish high school have decreasing job options. Gender differences are small in high school completion rates, with the biggest difference for African American women, who finish high school at slightly higher rates than African American men (USBC, 2002).

The percentage of ethnic minority students entering college increased between the 1970s and the late 1990s (USBC, 2002). By the year 2000, 64% of White and 56% of African American high school graduates attended college (USBC, 2002). The graduation rate showed greater discrepancies; about 10% of Hispanic Americans and 16% of African Americans earn college degrees, but 26% of Whites and 44% of Asian Americans do. Despite their growing number, fewer ethnic minority than White students finish high school well prepared to enter college (McCombs, 2000). Hispanic American, African American, and Native American students are not often among the highest achieving high school students, and they lack the academic records to be competitive at selective colleges. Indeed, these ethnic groups are more likely to enter 2-year than 4-year colleges (USBC, 2002). The percentage of ethnic minority students decreases as the number of years required for college degrees increases, resulting in a very low percentage of doctoral and professional degrees granted to people from ethnic minorities.

Ethnic minorities are underrepresented in college for all types of higher and professional education. The exception is Asian Americans, who are more numerous in college than in the population, especially in prestigious research universities (USDE, 2000). Other ethnic minority students are more likely to attend public than private schools, and financing is one reason for their low college attendance and their choice of 2-year rather than 4-year programs. The cost of college has increased rapidly (USBC, 2002), and minorities disproportionately live in poverty. Thus, even academically capable minority students may not be able to afford higher education. Ethnic minority students may be restricted to less expensive college options, even when their academic abilities and preparation are adequate to make them competitive.

The gender differences in high school graduation rates are small, but larger differences appear in college (USBC, 2002). Over the past 40 years, women have become more numerous on college campus (and at graduation ceremonies) than men. These differences are even more dramatic for ethnic minority women. Slightly more Asian American women than men attend college, substantially more Hispanic and Native American women do so, and the gender difference for African Americans is even larger.

The gender difference in advanced degrees produces differences in university faculties, in which ethnic minorities are also underrepresented (USBC, 2002). Despite years of pressure to include diversity not only in curriculum but also in faculty, African Americans, Hispanic Americans, and Native Americans are underrepresented among the faculty in U.S. colleges and universities. Using medical school faculty as an example, one study (Fang, Moy, Colburn, & Hurley, 2000) showed that minority faculty experienced lower rates of promotion than White faculty. Therefore, ethnic minorities are not common on university faculties and advance at slower rates than their White colleagues.

The overall picture of education is one of increasing diversity but not always increased educational opportunities for those diverse groups in the United States. Ethnic minority students have not enjoyed the rapid progress that women have in gaining access to college and professional training. Asian Americans are an exception, but Hispanic American, African American, and Native American students have to face many barriers to obtaining an education. Those barriers block the academic achievement of many, as reflected in the higher dropout rates and lower college attendance and graduation rates for these students.

Around the world, girls and women experience an educational disadvantage. Indeed, many girls never make it to school at all in some countries in sub-Saharan Africa and South Asia (Guttman, 2001). The gender gap in school enrollment is largest in sub-Saharan Africa, South Asia, and the Arab world (*WIN News,* 1999). During the 1990s, that gap decreased in many countries (such as Nepal, China, and Mauritania) but remained and even widened in others (such as Pakistan, Afghanistan, and Nigeria).

Of the 113 million children who are not attending elementary school worldwide, girls account for 60% (Guttman, 2001). They may be kidnapped and sold as wives, household workers, or sex workers while they are young enough to be in elementary school. Alternatively, they may be the victims of the tradition of educating boys but not girls. Most countries have official policies that include educating girls, but many of those countries are facing heavy debts and the burden of HIV infection, which drains money from educational efforts. However, societal attitudes that diminish the importance of education for girls are the underlying problem in many of these developing countries.

SUMMARY

Men and women have different experiences in education. Although Title IX of the Education Amendments of 1972 prohibits discrimination based on gender in schools, girls and boys do not receive the same treatment in schools. Beginning during the earliest school years and continuing throughout college and professional training, boys receive more attention and feedback about their performance in classroom work than girls do. Some of this attention is negative. Girls make better grades than boys, beginning in elementary school. During junior high school, both boys and girls become less confident of their abilities.

Until recently, girls pursued advanced courses in math and science less often than boys did in high school. The difference in number of math courses completed has disappeared, but girls are still less likely to take advanced physical science courses. Counselors convey higher career expectations to boys and fail to present the full range of career options to girls. Boys who enter vocational education programs are more likely to be steered toward lucrative skilled trades, whereas women in vocational education learn low-paying clerical skills. Athletics continues to be a way for boys to gain prestige, but the increase in sports participation among girls has led to greater acceptance of female athletes. Sexual harassment, especially from peers, becomes a problem for both girls and boys during high school. Gay and lesbian adolescents become targets of sexual harassment especially often, making school an unpleasant and even dangerous place for them.

Although women have not historically attended college in numbers comparable to men, that pattern has changed. Women now receive more undergraduate degrees than men do, but gender differences in choices of major persist, with a small percentage of science and engineering degrees and a large percentage of education and liberal arts degrees going to women. An increasing number of women are receiving advanced and professional degrees, however, and many majors are becoming less dominated by one gender.

The campus climate is less supportive of women's than men's achievements, both in the classroom and on the athletic field. Although Title IX of the Educational Amendments of 1972 also applies to athletics, women are less likely than men to be involved in college athletics, and equitable funding for women's athletics has become a source of controversy. Despite legal challenges, support for women's athletics is part of the law mandating equal opportunities in education, and this situation has resulted in a large increase in the number of women involved in sports.

Although achievement consists of a variety of attainments, studies of achievement have focused on career success rather than success in re-lationships or families. This emphasis has led to the portrayal of men as having a higher motivation for achievement than women. In considering women and achievement, the fear of success or the motivation to avoid success was once popular as a way to explain women's lower levels of achievement. Under this definition, women who exhibited fear of success acknowledged that negative as well as positive consequences would accompany success. Further studies have indicated that negative evaluations of people and predictions about the future may be related to the gender appropriateness of achievement situations. Men as well as women exhibit misgivings about achievements in gender-inappropriate occupations. The social consequences of achievement are a double bind for all women, but for women from ethnic minority groups, these problems are compounded by the desire to retain their ethnicity.

Contrary to widely publicized reports, girls do not experience a sharp decrease in confidence during adolescence, but boys and men show slightly greater self-esteem than girls and women from adolescence through middle adulthood. Women also exhibit less confidence in their ability to achieve than do men, but these gender differences in confidence depend more on the situation than on a general trait. Again, the gender typing of the situation plays a role in the confidence of both men and women, with each having more confidence in gender-typical compared to gender-atypical situations. The gender typing of the task also influences the attributions that women and men use to explain their performance, with both attributing success to internal, personal sources on gender-typed tasks and resorting to external, situational explanations for failure. Thus, gender role stereotypes are an important factor in achievement, with both men and women being influenced by their perceptions of the characteristics of the achievement situation.

Ethnic minorities in the United States face barriers to education. Over the past 40 years, high school graduation rates have increased for all groups, but African Americans, Hispanic Americans, and Native Americans graduate at lower rates than Asian Americans and Whites. This same disparity carries over into college, graduate, and professional training. Women from all ethnic groups attend college at higher rates than men from the same groups. Thus, at all levels, ethnic minorities experience educational disadvantages. Around the world, girls and women experience an educational disadvantage; a disproportionate number of girls do not go to school at all.

■ GLOSSARY

fear of success   negative consequences associated with success.

sexual harassment   unwanted sexual attention.

Title IX of the Education Amendments of 1972   the federal act that prohibited educational institutions that receive federal funds from discriminating on the basis of gender.

■ SUGGESTED READINGS

Connell, R. W. (1996). Teaching the boys: New research on masculinity, the gender strategies for schools. *Teachers College Record, 98,* 206–235.

The research and publicity on girls' treatment in schools has overlooked how schools can shortchange boys, too. Connell describes the problems that boys experience in school and how school can be an unfriendly place for them.

Hyde, Janet Shibley; & Kling, Kristen C. (2001). Women, motivation, and achievement. *Psychology of Women Quarterly, 25,* 364–378.

Hyde and Kling provide an excellent review of the research on motivation and achievement, with an emphasis on factors related to women. They consider models of achievement, the fear of success concept, educational achievement, and the testing controversy.

Jacobs, Jerry A. (1996). Gender inequality in higher education. *Annual Review of Sociology, 22,* 153–182.

This review provides an evaluation of access to higher education, along with a historical and cross-national comparison. The experience of attending college is also critically reviewed, as well as the gender differential in majors and students' likelihood to be the targets of sexual harassment.

12 CAREERS AND WORK

■ HEADLINE   The Gender Trap
The Mercury News (San Jose), December 9, 2001

Author, attorney, and political strategist Susan Estrich (2001) described the rising and falling career of Carleton (Carly) Fiorina, who was the first woman to head one of the top 20 companies of the Fortune 500 list. ". . . the high-profile and much-celebrated executive told reporters that gender had nothing to do with her success. But it might have everything to do with the reaction to her perceived failures" (p. 1D). Estrich contended that Fiorina may have been correct; gender may have had nothing to do with Fiorina's success. Her gender made her a media star when she was chosen to be CEO of Hewlett-Packard, whereas the same accomplishments would not have been notable for a male executive: "So when a man is chosen to run a major corporation, it's business as usual. When a woman is chosen, it's news precisely because there are so few" (Estrich, 2001, p. 1D).

That media spotlight was harsh when Hewlett-Packard experienced trouble. The attention became negative criticisms, which Estrich described as a trap, noting that "women on pedestals make tempting targets" (p. 1D). She argued that Fiorina may not have deserved either the credit or the blame that she received, but that women in prominent positions often receive both. Their prominence makes their successes and failures very visible.

Estrich recounted her experiences as a law student at Harvard over 20 years ago, when that school (and most others) had few female professors. Each new female professor received poor evaluations, which led to dismissal and the growing opinion that female professors were not as good as male professors. Estrich contended that all new professors were terrible, but being female made the women stand out for special criticism, just as today's female executives do. Estrich noted the solution: Hire more women so that each may be considered and judged on individual merit.

This solution is not on the horizon for CEOs in the United States, Canada, Australia, or Europe. In the United States, 4% of officers of Fortune 500 companies, 13% of senators, 14% of congressional representatives, 10% of governors, 2% of top military officers, and 5% of managing partners in law firms are women (Carli & Eagly, 2001). Each woman who achieves any of these goals receives the media attention that places her on a pedestal and into the gender trap.

Most women in the United States will not experience the type of gender trap that Carly Fiorina did because they will not climb the corporate ladder to the top. However, most women and men will choose and pursue a career, and the number of women who pursue paid employment was one of the most notable changes of the 20th century.

CAREERS

"Career, in its broadest sense, means 'life path' and thus includes all the roles a person plays throughout life" (Farmer & Sidney, 1985, p. 338). This definition places careers in a developmental framework and emphasizes the lifelong nature of career development and the many choices and roles that contribute to this path. Ideally, all people should choose a career on the basis of their interests, abilities, and potential contributions to society, but obstacles prevent the full development of both men's and women's potentials. Gender stereotyping is one of the obstacles.

Despite the encompassing social definition of career as the role people play throughout their lives, the study of career development has focused on the choices and patterns that men have taken, and only recently has women's career development received attention. Women's careers do not fit into the same framework as those of men, and men and women are likely to continue to have different career paths in the near future (Williams, 2000). One reason for this difference relates to the expectations about the types of careers each gender will occupy.

Although career choices are not as sharply gendered as in the past, most women and men continue to choose gender-traditional occupations. Another expectation is that wives' careers will be secondary to those of their husbands. If someone must stay home with a sick child or if one person must relocate due to job demands, the husband's career nearly always takes precedence, and the wife must accommodate her schedule and employment. These expectations tend to result in interruptions in the careers of women, who may take years away from employment to care for children or to support a husband's career before rejoining the workforce.

Women are more likely to hold part-time employment than men are—68% of part-time workers are women (U.S. Bureau of Labor Statistics, 2003). Part-time employment means not only lower salaries for women but also problems for them in career advancement. Men's careers are more likely to follow a smooth line of career choices during schooling, uninterrupted employment, and continuing career advancement throughout adulthood.

Homemaking is considered a legitimate career for women, but one that excludes them from the paid workforce. Homemaking is not directly comparable to paid work in a number of ways: It has no training requirements, no wages, no retirement benefits, no job security, and no opportunity for advancement (Betz, 1993). For most women, homemaking does not allow them to use and develop their abilities and talents: "This is not to discount the importance of childrearing, but only its insufficiency as a lifelong answer to the issue of self-realization" (Betz, 1993, p. 629).

Helen Astin (1984) formulated a model showing gender similarities and differences to explain career development for both women and men. Astin's model includes four components—motivation, expectations, gender role socialization, and opportunity.

She assumed that motivation was the same for men and women but that their expectations differed due to differing gender role socialization patterns. Both gender role socialization and opportunities create different outcomes in the workforce for men and women. Men have had the opportunity to participate in more highly paid, more prestigious, and a wider variety of work than women have. Astin contended that changes have occurred, which have given women greater freedom to choose careers dominated by men and which equalize the opportunities in those careers. Does research on motivation, expectations, gender role socialization, and opportunity support Astin's model? Do women have strong career motivations? Have opportunities for careers become more equal for women and men?

Exploration of children's and adolescents' career beliefs has revealed gender similarities and differences. A study of high-achieving adolescent girls (Watson, Quatman, & Edler, 2002) found that girls' career aspirations were as high as those of boys. Indeed, the two groups were indistinguishable in terms of either their ideal or realistic career aspirations, substantiating this factor in Astin's model. This strong motivation also applies to older women who are pursuing careers. A survey of adults in New Jersey (Sigel, 1996) included women of varying ages and educational levels ranging from high school dropouts to advanced professional degrees. The women in this study valued meaningful, rewarding work and showed ambition and dedication to their various careers. However, gender role socialization affects career beliefs, beginning when children are quite young.

Career Expectations and Gender Role Socialization

Career beliefs and expectations are not so equal for girls and boys; even preschool children have beliefs about the career differences of women and men (Levy, Sadovsky, & Troseth, 2000). They expressed a concept of female-dominated versus male-dominated occupations, believed that men were more competent at male-dominated and women more competent at female-dominated occupations, and these children said that women earn less money than men. During early adolescence, beliefs concerning competence and self-efficacy showed traditional gender differences that shaped these children's career choices over the next few years (Bandura, Barbaranelli, Caprata, & Pastorelli, 2001). Some evidence also suggests that older adolescents use gender-biased thinking when they evaluate their career choices (Correll, 2001).

Young women still have family- and child-related expectations, but the career expectations of college women changed between the 1940s and the 1970s (Konrad, 2003; Phillips & Imhoff, 1997; Komarovsky, 1982). In the 1940s, few college women planned to continue their careers after they married, but beginning in the 1970s, the opposite was true—very few planned to discontinue their careers after marriage. However, most women, regardless of their career plans, also anticipated marriage and children as part of their life goals. The requirements of combining family duties and paid work are probably factors in women's lower career aspirations (Phillips & Imhoff, 1997) and priorities for more flexible careers (Konrad, 2003).

These expectations about marriage and motherhood demonstrate what Joan Williams (2000) described as force fields that pull women toward domesticity and away from careers. Similar forces affect men, drawing them toward careers and away from family. Despite college students' beliefs that few difficulties will arise in combining career and family, research presents a different picture. Arlie Hochschild (1997) found the situation of families squeezed by a lack of time as employed parents devoted hours to work and resented spouses and children for the time they demanded.

One factor that created Hochschild's (1997) "time bind" for families was the movement of women into nontraditional careers. Women who work as managers and engineers were as devoted to their careers as the men who held these jobs and almost as reluctant to go home to household work and child care as men were. That is, when women pursue high-prestige careers, they are more likely to behave in the same career-driven ways that men do.

Those women who pursue careers in male-dominated fields tend to have values similar to the men in these careers, but acceptance of traditional gender roles is related to the likelihood of women being in occupations more traditional for women (Schutte, Malouff, Curtis, Lowry, & Luis, 1996). For example, women who value personal interaction with coworkers and providing care to others expressed less interest in science and technology careers because they perceived these fields as offering less of these valued experiences (Morgan, Isaac, & Sansone, 2001). In addition, more women than men held these values. Thus, women may have different reasons for choosing their careers than men do.

Gender segregation of occupations is so prominent that choosing certain occupations often places persons within gender roles strongly identified with these occupations, whereas other careers do not have similar role characteristics. For example, caring about others and taking care of others is associated with the female gender role (Cancian & Oliker, 2000), and the "caring professions" of teaching, nursing, and child-care work are overwhelmingly female.

Ethnicity also plays a role in career expectations. Compared with European American women, African American women are more likely to expect that they will be employed throughout their adult lives (Betz, 1993). Those expectations are consistent with history: African American women have been more likely than European American women to be the heads and sole supporters of their households. The proportion of African American women who enter professional occupations is higher than for European American women, but African American women are even more concentrated in traditionally female occupations, which influences their incomes.

In comparing Mexican American and European American high school students, both gender and ethnic differences appeared (McWhirter, 1994). Female students perceived more barriers to careers than male students did, and Mexican American students saw more barriers and had less confidence in their abilities to overcome these barriers than did European American students. For the young women, family-related problems were more common reasons for their lack of confidence than were their abilities, and the Mexican American students were more likely than the European American students to expect negative attitudes from their families should they attend college. The average ratings for the perception of barriers indicated uncertainty rather than pessimism, but ethnicity and gender both affected perception of barriers to careers.

The percentage of women in the U.S. workforce has risen to 46.6% of the total labor force (USBC, 2002; see "According to the Media" and "According to the Research"), yet employed women remain concentrated in occupations that are female dominated. Table 12.1 shows the percent of women in various occupations in 1983 and 2001. Women remain concentrated in a narrow range of clerical, service, or professional positions, such

TABLE 12.1 *Percentage of Women in Various Occupations, 1983 versus 2001*

Occupation	1983	2001
Managerial	41%	50%
Accountants and auditors	38	59
Public officials and administrators	39	51
Advertising, marketing, and public relations	22	39
Professional	48	53
Architects	13	23
Engineers	6	11
Lawyers and judges	16	29
Mathematics and computer scientists	29	30
Natural scientists	21	34
Nurses	96	93
Physicians	16	29
Teachers, college	36	43
Teachers, noncollege	71	75
Social workers	64	72
Technical	48	54
Health technicians	84	82
Science technicians	29	45
Administrative support	80	79
Records processing	82	81
Secretaries	99	98
File clerks	84	82
Sales	48	49
Mechanics	3	5
Production and skilled crafts	21	25
Construction	2	3
Labor	19	21
Service occupations	60	60
Household service	96	96
Firefighters	1	4
Police and detectives	9	18
Food preparation	63	57
Hairdressers	89	90
Machine operation	42	36
Farm workers	25	21

Source: Statistical Abstract of the United States, 2002 (122nd ed., pp. 381–383), by U.S. Bureau of the Census, 2002, Washington, DC: U.S. Government Printing Office.

▧ ACCORDING TO THE MEDIA . . .

Most Women Are Not Employed

Television programs frequently include characters' occupations as part of the plot, thus presenting a picture of occupations and the people who pursue those occupations. Content analyses of women on television in the early 1990s (Elasmar, Hasegawa, & Brain, 1999) and the decade of the 1990s (Signorielli & Kahlenberg, 2001) revealed that female major characters were more likely to have no job than to be employed—about 40% of female characters were not employed. Of those who were employed, the occupations of about 30% were unclear. Of the women on TV with clear occupations, 10% held professional jobs that were prestigious and glamorous. However, these characters tended to be minor rather than major characters. About 15% held jobs in the entertainment industry (such as model, musician, or actress), and 11% were portrayed as homemakers. However, women's jobs on television tended not to be the ones traditionally associated with women (Signorielli & Kahlenberg, 2001). Female characters were more likely to have a gender-neutral job (such as artist) or a traditionally male job rather than a traditionally female job.

Music videos share some of the characteristics of television entertainment shows in portraying more men than women with a designated occupation and in the level of gender stereotyping (Seidman, 1999). A large majority of the characters with occupations typically associated with men or women were played by an actor of that gender; music videos did not show gender-atypical characters in work situations. For example, all of the prostitutes were female, and all of the politicians were male. Not surprisingly, more women wore fewer clothes: Of the women, 33% were scantily clad, compared to 7% of the men. Some occupations appeared more often in music videos than on television programming, such as mechanics and manual laborers, but the gender stereotyping was similar in both media.

In examining the occupations of women on TV, the picture is not as gender stereotypical as it was in television of the 1970s and 1980s (Signorielli & Bacue, 1999). Women are more likely to appear in occupations traditionally dominated by men than they were in decades past. However, women's work is largely absent from television, and even women are less common on television than in the real world. Although the percentage of women on television increased between the 1970s and 1990s, the percentage of employed women on television did not (Signorielli & Bacue, 1999; Signorielli & Kahlenberg, 2001). Television characters and TV employment remain largely a man's world.

as clerical workers, secretaries, child-care workers, teachers, nurses, and social workers. An examination of that table reveals some changes, with an increased percentage of women in occupations dominated by men, but fewer decreases in the percent of women in female-dominated fields. That is, women are moving into male-dominated occupations at a higher rate than men are moving into female-dominated jobs. Even with these changes, a gender-segregated workforce persists, with the majority of employed women and men working in jobs occupied by others of the same gender. This gender segregation promotes traditional gender role identification and hinders the career development of both women and men.

Career Opportunities

Women and men do not have equal career opportunities on several counts. Different education and training create unequal preparation for careers, which is the first point for gen-

▓ ACCORDING TO THE RESEARCH . . .

Most Women Are Employed

The demographic picture of women and employment varies substantially from the television portrayal. On television, a minority of women is employed, whereas in the United States, employment rates for women are about 60% (USBC, 2002). Indeed, women have always been employed at a higher rate in real life than in screen life (Signorielli & Bacue, 1999).

In some respects, women's jobs are better in real life than on television. About 10% of female characters on television hold professional or managerial jobs, whereas the employment statistics reveal that women hold about 50% of such jobs (USBC, 2002). In other respects, the television versions of professional women's working lives are better than reality; television portrays the professional woman as a high-level executive with a prestigious job. Few women have those types of jobs—only 4% of high-level corporate executives and about 5% of managing partners in law firms are women (Carli & Eagly, 2001).

Television overrepresents some occupations and underrepresents others for both women and men. The reasons behind these deviations relate to the occupations' potential for drama and excitement. The jobs of lawyers, physicians, and law enforcement officers have good potential for interesting plots, so these occupations are overrepresented on television (Signorielli &

Kahlenberg, 2001). For example, over 13% of television characters are law enforcement officers, but only about 2% of working people pursue this occupation. In addition, female law enforcement officers are six times more common on television than in real life.

On television, women appear as often as men as in white-collar jobs and blue-collar jobs (Signorielli & Kahlenberg, 2001). Both the proportions and the gender distribution are inaccurate. About 11% of employed characters appeared in white-collar jobs such as managers, clerks, and salespeople, whereas over 40% of employed people have these types of jobs. Women are more likely than men to be white-collar workers. About 6% of male and female characters on TV had blue-collar jobs, but the figure is really about 36%. Men are more than twice as likely as women to have these jobs.

Women do not necessarily hold jobs traditionally associated with women on television—only 10 of the 68 job categories portrayed were jobs traditionally dominated by women (Signorielli & Bacue, 1999). This situation contrasts with the work that most women do, which continues to be predominantly in the fields traditionally associated with women, such as nurses, teachers, secretaries, clerks, and social workers. Thus, an accurate picture of women's employment is largely absent from television.

der inequity at work (see Chapter 11 for a review of these issues). The gender stereotyping that affects choices in education and training also influences hiring decisions. Discrimination in hiring represents a second point at which women are disadvantaged in careers (Gupta, 1993).

Discrimination in Hiring. Discrimination in hiring may be the primary factor in the gender gap in wages, but the problems with research on the hiring process make it the most difficult to document (Petersen, Saporta, & Seidel, 2000). Table 12.2 shows the gender gap in wages, and the differences are dramatic. For *every* occupational category, women earned less than men.

An examination of the wage differential between men and women who worked in a large private firm (Gerhart, 1990) showed that the women's salaries were 88% of the men's salaries, even after controlling for background, training, length of service with the company,

TABLE 12.2   *Weekly Earnings of Women and Men in Various Occupations, 2002*

Occupation	Women's Earnings	Men's Earnings
Executive and managerial	$ 756	$1,058
Lawyers and judges	1,206	1,615
Mathematics and computer science	945	1,165
Science technician	576	733
Engineer	1,011	1,180
Physician	947	1,626
Teacher, noncollege	720	828
Administrative support and clerical	488	583
Secretary	496	544
Sales	441	742
Mechanics	593	677
Production and skilled crafts	445	663
Construction	553	606
Labor	361	430
Food service	309	349
Protective service (firefighters, police, guards)	501	689
Other service (food, health care, cleaning, and personal services)	339	379
Machine operation	386	520
Handlers, helpers, and laborers	359	411
Farming, forestry, and fishing	308	376

Source: Labor force statistics from the "Current Population Survey, Annual Averages—Household Data 2002," Table 39. Retrieved July 28, 2003, from www.bls.gov/cps/home.htm#data.

and job title. This difference was attributable to inequitable initial salaries. When this factor was taken into account, the salary advancements were comparable. Consistent with these earlier figures, a more recent examination of hiring in a technology organization over a 10-year period (Petersen et al., 2000) revealed no gender discrimination in hiring decisions but an 11% difference in initial salary offers. The initial salary differences make it difficult for women's salaries to ever equal men's salaries.

Research on the gender difference in initial salaries has revealed that women expected lower initial salaries than men did (Heckert et al., 2002). This expectation held for college students in a variety of majors. In addition, women also expected to earn less than men expect at the peak of their earnings. Other research (Solnick, 2001) concentrated on negotiation skill and found that men were more effective than women in negotiating for money. Indeed, the gender of the negotiators made a substantial difference, and women fared more poorly when they negotiated with men; men had better outcomes when they negotiated with women than with other men. However, men got more money in all pairings. These findings suggest that women may be at a disadvantage in negotiations for initial salaries and may expect to earn less than men. Both situations may contribute to women's lower salaries.

Gender stereotypes are one source of discrimination in hiring, with both men and women subject to positive and negative discrimination on the basis of gender stereotypes (Martinko & Gardner, 1983; Pratto & Espinoza, 2001). The gender role of the job position is a major factor in discrimination: Men have the advantage in applying for "masculine" jobs, and women have a disadvantage. On the other hand, men can face negative discrimination when they apply for "feminine" jobs, whereas women can have the advantage. Specific, job-related information about applicants can overcome some gender stereotypes and can thus eliminate some discrimination, but the tendency toward gender stereotyping is a factor in hiring decisions.

Stereotyping also occurs on the basis of ethnicity and sexual orientation, which may affect hiring decisions and salary offers. One study (Pratto & Espinoza, 2001) found complex effects for gender and ethnicity in ratings of job applicants. In most cases, White applicants received higher ratings than African American or Hispanic American candidates with the same qualifications. A study of hiring discrimination for gay men and lesbians (Horvath & Ryan, 2003) found that heterosexual men received the highest ratings and heterosexual women the lowest. The gay men and lesbians received ratings between the heterosexuals. Therefore, men continue to have advantages in judgments about their suitability for jobs, even when their qualifications are no better than women's, and both ethnicity and sexual orientation are factors that form complex patterns of preference and bias.

Gender bias appeared in a study that concentrated on academic hiring and promotion (Steinpreis, Ritzke, & Anders, 1999). Academic psychologists who evaluated a résumé were more likely to endorse hiring when the résumé had a man's rather than a woman's name (although the résumés were identical in content). These evaluators also showed bias in commenting on qualifications for promotion, questioning the female but not the male professor's accomplishments. These biases appeared in the evaluations of both female and male academicians, indicating that discrimination in hiring and promotions continues to occur, even among academic psychologists.

Therefore, discrimination based on gender, and especially on the match between gender and gender stereotypes associated with the job, presents problems in making fair hiring decisions. Such discrimination is an important factor in the wage gap between men and women. Providing specific information that shows that applicants have some characteristics of the other gender can diminish stereotypical perceptions of these applicants and influence hiring. Unfortunately, gender stereotyping is resistant to change, and women experience more disadvantages than men because of such discrimination.

Barriers to Career Advancement.   The barriers to career advancement can come from situational and organizational as well as individual sources. One of the organizational sources is the **glass ceiling,** the invisible barrier that prevents women and ethnic minorities from advancing in organizations. Only 4% to 5% of senior-level managers in major corporations are women, and these women tend to be concentrated in jobs traditionally associated with women, such as human relations or communications (Dingell & Maloney, 2002). Women in corporate jobs often believe that they have hit the glass ceiling.

To study the situation of the glass ceiling and its effect on women's advancement in business, the Glass Ceiling Commission was established by the U.S. government in 1991. The results of studies of women and ethnic minorities in the corporate and business world paint a discouraging picture (Dingell & Maloney, 2002). Despite the view that advancements have occurred (such as the case of Carly Fiorina), women constitute proportionally fewer managers than men, even when the gender composition of the business is taken into consideration. Furthermore, female managers receive lower salaries than men, even when they do the same job.

Women's failure to advance to the highest levels of corporate success remains puzzling but not unique; women and ethnic minorities also advance more slowly in academic and scientific careers (Long & Fox, 1995). At one time, few women were qualified and experienced, and some evidence (Catalyst, 1996) suggests that male executives believe that situation still exists. The evidence indicates otherwise; many women have the credentials to be managers, executives, and CEOs. Women tend to believe that male stereotyping is responsible for their lack of advancement (Catalyst, 1996), and women reported experiences consistent with the career of Carly Fiorina, the CEO whose story was featured in the headline for this chapter (Estrich, 2001). Women are often in the spotlight because they are women rather than because of their accomplishments. When they fail, everyone notices. To succeed, female vice presidents reported the necessity of working harder and taking more risks than men in similar positions (Catalyst, 1996). Thus, men and women in business tend to see the glass ceiling differently, and women in corporate life believe that the glass ceiling is a real barrier to their advancement.

Ironically, women have no advantages in attaining higher positions in traditionally female-dominated fields. Indeed, men seem to have advantages in all types of jobs. The advantages that men have in female-dominated fields have been referred to as the *glass escalator* (Williams, 1992). This term conveys the image that some invisible force produces an easy ascent to higher positions, in contrast with the glass ceiling, which prevents women and minorities from reaching the highest levels of career achievement. Men who choose careers traditionally dominated by women face some discrimination from society in general, but these men's careers reflect a history of rapid promotion. These advantages may come as a result of the perception that men should not be in jobs that women usually perform, and thus men receive promotions to administrative or supervisory positions within that occupation.

For example, a male librarian described how happy and confident he had felt in his abilities as a children's librarian (Williams, 1992). Reading stories to children and helping them find books were part of his job, but many people mentioned to him that this was inappropriate work for a man, and he was transferred to another library and given the position of research librarian. When asked why he did not consider a discrimination lawsuit, the man reported that his new job was really a promotion to a more prestigious position, so he felt benefited rather than harmed by these clearly discriminatory actions. His experience is typical of men in female-dominated careers (Budig, 2002).

Gender role discrimination and occupational stereotypes provide the basis for both the glass ceiling and the glass escalator. In addition, the *sticky floor* is also a factor in

◼ GENDERED VOICES

I Never Felt Discriminated Against

A man who had gone to nursing school almost 30 years ago told me, "I decided to be a nurse when I was in the 10th grade, after I'd had surgery. The woman who lived across the street told me about the salaries of nurse-anesthetists, and the work interested me and the money sounded good. I don't remember my parents saying anything, my school counselor got information about nursing, and I didn't discuss it with my friends, so I don't recall any negative comments.

"During a career day at school, we had to choose the areas to attend, and I wrote down that I wanted to be a nurse. Much to my surprise, so did one of my friends, and neither of us knew that the other had thought about becoming nurses. One other guy wanted to be a surgeon, and we were the only three who had signed up for the health care option. The guy who wanted to be a surgeon was really mad at us, because he thought we were kidding about being nurses and were making fun of him.

"There were only two men in our nursing class. Now many men go into nursing, but then it was uncommon. There had been another guy about 10 years earlier and the two of us. That's it. I never felt discriminated against by either the teachers or the female students. Everybody was supportive and more than fair. My fraternity brothers were another story—they gave me a lot of static about majoring in nursing. The jokes were pretty good-natured, but there were a lot of jokes. I joke around a lot too, so it wasn't really a problem, but it was something that came up a lot.

"The women I have worked with were great. If anything, I think that being a man has been an advantage to me in my career. Rather than being discriminated against, I think that I was at some advantage. Maybe I got promotions and advancement faster than women, but those who chose me and recommended me were almost always women. I think I was competent and deserved the promotions, so I would have a hard time saying that I advanced in my career because I was a man, but I certainly never felt that it held me back."

I told him about the frequency of sexual harassment in jobs in which the gender ratio is far from equal and asked him if his female-dominated work situation had led to harassment. He replied, "Did I ever feel sexually harassed? That's hard to say. I never was put in the position of 'You do this or it's your job.' Never. But I've had my butt grabbed, and I've gotten a lot of offers. If that's harassment, then I guess I've been harassed, but I can't say that it really bothered me."

women's lower wages and problems in career advancement. The concept of a sticky floor contrasts with the glass ceiling as a means to describe low-status occupations with little opportunity for advancement. That is, occupations in which employees get stuck at the lowest levels. Many of the occupations dominated by women fit this description, including clerks, secretaries, beauticians, garment workers, and household service workers. Greater numbers of ethnic minority women tend to be concentrated in these low-level jobs, with both African American and Hispanic American women more likely to occupy blue-collar jobs than White women (USBC, 2002). Ethnic differences exist within blue-collar occupations; African American women are more likely to work in health service jobs, and Hispanic American women are more likely to be employed in manufacturing. All of these jobs have lower wages than jobs typically occupied by White women or by men.

Factors other than gender stereotyping and discrimination contribute to the gender gap in wages—different educational credentials, career choices, career schedules, and workplace climate. Women occupy jobs and pursue careers that are less prestigious and not as well paid as those that men occupy. For example, only 34.0% of lawyers and judges are women compared to 89.0% of nursing aides, orderlies, and attendants; only 36.0% of managers in marketing, advertising, and public relations are women compared with 98.6% of secretaries and stenographers (U.S. Bureau of Labor Statistics, 2003). In addition, women in science, engineering, and management tend to choose public institutions rather than private industry. These situations tend to have more egalitarian attitudes and better working climates for women, but the consequences are lower salaries.

The differences in women's and men's career development schedules also differentiate the genders in promotions and wages. Women are more likely than men to take time off from their careers to attend to family needs, such as staying home with young children. These employment gaps take women out of the workforce, pull them off the track to advancement, and slow their career progress (Dingell & Maloney, 2002). Employment gaps are even more damaging to men's career advancement plans (Schneer & Reitman, 1990), but women are more likely to interrupt their careers, so the overall impact of interrupted employment decreases women's wages and limits their opportunity for advancement more than it does for men.

What about those women who place a high priority on their careers? Does equal emphasis on work create equal rewards for women? Answers to those questions can come from women's satisfaction with their careers or from an assessment of their career progress. A group of successful male and female MBAs (people who have earned master's degrees in business administration) showed similar motivation, involvement, and enjoyment for work as well as similar tendencies to be "workaholics" (Burke, 1999). A study of the career progress of corporate men and women (Stroh, Brett, & Reilly, 1992) led to the conclusion that the same behavior did not result in the same success. "Although the women had done 'all the right stuff'—getting a similar education as the men, working in similar industries, not moving in and out of the workforce, not removing their names from consideration for a transfer more often—it was still not enough" (Stroh et al., 1992, p. 251). When women followed the traditionally male pattern of career advancement, they still did not advance at comparable rates. However, both women and men who did not do "all the right stuff" fared more poorly in terms of career progress than the women who did. If deviating from the standard pattern does not work and following the pattern does not work, then women have no way to succeed to the extent that men do.

Another factor in career advancement comes from the work climate and the informal social structure at work, which can help or hinder the advancement of employees. Women perceive their work environments as more hostile in terms of the informal social structure, standards they must meet for advancement, sexist attitudes, and the possibility for solving problems that arise at work (Murrell & James, 2001). For example, people working in business settings demonstrated their tendency to discriminate against women by choosing a man rather than a woman as the company representative for an important assignment, but choosing a woman for a less important assignment (Trentham & Larwood, 1998). Indeed, these businesspeople believed that they were conforming to the social norms for business by favoring men, even when the individuals themselves believed in equal treatment. This tendency to comply with the norm of discrimination burdens women in their career advancement.

Achievement-oriented women who pursue careers in male-dominated fields are in the minority, and minority status can handicap career advancement through isolation from the informal power structures (Kanter, 1977). When a minority member (either a woman or a member of an ethnic minority) enters the corporate world, the person becomes a **token** of the minority group. The token stands out, becoming more visible than other employees, and feels pressure to succeed and to reflect well on the ability of everyone in his or her minority group. Like Carly Fiorina, the female CEO in this chapter's headline story, the situation of the few women who are CEOs of Fortune 500 companies meets the definition of tokens.

As tokens try to fit into the existing corporate and social structure, the dominant group may work toward keeping them on the periphery. The process of excluding women and minorities may function either overtly or in a subtle manner (Benokraitis, 1997; Lorber, 1989). New workers either become part of the "inner circle" or not, and those who are not accepted never fit into the organization. As a result of this failure to fit in, these employees never gain the trust and confidence of coworkers (or in the case of Carly Fiorina, the media). Such mistrust can isolate tokens and prevent them from doing their job in the same way that other workers can. Women from ethnic minorities are at a special disadvantage because they are tokens in two ways (Murrell & James, 2001)

Tokens are also handicapped in forming mentoring relationships, the relationships between (usually) younger and less experienced and more experienced workers that offer valuable support in the form of friendship, advice, or even direct intervention in the organization to these less experienced employees. Mentor–protégé relationships tend to form within gender and ethnic lines. Neither women nor ethnic minorities are common in the upper echelons of organizations, and this situation places barriers on finding mentors (Murrell & James, 2001). Access to mentors can be an advantage for those who find them, and an impediment to advancement in the careers of those who do not.

For example, women and ethnic minority graduates from one MBA program were less likely to have mentors than were White men who had completed the same program (Dreher & Cox, 1996). Establishing a mentor relationship with a White man was advantageous. Those MBAs who did form such relationships earned over $16,000 more per year compared with those without mentors and those whose mentors were women or ethnic minorities. Therefore, women and minority employees are at a disadvantage and White men at an advantage in finding mentors who can further their careers.

The workplace environment and interactions in it affect performance and influence both colleagues' and supervisors' ratings of female workers. Management is a category that has been associated with men and has thus traditionally been considered male (Kanter, 1975). Despite a growing number of women entering management, the perception continues that management is a male position. Studies on perceptions of managers confirm the association of men and management. An early study (Heilman, Black, Martell, & Simon, 1989) found an association between men and management and negative stereotypes of women as managers. A later study (Deal & Stevenson, 1998) questioned college students about their perceptions of male and female managers. The male students expressed negative opinions of women in management, but the female students indicated significantly more positive perceptions of female managers. A more recent study (Willemsen, 2002) examined stereotyping of the category of managers and found that gender-neutral words were more strongly associated with successful managers than either feminine or masculine terms. However, participants still pictured the successful manager as a man.

A study of business managers (Rosenthal, 1996), however, showed no gender bias in managers' evaluations and explanations of their subordinates' performance. This finding of no gender bias in a field study is particularly optimistic because research participants were managers rather than students, and this research took place in organizations rather than in labs. Therefore, the existence of persistent stereotypes may be more of a factor for laboratory research than for ratings that appear as part of work settings with real people. Indeed, the opportunity to know persons allows managers to make ratings that are individual and specific rather than relying on stereotypes, as participants in laboratory research often must. This single finding does not overrule the possibility of gender bias operating in organizations, but it does suggest that knowing persons can allow some people to overcome the stereotype bias.

The gender wage gap decreased during the 1980s, mostly due to an increase in women training for and entering fields that paid better (Loury, 1997). Therefore, the choices are not as different as they once were, and wages have changed as a result. For college-educated women and men, the situation is not as discrepant as for the workforce in general (Hecker, 1998). The gender wage gap narrows and even disappears when comparing women and men who had completed the same college majors. This narrowing was even more prominent as a trend for younger workers, demonstrating that the changes in workforce composition have made a difference in closing the wage gap.

Therefore, women and ethnic minorities encounter several barriers to their career advancement. Many of those barriers relate to negative stereotypes of women and minorities, involving questions of their abilities, competence, and dedication to work. Even with similar qualifications and performance, few women and ethnic minorities attain the highest levels of career advancement, which suggests that discrimination is a deciding factor in the difference.

Balancing Career and Family.   Family demands influence career paths for both men and women. Although most people marry and have children, the historic association of women with household work and child care has made family concerns more of an issue for women's than men's careers. The association between women and domesticity has created a "force field" that pulls women toward household work and child care, which often decrease the amount of time they spend on their careers (Williams, 2000). This pull toward domesticity prevents women from fulfilling the "ideal worker" role, a worker able and willing to devote full time and overtime to work. Men who want to be involved with their families also fail as ideal workers and also may suffer penalties in their career advancement. The assumption still operates in most workplaces that workers will devote themselves to their careers and someone will be at home to support these ideal workers by taking care of household and children.

A large majority of people marry and have children, placing them in the situation of balancing work and family demands. Figure 12.1 shows the increase in employment for married women, including women with young children. Society, employers, and many husbands assume that women will be the ones who perform most household chores and become the primary caregivers for children. Arlie Hochschild (1997) studied women and men in a large, multinational corporation and found that, even when the company had a variety

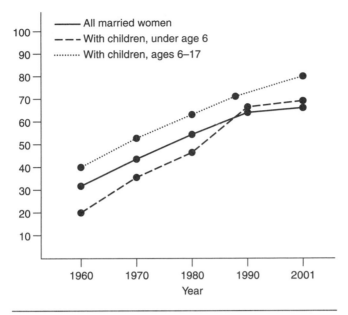

FIGURE 12.1 *Employment Trends for Married Women, Including Women with Children, 1960–2001*

Sources: Statistical Abstract of the United States: 1999 (119th ed., p. 417), by U.S. Bureau of the Census, 1999, Washington, DC: U.S. Government Printing Office; and *Statistical Abstract of the United States: 2002* (122nd ed., p. 373), by U.S. Bureau of the Census, 2002, Washington, DC: U.S. Government Printing Office.

of "family friendly" policies, the corporate climate pushed women toward domesticity and men toward career advancement. Thus, women who chose to concentrate on their careers were perceived as neglecting their families.

On the other hand, assumptions about men place them under suspicion when they do *not* concentrate on their careers (Riggs, 1997). Men's traditional role in families is breadwinner, which puts men into careers as a way of showing devotion to their families. Thus, traditional family demands take men away from their families while they devote time to careers. Therefore, the choice to spend time away from family has been (and remains) more socially approved for men than for women (Steil, 1995). Changes have occurred and continue to occur as men want to participate more fully in their children's lives (Adler, 1996). These desires to become active fathers as well as good providers can conflict. The most lucrative careers tend to be the ones that take the most time. When men work 80 hours a week, they have little time to attend Little League games.

What does it take to balance these demands? Several researchers have studied couples and companies to understand how some people manage this balancing act while others do not. Pepper Schwartz (1994) found that couples with children had a much more difficult time than those without children. The added demand of raising children coupled with the expectation that wives would be the primary caregivers prevented many couples from forming equitable relationships. Schwartz found that couples who had formed equal partnerships often had chosen to sacrifice high-prestige careers. For many such couples, the decision was a deliberate acknowledgment that current corporate, scientific, and academic careers require more than full-time devotion to the job.

Despite the conflicts and demands from family and work commitments, an increasing number of people fulfill these multiple roles. Some theories predict problems for the individuals who do, but research has not confirmed the harmful effects (Barnett & Hyde, 2001). To the contrary, people who have both employment and family tend to be psychologically and physically healthier and happier than people who do not occupy multiple roles. Career, marriage, and children are a balancing act, and overload and distress may occur. However, when people are employed, they have the opportunity to experience success, social support for others at work, and income. "Adding the worker role is beneficial to women, and adding or participating in family roles is beneficial for men" (Barnett & Hyde, 2001, p. 784).

GENDER ISSUES AT WORK

The gender gap in wages reflects the barriers that women face when entering and advancing in careers. Although women have entered male-dominated professions in greater numbers in the past decades than at any previous time, women remain underrepresented in the highest levels of their professions. Even when factors such as education, position, job tenure, and type of job are equated, women earn less money than men (Budig, 2002). About 25% of the wage gap between men and women is the result of gender segregation of occupations (Jacobs, 1989).

Gender Segregation on the Job

The gender-typical choices that most men and women make in careers have resulted in gender segregation in most jobs. That is, in most work situations the large majority of jobs are held by either men or women but not by an equal (or nearly equal) mix of both. These associations have created the perception that the jobs are gendered. Regardless of the job demands, some jobs have become so associated with either men or women as to be considered male occupations or female occupations. This process contributes to the differential value of occupations because both women and men value the type of work that men do more highly than the type of work that women do (Cohen & Huffman, 2003).

Women also occupy a less diversified range of occupations than men. Consequently, most employed women are concentrated in a few occupations, whereas men are employed in a wider variety of jobs. Over two thirds of women have jobs in clerical or professional fields, but the professional fields are those traditionally dominated by women—nursing and teaching (USBC, 2002). Women are most underrepresented in skilled blue-collar jobs, such as electricians, mechanics, and plumbers. (Refer to Table 12.1 for the percentages in the "construction," "mechanics," and "production and skilled crafts" categories.)

Changes over the past 20 years have not made a large impact on gender segregation on the job. Women have moved into male-dominated jobs at a much faster rate than men have moved into female-dominated work, leaving a high degree of gender segregation. The reasons for this pattern are largely economic: Male-dominated occupations pay better than female-dominated ones (Cohen & Huffman, 2003). Even when the educational and skills levels are controlled, jobs in female-dominated fields pay less than the equivalent jobs in male-dominated areas. Thus, women have an incentive to move into male-dominated jobs, and men have little incentive to seek jobs in female-dominated occupations.

The process of integrating either women or men into a gender-dominated workplace poses problems, especially during the early stages of the process. Studies of men and women in workplaces undergoing this process (Wharton & Baron, 1987, 1991) showed that men became significantly less satisfied with the gender-integrated work situations. Women, on the other hand, were most dissatisfied with work situations in which women were in the majority but the few men received preferential treatment. The dissatisfaction may be greatest at the beginning of the integration process (Allmendinger & Hackman, 1995), when either men or women dominate the workplace. When women held between 10% and 40% of positions within an organization, both genders were dissatisfied, and the organization did not function as effectively as it had previously. As the proportion of women increased toward 50%, many of the problems and conflicts diminished. When the workplace was integrated, no gender differences appeared in the perception of work-related demands (Hochwarter, Perrewe, & Dawkins, 1995). Although the integration process may create problems, those problems diminish when gender integration progresses.

Gender segregation is often more extreme in specific work situations than in any occupation as a whole (Groshen, 1991). For example, both men and women wait on tables, but some restaurants hire more men, whereas others hire more women to perform this job. Even people who choose occupations that are not dominated by one gender may work in companies or offices in which that occupation is gender segregated and thus, they will spend their time with same-gender colleagues. Gender segregation declined between 1970 and 1980 (Fields & Wolff, 1991), but the pattern of decrease was not consistent during the 1990s (Dolado, Felgueroso, & Jimeno, 2001). For younger, well-educated women, the gender gap diminished substantially. For others, especially for those with less education, gender segregation remains.

Although jobs are gender segregated for most workers, the workplace is likely to include both men and women, who, though they may hold different jobs, must work together in the same setting. For example, most secretaries are women, most managers are men, and most managers have secretaries. Thus, men and women often work together but not at the same job. Indeed, the work situations that allow for interaction between men and women often involve a power differential, with men having the more powerful positions and women the more subordinate.

Gender, Communication, and Power in the Workplace

Communication is a very important aspect of the workplace, and the ideal that women's style of communication may place them at a disadvantage can be traced to the 1970s. Robin Lakoff (1975) contended that "women's language" differs from "men's language," with women adopting a more tentative and deferential style of communication than men. She hypothesized that this style of speaking fails to convey the assertive, commanding qualities necessary for leadership, which makes women's speech style a handicap in their careers.

Would women be more successful at work if they talked like men? Early research (Wiley & Eskilson, 1985) indicated that a hesitant speech style is less successful, whether used by women or men, but neither style was unique to either. Elizabeth Aries's (1987, 1996) reviews on gender and communication confirmed these results: No distinctive patterns of communication are uniquely associated with success or even with women or men. That is, the hesitant speech style that Lakoff characterized as "women's language" and the assertive style that she identified as "men's language" are not specific to either. Although women and men may have different goals in speaking, the notion of a male versus a female way of talking is not supported by research. Even the tendency for men to interrupt more than women is small (Anderson & Leaper, 1998). Furthermore, the emphasis on group differences obscures more important individual differences. Gender-related differences in communication are complex, and both the setting and situation in which communication takes place are critical factors in men's and women's speech patterns.

Conversational style also reflects power, and power is one of the situational differences that affects speech. Speakers with more power speak differently than speakers with less power (Aries, 1987, 1996). Those in positions of power tend to use more assertive language. Work roles mirror social roles, giving women less power. Thus, aspects of the female role carry over into the workplace to produce **sex role spillover** (Nieva & Gutek, 1981), gender role characteristics that spill over into the workplace, creating stereotyping and a sexualized atmosphere. Barbara Gutek (1985) expanded the concept, emphasizing that sex role spillover focuses on gender role behavior that is irrelevant (or even an impediment) to the work role. Sex role spillover can take several different forms, including the expectation that women will be more nurturant or loyal than men, that women will occupy less powerful and subordinate positions, and that women will be sexual at work.

Power in the workplace is typically associated with leadership, and leaders simultaneously occupy both the leadership role and a gender role (Eagly & Johannesen-Schmidt, 2001). For men, the leadership role is consistent with the male gender role, but the dissimilarity between these two roles for women may create conflicts, both in female leaders and in their subordinates. For example, men's experiences with women are more likely to have been women as mothers, girlfriends, wives, daughters, and secretaries, but possibly not as professional colleagues or supervisors. When a man is faced with a woman who is his colleague or boss, he may rely on one of the other role relationships to guide his interaction with her. Although treating the new female account executive like his mother or his secretary may not be appropriate, these relationships are familiar and may be the chosen patterns. The new female account executive may also fall back on habitual patterns of interacting with men on the job, perpetuating inappropriate work behavior for everyone involved. On the other hand, her behavior may be shaped by the account executives she has known, most of whom were men, as well as her beliefs about how an executive should act. Thus, she may act like a male executive, enacting a version of the role with which she is most familiar.

Some evidence exists that women who occupy jobs most commonly filled by men adopt a male style of work-related behavior, and this behavior demonstrates how powerful situational demands can be. A review of the research on gender and leadership roles (Eagly, Johannesen-Schmidt, & van Engen, 2003; Eagly & Johnson, 1990) showed that both women and men who have attained managerial status in organizations tend to share similarities in leadership styles. Especially in male-dominated workplaces, male and female leaders exhibit similar, typically masculine leadership styles (Gardiner & Tiggemann, 1999). Male leaders described themselves as somewhat more aggressive, instrumental, and risk oriented than female leaders (Lewis & Fagenson-Eland, 1998), but their supervisors failed to see this difference. Thus, job requirements and the selection of people for the job make managers more alike than different, regardless of gender.

When women adopt the same power styles as men, they may not receive equally positive evaluations. Men are not more effective leaders than women (Eagly, Karau, & Makhijani, 1995), but their styles of leadership can be perceived as differing in effectiveness, depending on the extent to which the style matches the gender stereotype. Authoritative and even autocratic styles of management are common for men, but women are expected to be more "people oriented" and interpersonally sensitive. When managers exhibit different styles, the choice of autocratic versus democratic often corresponds to the male versus the female style (Eagly & Johnson, 1990).

In a comparison of leadership styles, women were more likely than men to adopt leadership behaviors that included motivating subordinates by example, showing optimism and excitement, attending to individual needs, and using rewards to change behavior (Eagly & Johannesen-Schmidt, 2001). The gender differences were small, but women's leadership behaviors were associated with positive outcomes, whereas some of the behaviors associated with male leadership were associated with less effective leadership, such as concentrating on negative behaviors and problems and waiting until problems were serious before taking action.

Despite their potential as good leaders, women do not receive the opportunity to develop this potential as often as men do, and when they do, they are subject to more careful scrutiny and criticism than men in comparable positions (Eagly & Karau, 2002). Indeed, a type of double standard seems to operate in the workplace in which women are held to different standards of competence and success than men are (Foschi, 2000). The story of Ann Hopkins provides a dramatic example of such this type of double standard (Fiske, Bersoff, Borgida, Deaux, & Heilman, 1991). Ann Hopkins was an employee of Price Waterhouse, and she was so successful that she was nominated for partner in that company, the only woman nominated that year. She was not chosen as a partner, and she became the object of criticism for being too aggressive and "macho" as well as for not being sufficiently feminine in her behavior and appearance. Hopkins sued the company for applying different criteria to its male and female employees, contending that gender stereotyping was a factor in their decision. Eventually, the U.S. Supreme Court agreed with these arguments and condemned the double bind that women face—they are penalized for using an aggressive, powerful style when only this style can lead to success.

If women are penalized for using the same methods to gain power that men use, how do women achieve power at work? Changing stereotypes is not easy, but people's behavior in real workplaces is often not as strongly influenced by stereotypes as that of people in laboratory situations. When people have the opportunity to interact and know each other on a personal basis, this information can override stereotypes (Eagly & Johannesen-Schmidt, 2001). People in organizations are often mutually dependent on each other for positive outcomes related to work, and this interdependence can build respect and recognition of competence (Goodwin & Fiske, 2001). In addition, when workers are accountable to some third party, such as an organizational hierarchy that supports female leaders, this situation can act to reduce bias throughout the organization. Thus, women can become and function as effective leaders in organizations, but many barriers exist to block their progress.

In summary, although research has failed to support the notion of different communication styles that are unique to women or men, it has shown that communication styles relate to the power of the speaker and the communication situation. The issues of gender, communication, and power also relate to adherence to stereotypical gender roles in the workplace, which gives power to men and places obstacles in the way of women's career advancement. Using habitual patterns of interaction between men and women in the workplace produces a power differential, with men having the advantage. When women use the same behaviors as men to exert power, they are often perceived as behaving inappropriately and are penalized. Women have the potential to be excellent leaders, but they face many barriers in achieving their potential.

The power difference between men's and women's positions offers not only the opportunity for men to be more successful at work but also the opportunity for men to sexually exploit the women who work for them. Although sexuality at work can also be interpreted as a power issue, the term **sexual harassment** is now used as the label for sexual exploitation in the workplace.

Sexual Harassment at Work

According to Barbara Gutek (1985), "sex role spillover facilitates the expression of sexuality at work to the extent that the sex object aspect of the female sex role and the sexual aggressor aspect of the male sex role carry over into the work setting" (p. 18); sexual harassment is a function of sex role spillover. Men and women also choose to enter sexual relationships in the workplace, making it difficult to distinguish between this type of sexuality and sexual harassment.

Sexual harassment became illegal as a form of gender discrimination in the United States through a court interpretation of Title VII of the 1964 Civil Rights Acts (Fitzgerald, Swan, & Magley, 1997). In 1980, the U.S. Equal Employment Opportunity Commission established guidelines on sexual harassment. The first form of sexual harassment to be recognized was **quid pro quo sexual harassment,** in which employers or supervisors demand sexual favors as a condition of employment or as a condition for promotion. This form of harassment involves a supervisor using threats or pressure toward a subordinate, making it a clear abuse of power. Men are more often supervisors and women more often subordinates, resulting in women as the common targets of this form of harassment.

In 1986, another form of sexual harassment was legally recognized in the United States—**hostile environment sexual harassment.** This concept of harassment is based on the notion that psychological harm or reduced effectiveness at work can result from unwanted sexual attention as well as from offensive or hostile behavior (Fitzgerald et al.,

1997). A third classification of sexual harassment is **gender harassment,** which occurs when people are subjected to offensive or hostile behavior because of their gender. This type of harassment is distinctive because it does not necessarily involve sexuality; rather, it involves hostile or disparaging remarks directed toward a person because of that person's gender. Table 12.3 gives examples of each type of sexual harassment.

The U.S. Supreme Court made a series of decisions that strengthened sexual harassment law, making lawsuits easier to win (Gould, 2000). During the 1990s, the number of cases filed with the Equal Employment Opportunity Commission more than doubled, and the monetary awards increased by more than fourfold (Simon, Scherer, & Rau, 1999). Since the mid-1990s, the number of complaints filed with the Equal Employment Opportunity Commission (EEOC, 2003) has remained stable, but the monetary compensation continued to rise. The court decisions extended protection against sexual harassment to men as well as women, and the percent of complaints filed by men is still increasing (although 85% of complaints are filed by women against men). Sexual harassment often receives comic treatment on television (Montemurro, 2003), on which such behavior is either

TABLE 12.3 *Examples of the Three Types of Sexual Harassment*

Quid Pro Quo Type

Demands for sex in exchange for hiring

Demands for sex in exchange for promotion or favorable job evaluation

Demands for sex to keep a job

Demands for sex to avoid being placed in an undesirable job

Hostile Environment Type

Sexual touching

Sexual comments and jokes

Displays of sexual material, such as drawings or photographs

Nonverbal sexual posturing, including sexual gestures

Personal remarks about sexuality

Sexually oriented comments about appearance

Discussions about a person in sexual terms in the person's presence, including comments phrased as though the person were not present

Gender Harassment Type

Degrading comments about the ability of women (or men)

Hostile comments about women's (or men's) behavior as a group; not confined to sexual comments

Insults directed toward women or men because of their gender, rather than because of any action or characteristic of the individual portrayed as the subject of jokes or omitted from the script entirely. The growing monetary awards and settlements have prompted real businesses to adopt attitudes different from those of TV sitcoms, and most companies in the United States have policies and training to prevent harassment.

Many countries also have laws and regulations that have been used to prohibit sexual harassment, and some countries have laws that specifically apply to sexual harassment (Barak, 1997). The United Kingdom, Canada, Australia, Israel, Austria, Ireland, and New Zealand have laws that prohibit sex discrimination or sexual harassment, and the establishment of the European Community led to additional laws. The cities of Berlin and Tokyo enacted regulations of their own rather than wait for Germany and Japan to pass legislation. Yet sexual harassment is a common experience throughout the world. For countries in which surveys have been done, the prevalence falls between 30% and 50%.

The forms of sexual harassment are not equal in frequency or in perceived severity; the hostile environment form is more common, but the quid pro quo form is perceived as more serious (Rotundo, Nguyen, & Sackett, 2001). Despite the perceived lack of severity of hostile environment sexual harassment, Louise Fitzgerald (1994) found that workplaces that spawn this type of harassment tend to also have the quid pro quo type, and a 1998 U.S.

▣ GENDERED VOICES

Hardly a Day Went By

In two stories I heard about sexual harassment, the behaviors of the two harassers were amazingly similar. Both harassers, a woman and a man, harassed a coworker. The behaviors of the targets were also very similar to each other.

A man told me, "I worked in a car dealership selling cars after I graduated, and one of the other salespeople was a woman—the only woman who was in sales. She sexually harassed the finance manager. It was blatant. She propositioned him in front of everybody, saying things like 'Let's go in the back room now,' and things much more vulgar.

"He seemed embarrassed and usually didn't reply; he tried to ignore her. He was married, and he never gave her any encouragement at all. She would go over and stand very close to him, never touching him, but standing close and making him uncomfortable. And she would proposition him; rarely a day went by when she didn't. The guy was clearly uncomfortable, but nobody ever did anything."

A young woman said, "I worked as a cashier in a discount store, and one of the department managers sexually harassed me. He would come over to the cash register where I was working, and he would proposition me. He made reasons to be close to me, and he kept saying what a good idea it would be for us to have sex. I didn't think it was such a good idea. I always said no, and I asked him to stop asking. His offers embarrassed me. Hardly a day went by without some sexual offer from him or some remark with sexual connotations. He never touched me or fondled me, but he made my job harder, and he embarrassed me.

"I complained to my supervisor, but she told me to just ignore him. He wasn't my boss, and he never made any threats or attacked me or anything. But I think that he shouldn't have been allowed to harass me the way he did. Nobody did one thing to stop him. I don't think that the store manager ever said a word."

Supreme Court decision agreed (Gould, 2000). Fitzgerald contended that all of the types of sexual harassment are interrelated, as Figure 12.2 shows. Fitzgerald emphasized environmental rather than personal factors in sexual harassment and reported that environments that allow insulting remarks and unwanted sexual attention also tend to be permissive of sexual coercion. Despite the separate legal definitions for the types of sexual harassment and the differences in frequency and their perceived severity, they often coexist.

Women are more frequently the targets of all sexual harassment, when defined in terms of *unwanted* sexual attention. However, both men and women are targets for sexual attention in the workplace (Gutek, 1985, 2001). Men and women receive a comparable number of sexual overtures, but women are more likely than men to judge this behavior as sexual harassment (Rotundo et al., 2001). These different standards are a factor in sexual harassment. For example, men and women disagree over whether repeated offers for dates constitute sexual harassment, with men finding this behavior less harassing than women do. Gutek (1985) found that the biggest gender difference concerning sexuality at work had to do with attitudes about sexual propositions. She found that two thirds of the men in her study said that they felt flattered by such propositions, but only 17% of women felt the same way. Indeed, over 60% of the women said that they would feel insulted by a sexual proposition at work. The main problem, however, comes from the lack of understanding of each other's perceptions; neither the men nor the women in Gutek's study were aware of the perceptions of the other gender. The men believed that the women felt flattered by sexual attention when in actuality a majority of the women felt insulted or angered.

If the sexual attention that men receive at work is often welcome, are men exempt from being the targets of sexual harassment? The legal definition did not specify the gender of the target, and a 1998 U.S. Supreme Court decision (*Oncale v. Sundowner Offshore*

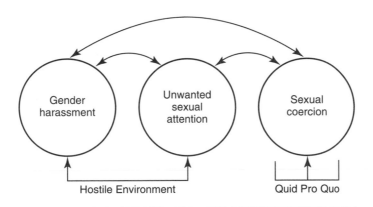

FIGURE 12.2 *A Model of Sexually Harassing Behaviors*

Source: From "But Was It Really Sexual Harassment? Legal, Behavioral, and Psychological Definitions of the Workplace Victimization of Women," by Louise F. Fitzgerald, Suzanne Swan, & Vicki J. Magley, 1997, in William O'Donohue (Ed.), *Sexual Harassment: Theory, Research, and Treatment* (p. 11). Copyright © 1997 by Allyn and Bacon. Reprinted by permission.

Services, Inc.) specified that men could be victims of sexual harassment. Reports of complaints to the EEOC (EEOC, 2003), surveys of employed men and women (Berdahl, Magley, & Waldo, 1996), and surveys of military personnel (DuBois, Knapp, Faley, & Kustis, 1998) revealed that sexual harassment with male targets was much less common than with female targets.

No men reported sexual coercion in the workplace study (Berdahl et al., 1996), but incidents of sexual hazing, including rape, occurred in the military study (DuBois et al., 1998). Gender harassment violations also occurred, with women using examples of such comments as "You men are all alike" and "Men have only one thing on their minds" (Berdahl et al., 1996, p. 540). In addition, several men mentioned a type of gender harassment that women did not. This type of harassment came from other men and involved comments about the target man not living up to standards of manliness by showing too much concern for or sympathy with women. For example, a man who failed to share a joke that is derogatory toward women might be censured by other men who enjoyed the joke. Indeed, the majority of complaints of sexual harassment of men designate another man as the harasser.

Although women often feel insulted and angered by sexual comments and propositions from supervisors and coworkers, they may have problems in labeling these behaviors as harassment (Gutek & Done, 2001). In addition, feeling harassed is not the same as experiencing a situation that meets the legal definition of sexual harassment. Therefore, the estimates about rates for harassment may be low if the figures are based on personal reports with a specific question about experiencing sexual harassment or high if the figures are based on personal judgments. When using a personal definition (Gutek & Done, 2001), between 35% and 50% of women have experienced sexual harassment at work. For men, at least 9% and up to 37% have experienced sexual harassment. However, most fail to report the harassment; some do not tell anyone, and only a small minority make use of their companies' policies to file a complaint.

Men who sexually harass women do not differ from employed men in general (Gutek, 1985, 2001), but an analysis of the situational as well as personal factors has been more useful in understanding those who harass (Pryor & Whalen, 1997; Gutek & Done, 2001). Men who are likely to sexually harass tend to view sex and power as linked, making them more likely to use their power at work to sexually exploit women who are their subordinates. In addition, some evidence (Done, 2000 in Gutek & Done, 2001) suggests that harassers of both genders have impulse control problems—they tend to act on rather than control their impulses to make sexual comments or overtures. Women who are targets of harassment differ in some ways from typical women in the workforce; they are more likely to be unmarried, younger than the average employed woman, and attractive. Women who initiate sexual relationships at work are much less likely to be perceived as harassing men than vice versa, and, like the women who are the targets of harassment, they are younger and more likely to be unmarried than the average employed woman. In cases of men who reported that they were sexually harassed, their harassers were similar both to the women who initiated sex at work and to the women who were targets of harassment—young, unmarried, and attractive.

Sexual harassment has both personal and professional effects. Women who are harassed in their workplaces are at increased risk for lowering of self-esteem and confidence, emotional consequences, depression, and even posttraumatic stress disorder (Gutek & Done, 2001). In addition, harassment decreased work satisfaction and commitment to the organization, which can lead to quitting the jobs or asking for transfers. In a survey of attorneys (Laband & Lentz, 1998), the experience of sexual harassment was associated with decreased job satisfaction and increased intentions to quit. Therefore, even among informed professionals, sexual harassment is a problem that can negatively affect women's careers. The effects on men's careers are not clear because so little research has concentrated on men's reactions to sexual harassment. However, men's experience of sexuality at work meets their definition of harassment less often than women's definition (Rotundo et al., 2001)

Perhaps the differences in consequences of sexuality at work explain the differences in perceptions of harassment: Why should men feel harassed by sex at work when they are very unlikely to experience negative consequences? Why should women welcome sexual attention at work when their esteem and careers are so much more likely to be harmed? Given an equal interest in sexual relationships with people at work, the unequal consequences of sexual behavior on careers suggests that men and women should have different views of sexuality at work—and they do.

CONSIDERING DIVERSITY

Diversity issues—more specifically, a lack of diversity—are evident in most workplaces. That lack of diversity may be traced to the concept of the "ideal worker." Many characteristics and circumstances can prevent a person from attaining that ideal (Williams, 2000). The model for the ideal worker is male, which presents problems for women who want to pursue careers. The ideal is also White, so ethnic minorities have disadvantages in hiring and career advancement. The image of the ideal worker is also able-bodied, which creates barriers for disabled people. Thus, many people in the workforce fail to meet this ideal in various ways. Despite the enormous changes that have made the current U.S. workforce more diverse than it has ever been, the assumption of White, male breadwinners continues to influence the cultural perception of workers, to the disadvantage of all the groups that fail to meet this description.

As a result, not only women but also ethnic minorities are less common among the upper ranks of corporate management, science, law, and technology. Figure 12.3 shows the underrepresentation and overrepresentation in various occupations held by women, African Americans, and Hispanic Americans. (The categories of African American and Hispanic American represent both men and women from these ethnic groups, not just women, so the percentages in the women category overlap with the other two categories.) The under- and overrepresentations appear in terms of deviations from the center line, which ties representation to the percentage of employed people in these groups: 46.6% women, 10.9% African American, and 12.2% Hispanic American. Thus, categories for which the bars deviate little from the center line indicate that individuals hold such jobs in about the same proportion as they participate in the workforce. Deviations indicate disproportionate numbers of women, African Americans, or Hispanic Americans in that occupation. For example, all three groups are underrepresented for most of the managerial and professional

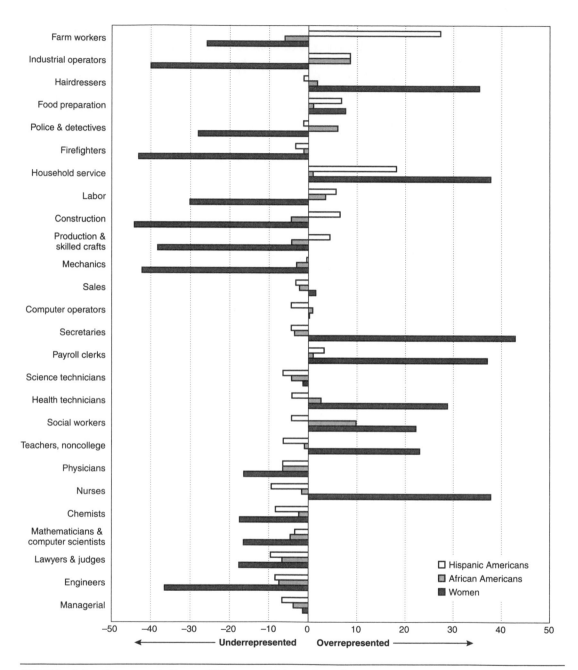

FIGURE 12.3 *Representation of Women, African Americans, and Hispanic Americans in Various Occupations*

Source: Statistical Abstract of the United States, 2002 (122nd ed., pp. 381–383), by U.S. Bureau of the Census. 2002, Washington, DC: U.S. Government Printing Office.

categories, meaning that women, African Americans, and Hispanic Americans do not occupy these prestigious, lucrative jobs as often as White men do. In contrast, women are overrepresented in the category of secretaries, and both African Americans and Hispanic Americans are overrepresented in the category of laborers. All three categories are overrepresented in household service. These jobs are premier examples of the "sticky floor," positions in which people get stuck at the bottom of the job hierarchy.

Some African Americans succeed in attaining the highest levels of career success. But the achievements of even these individuals are suspect, according to Stephen Carter (1991), who contended that African Americans have to work harder than Whites to achieve, and they receive less credit when they do. Part of the suspicion comes from the stereotyping of African Americans as less capable and less motivated than Whites. Additional suspicion comes from affirmative action, which gives ethnic minorities and women advantages in education and hiring to compensate for past (and, in many cases, continuing) discrimination. Many people believe that the only reason such individuals attend prestigious schools or get lucrative jobs is because of affirmative action. Affirmative action, Carter argued, allowed African Americans to enter elite schools and prestigious jobs, and the criteria for entry were lower for ethnic minorities than for others. The chances for advancement, however, were slimmer: "Once hired, people who are not white face difficulties in finding mentors, powerful institutional figures to smooth their paths; then they will naturally advance more slowly" (Carter, 1991, p. 64).

Later research (Biernat & Kobrynowicz, 1997) confirmed Carter's beliefs: Stereotypes influence judgments and evaluations of ability and performance in much the same way that Carter himself had experienced. When judging African Americans and women, participants set lower competency standards. Thus, it may be easier for ethnic minorities and women than for White men to stand out in a job interview or application process. The standards for judging performance were higher for African Americans and women than for White men, putting them in the position that Carter described—having to work twice as hard to be considered half as good.

Asian Americans are also subject to stereotyping, but this process can help them in certain careers. The stereotype holds that Asian Americans are hardworking, intelligent, and oriented toward science and technology, which pushes them toward careers in these areas, but hinders choices for other careers. Their success has ruled Asian Americans out of the category of "real" minorities, and workplace initiatives to diversify may thus exclude Asian Americans, leaving them at a disadvantage in terms of hiring and promotions (Ragaza, 1999).

Women and ethnic minorities are not the only groups at a disadvantage in the world of work. People with disabilities face prejudice and discrimination, and disabled women in the workforce encounter barriers on the basis of both their gender and their handicapping condition (Feist-Price & Khanna, 2003; McLain & Perkins, 1990). These biases result in these women's unemployment and underemployment. The unemployment rate among women with disabilities is 50% to 90%, and disabled women are more likely to be unemployed than disabled men. Furthermore, women with disabilities earn less; they earn 64 cents for each dollar able-bodied women earn and earn 44% less than men with disabilities earn. This high unemployment and underemployment result in poverty; these women's disabilities are more likely to bring their living standards below the poverty level. Women with disabilities have disadvantages compared not only to able-bodied women but also to men who have disabilities. Such women have the lowest percentage of employment compared to both able-bodied women and men with and without disabilities; they are "at the bottom of the work heap" (McLain & Perkins, 1990, p. 54).

■ SUMMARY

Career development has been associated with men, but women in industrialized countries now expect to pursue careers as well as have a family. Although career motivation is similar for men and women, social forces still pull women toward domesticity rather than toward careers. The limitations on women's careers come from their career choices, interruptions in their employment, and discrimination in hiring and promotion.

Career choices and preparation lead men into more prestigious, more lucrative, and a wider variety of occupations than women pursue. Women with high ability in math and science still do not pursue engineering, science, and technology careers at the same rate as talented men do. Different occupations are a big factor in the gender wage gap, with women pursuing careers that pay less than careers that men choose. Discrimination in hiring is a major factor in the wage gap between men and women, even when they choose the same careers. Specific, personal information about job applicants can partially overcome the gender stereotyping that affects hiring decisions, but the bias in favor of men is a factor that still exists. In addition, interruptions in employment affect careers negatively. This experience is more common to women, who more often interrupt their careers to devote time to families.

Women occupy a very small percentage of executive positions, often being blocked in their career progress by an invisible barrier called the glass ceiling, which limits women's careers throughout the world. Many factors have contributed to the formation of barriers to the advancement of women and ethnic minorities. The informal social structure in corporations excludes newcomers who differ from the majority. Thus, token women or minorities have difficulty being trusted and have trouble forming important mentoring relationships. Gender stereotypes influence perceptions of female managers' performance by making their competence difficult to acknowledge. Gender stereotypes can boost men in gender-typical careers, providing them with easier access to promotions. Even women who have comparable training, personal backgrounds, and performance do not advance in their careers as rapidly as men do, which shows evidence of discrimination in career advancement.

Gender-based interactions at work obstruct women from gaining power and from demonstrating their competence, as these characteristics are not part of the feminine stereotype. Women who fail to adhere to traditional standards of femininity can be penalized, but by following these "feminine" standards, women cannot succeed in the corporate world. Women can gain power at work, but they have to overcome many barriers to do so.

Balancing work and family is a task for both men and women, but the gender role for women holds that they, rather than men, should devote themselves to family concerns. These social expectations lead men toward and women away from career success by placing the burdens of household chores and child care on women. Ironically, taking care of their families by being the primary breadwinner takes men away from their families. Work and family both require time and effort, but research indicates that both employment and family are positive factors in health and well-being.

The workforce is gender segregated. Most men's and women's colleagues are the same gender as they are, and few occupations have an equal proportion of men and women. Even in occupations that are not gender segregated, job situations may be. However, women have moved into traditionally male-dominated fields more rapidly than men have moved into female-dominated jobs. Gender segregation on the job has resulted in certain jobs being associated with one gender, and this situation has resulted in spillover of male and female characteristics into the work environment. This gender role spillover tends to produce stereotypical patterns of interaction between men and women, rather than interaction between equal coworkers, bringing gender role stereotyping into the workplace.

Another consequence of gender stereotyping at work is sexuality and sexual harassment. Although illegal, both women and men are pressured for sexual favors from employers and supervisors and are subjected to unwanted sexual attention or hostile comments concerning characteristics and behaviors of their gender. Women are more likely than men to find sexual attention unwanted, possibly because they are more likely to be harmed by sexual relationships with coworkers. Women are more likely to label their experiences as sexual harassment than are men, especially for behaviors that fall into the hostile environment form of sexual harassment. Both men and women tend to agree that sexual coercion constitutes harassment.

Ethnic minorities also experience barriers to career success, and African Americans and Hispanic Americans are affected by stereotyping, discrimination in hiring and promotions, and gender segregation. Asian Americans are advantaged by their stereotypes in some ways, but restricted in other ways, especially in terms of job hiring and promotions. All ethnic minorities and women suffer from their discrepancy from the ideal worker model, which also poses a disadvantage for people with disabilities.

GLOSSARY

gender harassment a type of sexual harassment that occurs when people are subjected to offensive or hostile behavior because of their gender.

glass ceiling the invisible barrier that seems to prevent women and ethnic minorities from reaching the highest levels of their professions.

hostile environment sexual harassment the type of sexual harassment that occurs when employers allow offensive elements to exist in the work environment.

quid pro quo sexual harassment sexual harassment in the form of demands for sexual favors in exchange for employment or promotion.

sex role spillover the hypothesis that gender role characteristics spill over into the workplace, creating stereotyping and a sexualized atmosphere.

sexual harassment unwanted sexual attention.

token a symbol or example, in this case, of a minority group.

SUGGESTED READINGS

Gutek, Barbara. (2001). Women and paid work. *Psychology of Women Quarterly, 25,* 379–393.
Gutek compares the field of working women in 1981 with that of 2001, noting the changes that have occurred not only for women but also for research into careers, stereotyping, leadership, and sexual harassment.

Hochschild, Arlie Russell. (1997). *The time bind.* New York: Metropolitan Books.

Hochschild's study of workers in a large, multinational company presents the problems of balancing work and family and how work seems to be winning the time battle. Her book tells stories of women and men who have made various choices in combining the two, and of the problems they face from family and work as a result of their choices.

Murrell, Audrey J.; & James, Erika Hayes. (2001). Gender and diversity in organizations: Past, present, and future directions. *Sex Roles, 45,* 243–257.

As the title suggests, this review looks at the past, present, and future in examining gender and diversity in organizations. The article concentrates not only on women but also on ethnic minorities, especially ethnic minority women, and the barriers they face in developing careers.

Williams, Joan. (2000). *Unbending gender: Why family and work conflict and what to do about it.* New York: Oxford University Press.

Williams is an attorney who explores the social, psychological, and legal issues in balancing work and family concerns. Her analysis holds that forces push women and men toward traditional choices, and that individuals face overwhelming difficulties in departing from these traditions.

HEALTH AND FITNESS

"For as long as demographic records have existed in the United States, women have out-lived men. When flappers were big, a woman's life expectancy at birth was about two years more than a man's. Some 50 years later, when disco started taking over the land, the gap had expanded three-fold, to more than seven years" (Kreeger, 2002, p. 34). Karen Young Kreeger (2002) wrote about the gender difference in longevity, and the subtitle of her article suggests that "societal and lifestyle issues—not biology—appear to have the greatest influences on whether men or women live longer" (p. 34).

The notion that social and behavioral factors contribute to longevity pose questions about which conditions may be important for the longevity of men versus women. "In the 18th and part of the 19th centuries, for example, men probably outlived women because of the increased mortality of women during childbirth. In the early 20th century, the hyper-virulent flu that ravaged the population mortally affected more men than women. And, by the end of the 20th century, the life expectancy of both sexes started leveling off as more women became addicted to nicotine" (Kreeger, 2002, p. 34). Thus, beginning in the 1800s in the United States and in other industrialized countries, women have lived longer than men.

Despite the advantage in years, women are not necessarily healthier. The phrase "Women are sicker; men die quicker" (in Altman, 1997, p. 18) expresses this apparent con-tradiction. Women's poorer health is widely accepted, possibly because women make more doctor and hospital visits than men do. This situation leads to the acceptance of women's higher **morbidity,** that is, higher rate of illness. The health care system may be part of the reason why women are considered less healthy. Women receive more health care than men receive due to birth control and childbearing. During health care visits, providers may rou-tinely ask about other problems, prompting patients to become vigilant concerning prob-lems and to report problems that might otherwise be too minor to prompt doctor visits. Mentioning a problem leads to more health care. With more routine health care visits, women have more opportunities to experience situations that expand treatment.

The reasons for women's lower death rate, that is **mortality,** are also poorly under-stood. Women and men have different explanations for their varying life expectancies

(Wallace, 1996). Men attributed their shorter life spans to their greater physical labor and more stressful lives, whereas women reported that they live longer because they take better care of themselves. These opinions came from college students and not health experts, but the notion that health habits may play a role in longevity is the basis of Kreeger's (2002) headline story.

MORTALITY: NO EQUAL OPPORTUNITY

As the headline story related, women's advantage in life expectancy is not a recent development; this discrepancy has existed for over 100 years and is true throughout the world. Figure 13.1 highlights the longer life expectancy for women in the United States over the past 100 years and projected into the near future. Notice the increasing discrepancy between men and women in the first half of the 20th century and, as Kreeger's story pointed out, the recent narrowing of figures for women's survival. Also notice the difference between life expectancy for Whites and nonwhites, including the small discrepancies between men and women in the early 1900s, the advantage for Whites, and the increasing discrepancy in life expectancies for nonwhite women and men after 1910.

In addition, these gender differences are prominent in economically developed countries for each of the leading causes of death—cardiovascular disease, cancer, and accidents. These three causes of death account for about 64% of all deaths in the United States. For cardiovascular disease and cancer, men tend to die at younger ages than women, resulting in not only an excess of overall deaths of men, but also death at younger ages.

Cardiovascular Disease

Cardiovascular disease (CVD) includes a group of diseases involving the heart and circulatory system, some of which are life threatening and some of which are not. For example, angina pectoris is one of the disorders in this category; this disease causes shortness of breath, difficulty in performing physical activities, and chest pain, but it poses no immediate threat to life. On the other hand, myocardial infarction (heart attack) and stroke can be immediately fatal. Cardiovascular disease is the leading cause of deaths accounting for 36.5% of deaths in the United States in 2000 (National Center for Health Statistics [NCHS], 2002). Deaths from cardiovascular disease have decreased over the past 30 years, with deaths from stroke decreasing more rapidly than from heart disease.

As Table 13.1 shows, heart disease mortality for women and men does not differ greatly over the life span—women have more fatal strokes than men do, but men die from CVD at younger ages than women do. The discrepancy in heart disease deaths for men and women between ages 35 and 74 is especially dramatic, showing how much men are affected by premature death from CVD.

Cardiovascular disease is one of the **chronic diseases**—those health problems that develop over a period of time, often without noticeable symptoms, and persist over time without a complete recovery. Such diseases differ from acute conditions such as infectious diseases or accidents. Acute conditions have rapid onsets accompanied by specific

Years

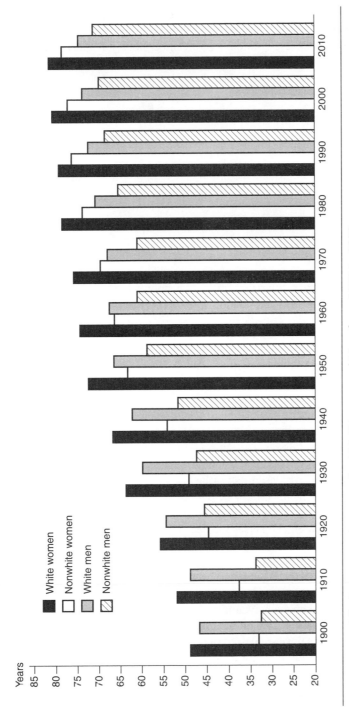

FIGURE 13.1 *Life Expectancy Increases for U.S. Women and Men from 1900 to 2010*

Sources: From *Historical Statistics of the United States, Colonial Times to 1970* (p. 55), by U.S. Bureau of the Census, 1975, Washington, DC: U.S. Government Printing Office; and *Statistical Abstract of the United States, 2002* (122nd ed., p. 78), by U.S. Bureau of the Census, 2002, Washington, DC: U.S. Government Printing Office.

TABLE 13.1 *U.S. Death Rates for Cardiovascular Disease in Men and Women, 2000 (rates per 100,000 population)*

Age Range	Women Stroke	Women Heart Disease	Men Stroke	Men Heart Disease
15–24	0.5	2.1	0.5	3.2
25–34	1.6	5.8	1.7	10.3
35–44	5.8	17.3	5.8	41.6
45–54	14.6	52.8	17.8	142.7
55–64	35.6	173.9	48.1	378.6
65–74	116.5	522.6	146.8	909.2
75–84	450.0	1,579.5	482.5	2,210.1
85+	1,637.4	6,013.7	1,408.3	6,100.8
All ages	73.2	260.2	48.1	256.1

Source: Health, United States, 2002, Tables 37 and 38, by National Center for Health Statistics, 2002, Hyattsville, MD: U.S. Government Printing Office.

symptoms, and people can recover completely. CVD develops over years but exhibits few symptoms until the condition is serious. For many people, heart attack is the first symptom of cardiovascular disease (Ellestad, 1996).

As with other chronic diseases, the causes of cardiovascular disease are not well understood. No infection or other specific agent appears to be responsible; instead, several physical conditions and behaviors are risk factors in the development of CVD. A **risk factor** refers to a condition associated with the increased probability that a disorder will develop. For example, high blood pressure is a risk factor for CVD; people with elevated blood pressure have an increased risk of heart attack and stroke.

Gender is a risk factor for CVD, with men at elevated risk to develop CVD before age 65. The source of this difference is unclear. The hormone estrogen was believed to play a protective role for premenopausal women, but recent research (Writing Group for the Women's Health Initiative Investigators, 2002) has questioned this assumption. If hormone levels were the only reason, then the gender differences in CVD would apply to all times and all societies. The current gender discrepancy is a fairly recent development; the gender gap was much smaller during the 1800s, began to widen during the 1920s, and has now begun to decrease (Nikiforov & Mamaev, 1998). These changes suggest factors other than biology are involved in this gender difference (Weidner, 2000).

Some authorities have suggested that behaviors associated with the male gender role may be dangerous (Courtenay, 2000a; Messner, 1997; Nicholas, 2000). A study that investigated the components of masculinity and femininity as they related to risk of heart attack (Helgeson, 1990) found that negative masculinity (such as aggression and hostility) was related to heart attack severity for both men and women. Lifestyle factors such as smoking and eating a high-fat diet are also risk factors for cardiovascular disease, and more men than women smoke and eat diets high in fat. However, lifestyle factors alone do not account for gender differences in CVD. In a study that statistically adjusted for lifestyle factors (Fried et al., 1998), men were still about twice as likely to experience CVD than women. Therefore, gender differences in CVD risk remain poorly understood.

Women who develop CVD have several disadvantages (Knox & Czajkowski, 1997), some of which relate to the disease itself, and some of which relate to women's treatment in the medical system. Since 1984, women have died of cardiovascular disease at higher rates than men. But women with CVD tend to be older and have more medical problems than men with CVD (Mark, 2000), which may produce treatment differences. Women experience differences in treatment for CVD for additional reasons, however. Physicians refer men who have symptoms of CVD for further testing, preventive interventions, and treatment more often than they refer women with similar symptoms (Hippisley-Cox, Pringle, Crown, Meal, & Wynn, 2001). A great deal of this difference in follow-up treatment is the hesitancy of physicians in the United States to refer African American women for additional testing (Mark, 2000). Thus, the bias may not be simply against women, and White women may receive treatment comparable to men.

In summary, cardiovascular disease, including heart disease and stroke, is the leading cause of death in the United States and other industrialized nations, accounting for about 36% of all deaths. Men die of heart disease at younger ages than women do, but overall, more women than men die of CVD. The death rates from both heart disease and stroke have fallen in the past 30 years, with strokes decreasing at a more rapid rate than heart disease. These gender differences in risk are not clearly understood, but both physiological and lifestyle differences between the two genders contribute to differences in risk.

Cancer

Cancer is the term applied to a variety of malignant neoplasms—tissues that have sustained uncontrolled growth that may form a tumor, as well as spread to other areas of the body. Most types of tissue can develop cancers. These growths are not restricted to human or even to animal tissues: Plants and all types of animals develop malignancies. Such uncontrolled tissue growth can become life threatening, and cancer is the second leading cause of death in the United States, accounting for about 23% of all deaths (NCHS, 2002).

Men have higher overall death rates from cancer than women do for most types of cancer and at most ages. Table 13.2 presents the mortality rates for women and men for various types of cancer at various ages. As the table shows, some gender differences exist. For example, women are much more likely to develop breast cancer than are men (although men do get breast cancer), and women have earlier mortality rates for cancer of the genitals and reproductive organs than men do. Lung cancer is the leading type of fatal cancer for both men and women, but more men than women die of lung cancer.

Cigarette smoking is a major factor in lung cancer death rates. Smoking takes time to cause health problems, so smoking differences among men and women in the past continue to appear in current health statistics. Until recently, men smoked at a much higher rate than women, but as Kreeger's (2002) headline story reported, women's increased use

TABLE 13.2   *U.S. Death Rates for Cancer in Women and Men by Age (rates per 100,00 population, averaged for years 1995–1999)*

Age Range	Women							
	Lung	Breast	Colon and Rectum	Cervix	Leukemias	Non-Hodgkins Lymphoma	Pancreas	Ovary
20–49	5.0	11.0	2.4	2.6	1.6	0.6	0.9	2.1
50–64	72.8	56.5	21.6	16.4	3.5	6.6	11.0	16.3
65–74	205.8	95.9	65.2	37.1	19.4	27.4	38.2	36.8
75+	236.3	151.4	164.0	117.5	46.4	57.7	75.8	53.1

All ages, all cancers: 171.4 per 100,000

Age Range	Men						
	Lung	Breast	Colon and Rectum	Prostate	Leukemias	Non-Hodgkins Lymphoma	Pancreas
20–49	7.2	—	2.9	0.6	2.2	2.7	1.5
50–64	127.1	0.5	32.3	2.9	10.5	14.1	18.4
65–74	404.4	1.1	102.7	100.0	37.7	39.8	52.1
75+	534.3	2.7	221.3	418.0	84.1	79.8	88.7

All ages, all cancers: 259.1 per 100,000

Source: Data from "Annual Report to the Nation on the Status of Cancer, 1973–1999, Featuring Implications of Age and Aging on U.S. Cancer Burden," by Brenda K. Edwards, Holly L. Howe, Lynn A. G. Ries, Michael J. Thun, Harry M. Rosenberg, Rosemary Yancik, Phyllis A. Wingo, Ahmedin Jemal, and Ellen Feigal, 2002, *Cancer, 94* (10), Table 4.

of tobacco is a factor in the narrowing of the gender gap in longevity. Women have begun to develop lung cancer at increased rates, whereas men's rates have leveled off. In 1986, lung cancer surpassed breast cancer as the leading cause of cancer deaths among women.

Use of tobacco products accounts for about 30% of cancers, and diet for another 30% to 40% (Doll & Peto, 1981; Willett, 1999). In addition to foods that contain known or suspected carcinogens, dietary components have been implicated in the development of cancer, especially a high-fat diet. A substantial amount of evidence indicates that people who eat a high-fat diet are at increased risk for cancers of the digestive tract, plus an elevated risk for breast cancer (Willett, 1999). On the average, women eat lower-fat diets than men, so this behavioral difference may explain part of the discrepancy in cancer death rates.

The "meat and potatoes" men may be at increased risk for cancer. The meat is much more of a risk than the potatoes; an increasing body of evidence indicates that high levels of animal-fat consumption increase the risk for several types of cancer (Courtenay, 2000a; Willett, 1999). Some dietary components increase risk, and others lower risk. For example,

☐ GENDERED VOICES

I Have Breast Cancer

An announcement of breast cancer is shocking but not unusual—unless the person is a man. That unusual situation happened to Robert Riter (1997), who noticed a lump in his breast. Like many people, Riter thought it was a cyst and that it would go away. When he started bleeding from his nipple, he sought medical advise and treatment. His treatment included a biopsy, which revealed a malignancy. Although breast cancer is rare among men, the disease affects over 1,000 men per year in the United States.

Riter's experience was both similar to and different from women's experience of breast cancer. Like many women, he had a mastectomy and chemotherapy. Unlike many women, losing the breast was not as traumatic an event for him. His greatest distress came from examining the survival statistics, which are virtually identical for men and women. Riter learned that his chances of surviving for 5 years were about 80%, but his likelihood of living 10 years was only about 60%.

Riter was the first man to join his area's support group for breast cancer survivors. "I'm probably not the only male in this area with the disease, but . . . men find it hard to discuss their prostate cancer, let alone a 'female' disease," he said (Riter, 1997, p. 14). He also encountered some surprised reactions, like the lab technician who questioned the referral slip with the diagnosis of breast cancer. He felt odd going to a "women's imaging center" to get a mammogram and he said, "My follow-up letter from the center was addressed to Ms. Robert Riter. The radiology tech did note that I had the hairiest chest she's ever seen in a mammogram room" (p. 14).

Riter noted that his experience with breast cancer had taught him more about women's health issues than he would otherwise have known, but having a life-threatening "female disease" was a difficult way for him to gain knowledge and empathy.

lycopene, folic acid, selenium, and vitamin E are all nutrients that seem to lower the risk of various cancers. People who eat diets high in these nutrients develop cancer at lower rates than people whose intake of these nutrients is lower. Therefore, food can raise or lower the risk for a variety of cancers, and women's diets tend to be healthier than men's diets.

Occupational exposure accounts for another 4% of cancer deaths (Doll & Peto, 1981). Men are at increased risk for cancer due to their exposure to workplace hazards (Courtenay, 2000a). Men are more likely than women to hold jobs that bring them into contact with carcinogens such as asbestos, benzene, and various petroleum products. Exposure to such substances may also be a factor in the difference in cancer deaths between women and men.

Sexual behavior and reproduction also contribute to the development of cancer, and about 7% of cancers are attributable to these factors (Doll & Peto, 1981). Women who have sexual intercourse at an early age and have many sexual partners are at elevated risk for cancers of the reproductive tract (Adami & Trichopoulos, 2002; Levy, 1985). However, women who complete pregnancies before age 20 are at decreased risk for breast cancer compared to women with later pregnancies and to women who do not bear children. Thus, early intercourse presents a risk for cancer, but early pregnancy is a protection against cancer.

Men's sexual behavior can place them at risk for cancer, but their behavior can also be a risk for their female sex partners (Courtenay, 2000a). Twice as many men as women engage in risky sexual behaviors. Men who are the receptive partner in unprotected anal intercourse are at increased risk for anal cancer as well as for infection with the human immunodeficiency virus (HIV), which is related to the development of acquired immune deficiency syndrome (AIDS). One of the diseases associated with AIDS is a form of cancer called Kaposi's sarcoma. Thus, receptive anal intercourse is a direct risk for anal cancer and an indirect risk for Kaposi's sarcoma. Men who have many sexual partners, especially those who have sex with prostitutes, endanger their female partners by elevating the women's risk for cervical cancer. In addition, poor genital hygiene in men is associated with increased risk of cervical cancer in their female sexual partners.

As Table 13.2 shows, women experience higher mortality rates from cancers of the genitals than men do until after age 65 years. Cancer of the genitals and reproductive tract plus breast cancer deaths account for the large proportion of women's cancer deaths during their early and middle-adult years. Indeed, before age 65, cancer is responsible for a greater proportion of women's deaths than is cardiovascular disease. The opposite pattern occurs for cardiovascular deaths among men, who are more vulnerable to premature death from CVD than from cancer.

Violent Deaths

Unintentional injuries (accidents) are the 4th, suicide the 10th, and homicide the 14th leading causes of death in the United States (USBC, 2002). Added together, these acts of violence account for about 6% of deaths in the United States. This number reflects a relatively high rate of violence compared to other industrialized, economically developed countries. Violent death rates are lower in Australia, Canada, Japan, most of the countries in western Europe, Scandinavia, and other countries scattered throughout the world (*Britannica Book of the Year,* 1999). Moreover, violent death is the leading cause of death for adolescents and young adults in the United States. Men are about three times more likely than women to die from violent deaths. This discrepancy holds for all ages, from birth until old age, but the differences are most pronounced early in life.

Ethnicity plays a major role in risk of violence. As Table 13.3 shows, African Americans in the United States are much more likely than European Americans or Hispanic Americans to die from accidents and homicides, but European Americans are more likely to die from motor vehicle crashes and suicide. African American men are disproportionately vulnerable to deaths from homicide, but gender differences are more prominent than ethnic differences.

The gender differences in risky behaviors account for the differences in violent deaths. Men tend to behave in ways that increase their risks, such as heavy alcohol use, low seat belt use, occupational risks, and illegal activities. Alcohol use increases the chances of accidents, suicide, and homicide (Courtenay, 2000a). By slowing responses and altering judgment, alcohol contributes to traffic crashes. People who have been drinking (even those who are not legally intoxicated) are more likely to be involved in fatal traffic accidents; about half of all traffic fatalities are related to alcohol. Seat belt use is an important factor in reducing traffic fatalities, and women are more likely than men to use seat belts (National Highway Traffic Safety Administration [NHTSA], 2000). For the same rea-

TABLE 13.3 *U.S. Death Rates from Accidents and Violence, 2000 (rates per 100,000 population)*

Cause	European American Women	Men	African American Women	Men	Hispanic American Women	Men
Motor vehicle accidents	10.2	21.6	8.5	23.4	7.7	22.4
Firearms-related accidents	2.8	16.0	4.2	37.5	1.9	15.8
Suicide	4.9	20.5	1.8	9.8	1.6	9.3
Homicide	1.9	3.6	7.5	38.6	3.0	14.9

Source: Health, United States, 2002, Tables 45, 46, 47, and 48, by National Center for Health Statistics, 2002, Hyattsville, MD: U.S. Government Printing Office.

sons that alcohol use increases the chances of traffic accidents, alcohol use is also related to deaths from falls, fires, and drownings as well as from boating, airplane, and industrial accidents. Intoxication also increases the chances of becoming a pedestrian victim of an auto accident (Courtenay, 2000a).

About 47% of adults in the United States drink alcohol, but less than 6% are heavy drinkers (Substance Abuse and Mental Health Services Administration [SAMHSA], 2001). Any amount of alcohol consumption can increase the risk of accidents, but heavy and binge drinking are especially risky. The gender differences in drinking are disappearing, but men are more than three times more likely to binge drink than women. In addition, drinking varies by age group, with younger adults being heavier drinkers. These gender and age differences in drinking patterns correspond to the differential risks of violent death. With the increases in women's drinking have come increases in problem drinking among women (Rodin & Ickovics, 1990). These changes have the potential to decrease the current female advantage in avoiding violent death.

Men are also more likely to hold dangerous jobs than women are (Courtenay, 2000a). In addition to exposure to hazardous materials, which increases the chances of cancer, men are more likely than women to have jobs that involve working around or operating dangerous machinery. Around 94% of the fatalities at work involve men. Therefore, occupational hazards and violence are substantial factors contributing to the gender difference in accidental deaths.

Men are more likely to commit suicide, but women are more likely to attempt suicide (U.S. Department of Health and Human Services [USDHHS], 2001b). This difference in suicide rates for men and women began to appear during the 1950s, increased during the 1960s, and began to decrease during the 1970s. The ratio of attempted to completed suicides is about 10 to 1. The main reason for the higher rates of completed suicides among men is that they tend to choose more lethal methods, such as guns and jumping from high places, whereas women more often attempt suicide by taking drugs. (No method is certain to be nonlethal, so any suicide attempt is serious.) The lethality of the methods chosen produces higher suicide rates among men, despite women's more frequent suicide attempts.

Chapter 8 described a gender difference in crime rate, explaining that men are more likely than women to commit crimes. This discrepancy is even greater for crimes involving violence, with men more likely to both perpetrate crimes and be victims of crime (USBC, 2002). The increase in lawbreaking among women in the past decades has not changed these figures, because this increase reflects primarily nonviolent crimes. Thus, homicide affects men to a larger degree than women and has an especially disproportionate impact on young African American men.

In summary, men are more often the victims of unintentional and intentional violence than are women. Men's increased risk comes from several sources, including their heavier use of alcohol, heightened risk of workplace accidents, greater success at committing suicide, and greater involvement in illegal activities. In addition, men are less likely to take protective measures, such as using seat belts. All of these causes of violent deaths put men at a survival disadvantage and account for some of women's survival advantage. Women, however, do not experience the same advantage when seeking health care; women experience greater morbidity than men and have more difficulty receiving treatment for serious conditions than men do.

THE HEALTH CARE SYSTEM

As the headline story for this chapter discussed, women live longer than men, but they are sick more often. Defining what constitutes being sick is not simple, but doctor visits, hospital admissions, restriction of activities, or reports of distress are some of the indicators; women meet any of these definitions of illness more often than men do (Chrisler, 2001). The combination of greater morbidity with lower mortality seems a contradiction, but sex and gender roles as well as physiology contribute to the situation. Women's reproduction and its medicalized treatment account for increased use of medical services among women—pregnancy and childbirth are functions that now receive medical attention, require medical appointments, and are cared for by hospitalization. Another possibility is that women are not as healthy as men, but that their health problems are less often life threatening, producing the combination of poorer health but longer lives. A third explanation involves the difference in gender roles related to seeking and receiving health care.

Gender Roles and Health Care

People seek and receive health care from a variety of formal and informal sources, and gender roles affect receiving help from each source. Traditional male and female gender roles differ in the amounts of vulnerability each is allowed and the permissibility of seeking help. One facet of the masculine role, the Sturdy Oak, holds that men are strong and invulnerable; this aspect of the role causes men to restrain from showing signs of physical illness or seeking medical care (Brannon, 1976). The traditional female role, on the other hand, allows and even encourages weakness and vulnerability for emotional and physical problems (Lorber, 1975). Adherence to traditional gender roles may, therefore, hinder men from seeking help for their symptoms, but elements of the traditional feminine gender role relate to greater distress for women as well as to their increased readiness to seek medical care. After women and men enter the health care system, they also receive different care.

Gender and Seeking Health Care. The decision to seek medical care is influenced by many factors, including the perception of symptoms and beliefs about the consequences of seeking or failing to seek treatment. People who feel healthy may enter the medical care system to receive routine exams, but many skip such screening procedures, finding it easy to ignore their health as long as they feel well. Men are more likely to avoid regular health care than women are (Courtenay, 2000a). Men are less likely than women to have regular physicians, sometimes avoiding checkups for years. Men explain these omissions in terms consistent with the masculine gender role, saying that they feel fine and thus do not need to consult physicians. This belief can be fatal; the first sign of heart disease can be a fatal heart attack, and many cancers do not produce symptoms in the early stages. Nonetheless, the belief that a lack of symptoms equals good health can lead men to avoid regular contacts with the health care system.

Women, on the other hand, find it more difficult to avoid the health care system, regardless of how well they may feel. Young women must seek medical advice to obtain many forms of contraception, especially birth control pills (Chrisler, 2001). These young women count in the statistics as having consulted physicians, although their medical visits involve no illness. Such medical consultations often include physical examinations that may reveal health problems that require additional treatment. For example, blood tests may reveal anemia, and blood pressure readings may show hypertension. Each of these conditions merits further treatment, which leads these women into additional physician visits and medication. Young men receive no comparable medical attention during young adulthood that might reveal physical problems, and these differences in treatment for healthy young men and women contribute to the statistics concerning gender differences in seeking health care.

The personal perception of symptoms is an important factor in seeking medical care. People who sense that their bodies are not working correctly are more likely to seek medical advice than are those who sense no problems. Perceiving symptoms, however, is not sufficient to lead people to make appointments with their physicians. Although some people readily seek professional medical advice and care, most people experience some reluctance to become part of the health care system.

This reluctance has many origins, including financial resources, convenience and accessibility of medical care, and personal considerations. Health care costs have risen faster than personal incomes, creating problems for many people in paying for health care. Scheduling of appointments and changing daily routines to keep these medical appointments are additional barriers. Anxiety about the diagnosis or treatment may keep people from seeking professional care; the diagnosis may be threatening, or the treatment may be painful or expensive, or both.

The factors that influence reluctance to seek medical care may not affect men and women equally. Women are more likely than men to be outside the paid workforce and to be employed on a part-time basis, whereas men are more likely to have the types of jobs that offer health insurance benefits. Employment situations can put women at a disadvantage in seeking health care, which leaves them with less money to pay for health care and to be without the health insurance that might cover their expenses (Ratcliff, 2002).

Unemployed women can receive these benefits if they are married to men who have good insurance plans. For both men and women in these situations, continued health insurance depends on the continued employment of the spouse and the continuation of the marriage. Not only can women lose their health insurance through divorce, but children can also lose insurance coverage due to their parents' divorce. Mothers are most often granted custody, and the children may lose their coverage unless their mothers have employment that includes these benefits. Thus, women and children are less likely to have health insurance than are men, making health care less accessible for them.

Men and women may have similar experiences of daily symptoms, but women are more likely to seek medical care for these symptoms. The reasons for this readiness may lie in two circumstances. Women are more sensitive to their body's signals than men are, making women more capable of reporting these physical symptoms (Pennebaker, 1982). In addition, their traditional gender role allows women to seek help more readily than men do.

Men and women also seek health care from different types of providers (Kane, 1991). Both women and men are more likely to consult pharmacists than any other category of health care professional, and women make more inquiries than men. Women may ask pharmacists for advice about over-the-counter remedies for their entire families, so the number of consultations may not reflect any gender difference in personal need. Men experience more injuries due to accidents and sports participation, so they are more likely to seek the services of physiotherapists than are women. On the other hand, women are more likely to seek the services of chiropractors or nutritionists. Women are also more likely to use alternative health care services, such as herbal medicine and acupuncture. None of these differences is large; thus, the types of health care professionals that men and women seek vary only to a small extent.

The different preferences in seeking medical care may be partly attributable to access to medical care, with women at a disadvantage due to their lower financial resources and poorer insurance coverage. Another difference may lie in women's greater sensitivity to symptoms, but a difference also exists in the willingness to report symptoms. These differences are consistent with the gender roles, with men denying and women accepting help.

Gender and Receiving Health Care.   After a person has contacted a health care professional and becomes part of the health care system, gender becomes a factor in treatment. Again, gender roles influence the behavior of both patient and practitioner. Although some patients and practitioners are coming to view their relationship as a collaboration, the traditional conceptualization of the patient–practitioner relationship has included the subordinate patient and the controlling practitioner. The patient role is thus more compatible with the stereotypically female than the stereotypically male role, whereas the practitioner role is more consistent with traditional masculinity. The combination of gender roles and patient–provider roles puts women at a disadvantage in both giving and receiving medical care; when they are patients, physicians tend to ignore women's descriptions of symptoms, and when they are physicians, patients have trouble recognizing their expertise (Chrisler, 2001).

Men seem to have more trouble adopting the patient role than women do. Being a patient requires a person to relinquish control and follow the advice or orders of the practitioner. Gender is not a reliable predictor of patient compliance (Brannon & Feist, 2004), but the combination of the demographic factors of gender, age, ethnic background, cultural norms, religion, and educational level relates to patients' compliance with physicians' treatment advice. For example, people who are part of a culture that trusts physicians and accepts their advice as the best way to get well are more likely to follow physicians' advice than are people from a culture that accepts herbalists as the preferred health care professionals. Therefore, gender is only one factor from among a configuration of variables that relates to compliance with medical advice. Indeed, the interaction between patient and practitioner is more important to the patient's willingness to follow health advice than a patient's personal characteristics, and gender often plays a role in that interaction.

The medical profession has been criticized for its treatment of female patients, and this criticism has taken several forms. The most radical form of criticism holds that women were healers throughout history but have been replaced by technological, male-dominated forms of healing, with dominant male physicians but subordinate female nurses (Ehrenreich & English, 1973). Other criticisms (Chrisler, 2001) have claimed that negative stereotypes of female patients have led to poorer levels of medical care for women than for men. Yet other criticisms (Tavris, 1992) have been brought against the use of men as the medical standard to which women are compared, claiming that omitting women from medical training and research leaves physicians ill-prepared to treat women.

Physicians often have stereotypical views of women, and these views influence their treatment of female patients (Chrisler, 2001). Medical school educational standards have promoted the view that women are emotional and incapable of providing accurate information about their bodies. Physicians tend to rely on gender stereotypes in treatment decisions when they do not have a positive impression of the patients (Di Caccavo & Reid, 1998). When they felt positively about their patients, physicians in this study made similar treatment decisions about women and men, but when their feelings were neutral or negative, gender stereotypes took over, and women received more prescriptions for psychoactive drugs (to treat "emotional problems"), whereas men received more referrals for additional services. An increasing percentage of physicians are women, and some evidence (Franks & Bertakis, 2003) indicates that female physicians spend more time with female patients and recommend preventive care more than male physicians do.

The view of "emotional females" may lead physicians to discount the information provided by female patients and to believe that women cannot participate in decisions concerning their own health and treatment. Some research (Benrud & Reddy, 1998) supports the view that people explain women's and men's health problems in different ways. The researchers manipulated the information such that the problems were the same for both genders, so the differences in attributions were not due to the type of problems, but to the use of stereotypes of women and men in making judgments. People saw women's health problems as the result of relatively uncontrollable biological and emotional factors, but judged men's problems as the result of controllable behavioral and situational factors. These attributions have the potential to make big differences in health care: Women's health problems may be viewed as "emotional problems," but men may receive blame for causing their own poor health through misbehavior.

Another criticism is aimed at a more subtle type of discrimination in medicine: the view that medical training represents men as the standard by which to measure all health concerns (Tavris, 1992). Physicians receive instruction in how to dissect and prescribe drugs for the standard patient, a 154-pound man. With men as the standard, women become the exception. Thus, any condition that men do not develop comes to be considered as deviant, including even the normal conditions associated with women's physiology—menstruation, pregnancy, and childbirth.

In addition to holding men as the standard in medicine, medical research routinely omitted women entirely; that is, many studies have failed to include women as research participants. The rationale for omitting women was that women bias the research because of their low rates of certain diseases, and their hormonal variations affected the action of drugs. For example, middle-aged women develop CVD at a rate lower than middle-aged men, so longitudinal studies that follow healthy people until they show signs of CVD would have to include many more women than men to obtain a group of women with this disorder. Using only male participants results in studies that are easier to complete, but these studies reveal nothing about CVD in women. Assuming that women are similar to men in their development of CVD is unwarranted, because women are excluded from these studies precisely because of their physical differences. A similar rationale applied to developing and testing new drugs, and a similar problem arose as a result: Omitting women from drug trials fails to establish the safety and effectiveness of drugs for women.

During the 1980s, the practice of excluding women from medical research received increasing criticism, and pressure mounted to give women's health additional emphasis. That pressure resulted in the creation of the Office of Research on Women's Health, a part of the National Institutes of Health (Kirschstein, 1991). This office's mission is to improve the prevention and treatment of diseases in women, and one of its first steps was to attempt to end the exclusion of women from medical research studies with the help of U.S. government sponsorship.

One of the research projects on women's health sponsored by this organization is the Women's Health Initiative (Blumenthal & Wood, 1997; Matthews et al., 1997). This study is designed to investigate factors involved with health problems experienced by older women, including CVD, cancer of the breast and digestive tract, and osteoporosis. The plan includes a 16-year longitudinal study with over 150,000 women, with both medication and psychosocial components of assessment and treatment.

Several reports of research from the Women's Health Initiative have made headlines. In July 2002, researchers announced that the effects of hormone replacement therapy for menopausal symptoms produced higher risks than benefits, and the trial was halted (Writing Group for the Women's Health Initiative Investigators, 2002). This finding came as a surprise because of the widespread assumption that hormone replacement therapy not only relieved the symptoms of menopause but also lowered the risk of heart disease. The results of this study indicated the opposite: Women taking the combination of estrogen and progestin experienced higher rates of breast cancer, heart disease, blood clots, and stroke than did women taking the placebo. Another surprising result from the Women's Health Initiative study on hormone replacement (Shumaker et al., 2003) showed that older women who take hormones increased their risk of developing Alzheimer's disease or other types of cognitive dementia. Again, the assumptions were that hormones protected against cognitive deficits in aging people, but the results showed otherwise. Therefore, results from the Women's Health Initiative have already made a difference in the knowledge and treatment of women.

Although medicine remains male dominated, men are not the focus of comparable health initiatives (Lee & Owens, 2002; Sabo, 2000). Indeed, men may not receive optimum or even adequate care. During childhood, parents are somewhat more likely to take their sons to the doctor than their daughters, but once men are responsible for seeking their own medical care, they tend to avoid regular medical care. Men seek care for their injuries, but not for regular exams and screening tests. Men were 70% of those in a survey who had not been to a physician in 5 years (Courtenay, 2000a). Men were less likely to have regular physicians than women, so getting an appointment to see a physician is a greater inconvenience for a man in that he must first find a physician.

Prostate cancer kills almost as many men as breast cancer kills women, yet many times more funds go toward breast cancer research than for prostate cancer (Stipp, 1996). Men have not mobilized to exert the type of political pressure that spurs funding in the same way that women have, leaving men's health issues with fewer vocal advocates (Sabo, 2000).

Some authorities (Schofield, Connell, Walker, Wood, & Butland, 2000) have argued that the division of health care into fields of women's health versus men's health will not best serve either. Indeed, the implication of labeling these specialty areas is that the differences between women and men are their main health concerns, when sexual and reproductive health are not the entirety of health care for either. These authorities recommended an integration so that the fields of women's and men's health can be seen in relation to each other and to the cultural and situational factors that influence both, such as family, work, poverty, and ethnicity.

In summary, the Sturdy Oak component of the male gender role may be a factor in men's avoiding health care; feelings of invulnerability and the belief that illness represents weakness lead men to ignore their health. Such avoidance can result in serious health problems that might be prevented or detected through routine physical exams. Men can avoid regular physical exams more easily than women can, because men typically do not have the same contacts with the health care system connected with reproduction or contraception that women of reproductive age have. Thus, men seldom use the health care system until they become ill, perhaps to the detriment of their health. Not only do reproduction and contraception concerns prompt women but not men to seek medical care during the reproductive years, but the differences in their reproductive systems also account for a large proportion of the gender difference in seeking and receiving health care.

Reproductive Health

Many of women's encounters with the health care system do not involve illness but occur as a result of contraception, pregnancy, childbirth, and menopause. In addition, sex and reproductive issues have an impact that extends to other aspects of functioning, affecting emotion, beliefs, and identity throughout the life span (Murphy, 2003). Although these functions were completed throughout history with little medical assistance, they became increasingly "medicalized" during the 19th and 20th centuries (Ehrenreich & English, 1973; Ratcliff, 2002). During this time, college education was largely restricted to men, who came to dominate the growing profession of medicine.

This expansion of medicine included attending women during childbirth, a role that had been performed by midwives. Childbirth was not the only function to gain medical attention; pregnancy came to be considered an appropriate area for regular medical care. The increasing number of contraceptive technologies during the 20th century depended almost exclusively on controlling women's rather than men's fertility, and physicians assumed control over access to contraception techniques such as birth control pills. During the middle of the 20th century, even menopause became a "disease" that could be "cured" by hormone replacement (Wilson, 1966). Thus, medical technologies came to be involved in all facets of women's reproductive health, from contraception during adolescence to hormone replacement after menopause.

Some critics have argued that access to the medical field has burdened women by forcing them to give birth in sterile, impersonal surroundings and subjecting them to increasingly large hospital bills for these services. According to this argument, birth is a natural process requiring no medical intervention. However, comparing statistics from undeveloped countries and from times in the United States before routine medical care during pregnancy and delivery, death could also be seen as a natural process. There is no question that technological medicine has dramatically cut both maternal and infant mortality (Kane, 1991). Nonetheless, women may receive too much treatment in some areas (as in too many hysterectomies or cesarean section deliveries) and too little in other respects (as in too little testing for heart disease or too little treatment for high cholesterol).

Women's more numerous consultations with health care professionals are due largely to their complex reproductive systems (Chrisler, 2001). Not only do women get pregnant and bear children, but also their reproductive organs are subject to a greater variety of problems than are male organs. Figures 13.2 and 13.3 show the female and male reproductive systems. Except for children under age 15 years, girls and women receive more treatment for problems related to their reproductive systems than boys and men do.

Both systems can develop problems during prenatal development, producing congenital conditions that are more common in boys than in girls. During infancy and early childhood, boys have more problems with their genitourinary system than girls do, requiring more hospital stays and physician consultations for these problems (Kane, 1991). Beginning at age 15 years, girls make more visits to health care professionals, and require more hospitalizations, regarding their reproductive systems. The majority of the physician visits and hospitalizations for women during their reproductive years involve contraception, pregnancy, and childbirth; most of these contacts with the health care system are not due to illness or health problems but because women's reproductive functions have come under medical supervision (Ratcliff, 2002).

Many of the methods of contraception for women—birth control pills, implants, intrauterine devices (IUDs), diaphragms, sterilization, abortion—not only require medical supervision but also increase health risks. For example, birth control pills provide very effective contraception, but women over age 35 years who take contraceptive pills have significantly

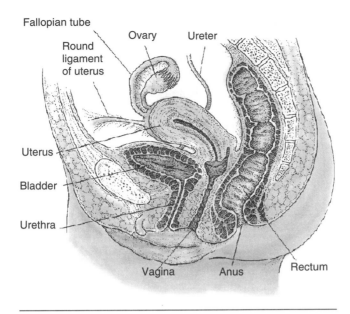

FIGURE 13.2   *Female Reproductive System*

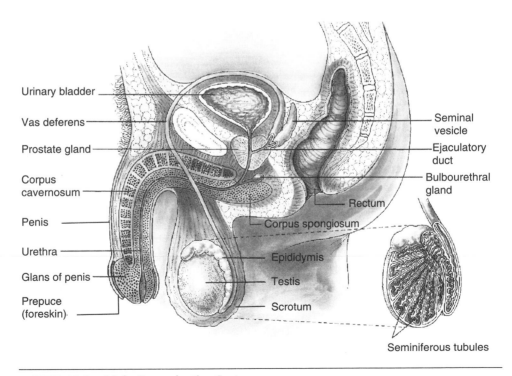

FIGURE 13.3   *Male Reproductive System*

369

increased risks of stroke, and smoking multiplies this risk. Therefore, contraception is not only more often a woman's responsibility but also more of a health threat to women.

Both men and women are subject to **sexually transmitted diseases (STDs),** infectious diseases that are spread through sexual contact. The infectious agents can be bacterial, viral, fungal, or parasitic, and many can be transmitted by vaginal, oral, or anal sexual activity. These bacterial infections include gonorrhea, syphilis, and chlamydia, and do not always produce symptoms; women are especially likely to be symptom free until advanced stages of the diseases. Although antibiotics can cure bacterial infections, people without symptoms may not receive treatment until their diseases are serious. Furthermore, delays in treatment allow infected persons to transmit the disease to others.

Delays in treatment are also likely to escalate the growth of the fungal and parasitic STDs. *Candidiasis albicans,* a yeast-like fungus, produces itching and swelling of the genitals. It can be transmitted through sexual intercourse, but this infection is not always an STD; it is more common in women who take contraceptive pills or who are pregnant or diabetic. These conditions alter the chemistry of the vagina, allowing this fungus to grow at a rapid rate, producing annoying and painful symptoms. Chemical treatments exist to control this type of infection. Trichomonia is a one-celled parasite that can infect the vagina in women and the urethra in men. It is almost always sexually transmitted, and an effective drug treatment exists.

No drugs exist to cure viral diseases. Thus, the viral STDs pose an even more serious problem than other types of STDs. The human immunodeficiency virus (HIV) is the virus that produces acquired immune deficiency syndrome (AIDS), a virus that can be sexually transmitted. The virus damages the immune system, leaving the body open to a variety of opportunistic diseases that eventually lead to death. Years may pass between time of infection and the development of symptoms, allowing infected persons to be unaware of the presence of the condition and able to unknowingly transmit the infection to others.

Genital herpes, viral hepatitis, and genital warts are also viral STDs. Evidence has mounted that the human papillomavirus that causes genital warts is the cause of cervical cancer (Bosch, Lorincz, Munoz, Meijer, & Shah, 2002). Genital warts can sometimes be surgically removed, and researchers are working toward a vaccine for this virus, which should drastically reduce cases of cervical cancer. Several medications exist to manage the symptoms of herpes infections. Like other viral infections, these STDs are difficult to manage and are presently without a cure. In addition, infection with any STD makes a person more vulnerable to HIV infection because genital lesions allow HIV an easy route for infection.

Not all medical problems of the reproductive organs are related to reproduction; that is, these organs can be the site of disease and cancer. Again, women are more likely than men to seek health care concerning problems with their reproductive organs. Although women are at greater risk for cancer of organs in the reproductive system than men are throughout young and middle adulthood, men are most likely to develop testicular cancer between ages 15 and 34 years (Parker, 1997). This form of cancer is quite rare, but rates are increasing; men are most likely to develop this form of cancer during the years when they tend to avoid regular physical checkups. A man may have no regular physician to tell about the lump he has detected on a testicle, and the tumor may go untreated for a dangerously long period. This form of cancer is rarely fatal if treated early, but fatality rates rise sharply with delays in treatment, going from a 90% survival rate to only a 25% survival rate. Thus, this rare form of cancer that affects men in their 20s and 30s may be fatal more often than it would be if men gave more attention to their health.

Prostate cancer is much more common than testicular cancer, and it tends to develop in older men. This form of cancer is not common until after age 75 years, when it increases sharply (refer back to Table 13.2). Even without malignancy, prostate enlargement, which begins during puberty, can cause problems, such as difficulty during urination that can require surgery. Malignant tumors of the prostate typically are small and grow slowly, and many elderly men die *with* rather than *from* prostate cancer (Stipp, 1996). The development and use of a diagnostic test, the prostate specific antigen test, has allowed earlier diagnosis, and men are beginning to mobilize as advocates for improved treatment.

Endometrial cancer affects the uterine lining, but women can also develop cancer of the cervix, ovaries, vulva, vagina, and Fallopian tubes. None of these sites is the most common site for cancer—the breast is. About one in nine women will develop breast cancer. (Even so, lung cancer is the leading cause of cancer death for both men and women due to its high fatality rate.) From ages 15 to 45, cancers of the reproductive system are a major cause of mortality for women but not for men.

During menopause, women lose their fertility; they cease ovulation and menstruation, and their production of estrogen and progesterone declines. Some women experience uncomfortable symptoms associated with menopause; the most common of these is the "hot flash," a sudden feeling of heat and skin flushing. These feelings may be uncomfortable and embarrassing but are not health threatening. Only 10% of menopausal women experience serious symptoms associated with menopause (Livingston, 1999). Hormone replacement therapy can alleviate the symptoms, but findings from the Women's Health Initiative (Writing Group for the Women's Health Initiative Investigators, 2002; Shumaker et al., 2003) have indicated that hormone replacement raises the risk for breast cancer, blood clots, cardiovascular disease, and memory deficits. These findings led many women to reconsider this therapy and to ask more critical questions and make more informed choices. However, these findings confirm the criticisms that women have been overtreated for menopause.

Men's hormone production also drops with aging, but they undergo no symptoms as visible as those of women during menopause. The decrease in hormone production in men results in the decline, but not the end, of their fertility. Men who lose the ability to get erections may receive hormone replacements, but many fewer men than women receive analogous hormone replacement therapy.

Thus, treatment for malignancies of the reproductive system accounts for only a small portion of the reproductive health care received by women, but for a larger portion of that received by men. Women not only get pregnant and bear children, but they also have the majority of responsibility for contraception. In addition, menstruation is often painful, and some women experience pain sufficiently serious to prompt them to consult health care professionals. The decline in hormone production associated with menopause also causes some women to seek medical treatment. Therefore, a great deal of the added health care received by women is due to their reproductive system needs, but this is only part of the reason for women's greater number of contacts with the health care system.

GENDER, LIFESTYLE, AND HEALTH

Men have shorter average life spans than women in all developed and most undeveloped countries. The gender gap in mortality is not static but has varied over time. Coexisting with this advantage, women are more likely to use health care and to report symptoms of illness. Both men's shorter lives and women's poorer health may be, as women believe (Wallace, 1996), related to their lifestyles. That is, men may lose years from their life span by their behaviors, and factors in women's lives may increase their morbidity. As the headline story for this chapter (Kreeger, 2002) suggests, men's lifestyle choices and occupational health risks may be significant factors in shortening their lives. Many of these risky behaviors are associated with the male gender role, which may be dangerous to men's health (Courtenay, 2000a; Messner, 1997).

The female gender role may likewise endanger health. Women's role as nurturer presents both benefits and drawbacks (Barnett & Hyde, 2001). Offering and receiving social support is an important factor in health, but when people take care of others better than themselves, then the role of nurturer becomes a health deficit. The demands of providing social support and nurturant care can be emotionally and physically draining, but may not guarantee receiving the same quality of care given. Women are more likely than men to be in such a situation.

Therefore, both traditional gender roles carry health risks. Women's morbidity is a factor that significantly decreases the quality of their lives (Kaplan, Anderson, & Wingard, 1991), but their more frequent illnesses are usually not ones that threaten their lives. Men, on the other hand, tend to experience health problems that are more likely to be life threatening. In other words, "One sex is 'sicker' in the short run, and the other in the long run" (Verbrugge, 1985, p. 163). The causes of death, however, are similar. Two behaviors that relate to health and longevity are eating and exercising, and these behaviors show gender-related differences.

Eating

Everyone eats, but people vary in their eating patterns and in the meanings they attach to eating (Rozin, 1999; Rozin, Bauer, & Catanese, 2003). Women's relationship with food is especially complex; women use food as comfort, but they also show more concern with eating to control weight and are more likely to diet than men. This concern with weight and their attempts to restrict food intake lead women to hold different attitudes toward eating than men do. Indeed, men's and women's brains do not respond to hunger and satiation in exactly the same ways (Del Parigi et al., 2002). Although the brain activation in response to hunger and eating were far more similar than different, some areas of brain activity differed for women and men.

Gender differences in eating patterns start during early adolescence (Rolls, Fedoroff, & Guthrie, 1991) and become greater during the teen years. Figure 13.4 shows the changes in concerns about weight from fifth through ninth grades. Adolescent boys, on the average, eat enough food to obtain the required calories, but adolescent girls restrict their caloric in-

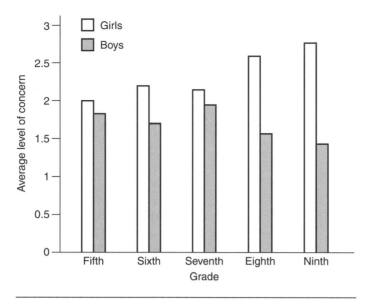

FIGURE 13.4 *Gender Differences in Young Adolescents' Concerns about Weight and Eating, by Grade*

Source: Reprinted by permission of Elsevier Science from "Weight and Eating Concerns Among Pre- and Young Adolescent Boys and Girls," by M. H. Richards, R. C. Casper, and R. Larson, *Journal of Adolescent Health, 11,* pp. 203–209, Copyright © 1990 by The Society for Adolescent Medicine.

take to the point of risk for nutritional inadequacies. Adult women also eat less than adult men, but the discrepancy is not as great as during adolescence. Nonetheless, women may eat too little to receive adequate nutrition.

Not only do men eat more than women, but also the eating patterns of each conform to the expectations of their respective gender roles. Eating less and taking smaller bites may relate to efforts to appear feminine. Eating style can affect social perception, including impressions of femininity and personal concern about appearance (Chaiken & Pliner, 1987). In studies that paired female and male participants with same- and other-gender partners to snack and talk, women showed a tendency to eat less when paired with an attractive male partner but not with an unattractive male or with a female partner (Mori, Chaiken, & Pliner, 1987). Men, too, seem subject to the pressures to eat less to create a social impression (Pliner & Chaiken, 1990). Women's eating is motivated by the desire to appear feminine as well as the desire to give a good social impression. Thus, women have two constraints on their social eating, whereas men have only one. Therefore, women and men eat somewhat differently, partly due to men's greater caloric requirements and partly due to the impression that women may wish to convey through their eating style.

Difference in eating styles is more than a way to make an impression; concerns with food and eating are a pervasive concern among young women (Rozin et al., 2003). Women have more body fat than men, but the ideal body image for women demands thinness. Thus, women often believe that they must diet to achieve the desired weight. Extreme concerns with weight and dieting can produce abnormal eating habits and serious eating disorders. A growing consensus holds that body image and eating disorders are linked; an unattainably thin body image can prompt these unhealthy eating patterns, and women are more likely than men to be concerned, even obsessed, with body shape.

Body Image.   The image of what constitutes an attractive female or male body currently emphasizes thinness for women and muscularity for men (see "According to the Media" and "According to the Research"). The contemporary ideal body image for women has developed over the past 100 years (Chernin, 1978; Wooley, 1994). In the past, plumpness was the ideal for women, signifying their health and wealth, but that ideal has faded. The thin image arose during the early part of the 20th century, signifying a departure from the plump

ACCORDING TO THE MEDIA . . .

Appearance Is Paramount, and Women Must Be Thin and Men Must Be Muscular to Be Attractive

Media portrayals of beauty influence the images of how women and men want to look, and appearance is very important in all the media. On television, appearance is the basis for comments from both male and female characters, but one analysis (Lauzen & Dozier, 2002) found that female characters are the recipients of twice as many comments about their appearance as male characters. Men are also the targets of comments about appearance, which tend to be negative if they are overweight (Fouts & Vaughan, 2002). Indeed, remarks to overweight male characters are the source of laughter from the audience. However, being overweight is not common on television; only 10% of female characters are overweight, but 31% are underweight, and 17% of male characters are overweight but only 12% are underweight (Fitzgerald, 2002).

Examinations of portrayals of magazine images also reflect the thin ideal for women and the muscular ideal for men. In addition, the examples of attractive women have gotten thinner over the past years. One example of this trend appeared in analyses of the weight of *Playboy* centerfolds. Between 1959 and 1978, centerfolds became thinner (Garner, Garfinkel, Schwartz, & Thompson, 1980), but did not continue to

decline after 1979 (Spitzer, Henderson, and Zivian, 1999). However, 99% of the centerfolds fell into the category indicating underweight, even to an extent that suggested anorexia.

Other magazines also portray attractive women as very thin. Women who appeared in women's fashion magazines have always been thin, but between 1972 and 2002, those models became thinner (*Marketing to Women*, 2002). By 2002, 70% of models were in the category of "very thin." Even models in the "plus size" advertisements were actually thinner than the average woman in the United States. Therefore, magazines portray a version of the female form that less than 5% of women can attain.

Men do not receive as many compliments about their appearance as women on television do (Lauzen & Dozier, 2002), but they are the targets of far more insults. In magazines, portrayals of men have become more sexualized over the past 15 years (Rohlinger, 2002). An analysis of *Playgirl* centerfolds from 1986 to 1996 (Spitzer et al., 1999) showed an increase in weight for these men. The increase represented muscle, not fat. Again, the ideal in the media is extreme, and most men cannot meet this unreasonable ideal.

image of traditional femininity. The thin ideal originated with the upper classes but has spread (with varying severity) to all socioeconomic classes and diverse ethnic groups, including African Americans and Hispanic Americans (Bay-Cheng, Zucker, Stewart, & Pomerleau, 2002; Miller et al., 2000), Asian Americans (Barnett, Keel, & Conoscenti, 2001), and Native Americans (LaFromboise, Berman, & Sohi, 1994). A greater concern with thinness also exists among women in many countries (Rozin, Fischler, Imada, Sarubin, & Wrzesniewski, 1999). Thus, the thin ideal has become widespread, and women are concerned with not meeting this ideal.

Overweight is a stigma for men as well as for women and extends to children. Body image discontentment appears even in preadolescent children (Lowes & Tiggemann, 2003). As young as age 6 or 7, both girls and boys chose an ideal body thinner than their own, but girls made more extreme choices. Both boys and girls attend to media models and peers in judging their own bodies during early adolescence and make comparisons to both

 ACCORDING TO THE RESEARCH . . .

Despite Media Images, Both Women and Men Have Gotten Heavier

Media images of thin women and muscular men influence how people want to look. This influence begins early, affecting both girls and boys during early adolescence (Field et al., 2001). Preadolescents and adolescents who reported that they cared about looking like same-gender characters in the media were more likely to be dieting a year later than girls and boys who did not attend so closely to media images. For college students, the media influence extends to specific body parts: College students who watched a lot of television had ideal measurements for hips, waists, and busts. Furthermore, those who were most influenced by the media were most receptive to the notion of surgical intervention with liposuction or breast implants to achieve these ideals (Harrison, 2003). For adults, media images were an influence for body image dissatisfaction among women but not men (Palladino Green & Pritchard, 2003).

During the time that the media promoted and women and men came to accept the thin and muscular ideal bodies for women and men, both became heavier (NCHS, 2002). The percentage of overweight U.S. residents increased from 47% during the 1970s to 65% in 2000; the number of overweight Canadians also increased during this time (Spitzer et al., 1999). "The ideal female weight, represented by actresses, models, and Miss Americas, has progressively decreased to that of the thinnest 5% to 10% of American women. Consequently, 90% to 95% of American women feel that they don't 'measure up' " (Seid, 1994, p. 8). The vast majority of women do not (and cannot) meet the standards presented as ideal, resulting in a norm of discontent.

The result of that dissatisfaction is depression, guilt, a growing number of eating disorders, and an increasing tendency to visit the plastic surgeon. Some adolescents who use media images as a standard for their own bodies resort to extreme dieting, which relates to developing anorexia (Fitzgerald, 2002). In addition, the number of body-sculpting plastic surgeries increased dramatically during the 1990s; liposuction is now the most common of the plastic surgery procedures (*U.S. News & World Report,* 2001). An increasing number of adolescents are seeking this remedy for their dissatisfactions with their bodies (Diclementi, 2001). Unfortunately, this solution carries safety risks and may not yield the expected results. As the title of one article on weight summarized: "Nobody's satisfied" (Raudenbush & Zellner, 1997), and the dissatisfaction has spread to both men and women.

these sources (Jones, 2001). These results suggest that body image and dissatisfaction begin during preadolescence and become established during early adolescence.

Men and boys who see themselves as overweight want to lose weight (Grogan & Richards, 2002), but being too heavy is not the typical male problem. A different ideal body image exists for men—they are under pressure to conform to an ideal of muscularity. Adolescent boys (McCreary & Sasse, 2000), college men (Morrison, Morrison, & Hopkins, 2003), and adults (Olivardia, Pope, & Phillips, 2000) expressed the desire to be more muscular rather than thinner. Boys and college men were more likely than girls and women to enact their attitudes about muscularity by working out with weights and to eat to increase bulk. The desire to increase muscularity may also be expressed by taking anabolic steroids, drugs that can help increase muscle mass (Courtenay, 2000a). Unfortunately, these drugs have many negative side effects that can present physical and psychological risks.

Early research (Fallon & Rozin, 1985) indicated that women perceived the ideal female body as thinner than their own, and they believed that men found thinner female bodies attractive. However, men's preference was not as thin as the women believed. Later research (Furnham, Dias, & McClelland, 1998) showed that ratings of attractiveness were not unique to any weight, but the body shape was; the important contributors were the ratio of waist size to hip size, breast size, and weight. These factors combined in ways that were not surprising: Smaller waists and larger breasts contributed to high attractiveness ratings. A recent study (Harrison, 2003) that investigated ratings of ideal body proportions extended these earlier findings. This study measured the influence of watching television featuring thin women and determined that these models were influential. Women who watched more such television programming tended to rate the ideal body as one with a small waist, slim hips, and moderately large breasts. Men's views of the ideal female body were similar to women's ratings.

Although men have experienced fewer problems with body image than women have, that situation is changing, and men are also subject to pressures to attain the ideal body (Olivardia et al., 2000). Men are not as subject to media influences as women (Lee & Owens, 2002), but men are dieting, working out, and seeking surgery in increasing numbers (Olivardia et al., 2000). Women's ratings also contribute to this pressure, and one study of size (Maisey, Vale, Cornelissen, & Tovee, 1999) found that women's ratings of men's body attractiveness showed a strong preference for a large upper body compared to waist and hip.

Therefore, both women and men are subjected to pressures to have bodies that conform to the ideal, but the methods for achieving these changes differ. If these messages are effective, men and women would be likely to take different strategies to achieve their ideal bodies: Women would be more likely to experience eating disorders, whereas men would be more likely to encounter exercise-related problems.

Eating Disorders.   Anorexia nervosa and bulimia are two eating disorders that have received a great deal of publicity, but these two disorders lie at the extreme on a continuum of eating problems that includes dieting (Polivy & Herman, 2002). Indeed, dieting is related to the development of the more serious eating disorders of anorexia and bulimia. **Anorexia nervosa** is a disorder caused by self-starvation in pursuit of thinness, and **bu-**

limia consists of binge eating followed by some method of purging (induced vomiting or excessive laxative use).

Dieting, anorexia, and bulimia are all more common among women than men. A survey of high school students (Grunbaum et al., 2002) and adult women and men (Serdula et al., 1999) showed that dieting was more common among women. About 70% of the girls and 80% of the women were either trying to lose or trying not to gain weight, compared to about 30% of the boys in high school and two thirds of the men. The gender distribution is even more divergent for eating disorders, and around 90% of people who are treated for eating disorders are women (Menaster, 2002). However, some research (Woodside et al., 2001) has suggested that this figure represents an underestimate for men, who fail to receive diagnosis and treatment but experience eating disorders nonetheless.

Women may also avoid diagnosis and treatment, so the statistics based on treatment for eating disorders may also be underestimates for them. Only 0.5% of women and one-tenth as many men receive a diagnosis of anorexia; between 1.0% and 3.0% of women and 0.2% of men are diagnosed as bulimic (American Psychiatric Association, 2000). Studies that question people about their eating habits, however, have found higher percentages of people who show symptoms of these disorders. For example, a survey of high school students (Grunbaum et al., 2002) reported that 7.8% of girls and 2.9% of boys said that they had vomited or used laxatives to lose or to prevent gaining weight. Both strategies are symptoms of bulimia. A survey of eating attitudes and behaviors in college students (Nelson, Hughes, Katz, & Searight, 1999) revealed that 20% of the women and 10% of the men showed symptoms of anorexia. Thus, these eating disorders may be more common than the treatment figures reflect.

Several factors relate to the development of eating disorders. As the rates of anorexia and bulimia suggest, both gender and age are factors, with women at a higher risk than men, and young women more subject to eating problems than older women. Social class was once a major factor, but pressures for thinness now occur in all social classes and among all ethnic groups (Polivy & Herman, 2002). Occupation is also a factor, with young women who are in modeling or dance school more likely to have eating disorders than comparable young women whose careers do not demand thinness (Garner & Garfinkel, 1980). For men, pressures from occupation or athletics exert similar effects with wrestlers, runners, bodybuilders, rowers, and jockeys at specific risk (Menaster, 2002). For athletes, intensity of training is a factor, and high-mileage runners have a greater chance of showing symptoms of eating disorders than those who run less (Kiernan, Rodin, Brownell, Wilmore, & Crandall, 1992).

Sexual orientation is also related to disordered eating in men. Gay men expressed higher body dissatisfaction than heterosexual men (Lakkis, Ricciardelli, & Williams, 1999), and the preference for thinness is a risk for eating disorders. About a fourth of men who are anorexic are gay (Seligmann, 1994). Regardless of gender or sexual orientation, symptoms and behaviors are similar for those with the same eating disorder (Woodside et al., 2001).

The underlying causes of eating disorders are not understood, mainly because research capable of identifying causes is difficult to conduct on this topic (Polivy & Herman, 2002). Thus researchers have identified risks and have attempted to build theories. Societal conditions that emphasize weight are related to the development of eating disorders, so several social factors are risks for eating disorders. When the media highlight specific body types and family and peers pressure young people to strive for a particular weight, body image dissatisfaction increases. Being dissatisfied with one's body is a necessary component for developing an eating disorder. However, these societal conditions are not sufficient to cause eating disorders. According to Janet Polivy and Peter Herman (2002), individuals must also come to see eating and weight control as solutions to their personal problems, and certain research (Evans, 2003) indicates that some women believe in a link between weight and happiness. The combination of body dissatisfaction and the belief that eating and weight control are keys to solving one's problems lays the foundation for eating disorders.

Both anorexia and bulimia are serious disorders, but anorexia is more likely to be life threatening. Indeed, anorexia has the highest mortality rate of any psychiatric disorder; between 5% and 15% of anorexics starve themselves to death (Brown, Mehler, & Harris, 2000). Furthermore, treatment for anorexia is difficult. Anorexics often fail to cooperate with their treatment and persist in their desire to lose weight—even at the risk of their lives. Bulimia is more easily treated because bulimics typically feel guilty about their binge eating and purging, and thus they want to change their behavior. Therapy can fail with both disorders, resulting in persistent eating problems that can lead to permanent damage to health.

GENDERED VOICES

I'm Afraid Some of Them Are Not Going to Be Around

"I'm afraid some of them are not going to be around," a 14-year-old dancer told her mother concerning other dancers who showed symptoms of anorexia. The dancers in her classes were encouraged to be thin, and the girl believed that several were in danger; they were so thin that she had considered them in danger of dying. Her mother was angry because she believed that the instructor was encouraging unhealthy eating in students, by telling her normal-weight daughter that she needed to lose weight. The girl knew that she was heavier than many of the other dancers, but she believed that they had the problem, not her.

She had begun to hear criticisms about her weight when she was 12, and she started to become self-conscious about it, but she had resisted dieting, partly because she thought the other girls were too thin and partly because she didn't want to change her eating habits. She had also received conflicting messages about her weight, with her mother and others telling her that she wasn't too heavy, her dance teacher telling her that she needed to be thinner, and her classmates dieting to the point of anorexia.

Another girl's story confirmed the prevalence of weight consciousness among early adolescents. This 12-year-old came home from school one day and told her mother that when they had gone swimming for gym class, most of the girls had gone into the pool with their T-shirts over their bathing suits. She didn't understand why they had done so; a wet T-shirt made swimming more difficult. When she asked one why she had kept her shirt on, the other girl said, "Because I'm so fat. I don't want anyone to see me in a bathing suit." The 12-year-old told her mother, "But they're not fat." She considered her classmates' perceptions of their bodies very odd. Judging from the number of girls who had been reluctant to be seen in their bathing suits, her classmates' distorted perception was more common than her accurate assessment of what was normal and what constituted overweight.

Eating disorders, then, may be the result of concerns with body image and exaggerated attempts to achieve thinness. Because their ideal body images are thin, women are more likely than men to develop eating disorders. Over the past several decades, both men and women have begun to feel increased pressure to attain and maintain attractive bodies, and women tend to try to achieve this goal through dieting and, to a lesser extent, through exercise; men on the other hand, use exercise as a primary means and dieting as a secondary means of shaping their bodies.

Exercise and Fitness

Exercise is a factor in the weight maintenance equation. To maintain a steady body weight, the energy (calories) from food consumed must equal body energy expenditures. Such expenditures come from the energy required to maintain basal metabolism and from the energy required for physical activity. Increases in physical activity require more calories, or weight loss occurs. Thus, increases in physical activity can produce weight loss.

As noted earlier, men are more likely to exercise and women are more likely to diet as their main strategies to lose weight. When dieters eat less, their basal metabolism slows, and their bodies require fewer calories, which protects against starvation but makes weight loss difficult (Pinel, 2003). To overcome this problem, the dieter must eat even less, increasing the chances of nutritional deficits and the difficulties in maintaining the diet. Thus, dieting is not only difficult, it also is not as effective for weight control as dieting plus exercise.

Increased concern with body image and the growing evidence that dieting may not be a good weight control strategy has led to an increased emphasis on exercise. Weight control, however, is a minor factor in considering the benefits of exercise; physical activity is a basic part of life. The amount of physical activity varies from person to person and from time to time, but people are physically active creatures.

However, the circumstances of contemporary life do not guarantee much physical activity. Most jobs in technological societies do not require a high level of physical effort. Some people enjoy exercise and participate in various types of leisure-time activities that require a great deal of physical effort, whereas others prefer television or other sedentary activities as a way to spend their leisure time. Differences in job and leisure-time activities show gender differences, with women being less likely to engage in physical activity than men, but the overall difference is very small (USBC, 2002).

During the preschool years, boys are more active than girls. Throughout childhood, boys are more likely to engage in physical activities requiring gross motor skills that use the large muscles of the body. Boys' preferences for baseball, football, soccer, and basketball put them into more active situations than many girls' games require. Girls and boys do not play together often during childhood, decreasing the chances that girls will participate in many games and sports involving vigorous activity. Girls who do, however, are more likely to become college athletes than girls who engage in more traditional play activities (Giuliano, Popp, & Knight, 2000). (See Chapter 9 for a discussion of gender segregation and friendships during childhood and Chapter 11 for a consideration of athletics in schools.)

Watching television and playing computer games have become popular recreational activities for children and adolescents. The computer game market was dominated initially by games aimed at boys, but companies began to market games that girls liked (Gardyn, 2003). Now, 65% of both male and female college students play video or computer games regularly, and about 70% of those students have played since elementary school. Regardless of the content, computer games can take the place of more active games and decrease the physical activity of both boys and girls.

Although children with athletic talent are encouraged to participate in sports, the emphasis on sports may leave the majority of children without adequate encouragement to be active. Many children of both genders avoid physical activity and concentrate on sedentary activities. Not having the ability to excel, they shun exercise, resulting in poor fitness and an increased probability of obesity (Berkey, Rockett, Gillman, & Colditz, 2003).

Gender differences in exercising increase during adolescence, with girls decreasing and boys increasing their participation in athletics. The traditional gender roles hold that women should look slender and dainty and should feel reluctant to compete. Men, on the other hand, should look muscular and strong and should feel eager to compete. Athletic participation, with its emphasis on size, strength, and competition, is more compatible with the male than the female gender role. Adolescents feel the pressures to adopt these gender roles; thus, boys are urged to "try out" for sports, whereas girls may not receive similar encouragement.

Title IX of the Education Amendments of 1972 prohibited sex discrimination in education, which included support for school athletics. The subsequent development of athletic programs for high school girls and college women has changed opportunities and attitudes toward women's athletics. Many more women now participate in athletics, establishing a pattern of physical activity that, like men's, can carry over into adulthood and provide long-term health benefits.

A growing body of research evidence indicates that exercise provides physical and psychological benefits to both men and women (Blair, Cheng, & Holder, 2001; Oguma, Sesso, Paffenbarger, & Lee, 2002). The benefits of physical activity seem particularly strong in terms of lowering the risk of cardiovascular disease (heart attack and stroke), but exercise also lowers the risk for several cancers, helps to prevent and to control diabetes, assists people in sleeping better, lowers depression, reduces anxiety, and buffers against stress (Brannon & Feist, 2004). In addition, physical activity guards against **osteoporosis,** the process of bone demineralization. This disorder affects older individuals and is more common among women than men. Orthopedic problems such as fractures are common and can lead to decreased mobility, which is a major factor in decreased quality of life for the elderly (Robine & Ritchie, 1991). Exercise slows and may reverse this process. Therefore, a regular program of physical activity offers many health benefits throughout the life span.

Men's greater sports participation during adolescence makes them more likely than women to continue this athletic activity throughout their lives, but this background is no guarantee of an active lifestyle. After they leave school, men become less likely to continue with physical activity, falling into the dominant pattern of desk jobs and sedentary hobbies.

Pressures on women to be thin have extended to fitness, with an increasing number of articles in women's magazines (Weisman, Gray, Mosimann, & Ahrens, 1992) and messages on magazine covers (Malkin, Wornian, & Chrisler, 1999) urging women to achieve thinness not only through diet but also through exercise. This message has gotten through to women; a study that investigated reasons for exercising (Strelan, Mehaffey, & Tiggemann, 2003) found that young women's exercising may be so concentrated on appearance that their participation signals a problem in body image rather than a positive health habit. This finding is consistent with the messages aimed at women to exercise as part of weight control and body shaping rather than health promotion.

A relationship exists between exercise and eating disorders, but this relationship is complex and involves gender. People who are anorexic (usually women) are often overly concerned about exercising and may work out for hours per day in attempts to lose weight. Some people who exercise excessively (usually men) also have some eating disorder (Hausenblas & Symons Downs, 2002). Not all anorexics exercise obsessively, nor do all committed exercisers have eating disorders, but there is some concordance between these two extreme behaviors.

In this framework, men's exercise motivations may also be symptomatic of body image problems. The drive to develop muscularity can lead boys and men to exercise excessively (McCreary & Sasse, 2000; Olivardia et al., 2000), which can lead to injury. Boys and men may be motivated to be muscular in a gender-stereotypical counterpart to girls and women, who are motivated to be thin. Exercise may allow both women and men to achieve fitness, but exercise may also provide a format for enacting body image dissatisfaction and unrealistic weight concerns. Therefore, despite the benefits of exercise, overcommitment to exercise is not always healthy.

In summary, exercise can be a healthy habit that provides a number of physical and psychological benefits. Although men are more likely to have a background in sports, both women and men may pursue exercise for a variety of reasons. Men are more likely to use exercise as a way to shape their bodies, and women are more likely to use exercise as an adjunct to dieting to lose weight. Both of these goals may be the basis for pathological exercising, but moderate exercise is a factor in a healthy lifestyle, with men more likely to be physically active than women.

CONSIDERING DIVERSITY

Health and mortality figures from around the world and within the United States reflect the influence of ethnicity and the economic conditions that are often related to ethnicity. One way to analyze world economies is the division into developed (or industrialized) countries, developing countries, and undeveloped countries. The economics of life in these countries also affects death in these countries (Seale, 2000). As Table 13.4 shows, life expectancy is longer in industrialized countries than in developing or undeveloped countries. In addition, the causes of death vary. In developed countries, leading causes of death are the chronic diseases (cardiovascular disease [CVD] and cancer) that are more common among older people. People in industrialized countries live long enough to develop these diseases. The death rates for CVD and cancer are much lower for the developing countries because many people do not live to the ages when these diseases become common. In undeveloped countries, mortality is high from infectious and parasitic diseases, which are fatal for infants and young children more often than for other age groups. High mortality for infants and children lowers life expectancy and typically occurs in poor countries with inadequate nutrition and medical care.

As Table 13.4 illustrates, life expectancy and causes of death vary enormously throughout the world, but the gender gap in favor of women in life expectancy appears everywhere. That gap is larger in industrialized countries (5 to 8 years) and much smaller

TABLE 13.4 *Average Life Expectancies, Infant Mortality, and Causes of Death for Developed, Developing, and Undeveloped Countries*

Country	Life Expectancy Men	Life Expectancy Women	Infant Mortality (per 1,000)	Circulatory Diseases	Cancer	Accident/ Violence	Infectious/ Parasitic
Developed Countries							
Australia	77	83	6.0	296.0	190.0	41.0	6.0
Canada	76	83	5.1	264.8	195.6	43.5	8.3
France	75	83	4.8	288.2	207.7	76.1	12.8
Germany	75	81	4.8	525.7	260.7	48.6	7.4
Japan	77	84	3.4	237.7	220.4	52.4	14.6
Sweden	77	83	3.5	525.5	234.6	48.9	8.6
United Kingdom	76	81	5.6	442.1	261.2	55.9	6.8
United States	74	80	6.9	354.4	201.6	55.9	19.6
Developing Countries							
Brazil	67	75	38.0	159.0	65.9	75.9	33.5
Iran	68	71	30.0	304.0	61.0	108.0	34.0
Mexico	69	75	26.2	106.8	52.9	62.4	22.0
Thailand	69	74	18.0	89.8	49.0	73.8	27.6
Undeveloped Countries							
Angola	36	38	195.8	diarrheal diseases, 25.8%; malaria, 19%; cholera, 7%			
Bangladesh	61	61	73.0	typhoid, 19.8%; tetanus, 10%; tuberculosis, 8.7%			
Haiti	50	53	97.1	11.9	malnutrition, 8.5		46
Laos	52	56	91.0	includes bronchitis, influenza, malaria, diarrhea			
Zimbabwe	39	36	62.3	40.9	28.4	44.4	64.7

Sources: Causes of death from *Britannica Book of the Year, 2002,* 2002, Chicago: Encyclopedia Britannica; life expectancies from *The World Factbook 2002,* by Central Intelligence Agency, 2002, Washington, DC: U.S. Government Printing Office.

in undeveloped countries (a few months to 4 years). In some of the undeveloped countries, maternal mortality is high because of problems related to pregnancy and childbirth. In several countries in sub-Saharan Africa, HIV infection is the leading cause of death and affects a similar number of women and men. Several of these countries have experienced a decreased life expectancy over the past few years (*Population Reports,* 2001).

Another practice that can decrease the survival advantage for girls and women is *son preference*—that is, the preference for sons over daughters. Son preference can lead to the murder of infant girls or the abortion of female fetuses (Satpathy & Mishra, 2000), but more often it is expressed through preferential treatment for sons, including better feeding and medical attention, and the neglect of daughters. In countries where girls and boys receive more equal treatment during infancy and childhood, girls have a survival advantage over boys, as women do when compared to men. Thus, the female survival advantage holds across many cultures. However, the life expectancy varies more than the magnitude of the gender gap, which indicates that social factors are important in life expectancy.

Worldwide, men are more vulnerable to disease and death in patterns similar to those in the United States: Men's rate of CVD death is higher than that of women of comparable age, they use tobacco at a higher rate, and they engage in risky behaviors that increase their vulnerability to violent death. In countries in which the death rate for CVD is high, the gender gap is larger than in countries with fewer deaths from this cause. The countries in eastern Europe, including those that were part of the Soviet Union, have a particularly high rate of CVD, and this rate has increased since the breakup of the Soviet Union (Weidner, 2000). The rise has affected those people most vulnerable to CVD—middle-aged men. The increase in Russia has been over 30%, the life expectancy in Russia has declined, and the gender gap in life expectancy has increased. The CVD death rate in Russia is about 500 per 100,000 population for men, but only 80 per 100,000 for women; the life expectancy is 59 and 72, respectively. The reasons for this dramatic increase in CVD are somewhat mysterious, but one hypothesis (Weidner, 2000) holds that psychosocial factors such as stress, economic uncertainty, inadequate social support, and depression are the basis of the problem.

The gender gap in life expectancy is not predicted to decline in the near future, nor are other causes of disease to which men are particularly vulnerable. An analysis of mortality statistics allowed researchers (Murray & Lopez, 1997) to predict death rates in the year 2020, and those predictions included no reversal of the epidemic CVD death rate among men in eastern Europe. In addition, those predictions included an increase in tobacco-related deaths and deaths due to violence, all of which affect men to a greater extent than women. Life expectancy will likely increase because infectious diseases are predicted to decline, but would benefit women more than men, which would increase the gender gap.

The United States is among the industrialized nations, but some ethnic groups in the United States have patterns of disease and death that look more like those of developing countries. The underlying reasons for these health disadvantages include poverty and discrimination, both of which affect living conditions and access to medical care. The provision of health insurance through employment or through private policies results in decreased access and often poor-quality medical care for poor people. Ethnic minority groups are affected by these circumstances more than White people are (NCHS, 2002).

African Americans have higher infant mortality rates and shorter life expectancies than other ethnic groups in the United States. The infant mortality rate for African Americans is 14.6 deaths per 1,000 live births compared to a rate for Whites of 5.8 per 1,000 (USBC, 2002). That is, African American babies die at a rate comparable to those in Kuwait, Costa Rica, and Bulgaria, whereas infant mortality for White babies is comparable to that of wealthy, developed countries. Other health indicators for African Americans show that they have a shorter life expectancy and a higher rate of several diseases, including cardiovascular disease, diabetes, and liver disease. African Americans also die from violence more often than Whites do—68.8 versus 45.8 per 100,000. Young men are especially likely to be the victims of unintentional and intentional injuries.

Hispanic Americans are disadvantaged by conditions similar to African Americans, but their mortality rates are more similar to non-Hispanic Whites than to African Americans. Young Hispanic American men are at elevated risk for injuries and death due to violence (Hummer, Rogers, Amir, Forbes, & Frisbie, 2000), but deaths due to cardiovascular diseases and cancer are lower than for non-Hispanic Whites. The overall death rate for Hispanics was comparable to that of non-Hispanic European Americans.

Native Americans experience a pattern of health problems that varies from other ethnic groups. Poverty and poor living conditions are major problems for the health of Native Americans, and their access to medical care is often through the Indian Health Service, which provides free medical care to Native Americans who live on reservations or in areas covered by the service (Weitz, 2001). This limitation restricts health care of many Native Americans. Infant mortality is higher for Native Americans than for Whites, but lower than that for African Americans (NCHS, 2002). Youth violence is a bigger problem among Native Americans than any other ethnic group. Native Americans also have a genetic predisposition for developing diabetes, and their levels of alcohol abuse contribute to liver disease, violent deaths, and fetal alcohol syndrome.

As a group, Asian Americans experience health advantages rather than disadvantages when compared to all other ethnic groups in the United States. Infant mortality rates for Chinese Americans, Japanese Americans, and Filipino Americans are among the best in the world (USDHHS, 2000). For Asian Americans as a group, CVD death rates and deaths from violence are about half of those for European Americans, and rate of cancer deaths is lower.

Therefore, some ethnic groups within the United States have health disadvantages whereas others have advantages. The health of non-Hispanic Whites and Asian Americans compares favorably with the industrialized nations throughout the world. For African Americans and Native Americans, health care and health indicators are comparable to those of developing nations.

SUMMARY

Women live longer than men. This gender difference has existed in most countries and during most time periods. In economically developed countries such as the United States, Canada, Australia, and the countries of Scandinavia and western Europe, deaths from cardiovascular disease, cancer, and accidents account for the majority of deaths. Men die of these causes at younger ages than women, creating a gender gap in longevity.

Cardiovascular disease (CVD) refers to diseases of the heart and circulatory system. Although not all CVD is life threatening, heart attack and stroke account for almost half of the deaths in the United States. Men are more likely to die of CVD than women are before the age of 65 years, but the total mortality is similar for the two. Women with CVD may not have their symptom reports taken as seriously as men with similar symptoms, which suggests a treatment bias on the part of physicians.

Cancer is the second most common cause of death, and men are more likely than women to die from this cause. Lung cancer, the deadliest form of cancer for both men and women, is strongly related to cigarette smoking. Until recently, men have smoked at a substantially higher rate than women. With the rise in women's smoking, their lung cancer rates have increased and will continue to do so. Both women and men develop cancer of the reproductive organs, but women are more likely to die of such cancers, especially before age 65 years.

The gender difference in violent deaths is large; men die of unintentional injuries, suicides, and homicides at higher rates than women. The male gender role, which holds that men are supposed to be reckless and aggressive, may play a part in the high death rates from these causes. Men's greater prevalence of heavy alcohol use increases their chances of dying of any of these violent causes. Violent deaths also vary from country to country, with the United States having one of the higher rates of violent deaths. Within the United States, different ethnic groups are not equally affected by violence—African Americans are especially vulnerable to violent death.

Although women live longer than men, women also seek health care more often. The female gender role allows and even encourages vulnerability to illness, but the male gender role

discourages the acceptance of any weakness, including illness. Women's sensitivity to physical symptoms tends to boost health care seeking, but their access to health care is diminished by lower rates of employment, lower salaries, and lower insurance coverage.

The interaction of gender roles of the patient and health care provider has an impact on the type of health care patients receive. Physicians have been the target of criticism concerning their treatment of female patients; three of these include being reluctant to believe female patients, using men as a standard against which all patients are judged, and omitting women from medical research. Concern over these problems has prompted the founding of the Office of Women's Health and the Women's Health Initiative. This Initiative includes a series of studies, several of which have already made important contributions to knowledge of the risks of hormone replacement therapy after menopause.

Reproductive health is a major reason for the gender difference in receiving health care. Women not only become involved in the health care system due to pregnancy and childbirth, but contraception and menopause are also reasons for consulting physicians. Both women and men are affected by sexually transmitted diseases and disorders of the reproductive organs. Both develop cancer of the genitals, and among women, breast cancer is the most frequent (but not the deadliest) cancer.

Lifestyle differences may account for some of the gender differences in morbidity and mortality. Eating and exercising are behaviors that relate to health. The thin body has become such a widespread ideal among women that dieting is now a way of life for millions of women. Because they cannot be as thin as the ideal, women develop body image problems and are more prone to eating disorders such as anorexia nervosa and bulimia. Men also experience body image dissatisfaction, but they tend to feel insufficiently muscular and are more likely to attempt to alter their bodies through exercise rather than through dieting.

Exercise can be a positive factor for fitness and weight control, and men are more likely to participate in sports and physical activity than women are. The passage of Title IX of the Education Amendments of 1972 removed some barriers that prevented women from participating in athletics, and increasingly positive publicity for female athletes encourages girls to become athletic. In an increasingly technological and sedentary society, most men and women must use their leisure time to pursue fitness. Athletic activities can build fitness and contribute to health, but ex-

cessive exercise can also be symptomatic of body image problems.

Life expectancy and health vary around the world, and economic factors contribute heavily to this variation. Wealthy, industrialized nations have longer life expectancies and the problems associated with long life—high rates of cardiovascular disease and cancer. Poor, undeveloped countries have shorter life expectancies and the problems associated with poverty—high infant mortality and death from infectious diseases. Within the United States, Asian Americans and European Americans have longer life expectancies and better health than African Americans and Native Americans.

▣ GLOSSARY

anorexia nervosa   an eating disorder consisting of self-starvation in pursuit of thinness.

bulimia   an eating disorder consisting of binge eating, followed by some method of purging, either by induced vomiting or excessive laxative use.

cardiovascular disease (CVD)   a group of diseases involving the heart and circulatory system, some of which are life threatening; heart attack and stroke are the most common.

chronic diseases   health problems that develop over a period of time, often without noticeable symptoms, and persist over time without a complete recovery.

morbidity   illness.

mortality   death.

osteoporosis   the process of bone demineralization, resulting in greater likelihood of orthopedic problems and injuries.

risk factor   any condition or factor that increases the probability that an illness will develop.

sexually transmitted diseases (STDs)   infectious diseases that are spread through sexual contact, including bacterial infections, viral infections, fungal infections, and parasitic infections.

▣ SUGGESTED READINGS

Brumberg, Joan Jacobs. (1997). *The body project.* New York: Random House.
   Brumberg explores the contemporary obsession with the body and how this emphasis affects girls and their relationship with their bodies.

Chrisler, Joan C. (2001). Gendered bodies and physical health. In Rhoda K. Unger (Ed.), *Handbook of psychology of women and gender* (pp. 289–302). New York: Wiley.
   Chrisler presents a relatively brief but fairly comprehensive summary of women's experience with illness and with the health care system. In addition, she discusses the health risks involved with the pursuit of beauty.

Courtenay, Will H. (2000). Behavioral factors associated with disease, injury, and death among men: Evidence and implications for prevention. *Journal of Men's Studies, 9,* 81–142.
   Courtenay presents a lengthy, excellent summary of men's behaviors that contribute to the gender gap in mortality.

Weidner, Gerdi. (2000). Why do men get more heart disease than women? An international perspective. *Journal of American College Health, 48,* 291–294.
   This short, provocative article focuses on the gender gap in cardiovascular disease on an international level and touches on many of the issues that differentiate men's and women's health.

14 STRESS, COPING, AND PSYCHOPATHOLOGY

HEADLINE Who Has the Most Stress?
Ladies Home Journal, March 2000

Everyone encounters stress, but people have different experiences with stress and cope with their stresses with varying effectiveness. Kathryn Casey (2000) and *Ladies Home Journal* investigated the stress levels of five women throughout a typical day to determine how their stress varied and how they coped. The women included a married mother who had left her job as a physical therapist to stay home and care for her four young children, a married hairdresser who had one young daughter, an unmarried nurse with no children, a married teacher with an infant daughter, and a film executive with teenage children whose husband was her business partner. Casey reported on their perceptions of the stresses they encountered, but each also wore a heart rate monitor to give a physiological measurement of her reactions to the stresses of the day.

These two different strategies for assessing stress point to one of the difficulties in studying stress—its definition. When people report that they feel stressed, they may be considering the event or their own feelings. When their bodies react, a number of physiological changes occur, including an increase in heart rate. However, for the physiological reactions to occur, people must perceive an event as arousing, so perception is a critical factor in the experience of stress. **Stress** has been defined in many ways, but when circumstances place people in situations that tax or exceed their resources and endanger their well-being, they feel stressed (Lazarus & Folkman, 1984). People who are stressed typically experience both a feeling of the stress and a physiological reaction; the feelings are easier to deny or ignore than the physiology.

The women in Casey's story varied in marital status, number and age of children, employment, and economic status of the family, so they provided good examples of how these factors operate to produce stress and how people's perceptions of the stresses in their lives may be inaccurate. For example, the homemaker had quit her job to stay home with her four children, and she believed that giving up her job would make for low stress levels. Her heart rate monitor told another story. Caring for her children, especially when they squabbled, raised her heart rate into the high range, and she was not coping effectively.

The hairdresser combined her job with caring for her 6-year-old daughter, without much help from her husband. She expressed feelings that mirror those of many women:

"At work, I worry that I don't spend enough time at home. At home, I'm stressed because I can't finish everything I want to" (in Casey, 2000, p. 153). She rated her stress level as moderate, but the heart rate monitor showed very high levels of stress, and an assessment of her daily routine showed poor coping skills. The woman whom many would rate as having the most stressful life was the nurse. She was unmarried, with no children, and worked 12-hour shifts in a busy trauma center emergency room. However, the most stressful event of her day was the commute to work and not the crowded, life-and-death work environment. Her job included many difficult situations, but her coping skills were very good, and she felt competent and in control.

Work was also not the most stressful time of the day for the teacher—instead, caring for her infant daughter was, especially getting up during the night to do so. Her husband was also a teacher and actively involved with child care. She rated her stress levels as moderately high, but her heart rates were lower than either of the other women who cared for children. The film executive rated her stress as high, and both her job and family life included several situations that most people consider stressful. Both she and her husband had teenage children from prior marriages, and their blended family's rotating custody schedule and relationships with former spouses were sources of stress. In addition, the demands of running a business turn up the pressure. Despite her perception of high stress, her monitor ratings showed low to moderate levels, and the analysis of her reactions reflected good coping skills. Her highest heart rate occurred when she read an e-mail from her husband's former wife.

These women's experiences illustrate how job and family situations produce stress, how children can add to stress levels, and how employment is often not the main source of stress in women's lives. Are these women typical? Do the differences in men's work and family lives produce different patterns of stress for men? What types of problems develop for people who cannot cope?

STRESS AND COPING

Explanations for psychological problems have ranged from demonic possession to genetic vulnerability. The belief that madness results from possession has faded, but many authorities accept that some mental disorders, including depression and schizophrenia, have a genetic component. The variability in diagnoses, however, is too large to be accounted for by genetics. Therefore, the search for risk factors for mental disorders has focused on life circumstances and stresses.

Stress is an inevitable part of life, so searching for the stresses that relate to the development of mental disorders becomes a complex task. Researchers cannot simply identify sources of stress but must, as did the headline article, investigate how people perceive various stressors and how they cope with the resulting stress in their lives.

Sources of Stress for Men and Women

The basic physiological reaction to stress is similar for men and women (Taylor et al., 2000), but sources of stress vary. As Chapters 9 and 12 explored, the many combinations of marriage, parenthood, and employment provide women and men with complex roles. Men have traditionally occupied the breadwinner role and have not been involved with providing much in the way of housekeeping or child care; that situation has changed, and women are pressuring men to become more actively involved in household work and caring for children. That pressure may be one source of stress for men. Research has explored the ramifications of occupying the multiple roles of spouse, parent, and employee. As the women in the headline story showed, fulfilling these roles may be stressful and thus related to the development of problems.

Experiences with violence provide an additional reason for gender differences with stress. As Chapter 8 presented, men are more likely to be the perpetrators as well as the victims of violence. However, women are much more likely to be the targets of sexual abuse and violence in families, which places them at risk for the aftermath of such violence. Poverty, sexism, and gender discrimination are also potential sources of stress that have different impacts on women and men. How do these life experiences relate to the development of mental disorders—and are the gender differences in mental disorders related to these life experiences?

Family Roles.   The gender differences in family roles revolve around marriage, parenthood, and employment. Marriage roles may be analyzed into "his" and "hers," and Jessie Bernard (1972) contended that "his" tends to be more beneficial than "hers." During the time that Bernard proposed that marriage was a danger to women, most women fulfilled the role of spouse and parent but not employee, whereas men typically occupied all three roles. Those circumstances have changed. Currently, a majority of women are employed, so role occupancy has become more similar for women and men. More recent research from Australia (de Vaus, 2002) and from the United States (Hetherington & Kelly, 2002; Sachs-Ericsson & Ciarlo, 2000) indicated that many of the gender differences have become smaller.

For example, being married was a mental health advantage to both wives and husbands in both countries. Indeed, married people showed lower levels of mental disorders for almost every category of problem than people who were not married. In the United States, unmarried men were at higher risk for mental health problems than unmarried women (Hetherington & Kelly, 2002; Sachs-Ericsson & Ciarlo, 2000), but in Australia, the two groups showed similar rates of disorders (de Vaus, 2002). Husbands and wives were equally benefited by marriage in Australia, but in the United States, husbands experienced fewer mental health problems than wives (Sachs-Ericsson & Ciarlo, 2000).

These studies also showed that roles other than marriage may raise or lower the risk for mental disorders. Being employed was a positive factor for men and women in both countries. Indeed, the combination of marriage and employment was associated with low levels of mental health problems, and being both unmarried and unemployed raised the risks (de Vaus, 2002; Sachs-Ericsson & Ciarlo, 2000). Adding the role of parent did not increase the risk of mental health problems for married people, but unmarried women with children were at increased risk in both countries. In the United States, men who occupied all three roles— spouse, parent, and employee—showed the lowest risk for mental problems of any group.

As these studies demonstrate, these three family roles have the potential to improve mental health, but some combinations of roles present benefits and others pose risks for mental health problems. Being unhappily married was a mental health risk for both women and men, but women were affected more strongly than men (Whisman, 1999). That is, marriage may be beneficial but not all marriages are equally so. Satisfaction and feelings of support from a spouse make a difference (Hughes & Galinsky, 1994). One of the women in the headline article for this chapter had left her job to care for her four children, and her life was more stressful than she had thought. Another of the women combined full-time employment with caring for her young daughter. These women did not have much assistance from their husbands, which tended to make their child care duties more stressful. When employed mothers experience little strain in either role, they are at a low risk for depression, like the film executive and the teacher in the headline story. When married, employed mothers experience strain in each role; their risk for mental health problems increases. When family demands are equal for employed men and women, they have comparable rates of depression and anxiety disorders. When the burdens of family care fall disproportionately on women, these women's social circumstances pose risks for the development of depression.

Women have fewer mental health problems when they are employed, but their husbands may not. The shift in power that accompanies wives' employment may pose problems for their husbands, especially if husbands are unemployed (Hetherington & Kelly, 2002). When husbands are not fulfilling their role as breadwinner, they are at risk for depression and substance abuse problems (de Vaus, 2002). If the wife's employment leads to a decrease in the husband's relative contribution to family income and an increase in his share of domestic duties, husbands often feel stressed, and their mental health may suffer. Thus, men also may experience conflict and pressures related to their family roles that influence their mental health.

Although most research on stresses in men's lives has concentrated on job-related stress and its effects, family roles may contribute to feelings of distress or well-being (Barnett, Marshall, & Pleck, 1992; Larson & Richards, 1994). Men tend to feel more stressed at work and more relaxed at home (Larson & Richards, 1994), thus their family relationships are important. Satisfaction with family life can buffer men against the stresses of the workplace.

High commitment to the breadwinner role can be a source of strain for men, and again, spousal support is a critical factor (Greenberger & O'Neil, 1993). Women also experience strain from a lack of support, especially when husbands spend many hours on their jobs and when they feel their husbands and neighbors are not supportive of their employment and parenting efforts. Thus, both partners may experience role strain related to parenting and work, and lack of support is an important factor in the equation. Therefore, the relationship between family roles and mental health is quite complex. Table 14.1 presents some of the influences of various roles on psychological health.

Violence.   Violence researcher Mary Koss wrote, "Experiencing violence transforms people into victims and changes their lives forever. Once victimized one can never feel quite as invulnerable" (Koss, 1990, p. 374). Men and women may both be the victims of violence, but their experiences tend to differ. As discussed earlier, men are more frequently the perpetrators as well as the victims of violence. When women are the targets, their victimization may be especially traumatic, because women are more likely to be the victims

TABLE 14.1 *Influences of Various Roles on Psychological Health*

Role	Affects	Consequences
Caregiving	Women more than men	Stress; emotional and physical exhaustion
Marriage	Both genders	Positive
Parenthood	Both genders	Depends on other roles occupied and the support available
Child caregiving	Women more than men	At risk for mental and physical health problems
Employment	Both genders	Positive
Homemaker role	Women	At risk for depression
Breadwinner role	Men more than women	At risk for mental health problems
Employed wife	Men	At risk for mental health problems

of violence by family and friends than by strangers (Pimlott-Kubiak & Cortina, 2003). Furthermore, women are more likely to be injured in violent encounters by persons they know (Dutton, Haywood, & El-Bayoumi, 1997).

The risk to physical health is apparent, but a growing body of research has implicated violence as a risk to mental health. Much of this research has concentrated on intimate violence in families—namely, childhood sexual abuse, rape, and marital violence. Although women are more often the victims of intimate abuse, men who are similarly victimized show comparable effects. A history of violence is related to the development of a wide variety of psychological problems.

The American Psychological Association established a Task Force on Male Violence Against Women in 1991 (Goodman, Koss, Fitzgerald, Russo, & Keita, 1993). This task force estimated that between 21% and 34% of women in the United States are physically assaulted by men who have close relationships with them, and between 14% and 25% of adult women will be raped at some time during their lives. Although these (and other) types of violence have declined in the years since these reports (Rennison, 2003), these figures suggest that male violence toward women puts a great many women at risk for mental disorders.

A body of research implicates violence as a risk for mental health. A meta-analysis of research on intimate partner violence (Golding, 1999) revealed that a history of such violence increases the risk for depression, suicide, posttraumatic stress disorder, and substance abuse for women. Almost half of the women in the studies showed some type of mental health problem, demonstrating a greatly elevated risk. A study that included a large, representative sample of men and women (Pimlott-Kubiak & Cortina, 2003) also found a significant relationship between being the target of violence and several types of psychopathology. Although this study showed that men and women were equally vulnerable to mental disorders when they had experienced violence, the results indicated different patterns of victimization. Table 14.2 shows the gender differences in these experiences.

Violence may be not only a significant contributor to the prevalence of depression among women but also a main factor that accounts for the gender difference in this disorder (Cutler & Nolen-Hoeksema, 1991; Wise, Zierler, Krieger, & Harlow, 2001). Childhood

TABLE 14. 2   *Patterns of Violence Victimization for Women and Men*

Type of Violence	Women	Men
Physical assault (during adulthood)	31%	45%
Physical assault (during childhood)	40	54
Emotional abuse (during adulthood)	51	48
Sexual violence (lifetime)	18	3
Stalking	32	26

Source: Data from "Gender, Victimization, and Outcomes: Reconceptualizing Risk" by S. Pimlott-Kubiak and L. M. Cortina, 2003, *Journal of Consulting and Clinical Psychology, 71,* pp. 528–539.

sexual abuse is more common for girls than boys, and evidence links childhood sexual abuse with anxiety, depression, and low self-esteem. Support for this relationship has come from two studies that compared women who were sexually abused as children to those with no history of sexual abuse (Wise et al., 2001; Yama, Tovey, & Fogas, 1993). The results from both studies demonstrated that this type of childhood abuse has lasting effects for the development of anxiety and depression.

Other research has shown that sexual abuse at any age increases the risk for a variety of mental disorders, and this risk applies to both men and women (Burnam et al., 1988; Koss, Bailey, Yuan, Herrera, & Lichter, 2003; Pimlott-Kubiak & Cortina, 2003). Being a victim of sexual abuse increases the chances of depression, posttraumatic stress disorder, substance abuse or dependence, phobic disorder, panic disorder, and obsessive-compulsive disorder, with the magnitude of increase reaching between two and four times that of men or women who have not been abused. Childhood abuse may be more of a danger than abuse during adulthood, but both pose risks. These studies found no gender difference in likelihood of developing psychological problems following abuse, but men were more likely to experience drug and alcohol problems and women were more likely to experience depression. Sexual victimization clearly increased the risk for a variety of problems for both genders, but women's more frequent victimization means they have greater risks.

Violence in the form of criminal victimization also relates to the development of psychological disorders, especially posttraumatic stress disorder (PTSD) (Koss et al., 2003; Resnick, Kilpatrick, Best, & Kramer, 1992). Those women who were victims of crimes involving violence or the threat of extreme violence were much more likely to develop symptoms of PTSD than women who were the victims of less violent crimes. However, all crime victims showed elevated risks of PTSD, demonstrating the psychological risks of criminal victimization. Direct involvement with violence is not necessary for the development of problems; exposure to violence is also a risk. For example, inner-city adolescents exposed to violence (an average of five incidents within the year of the study) also had elevated risks for PTSD (Mazza & Reynolds, 1999). Thus, exposure to as well as the experience of violence are risks to mental health.

The evidence for the relationship between violence and mental disorders is much more straightforward than risks from the various family roles: Violence increases the risk for several mental disorders. Childhood victimization is especially harmful. Women are more likely to be the targets of childhood sexual abuse and rape, two types of violence that research has related to psychological disorders, but men who are victimized are at comparably elevated risk of such problems.

Poverty.   Poverty also presents a risk for mental disorders for women, men, and children (Attar, Guerra, & Tolan, 1994; Belle & Doucet, 2003). Those who live in poverty are at least two and a half times more likely to receive diagnoses of mental disorders than those who are not poor. The discrepancy between lowest and highest income groups is sharper in the United States than in other industrialized countries, and this difference may be a factor in health status (Wilkinson, 1996). Long life expectancies and low rates of disease are more strongly related to egalitarianism in societies than to income across societies. That is, among industrialized nations, those societies that are most egalitarian have longer life expectancies than countries like the United States, with its extreme difference between wealthy and poor people. These health risks extend to mental health, and this pattern appears across the United States in states with more extreme income inequalities (Kahn, Wise, Kennedy, & Kawachi, 2000).

Life circumstances associated with poverty are also associated with poor mental health (Belle & Doucet, 2003). That is, not only does low income create many stresses, but unemployment or underemployment, divorce, single parenthood, problems in access to services, and lack of power and resources are all sources of stress that are associated with poverty and contribute to poor mental health. In addition, low income can lead to a host of problems, such as poor housing in high-crime neighborhoods, which exposes poor people to greater risks of violence and other community dangers. Thus poverty has an indirect as well as a direct link to risks that increase the likelihood for problems.

Poverty affects women and ethnic minority families more than other groups (Belle & Doucet, 2003). Single mothers are more likely to be poor than any other demographic group, not only affecting their mental and physical health but also placing their children at risk. Poverty has a negative impact on the ability to cope, depriving people of the ability to deal with other problems that can produce stress. Lack of money limits opportunities and choices, putting people in positions of dependency on government bureaucracy for housing, health care, food, and other essentials. The economically advantaged may be able to extricate themselves from problem situations and relationships that poor people cannot avoid. Both problem situations and the lack of any control over them can produce stress.

Discrimination.   In addition to poverty and violence, a community study of mental health functioning (Hendryx & Ahern, 1997) identified racism as a factor related to lower levels of mental health functioning. Using the Schedule of Racist Events (Landrine & Klonoff, 1996), a sample of African Americans reported a high incidence of racist discrimination within the year before the study, and 100% reported having experienced racist discrimination during their lives. The study also examined the stressful effects of the experience of racist discrimination and found that a positive relationship existed between experiences of racist discrimination and psychiatric symptoms.

Sexist discrimination is also a source of stress. The large traumas such as childhood sexual abuse and criminal victimization can produce problems; however, so can being subject to frequent discrimination and harassment, such as being denied a job or promotion or having to listen to sexist jokes. A national survey of U.S. residents (Kessler, Mickelson, & Williams, 1999) revealed that the experience of discrimination was common—33.5% of the participants reported some incidence of major discrimination, and 60.9% said that they had experienced less serious discrimination. This survey included all types of discrimination and focused on participants' perception of the extent and severity of discrimination. This study showed a substantial relationship between perceptions of discrimination and mental health problems.

The experience of sexist discrimination has also been related to mental health problems. In one study (Landrine, Klonoff, Gibbs, Manning, & Lund, 1995), the experience of sexist discrimination related to psychological distress in women and predicted some symptoms better than more general measures of stress. In a later study (Klonoff, Landrine, & Campbell, 2000), women who experienced a high amount of sexist discrimination exhibited more depression, anxiety, and physical complaints than women who experienced lower levels of sexist treatment. Indeed, the women whose experience with sexism was low showed symptom levels comparable to the men in the study.

To explain how discrimination might influence mental health, Jennifer Katz and her colleagues (Katz, Joiner, & Kwon, 2002) proposed and tested a model for ways in which being a member of a devalued group might affect mental health. One route is through the internalization of negative beliefs about one's group, which may affect self-concept and feelings of worth. A second route may act through discrimination based on membership in the devalued group, and a third route may operate through the behaviors that people in devalued groups exhibit as a result of their identification with the groups. Katz et al. (2002) found support for each of these three routes as possible pathways through which being female, lesbian, gay, or a member of a devalued ethnic minority group may affect mental health.

Thus, the experience of sexism may be a substantial factor in the greater number of psychiatric symptoms among women. Adding this factor to other sources of stress may help explain why women experience greater levels of distress than men do.

Coping Resources and Strategies

The number and intensity of stressors are important factors in any resulting problems, but resources and strategies for coping are even more important. Those who have resources to cope with the stresses in their lives may not perceive the situations as stressful. One theory of stress (Lazarus & Folkman, 1984) proposed that each person's appraisal of a potentially stressful situation varies according to his or her perception of the personal importance of the situation plus personal resources to deal with the situation. Those who do not have (or believe that they do not have) the resources to cope with events in their lives are vulnerable to stress, whereas similar experiences but better resources lead others to experience less stress. Thus, stress varies according to perception, which depends on the evaluation of resources for coping.

The resources for coping may differ for women and men; men often have more power and greater financial resources than women have. Power and money certainly offer advantages for avoiding many of life's problems and for dealing with others. For example, the loss of a job may be more stressful for a single mother of two with only a high school education and skilled as a salesclerk than for a married male engineer with an employed wife and a sizable savings account. Neither of these jobless people will avoid stress; losing a job is stressful for almost everyone. However, the engineer has social and material resources for dealing with his situation that the salesclerk lacks.

One of the most important differences between the male engineer and the female salesclerk is the social support the engineer has in the form of his family. The salesclerk may receive support from her children, but she must also offer them care and support. Women's roles generally carry obligations for providing support for others, whereas men's roles more often provide them with emotional support (Belle & Doucet, 2003; Gove, 1984). Receiving support is a large advantage in coping with stress, but providing care for others can be stressful. As Deborah Belle and Joanne Doucet (2003, p. 103) commented, ". . . social networks can serve as conduits of stress, just as they can serve as sources of social support." Thus, involvement in social relationships offers advantages and costs.

Social Support.   **Social support** is more than a matter of social relationships or social contacts; support implies providing emotional and material resources. Four different elements of social support are emotional concern, instrumental aid (such as money or other assistance), information and advice, and feedback (House, 1984). A person with few contacts with other people is more likely to be socially isolated than the person with many contacts, but social support requires more than contact or acquaintanceship. People who have a high amount of social support have a wide network of people on whom they can count for emotional and material support. Poor quality of support and small network size both relate to the development of anxiety and depression (Vandervoort, 1999).

As discussed in the "Friendships" section of Chapter 9, women are more likely than men to form friendships that include emotional intimacy, which may give them the advantage in creating networks that provide them with social support. Men's friendships tend to be activity oriented, which may offer them the material support but lack the emotional intimacy that is an important component of social support. Men's social support often comes from their relationships with women, on whom men tend to rely for emotional support as well as for many aspects of physical care. Single and divorced men are at greater risk for mental health problems than married men (de Vaus, 2002; Sachs-Ericsson & Ciarlo, 2000), again suggesting the importance of social support. Those at greater risk typically have less social support, and those at lesser risk typically have more sources of social support.

The breadth and strength of social networks vary with ethnicity as well as with gender (Aranda, Castaneda, Lee, & Sobel, 2001; Renzetti & Curran, 1992). Some ethnic groups maintain close family relationships, whereas in other ethnic groups, increased mobility and small families decrease the chances of having close friends. Hispanic, African, and Asian American families often experience extended family groupings, meaning grandparents, parents, children, and other relatives who live in close proximity. This pattern differs from the isolated nuclear family typical of many (but by no means all) European Americans, with resulting advantages and disadvantages. The advantages of an extended family include a wider range of people who offer their emotional and material support and advice. The disadvantages include many demands for emotional and material support (Belle & Doucet, 2003). If these other family members are poor (and members of ethnic minorities are more likely to be poor than members of the dominant ethnic group), then being part of a support network can lead to many demands and obligations. Thus, being part of an extended family network can provide social support, but it can also impose social costs, and these advantages and disadvantages operate within a social context that includes income and ethnicity.

Coping Strategies.   **Coping** is the process of changing thoughts and behaviors to manage situations that involve potential stressors (Lazarus & Folkman, 1984). How people deal with the events in their lives makes a critical difference in the amount of stress they experience, so having coping strategies is an essential factor in relieving part of the stress. These management strategies vary among people and situations, and these differences may distinguish among people who feel more or less stress. Table 14.3 lists coping strategies and gives examples of each.

The role of gender in coping with stress is not clear. Several models hold that gender-related differences exist, but research has not furnished results that fully clarify these varying views. One view (Taylor et al., 2000) holds that women react to stress in ways that differ from men's reactions. That is, the "fight or flight" reaction is more typical of men, whereas women's reactions to stressful situations can be described as "tend and befriend." This view

TABLE 14.3   *Examples of Coping Strategies*

Coping Strategy	*Behaviors That Exemplify This Strategy*
Seeking social support	Talk to someone who could help Talk to someone who has experienced similar problems Talk to friends or family who will sympathize
Problem-focused	Analyze the situation Plan a strategy to solve the problem Take action to get rid of the problem Concentrate on the problem
Emotion-focused	Become upset Express negative feelings
Denial	Refuse to accept the reality of the problem Try to ignore the problem
Turn to religion	Seek God's help Pray
Disengagement	Work on other activities Sleep more than usual Engage in distracting activities Consume alcohol or other drugs

ties together women's role as caregivers with neurohormonal reactions and evolutionary history, predicting that women's primary coping strategy will be seeking social support.

Views of gender-related differences in coping include the socialization view, which holds that women and men are socialized to react to stress differently (women with emotional coping and men with active, problem-solving strategies) and the structural view, which holds that gender-related differences in coping come from the different stressful situations women and men encounter (Ptacek, Smith, & Zanas, 1992). The evolutionary approach represents a third view of gender differences in coping, and one comment (Geary & Flinn, 2002) proposed that men also "tend and befriend" under some stressful circumstances.

Examining the research, more evidence exists for gender differences in the experience of stress than for differences in coping. In a study of Canadian college students (Day & Livingstone, 2003), female students rated situations as more stressful than male students did. Consistent with the tend-and-befriend view, women are more likely than men to seek social support when they experience stress (Taylor et al., 2000). Consistent with the socialization view, men in one study (Folkman & Lazarus, 1980) were more likely to report experiencing stressful situations at work and using problem-focused coping strategies for those situations. However, the men in this study were more likely to be employed than the women, and no difference appeared for the frequency of emotion-focused coping.

Studies have attempted to assess coping strategies for men and women in comparable situations, and the results have shown more similarity than difference in coping, with the exception that women tend to use social support more than men. A study of college students (Lengua & Stormshak, 2000) showed no gender differences for active, problem-focused, or avoidant coping, but the women in this study were more likely to seek social support than the men. Examining coping strategies among adolescents in Hungary (Piko, 2001) showed that girls were more likely than boys to seek social support, but boys who used this strategy showed fewer mental health problems than boys who used other coping strategies. In a study of workplace stress (Gianakos, 2002), women were more likely to use active coping strategies than men, and both sought social support, but men tended to rely on their workplace social networks whereas women relied on their family social networks for support. A study with industrial workers (Fontenot & Brannon, 1991) found that both men and women used similar coping strategies in similar situations, but significant situational differences appeared. Both women and men said that personal conflict situations were more likely to prompt emotion-focused coping and that task-related stress situations were more likely to elicit problem-focused coping strategies. These findings suggest that specific situations were more likely than gender to be the source of differences in coping efforts.

Another possibility is that the gender difference in coping does not really exist. A study that used two methods to measure coping (Porter et al., 2000) pointed to this possibility. This study asked male and female participants to fill out questionnaires about their coping strategies, but these participants also carried electronic diaries that prompted them to make a report every 40 minutes concerning their stress and coping. The reports showed no gender differences, but the questionnaires did. This result brings up the possibility that reports of gender differences in coping are biased by gender role stereotypes, and the few gender differences in coping may be research artifacts rather than genuine differences.

Therefore, situational factors and gender roles may be more important factors in coping than sex or personality traits. If so, gender differences in coping may be fairly large because men's and women's lives show many situational differences. Also, gender roles place women in more tend-and-befriend situations. Therefore, the stresses related to women's and men's lives continue to vary, and so do their coping strategies. The tendency of women to define more events as stressful, combined with stressors that occur more frequently in their lives, may account for some of the differences in behavior problems. Other possibilities for the source of these differences lie in the criteria and in the processes used to diagnose mental and behavioral disorders.

DIAGNOSES OF MENTAL DISORDERS

Before a sick person can receive appropriate treatment, the person must receive a **diagnosis,** a statement of the classification of a physical or psychological problem. Without a diagnosis, treatment would be haphazard and not connected with the problem. Thus, classification of both physical and mental problems is an essential step in receiving proper care. A good clinical classification system has several characteristics (Sarason & Sarason, 2001). Specifically, such a system should provide information about the cause of the condition, enable clinicians to make predictions about the course of the disorder, and suggest a course of treatment as well as methods of prevention. In addition, a system of classification should provide a set of common terminology for professionals to communicate among themselves. No system of diagnosis meets these goals perfectly, but the goals are common to the diagnosis of physical and mental problems.

Diagnosis is not a simple task; it consists of matching information about what constitutes a disorder against a description of symptoms. Because any person's symptoms will not match the textbook description of a disorder, clinicians' personal judgment is always a factor in the diagnostic process. This judgment provides for the possibility that personal bias can enter the diagnostic process.

Diagnosis is a necessary part of treatment, offering patients disadvantages as well as advantages (Sarason & Sarason, 2001). The advantages include providing an accepted standard that allows reliable diagnosis of the same problem by different clinicians. One of the problems involves labeling—the need to apply a label to the diagnosis. With mental disorders, many labels carry a stigma, and people who have been labeled with diagnoses of mental disorders may be the targets of discrimination. Furthermore, labeling also puts people into categories, and grouping people tends to magnify the similarities and obscure the individual differences of those within a category.

The diagnosis of mental disorders dates back to the time of Hippocrates, who used a simple four-category classification—mania, epilepsy, melancholia, and paranoia (Lerman, 1996). During the late 19th century, interest in mental disorders increased, and in 1917 the National Committee for Mental Hygiene in the United States published a manual to aid in diagnosis. Currently, two systems exist for the classification of mental disorders—the International Classification of Diseases (ICD) of the World Health Organization and the *Diagnostic and Statistical Manual of Mental Disorders (DSM)* of the American Psychiatric

Association. With the publication of the fourth edition of the *DSM,* the two systems became more compatible, but the *DSM* remains oriented to psychiatric diagnosis.

The *DSM* Classification System

The *Diagnostic and Statistical Manual of Mental Disorders (DSM)* of the American Psychiatric Association has become the standard for professionals who provide mental health care, especially in North America. Both the first version of the manual (1952) and the second edition (1968) were relatively brief and strongly influenced by psychoanalytic theory (Sarason & Sarason, 2001). Diagnosis required the clinician to understand the patients' internal, unobservable psychological processes. Understandably, these schemes of classification led to a great deal of variation in diagnoses.

The third edition of the *DSM* appeared in 1980 and represented a substantial revision. The goal was to create a description-based system of classification for mental disorders that would lead clinicians to make reliable judgments. A relatively minor revision of the *DSM-III* appeared in 1987. The *DSM-IV,* which appeared in 1994, contained no major changes but allowed for greater compatibility with the ICD, and in 2000 a text revision of *DSM-IV* appeared, enlarging the text descriptions but leaving the diagnostic categories unchanged.

The system of the *DSM* consists of five dimensions, or *axes,* which allow for comprehensive physical, psychological, and social diagnoses. The first three axes provide the diagnosis, and the two other axes provide an evaluation of stressors and overall functioning. The manual contains over 240 different diagnoses along with descriptions of the symptoms that characterize the disorders. Information also appears concerning typical age of onset, course of the disorder, and gender ratio of the disorder; that is, how common the problem appears in men compared to women. In addition, the manual also contains information concerning a comparison of other, similar disorders so that clinicians can distinguish among disorders that have similar symptoms.

Axis I describes the major clinical disorders, such as schizophrenia, depression, and anxiety disorders, among others. Axis II includes mental retardation and personality disorders, such as antisocial personality, histrionic personality, and dependent personality disorders. Axis III contains a classification of physical disorders and is compatible with the ICD diagnosis system. Axis IV allows for reporting of psychosocial and environmental problems related to the diagnosis of psychopathology, including events such as death of a loved one, problems in school, homelessness, or loss of a job. Axis V provides an overall rating of functioning on the Global Assessment of Functioning Scale, which takes psychological, social, and occupational functioning into account. Diagnosis includes a rating on each of the five axes.

For example, a diagnosis on Axis I might be **posttraumatic stress disorder (PTSD),** a subclassification within the category of anxiety disorders. The *DSM-IV-TR* describes the diagnosis for this disorder as composed of several criteria. To be diagnosed with posttraumatic stress disorder, the person must meet five criteria: (1) "the person experienced, witnessed, or was confronted with an event or events that involved actual or threatened death or serious injury, or a threat to the physical integrity of self or others . . . [and] the person's response involved intense fear, helplessness, or horror" (American Psychiatric Association,

2000, p. 467); (2) reexperience of the event in some form; (3) avoidance of stimuli associated with the traumatic event or numbing of responsiveness; (4) increased arousal, such as irritability, difficulty concentrating, or hypervigilance; and (5) duration of at least 1 month.

The combination of these criteria must be present and must produce "clinically significant distress or impairment in social, occupational, or other important areas of functioning" (American Psychiatric Association, 2000, p. 468) before a diagnosis of PTSD can be made. The *DSM-IV-TR* offers guidelines to the clinician for the different forms of reexperiencing the event, the types of avoidance and numbing that might occur, and the symptoms of increased arousal that accompany PTSD.

In addition, the manual includes examples of the types of unusual events that might precipitate PTSD, examples of the behaviors of affected individuals, and descriptions of disorders that often accompany PTSD. Depression and substance-related disorders often coincide with PTSD, sometimes preceding and sometimes developing after the traumatic stress. If evidence of these disorders exists, the clinician should diagnose all of the conditions. Although the *DSM* provides the gender ratio for many diagnoses, no such information appears for PTSD.

For a person with a diagnosis of PTSD on Axis I, the Axis II diagnosis might or might not indicate pathology. That is, an Axis I diagnosis of a certain clinical disorder does not necessarily coincide with a problem in the developmental and personality disorders described on Axis II. Nor does one prohibit the other. The clinical disorders on Axis I and the personality disorders on Axis II may be related, but the diagnoses are made according to separate criteria. Thus, many people who receive a diagnosis of PTSD have no other conditions that predispose them to the disorder and might receive diagnoses of "no problem" on Axis II (Sarason & Sarason, 2001). Alternatively, people with PTSD might have other separate developmental or personality disorders, which may relate to the PTSD. Some personality disorders, such as paranoid personality disorder, would tend to worsen PTSD.

If the person with a diagnosis of PTSD has developed the disorder as a result of a combat experience or rape, then the person may also have physical injuries that stem from the same situation. The distinction between symptoms produced by PTSD and physical injury such as brain damage may be particularly difficult to distinguish during diagnosis (O'Donnell, Creamer, Bryant, Schnyder, & Shalev, 2003). The Axis III diagnosis would note injuries or other physical conditions that could affect the person's psychological functioning.

Axis IV gives the clinician an opportunity to note any social and environmental problems that might affect the development, recurrence, or exacerbation of mental disorders. The *DSM-IV-TR* instructs clinicians to note as many of these problems as are relevant and that have occurred within the prior year. PTSD is an exception, however; these events may have occurred more than a year before diagnosis and still be relevant to the problem.

Axis V allows the clinician to rate the person on the Global Assessment of Functioning Scale, based on overall psychological, social, and occupational functioning (excluding physical and environmental limitations). This scale ranges from 1 to 100, with low numbers indicating a low level of functioning and high numbers indicating less impairment. For example, a person with PTSD resulting from combat experiences might also show alcohol abuse, sleep problems, sensitivity to loud noises, and outbursts of violence with little provocation. Such a person would probably receive a global assessment rating between 50 and 60, indicating moderate difficulty in social and occupational functioning. But PTSD can produce symptoms that result in more or fewer problems in functioning.

The *DSM-III, DSM-III-R, DSM-IV,* and *DSM-IV-TR* represent improvements over the earlier versions of the *DSM*. The extensive descriptions of problem behavior allow clinicians to match patients' symptoms to the descriptions without relying on unobservable, internal psychological processes. Despite this advantage, the system has sparked heated controversy. Criticisms include a lack of research support, adding and deleting diagnoses for political rather than scientific reasons, and adding diagnoses that may not be abnormal (Kutchins & Kirk, 1997; Marecek, 2001). The lists of behaviors that serve as criteria for each diagnostic category give the impression of objectivity, but little research supports these criteria (Lerman, 1996). Therefore, the impression of objectivity is an illusion.

Criticism has also arisen concerning the *DSM*'s inclusiveness; some of the diagnostic categories describe behaviors that are arguably within the normal range. For example, nicotine dependence and nicotine withdrawal are diagnoses applied to smokers and smokers who have quit, respectively. Applying diagnoses in such cases implies that these behaviors represent diagnosable mental disorders. Many people, including mental health care professionals, disagree with the extension of diagnostic classifications to behaviors that fall within the range of normal for many people.

Gender Inequity in the Diagnosis of Mental Disorders

Criticisms of the multiaxial system of the *DSM* appeared immediately following its release in 1980. Some of these criticisms concerned gender bias in this diagnostic system. A number of critics (Kaplan, 1983a, 1983b; Lerman, 1996; Marecek, 2001) have asserted that the *DSM* system includes descriptions of disorders that make women likely to be diagnosed with problem behavior, even when the behavior is not due to any pathology. Indeed, the assumption that men provide a standard makes it likely that any behavior found more commonly in women will be viewed as pathological. The process of diagnosis is influenced by social values, and generally "professionals have used male-based norms to define healthy versus pathological behavior" (Cook, Warnke, & Dupuy, 1993, pp. 312–313). This bias has resulted in behaviors such as independence and assertiveness considered to be important for healthy mental functioning, whereas emotional expressiveness may be considered the sign of a problem.

The *DSM* system has also received criticism for its failure to consider the life circumstances and culture of those receiving diagnoses (Lerman, 1996; Marecek, 2001). Both versions of the fourth edition of DSM made specific efforts to sensitize clinicians to the importance of cultural factors in diagnosis, but some critics (Dana, 2001) have contended that these efforts have not gone far enough. Despite the warnings about cultural factors in behavior, the conceptualization of diagnosis for behavior problems focuses on personal behavior. This focus assumes that disorders reside within the person, and that the person's circumstances, although possibly relevant, are not the source of the problem. Thus, if a battered woman experiences distress or depression, she will still be diagnosed by her symptoms as having depression or one of the anxiety disorders. The violence of her home life may be taken into account; however, even though the symptoms warrant a diagnosis of mental disorder, that diagnosis is given to her, not to her batterer or her home circumstances. Thus, people may receive diagnoses and then treatment for depression or substance abuse disorder without addressing the social context of the problem and without the clinician considering it appropriate to do so. A survey of clinical psychology interns (Middaugh, 1994) showed that 19% of male (but only 5% of female) interns believed that female clients must learn to adjust to their life circumstances. Although these percentages indicate that a minority of clinicians holds such attitudes, this minority holds women responsible for the behavior of others.

As noted in Chapter 13, the normal female functions of reproduction and childbearing have become "medicalized," as have other conditions that should fall within the range of normal. This criticism applies to **premenstrual dysphoric disorder (PMDD),** the diagnosis applied to symptoms that are very similar to premenstrual syndrome (PMS) (Marecek, 2001). A diagnostic category limited only to women is destined to provoke controversy; such controversy has continued with the publication of the *DSM-IV* and its inclusion of PMDD.

In 1972, Phyllis Chesler proposed that diagnosis of mental disorders is fundamentally gender biased. Chesler contended that women who overconform or underconform to the traditional feminine gender role are subject to diagnosis; if they are either too aggressive or too submissive, they are deviant. Although Chesler's argument centered on the diagnosis of women's problems, the rationale can also extend to men. Those men who fail to conform to the male gender role may be at increased risk for diagnosis. One study (Rosenfield, 1982) offered confirmation for Chesler's contention by demonstrating that gender role stereotypes relate to psychiatric diagnosis. Women and men who showed signs of psychopathology that were more typical of the other gender were more likely to be judged as candidates for hospitalization than were those who showed gender-typical disorders. Men with depression or anxiety disorders, and women with personality disorders or substance abuse problems—patients displaying "deviant" deviance—were judged more likely to be candidates for hospitalization than were men who showed substance abuse disorders or women who showed depression—the more "normal" disorders for those genders.

Criticisms of gender bias have been more frequent for the Axis II personality disorders than for Axis I disorders. Part of the criticism has focused on the poorer research sup-

GENDERED VOICES

I Think I Have It

Male psychologist: "Have you read the new description of PMS that will appear in the fourth edition of the *DSM*? I'm really very concerned."

Female psychologist: "Yes, I have. *Premenstrual dysphoric disorder* will replace *late luteal phase dysphoric disorder*. I'm concerned, too. It's supposed to appear in

the main body of the classification under mood disorders, and I understand that the treatment will be antidepressant drugs. It's been very controversial, and I think that this move will keep it that way. What bothers you?"

Male psychologist: "According to my reading of the diagnostic criteria, I think I have it."

port for the personality disorders: "The claims to a scientific basis for these diagnoses hang upon an extremely slender thread" (Brown, 1992, p. 215). Other criticism has aimed at the possible gender, ethnic, and social class biases for these disorders, and the *DSM-IV* warned clinicians that they "must be cautious not to overdiagnose or underdiagnose certain Personality Disorders in females or in males because of social stereotypes about typical gender roles and behaviors" (American Psychiatric Association, 2000, p. 688).

The *DSM* warning is warranted; the differential diagnosis for mental disorders can be conceptualized by viewing personality disorders as extensions of gender role stereotypes. For example, **schizotypal personality disorder** is characterized by "a pervasive pattern of social and interpersonal deficits marked by acute discomfort with, and reduced capacity for, close relationships as well as cognitive or perceptual distortions and eccentricities of behavior" (American Psychiatric Association, 2000, p. 697). **Antisocial personality disorder** appears as a "pervasive pattern of disregard for, and violation of, the rights of others" (p. 701), including lying, fighting, stealing, and physical cruelty. Both these personality disorders include exaggerations of the traditional male gender role (Brannon, 1976). Indifference to social relationships resembles the Sturdy Oak facet of the role, with its emphasis on self-reliance and lack of emotion. Elements of antisocial personality disorder resemble the Give 'Em Hell facet, with its emphasis on dominance and aggression.

Dependent personality disorder features "a pervasive and excessive need to be taken care of that leads to submissive and clinging behavior and fears of separation" (American Psychiatric Association, 2000, p. 721), which is an exaggeration of stereotypical feminine behavior. Table 14.4 shows some of the personality disorders, along with their prevalence and the gender-related differences in their diagnosis. An examination of the diagnostic criteria for personality disorders (Funtowicz & Widiger, 1999) revealed that the

TABLE 14.4 *Prevalence of and Gender-Related Differences in Personality Disorders*

Disorder	Estimated Rate in General Population	Gender Difference
Paranoid	0.5–2.5%	More common among men in clinical populations
Antisocial	3% men 1% women	More common among men in both general and clinical populations
Avoidant	0.5–1.0%	Equally frequent in women and men
Borderline	2%	More common in women—75% of those diagnosed are women
Histrionic	2–3%	More commonly diagnosed in women
Narcissistic	<1%	More common among men—50–75% are men
Dependent	Most common of personality disorders	More commonly diagnosed in women
Schizotypal	3%	Slightly more common in men

Source: Based on *Diagnostic and Statistical Manual of Mental Disorders* (4th ed., Text Revision), by American Psychiatric Association, 2000, Washington, DC: Author.

categories that seem to be exaggerations of the female gender role do not contain a lower threshold of pathology than the stereotypically male categories. Thus, these Axis II diagnoses do not discriminate against women more than against men, but the entire group of diagnoses varies in the degree of psychopathology necessary for a diagnosis; some require low levels of pathology.

Both the gender bias for several personality disorders and the ease of diagnosis became apparent in several studies. Not only clinical psychologists and psychiatrists (Landrine, 1987) but also college students (Landrine, 1989) were able to match descriptions of stereotypical cases to the various personality disorders. For example, participants assigned a diagnosis of antisocial personality disorder to the description of a lower-class man, the single middle-class woman was identified as histrionic, and the married middle-class woman received a diagnosis of dependent personality disorder. Only the married upper-class man was without pathology. Given descriptions of the personality disorders, college students were able to supply demographic information that was similarly stereotypical. Thus, both professionals and university students perceive consistent gender and social class patterns associated with the personality disorders, which correspond to the frequency of such diagnoses.

A more fundamental criticism of diagnoses of mental disorders revolves around the concern that women will be considered less psychologically healthy than men because in any system, men constitute the standard for what is mentally healthy (Bem, 1993b). An early study (Broverman, Broverman, Clarkson, Rosenkrantz, & Vogel, 1970) laid the foundation for the concerns over gender bias in the clinical diagnosis of mental disorders by asking what constitutes a well-adjusted, healthy adult. The results showed that clinically trained psychologists, psychiatrists, and social workers described a well-adjusted, healthy person in different terms than a well-adjusted, healthy woman. For example, such stereotypically feminine traits as dependence and emotionality are not part of the concept for adult mental health. These researchers contended that the discrepancy between the ideal of mental health for a woman and that for an adult reflected a double standard. However, later studies (Phillips & Gilroy, 1985; Wood, Garb, Lilienfeld, & Nezworski, 2002) have revealed no significant gender-related differences for standards of mental health.

Even without overall bias within the system, gender and ethnic biases may enter the diagnosis process through clinicians' personal biases and their influence on the decision about pathology (Wood, Garb, et al., 2002). This process may include two types of judgment errors—overdiagnosis and underdiagnosis (López, 1989). The most commonly studied form of diagnostic bias has been *overdiagnosis,* identifying people as having disorders when they do not. *Underdiagnosis* is the mistake of failing to identify problems by overlooking symptoms. Both present problems for patients by identifying problems in people who have no pathology and by failing to diagnose problems in others who have mental disorders.

Research on under- and overdiagnosis has confirmed their existence but has also found a pattern of gender bias (Redman, Webb, Hennrikus, Gordon, & Sanson-Fisher, 1991). Overdiagnosis was more common for female patients, and underdiagnosis was more common for male patients. These gender differences appeared when contrasting the diagnoses on standardized assessment of psychological disturbance with physicians' clinical judgment of the degree of disturbance. The standardized assessment showed a similar number of men and women as psychologically disturbed, but the physicians did not. Instead, physicians showed a tendency to underrate the psychological disturbances of men and to overrate those of women. A later review (Wood, Garb, et al., 2002) confirmed the tendency to both overdiagnose and underdiagnose certain psychological problems, but concluded that these problems occur more often for cultural differences than for gender.

Therefore, both the *DSM* system and the process of diagnosis contain the potential for bias. The *DSM* contains descriptions of disorders that allow clinicians to decide which diagnosis is appropriate for a particular person. These diagnoses are included in the *DSM* through a committee decision that may be motivated by social or political reasons rather than accuracy or scientific research. The descriptions of several diagnoses seem like exaggerations of gender stereotypes, and the number of women and men who receive these diagnoses vary. In addition, clinicians may find it difficult to keep their personal beliefs from intruding into the diagnosis process, providing another route for gender and cultural bias in the diagnosis of mental disorders.

GENDER COMPARISONS IN PSYCHOPATHOLOGY

Chapter 13 presented information about gender differences in seeking health care, showing that women are more likely than men to seek health care. This tendency also applies to psychological problems. Data from large-scale surveys of mental health problems (Kessler, Brown, & Broman, 1981; Substance Abuse and Mental Health Services Administration [SAMSHA], 2002) showed that women seek mental health care more often than men do. Several possibilities exist for this difference, including women's tendency to interpret problems as mental health problems (Kessler et al., 1981). Women's help-seeking is responsible for between 10% and 28% of the gender difference in treatment.

The circumstances that bring women and men to treatment vary. Women are more likely than men to consult general physicians about mental health problems, which opens the possibility for additional mental health consultations. Men do not make as many physician visits as women (see Chapter 13), so a comparable number of opportunities do not arise for them. The overall rate of hospitalization for mental disorders is somewhat higher for women (USBC, 2002), but the difference occurs primarily in older people. For men and women in other age groups, men have slightly higher hospitalization rates and longer stays than women.

Not all disorders show gender differences, but several do. Anxiety disorders, depression, and substance abuse disorders are among those problems that show marked gender differences, whereas schizophrenia and bipolar disorder are more evenly distributed between women and men.

Depression

The clinical diagnosis of *depression* varies from the popular conception of minor, temporary, low mood; depression is a severe, debilitating disorder that affects all aspects of functioning. In the *DSM* system, depression is classified as a type of mood disorder and appears as a diagnosis on Axis I. Two subclassifications of depressive disorders exist—major depression and dysthymia.

Symptoms of **major depression** include dissatisfaction and anxiety, loss of interest and loss of pleasure, feelings of helplessness and hopelessness, changes in sleep or eating habits, and difficulty in concentrating. These symptoms must persist for at least 2 weeks to warrant a diagnosis of major depression. **Dysthymia** is milder than major depression and tends to be a chronic condition that may last for years. This diagnosis applies to people who chronically experience depressed mood, loss of interest, or other symptoms of depression, much as they would a personality trait. Major depression and dysthymia can co-occur or can exist separately.

Table 14.5 shows the prevalence of and gender-related differences in mood disorders. The ratio of major depression in women compared with that in men is about 2 to 1, considering either the figures obtained from treatment or those from community surveys (Culbertson, 1997; Kessler, 2003). These numbers apply to many (but not all) societies around the world, and the explanations for these figures have included biological as well as social and cognitive theories. The biological theories rely on the differences in reproductive hormones to account for gender differences in depression, but simple versions of hormonal theories have very little clear support (Nolen-Hoeksema, 2001).

Reproductive hormones may play some role in depression for both women and men. Jill Cyranowski and her colleagues (Cyranowski, Frank, Young, & Shear, 2000) hypothesized that hormones associated with the onset of puberty, girls' needs for affiliation, and negative life events combine to make girls and women more vulnerable to depression. Alan Booth and his colleagues (Booth, Johnson, & Granger, 1999) researched the connection between testosterone and depression in men and found a complex relationship. For men with low testosterone levels, the lower their hormone level, the higher their rate of depression. For men with high testosterone levels, the relationship between the two factors was positive: The higher the hormone level, the higher the rate of depression. Booth et al. hypothesized that the relationship of negative life events and high testosterone is the basis of this association; men with high testosterone are more likely to exhibit antisocial, employment, and marriage problems, which are all risk factors for mental health problems. Therefore, hormones may be a factor in depression, but their role is quite complex, not clearly established, and not restricted to women.

TABLE 14.5 *Prevalence of and Gender-Related Differences in Mood Disorders*

Disorder	Estimated Rate in General Population	Gender Difference
Major depression	10–25% for women 5–9% for men	More common in women, with a ratio of 2:1
Dysthymia	3%	More common in women, with a ratio of 2–3:1
Bipolar disorder	0.4–1.6%	No difference

Source: Based on *Diagnostic and Statistical Manual of Mental Disorders* (4th ed., Text Revision), by American Psychiatric Association, 2000, Washington, DC: Author.

Although most societies show a ratio of female to male depression similar to that of the United States, gender differences in depression do not occur during childhood (Twenge & Nolen-Hoeksema, 2002) but begin during adolescence (Wade, Cairney, & Pevalin, 2002). In addition, several rural, nonmodern cultures have similar rates of depression in women and men. Among these cultures are the old-order Amish, a rural farming society in the United States. In addition, university students, the elderly, and the bereaved show no gender differences in rates of depression. These exceptions suggest a strong situational component for the gender differences in depression, and a number of researchers have pinpointed social and family roles as the source of this difference. (See the "Family Roles" section earlier in this chapter for a review of the gender differences in stress.)

Alternative explanations for gender differences in depression come from differences in the use of cognitive strategies for dealing with distressing events. Susan Nolen-Hoeksema and her colleagues (Nolen-Hoeksema, 2001; Nolen-Hoeksema & Jackson, 2001; Nolen-Hoeksema, Larson, & Grayson, 1999) proposed that the gender differences in depression come from a combination of differences in negative experiences, feelings of mastery, and strategies for dealing with negative feelings. Women have more negative experiences, lower feelings of mastery, and tend to ruminate on their feelings. Dwelling on problems and negative feelings tends to amplify the feelings, which can lead to depression. Rather than ruminate, men tend to take action, which may not solve problems but does provide distraction. Figure 14.1 shows the complex relationship among these factors. This pattern of interrelationships appeared in a large community study and suggested that women may become involved in a cycle of stress from negative events, low feelings of mastery, rumination, and depression. The relationship between rumination as a style of coping and the development of depression also appeared in a study of adolescents (Broderick & Korteland, 2002).

Another cognitive explanation for women's higher rates of depression is that their genuine emotions, goals, and desires become suppressed (Jack, 1991, 1999). According to this view, women are more prone to depression because society devalues women and the feminine, placing women in a position in which they must deny who they really are to get along in the world and to maintain their relationships; when women lose their sense of self, they become depressed. Research support for this view is mixed. Several studies have confirmed that scores on Silencing the Self Scale relate to depression (Carr, Gilroy, & Sherman, 1996; Gratch, Bassett, & Attra, 1995; Page, Stevens, & Galvin, 1996), but not for everyone. This relationship was true for European American women, but not for African American women (Carr et al., 1996). In studies that included men (Duarte & Thompson, 1999; Gratch et al., 1995; Page et al., 1996), the relationship between self-silencing and depression was significant, and men showed higher self-silencing scores than women did. In a factor analysis (Cramer & Thoms, 2003), the factor structure of the Silencing the Self Scale was similar for women and men. This finding and the results that indicate that men's scores are higher than women's pose problems for this view of depression—this view holds that women (not men) experience circumstances that lead to their higher rate of depression. Thus, these gender similarities cast doubt on this view.

Although gender differences exist in the diagnosis of depression, perhaps no differences occur in the frequency of negative mood (Nolen-Hoeksema, 1987; Sachs-Ericsson & Ciarlo, 2000). That is, women and men may experience the negative feelings that underlie

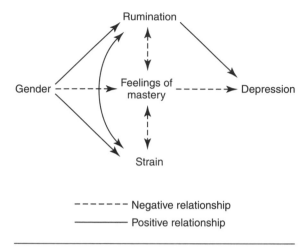

FIGURE 14.1 *Effects of Gender, Rumination, Strain, and Feelings of Mastery on Depression*

Source: Adapted from "Explaining the Gender Difference in Depressive Symptoms," by S. Nolen-Hoeksema, J. Larson, and C. Grayson, 1999, *Journal of Personality and Social Psychology, 77*, p. 1067. Copyright 1999 by the American Psychological Association. Adapted by permission of Susan Nolen-Hoeksema.

depression at similar rates, but they express their feelings differently. Women tend to turn their negative feelings inward, whereas men tend to take action. In women, the feelings produce symptoms consistent with the female gender role and hence with the *DSM* diagnostic criteria for depression. In men, the feelings produce symptoms such as substance abuse, risk taking, and violence.

Support for this conception comes from a study that examined symptoms among high school seniors (Casper, Belanoff, & Offer, 1996). The young men reported anger as their most common problem, whereas the young women listed sadness. Therefore, the symptoms of depression may be seen as an expression of gender role socialization for women, but men exhibit different symptoms that receive other diagnoses.

In summary, two types of depression appear in the *DSM* classification—major depression and dysthymia. Women from many cultures are more likely than men to report symptoms of and receive treatment for depressive disorders at a ratio of approximately 2 to 1. Several explanations exist for this gender difference, including factors that make women vulnerable to depression, such as family role differences, personal control differences, and cognitive differences in coping with negative events. Another view holds that the gender differences in depression are a product of the ways in which women and men deal with distress. Women become passive, expressing symptoms of depression, and men become active, expressing symptoms of risk taking, violence, drug use, or some combination of these three behaviors.

Substance-Related Disorders

Substance-related disorders involve the use of **psychoactive substances,** drugs that affect thoughts, emotions, and behavior. Examples include alcohol, amphetamines, marijuana (cannabis), cocaine, hallucinogens, opiates, sedatives, and hypnotics. In order to be diagnosed as having one of the types of substance-related disorders, the person not only must use the drug but also must exhibit a strong desire to use the substance and experience problems in social or occupational functioning due to drug use.

Alcohol is the most frequently used and abused substance, and men drink more than women in the categories of light, moderate, and heavy drinking (SAMSHA, 2002). Indeed, drinking and drunkenness are associated with the male, and not the female, gender role (Caparo, 2000). People expect men to drink beer and to get drunk, but the same expectation does not apply to women. Indeed, women (and especially feminine women) are not expected to drink beer (but are expected to drink wine) and should *not* get drunk (Landrine, Bardwell, & Dean, 1988).

Alcohol is not equally intoxicating for men and women. Women tend to weigh less than men, and body weight affects intoxication, meaning that each drink has a greater effect on a smaller person. In addition, some research has indicated that women's metabolism of alcohol produces a higher alcohol concentration in their blood compared to that in men's blood, even with the body-weight factor taken into account (Mumenthaler & Taylor, 1999). Both these factors result in greater risks to women who drink moderately or heavily than to men who do so. Because fewer women than men are heavy drinkers, however, men are more likely than women to experience the problems associated with heavy drinking, including the health risks and social problems associated with alcohol abuse.

A variety of evidence suggests that drinking is related to depression, in both men and women. Alcohol and other substance abuse disorders often co-occur, but the direction of the relationship has not been clear. Several longitudinal studies have demonstrated that some people use drinking (and probably other substances) as a strategy of avoidant coping (Holahan, Moos, Holahan, Cronkite, & Randall, 2001, 2003). In both a group of community adults (Holahan et al., 2001) and in a group of people diagnosed with depression (Holahan et al., 2003), the association between drinking and depression appeared. For the individuals diagnosed as depressed (Holahan et al., 2003), 43% of those who used the strategy of drinking to cope with stress and problems escalated their drinking or developed alcohol-related problems over the 10 years of the study. Thus, the drinking-to-cope strategy constitutes a risk of alcohol problems for depressed people. In the community sample (Holahan et al., 2001), people who reported that they used drinking as a way to cope tended to escalate their drinking and were more likely to develop problem drinking over the 10-year period of the study than people who drank for other reasons. Therefore, the link between drinking and depression may be through the strategy of drinking to cope with stress and problems.

Illegal drug use is also higher among men than women, with men more likely than women to use and abuse drugs such as heroin, amphetamines, cocaine, and marijuana—a pattern that parallels their alcohol use (SAMHSA, 2002). On the other hand, women are more likely to use prescription tranquilizers and sedatives. That is, women are more likely to describe symptoms to physicians, which leads to their diagnoses of having mental disorders treatable by drugs (Travis & Compton, 2001). The higher rate of prescription drug use by women and the greater use of illegal drugs by men result in similar rates but different patterns of substance use. Table 14.6 summarizes the prevalence of and gender-related differences in substance use.

Men's drug use is more apt to be illegal, making them more likely to receive diagnoses because of their drug use. This diagnosis difference may not reflect much of a differential tendency in substance use: "The sex differences in the use of alcohol and prescription psychotropics are not inconsistent with the hypothesis that men and women are equally likely to resort to substance use for coping, and that the sex difference is merely in the choice of substances" (Biener, 1987, p. 336). Perhaps women might also resort to illegal drug use if physicians were less willing to prescribe drugs for them.

In summary, the research indicates that a relationship exists between depression and drinking. The tendency to drink more heavily when depressed is stronger among men but not exclusive to them. Perhaps men choose this strategy for dealing with negative feelings more often than women do, so this difference in dealing with negative feelings may account for some of the gender differences in depression and substance abuse disorders. The overall pattern of drug use for men and women probably differs little, but women tend to use legal prescription drugs, whereas men's drug use is more likely to come in the form of alcohol and illegal drugs.

TABLE 14.6   *Prevalence of and Gender-Related Differences in Substance-Related Disorders*

Disorder	Estimated Rate in General Population	Gender Difference
Alcohol dependence	5%	More common in men, with a ratio as high as 5:1, varying with age and cultural background
Amphetamine dependence	Possibly as high as 1.5%	More common in men, with a 3:1 or 4:1 ratio
Cannabis	1.2%	More common in men
Cocaine	0.2%	More common in men, with a 1.5–2:1 ratio
Hallucinogens	0.1%	More common in men, with a 3:1 ratio
Opiates	2%	More common in men, with a ratio of 1.5–3:1
Sedatives, hypnotics, or anxiolytics	<1%	Women are at higher risk

Source: Based on *Diagnostic and Statistical Manual of Mental Disorders* (4th ed., Text Revision), by American Psychiatric Association, 2000, Washington, DC: Author.

Anxiety Disorders

The group of disorders labeled anxiety disorders includes panic attack, phobias, obsessive-compulsive disorder, and posttraumatic stress disorder, all involving features of anxiety and avoidance of problem situations. A survey of over 18,000 people indicated that anxiety disorders affect more than 7% of adults in the United States (Regier, Narrow, & Rae, 1990). No gender differences exist for some types of anxiety disorders, but other types appear much more often in women than in men.

Panic attack is characterized by periods of intense fear that occur without any fear-provoking situation. These attacks are typically accompanied by physical symptoms of distress, such as sweating, dizziness, and shortness of breath. This disorder is about equally common in women and men, but panic disorder with **agoraphobia** is about twice as common in women. "The essential feature of agoraphobia is anxiety about being in places or situations from which escape might be difficult (or embarrassing) or in which help may not be available in the event of having a panic attack . . . or panic-like symptoms" (American Psychiatric Association, 2000, p. 432). These feelings of anxiety lead people to avoid the situations that might provoke such feelings.

Agoraphobia can also occur without panic disorder, and women are also more likely to have this disorder (American Psychiatric Association, 2000; Carlbring, Gustafsson, Ekselius, & Andersson, 2002). Other **phobias,** unreasonable fears concerning some object or situation, constitute a second category of anxiety disorder. *Social phobias* appear as persistent fears of certain social situations, such as speaking in public, in which the person is judged by others or in which the person may do something embarrassing. The American Psychiatric Association (2000) stated that women in the general population are more likely to have social phobias, but in clinical populations, the gender ratio is either closer to equal, or men predominate. *Specific phobias,* fears of some object or situation other than anticipating a panic attack or being in a certain social situation, are more common among women.

Obsessive-compulsive disorder is the combination of obsession, which refers to recurrent, intrusive thoughts about something the person would prefer to ignore, and compulsion, which refers to repetitive behaviors intended to ease anxiety. To receive this diagnosis, a person must be distressed by the obsessive thoughts and must spend over an hour per day on the compulsive behaviors. According to the *DSM-IV-TR* (American Psychiatric Association, 2000), this pattern of behavior is equally common in women and men but more common among boys than girls. Other research (Fireman, Koran, Leventhal, & Jacobson, 2001) has confirmed the gender difference for children but found obsessive-compulsive disorder more common among adult women than men.

Posttraumatic stress disorder (PTSD) (defined and discussed earlier in this chapter) was originally applied to men who suffered lasting effects from their war experiences. As research accumulated on PTSD, its wider application became evident. Now the diagnosis is given to people experiencing the prolonged aftereffects of many different types of trauma, including natural disasters, accidents, and violent crime as well as military combat. A random sample of women revealed that over 12% met the criteria for PTSD, a much higher percentage than previous estimates (Resnick, Kilpatrick, Dansky, Saunders, & Best, 1993). Both a community survey (Stein, Walker, & Forde, 2000) and a study of 16- to

22-year-olds (Cuffe et al., 1998) showed that women were more likely than men to develop PTSD, possibly because of the varieties of trauma and violence to which they are victim (Pimlott-Kubiak & Cortina, 2003).

Table 14.7 summarizes the prevalence figures presented in *DSM-IV-TR* and the differences associated with gender for these disorders. Overall, more women than men receive diagnoses of some type of anxiety disorder, indicating that agoraphobia and specific phobias are sufficiently common to cause women to dominate this category.

Women with anxiety disorders experience more severe symptoms than men with anxiety disorders do. Anxiety and fear are more characteristic of the female gender role than of the stereotypical male role. The match between gender role traits and mental disorders that appears in personality disorders (Landrine, 1987, 1989) may also apply to anxiety disorders and may constitute an explanation for the higher overall rate of anxiety disorders among women. The gender differences among the different anxiety disorders suggest varying gender-related ways of expressing anxiety.

Other Disorders

Several important classifications of mental disorders show few or no gender differences in prevalence, but men and women with these disorders may not exhibit identical symptoms or the same time course of the disorder. For example, **schizophrenia**—a serious and complex disorder involving thought disturbances, problems in personal relationships, and possibly hallucinations—has been diagnosed with almost equally frequency in women and men.

This equal prevalence does not require that men and women have identical experiences with the disorder, and they do not. Several studies (Kalisz & Cechnicki, 2002; Usall et al., 2001) have found that male schizophrenics were younger than female schizophrenics at the time of their diagnosis, men were less likely to be married than women, and

TABLE 14.7 *Prevalence of and Gender-Related Differences in Anxiety Disorders*

Disorder	Estimated Rate in General Population	Gender Difference
Panic attack with and without agoraphobia	1–3.5%	More common in women, with a ratio of 2–3:1
Specific phobias	4–8.8%	More common in women, with a ratio of 2:1
Social phobias	2–20%	More common in women in general population; more common in men in clinical settings
Obsessive-compulsive disorder	0.5–2.1%	No difference
Posttraumatic stress disorder	8%	Not specified in *DSM-IV*

Source: Based on *Diagnostic and Statistical Manual of Mental Disorders* (4th ed., Text Revision), by American Psychiatric Association, 2000, Washington, DC: Author.

women's social functioning was better than men's. The severity of symptoms tended to be similar, but men were more likely than women to have been hospitalized in the year before the study. Despite these advantages for women, they tend to have more severe symptoms than men as both age (Seeman, 2003). Despite these differences, male and female schizophrenics exhibited more similarities than differences. (See "According to the Media" and "According to the Research," which present media confusion about schizophrenia.)

Bipolar disorder is one of the mood disorders, along with major depression and dysthymia (see Table 14.5). Bipolar disorder is characterized by periods of mania, high activity, and elevated mood alternating with periods of depression. These drastically different mood states change in a cyclic fashion such that the affected person experiences both mania and depression over a period of weeks or months, usually interspersed with periods of normal moods. Unlike the other two mood disorders, bipolar disorder shows no gender differences in prevalence (American Psychiatric Association, 2000). However, women may manifest symptoms somewhat differently, especially in cycling from manic to depressed more rapidly (Amsterdam, Brunswick, & O'Reardon, 2002).

The **somatoform disorders** show some gender differences. This classification of disorders includes problems with physical symptoms of disease, but no identifiable physical basis for those symptoms. As a group, women are more likely to receive the diagnosis of somatoform disorder, but some of the disorders within this classification show no and others show large gender differences. *Conversion disorder,* the loss of physical function without any physical basis for the disability, was originally called *hysteria.* In the late 1800s, this disorder was so strongly associated with women that the extension of the label to men was controversial. The *DSM-IV-TR* (American Psychiatric Association, 2000) listed conversion disorder as substantially more common in women than in men.

Another of the somatoform disorders is *somatization disorder,* the recurrence of physical complaints and the seeking of medical attention without receiving any diagnosis of a physical problem. These complaints are often dramatic or exaggerated, and the affected person seeks care from many medical professionals. Women account for 95% of somatization disorder patients (Tomasson, Kent, & Coryell, 1991). The diagnosis is rare for men in the United States, but in other cultures, men develop this disorder (American Psychiatric Association, 2000).

The *DSM-IV-TR* cautions that physical disorders that involve many variable symptoms can erroneously lead to the diagnosis of somatization disorder. Given physicians' tendency to dismiss the physical complaints of women and attribute those complaints to emotional problems (see Chapter 13), this diagnosis may be erroneously applied to women who have physical rather than mental problems. Indeed, physical and psychiatric disorders share many symptoms, and diagnostic bias can cause women to receive psychiatric diagnoses when they actually have physical disorders (Klonoff & Landrine, 1997).

Sexual disorders consist of two groups of disorders, paraphilias and sexual dysfunctions. **Paraphilias** are characterized by intense sexual feelings in response to objects or situations, such as nonhuman objects, children, nonconsenting persons, or even the suffering of self or others. The nonhuman objects include animals or items of clothing, and the situations include exposing one's genitals to strangers, fondling strangers in public places, observing sexual activities, or dressing in gender-inappropriate clothing. Sexual masochism—experiencing pleasure from receiving pain or humiliation—and

⧉ ACCORDING TO THE MEDIA . . .

Multiple Personality Disorder Creates Violent Men

In the movies, dissociative identity disorder (DID) is a popular plot device, but DID is referred to by the older term *multiple personality disorder* and often confused with schizophrenia (Byrne, 2001). In *Me, Myself and Irene* (2000), Jim Carrey's character is called a "schizo" whose split personalities both fall for the same woman. This movie was a comedy, but DID is usually not played for laughs; instead, movies featuring characters with DID either dramatize a case study of an individual with DID or present a fictional character as part of a plot revolving around this character's disorder. The former movies usually feature female characters; the latter more often show men with DID.

The fictionalized case studies of DID include *The Three Faces of Eve* (1957), *Sybil* (1976), and *Voices Within: The Lives of Trudi Chase* (1990). All of these movies presented stories based on women who had experienced the symptoms typical of this disorder, in-

cluding childhood trauma; memory "blackouts" during which alternate personalities dominate; and a core personality that is passive, dependent, and plagued by feelings of guilt and depression (American Psychiatric Association, 2000). These fictionalized stories also contain a number of inaccuracies, but the movies in which DID is a plot device portray individuals with dissociative personality disorder who are typically male and violent. In movies such as *Psycho* (1960), *Raising Cain* (1992), *Primal Fear* (1996), and *Fight Club* (1999), men with DID commit murder (or try to get away with murder). Even in the movies that present fictional female characters with DID such as *Dressed to Kill* (1980) and *Never Talk to Strangers* (1995), these female characters are killers. These movies send the message of "hidden evil in the person tainted with mental illness" (Byrne, 2001, p. 27).

sexual sadism—experiencing pleasure from inflicting pain or humiliation on one's sexual partner—are also among the paraphilias. About 5% of sexual masochists are women (American Psychiatric Association, 2000), and this disorder is the most common paraphilia among women, which indicates that women are rarely diagnosed with these disorders.

Sexual dysfunctions, the other subcategory of sexual disorders, consist of abnormally low (or high) levels of sexual desire, or difficulty achieving arousal or orgasm. Women are more likely to receive diagnoses indicating abnormally low levels of sexual desire or inhibited orgasm, but men also experience these sexual problems. A summary of the prevalence of and gender-related differences in schizophrenia, somatoform, and sexual disorders appears in Table 14.8.

When people receive diagnoses of abnormally low (or high) sexual interest or activity, these diagnoses require a standard of comparison, which may be their previous behavior as compared with their currently decreased (or increased) interest. The standard can also be the clinician's judgment about what is normal, and this standard may be biased or arbitrary. Despite warnings in the *DSM* concerning other physical or behavioral problems that can produce sexual dysfunctions, the possibility exists that patients may be held to some arbitrary standard of what constitutes normal levels of sexual activity, and they may be diagnosed on the basis of behavior that is deviant merely by definition.

ACCORDING TO THE RESEARCH . . .

People with Dissociative Identity Disorder Are Usually Nonviolent Women

The movie portrayals of multiple personalities as killers offer screenwriters an easy way to show bizarre, violent behavior, but these media images depart from typical cases in many ways. First, the term *multiple personality disorder* is no longer the one used to describe this disorder. The current term is *dissociative identity disorder* (DID). This disorder was rarely diagnosed until the 1980s, and its increase has made it controversial (American Psychiatric Association, 2000). However, the disorder has always been distinct from schizophrenia, which is much more common, affecting about 1% of the population.

An even greater inaccuracy is the portrayal of individuals with DID as violent. "Confusing schizophrenia with DID is unfortunate, but the violence these films depict adds misunderstanding to misinformation. That misunderstanding equates 'split personality' with 'nice guy/murderer'" (Byrne, 2001, p. 27). Even Jim Carrey in *Me, Myself, and Irene* (2000) had a violent (but comic)

personality that got into a fight with himself, as did Edward Norton's character in *Fight Club* (1999). However, that character was also a murderer.

Research on the influence of media portrayals of people with mental illness has revealed that these depictions have the power to influence people's attitudes and behaviors. The association of mental disorders and violence in the media is exaggerated; characters with mental illness are 10 to 20 times more likely to be violent than actual mental patients or former mental patients (Diefenbach, 1997). In addition, a study with college students showed a relationship between negative attitudes toward the mentally ill and watching portrayals of mental disorders on television (Granello & Pauley, 2000). Therefore, the inaccurate depictions of DID in the media serve not only to convey inaccurate information but also to perpetuate the stigma associated with mental illness.

In summary, several mental disorders show patterns of gender differences, and some disorders that have no overall discrepancy in prevalence do show gender differences in onset or experience. The most dramatic gender differences occur for anxiety and somatoform disorders—diagnoses overwhelmingly given to women—and sexual paraphilias—diagnoses overwhelmingly given to men. Schizophrenia and bipolar disorder show no gender difference in prevalence, but male schizophrenics show some behavioral differences compared to female schizophrenics. The gender differences in bipolar disorder relate to rapidity of cycling, with women more likely to cycle rapidly.

Although psychopathology constitutes more than exaggerated gender role behavior, all gender differences in mental disorders lend themselves to interpretations through a lens of gender. People tend to exhibit pathology related to their gender roles; that is, women show signs of weakness and physical complaints, whereas men show violence and unusual sexuality. These behaviors are consistent with traditional gender roles. The patterns in rates of mental disorders for men and women reflect the power of gender roles. The most common patterns of disorder for both men and women show consistencies with what are considered to be appropriate gender-related behaviors. When violations of gender roles occur, clinicians are likely to perceive that these patients have more severe problems than patients who exhibit psychopathology consistent with their gender roles.

The Doctor Wouldn't Listen

The case of a young woman who was in one of my classes is a good example of a woman whose physician failed to take her complaints seriously. This young woman felt unwell, experiencing a variety of symptoms including chest pain, abdominal pain, and lack of energy. She consulted her physician, who had been her family's doctor since she was a child. He asked her about her symptoms and about her life. She described how she felt and where it hurt, along with the stresses and problems she had recently experienced: Her parents were getting divorced, and she felt so tired that school was difficult to manage. The physician said that she was experiencing stress and told her to relax, assuring her that she would feel better.

She tried but felt no better. After several visits, the woman was convinced that she had a problem that the physician was missing, and he was equally convinced that she had a mental problem that she failed to ac-

knowledge. She consulted another physician, who might have behaved much as the first did, but instead, the physician did a series of tests that revealed a kidney tumor, which required immediate surgery. Her many symptoms and the stresses in her life were consistent with a number of diagnoses, but her family physician failed to take her physical complaints seriously, insisting that she was experiencing psychological distress rather than organically based physical problems.

This woman's experience is by no means unique. Men may also be erroneously diagnosed in a medical examination, but the overwhelming majority of horror stories of physical problems diagnosed as psychological disorders come from women who have experienced biased diagnosis and treatment. Therefore, biased diagnosis may be the source of some of the gender differences in somatization disorder.

TABLE 14.8 *Prevalence of and Gender-Related Differences in Rate of Selected Axis I Disorders*

Disorder	Estimated Rate in General Population	Gender Difference
Schizophrenia	0.5–1.5%	Slightly higher rate in men
Somatoform disorders		
Conversion disorder	11–500 per 100,000	More common in women, with a ratio of 2–10:1
Somatization disorder	0.2–2% in women < 0.2% in men	Rarely diagnosed in men in the United States
Body dysmorphic disorder	Unknown	Equally common in men and women
Dissociative identity disorder	Controversial	More common in women, with a ratio of 3–9:1
Sexual dysfunction		
Paraphilias	No estimate	Rarely diagnosed in women, with the ratio of men to women at 20:1

Source: Based on *Diagnostic and Statistical Manual of Mental Disorders* (4th ed., Text Revision), by American Psychiatric Association, 2000, Washington, DC: Author.

CONSIDERING DIVERSITY

Gender stereotypes are not the only possibility for biased diagnosis with the *DSM* system; ethnic stereotypes can also influence the labeling of mental disorders. The *DSM* system represents the summary of the American Psychiatric Association's evaluation of mental disorders, and the psychiatrists who compose this organization are mostly male and mostly White. As previous sections of this chapter have proposed, the descriptions of categories within the *DSM* system have received criticisms for including gender and ethnically biased components. The *DSM* system has also been criticized for containing a western bias, which may be a problem for people from different cultures who live in a western country.

The latest edition of the *DSM* (American Psychiatric Association, 2000) contains repeated warnings to clinicians to be sensitive to culture when making diagnoses. The diagnostic categories correspond to symptoms that people manifest in cultures around the world (U.S. Department of Health and Human Services [USDHHS], 2001a), but an appendix of the *DSM* describes *culture-bound syndromes,* patterns of abnormal behavior that are unique to a specific cultural group. For example, *ghost sickness* is a disorder recognized by several Native American tribes and consists of a preoccupation with death or a specific deceased person. The symptoms include nightmares, dizziness, anxiety, confusion, and even hallucinations. *Ataque de nervios* is a disorder experienced in Latin American and Mediterranean cultures and includes symptoms of uncontrollable shouting and crying, fainting episodes, a sensation of heat that rises within the body, and aggressive outbursts. These behaviors are usually precipitated by some stressful event, and the affected person (who is usually a woman) may have no memory afterward of the events that occurred during the *ataque.* Neither ghost sickness nor *ataque de nervios* fits within a diagnostic category of the DSM, and clinicians who are following the guidelines to be sensitive to culture should be familiar with and consider these syndromes when making diagnoses.

Research on clinician bias has suggested that the cultural sensitivity recommended by the *DSM* may not occur as often as it should (Wood, Garb, et al., 2002). When comparing the diagnosis made by a clinician to the diagnosis by a standardized assessment, the agreement was better for White than for non-White clients. This finding suggests that clinicians are influenced by the ethnicity of clients in making diagnoses, and a study (Trierweiler et al., 2000) that examined diagnoses of schizophrenia for African Americans confirmed the presence of bias. This diagnosis bias may be responsible for the findings that people of African descent receive more diagnoses of schizophrenia than White people both in the United States (Trierweiler et al., 2000) and in the United Kingdom (Boydell et al., 2001). The reports of symptoms varied between African Americans and Whites (Trierweiler et al., 2000), but even when African Americans reported symptoms consistent with depression, the tendency was to diagnose them as schizophrenic.

Another naturalistic study of over 26,000 African American, Mexican American, Vietnamese American, Philippino American, and European American clients of a county mental health agency (Flaskerud & Hu, 1992) found fewer ethnic differences in psychiatric diagnoses and treatment than were expected. The relationship between ethnic background and psychiatric diagnosis showed differences for ethnic background in certain categories of diagnosis, but few differences in overall rates. Those differences included a greater proportion of African American and Asian American clients receiving diagnoses of serious mental disorders compared with European American clients, who, in turn, received more of these diagnoses than Hispanic clients did. Asian American clients were less likely than any other ethnic group to receive diagnoses involving substance abuse. Surprisingly, these researchers failed to find any differences in diagnoses relating to social class.

Other research has identified both ethnicity and social class as factors in psychiatric disorders as well as in access to treatment (USDHHS, 2001a). After controlling for several factors including socioeconomic level, the difference in rates of diagnosed mental illness between African Americans and White Americans disappeared. However, educational and income levels are lower for African Americans and Hispanic Americans than Whites, and thus these two factors relate to the risk of mental illness. Without statistical controls for these factors, they make a significant difference in risk for mental health problems.

Looking beyond the United States, similarities appear in psychopathology and in the factors related to its development around the world. However, different countries show different rates of problems (WHO International Consortium in Psychiatric Epidemiology, 2000). For example, a much higher percentage of people in the United States and the Netherlands (over 40%) reported some type of serious psychological problem during their lifetime than did people in Mexico (20%) or Turkey (12%).

The factors that relate to the development of mental disorders in the United States also operate throughout the world, including the disproportionate hazard to women (Desjarlais, Eisenberg, Good, & Kleinman, 1995). Inequitable treatment in family relationships, poverty and economic discrimination, and violence exert a negative impact on women, putting them at risk. Both women and men who live in war-torn areas are at increased risk for PTSD as a result of the violence in their countries, and women's lack of education, limited access to good jobs, and dependence on men for survival place women at risk for depression and anxiety disorders, which are more common diagnoses for women than for men throughout much of the world. Like men in the United States, men throughout the world receive more diagnoses of drug and alcohol abuse, suggesting that the gender role's pressures that prompt U.S. men to cope with negative feelings by alcohol and drug use operate in many cultures. As in the United States, psychopathology tends to follow gender role patterns.

SUMMARY

Women experience more stress than men, and women's roles are the most probable sources of these differences. Women's roles often obligate them to provide physical and emotional care for their families, but they may not receive as much social support as they give. An increasing body of evidence has implicated violence as a factor contributing to a variety of mental disorders. Al-

though men are the more common targets of violent crime, women are more commonly the victims of intimate violence, including childhood sexual abuse, rape, and spouse battering. Poverty is also a source of stress that disproportionately affects women and ethnic minorities, both of whom have higher rates of mental disorders than White men. Discrimination is a pervasive experience that increases stress in the lives of both ethnic minorities and women.

Comparisons of women's and men's coping strategies have been complicated by the need to examine differences in stressful situations in their lives. Studies that fail to control for these factors tend to support the stereotypical view that women use emotion-focused techniques more often and men use problem-focused coping. Not only do situational factors affect coping, but also women and men seem ready to report the use of gender-stereotypical coping strategies, which suggests that self-report studies are biased.

Gender differences in patterns of psychopathology have been the source of accusations of gender bias in construction of categories and in the process of diagnosis. These criticisms have centered around the *Diagnostic and Statistical Manual of Mental Disorders (DSM)* of the American Psychiatric Association. This publication contains a descriptive, multiaxial system for assigning diagnoses to people's behavioral problems. Using the *DSM* system, clinicians match each patient's symptoms against a description and make diagnoses on each of five axes. Axis I contains descriptions of the major clinical disorders, Axis II describes mental retardation and personality disorders, and Axis III provides a diagnosis of physical conditions. Axis IV contains a listing for the stressors in the person's life, and Axis V allows for an overall rating of level of functioning.

Women's higher rate of treatment and the gender differences in some categories of disorders have led some critics to argue that there is gender bias in the *DSM,* especially in the personality disorder diagnoses that appear on Axis II. The descriptions of these disorders appear to exaggerate traits of the female and male gender roles, and the expected gender differences appear.

The clinicians who apply the criteria may also be biased, holding men as the standard for both women's and men's mental health. Early research indicated that clinicians value masculine traits above feminine ones. These biases may be weakening, but physicians are more likely to overdiagnose women's and underdiagnose men's mental disorders. Although clinicians may not be personally prejudiced, their limited attention to gender and ethnic information can lead them to use this information in biased ways in their diagnoses, creating differences in the numbers of women and men who are given various diagnoses.

Many categories of mental disorders show few gender differences, but major depression and substance-related disorders show marked gender differences, with women being more often diagnosed with depression and men more often diagnosed with substance abuse problems. Various explanations for these differences exist, but one explanation holds that the gender differences in these two behavior problems reflect differences in expressing similar underlying, negative feelings: Women express their negative feelings in the form of depression, whereas men express their negative feelings in the form of alcohol and drug abuse.

Other mental disorders show few gender differences in prevalence, such as obsessive-compulsive disorder, schizophrenia, and bipolar disorder. Those disorders that do tend to fall along gender stereotypical lines, such as phobias, which are more common among women, and paraphilias, which are far more common among men. Therefore, the patterns of abnormal behavior reflect aspects of the gender roles of women and men.

Ethnic bias may also affect diagnosis of mental disorders, and several ethnic groups in the United States receive diagnoses at higher rates than Whites do. People in these ethnic groups tend to be more burdened with risks such as poverty, violence, and discrimination. Patterns of gender difference exist throughout the world, but so do the factors that relate to the development of mental disorders, including stresses in family life, poverty, violence, and discrimination.

GLOSSARY

agoraphobia   a phobic disorder characterized by anxiety about being in places or situations in which escape might be difficult or embarrassing.

antisocial personality disorder   a personality disorder that is characterized by irresponsible and antisocial behavior such as lying, fighting, stealing, and physical cruelty.

bipolar disorder   one of the mood disorders, characterized by periods of mania, high activity, and elevated mood alternating with depression.

coping   the process of changing thoughts and behaviors to manage situations that involve potential stressors.

dependent personality disorder   a type of personality disorder that features excessive desires to be cared for combined with submissive, clinging behaviors and fear of separation.

diagnosis   classification of a physical or psychological problem.

dysthymia   diagnosis within the category of mood disorders that is applied to milder but chronic symptoms of depression, including depressed mood, loss of interest and pleasure, or other symptoms over an extended period, often for months or years.

major depression   diagnosis within the category of mood disorders that is applied to severe symptoms of depression, such as dissatisfaction and anxiety, loss of interest and pleasure, feelings of helplessness and hopelessness, changes in eating or sleep habits, and difficulty concentrating.

obsessive-compulsive disorder   the combination of obsession (recurrent, intrusive thoughts about something the person would prefer to ignore) and compulsion (repetitive behaviors intended to prevent anxiety).

panic attack   one of the anxiety disorders, characterized by periods of intense fear that occur without any fear-provoking situation and accompanied by physical signals of distress.

paraphilias   a type of sexual disorder characterized by intense sexual feelings in response to objects or situations that are unusual.

phobias   unreasonable fears concerning some object or situation.

posttraumatic stress disorder (PTSD)   one type of anxiety disorder that involves the experience of some distressing event outside the range of normal human experience, the reexperience of the event, avoidance of stimuli associated with the event, and increased sensitivity to associated experiences. These symptoms must persist for at least one month.

premenstrual dysphoric disorder (PMDD)   a controversial diagnostic category that appears in an appendix of *DSM-IV*. Its symptoms are those of premenstrual syndrome, and the broad description of these symptoms presents the possibility that vast numbers of women could be diagnosed as mentally ill.

psychoactive substances   drugs that affect thoughts, emotions, and behavior.

schizophrenia   a serious and complex disorder involving thought disturbances, problems in personal relationships, and possibly hallucinations.

schizotypal personality disorder   a personality disorder characterized by "pervasive pattern of social and interpersonal deficits marked by acute discomfort with, and reduced capacity for, close relationships as well as cognitive or perceptual distortions and eccentricities of behavior."

sexual dysfunctions   a subcategory of the sexual disorders that includes problems with low or high level of sexual desire, or difficulty achieving arousal or orgasm.

social support   receipt of emotional and material resources from friends and family members.

somatoform disorders   a classification of disorders that includes problems with physical symptoms of disease but with no physical basis for these symptoms.

stress   a response that occurs when circumstances place people in situations that tax or exceed their resources and endanger their well-being.

SUGGESTED READINGS

Brooks, Gary R. (2001). Masculinity and men's mental health. *Journal of American College Health, 49,* 285–297.

Brooks discusses the "dark side of masculinity" and how fulfilling the masculine gender role may be a danger to men's mental health but also a problem for women.

Lerman, Hannah. (1996). *Pigeonholing women's misery: A history and critical analysis of the psychodiagnosis of women in the twentieth century.* New York: Basic Books.

Lerman's provocative book includes a historical review of the diagnostic process and many varieties of criticism of the ways that women's distress has been categorized.

Marecek, Jeanne. (2001). Disorderly constructs: Feminist frameworks for clinical psychology. In Rhoda K. Unger (Ed.), *Handbook of the psychology of women and gender* (pp. 303–316). New York: Wiley.

Marecek's review of feminist clinical psychology is arranged around five themes that allow her to discuss the clinical bias against women, the disorders that occur in a higher prevalence in women, theories of women's difference, the relationship between social context and disorders, and feminist therapy.

Nolen-Hoeksema, Susan. (2001). Gender differences in depression. *Current Directions in Psychological Science, 10,* 173–176.

This brief article summarizes Nolen-Hoeksema's theory and research concerning the role of rumination in the development of depression and how women are more likely to use this cognitive coping strategy.

Vandervoort, Debra. (1999). Quality of social support in mental and physical health. *Current Psychology, 18,* 205–222.

Vandervoort thoroughly reviews the research on social support and its relationship to both mental and physical health.

15 TREATMENT FOR MENTAL DISORDERS

Talking about feelings, emotions, and problems are the core of psychotherapy, but these activities are often unappealing to men. Yet Tony Soprano, the lead character in the HBO series *The Sopranos,* may have prompted some change in that attitude (Philadelphia, 2001). In the first episode of the series, Tony waited for Dr. Jennifer Melfi, who talked to him about the panic attacks he had experienced and asked him about his view of the cause. Tony's discomfort was obvious, but he persisted with his therapy.

Tony's initial reluctance to consult a therapist and his discomfort in the first session were typical of not only most men but most people. His behavior may have made an impact outside the fictional world of gangsters in New Jersey. According to Desa Philadelphia's (2001) article, his acceptance of therapy may have influenced other "tough guys" to bring their problems to a therapist. Psychotherapists quoted in Philadelphia's article said they are seeing more male patients, and almost everyone talks about Tony Soprano.

Tony's therapist, Dr. Jennifer Melfi, is a psychiatrist who prescribed drugs for Tony in addition to conducting therapy sessions. Prescribing Prozac is common among psychiatrists, but conducting lengthy therapy sessions is more typical of the treatment Tony would receive from a psychologist. A psychologist would not be able to prescribe Prozac in most states in the United States because this treatment is restricted to physicians. However, psychologists use a variety of therapy approaches to help people with problems, and Tony's reluctance to seek psychotherapy reflects the gender differences in attitudes toward counseling. However, women's acceptance of therapy does not mean that they always receive good care.

APPROACHES TO THERAPY

Formal psychological treatment for mental disorders or behavior problems has a relatively short history, and throughout that history, source of problems. Until the middle of the 19th century, the dominant belief was that abnormal and socially unacceptable behavior was a moral or spiritual problem, and few treatment procedures existed for people with mental disorders (Russell, 1995). The reconceptualization of mental disorders from possession by demons or moral deficiencies to problems in mental functioning came about during the 19th and early 20th centuries, and medicine became the model for understanding these problems. With the growing acceptance of mental illness as analogous to physical illness, medical researchers began to seek methods of treatment for abnormal behavior.

Therapies for the treatment of mental disorders arose and became part of psychiatry and psychology. The earliest modern therapy was **psychoanalysis,** Freud's version of talk-based treatment for psychological problems, although other therapists who were dissatisfied with psychoanalysis devised alternative talk-based therapies. The proliferation of treatment for behavior problems came to include **behavior modification,** a technique based on operant conditioning applied to changing undesirable behavior. Like Dr. Melfi on *The Sopranos,* psychiatrists use psychoactive drugs in the treatment of behavior problems—sometimes instead of, and sometimes in addition to, psychotherapy. Therefore, a variety of treatments for people with mental disorders now exists.

Psychoanalysis

Sigmund Freud was among the early researchers who investigated causes of and sought cures for mental disorders. He developed a system of therapy that has influenced treatment as well as contemporary thinking about mental disorders. Psychoanalysis is a talk-based approach geared toward understanding and alleviating psychological problems that was part of Freud's comprehensive theory of personality development and functioning. (Chapter 5 presented the Freudian approach to personality development.) Freud believed that psychological problems develop when people are incapable of dealing with problems and use **repression** to push problematic material into the region of the unconscious. The unconscious does not function rationally, so repressed material has the potential to remain in the unconscious throughout childhood and adulthood and can produce problems at any time.

Psychoanalysts attempt to help patients resolve their problems by bringing unconscious material to consciousness so that patients may deal with these problems rationally. Once patients gain insight into the source of their conflicts, Freud believed that the conflict would disappear. Therefore, bringing repressed material to consciousness was a goal of psychoanalysis. Table 15.1 summarizes the elements of psychoanalytic therapy.

Although Freud and his colleagues were physicians, psychoanalysis developed as a psychological treatment for mental disorders; the source of mental disorders was psychological, and the treatment was accomplished through talking about the problems. Medically based treatments for mental disorders also developed, but talked-based psychotherapy remains a prominent approach to the treatment of problem behavior.

Dissatisfaction with some aspects of psychoanalysis prompted the development of other therapies, but they were also based on talking about problems. Karen Horney (1939) was one of the psychoanalysts who protested the Freudian view of women and offered alternative approaches to dealing with psychological problems. Her theory and therapeutic interventions are the basis for a contemporary talk-based therapy (Westkott, 1997). (See Chapter 5 for more about Freud's theory and Horney's alternatives to Freudian theory.)

TABLE 15.1 *Elements of Psychoanalytic Therapy*

Category	Description
Underlying source of problems	Childhood trauma plus insufficient ego to deal with trauma
Cause of problems	Repression of unconscious conflict
Immediate source of problems	Repressed material escapes from unconscious
Goal of therapy	To bring repressed material to consciousness
Techniques	Talking, free association, dream analysis
Practitioners	Psychoanalysts (who are usually psychiatrists)

Other alternative therapies originated with Carl Rogers (1951), who developed a humanistic approach to therapy called client-centered therapy, and Albert Ellis (1962), who developed a cognitive therapy called rational-emotive therapy. These therapists objected to the emphasis on the unconscious in psychoanalysis and offered therapies that emphasized coping with current life problems rather than exploring developmental trauma from childhood.

Humanistic Therapies

The psychoanalytic view of human nature is rather pessimistic, holding that psychological development is filled with potentially debilitating problems and that few people develop into healthy adults. In contrast to psychoanalysis, humanistic theories of personality hold a more optimistic view: People are innately drawn toward fulfilling their human potential. If they fail, the reasons lie in their circumstances and in their environments, which somehow prevent the complete development of their full potentials. This context-sensitive, optimistic view of humanity is reflected in Carl Rogers's client-centered therapy and Frederick (Fritz) Perls's Gestalt therapy.

Rogers (1951, 1961, 1980) proposed that human development follows a natural course toward health unless events impede this development. Rogers believed that problems originate from distortions in self-concept, and these distortions arise from a lack of acceptance of true feelings. When children get messages that the feelings they experience are unacceptable, they begin to deny these feelings. Lack of acceptance of feelings leads to inaccuracies in self-concept and interferes with many facets of development.

Client-centered therapy seeks to help people develop their full potential by providing a safe therapeutic environment (Kaplan & Yasinski, 1980). To form a relationship with an empathic, acceptant, and genuine counselor is of primary importance. Thus, client-centered counselors offer three conditions to their clients—unconditional acceptance, empathy, and congruence. The most important of these is congruence: "To be congruent means to be real or genuine, to be whole or integrated, to be what one truly is" (Feist & Feist, 2002, p. 474). These three conditions are essential for clients to experience growth, and all three arise from clients' relationship with the counselor. Given these three conditions, the process of therapy occurs.

A major goal of client-centered therapy is to eliminate discrepancies between clients' actual feelings and the feelings they recognize. By coming to recognize their true feelings—including negative feelings—clients can accept themselves. That is, clients develop congruence during the course of successful client-centered therapy. In addition, they become open to change and new experiences, develop a freshness of attitude, and come to trust in themselves.

The counselor does not work directly on changing clients, who must do that for themselves. The counselor's job is to provide clients with therapeutic relationships so that clients can reclaim their abilities to move toward personal growth and development. The focus is on allowing clients to think in undistorted ways, assuming that behavior changes will follow.

Gestalt therapy, another humanistic therapy, has similarities to client-centered therapy. Perls (1969), the originator of this therapy, believed that psychological problems come from feelings of not being whole, so he named his therapy *gestalt,* after the German word for whole. The failure to acknowledge their emotions leads people to this feeling of not being whole; they have a sense that parts of themselves have been psychologically disowned. Gestalt therapy seeks to help clients become whole again by allowing them to recognize and express their emotions, and Gestalt therapists use a variety of techniques oriented around understanding and integrating emotions to further this goal.

The humanistic therapies all share the view that fulfillment is a natural goal that people can reach, but barriers exist that block psychological growth. Humanistic therapists attempt to provide an atmosphere that permits clients to move in the natural direction of self-enhancement. Table 15.2 summarizes the elements of humanistic therapy.

Cognitive Therapy

Clients' thoughts are important in humanistic therapy, but these thought processes are the major focus in cognitive therapy. Cognitive therapists believe that thought processes are

TABLE 15.2   *Elements of Humanistic Therapy*

Category	Description
Underlying source of problems	Discrepancy between genuine feelings and acknowledged emotions; feelings of not being whole
Cause of problems	Blockage of development toward full potential
Immediate source of problems	The problem that prompts a client to seek therapy
Goal of therapy	To provide an atmosphere that allows clients to move toward personal growth
Techniques	Empathic listening, providing unconditional positive regard, showing congruence
Practitioners	Psychologists, social workers, counselors

the basis of feelings and behavior; they create psychological problems and also provide the potential for alleviating those problems. Behavior and emotions follow from cognition, so changes in cognition provide the foundation for changes in behavior.

Ellis (1962) developed rational-emotive therapy, one of the earliest cognitive therapies, in response to what he saw as the failure of psychoanalysis to solve people's problems. Ellis objected to both the length and nondirective nature of psychoanalysis, insisting instead that therapists should set goals and that therapy should be brief and problem oriented.

Rational-emotive therapy views psychological problems as a result of people's irrational beliefs. Such beliefs lead people to unrealistic views of themselves and the world, and when these expectations go unmet, people make themselves miserable. Rational-emotive therapy attempts to change these irrational thoughts and assumes that a change in cognitions will produce changes in emotions and behavior. Correcting these irrational beliefs is the basic goal of rational-emotive therapy.

Aaron Beck (1985) developed a cognitive therapy specifically for depression, which concentrates on the distorted, self-defeating thoughts that accompany depression. Beck contended that depressed people overgeneralize personal failures into the belief that they are worthless, and that they explain positive occurrences as exceptions to the general rule of failure. Depressed people also magnify the enormity of negative events, seeing these events as catastrophic and unchangeable. Selective perception is another cognition that adds to depression, causing depressed people to notice the negative elements of their surroundings and ignore the positive ones. These distortions of thinking magnify and maintain negative cognitions and thus perpetuate depression.

Beck's cognitive therapy attempts to help clients change their negative thinking patterns by testing the beliefs to evaluate their validity. Rational-emotive therapy attempts to confront irrational beliefs with logic, but Beck's cognitive therapy is less directive and more experiential. Rather than arguing against such cognitions, Beck might formulate ways for clients to evaluate their thought processes and test their accuracy. Lack of pleasure is often a prominent component of depression, and Beck's cognitive therapy urges depressed people to introduce pleasurable experiences into their lives.

Table 15.3 summarizes cognitive therapies. These therapies, such as Beck's cognitive therapy, assume that cognitions underlie psychological problems and that changing cognitions will change behavior. Rather than concentrating on behavior itself, these therapies concentrate on thoughts. Another therapeutic orientation takes an alternative approach—behavior modification emphasizes behavior rather than cognitions.

Behavior Modification

Behavior modification arose from laboratory research in psychology on the process of learning. In exploring learning principles, researchers discovered that the principles of operant conditioning—reinforcement and punishment—are powerful forces in determining behavior. Not only do these principles apply to the nonhuman animals commonly used in laboratories, but they also apply to humans and their complex behaviors. As applied to behavior problems, behavior modification theory holds that such behaviors are learned and

TABLE 15.3 *Elements of Cognitive Therapy*

Category	Description
Underlying source of problems	Irrational beliefs
Cause of problems	Application of irrational beliefs to personal circumstances
Immediate source of problems	The problem that brings a person to therapy
Goal of therapy	To change irrational beliefs to more rational beliefs
Techniques	Confronting and disputing irrational beliefs; testing the validity of negative cognitions
Practitioners	Psychologists, social workers, counselors

maintained by reinforcement and punishment, and application of these two principles can change unacceptable behavior.

Behavior modification strives to replace inappropriate or deviant behaviors with other healthier behavior patterns through operant conditioning. Although both have been used in behavior modification programs, reinforcement for desirable behavior is more common than punishment for undesirable behavior.

Behavior modification is more specific and task oriented than talk-based psychotherapies are. For example, behavior modification is often the choice for various skills training, such as developing assertiveness, dealing with phobias, or changing eating patterns. In such programs, a client learns to replace maladaptive behaviors with other responses that are adaptive and acceptable in specific situations. Women are the most common clients for behavior modification because they are the ones who most often seek treatment for assertiveness problems, eating disorders, depression, and phobias.

Cognitive behavior therapy is a variation of behavior modification that incorporates the concept that cognition is an important factor in behavior, and the application of principles of reinforcement is used to bring about behavioral changes (Fodor, 1988). As with behavior modification, this therapeutic approach assumes that problems are the result of learned patterns of maladaptive behavior.

The process of cognitive behavior therapy typically differs from behavior modification in several ways, however. Rather than concentrating on behavior and ignoring internal cognitive processes, cognitive behavior therapy attempts to change thought patterns and thereby change behavior. This therapy tends to be more collaborative than behavior modification, with the client playing an active role. Client and therapist cooperate to establish goals, and the client, rather than the therapist, may monitor and reward the desired behavior. Table 15.4 summarizes behavior modification and cognitive behavior therapy.

Behavior modification and cognitive behavior therapy have been used as alternatives to more traditional therapies and differ from the psychoanalytic and humanistic approaches. The behavior modification approach emphasizes specific problems and the need to analyze the behavior that contributes to the problem. This behavior-oriented emphasis

TABLE 15.4 *Elements of Behavior Modification and Cognitive Behavior Therapy*

Category	Description
Underlying source of problems	None
Cause of problems	Behavior that is not adaptive or successful in specific situations
Immediate source of problems	The problem that brings a person to therapy
Goal of therapy	To change behavior (or cognitions that underlie behavior) to more acceptable alternative behaviors
Techniques	Reinforcement for acceptable behaviors, desensitization for phobias, assertiveness training
Practitioners	Psychologists, social workers, counselors

is also important in knowing when and how to apply reinforcement to change maladaptive to more adaptive behaviors. Therefore, behavior modification and cognitive behavior therapy represent different approaches to understanding and treating problem behavior.

Some therapists use behavior modification and cognitive behavior therapy with all clients and for all problems. Many therapists, however, take a more eclectic approach, using a variety of techniques rather than adhering to a single therapy orientation. These therapists argue that an eclectic approach offers them the opportunity to choose from a variety of approaches, fitting the problem and the client to the approach.

Medical Therapies

Talk-based psychotherapies and behavior modification are practiced by psychologists, social workers, counselors, and psychiatrists, but psychiatrists and other physicians can also use medical therapies for behavior problems. Psychoactive drugs are the most common of the medical therapies, but **electroconvulsive therapy** is also a medical approach to behavior problems. These medical therapies take the approach of altering brain functioning in order to change thoughts and behavior, but the exact mechanisms of the therapeutic benefits for both psychoactive drugs and electroconvulsive therapy are not completely understood. Nonetheless, physicians may use these therapies in conjunction with psychotherapy or alone.

Since the 1950s, both the use of and the number of psychoactive drugs have increased. Psychiatrists now use psychoactive drugs to treat schizophrenia, depression, and anxiety disorders. Women receive more drug prescriptions than men, and this difference is higher for both psychoactive as well as other types of drugs. Over 30 years ago, a review of the patterns of prescription psychoactive drug use in Canada, the United States, and the United Kingdom showed a consistently higher rate of use for women (Cooperstock, 1970). In addition, this review revealed evidence for both differences and similarities in patterns of drug use. The similarities included a higher rate of use for both women and men not in the workforce. The differences included a greater use of tranquilizers by women during early adulthood and middle age, compared to men's use of tranquilizers, which peaked at older ages.

Since that review, the prescription of psychoactive drugs has increased for both men and women, but the pattern remains similar (Ashton, 1991; Simoni-Wastila, 2000). The trend in psychiatry is toward a greater use of drug therapy and a decline in talk-based therapy, which makes Dr. Melfi's treatment of Tony Soprano unusual. New drugs continue to appear for the treatment of schizophrenia, anxiety disorders, and depression, and women in North America and Europe have been prescribed psychoactive drugs 1.5 to 2 times more often than men.

The use of electrical shock to alter behavior became common during the 1940s and remains in use today. This therapy involves delivering electric shocks to the brain, and the resulting convulsions have a therapeutic effect. Although the reasons for the beneficial effects remain unclear and serious side effects can occur, electroconvulsive therapy is now used almost exclusively for depression in patients who have failed to respond to antidepressant drugs (U.S. Department of Health and Human Services [USDHHS], 1999). Because a majority of the cases of depression occur in women, they are the most frequent recipients of this therapy.

Table 15.5 summarizes medical therapies. Despite the growth of medically based treatments for behavior problems, this approach is controversial. Drugs and electroconvulsive shock alter behavior and sometimes bring about substantial improvements, but side effects are a serious risk. In addition, these therapies decrease or diminish the severity of symptoms but do not cure mental disorders. These effects can be beneficial, but not permanent; the symptoms tend to reappear when patients stop taking the drugs, and the therapeutic effects of electroconvulsive therapy rarely last for more than a few months (USDHHS, 1999). Psychoactive drugs, like other drugs, can cause serious side effects, and electroconvulsive therapy typically produces some memory loss. The benefits of medical treatments can outweigh the risks for some people, but the risks exist.

Accusations of Gender Bias in Therapy

Psychoanalysis (and the Freudian theory and on which it is based) have come under heavy criticism for their sexism. One type of criticism is that this traditional therapy was designed primarily by men to treat women (Levant, 1990). The cultural views of gender roles during

TABLE 15.5   *Elements of Medical Therapies*

Category	Description
Underlying source of problems	Biological or biochemical abnormalities
Cause of problems	Chemical or biological malfunction in brain
Immediate source of problems	The problem that brings a person to therapy
Goal of therapy	To change biological functioning
Techniques	Psychoactive drugs, surgery, electroconvulsive therapy
Practitioners	Psychiatrists and other physicians

the late 1800s came to be incorporated into psychoanalysis, so the cases treated by Freud and his colleagues reflect men's views of women and their problems during that era. Freud's behavior in treating Dora, one of his most famous case studies, exemplified his mistreatment of female patients and the sexism of his system (Hare-Mustin, 1983); he refused to listen to or believe her and treated her as a child. Critics have long argued that psychotherapy in general and psychoanalysis in particular have failed to meet the needs of female patients, as they failed Dora.

The American Psychological Association's Task Force on Sex Bias and Sex-Role Stereotyping in Psychotherapeutic Practice (Brodsky & Holroyd, 1975) listed the sexist use of psychoanalytic concepts as one of the four main causes of gender bias in therapy. The gender bias in psychoanalysis comes from conceptualizing men as the standard and making female development an inferior variation of male development. In psychoanalytic theory, girls' perception of their gender inadequacy is a critical element in personality development; women were a deviation that could never meet the male standard. To critics, this view is inherently gender biased, and the bias extends not only to psychoanalytic therapy but also to all of the other therapies that have accepted Freudian concepts. This criticism extends to some (but not all) of the other talk-based psychotherapies.

Neither humanistic nor cognitive therapy is inherently gender biased in the way that psychoanalysis is, but both emphasize personal rather than social and environmental factors in functioning (Lerman, 1992). Such neglect makes client-centered counseling inadequate for women due to its emphasis on the individual and its failure to take the social and political aspects of personal problems into account (Worell & Remer, 2003). By stressing the individual and orienting counseling toward the "here and now," women can be made to accept responsibility for the problem behavior of others, thus intensifying, rather than diminishing, their problems.

The practices of humanistic and cognitive therapy can become gender biased if therapists apply their own personal values to therapy situations (Hawtin & Moore, 1998). Although not part of the therapy process, therapists might impose their personal values when they encourage their clients to adhere to traditional gender roles as a way to handle their problems. Such therapists may encourage clients to adopt more traditional gender roles, and such actions are sexist.

Behavior modification is value free and has no theoretical component related to gender. Any behavior can be the target for modification, however, and the choice of which behaviors to encourage or discourage can reflect traditional or nontraditional values. Although behavior modification is not inherently gender biased, its practice can also be sexist (Blechman, 1980). Critics (Kantrowitz & Ballou, 1992) fear that behavior modification can be and has been used to enforce women's conformity rather than their personal development.

Medical therapies have also been the target of criticisms of sexist bias. As Chapter 13 detailed, women and men receive different levels of treatment in the health care system. Physicians tend to take men's symptom reports more seriously than similar reports from women, and they tend to attribute women's complaints to psychological rather than physical causes. This tendency toward overdiagnosis of women and underdiagnosis of men results in inappropriate psychological treatment for women and a lack of appropriate psychological treatment for men.

Women are more likely to receive prescriptions for psychoactive drugs than men are, a pattern that has persisted since the 1960s (Ashton, 1991; Cooperstock, 1970). Some of these prescriptions are unnecessary, and both women and men may be overmedicated with psychoactive drugs (Ashton, 1991). Table 15.6 summarizes the potential sources of bias in the various types of therapy.

In an early and vehement indictment of gender bias in diagnosis and therapy, Phyllis Chesler (1972) argued that diagnosis has been used to identify women who deviate from their traditional gender roles and that therapy has been used to restore women to those roles. Chesler contended that women experience problems when they either conform too little or too much to traditional gender roles, and that therapy is a process used to reimpose the traditional feminine role. Women may behave in many deviant ways, but when they fail to be subservient and domestic, they are sometimes labeled as needing therapy.

This therapy may be of any variety, but according to Chesler, all therapies seek to restore women to the traditional female gender role. One of the respondents to a survey by the American Psychological Association (APA Task Force on Sex Bias and Sex-Role Stereotyping in Psychotherapeutic Practice, 1978) confirmed Chesler's view by saying, "I have had women report to me that they could not continue in therapy because the objective seemed to be for them to learn to adjust better to their roles as wives, mothers, daughters (underlings of one kind or another), and they needed to become free persons" (p. 1122).

By surveying female psychologists, the APA Task Force (Brodsky & Holroyd, 1975) determined that sexist bias exists in four main areas of the practice of psychotherapy. As mentioned previously, sexist use of psychoanalytic concepts was one of the four. The other areas included fostering traditional gender roles, including having biased expectations concerning women; devaluing women's potential; and responding to women as sex objects, including therapists' sexual exploitation of clients.

Men are also subject to gender bias in therapy when practitioners urge the adoption of gender-typical behaviors. When a male patient in one study described a lifestyle that included providing housework and child care, therapists tended to concentrate on these

TABLE 15.6 *Sources of Gender Bias in Therapies for Behavior Problems*

Type of Therapy	Source of Potential Gender Bias
Psychoanalysis	Psychoanalytic theory assumes that women are inferior.
Humanistic	Therapists may apply personal standards that are sexist; therapy focuses on the individual and ignores the social context of personal problems.
Cognitive	Therapists may apply personal standards that are sexist; therapy fails to address the social context of personal problems.
Behavior modification	Therapists may choose to reinforce traditional gender-related behaviors.
Medical	Women and men are diagnosed and treated according to stereotypical and traditional values.

atypical behaviors, emphasizing the gender role as a potential source of problems (Robertson & Fitzgerald, 1990). A second male patient who described his role as more typical of a breadwinner received no comments on his gender role behaviors as a potential source of problems. A more recent study (Guanipa & Woolley, 2000) confirmed the existence of this type of gender bias in marriage and family therapy.

Counselors are likely to view both men and women stereotypically in terms of emotionality: women as overly emotional and men as lacking in emotion (Heesacker et al., 1999). These views influence the process of counseling when therapists blame husbands rather than wives for marital problems and when therapists set goals consistent with their stereotypes. Such a bias appeared in a study (Fowers, Applegate, Tredinnick, & Slusher, 1996) in which therapists did not encourage men to develop their expressiveness as much as they encouraged women to do so. An examination of the content of master lectures in family therapy practice (Haddock, MacPhee, & Zimmerman, 2001) revealed that only 3% of the time was devoted to feminist concepts and stereotypical and even overtly sexist statements occurred, such as blaming women for family problems and endorsing traditional rather than egalitarian family roles. Therefore, evidence exists that the practice of therapy is not value free, and that therapy tends to work toward preserving traditional values, especially for men.

GENDER ISSUES IN THERAPY

Besides therapist bias, treatment presents several other gender issues. One issue is the suitability of various types of therapy for women or men. Although women more often seek counseling and psychotherapy and tend to be better at the therapy tasks involved, their needs may not be met by the process itself. The gender bias in psychoanalytic approaches and the potential for gender bias in other therapies have presented important issues for therapy, and several alternative approaches have endeavored to correct these biases.

Recognizing the potential for bias in therapy has led to the notion that good therapy should be nonsexist (APA Task Force on Sex Bias, 1978), and professionals have worked toward the principles underlying nonsexist therapy. Feminist alternatives to therapy arose from the belief that ignoring gender issues does not make therapy gender fair. The contention that nonsexist therapy is not an adequate answer to the gender bias in therapy prompted the development of therapies that are specifically feminist and oriented toward women's problems as well as practiced exclusively by women. "The sexism in so-called nonsexist brands of psychotherapy may be less blatant, but any approach to psychotherapy that conceptualizes women's social problems as personal pathology and promotes 'cures' for women's distress primarily through individual personal change strengthens the patriarchal status quo" (Rawlings, 1993, p. 90).

Feminist Therapy

A review of the history of feminist therapy (Enns, 1997) traced it to the early 1970s and the women's rights movement. Women, both inside and outside the mental health care professions, began to criticize therapy for its traditional goals and for its power in maintaining the status quo for women. Some women in professions that provide mental health care then responded by attempting to combine feminist goals with therapy; their results diverge from traditional therapy in several ways.

Four principles underlie the practice of feminist therapy (Worell & Remer, 2003). The first principle is that personal and social identities are interdependent. That is, each individual occupies several social identities (such as gender, ethnicity, sexual orientation, and physical abilities) that exist within society; all these identities influence and interact with personal identity. The second principle is borrowed from the feminist movement and states that "the personal is political." That is, personal experience is embedded within the social and political structure of the society, making the problems of any individual woman a reflection of the wider society. The first two principles have a close relationship.

Feminist therapy strives to enact these two principles in several ways. Clients explore the influence of social roles on their individual behaviors, examining the difference between what they have been taught about appropriate behavior and what is actually appropriate. During feminist therapy, women have a forum for validating their experiences as women, including the situations and problems that are unique to women. Feminist therapists help clients reframe their problems and understand that their symptoms are a reflection of the society in which they live (Worell & Remer, 2003).

Feminist therapy is political, striving to bring about change in society. The early feminist therapists were politically active in the women's movement; indeed, such activity was a requirement for declaring oneself a feminist therapist. These therapists sought to bring about changes in the status of women and advocated political activism for their clients. Their position was that significant change was not possible in women's lives through personal changes in psychological adjustment; only change in society and in women's roles would lead to beneficial changes for women. Contemporary feminist psychotherapists may not emphasize the political as strongly as the founders did (Morrow & Hawxhurst, 1998), but feminist therapists have tried to maintain the emphasis on politics by continuing to discuss power issues as part of their therapy sessions (Marecek & Kravetz, 1998).

The third principle of feminist therapy states that therapists and clients should form an egalitarian relationship rather than the traditional therapeutic relationship in which therapists are powerful and dominant and clients are subordinate. This principle ensures that clients understand the types of therapy that they will receive and that they know about the options for other sources of assistance (Worell & Remer, 2003). This level of informed consent represents a consumer orientation to therapy, and feminist therapy tries to promote such an orientation.

The equal relationship between client and therapist also aims to "demystify" the therapist as a person who has special knowledge and power (Gilbert, 1980). The rationale for this position lies in the attempt to counter the typical subordinate position that women occupy and to promote the belief that feminist therapy is an appropriate place for women to begin to feel a sense of personal power. Research (Simi & Mahalik, 1997) has indicated that feminist therapists endorse more openness and self-disclosure with their patients than do psychodynamic and other therapists.

Feminist therapists participate in therapy by modeling appropriate behaviors for their female clients and by sharing personal experiences with their clients. This degree of personal openness and the advocacy of political activity on the part of the therapist differentiate the role of feminist therapists from therapists in most traditional therapies. Feminist therapists consider these differences essential to their approach.

The fourth principle states that women's perspectives are valued. Feminist therapists believe that women's viewpoint has not been valued or heard and that both value and voice can help women grow and become empowered: "Feminist therapists believe that women need to reject androcentric definitions of womanhood, to learn to value their personal characteristics, and to validate their own, woman-centered views of the world" (Worell & Remer, 2003, p. 74). Table 15.7 lists the four principles of feminist therapy.

Theoretical Orientations of Feminist Therapy.   Feminist therapists hold a variety of theoretical orientations. Indeed, feminist therapists have followed theories as diverse as psychoanalysis and behavior modification and all varieties of humanistic and cognitive therapies. The goals of feminist therapy differ somewhat, depending on the orientation of the therapist, and a common element of all feminist therapists is their striving to modify therapy techniques to make them more compatible with feminist goals (Hill & Ballou, 1998). These efforts have produced similarities in the goals of all feminist therapy: "The emphasis becomes growth rather than adjustment or remediation, development rather than blame or illness" (Cammaert & Larsen, 1988, p. 23).

With the amount of criticism of psychoanalysis for its sexism, it is ironic that psychoanalytic therapy is the orientation adopted by many feminist therapists. Revisions to traditional psychoanalytic theory have made it an acceptable basis for feminist therapy (Daugherty & Lees, 1988), but the fit between psychoanalytic theory and feminist goals may not be an entirely comfortable one (Burack, 1998). These revisions retain the emphasis on early childhood development and the importance of unconscious forces in personality development and functioning but include the revised view from feminist psychoanalytic theorists (Chodorow, 1978; Dinnerstein, 1976). Both traditional and feminist versions of psychoanalysis have as their goal the process of uncovering unconscious conflicts and bringing this material to consciousness so that clients can make more reasonable decisions about their behaviors. Feminist psychoanalytic therapists share the principles of feminist therapy, conveying their feminist values to their clients and attempting to build egalitarian counseling relationships.

TABLE 15.7   *Four Principles of Feminist Therapy*

Principle 1—Personal and social identities are interdependent.

Principle 2—The personal is political.

Principle 3—Relationships between therapists and clients are egalitarian.

Principle 4—Women's perspectives are valued.

Source: Based on *Feminist Perspectives in Therapy: Empowering Diverse Women* (2nd ed., pp. 66–75), by Judith Worell & Pamela Remer, 2003. New York: Wiley.

Feminist adaptations of cognitive, behavioral, and cognitive behavior therapy are easier than feminist adaptations of psychoanalysis. This family of therapies includes techniques that have been evaluated as effective for a range of problems (Chambless & Ollendick, 2001). Behavior modification treatments are common and effective for phobias, substance abuse problems, eating disorders, and depression. Cognitive behavior therapy is the integration of behavioral and cognitive therapy with research from cognitive and social psychology. During the 1970s, when feminist therapy arose, cognitive behavior therapy also gained prominence, and the goals of feminist theory were integrated into this therapy. The cognitive component of this therapy was especially compatible with feminist therapy; the goals of analyzing the social system and restructuring thought processes are consistent with an understanding of the personal as political (Worell & Remer, 2003).

For example, a woman who is stressed by her work situation might be urged to consider her company's corporate culture and the difficulties that many women experience in obtaining promotions rather than blaming herself for failure. Cognitive behavior therapy has social learning theory as its basis, with its view that the environment shapes behavior. This position is compatible with feminist therapy's view that the social context of behavior is essential to understanding the behavior.

Cognitive behavioral therapy is applicable to a wide variety of problems and has been evaluated as effective for this wide range of problems, including depression, stress and anxiety disorders, relapse prevention for substance abuse problems, sexual dysfunctions, paraphilias, and some personality disorders (Chambless & Ollendick, 2001).

Clients of Feminist Therapy. During the early years of feminist therapy, the majority of clients were White middle-class women—a demographic description that matches many of the clients who seek therapy. Questions arose over the suitability of feminist therapy for all women: After all, some women who seek therapy do not endorse feminist goals, and many are not White or middle class. Some people who seek therapy are men. Is feminist therapy appropriate for all women? And is it ever appropriate for men?

Early studies of feminist therapy evaluated the clients and problems for which this approach was suited. One study compared feminist and traditional therapy (Marecek, Kravetz, & Finn, 1979) and found that feminist therapy was more helpful to those who identified themselves as part of the women's movement, but women who did not also benefited. Other studies examined the feminist orientation of the counselor (Enns & Hackett, 1990; Hackett, Enns, & Zetzer, 1992) and found that women showed some reluctance to see radical feminist therapists but preferred more moderate feminist therapists over traditional or nonsexist therapists.

As feminist therapy developed, practitioners and researchers focused on prevention and empowerment as well as reducing specific symptoms and problems (Worell, 2001; Worell & Johnson, 2001). Practitioners use specific therapy approaches and techniques, and the effectiveness of these approaches varies (Chambless & Ollendick, 2001). However, in order to be successful within the goals of feminist therapy, therapists must achieve political as well as personal goals. These criteria create an almost unattainable definition of success for feminist therapy and make the assessment of effectiveness very difficult. Considering the goal of creating empowerment, some research (Cummings, 2000) has demonstrated the achievement of this goal. In addition, practitioners and clients of feminist therapy were able to identify the distinct elements of feminist therapy, such as empowerment for women and valuing women's point of view (Worell & Johnson, 2001).

Although men may seem to be unlikely clients for feminist therapy, this approach holds potential benefits for men (Johnson, 2001; Walker, 2001). Traditional therapy adheres to a gendered model of mental health, but many feminist therapists adhere to a model that holds both masculine and feminine characteristics as beneficial to mental health. Research has demonstrated the risks of extreme instrumental traits (Helgeson, 1994; Saragovi, Koestner, Di Dio, & Aubé, 1997) and the mental health benefits for men to develop their expressiveness (Sharpe, Heppner, & Dixon, 1995). Feminist therapists have the theoretical orientation and the experience to help men make these changes. In addition, their experiences with female clients and their emotional issues has given feminist therapists valuable background that allows them to help male clients who are experiencing similar pain (Johnson, 2001; Walker, 2001).

By taking this approach with male clients, feminist therapists attempt to develop relationship skills, appropriate emotionality, empathy, and communication skills—skills that men often lack due to their masculine socialization. Feminist therapy with men also works toward altering views of gender roles and seeks to change men's attitudes concerning what is appropriate for both women and men (Szymanski, Baird, & Kornman, 2002). By examining and questioning traditional gender roles, feminist therapy with men upholds the principle that the personal is political, one of the basic principles of feminist therapy. Most feminist therapists, however, believe that the practice of feminist therapy is restricted to women. Male therapists who adopt the principles of feminist therapy are labeled "profeminist." However, a survey of practicing psychotherapists (Szymanski et al., 2002) revealed that 24% of male therapists identified themselves as feminist therapists. With either male or female therapists, male clients in feminist therapy can find both appropriate modeling and support through participation in group therapy.

Therefore, feminist therapy is appropriate for a wide range of people. From its beginnings as a radical therapy for women who were discontent with traditional therapy (both as therapists and as clients), feminist therapy has broadened its scope and clientele. Both women and men can benefit from feminist therapy by learning to develop their potential and becoming empowered in domains outside traditional gender roles.

Therapy with Men

Tony Soprano, the lead character in the HBO series *The Sopranos,* was reluctant to make an appointment with a psychiatrist, but tests by his family physician revealed no neurological basis for his blackouts, so panic attacks were a possibility. His therapy was an important part of the script, and Desa Philadelphia's headline story (2001) reported that his acceptance of therapy made it more acceptable for "tough guys" to seek therapy. If this trend is significant, it will constitute a reversal of an overwhelming gender difference; men of different ages, ethnic backgrounds, and nationalities have been less likely than women to seek psychiatric, psychotherapy, or counseling services (Addis & Mahalik, 2003).

Considering men's traditional gender role, their reluctance is no surprise—the demands of therapy and the therapy situation diverge from traditional masculine behavior (Brooks, 1998, 2001). The masculine gender role demands that men hide their vulnerabilities, whereas counseling calls for disclosing them. Counseling urges clients to share their problems with other persons, and men have been socialized to hide their problems and approach problem solving in an intellectual rather than an emotional way. Therapy emphasizes behaviors associated with the feminine rather than the masculine role. Men who show emotion, express their vulnerability, and seek help from others fail to fit the masculine gender role, but all of these behaviors are necessary for psychotherapy.

Both clients and counselors experience difficulties in the counseling process due to male clients' stereotypically masculine behavior. Indeed, men may be in therapy because of their attitudes and unacceptable behavior associated with masculinity (Mahalik, Good, & Englar-Carlson, 2003). These men may have followed the "Strong-but-Silent" or the "Tough Guy" script and become emotionally distant and uncommunicative. They may have followed the "Give 'Em Hell" script and battered their partners or children. They may have carried out parts of the "Playboy" script and experienced relationship problems or committed sexual violence. They may have enacted the "Winner" script and worked 80-hour weeks to adhere to their definition of success and developed a stress-related disorder. These men tend to be resistant to the therapy process, and therapists may be unacceptant of such clients. Thus, men not only may avoid counseling but also have difficulties with the process when they attempt it. Table 15.8 presents some of the barriers that can deter men from seeking and succeeding in counseling.

Psychological services can be made more approachable for men through changing the description of those services (Robertson & Fitzgerald, 1992; Rochlen, Blazina, & Raghunathan, 2002). Advertising services through brochures in terms of classes, workshops, seminars, and videotapes made traditional men consider these services as more attractive than when the services were presented as counseling. Thus, it is possible to frame counseling so that it is more appealing to men and more compatible with masculine values.

TABLE 15.8 *Barriers to Counseling Men*

Help-seeking is discouraged by elements of the masculine gender role:
- Men should not require help.
- Men should deny and suppress their emotions.
- Men should not express their vulnerability.

Therapy often takes a talk-based rather than an action-based or intellectual approach to problem solving.

Emotional sharing is difficult for many men.

Men may believe that counselors are biased against men's needs.

Psychology has responded by addressing women's needs better than it does men's needs.

Presentation of psychological services may be in a format that does not appeal to men.

Counseling offers advantages for men: "Men need counseling because many of them are unhappy, dissatisfied with their lives, and damaged by their roles" (Scher, 1981, p. 199). Men need help in relinquishing some of the negative elements of the masculine role so that they can learn to understand the value of being in touch with their emotions, ask for assistance when they need it, and encourage freedom from constraining gender roles in themselves and in others.

Gender-Sensitive Therapies

Good therapy must be nonsexist. The APA Task Force on Sex Bias and Sex-Role Stereo-typing in Psychotherapeutic Practice (1978) recognized the need for nonsexist therapy, but therapists have disagreed over how to achieve this goal. Will vigilance against sexism be an adequate approach to making therapy gender fair, or will it be necessary to add elements to therapies to achieve this goal? Those who follow feminist therapy believe that ignoring gender or removing objectionable elements is not sufficient to make a therapy gender fair; a therapeutic approach must include some stated goals oriented around achieving social and personal equity.

Gender aware therapy (GAT) is an attempt to integrate concepts of male and female gender development with the revised attitudes toward psychotherapy proposed by feminist therapists (Good, Gilbert, & Scher, 1990). This therapy approach has both similarities to and differences from nonsexist and feminist therapies. This approach acknowledges that society's conception of mental health is changing to a more androgynous standard in which conforming to traditional standards is no longer a desirable goal for either gender. Gender aware therapy has its foundation in feminist therapy but extended principles of gender fairness to a therapy that could apply to men or women by including five principles as an integral aspect of counseling and mental health. Table 15.9 presents these five points.

Gender aware therapy has not become the dominant approach to gender-sensitive counseling. Instead, feminist therapy has continued as the major approach to dealing with gender issues in counseling for women, and new therapies for men have arisen. Gary Brooks (1998, 2001) has proposed a gender-sensitive approach for counseling with traditional men that he described with the acronym MASTERY. Table 15.10 lists these principles, along with a brief description of how therapists can enact them.

TABLE 15.9 *Five Principles of Gender Aware Therapy*

1. Regard the conception of gender as an integral aspect of counseling and mental health.
2. Consider problems within their societal context.
3. Actively seek to change gender injustice experienced by women and men.
4. Emphasize development of collaborative therapeutic relationships.
5. Respect clients' freedom to choose.

Source: Based on "Gender Aware Therapy: A Synthesis of Feminist Therapy and Knowledge about Gender," by G. E. Good, L. A. Gilbert, and M. Scher, 1990, *Journal of Counseling & Development, 68,* p. 377.

TABLE 15.10 *Principles of Gender-Sensitive Counseling with Men: MASTERY*

Monitor Personal Reactions to Men and Male Behavior Styles—Therapists may have negative reactions to men's behaviors and should develop empathy with their clients to help them change.

Assume That the Male Client Is Feeling Pain—Even though men may be privileged in society, their strain at maintaining the male gender role causes pain.

See the Male Client's Problems in Gender Context—Understand and help clients understand that their behavior occurs in a cultural context with gendered roles.

Transmit Empathy and Understanding—Convey compassion and understanding; if possible, urge clients to become part of a men's group so that they can see they are not alone in their feelings.

Empower Men to Change—Understanding is not enough; therapists must challenge men to make positive changes in their lives.

Respect Resistance—Accept that men in therapy are not eager to change and that change is difficult.

Yield Some Control to the Larger System—Accept that many social forces push men toward traditionality, making therapeutic change slow and difficult.

Source: Based on *A New Psychotherapy for Traditional Men,* by Gary R. Brooks, 1998, San Francisco, CA: Jossey-Bass.

A comparison of Tables 15.7, 15.9, and 15.10 reveals many commonalities in the goals of feminist therapy, gender aware therapy, and Brooks's MASTERY approach to counseling with traditional men. All of these approaches strive to be nonsexist, not by ignoring gender issues, but by finding ways to redefine gender roles, personal goals, and personal relationships. All draw attention to the social context of problem behavior, define an egalitarian relationship between client and therapist, and cultivate respect for clients' views and values. Feminist therapy and the MASTERY approach both urge political and social action to change gender roles. Therefore, sensitivity to gender-related issues is an important goal to several therapy approaches, and therapists have choices in selecting how to accomplish the goals of nonsexist therapy.

SEXUAL EXPLOITATION IN THERAPY

The preponderance of female clients and male therapists poses a situation in which gender is nearly always either an overt or covert issue in the therapy process (see "According to the Media" and "According to the Research"). The APA Task Force on Sex Bias and Sex-Role Stereotyping in Psychotherapeutic Practice (Brodsky & Holroyd, 1975) identified the treatment of clients as sex objects as a gender-related problem in psychotherapy. Erotic or sexual behavior with clients is included in this category. Unfortunately, sex between therapist and client is not unusual. Beginning with the founding fathers of psychoanalytic therapy and continuing today, some clients are sexually exploited by the therapists to whom they come for help.

During the 1970s, a survey of licensed psychologists in clinical practice (Holroyd & Brodsky, 1977) disclosed attitudes toward sexual and nonsexual physical contact with

ACCORDING TO THE MEDIA . . .

Male Therapists Are Crazy or Evil, and Female Therapists Have Sex with Their Patients

The image of psychotherapists in movies is often vague and usually not flattering. The profession of therapists is often left unclear—whether they are psychiatrists, psychologists, psychoanalysts, psychiatric social workers, or some other profession (Greenberg, 1992). In addition, therapists are portrayed in unflattering ways. Therapists in the movies usually fall into one of three categories: Dr. Dippy, Dr. Evil, or Dr. Wonderful (Schneider, 1987). Dr. Dippy first appeared in a short film in 1906 as the therapist who was crazier than the patients, and about 35% of movie therapists fit into this category. Dr. Evil also appeared early in film history in a 1908 movie, *The Criminal Hypnotist,* and about 15% of movie therapists (excluding those in horror movies) have harmful motives. Dr. Wonderful is the ideal therapist—effective, caring, and available. These Dr. Wonderfuls devote large amounts of time to their on-screen patients doing talk-based therapy and rarely asking for payment. The psychiatrist in *Ordinary People* (1980) and the counselor in *Good Will Hunting* (1998) are good examples of Dr. Wonderful. About 22% of movie therapists fall into this category.

Female therapists are more likely to be Dr. Wonderful than Dr. Evil or Dr. Dippy, but their screen portrayals differ from male therapists. Female therapists are likely to be single or unhappy in their marriages, and in the movies, female therapists often "help" their male patients by becoming their lovers (Gabbard, 2000). In *Spellbound* (1945), Ingrid Bergman portrayed a competent but sexually repressed psychiatrist who fell in love with Gregory Peck's amnesiac character. More recently, movies such as *The Prince of Tides* (1991), *Basic Instinct* (1992), and *Twelve Monkeys* (1995) depicted female therapists who formed sexual relationships with their clients. One analysis (Gabbard & Gabbard, 1999) had trouble finding a movie female therapist who had a relationship with anyone *except* a patient or former patient.

In the movies, female therapists who have sex with their patients do not seem to violate any rules or suffer any negative consequences. The patients sustain no harm, and the therapists experience benefits by "finding their femininity" (Gabbard, 2000) and often by abandoning their professional careers (Greenberg, 1992). When male therapists have sex with their patients, the relationship is usually more problematic, but again, the extent to which such behavior violates codes of professional conduct and the harm that comes to patients remains off screen.

clients. Nonsexual physical contact was acceptable under some circumstances to 27% of the therapists, but a large majority of the therapists reported that erotic contact between clients and therapists would *not* be beneficial to clients. Significantly more female than male therapists (88% versus 70%) believed that such contact would not be a beneficial component of therapy, and a large majority of the therapists who reported that they had engaged in such behavior were men. Factors that contribute to therapists' willingness to enter into sexual relationships with their clients are their lack of preparation for sexual attraction to clients and their denial of the harm that such relationships can exert (Pope, 1988, 2000). Another factor that increases the risk of sexual exploitation is the history of sexual abuse in therapists' backgrounds; therapists who have been the victims of childhood sexual abuse are at increased risk of sexually exploiting their clients (Jackson & Nuttall, 2001)

ACCORDING TO THE RESEARCH . . .

Male Therapists Are More Likely Than Female Therapists to Form Sexual Relationships with Patients

Movie portrayals of therapists are inaccurate in a number of ways. Therapists are not as dramatic as movie portrayals; very few therapists match the flamboyant behavior of Dr. Dippy, Dr. Evil, or even Dr. Wonderful. Effective, concerned therapists exist, but the ideal of a psychiatrist providing the amount of talk-based treatment that Dr. Wonderfuls dispense is not realistic (Gabbard, 2000). Drug treatments have replaced psychotherapy for most psychiatrists, making Dr. Jennifer Melfi—Tony Soprano's psychiatrist—unrealistic. Of course, all types of therapists charge for their services, which makes them different from the media therapists.

Research also indicates that sexual relationships with patients are substantially different than the movies depict. In an early study (Holroyd & Brodsky, 1977), a significant gender difference appeared in the percentage of therapists who reported any type of sexual contact with clients—10.9% of male therapists and 1.9% of female therapists had some kind of sexual contact. When considering only those therapists who admitted having intercourse with past or present clients, the survey showed that 8.1% of the male therapists and 1% of the female therapists acknowledged this behavior. Of those therapists who admitted at least one sexual rela-

tionship with a patient, 80% acknowledged more than one such relationship. This figure suggests that some therapists have formed a pattern of habitual sexual exploitation of their patients. In the movies, sexual relationships are usually the result of two people falling in love rather than a powerful therapist exploiting a vulnerable patient.

Research indicates that another pattern of sexual relationship occurs as a series of steps of violations of the boundary between client and therapist (Simon, 1999). That is, therapists begin to behave in ways that are more intimate and personal, which eventually leads to sex. This situation is more likely to occur in gradual steps, with clients who are victims of childhood sexual abuse, and with therapists who are in a sole private practice, rather than to occur in other configurations of clients and therapists (Somer & Saadon, 1999). This picture of sexually exploitative therapists contrasts sharply with the movie portrayal: Therapists who form sexual relationships with their clients are more often male than female, tend to engage in a series of exploitative relationships, often prey on vulnerable clients, and understand that their behavior is a violation of their code of professional conduct.

The possibility of sexual attraction on the part of clients toward therapists and for therapists toward clients is an important concept in psychoanalytical treatment, but the knowledge of this possibility did not deter several prominent early psychotherapists from forming sexual relationships with their patients. Other counseling theories do not include the likelihood of mutual attraction between therapist and client; thus therapists adhering to other approaches were not prepared to deal with the possibility that they may develop sexual feelings for their clients (Pope, 1988). Most professionals considered such relationships unacceptable and unprofessional. This attitude was a component in the denial of the existence of therapist–client sex. Initially, journals were reluctant to publish articles, and conventions were unwilling to feature presentations on the topic (Pope, 1988).

During the 1990s, sexual relationships between therapists and clients became a widely publicized issue, and the helping professions began to address this problem. Therapists receive training concerning ethics and the unacceptability of sexual contact with their clients, but the emphasis is usually on the unacceptability of such behavior, rather than on how to deal with sexual feelings that therapists may experience. A survey of psychology internship programs (Samuel & Gorton, 1998) showed that 99% of programs provided some training on this topic. However, only about half of the graduates of counseling psychology programs remembered how their programs addressed this issue, and only 60% of that half thought that their program's training was adequate (Blanchard & Lichtenberg, 1998).

Although some therapists believe that personal and sexual relationships with clients are therapeutic for clients, research indicates otherwise. A variety of negative effects befall clients who have participated in sexual relationships with their therapists (Luepker, 1999; Pope, 1988). Clients may not exhibit any immediate negative effects of sexual intimacy with their therapists, but evidence indicates that at least 90% will eventually experience negative effects. These effects include posttraumatic stress disorder, depression, suicide, substance abuse, disrupted personal relationships, and career problems. The effects are

◼ GENDERED VOICES

Of Course I've Felt Attracted to My Clients

Both a counseling intern and a counselor with 30 years of experience told me, "Of course I've felt attracted to some of my clients. I think it's almost inevitable." Both reported that the attraction made them very aware of the nature of the counseling relationship and how inappropriate these feelings were. Both also became very conscious about behaving so as to conceal signs of their attraction, because it was considered professionally unacceptable.

"Part of our training includes the ethical unacceptability of any type of personal relationship with clients, especially any sexual relationship. It's completely unacceptable," the counseling intern said. "So feeling attracted to a client raised flags and made me aware that I needed to be very careful about what I did. I didn't want to convey my feelings to my client, and I didn't want to let my feelings affect my counseling. It's a difficult situation and an inevitable conflict, I think."

The veteran counselor agreed. "It's practically inevitable, although I have been sexually attracted to very few of my clients. When I felt attracted, those feelings made counseling more difficult. I tried to conceal how I felt, which is dishonest, while remaining honest in all other respects. And I tried very hard to do a good job in counseling the client. It made the counseling relationship more difficult."

"Nothing in our training taught me how to deal with these feelings," the intern said. "A great deal was oriented toward the ethics of counseling, but not how to handle my feelings or situations in which clients express some attraction for me. It was all 'Don't do that,' but nothing about what to do. I wouldn't feel comfortable talking to my supervisor about my feelings because of the ethical prohibition. I know it's unreasonable to imagine that counselors won't feel attracted to clients, but it's so forbidden that I feel I shouldn't have or admit to the attraction. I know that I will think about how to avoid letting any client know about my attraction, but teaching me how to deal with such feelings and what to do—no, that was lacking in my training."

The experienced counselor said that his training included how to deal with clients' attraction to him but not his toward clients. "The whole issue of sexual exploitation of clients hadn't been publicized or addressed in counselor training, so those issues were not part of my training."

stronger when the relationship occurs concurrently with therapy, but clients who begin relationships with their therapists after the termination of therapy are still at risk.

The therapist–client relationship is one of trust and intimacy, but when sexual intimacy becomes part of the relationship, a betrayal of the client's trust has occurred. Thus, impaired ability to trust is a potential lifelong problem (Pope, 1988). This situation often leaves clients feeling ambivalent; they experience rage and a longing to escape combined with a fear of separation from the therapist. Sexually exploited clients may also feel guilt, isolation, emptiness, and sexual confusion. In addition, they have trouble finding help, contacting an average of 2.36 professionals before finding assistance they consider satisfactory (Luepker, 1999). Therefore, clients often experience a variety of serious problems after sexual involvement with their therapists and seek subsequent help for problems.

The growing awareness of the sexual exploitation of clients by therapists has produced changes in the codes of ethics for all of the professions that provide mental health care (Lazarus, 2003; Vasquez & Kitchener, 1988). The ethical codes that govern psychiatrists, psychologists, social workers, and marriage and family therapists all specifically prohibit sexual activity between therapists and clients.

Violations of sexual boundaries have been the most common of the ethical complaints against therapists (Gross, 2003). The typical situation involves a male therapist who forms a sexual relationship with a female client who is approximately 10 years younger than he is. This typical therapist has been the target of prior ethical complaints, but he is also at increased risk to have been involved in a sexual relationship with a teacher or supervisor. Thus, sexual exploitation during therapy may be part of a chain of sexual abuse.

THE SELF-HELP MOVEMENT

A growing lack of confidence in psychotherapy, mounting awareness of sexual exploitation of clients, and increased cost have led to reluctance to seek therapy on the part of thousands of people with personal problems. "Across the country, in hospitals, churches, empty offices, and even shopping malls, small groups of individuals assemble to cope collectively with their unique challenges" (Davison, Pennebaker, & Dickerson, 2000, p. 205). People in self-help groups meet to share similar problems, and in the process, they receive emotional support as well as information that can assist in helping them cope.

Self-help groups began to proliferate during the 1980s. The 1987 Surgeon General's Workshop on Self-Help and Public Health brought the benefits of self-help groups to the attention of an increased number of health care providers (Hedrick, 1995). In 1992, the number of self-help groups was more than 500,000, and over 7 million people were involved. By the end of the 1990s, the number of people in the United States who would be involved in some type of self-help group at some time during their lives was estimated at 25 million, a number that exceeded those in other types of therapy programs (Davison et al., 2000). The United States is not unique in this proliferation; self-help groups exist in growing numbers in all industrialized countries and in most other countries in the world (Katz, 1993).

The prototype for the self-help movement is Alcoholics Anonymous (AA). Founded in 1935 by two alcoholics who had stopped drinking, AA proclaimed that people with drinking problems could stay sober through the social support of others with similar problems (Robinson, 1979). The format is a meeting in which people acknowledge their alcoholism and seek the support of others to continue in the struggle to abstain from drinking, one day at a time. This approach to dealing with problem drinking has been enormously influential, both in the treatment of problem drinking and in the formation of other self-help support groups. For example, addictions and other compulsive disorders were the concerns of early support groups such as Narcotics Anonymous, Gamblers Anonymous, and Overeaters Anonymous, but support groups now exist for a wide variety of problems, including mental disorders, physical diseases, and people living with or involved in providing care for people with mental or physical problems. "There are groups for almost every serious medical problem and almost every presenting problem that clinicians confront, plus groups for dozens of conditions virtually unserved by therapists" (Jacobs & Goodman, 1989, p. 537).

The philosophy of the self-help approach is that people with similar problems can offer each other social support and information, which can be helpful and beneficial. Rather than consisting of therapists who direct the therapy and clients who take direction, self-help and support groups may not involve professional therapists and may have no designated leaders (Gartner & Riessman, 1998). Other groups have professionals who consult or even participate in meetings (Davison et al., 2000). Groups vary in size from a few members who have formed their own group to large, nationally affiliated groups, and they vary in organization from no specified format to one that is tightly scripted (Gartner & Riessman, 1998). Although the concerns of people in these groups vary, the underlying philosophies are similar.

The success of self-help groups is due in part to the comfort that people feel from being with others whose experience is similar (Gartner & Riessman, 1998). Because individuals in these groups are similar, empathy is facilitated. The similarities among participants may be an important factor that draws people to support groups, especially for people with certain problems. For example, people with AIDS are 250 times more likely to join a support group than people with hypertension, and breast cancer has about 40 times as many support groups as heart disease (Davison et al., 2000). For disorders that have a social stigma or visible effects, support groups of similar others may be especially helpful.

The financial advantages of self-help groups are another factor in the growth of this approach. These groups may charge participants a minimal fee, although many of them charge nothing. With the growing emphasis on cost containment, health care professionals have begun to promote cooperation between medicine and self-help groups as one way to contain treatment costs (Wituk, Shepherd, Slavich, Warren, & Meissen, 2000).

Free therapy is certainly cost-effective, but is it effective? Although research has not compared the effectiveness of self-help to traditional therapy (Christensen & Jacobson, 1994), some studies have attempted to assess the value of self-help. Problems arise from participants who are involved in multiple types of therapy, which makes assessment of the self-help component difficult. However, research has revealed some evidence for the effectiveness for self-help groups. An analysis of bibliotherapy, providing people with reading materials, for people with drinking problems (Apodaca & Miller, 2003) indicated that reading about reducing problem drinking was moderately successful in helping decrease drinking compared to no type of intervention. Also, a one-year follow-up assessment of people treated for substance abuse disorders (Moos, Schaefer, Andrassy, & Moos, 2001) found that those who participated in self-help group meetings were functioning better than those who attended no such meetings. Thus, self-help may provide some benefits, boost the benefits of therapy, or both.

Self-help groups may function to alter cognitions, which change behavior (Dijkstra & De Vries, 2001). That is, when self-help groups are effective in bringing about therapeutic change, they do so in ways that are similar to therapist-assisted change. These results suggest that specific information about changing behavior and providing ways to bring about changes are important components, regardless of the therapy format. Furthermore, groups that provide social and emotional support may be valuable but perhaps not always therapeutic.

The cost difference between self-help and traditional therapy makes self-help attractive to a wide range of participants. The ease of access to support groups is another attractive feature, and the growing accessibility of the Internet has created an even more accessible form of self-help: online support groups.

Online Support Groups

Internet sites are available for a number of problems, allowing people without easy access to groups in their hometowns to meet in cyberspace. Preliminary evidence (Weinberg, Uken, Schmale, & Adamek, 1995) indicated that participants in online self-help groups receive some of the same benefits that other participants obtain. Later research has examined the participants and types of problems in online groups, the patterns of support that develop on line, and the differences from and similarities to face-to-face support groups.

The formation of online groups differs from face-to-face groups. Support groups may consist of only a few people, or as many as a few dozen, but online groups may have thousands of members (Galegher, Sproull, & Kiesler, 1998). No meetings take place, but participants can enter discussions 24 hours a day, 7 days a week. Most online groups have no designated leader, but at least one site has attempted to provide the "best of both worlds" by combining the online format with a mental health professional as the host (Hsuing, 2000). People can actively participate by posting comments and asking questions, or they may "lurk," reading the posted interactions but not offering comments themselves. Participants often use created names, which makes online interaction anonymous. Thus, the format for online support groups shows clear differences from other support groups.

The types of problems that prompt people to seek support on the Internet vary somewhat from those that bring people to face-to-face support groups (Davison et al., 2000). Rare and debilitating conditions are frequent topics on the Internet because sufficiently many people can meet on line to form a group. Conditions such as chronic fatigue syndrome and multiple sclerosis seem well suited to online support—people with these conditions have problems that impair them from going to meetings, but online access is possible. People who have problems with oral speech can use a computer to communicate in a medium they can master and at their own pace (Finn, 1999). For example, those with hearing impairment benefited from their involvement in an online group (Cummings, Sproull, & Kiesler, 2002).

The problems of participants in online support groups tend to center on physical health, but behavioral problems such as depression, anxiety disorders, and attention deficit disorder are also common topics. An assessment on an online support group for depressed people (Houston, Cooper, & Ford, 2002) indicated that these participants had low social support from other sources in their lives and that those who used the online group more often were more likely to have a resolution to their depression problems than those who participated less.

Alcohol and substance abuse treatment form a large segment of the face-to-face support groups, but these problems are not as prominent in online support groups (Davison et al., 2000). However, a survey of those who participated in such services (Hall & Tidwell, 2003) indicated that people from many ethnic and age groups participated in a variety of Internet recovery services. In addition, cancer, diabetes, and AIDS bring people together on line as well as in person to share information and emotional support.

The same support processes that occur in face-to-face groups also take place on line (Finn, 1999). That is, online support groups also share information, work toward mutual problem solving, allow expressions of emotion, and show support and empathy. An analysis of the processes in online support groups (Finn, 1999) showed that the majority of messages (55%) could be classified as emotional or social exchanges, and 21% of messages showed empathy. Although participants exchanged a great deal of practical information, the main function of these groups was emotional support. Thus, online support groups show similarities to face-to-face groups in providing a format for the exchange of emotional support and practical advice from similar others.

The gender interactions in online groups may differ from face-to-face groups. One possibility is that online anonymity might free people from gender-bound rules of interaction, but a study on this topic (Postmes & Spears, 2002) found otherwise. When participants had no information about the gender of another, they tended to rely on gender stereotypes to guide their interaction more than when they knew the gender of others. When a topic fit with a masculine stereotype, men dominated the interactions, and similarly, when the topic was stereotypically feminine, women dominated. Therefore, gender issues in therapy and self-help carry over into cyberspace.

Gender Issues in Self-Help

Just as women are more likely to seek therapy, women are also more likely than men to participate in self-help groups. More than two thirds of those who attend support groups are women (Galegher et al., 1998). However, men are more likely than women to use the Internet, and men use online support groups more than women do. Although depression is more common among women and online support groups for depression are plentiful, only 40% of those who posted comments in such groups were women. This finding suggests that the Internet may furnish a forum in which men feel more comfortable in seeking help than they do in formal therapy or in face-to-face support groups.

Gender issues are often prominent in self-help groups because many such groups are formed around women's or men's issues. Consciousness-raising groups originated as a way for women to share their unique experiences, explore the similarities of their lives, and increase interaction with other women (Morgan, 1970). These groups began to form in the mid-1960s as part of the women's movement; thus, the aims of these groups were political as well as personal. The early emphasis on political ideology shifted to personal development (Kravetz, 1978). Instead of political activism, the most important goals became a sharing of thoughts and feelings about being women, learning about other women's experiences, increasing self-awareness, receiving emotional support, and examining the traditional gender role for women. Participants rated the groups as very successful in helping them to attain these goals, and the majority of participants encouraged other women to join groups. The personal changes experienced by women during consciousness-raising groups were likely to have been therapeutic, leading to these groups' becoming substitutes for or adjuncts to therapy (Enns, 1992).

The men's movement has also devised group meetings for men to share their concerns (Andronico, 2001). In the 1970s, men's groups were similar to early women's consciousness-raising groups, with the purpose of making members more sensitive to the politics and the disadvantages of their gender role. Both concentrated on the social inequities women had experienced and how rigid gender roles had harmed men as well as women. Men sought to understand how they had participated in and had been harmed by society's mandates for their behavior.

In the 1980s, the goals of the men's movement began to diverge from those of the women's movement (Faludi, 1991). Men's oppression became the theme of many men's groups during that decade, and men sought to redefine masculinity (Andronico, 2001; Bly, 1990). The format for this discovery is often in groups in which men discuss and explore their own experiences and problems with society's definition of masculinity. Men's groups have a greater diversity than women's consciousness-raising groups, but fewer men's groups exist. Women's groups tend to be oriented toward sensitizing women to the political goals of feminism, but men's groups have a variety of possible goals. Some men's groups have political goals, such as groups organized around gay rights, divorce, or custody rights; others supplement therapy for substance abuse; still others explore social conceptions of masculinity and ways to bring about positive personal and social changes. Unlike traditional psychotherapy, both women's and men's groups share the goals of reexamining gender roles and seeking possible avenues of change.

CONSIDERING DIVERSITY

Based on an examination of mental illness and treatment throughout the world, Robert Desjarlais and his colleagues (1995, p. 51) concluded

> how illness is understood and responded to actually shapes the illness itself, organizing symptoms, interpretations, and care-seeking activities in behavioral pathways that differ

across societies and ethnic groups. . . . Every local system of medical knowledge and healing must cope with prolonged sadness and withdrawal, with violence and irrational anger, and with seizures, emotional distress, and acute and chronic forms of madness.

The views of different cultures often vary from those in the United States and western Europe by failing to make the distinction between physical and mental illness, which produces differences in treatments as well as in diagnoses.

Many people in Asia, Africa, and Latin America have views of treatment that are not compatible with psychiatric treatments involving drugs and psychotherapy. In these cultures, healing processes include folk healers, ritual dramas, herbal medicine, and possession rituals (Desjarlais et al., 1995). In some cultures, professionals using drugs and psychotherapy have little success in treating people because the individuals receiving treatment do not share the same views about their problems that the therapist holds, and they have no confidence in these therapies. For example, the Yolmo Sherpa of Nepal experience a disorder symptomized by a loss of energy; a loss of interest in eating, working, and socializing; sleep problems; and feelings of "dullness." In the United States, these symptoms would probably result in a diagnosis of depression, but the Yolmo believe that these symptoms occur because one of their spirits has left the body and wanders around the countryside. The treatment involves a lengthy and elaborate ritual performed by a shaman, who tracks the lost spirit and helps it return to the afflicted person. For the Yolmo, this course of treatment is a better choice and probably more effective than antidepressant drugs.

Every society has ways of treating behavioral problems, but conflicts arise when a society consists of various groups with differing views of the sources and appropriate treatments for problems. On a worldwide basis, this conflict has occurred when western treatment has been imposed on cultures that hold different views. Creating a mental health care system seems to be a worthy goal, but that system may not serve the people who receive the services. In most countries in Asia, Africa, and Latin America, providers must make adaptations to the culture for treatment to be effective (Desjarlais et al., 1995).

In the United States and Canada, people from many different ethnic groups receive treatment from mental health care professionals, yet this treatment may be as incompatible with their cultural beliefs as the same treatments would be in Asia, Africa, and Latin America. Effective treatment requires adaptations to the clients' culture and beliefs. The mixture of ethnic groups in the United States and Canada creates a challenge for those who provide mental health care.

A special report on mental health and care for the United States (USDHHS, 2001a, p. 3) concluded that "Racial and ethnic minorities have less access to mental health services than do whites. They are less likely to receive needed care. When they receive care, it is more likely to be poor in quality." This discrepancy means that "*racial and ethnic minorities bear a greater burden from unmet mental health needs and suffer a great loss to their overall health and productivity*" (emphasis in original). Issues of inaccessibility of services, mistrust of health care professionals, and stigma associated with treatment create problems for ethnic minorities in the United States. Perhaps in response to these barriers, ethnic minorities have been less willing than Whites to seek mental health care, including self-help groups (USDHHS, 1999). However, African Americans and Native Americans are disproportionately represented in psychiatric hospitals (USDHHS, 1999), which suggests that these groups are more likely to be subjected to involuntary treatment.

Feminist therapy may provide a model for therapy that is sensitive to the concerns of ethnic minority clients (Mays & Comas-Díaz, 1988; Raja, 1998). Indeed, the desire to include diverse clients has been a goal for many feminist therapists (Comas-Díaz & Greene, 1994; Worell & Remer, 2003). The sensitivity to environmental factors and the recognition of the impact of social reality on psychological functioning make feminist therapy better suited to ethnic minority clients than therapies that conceptualize problems as personal and internal. Feminist therapy offers African American (Greene, 1994; Hall & Greene, 2003), Native American (LaFromboise, Berman, & Sohi, 1994), Asian American (Bradshaw, 1994), and Hispanic American (Vasquez, 1994) women a method to help them feel empowered, to give them skills to solve their problems, and to furnish opportunities to change society. By allowing these clients to center on family and community, feminist therapy can be useful to clients who are ethnic minorities.

Cultural sensitivity is also important in counseling with men from different ethnic groups. African American, Hispanic American, and Asian American men may be even more reluctant to seek therapy than White men. Their ethnic groups' conceptualizations about help-seeking and masculinity may be even stronger than for White men, exerting pressure against seeking care. For example, Hispanic men may be influenced by the concept of machismo (Casas, Turner, & Ruiz de Esparza, 2001), which calls for independence and toughness. They may struggle with ethnic stereotyping and discrimination as well a living up to the standards of their culture's concept of masculinity. Asian men (Sue, 2001) and African American men (Caldwell & White, 2001) experience similar struggles with stereotyping and discrimination. All use mental health services at lower rates than White men (USDHHS, 2001a), leaving men in these ethnic groups underserved.

Sexual orientation is another diversity issue, and the mental health care system has a history of failing to offer appropriate treatment to lesbians, gay men, and bisexuals. The emphasis on the social environment as a factor in psychological problems makes feminist therapy "one of few models of behavior change that intentionally perceives the variability of sexual orientations in human beings as a simple fact, rather than a matter for concern and intervention" (Brown, 1988, p. 206). Since that statement in 1988, other gender-sensitive therapies have met the criterion of accepting sexual orientation as a circumstance in people's lives rather than as a problem to be treated. Feminist therapy and other gender-sensitive therapies are obvious choices for helping lesbians and gay men in accepting their sexual orientation. In addition, gender-sensitive therapy is especially important for lesbians, gay men, and bisexuals, who may otherwise receive treatment for their sexual orientation rather than for the cause of their distress. An insensitive therapist may assume that their problem is related to their sexual orientation, and this biased assumption will result in inappropriate treatment. Thus, feminist or other gender-sensitive therapy is a good choice for lesbians, gays, and bisexuals.

■ SUMMARY

Psychoanalysis, the treatment based on Freud's conceptualization of personality development, was an early form of treatment for mental disorders. This therapy uses talk to help people bring unconscious material to consciousness, but dissatisfaction with the theory and practice of psychoanalysis prompted the development of alternative talk-based therapies. These alternatives included the humanistic approach to therapy, which attempts to help people fulfill their potential by accepting their emotions and feelings. Cognitive therapy focuses on thoughts and holds that changing irrational and self-defeating thoughts will produce a change in behavior. Behavior modification centers on applying the principles of operant conditioning to alter undesirable behaviors. Cognitive behavior therapy is a blending of cognitive therapy and behavior modification that attempts to alter cognitions and establish different behaviors.

Medical therapies are also used to treat behavior problems, including psychoactive drugs and electroconvulsive therapy. Psychoactive drugs are increasing in use, and women receive more prescriptions for psychoactive drugs than men do. Once used for many mental disorders, electroconvulsive therapy is now used largely for depression that has not responded to antidepressant drugs.

Charges of gender bias extend to all therapies. Psychoanalysis holds men as the standard for psychological development, a standard that women can never attain. Humanistic, cognitive, behavior modification, and cognitive behavior modification therapies are not inherently gender biased, but each offers a format in which therapists can impose their values. In addition, all concentrate on the individual and ignore the social and political aspects of problems. Research indicates that therapists focus on departures from traditional gender roles in their recommendations for treatment, and that therapy can be used to enforce traditional gender roles.

Nonsexist therapy was created in an attempt to remove the gender bias in therapy, but many female therapists believed that therapy should promote feminist goals. Feminist therapists hold that personal problems are reflections of wider social problems, strive to maintain equality in the relationship between client and therapist, and value the views of women as ways to empower their clients and help them bring about positive changes. From its initial position of political activism, feminist therapy has expanded to a wide variety of clients, including men.

In general, men are less often therapy clients than women are. Men's reluctance to seek therapy relates to the masculine gender role, and men with more traditional values are less willing to seek help than men with less traditional values. Men find it difficult to accomplish the goals of therapy, which often include discussing emotions or acknowledging vulnerability. Therapies to help traditional men are among the gender-sensitive therapies developed in recent years. Another gender-sensitive therapy is gender aware therapy that integrates an awareness of the impact of gender with encouragements to men and women to find what is right for them.

A growing number of complaints of gender bias in therapy has led the American Psychological Association to survey female psychologists about their experiences. The results of this survey revealed four areas of concern: (1) using sexist psychoanalytic concepts, (2) fostering traditional gender roles, (3) diminished expectations for female clients, and (4) treating women as sex objects, including having sex with clients.

Surveys of therapists have revealed that the sexual exploitation of clients by therapists occurs with between 9% and 12% of male therapists and between 2% and 3% of female therapists. The prevalence of this problem has led professional associations to include prohibitions against sexual relationships with clients, but this section nevertheless remains the most commonly violated of any of the ethical codes. A growing body of evidence indicates that intimate relationships with therapists do long-lasting harm to clients.

Rather than seeking therapy from professionals, a growing number of people join self-help groups. These groups mushroomed during the 1980s, and over 25 million people in the United States will participate in a self-help group at some time in their lives. Originating with the model of Alcoholics Anonymous, these groups offer emotional support and access to information from others who share the same type of problem. The low cost of self-help groups is attractive, and a growing number of people seek this form of support for a wide variety of problems.

The increase in access to the Internet has led to the development of online support groups. These groups share many similarities with other support groups, but they are available to a wider group of participants. Men are more likely to participate in the online format for self-help than in face-to-face groups. Both in online and face-to-face groups, gender is a consideration. Groups may be organized around gender-related issues, and even Internet anonymity does not erase gender stereotypes.

People in Asia, Africa, and Latin America may not have the same views of psychopathology as people in the United States and western Europe and thus may not readily accept psychotherapy or medical treatments for behavior problems. Treatment must be compatible with a culture to be accepted and successful, and providing culturally appropriate treatment presents challenges on a worldwide basis as well as in ethnically diverse societies such as the United States. With its emphasis on social context, feminist therapy or other gender-sensitive therapies are appropriate for people from a variety of cultures as well as for gays, lesbians, and bisexuals.

GLOSSARY

behavior modification   the application of principles of operant conditioning to behavior, with the goal of changing undesirable behavior to more acceptable alternatives.

electroconvulsive therapy   the application to the brain of electric current sufficient to induce a convulsion, which for unknown reasons produces therapeutic effects.

psychoanalysis   Freud's talk-based treatment for psychological problems that consists of attempts to bring unconscious material to consciousness.

repression   a defense mechanism used to push troubling material from the conscious into the unconscious.

SUGGESTED READINGS

Brooks, Gary R. (1998). *A new psychotherapy for traditional men.* San Francisco, CA: Jossey-Bass.
Brooks discusses the barriers that men face in therapy, men's needs for therapy, and how he came to change his approach as a therapist so that he could provide effective therapy to traditional men.

Pope, Kenneth S. (2000). Therapists' sexual feelings and behaviors: Research, trends, and quandaries. In Lenore T. Szuchman, & Frank Muscarella (Eds.), *Psychological perspectives on human sexuality* (pp. 603–658). New York: Wiley.

Pope reviews the research on prevalence of sexual contact among therapists and clients, details the evidence concerning the damage done to clients, and suggests ways to recognize therapists who are at risk and how to manage this problem.

Substance Abuse and Mental Health Services Administration (SAMHSA). (2003). *The NHSDA Report: Treatment among adults with serious mental illness.* Retrieved Aug. 5, 2003, from www.samhsa.gov/oas/2k3/SMIadultTX/SMIadultTX.cfm.

This brief U.S. government agency report presents statistics on barriers to treatment, including demographic and ethnicity differences in access to treatment for mental disorders.

Worell, Judith; & Johnson, Dawn. (2001). Therapy with women: Feminist frameworks. In Rhoda K. Unger (Ed.), *Handbook of the psychology of women and gender* (pp. 317–329). New York: Wiley.
Worell and Johnson trace the history of therapy with women, beginning with the dissatisfaction with sexist treatment and progressing through the variations of feminist therapies.

16 How Different?

Men and women have declared a cease-fire in the war that raged between the sexes through much of the last half of this [the 20th] century. In its place, they face common new enemies—the stress, lack of time and financial pressure of modern life. . . .

But rather than emphasizing their differences and blaming many of life's problems on each other, men and women share a sense of conflict and confusion about how to make it all work under today's pressures. To a large extent, the politics of resentment have become the politics of fatigue. (Morin & Rosenfeld, 1998, p. A1)

In a series of articles in the *Washington Post,* Richard Morin and Megan Rosenfeld (1998) reported on a national survey on the status and sentiments of women and men concerning work, families, relationships, and the problems of juggling them all. This survey showed that most women and men believe that increasing gender equity has benefited both, but both also agree that the transitions have not been smooth. This survey concentrated on the problems in working out new ways to handle work and family life, and a recurring theme was the difficulties in balancing the multiple roles that have become the rule for modern life.

MULTIPLE ROLES HAVE BECOME THE RULE

The traditional assumptions hold that women will choose jobs to support themselves until they marry, but will make marriage their primary careers, and men will devote themselves to careers while remaining marginally involved in family life. These stereotypical assumptions no longer hold for an increasing number of women and men. Like the women and men that Morin and Rosenfeld reported on in the headline story, a growing number of women pursue careers on a full-time, uninterrupted basis. As a result, many men no longer provide the sole support for their families. The *Washington Post* survey reflected the importance of "building successful marriages, raising children and leading satisfying lives"

(Morin & Rosenfeld, 1998, p. A1). But both men and women find it difficult to find the time to devote to marriage and family with the job demands that each experiences.

Their problems stem from social expectations and the fixed gender roles that these expectations bring. Despite joining the workforce of paid employment, women still are expected (and expect themselves) to occupy the role of wife and mother, including performing a majority of the household and family work. Men have experienced fewer changes in their roles, but men are beginning to participate more in household work and child care (Coltrane, 2000). The increasing number of employed women has led to increased acceptance of women in the workforce in addition to their role in the family, but men's roles have not undergone comparable changes and remain centered on the role of breadwinner. This expectation leaves men who want to be involved in household work and child care without social support for their choice, a situation that the participants in the *Washington Post* survey mentioned repeatedly; men who want to be involved in family life have few successful models. Instead, they have television commercials that ridicule men's efforts to do household work (Crain, 2001).

Both men and women may be dissatisfied with the inequity in household work, and they are working toward a more equitable division but have not managed to find one (Coltrane, 2000). Gender stereotypes push men toward "men's work" around the house, including mowing the lawn, shoveling snow, and taking out the trash, whereas women still perform the most time-consuming chores such as grocery shopping, food preparation and cleanup, and the majority of child care. Even when partners plan an equitable sharing of household work, they have difficulty implementing these plans, almost as though there is no "blueprint" for equal involvement.

Some jobs are especially problematic. High-level managerial and professional careers require long hours and extraordinary dedication. The corporate, male-dominated careers that women began entering in somewhat larger numbers during the 1970s have not changed to accommodate women's family duties (Hochschild, 1997). Men provided the model for these careers—men who had wives to provide a support system for their husbands' careers. These wives offered not only emotional support at home but also social support in the public functions of the organization (Williams, 2000). That is, the "corporate wife" joins auxiliaries, organizes social functions, and boosts her husband's career. Women too need "wives" to provide this support, but few husbands are willing to be the homemakers who offer support to successful female breadwinners.

An increasing number of men have taken the role of at-home support for employed wives (Tyre et al., 2003). A few men have chosen to be "Mr. Mom" and to devote time to being with their children. Their own success and their wives' career orientation and success may allow an easy reversal of the traditional roles, with women as breadwinners and men as caregivers. However, many of these husbands have taken this role as a result of the loss of their jobs, making their wives involuntary breadwinners and creating tensions in their marriages. Many of these couples discovered that, even in companies that have "family friendly" policies, two high-power careers do not mix with having children.

Pepper Schwartz (1994) studied couples who had managed to construct marriages in which each shared equitably in family life, and she contrasted these couples with more traditional marriages. One factor that distinguished these two types of couples was level of

◼ GENDERED VOICES

I've Had This Conversation Before

Melinda was a single mother with a 2-year-old son who told me about her experiences with the woman she had hired to care for her son. She considered herself and her son extremely fortunate; the nanny was a retired pediatric nurse, ideally qualified to be a nanny, and a wonderful person. Like many mothers with careers, Melinda felt less than enthusiastic at the thought of leaving her son in the care of someone else, and she felt fortunate not only to be able to afford a full-time, live-in nanny, but also to have found a great person. Indeed, they had become like a family.

Melinda's business career was demanding but fulfilling. She had worked as a secretary during the time that she was married, but she had divorced and pursued a sales and management career and had become successful. Like other women with demanding and fulfilling careers, she worked long and sometimes irregular hours.

Her son's nanny took care of him and the house, cooking dinner for herself and the child. She said that she could easily cook for Melinda as well; she would be glad to do so, but Melinda needed to be home to eat with them.

Melinda explained that she didn't always know when she would need to work late, and she couldn't be sure about being home in time for dinner every night. "But that doesn't matter. If I'm late, just leave my dinner. It's no big deal." The nanny said that it was a big deal; she didn't want to cook dinner and have her be late and have cold food. It just wasn't right. Melinda thought, "I've had this conversation before—when I was married. Only this time I'm being the 'husband,' and last time I was the wife. My husband said all the things I'm saying and gave all the excuses I'm giving, and I said the words I'm hearing from my nanny." Melinda was now the "husband."

employment: Few fast-track careers appeared among the marriages in which the partners shared equally. Schwartz found that these couples "maintain their relationship goals by folding work into the relationship rather than vice versa" (1994, p. 181). For both men and women, the relationship was more important than career. By making their relationship and home life primary, these couples have expanded the role for men, making them into full participants in their wives' and children's lives.

What are the consequences of multiple roles for men and women? Several models hypothesize different consequences of multiple roles (Barnett & Hyde, 2001). The *functionalist* holds that families function best when men concentrate on their jobs and women specialize on caring for home and children. This view dates back to the 1950s, when this family configuration was common and deviations were considered less than ideal. In this view, multiple roles lead to role conflict because people who try to fulfill many roles experience conflict when the multiple roles produce stress in their lives. An alternative model, the *psychoanalytic* view holds that boys develop a sense of autonomy that suits them to pursue accomplishments in the outside world, but girls do not. Thus women are unsuited for paid employment but well suited to domesticity and child care. This model also envisions a sharp division of gender roles and varying suitability for paid employment. Individuals who pursue unsuitable goals should experience problems. The view from *evolutionary* psychology also holds that women and men are inherently propelled toward different work and family roles by their evolutionary heritage. For example, one hypothesis drawn from this view is that women who have less contact with their families will experience more depression and mental health problems than those who stay in close contact. The *role expansion model* emphasizes the direct and indirect benefits of employment for women, proposing that the monetary benefits, the satisfaction of fulfilling several roles, and the protection of occupying several different roles will be beneficial. Table 16.1 shows these four models and the position of each on the effects of multiple roles.

Research supports the advantages of multiple roles, especially the benefits that come from employment. These benefits apply to women and men (Barnett & Hyde, 2001; de Vaus, 2002; Sachs-Ericsson & Ciarlo, 2000). Employment may cause stress, but its impact is similar for men and women and does not harm women more than men. Indeed, multiple roles *decreased* psychological distress in businesswomen, suggesting that the benefits of paid employment outweigh the stresses of fulfilling multiple roles (Abrams & Jones, 1994). Considering the economic and power benefits, women gain many advantages from paid employment.

Women's balance of career, household work, and child care may, indeed, produce stress, but the amount of support they receive is a mediating factor (Barnett & Hyde, 2001). For women with young children and no partner, their multiple roles of mother, head of household, and employee may be stressful, and these women tend to have more mental health problems than women with partners (Sachs-Ericsson & Ciarlo, 2000). For men, participation in child care and family chores increased fathers' feelings of competence as parents, and men tended to feel less stressed at home than at work (Larson & Richards, 1994). Employed, married men with children had fewer mental health problems than any other combination of demographic characteristics for people in the United States (Sachs-Ericsson & Ciarlo, 2000).

Although multiple roles have become the rule and evidence exists of the benefits of multiple roles, these changes have created stresses, especially in the transition to women in the workforce and men to household work and child care. As the couples in the *Washington Post* survey (Morin & Rosenfeld, 1998) indicated, the benefits were greater than the

TABLE 16.1   *Four Models for Multiple Role Occupancy*

Model	Result of Multiple Roles	Benefits
Functionalist	Conflict—Men should be breadwinners, and women should take care of household	None
Psychoanalytic	Conflict—Men are suited to the outside world and women to home	None
Evolutionary	Conflict and depression—"Natural" roles of breadwinning and homemaking are genetically programmed	None
Expansionist	Enhancement—Both men and women are healthier and more satisfied when they occupy roles of partner and employee	Direct and Indirect

Source: Based on "Women, Men, Work, and Family: An Expansionist Theory," by Rosalind Chait Barnett and Janet Hyde, 2001, *American Psychologist, 56,* pp. 782–785.

drawbacks, but the growing equity in their relationships produced more work for women, who now work more hours in paid employment, and for men, who now work more hours performing household work and child care. Are these changes what women and men really want?

WHAT DO WOMEN WANT? WHAT DO MEN WANT?

Questioning what women want became popular after Sigmund Freud asked the question of Marie Bonaparte in the 1930s (Jones, 1955). His version of the question, as many others have been, was an exasperated plea prompted by a genuine lack of understanding of women's motivations (Feist & Feist, 2002). Other men have contended that women's goals are unreasonable rather than mysterious. Are women's motives so troublesome and difficult to understand? How different are the things that women and men want?

Men's motives have not been subject to the same degree of scrutiny, but the changes in women's roles have forced men to examine their own lives to consider what they want. Much of this examination has centered on what men want from women and the difficulties that changes in women's lives have created for men. Do men want traditional women, "new" women, or some combination?

Have Women Become More Like Men?

"Why can't a woman be more like a man?" was the title of a song in the musical play *My Fair Lady* (Lerner & Loewe, 1956). Henry Higgins sang about how unreasonable women were in comparison to men, and as he longed for women and men to be more similar, he was voicing the stereotypical belief that women and men differ in many ways. Although this view was common at the time the musical appeared (and for some people, is accepted even now), the differences between genders may have been exaggerations. Gender differences may not have been as large as people believed, but these beliefs have been perpetrated by focusing on the differences and maintaining the dichotomy by conceptualizing an "opposite" sex.

Women have begun to take the opportunity to pursue some of the goals that were once reserved for men, most notably paid employment. If large differences once existed between men and women, perhaps the intervening years have allowed Higgins's wish to come true. Have women become more like men? And if this wish has come true, what do men think of these changes?

Higgins's wishes centered around emotionality; he listed negative emotions for women and positive ones for men. Of course, Higgins himself deviated from this ideal quite a bit, and his notion of emotional women failed to take into account the context of emotional expression (Shields, 2002). Women may report more emotional intensity than men do, but a willingness to report emotion is tied to gendered stereotypes of emotionality. Girls and boys spend years learning how to perform emotion in gendered ways according to the display rules of their culture. These social rules for displaying emotion shape the gender differences in emotionality.

Rather than women becoming more like men, the opposite trend has appeared in relationships; the typical feminine style of intimacy has become the standard for both men and women (Cancian, 1986). Although men often feel uncomfortable in sharing emotions with others, especially with other men, a growing number of men are seeking this style of relationship. Pressure for men to become more emotionally intimate has occurred in friendships, marriages, and other committed love relationships. Thus, women have not become more like men in this respect, but instead, men are feeling the pressure to become more like women.

Sexual behavior continues to show some gender differences. Some of those differences have decreased, but those that remain may be important. When Alfred Kinsey and his colleagues (1948, 1953) conducted their surveys in the 1930s and 1940s, women reported more sexual activity and enjoyment than the popular image of women portrayed, but the double standard for sexual behavior constrained women from expressing their sexuality. Women were less likely to masturbate and to have intercourse outside marriage than men were. Later surveys (Janus & Janus, 1993; Laumann et al., 1994) have shown a decrease in the differences.

Differences in sexuality may have a significant impact on heterosexual relationships (Hyde, 1996). Women now endorse a greater variety of sexual behaviors and are likely to have their first sexual intercourse at younger ages than in previous decades, but men masturbate more and favor casual sex more than women do. The implications of these differences may be larger than the differences themselves (Hyde, 1996).

For example, women's lower rate of masturbation may relate to their difficulties in having orgasms during sex with their partners, a problem that prompts many couples to seek therapy and many others to experience conflict in their sexual relationships (Hyde, 1996). (The advice of sex therapists often includes masturbation to learn how to have orgasms.) The difference in attitudes toward casual sex has a large influence on many relationships. When men and women bring different attitudes about commitment to sexual relationships, their varying standards can result in jealousy and conflict.

Changes in sexual attitudes have allowed women to explore their sexuality. Women made substantial changes in their sexual attitudes and behavior between the 1930s and the 1970s (Laumann et al., 1994). The conservatism of the 1980s and the growing fear of AIDS produced some decrease in the willingness for sexual exploration in both men and women, but women's exploration of their sexuality has taken them in directions that were not necessarily compatible with men's sexual preferences. Indeed, increased acceptance of sexuality other than intercourse led women to be less sexually dependent on men. This decreased dependence has become a source of men's discontent. Women have become more sexual, but not like men, and not necessarily to men's liking.

Women have become more like men in terms of their achievements: Educational differences between men and women have reversed, and women now receive more college degrees than men. Differences still persist in several areas of training and in the advanced and professional degrees awarded, but the gender gap is closing in training for prestigious careers such as law, business, and medicine. Women's gains may overcome men's current advantage, and more women than men will be qualified for high-status jobs in the future (Tiger, 2000).

Interviews with women about their achievements in one study revealed a picture of women who are proud of their progress in careers and who believe that they have fought and succeeded in gaining recognition (Sigel, 1996). Not only professional women but also working-class women expressed pride in women's accomplishments. Talking to men provided a different view: Men saw the changes in terms of letting women have more opportunities. This difference in view is very revealing, with each gender taking credit for the changes and seeing its own gender as responsible for those changes.

Employment gives women more economic advantages but also produces greater demands. Some of the older women in the *Washington Post* survey (Morin & Rosenfeld, 1998) reported that their employed daughters worked harder at home than they had during the 1950s. Many women see employment as a necessity rather than an option. Although some women have sought employment out of a desire for personal fulfillment, economic necessity is the reason that most women join the workforce. The degree to which women are satisfied with their employment varies according to the support they receive from their families as well as the support from their colleagues and supervisors on the job. Women whose husbands provide little assistance and emotional support for their employment are less satisfied than women with more supportive families.

In needing and providing support, women and men are now similar, but these similarities represent changes in their traditional roles. Female homemakers were the traditional caregivers, but employed women need to *receive* support from, as well as *provide* support to, their families. In the past, male breadwinners could expect the support of their wives, but they are now expected to provide their wives with emotional support and also help with household work. Through these changes, women and men have become more alike, but an increase in household chores was probably not what men like Henry Higgins had in mind.

Both women and men need the support of the other to be able to fulfill their dependency needs (Eichenbaum & Orbach, 1983). Men and women have similar needs, but the chances of fulfillment are usually not the same. Despite the helplessness and passivity some women display, they do not have someone on whom they can rely for emotional support, leaving dependency needs unmet. The lack of compatibility between meeting their own dependency needs and adopting the male gender role can make men feel ashamed of their dependency needs. In the past, men have been able to rely on women for emotional support, and women's increasing requests for emotional support from men can be an unwelcome change for many men.

These decreases in gender differences support the evidence that women and men have become more similar in education, employment, sexual attitudes and behavior, smoking rates, and athletic competition. The changes have occurred mostly in women, however. Whereas women have become more like men, men generally have not begun to adopt the positive aspects of women's behavior. This one-way change is not surprising when considering the situations that have produced the changes. Women have moved into the educational and employment worlds formerly occupied by men, but for the most part, men have not made corresponding moves into women's worlds. Thus, men encounter few, and women encounter many, situations that encourage the adoption of a more flexible style.

Despite superficial endorsement of the virtues of the traditional feminine role of homemaker and mother, society has accorded little value to nurturing skills or other traditional feminine behaviors (Cancian & Oliker, 2000). Men's traditional masculine style of assertive, independent, agentic behavior has set the mold for behavior in a variety of situations. Women who enter these situations tend to adopt the style of the situation, which is usually agentic rather than communal. Society's value of masculine over feminine traits results in women receiving rewards for adopting such active, instrumental behaviors and men receiving little encouragement for becoming more expressive or communal in their behavior. Thus, women have more freedom to become androgynous by combining the positive aspects of masculinity with the expressive, communal behaviors of femininity, but men have less encouragement to become more androgynous.

How do women feel about these changes? According to Susan Faludi (1991), a great deal of media attention has focused on the negative effects of the changes in women's lives. Faludi contended that the negative publicity about women's increased economic and sexual independence represents a reaction against these changes, and that the stories misrepresent women's actual feelings; women would like more opportunities rather than a return to traditional gender roles. These media reports tend to focus on interviews with selected discontented women rather than presenting studies with more representative samples. Women in a survey and interview study (Sigel, 1996) as well as women in the *Washington Post* survey (Morin & Rosenfeld, 1998) confirmed this view. Some women (and men) believe that family life would be better if someone were able to stay at home and take care of children, but a majority of women and men believe that going back to the gender roles of the 1950s is impossible and undesirable.

Men see more disadvantages to the changes in gender roles for men than women do for the changes for women. Faludi (1999) also examined contemporary men and masculinity, and found many problems. The traditional models of masculinity no longer seem either valid or available. Men's role as breadwinner is compromised by the decreasing availability of good jobs and the increasing number of employed women who can provide for themselves. A culture that seemed to revolve around boys and men stopped doing so, and women's concerns became preeminent. Many men to whom Faludi spoke voiced feelings of lack of control and isolation from family, work, and society. Faludi concluded that men have been led to expect privileges that they no longer have, leaving them feeling (as the title of one of her books indicates) "stiffed."

Henry Higgins's wish may have come true. Women have, indeed, become more like men, but the changes are not everything that he (and men like him) had hoped for. Most people find change difficult and anxiety provoking, and changes in expectations for men and women have come about very rapidly. Indeed, the changes have occurred faster than social institutions have been able to change to accommodate them. People have few models to emulate in adopting new gender roles, and they live in a society that pressures them to be more traditional. When gender roles were narrowly defined, everyone knew what to do. Although the rules were unquestionably restrictive, preventing people from performing gender-inappropriate activities, the roles were at least clear. Greater flexibility has produced uncertainty as well as options. Older men and women tend to feel less positively about the changes than younger men and women (Morin & Rosenfeld, 1998).

The power and privilege of men's traditional gender role put men in a position of having more to lose through change than women do, and men are less content than women with the changes that have occurred. Although some men have welcomed the opportunities to form more intimate relationships with friends and partners and to be involved in their children's lives, many others have resisted making changes or have found themselves not knowing how to enact the changes they want to make. Few men want some of the new options, such as careers as elementary school teachers or secretaries. Employed wives bring home incomes that may be very attractive, but few men welcome the prospect of having more household chores. Therefore, many men have not gotten what they wanted as women have become more like men.

Women too may not be entirely satisfied with the changes in their lives. As the many polls indicate, the majority of women favor more equal treatment in politics and jobs, but they too may resist making other changes in the roles and underlying assumptions about their relationships with men, their sexuality, and their children. Women become less interested in change when "it requires profound individual change as well, posing an unsettling challenge that well-adjusted people instinctively avoid. Why question norms of sex and character to which you've more or less successfully adapted?" (Kaminer, 1993, p. 51). Women do not want to lose their femininity in gaining equal rights, and they do not want to give up relationships with men (Sigel, 1996).

Some women long for a return to traditionalism, but that longing is stronger in men, who believe that changes in gender roles have caused them to lose more and gain less than women have. Women tend to complain, not about what they have lost, but about what they have gained—the equivalent of two full-time jobs. Men tend to complain about what they have lost—services and subservience. Table 16.2 summarizes some of these changes.

Why Can't a Man be More Like a Woman?

Men have not embraced the changes in gender roles and behaviors that have occurred in the past 25 years to the extent that women have. Study after study have found that men hold more rigid gender stereotypes than women do (see Chapter 7). Traditional men see no advantages for themselves in women's greater freedom. Indeed, these men feel the competition for grades and jobs, and they resent the presence of women in the workplace. Traditional men have stereotypical attitudes toward their own gender role and prefer women to adhere to traditional femininity. These men do not feel the appeal of expanding their gender role to include behaviors traditionally reserved for women, so they see nothing but disadvantages connected with changing gender roles.

The *Washington Post* survey (Morin & Rosenfeld, 1998) revealed that age is an important factor in men's attitudes toward changing roles. Traditional men were more likely to be older. Many men may be considered to be in transition between traditional views of male dominance and embracing new roles for women and for men. These men tend to see the progress but also acknowledge that progress has come with problems, saying that changes in women's and men's roles have made a lot of people's lives better but some people's worse. These men are likely to be sympathetic to individual women but unlikely to embrace women's issues.

TABLE 16.2   *Ways Men and Women Have Changed over Past 30 Years*

Women Have Become More Like Men In	
Education	• Women earned 57% of bachelor's, 58% of master's, and 44% of all doctoral degrees granted in 2000 (USBC, 2002)
Employment	• 47% of workforce is female (USBC, 2002)
Earnings	• Women earn 77¢ for every $1 earned by men (up from 59¢ in 1970s) (U.S. Bureau of Labor Statistics, 2003)
Sexual attitudes and behaviors	• Age of first intercourse is similar for girls and boys in ethnic groups in United States except for African Americans (Upchurch et al., 1998) • 88% of men and 81% of women engage in premarital sex (Christopher & Sprecher, 2000) • 98.9% of men and 99.2% of women want to settle down with one sexual partner at some time during their lives (Pedersen et al., 2002) • Large majority of men and women find extramarital sex unacceptable (Laumann et al., 1994)
Physical activity	• 25.5% of women and 27.0% of men are adequately physically active (USBC, 2002)

Men Have Become More Like Women in	
Forming intimate relationships	• Women's talk-based style of intimacy has become the standard (Cancian, 1986)
Smoking rate	• 25% of men and 21% of women currently smoke cigarettes (USBC, 2002)
Dieting	• 67% of men and 80% of women are dieting or trying not to gain weight (Serdula et al., 1999)

Younger men were especially likely to endorse equality for women. Women reported that men were beginning to "get it" concerning the discrimination and difficulties that women face. Very few of these men are actively involved in the profeminist men's movement, and few of them would consider themselves feminist in their views, but most men and women see that going back to traditional roles and behaviors is not likely.

But how far do we want the transition to go? Women have become more like men, but men have more often declined than accepted opportunities to become more like women. That is, women have developed a more instrumental orientation, but many men have failed to develop their expressive skills. The asymmetry of these changes may have created a situation in which women want men to change. Women are asking Henry Higgins's question from their own point of view: "Why can't a man be more like a woman?"

This question exists in two versions, one social and one personal. The first version applies to the question as a social one, challenging the wisdom of continuing to use men and masculine values as the preferred style. For example, what makes the hierarchical, directive (sometimes autocratic) style of leadership that men typically use preferable to the cooperative, democratic style women typically use? What is wrong with emphasizing relationships and being emotionally expressive? Why can't men accept the value of the feminine style? Why are men considered the standard and women the exception (Bem, 1993b)? The second version of the question is more personal, challenging men to include more expressiveness in personal relationships and to participate more fully in "women's work," that is, household work and child care. Women contend that both society at large, as well as their individual lives, would profit from men accepting the value of men becoming a bit more like women.

Some evidence exists to indicate that people have no problems accepting the value of the communal qualities associated with women. Alice Eagly and her colleagues (Eagly & Johannesen-Schmidt, 2001; Eagly, Mladinic, & Otto, 1991) investigated evaluations of men and women, finding that women received more positive personal evaluations than men did. People think of women as a social category in very positive terms, but not necessarily when women exhibit these qualities in positions traditionally held by men. As Eagly et al. (1991) put it, "Although people evidently think that these qualities are wonderful human attributes, they may value them more in close relationships than in highly paid sectors of the workforce" (p. 213). Thus, the evidence concerning positive attitudes about women does not ensure the social acceptance of their style in roles other than traditional ones, despite evidence that these behaviors foster positive workplace outcomes (Eagly & Johannesen-Schmidt, 2001).

Some men have recognized the value of developing greater emotional expressiveness and have attempted to make changes in their behavior. Although these men believe that women and men should have equal power in relationships and equal access to education and careers, they may find these principles difficult to incorporate into their lives. Society offers few models of couples who develop equal relationships, but many examples of traditional couples. However, couples are attempting to build new ways of living together and raising children, with both partners contributing in the workforce and at home. Indeed, according to the *Washington Post* survey (Morin & Rosenfeld, 1998), a good marriage and family life was a top priority for both women and men, and many saw the advantages of equity in achieving these goals.

What are the prospects for men becoming more like women? And how would women feel if they did? Currently, the rewards for men who adopt more expressive behaviors are not as great as for women who become more instrumental, which leads to the prediction that men may not change as much as women have. If the men who are involved in the men's movement provide any omen of changes to come, then men have little interest in adopting very many feminine qualities. Leaders in the men's movement, such as Sam Keen (1991) and Robert Bly (1990, 1994), have urged men to explore their masculinity and make changes in their attitudes and behavior, but their recommendations do not include listening to women to know what changes to make. The men's movement concept of authentic masculinity includes increased expressiveness and responsibility, making this view of what men should become correspond to the changes that many women want.

However, women do not want men to be like women (Bloom, 2002). Women see the benefits of breaking the stereotypes, both for themselves and for men. Indeed, many examples exist of individuals who easily break these rules, such as the men who do most of the cooking and women who repair automobiles. The ideals have changed so that the ideal for women as well as men is strong, smart, and self-reliant and the ideal for men as well as women is sensitive and affectionate. But this androgyny goes only so far. Parents do not want girls to become so strong, smart, and self-reliant that they have trouble getting invited to the prom, or boys to become so sensitive that they are taunted and bullied. The gender lines may not be drawn where they were, but the lines still exist.

WHERE ARE THE DIFFERENCES?

One of the places where differences exist between the genders is in the theories used to explain psychological factors related to gender. The traditional dichotomy for theories of gender is the biological view versus the environmental view—attributing differences to either nature or nurture. Although these opposing points of view have influenced research in gender, another approach now encompasses the nature–nurture debate in gender—the maximalist versus the minimalist positions.

The maximalist view holds that men and women have large differences, whereas the minimalist view holds that the differences between men and women are small compared to their similarities. The older versions of maximalist theory are biologically based, emphasizing differences, and offering genetic or hormonal explanations for behavior as well as for anatomy. These theorists tend to accept biological explanations as evidence of unchanging, fixed patterns of behavior. Thus, the biological explanation includes inevitable differences. These theorists tend to rationalize the disadvantaged social position of women (and often of ethnic minorities) by citing biological programming as the source of differences. Naomi Weisstein (1982, p. 41) summarized this position by saying, "Men are biologically suited to their life of power, pleasure, and privilege, and women must accept subordination, sacrifice, and submission. It's in the genes. Go fight city hall."

Not surprisingly, feminist scholars have disputed the biological basis of behavioral differences between men and women, proposing that social experiences produce differences in learning and thus in behavior. According to this view, social learning and situations, not biology, form the basis for psychological gender differences. This approach holds that behavior varies according to circumstances and surroundings, and these theorists attribute gender differences to the different situations that women and men typically encounter. Those who hold this view tend to be minimalists, accepting few essential differences between men and women.

Newer versions of the maximalist position also rely on social learning to explain gender differences. Although these theorists see the differences between women's and men's behavior as learned, they believe that the differences are large and persistent. Many of these maximalist theorists are cultural feminists, advocating the superiority of women's style and characteristics. Rather than accepting the differences as deficiencies, they promote the female version as the better alternative.

These theorists (including Gilligan, Chodorow, and Tannen) are appealing to some women because "they offer a flattering account of traits for which they have historically been castigated" (Pollitt, 1992, p. 802). This view is a modernized version of the Doctrine of the Two Spheres, the Victorian view that women were moral, pure, spiritual, emotional, and intellectually inferior. Unfortunately, the virtues that these maximalists idealize help rationalize the continued subordination of women. What's more, the popularity of this view is ironic, given that the roles of women and men are more similar than they have been at any time during the history of the West.

Both maximalists and minimalists look at the same research and find evidence to support their positions. The ability to maintain different interpretations of the same information highlights the constructed nature of theories; that is, those who support one view or the other have constructed their position in accordance with their beliefs about gender. Building and maintaining a theoretical position requires examining the research evidence, but theory goes beyond evidence. Therefore, it is possible for theorists to maintain discrepant positions with regard to gender differences, with some theorists holding maximalist and others minimalist positions.

Theories are not the only place that gender differences exist; gender-related differences also exist in behavior. The extent of gender-related differences, however, depends on the type of study considered. In considering studies on ability, few gender differences have appeared. In considering the choices that men and women have made about what to do in their lives, the gender differences are larger.

Differences in Ability

Considering the many comparisons of abilities of women and men, the gender differences are largest for physical strength. This difference relates to size and muscle mass, with men being significantly larger and stronger than women. The differences among individuals are also large; some women are stronger than other women, and some men stronger than other men. However, gender differences are larger than individual differences, making gender a good predictor of strength.

In the past, physical strength made a great deal of difference for a variety of activities, especially in the world of paid employment. Currently, few positions of prestige and power require strength, but the legacy of this position persists. In a survey and interview study of gender issues (Sigel, 1996), several men expressed the opinion that men should be paid more than women because men's jobs require more strength. Despite the high levels of skills that secretaries might need, they should receive less money, according to this view, because their jobs do not require heavy labor. The requirements for physical labor were also mentioned as a reason why men should not be expected to share household work or child care—they had already done physical labor and should not be expected to do more at home.

Gender is a very poor predictor of mental abilities. In both verbal abilities and mathematical abilities, only small gender differences exist. Despite the widespread belief that men have superior mathematical abilities and women have superior verbal abilities, the technique of meta-analysis has revealed that the gender differences are small (Hyde, 1996;

Hyde, Fennema, & Lamon, 1990; Hyde & Linn, 1988). The largest difference in cognitive abilities is in one type of spatial task, the mental rotation task, and in writing. Men have a large advantage in mental rotation, and women have a large advantage in writing ability, but other spatial and verbal tasks show a mixed pattern of advantages for men or women.

Research conducted in laboratory settings often shows few if any gender differences. When men and women are put into situations without gender-related cues, their behavior tends to be quite similar. For example, a literature review (Frodi, Macaulay, & Thome, 1977) and meta-analyses (Bettencourt & Miller, 1996; Eagly & Steffen, 1986; Knight, Guthrie, Page, & Fabes, 2002) of aggression have shown that women and men are similar in their willingness to behave aggressively in laboratory situations, but outside the laboratory, gender differences appear. One prominent difference is the type of aggression; men tend to choose direct confrontation whereas women are more likely to use an indirect strategy of causing harm.

Thus, the evidence about gender differences in abilities indicates a few large differences and many more small differences. Table 16.3 summarizes these few differences. When examining the behavioral choices that men and women make, gender differences are larger than when considering abilities.

TABLE 16.3   *Where Are the Differences?*

Differences between Men and Women Are Large In	
Size	• Men are larger than women
Strength	• Men are stronger than women, especially in terms of upper-body strength
Mental rotation ability	• Men are much better at mentally rotating figures in space than women are
Writing ability	• Women are better at writing than men are
Size of sexually dimorphic nucleus	• The sexually dimorphic nucleus is a brain structure that is larger in men, but its function is not currently understood
Gender flexibility	• Girls and women stereotype less and have more liberal attitudes about gender roles than boys and men do
Crime rate	• 77.5% of those arrested for crimes are men; 22.5% are women (FBI, 2002)
Sexual attitudes and behavior	• Men masturbate more than women (and feel less guilty about it) • Men are more acceptant of casual premarital sex than are women
Overweight	• 65% of men but only 48% of women in United States are overweight (USBC, 2002)
Strategy of dealing with negative feelings	• Women are diagnosed with depression twice as often as men (APA, 2000) • Men are diagnosed with substance abuse disorders at ratios of 3–5:1 compared to women (APA, 2000)

Differences in Choices

Women and men make different choices about important facets of their lives, and these choices reflect the behaviors that are encouraged for each gender. Saying that women make different choices than men implies that these choices are voluntary and freely made, but such is not the case. As Joan Williams (2000) described the situation, women and men are propelled by force fields that push them toward certain options and away from others, making the traditional choices the only available options for many individuals. Many barriers that prevented women and men from attempting some activities seem to have fallen away, but constraints remain in the form of expectations and encouragement. These choices are more important than abilities in determining what happens in people's lives. The gender differences that exist in education, employment, family life, relationships, sexuality, emotionality, health-related behaviors, body image, and behavior problems reflect these different choices and the expectations that foster them.

Although men and women have similar mathematical ability and now have similar preparation in terms of courses completed in high school (Bae, Choy, Geddes, Sable, & Snyder, 2000), young men are more likely than women to pursue careers that rely on math. Even women who complete the courses required for a good math background do not choose science and engineering careers as often as men do (Ayalon, 2003). These discrepancies are larger than the differences in abilities would suggest: Fewer women enter mathematics and engineering than women who have the ability to do so (Hyde, 1996).

The expectation that men will pursue careers consistent with the breadwinner role and that women will seek careers compatible with family duties eliminates many options for each. Men are limited in their family involvement by careers that require dedication and long hours. Men do not receive encouragement when they make different choices, such as allotting time to family life by choosing part-time employment or by choosing to be homemakers. Indeed, this choice is considered deviant, and men who have made such decisions are encouraged to reconsider (Guanipa & Woolley, 2000; Robertson & Fitzgerald, 1990).

The movement of women into the paid workforce has increased their options in some ways but not in others. Women have more choices than men do concerning employment or homemaking—women may be homemakers or employed, or alternate the two, but men are still expected to be employed. However, the expectation is coming to be that women will be employed in addition to having a husband and children (Granrose & Kaplan, 1996; Konrad, 2003; Phillips & Imhoff, 1997). Women who have chosen to have a career and family experience the strains of juggling roles as they work to develop their careers, find adequate child care, and make time for children and husbands. Women who have chosen to be homemakers feel that their choice is not as well accepted or respected as the choice of pursuing paid employment, but they feel that the job they are doing is essential for their children's well-being. Women who have paid employment but would rather be homemakers, and those who had expected to pursue careers but are instead homemakers, face conflict between their expectations and their actual lives (Granrose & Kaplan, 1996). The change in patterns of employment for women has resulted in additional role responsibilities as well as an additional option.

Men and women tend to choose different styles of friendships, and this difference is clearly a choice. That is, most women and men are capable of adopting the style of friendship more common in the other gender. A woman can be "one of the boys," and a man can adopt the emotionally intimate friendship pattern more common among women, but each tends to choose a gender-typical style of relating to others. This choice gives women more intimate friendships with other women than with men, and it prevents men from forming intimate friendships with other men (and possibly with women). Friendships are one source of social support that brings advantages for physical and mental health. Women's style of friendship tends to provide more emotional support, whereas men's style of friendship tends to offer more material support. The advantages of social support come from both types of support and extend to both women and men.

Women's choice of achieving intimacy through emotional sharing and talk has become the accepted style for love relationships (Cancian, 1986), and men may feel deficient if they are not adept at this type of relating. Men's attempts to establish intimacy through sexual activity are not entirely compatible with women's choice to create intimacy through talk and sharing feelings. Thus, sexuality may have different meanings for women and men. Even with comparable levels of desire, men and women make different choices concerning expression of their sexuality.

Different choices also appear to be related to the varying life expectancies of men and women, with women choosing healthier and safer lifestyles in terms of their use of health care services, diet, alcohol intake, and seat belt use. On the other hand, men tend to make better choices by exercising and avoiding unhealthy dieting. Both patterns match the interpretation that men's and women's health-related behaviors are oriented toward maintaining their gender roles. Much of women's health-related behavior is not oriented toward health, but due to their concern over weight and thinness. Likewise, men exercise to attain a muscular appearance and choose risky health-related behaviors, which match the Give 'Em Hell component of the masculine gender role.

Men's and women's strategies for handling negative feelings can lead to different outcomes. These differences appear both in statistics on violence and in rates of various types of psychopathology. The display rules for emotion allow (and perhaps even encourage) men to openly express anger, leading to more acts of violence and crime committed by men. Women are encouraged to restrict their displays of anger, leading not to a decrease in the experience of anger, but to differences in the expression of anger. One difference is that women often cry when they are angry, whereas men typically do not.

Different choices for dealing with negative feelings may be reflected in the statistics on psychiatric diagnosis. Women are more likely to receive the diagnosis of depression than men are, but men are more likely to drink alcohol and use other illicit psychoactive substances than women are. Some evidence exists that a pattern of avoidant coping involving alcohol use is related to developing depression (Holahan, Moos, Holahan, Cronkite, & Randall, 2001, 2003), which may be a more common strategy for men. Ruminating over negative events is also related to developing depression (Nolen-Hoeksema, 2001; Nolen-Hoeksema & Jackson, 2001; Nolen-Hoeksema, Larson, & Grayson, 1999), but this strategy is more common among women. These different choices produce apparent differences in psychopathology, but may not indicate a difference in the experience of negative emotions.

The expression of psychopathology tends to fall along gender-stereotypical lines (Chesler, 1972; Rosenfield, 1982). The categories of psychopathology most common among women fall into the feminine gender role, but are exaggerated versions of the role: being dependent (dependent personality disorder), passive (major depression), self-sacrificing (self-defeating personality disorder), fearful (agoraphobia), and emotional (histrionic personality disorder). Likewise, men experience psychopathology that seems to have formed around elements of the masculine gender role, but exaggerates these traits: being irresponsible, untruthful, and violent (antisocial personality disorder), reckless (psychoactive substance abuse disorder), and inappropriately sexual (paraphilias). Although these patterns may not represent intentional choices, they exist as reflections of gender-typical differences.

The choices that men and women make tend to fall along the lines sanctioned by tradition. Men's choices and women's choices tend to keep men and women each in their own category, which creates two domains—male and female—with limited "visitation privileges" from one to the other. Yet these two domains are not different planets, as the best-selling book *Men Are from Mars, Women Are from Venus* (Gray, 1992) suggested. Rather, "the truth is, there is only one culture, and it shapes each sex in distinct but mutually dependent ways in order to reproduce itself" (Pollitt, 1992, p. 806).

The freedom to make cross-gender choices is still limited. An argument has been made that there are benefits derived from perpetuating gender categories. Although such categorization may be convenient to each gender, it limits options to only those two well-defined choices. This limitation shares the problem posed by all stereotyping: These choices ignore the inherent complexity of individual differences and fail to allow for a wide range of individual choices. The benefit of convenience is outweighed by the cost of the limitations. The abilities of men and women demand an equally wide range of choices—wider than the choices that are available in the bipolar classification of traditional gender roles.

Is a peace plan possible for the gender war? Have the forays into each other's worlds increased understanding and empathy? The results from the *Washington Post* survey (Morin & Rosenfeld, 1998) suggested a move in that direction. Unlike earlier surveys (Sigel, 1996) that had reported continued discrimination against women and little attention to gender issues by men, this more recent survey included many reports of men who were dedicated to family involvement, discouraging sexual harassment in the workplace, respecting their female colleagues, and doing the laundry. Some men continue to complain about "the good old days" when women "knew their place," but these men are becoming less common and less vocal. After about a generation of sharing the workplace and attempting to forge equally shared personal partnerships, changes have taken place.

The quest for gender equity is by no means finished. The gender gap remains in wages and in household work. A new gender gap has appeared in education, with men lagging behind women. But as Morin and Rosenfeld's (1998) headline article suggested, women and men are coming to perceive the pressures of modern life as the enemy instead of each other. Many couples have worked out equitable plans for living together and have built satisfying personal relationships (Schwartz, 1994). Building such relationships often requires analyzing the underlying assumptions connected with gender roles and finding ways to overcome the roles that society dictates for women and men. Equity is still elusive, but an increasing number of couples are trying for a peace plan for themselves.

For society, peace in the gender war is not so close. As the couples in the *Washington Post* survey (Morin & Rosenfeld, 1998) mentioned, modern society is filled with barriers that make successful romantic partnerships, raising children, and leading satisfying lives difficult to attain. The traditional assumptions about women's and men's roles are one type of barrier. Despite many people's willingness to make individual exceptions, the rules still exist. As Williams (2000) described, these rules about gender roles exert force fields that push women and men toward traditional roles. Those roles include the type of oppositional thinking that helps to perpetuate the gender war.

■ SUMMARY

The roles that men and women occupy have undergone changes in the past three decades, allowing women to move into careers that had formerly been the province of men. As women began to acquire careers and salaries comparable with men's, some men began to imagine that women would become more like them, which would make relating to each other easier. Some of these men have been disappointed, because women have made changes in their lives, but not always the changes that men had in mind.

The changes in women's employment have been additive rather than substitutive; that is, most women who are employed outside their homes also have family work to do when at home. Thus, most women are now employees, wives, and mothers. These multiple roles present stress in women's lives but also offer rewards. Research indicates that the rewards outweigh the stresses for most women. Men also occupy multiple roles as employees, husbands, and fathers. Although today's men do more household work than their fathers, they do less than their wives. Research indicates that men find multiple roles rewarding, and many men are trying to build equitable relationships with their wives and active roles in their families.

Men have long wondered what women want and have expressed the desire for women to behave in ways more similar to men. Gender differences may never have been as large as many people imagined, but men have gotten their wish in several respects: Women's behavior has changed to become more like men's behavior in terms of education and occupation. Men, however, did not envision competition from women at work as a desirable outcome of gender similarity, but as women have moved into the worlds of higher education and paid employment, they have assumed roles and behaviors required by these situations. Men and women have become more alike in terms of education, employment, sexual attitudes and behavior, athletic competition, and rates of smoking. Few gender differences exist in experiencing emotion, but differences remain in how emotions are displayed. Men have become more like women, however, in their style of forming close personal relationships and are beginning to explore the rewards of opening up to emotional sharing and talk.

Although the changes in women's lives have prompted men to change, these alterations have not been equal to the ones that women have experienced. A combination of the devaluation of traditionally feminine behaviors and the value placed on the activities that men perform has pushed women toward change. Some men dislike these changes and long once again for traditional roles for both, but a larger number of men are willing to adapt to changing gender roles.

Women also wish for changes in men; they want men to accept and adopt some of the characteristics typical of women. Women would like for men to accept the validity of the feminine approach and to feel comfortable in adopting positive behaviors traditionally associated with women. One of these desired changes has occurred to some extent—the change in ways to communicate in intimate relationships. Women would like for men to be more emotionally expressive and to communicate intimate thoughts and feelings to their partners. Women would also like for men to become more active with their families, sharing household work and child care.

If women have become more like men in a number of ways, and if men have become more like women in some ways, how many gender differences remain? Differences continue in theories, with maximalist theories advocating that differences exist between the genders, and minimalist theories arguing for more similarities than differences.

Research on gender and ability has revealed relatively few differences. The largest of these differences in ability lies in men's greater physical strength, but few differences exist when measuring other abilities in laboratory situations. When examining the choices that men and women make concerning how to live their lives, larger gender differences appear. Indeed, the difference in choices may promote the idea that greater differences exist than research has confirmed.

The choices that women and men make tend to preserve well-defined gender roles rather than allow people to make freer choices and develop the most satisfying lives. Strict enforcement of gender-related behaviors may simplify rules of conduct, but preserving this dichotomy extracts a high price for individual women and men. On an individual level, peace between women and men is possible, and many couples have built relationships that allow them to participate fully in the workforce, household work, child care, and each other's lives. On a societal level, the gender wars will be more difficult to end because the widespread acceptance of inflexible gender roles is a societal-level issue.

SUGGESTED READINGS

Barnett, Rosalind Chait; & Hyde, Janet Shibley. (2001). Women, men, work, and family: An expansionist theory. *American Psychologist, 56,* 781-796.
Barnett and Hyde review the models and the evidence concerning the conflict between family and employment obligations. They suggest a model that is consistent with the benefits of occupying multiple roles.

Faludi, Susan. (1999). *Stiffed: The betrayal of the American man.* New York: Morrow.
Faludi's book about men takes a sympathetic look at the dilemmas that men face in fulfilling the demands of their several roles. By examining many men in various situations, Faludi hears men's concerns and problems.

Schwartz, Pepper. (1994). *Peer marriage: How love between equals really work.* New York: Free Press.
Schwartz examines couples' relationships, focusing on couples who have managed to construct marriage relationships in which both members are peers. Her report reveals the problems and advantages of working toward such relationships.

REFERENCES

Aboud, Frances E.; Mendelson, Morton J; & Purdy, Kelly T. (2003). Cross-race peer relations and friendship quality. *International Journal of Behavioral Development, 27,* 165–173.

Abrams, Leslie R.; & Jones, Russell W. (1994, August). *The contribution of social roles to psychological distress in businesswomen.* Paper presented at the 102nd annual convention of the American Psychological Association, Los Angeles, CA.

Adami, Hans-Olov; & Trichopoulos, Dimitrios. (2002). Cervical cancer and the elusive male factor. *New England Journal of Medicine, 346,* 1160–1161.

Addis, Michael E.; & Mahalik, James R. (2003). Men, masculinity, and the contexts of help seeking. *American Psychologist, 58,* 5–14.

Adler, Jerry. (1996, June 17). Building a better dad. *Newsweek, 127* (25), 58–64.

Ajram, K. (1992). *Setting the record straight: The miracle of Islamic science.* Retrieved April 28, 2003, from www.cyberistan.org/islamic/sciencehistory.htm.

Akiyama, Hiroko; Elliott, Kathryn; & Antonucci, Toni C. (1996). Same-sex and cross-sex relationships. *Journals of Gerontology, Series B, 51,* 374–382.

Alfieri, Thomas; Ruble, Diane N.; & Higgins, E. Tory. (1996). Gender stereotypes during adolescence: Developmental changes and the transition to junior high school. *Developmental Psychology, 32,* 1129–1137.

Allen, Bem P. (1995). Gender stereotypes are not accurate: A replication of Martin (1987) using diagnostic vs. self-report and behavioral criteria. (C. L. Martin's article, *Journal of Personality and Social Psychology,* vol. 52, p. 489, 1987) *Sex Roles, 32,* 583–600.

Allen, Elizabeth Sandin; Baucom, Donald H.; Burnett, Charles K.; Epstein, Norman; & Rankin-Esquer, Lynn A. (2001). Decision-making power, autonomy, and communication in remarried spouses compared with first-married spouses. *Family Relations, 50,* 326–334.

Allmendinger, Jutta; & Hackman, J. Richard. (1995). The more, the better? A four-nation study of the inclusion of women in symphony orchestras. *Social Forces, 74,* 423–460.

Allport, Gordon W. (1954). *The nature of prejudice.* Reading, MA: Addison-Wesley.

Altman, Lawrence K. (1997, June 22). Is the longer life the healthier one? *New York Times,* Section 14 (Women's Health), p. 18.

American Academy of Pediatrics. (2003). *Media matters: A national media education campaign.* Retrieved June 28, 2003, from www.aap.org/advocacy/mmcamp. htm.

American Association of University Women (AAUW). (1992). *The AAUW report: How schools shortchange girls.* Washington, DC: American Association of University Women Education Foundation and National Educational Association.

American Association of University Women (AAUW). (1993). *Hostile hallways: The AAUW survey on sexual harassment in America's schools.* Washington, DC: American Association of University Women Educational Foundation.

American Association of University Women Educational Foundation. (2001). *Hostile hallways: Bullying, teasing and sexual harassment in school.* Washington, DC: Author.

American Demographics. (2002). Sex and the city. *American Demographics, 24* (10), 11–12.

American Psychiatric Association (APA). (2000). *Diagnostic and statistical manual of mental disorders* (4th ed., Text revision). Washington, DC: Author.

American Psychological Association (APA) Task Force on Sex Bias and Sex-Role Stereotyping in Psychotherapeutic Practice. (1978). Guidelines for therapy with women. *American Psychologist, 33,* 1122–1123.

Amponsah, Benjamin; & Krekling, Sturla. (1997). Sex differences in visual-spatial performance among Ghanian and Norwegian adults. *Journal of Cross-Cultural Psychology, 28,* 81–92.

Amsterdam, Jay D.; Brunswick, David J.; & O'Reardon, John. (2002). Bipolar disorder in women. *Psychiatric Annals, 32,* 397–404.

Andersen, Arnold E.; & DiDomenico, Lisa. (1992). Diet vs. shape content of popular male and female magazines: A dose–response relationship to the incidence of eating disorders? *International Journal of Eating Disorders, 11,* 283–287.

Anderson, Craig A.; & Bushman, Brad J. (2002). Human aggression. *Annual Review of Psychology, 53,* 27–52.

Anderson, Elizabeth. (2002, Fall). Feminist epistemology and philosophy of science. In Edward N. Zalta (Ed.), *The Stanford Encyclopedia of Philosophy.* Retrieved April 28, 2003, from http://plato.stanford.edu/archives/fall2002/entries/feminism-epistemology.

Anderson, Kristin J; & Leaper, Campbell. (1998). Meta-analyses of gender effects on conversational interruption: Who, what, when, where, and how. *Sex Roles, 39,* 225–252.

Andronico, Michael P. (2001). Mythopoetic and weekend retreats to facilitate men's growth. In Gary R. Brooks & Glenn E. Good (Eds.), *The new handbook of psychotherapy and counseling with men: A comprehensive guide to settings, problems, and treatment approaches* (pp. 664–682). San Francisco, CA: Jossey-Bass.

Aneshensel, Carol S.; Frerichs, Ralph R.; & Clark, Virginia A. (1981). Family roles and sex differences in depression. *Journal of Health and Social Behavior, 22,* 379–393.

Angier, Natalie. (1999). *Woman: An intimate geography.* Boston: Houghton Mifflin.

Antill, John K. (1983). Sex role complementarity versus similarity in married couples. *Journal of Personality and Social Psychology, 45,* 145–155.

Antill, John K.; Goodnow, Jacqueline J.; Russell, Graeme; & Cotton, Sandra. (1996). The influence of parents and family context on children's involvement in household tasks. *Sex Roles, 34,* 215–236.

Apgar, Barbara. (2000). Premenstrual syndrome and the placebo response. *American Family Physician, 61,* 850.

Apodaca, Timothy R.; & Miller, William R. (2003). A meta-analysis of the effectiveness of bibliotherapy for alcohol problems. *Journal of Clinical Psychology, 59,* 289–304.

Aranda, Maria P.; Castaneda, Irma; Lee, Pey-Jiuan; & Sobel, Eugene. (2001). Stress, social support, and coping as predictors of depressive symptoms: Gender differences among Mexican Americans. *Social Work Research, 25,* 37–48.

Archer, John. (2000). Sex differences in aggression between heterosexual partners: A meta-analytic review. *Psychological Bulletin, 126,* 651–680.

Aries, Elizabeth. (1987). Gender and communication. In Phillip Shaver & Clyde Hendrick (Eds.), *Sex and gender* (pp. 149–176). Newbury Park, CA: Sage.

Aries, Elizabeth. (1996). *Men and women in interaction.* New York: Oxford University Press.

Armesto, Jorge C. (2002). Developmental and contextual factors that influence gay fathers' parental competence: A review of the literature. *Psychology of Men & Masculinity, 3,* 67–78.

Arnot, Madeline. (2000). Gender relations and schooling in the new century: Conflicts and challenges. *Compare: A Journal of Comparative Education, 30,* 293–302.

Aronson, Amy; & Kimmel, Michael. (1997). The children's hour. *Tikkun, 12,* 32–33.

Ashton, Heather. (1991). Psychotropic-drug prescribing for women. *British Journal of Psychiatry, 158* (Suppl. 10), 30–35.

Astin, Helen S. (1984). The meaning of work in women's lives: A sociopsychological model of career choice and work behavior. *Counseling Psychologist, 12,* 117–126.

Attar, Beth K.; Guerra, Nancy G.; & Tolan, Patrick H. (1994). Neighborhood disadvantage, stressful life events, and adjustment in urban elementary-school children. *Journal of Clinical Child Psychology, 23,* 391–400.

Averill, James R. (1982). *Anger and aggression: An essay on emotion.* New York: Springer-Verlag.

Ayalon, Hanna. (2003). Women and men go to university: Mathematical background and gender differences in choice of field in higher education. *Sex Roles, 48,* 277–290.

Bae, Yupin; Choy, Susan; Geddes, Claire; Sable, Jennifer; & Snyder, Thomas. (2000). *Trends in educational equity for girls and women.* Washington, DC: U.S. Department of Education, National Center for Education Statistics.

Baenninger, Maryann; & Newcombe, Nora. (1989). A role of experience in spatial test performance: A meta-analysis. *Sex Roles, 20,* 327–343.

Bagley, Christopher; & King, Kathleen. (1990). *Child sexual abuse: The search for healing.* London: Tavistock/Routledge.

Bailey, J. Michael; Bechtold, Kathleen T.; & Berenbaum, Sheri A. (2002). Who are tomboys and why should we study them? *Archives of Sexual Behavior, 31,* 333–341.

Bailey, J. Michael; Dunne, Michael P.; & Martin, Nicholas G. (2000). Genetic and environmental influences on sexual orientation and its correlates in an Australian twin sample. *Journal of Personality and Social Psychology, 78,* 524–536.

Bakan, David. (1966). *The duality of human existence.* Chicago: Rand McNally.

Baldwin, John D.; & Baldwin, Janice I. (1997). Gender differences in sexual interest. *Archives of Sexual Behavior, 26,* 181–210.

Ball, Richard E.; & Robbins, Lynn. (1986). Marital status and life satisfaction among Black Americans. *Journal of Marriage and the Family, 48,* 389–394.

Bancroft, John. (2002). Biological factors in human sexuality. *Journal of Sex Research, 39,* 15–21.

Bandura, Albert. (1986). *Social foundations of thought and action: A social cognitive theory.* Englewood Cliffs, NJ: Prentice-Hall.

Bandura, Albert; Barbaranelli, Claudio; Caprata, Gian Vittorio; & Pastorelli, Concettta. (2001). Self-efficacy beliefs as shapers of children's aspirations and career trajectories. *Child Development, 72,* 187–206.

Banks, Terry; & Dabbs, James M., Jr. (1996). Salivary testosterone and cortisol in delinquent and violent urban subcultures. *Journal of Social Psychology, 136,* 49–56.

Bankston, Carl L., III; & Zhou, Min. (2002). Being well vs. doing well: Self-esteem and school performance among immigrant and nonimmigrant racial and ethnic groups. *International Migration Review, 36,* 389–415.

Barak, Azy. (1997). Cross-cultural perspectives on sexual harassment. In William O'Donohue (Ed.), *Sexual harassment: Theory, research, and treatment* (pp. 263–300). Boston: Allyn and Bacon.

Barner, Mark R. (1999). Sex-role stereotyping in FCC-mandated children's educational television. *Journal of Broadcasting & Electronic Media, 43,* 551–564.

Barnett, Heather L.; Keel, Pamela K.; & Conoscenti, Lauren M. (2001). Body type preferences in Asian and Caucasian college students. *Sex Roles, 45,* 867–878.

Barnett, Rosalind Chait; & Hyde, Janet Shibley. (2001). Women, men, work, and family: An expansionist theory. *American Psychologist, 56,* 781–796.

Barnett, Rosalind C.; Marshall, Nancy L.; & Pleck, Joseph H. (1992). Men's multiple roles and their relationship to men's psychological distress. *Journal of Marriage and the Family, 54,* 358–367.

Bartkowski, John P. (2000). Breaking walls, raising fences: Masculinity, intimacy, and accountability among the Promise Keepers. *Sociology of Religion, 61,* 33–54.

Bartlett, Nancy H.; Vasey, Paul L.; & Bukowski, William M. (2000). Is gender identity disorder in children a mental disorder? *Sex Roles, 43,* 753–785.

Basow, Susan A.; & Rubenfeld, Kimberly. (2003). "Troubles talk": Effects of gender and gender-typing. *Sex Roles, 48,* 183–187.

Baumeister, Roy F. (1988). Should we stop studying sex differences altogether? *American Psychologist, 43,* 1092–1095.

Baumeister, Roy F. (2000). Gender differences in erotic plasticity: The female sex drive as socially flexible and responsive. *Psychological Bulletin, 126,* 347–374.

Baumli, Francis; & Williamson, Tom. (1997). *History of the men's movement.* National Coalition of Free Men. Retrieved March 31, 2003, from www.ncfm.org.

Baxter, L. C.; Saykin, A. J.; Flashman, L. A.; Johnson, S. C.; Guerin, S. J.; Babcock, D. R.; & Wishart, H. A. (2003). Sex differences in semantic language processing: A functional MRI study. *Brain and Language, 84,* 264–272.

Bay-Cheng, Laina; Zucker, Alyssa N.; Stewart, Abigail J.; & Pomerleau, Cynthia S. (2002). Linking femininity, weight concern, and mental health among Latina, black, and White women. *Psychology of Women Quarterly, 26,* 36–45.

Bazzini, Doris G.; McIntosh, William D.; Smith, Stephen M.; Cook, Sabrina; & Harris, Caleigh. (1997). The aging woman in popular film: Underrepresented, unattractive, unfriendly, and unintelligent. *Sex Roles, 36,* 531–543.

Beal, Carole R.; & Lockhart, Maria E. (1989). The effect of proper name and appearance changes on children's reasoning about gender constancy. *International Journal of Behavioral Development, 12,* 195–205.

Beausang, Carol C.; & Razor, Anita G. (2000). Young western women's experiences of menarche and menstruation. *Health Care for Women International, 21,* 517–528.

Beck, Aaron T. (1985). *Anxiety disorders and phobias: A cognitive perspective.* New York: Basic Books.

Begley, Sharon. (1997, April 21). The science wars. *Newsweek, 129* (16), 54–57.

Begley, Sharon. (2000, November 6). The stereotype trap. *Newsweek, 136* (19), 66–68.

Belle, Deborah; & Doucet, Joanne. (2003). Poverty, inequality, and discrimination as sources of depression among U.S. women. *Psychology of Women Quarterly, 27,* 101–113.

Bem, Daryl. (1996). Exotic becomes erotic: A developmental theory of sexual orientation. *Psychological Review, 103*, 320–335.

Bem, Daryl J. (2000). Exotic becomes erotic: Interpreting the biological correlates of sexual orientation. *Archives of Sexual Behavior, 29*, 531–548.

Bem, Sandra Lipsitz. (1974). The measurement of psychological androgyny. *Journal of Consulting and Clinical Psychology, 42*, 155–162.

Bem, Sandra Lipsitz. (1981a). Gender schema theory: A cognitive account of sex-typing. *Psychological Review, 88*, 354–364.

Bem, Sandra Lipsitz. (1981b). *Scoring guide for the Bem Sex-Role Inventory.* Palo Alto, CA: Consulting Psychologists Press.

Bem, Sandra Lipsitz. (1985). Androgyny and gender schema theory: A conceptual and empirical integration. In Theo B. Sonderegger (Ed.), *Nebraska Symposium on Motivation, 1984: Psychology and gender* (pp. 179–226). Lincoln, NE: University of Nebraska Press.

Bem, Sandra Lipsitz. (1987). Gender schema theory and its implications for child development: Raising gender-aschematic children in a gender-schematic society. In Mary Roth Walsh (Ed.), *The psychology of women: Ongoing debates* (pp. 226–245). New Haven, CT: Yale University Press.

Bem, Sandra Lipsitz. (1989). Genital knowledge and gender constancy in preschool children. *Child Development, 60*, 649–662.

Bem, Sandra Lipsitz. (1993a). Is there a place in psychology for a feminist analysis of the social context? *Feminism & Psychology, 3*, 230–234.

Bem, Sandra Lipsitz. (1993b). *The lenses of gender.* New Haven, CT: Yale University Press.

Benbow, Camilla Persson; Lubinski, David; Shea, Daniel L.; & Eftekhari-Sanjani, Hossain. (2000). Sex differences in mathematical reasoning ability at age 13: Their status 20 years later. *Psychological Science, 11*, 474–480.

Benbow, Camilla Persson; & Stanley, Julian C. (1980). Sex differences in mathematical ability: Fact or artifact? *Science, 210*, 1262–1264.

Benbow, Camilla Persson; & Stanley, Julian C. (1983). Sex differences in mathematical reasoning ability: More facts. *Science, 222*, 1029–1031.

Benderly, Beryl Lieff. (1987). *The myth of two minds.* New York: Doubleday.

Benderly, Beryl Lieff. (1989, November). Don't believe everything you read. . . . *Psychology Today*, pp. 67–69.

Benenson, Joyce F.; Morash, Deanna; & Petrakos, Harriet. (1998). Gender differences in emotional closeness between preschool children and their mothers. *Sex Roles, 38*, 975–986.

Benokraitis, Nijole V. (1997). Sex discrimination in the 21st century. In Nijole V. Benokraitis (Ed.), *Subtle sexism* (pp. 5–33). Thousand Oaks, CA: Sage.

Benrud, Lisa M.; & Reddy, Diane M. (1998). Differential explanations of illness in women and men. *Sex Roles, 38*, 375–386.

Berdahl, Jennifer L.; Magley, Vicki J.; & Waldo, Craig R. (1996). The sexual harassment of men? Exploring the concept with theory and data. *Psychology of Women Quarterly, 20*, 527–547.

Berenbaum, Sheri A.; & Bailey, J. Michael. (2003). Effects on gender identity of prenatal androgens and genital appearance: Evidence from girls with congenital adrenal hyperplasia. *The Journal of Clinical Endocrinology & Metabolism, 88*, 1102–1106.

Berenbaum, Sheri A.; & Hines, Melissa. (1992). Early androgens are related to childhood sex-typed toy preferences. *Psychological Science, 3*, 203–206.

Berenbaum, Sheri A.; & Snyder, Elizabeth. (1995). Early hormonal influences on childhood sex-typed activity and playmate preferences: Implications for the development of sexual orientation. *Developmental Psychology, 31*, 31–42.

Bereska, Tami M. (2003). The changing boys' world in the 20th century: Reality and "fiction." *Journal of Men's Studies, 11*, 157–174.

Berg, Nathan; & Lien, Donald. (2002). Measuring the effect of sexual orientation on income: Evidence of discrimination? *Contemporary Economic Policy, 20*, 394–414.

Berkey, Catherine S.; Rockett, Helaine R. H.; Gillman, Matthew W.; & Colditz, Graham A. (2003). One-year changes in activity and in inactivity among 10- to 15-year-old boys and girls: Relationship to change in body mass index. *Pediatrics, 111*, 836–842.

Berman, Phyllis W. (1980). Are women more responsive than men to the young? A review of developmental and situational variables. *Psychological Bulletin, 88*, 668–695.

Bernard, Jessie. (1972). *The future of marriage.* New York: World Publishing.

Bernard, Jessie. (1981). The good-provider role: Its rise and fall. *American Psychologist, 36*, 1–12.

Berndt, Thomas J. (1982). The features and effects of friendship in early adolescence. *Child Development, 53*, 1447–1460.

Berndt, Thomas J. (2002). Friendship quality and social development. *Current Directions in Psychological Science, 11,* 7–10.

Bernstein, Dan. (1999). Introduction. In Dan Bernstein (Ed.), *Nebraska Symposium on Motivation, 1999: Gender and motivation* (pp. vii–xxiii). Lincoln, NE: University of Nebraska Press.

Bettencourt, B. Ann; & Miller, Norman. (1996). Gender differences in aggression as a function of provocation: A meta-analysis. *Psychological Bulletin, 119,* 422–447.

Betz, Nancy. (1993). Women's career development. In Florence L. Denmark & Michele A. Paludi (Eds.), *Psychology of women: A handbook of issues and theories* (pp. 627–684). Westport, CT: Greenwood Press.

Beyer, Sylvia. (1998). Gender differences in self- perception and negative recall biases. *Sex Roles, 38,* 103–133.

Beyer, Sylvia. (1999). The accuracy of academic gender stereotypes. *Sex Roles, 41,* 297–306.

Beyer, Sylvia. (2002). The effects of gender, dysphoria, and performance feedback on the accuracy of self-evaluations. *Sex Roles, 47,* 453–464.

Bickel, Janet. (2001). Gender equity in undergraduate medical education: A status report. *Journal of Women's Health and Gender-Based Medicine, 10,* 261–270.

Biener, Lois. (1987). Gender differences in the use of substances for coping. In Rosalind C. Barnett, Lois Biener, & Grace K. Baruch (Eds.), *Gender and stress* (pp. 330–349). New York: Free Press.

Biernat, Monica. (1991). Gender stereotypes and the relationship between masculinity and femininity: A developmental analysis. *Journal of Personality and Social Psychology, 61,* 351–365.

Biernat, Monica; & Kobrynowicz, Diane. (1997). Gender- and race-based standards of competence: Lower minimum standards but higher ability standards for devalued groups. *Journal of Personality and Social Psychology, 72,* 544–557.

Bigler, Rebecca S. (1997). Conceptual and methodological issues in the measurement of children's sex typing. *Psychology of Women Quarterly, 21,* 53–69.

Bing, Janet. (1999). Brain sex: How the media report and distort brain research. *Women and Language, 22,* 4–12.

Bjorkqvist, Kaj. (1994). Sex differences in physical, verbal, and indirect aggression: A review of recent research, *Sex Roles, 30,* 177–188.

Blackwood, Evelyn. (2000). Culture and women's sexualities. *Journal of Social Issues, 56,* 223–238.

Blair, Steven N.; Cheng, Yiling; & Holder, J. Scott. (2001). Is physical activity or physical fitness more important in defining health benefits? *Medicine and Science in Sports & Exercise, 33,* S379–S399.

Blakemore, Judith E. Owen. (1998). The influence of gender and parental attitudes on preschool children's interest in babies: Observations in natural settings. *Sex Roles, 38,* 73–94.

Blakemore, Judith E. Owen. (2003). Children's beliefs about violating gender norms: Boys shouldn't look like girls, and girls shouldn't act like boys. *Sex Roles, 48,* 411–419.

Blanchard, Christy A.; & Lichtenberg, James W. (1998). Counseling psychologists' training to deal with their sexual feelings in therapy. *Counseling Psychologist, 26,* 624–639.

Blechman, Elaine A. (1980). Behavior therapies. In Annette M. Brodsky & Rachel Hare-Mustin (Eds.), *Women and psychotherapy* (pp. 217–244). New York: Guilford Press.

Blechman, Elaine A.; Clay, Connie J.; Kipke, Michele D.; & Bickel, Warren K. (1988). The premenstrual experience. In Elaine A. Blechman & Kelly D. Brownell (Eds.), *Handbook of behavioral medicine for women* (pp. 80–91). New York: Pergamon Press.

Blieszner, Rosemary. (2000). Close relationships in old age. In Clyde Hendrick & Susan S. Hendrick (Eds.), *Close relationships: A sourcebook* (pp. 85–95). Thousand Oaks, CA: Sage.

Bloom, Amy. (2002, October). Why can't a woman be more like a man? And vice versa. *O, The Oprah Magazine, 3* (10), 113+.

Blumenthal, Susan J.; & Wood, Susan F. (1997). Women's health care: Federal initiatives, policies, and directions. In Sheryle J. Gallant, Gwendolyn Puryear Keita, & Reneé Royak-Schaler (Eds.), *Health care for women: Psychological, social, and behavioral influences* (pp. 3–10). Washington, DC: American Psychological Association.

Blumstein, Philip; & Schwartz, Pepper. (1983). *American couples.* New York: Pocket Books.

Blustain, Sarah. (2000, November/December). The new gender wars. *Psychology Today, 33,* 42–45, 48–49.

Bly, Robert. (1990). *Iron John.* Reading, MA: Addison-Wesley.

Bly, Robert. (1994, August). *Where are men now?* Paper presented at the 102nd annual convention of the American Psychological Association, Los Angeles, CA.

Bobo, Lawrence D. (1999). Prejudice as group position: Microfoundations of a sociological approach to racism and race relations. *Journal of Social Issues, 55,* 445–472.

Bohan, Janis S. (1996). *Psychology and sexual orientation: Coming to terms.* New York: Routledge.

Bonds-Raacke, Jennifer M.; Bearden, Erica S.; Carriere, Noelle J.; Anderson, Ellen M.; & Nicks, Sandra D. (2001). Engaging distortions: Are we idealizing marriage? *Journal of Psychology, 135,* 179–184.

Bonvillain, Nancy. (1998). *Women and men: Cultural constructs of gender* (2nd ed.). Upper Saddle River, NJ: Prentice Hall.

Booth, Alan; Johnson, David R.; & Granger, Douglas A. (1999). Testosterone and men's depression: The role of social behavior. *Journal of Health and Social Behavior, 40,* 130–140.

Booth, Alan; Johnson, David R.; Granger, Douglas A.; Crouter, Ann C.; & McHale, Susan. (2003). Testosterone and child and adolescent adjustment: The moderating role of parent–child relationships. *Developmental Psychology, 39,* 85–98.

Booth, Alan; Shelley, Greg; Mazur, Allan; Tharp, Gerry; & Kittok, Roger. (1989). Testosterone, and winning and losing in human competition. *Hormones and Behavior, 23,* 556–571.

Bosch, F. X.; Lorincz, A.; Munoz, N.; Meijer, C. J. M.; & Shah, K. V. (2002). The causal relation between human papillomavirus and cervical cancer. *Journal of Clinical Pathology, 55,* 244–265.

Boston, Martha B.; & Levy, Gary D. (1991). Changes in differences in preschoolers' understanding of gender scripts. *Cognitive Development, 6,* 417–432.

Botkin, Darla R.; Weeks, M. O'Neal; & Morris, Jeanette E. (2000). Changing marriage role expectations: 1961–1996. *Sex Roles, 42,* 933–942.

Boydell, J.; van Os, J.; McKenzie, K.; Allardyce, J.; Goel, R.; McCreadie, R. G.; & Murray, R. M. (2001). Incidence of schizophrenia in ethnic minorities in London: Ecological study into interactions with environment. *British Medical Journal, 323,* 1336–1338.

Bradley, Susan J.; Oliver, Gillian D.; Chernick, A. B.; & Zucker, Kenneth J. (1998). Experiment of nurture: Ablatio penis at 2 months, sex reassignment at 7 months, and a psychosexual follow-up in young adulthood. *Pediatrics, 102,* 131–132.

Bradshaw, Carla K. (1994). Asian and Asian American women: Historical and political considerations in psychotherapy. In Lillian Comas-Díaz & Beverly Greene (Eds.), *Women of color: Integrating ethnic and gender identities in psychotherapy* (pp. 72–113). New York: Guilford Press.

Brannon, Linda; & Feist, Jess. (2004). *Health psychology: An introduction to behavior and health* (5th ed.). Belmont, CA: Wadsworth.

Brannon, Robert. (1976). The male sex role: Our culture's blueprint of manhood and what it's done for us lately. In Deborah S. David & Robert Brannon (Eds.), *The forty-nine percent majority* (pp. 1–45). Reading, MA: Addison-Wesley.

Brecher, Edward M. (1969). *The sex researchers.* Boston: Little, Brown.

Breedlove, S. Marc. (1994). Sexual differentiation of the human nervous system. *Annual Review of Psychology, 45,* 389–418.

Brendgen, Mara; Vitaro, Frank; Doyle, Anna Beth; Markiewicz, Dorothy; & Bukowski, William M. (2002). Same-sex peer relations and romantic relationships during early adolescence: Interactive links to emotional, behavioral, and academic adjustment. *Merrill-Palmer Quarterly, 48,* 77–103.

Britannica Book of the Year, 1999. (1999). Chicago: Encyclopedia Britannica.

Broderick, Patricia C.; & Korteland, Constance. (2002). Coping style and depression in early adolescence: Relationships to gender, gender role, and implicit beliefs. *Sex Roles, 46,* 201–213.

Brodsky, Annette; & Holroyd, Jean. (1975). Report of the Task Force on Sex Bias and Sex-Role Stereotyping in Psychotherapeutic Practice. *American Psychologist, 30,* 1169–1175.

Brooks, Gary R. (1998). *A new psychotherapy for traditional men.* San Francisco, CA: Jossey-Bass.

Brooks, Gary R. (2001). Masculinity and men's mental health. *Journal of American College Health, 49,* 285–297.

Brooks-Gunn, Jeanne; & Furstenberg, Frank F., Jr. (1989). Adolescent sexual behavior. *American Psychologist, 44,* 249–257.

Broverman, Inge K.; Broverman, Donald M.; Clarkson, Frank E.; Rosenkrantz, Paul S.; & Vogel, Susan R. (1970). Sex-role stereotypes and clinical judgments of mental health. *Journal of Consulting and Clinical Psychology, 34,* 1–7.

Broverman, Inge K.; Vogel, Susan Raymond; Broverman, Donald M.; Clarkson, Frank E.; & Rosenkrantz, Paul S. (1972). Sex-role stereotypes: A current appraisal. *Journal of Social Issues, 28* (2), 59–78.

Brown, Jeffrey M.; Mehler, Philip S.; & Harris, R. Hill. (2000). Medical complications occurring in adolescents with anorexia nervosa. *Western Journal of Medicine, 172,* 189–193.

Brown, Laura B.; Uebelacker, Lisa; & Heatherington, Laurie. (1998). Men, women, and the self-presentation of achievement. *Sex Roles, 38,* 253–268.

Brown, Laura S. (1988). Feminist therapy with lesbians and gay men. In Mary Ann Dutton Douglas &

Lenore E. A. Walker (Eds.), *Feminist psychotherapies: Integration of therapeutic and feminist systems* (pp. 206–227). Norwood, NJ: Ablex.

Brown, Laura S. (1992). A feminist critique of personality disorders. In Laura S. Brown & Mary Ballou (Eds.), *Personality and psychopathology: Feminist reappraisals* (pp. 206–228). New York: Guilford Press.

Brown, Susan L.; & Booth, Alan. (1996). Cohabitation versus marriage: A comparison of relationship quality. *Journal of Marriage and the Family, 58,* 668–678.

Browne, Beverly A. (1998). Gender stereotypes in advertising on children's television in the 1990s: A cross-national analysis. *Journal of Advertising, 27,* 83–96.

Brumberg, Joan Jacobs. (1997). *The body project.* New York: Random House.

Bryant, Alyssa N. (2003). Changes in attitudes toward women's roles: Predicting gender-role traditionalism among college students. *Sex Roles, 48,* 131–142.

Bryant, Anne. (1995, March). Sexual harassment in school takes it toll. *USA Today Magazine, 123,* 40–41.

Budig, Michelle J. (2002). Male advantage and the gender composition of jobs: Who rides the glass escalator? *Social Problems, 49,* 258–277.

Bukowski, William M.; Gauze, Cyma; Hoza, Betsy; & Newcomb, Andrew F. (1993). Differences and consistency between same-sex and other-sex peer relationships during early adolescence. *Developmental Psychology, 29,* 255–263.

Buntaine, Roberta L.; & Costenbader, Virginia K. (1997). Self-reported differences in the experience and expression of anger between girls and boys. *Sex Roles, 36,* 625–637.

Burack, Cynthia. (1998). Feminist psychoanalysis: The uneasy intimacy of feminism and psychoanalysis. In Paul Marcus & Alan Rosenberg (Eds.), *Psychoanalytic versions of the human condition: Philosophies of life and their impact on practice* (pp. 392–411). New York: New York University Press.

Burge, Penny L.; & Culver, Steven M. (1990). Sexism, legislative power, and vocational education. In Susan L. Gabriel & Isaiah Smithson (Eds.), *Gender in the classroom: Power and pedagogy* (pp. 160–175). Urbana, IL: University of Illinois Press.

Burke, Ronald J. (1999). Workaholism in organizations: Gender differences. *Sex Roles, 41,* 333–346.

Burnam, M. Audrey; Stein, Judith A.; Golding, Jacqueline M.; Siegel, Judith M.; Sorenson, Susan B.; Forsythe, Alan B.; & Telles, Cynthia A. (1988). Sexual assault and mental disorders in a community population. *Journal of Consulting and Clinical Psychology, 56,* 843–850.

Burns, Sheila L.; Peterson, Holly; Bass, Hope; & Pascoe, Neil. (2002). Gender differences on a mental rotation task: The effects of stereotype threat. *Michigan Academician, 34,* 84–85.

Burr, Ryan. (2002, May 21). Her true face in the mirror. *Kent County Times.* Retrieved December 5, 2003, from www.tomfronczak.com/trans.htm.

Burt, Keith B., & Scott, Jacqueline. (2002). Parent and adolescent gender role attitudes in 1990s Great Britain. *Sex Roles, 46,* 239–245.

Burton, Vanessa. (2000). How real is *Sex and the City*? Retrieved July 28, 2003, from www.askmen.com/love/vanessa_60/68_love_secrets.html.

Burton, Velmer S., Jr.; Cullen, Francis T.; Evans, T. David; Alarid, Leanne Fiftal; & Dunaway, R. Gregory. (1998). Gender, self-control, and crime. *Journal of Research in Crime and Delinquency, 35,* 123–147.

Bush, Diane M.; & Simmons, R. G. (1987). Gender and coping with the entry into early adolescence. In Rosalind C. Barnett, Lois Biener, & Grace K. Baruch (Eds.), *Gender and stress* (pp. 185–217). New York: Free Press.

Business Week. (1999, September 27). Ethnic gaps on campus. *Business Week, 3648,* 34.

Buss, David M. (1994). *The evolution of desire.* New York: Basic Books.

Buss, David M. (1996). Sexual conflict: Evolutionary insights into feminism and the "battle of the sexes." In David M. Buss & Neil M. Malamuth (Eds.), *Sex, power, conflict: Evolutionary and feminist perspectives* (pp. 296–318). New York: Oxford University Press.

Buss, David M.; Shackelford, Todd K.; Kirkpatrick, Lee A.; & Larsen, Randy J. (2001). A half century of mate preferences: The cultural evolution of values. *Journal of Marriage and Family, 63,* 491–503.

Bussey, Kay; & Bandura, Albert. (1984). Influence of gender constancy and social power on sex-linked modeling. *Journal of Personality and Social Psychology, 47,* 1292–1302.

Bussey, Kay; & Bandura, Albert. (1992). Self-regulatory mechanisms governing gender development. *Child Development, 63,* 1236–1250.

Bussey, Kay; & Bandura, Albert. (1999). Social cognitive theory of gender development and differentiation. *Psychological Review, 106,* 676–713.

Byne, William. (1997). Why we cannot conclude that sexual orientation is primarily a biological phenomenon. *Journal of Homosexuality, 34,* 73–80.

Byne, William; Tobet, S.; Mattiace, L. A.; Lasco, M. S.; Kemether, E.; Edgar, M. A.; Morgello, S.; Buchsbaum, M. S.; & Jones, L. B. (2001). The interstitial nuclei of the human anterior hypothalamus: An investigation of variation with sex, sexual orientation, and HIV status. *Hormones and Behavior, 40,* 86–92.

Byne, Peter. (2001). The butler(s) DID it—Dissociative identity disorder in cinema. *Journal of Medical Ethics: Medical Humanities, 27,* 26–29.

Cairns, Robert B.; Cairns, Beverley D.; Neckerman, Holly J.; Ferguson, Lynda L.; & Gariépy, Jean-Louis. (1989). Growth and aggression: 1. Childhood to early adolescence. *Developmental Psychology, 25,* 320–330.

Caldwell, Leon D.; & White, Joseph L. (2001). African-centered therapeutic and counseling interventions for African American males. In Gary R. Brooks & Glen E. Good (Eds.), *The new handbook of psychotherapy and counseling with men: A comprehensive guide to settings, problems, and treatment approaches* (pp. 735–753). San Francisco, CA: Jossey-Bass.

Caldwell, Mayta A.; & Peplau, Letitia Anne. (1982). Sex differences in same-sex friendship. *Sex Roles, 8,* 721–732.

Cammaert, Lorna P.; & Larsen, Carolyn C. (1988). Feminist frameworks of psychotherapy. In Mary Ann Dutton Douglas & Lenore E. A. Walker (Eds.), *Feminist psychotherapies: Integration of therapeutic and feminist systems* (pp. 12–36). Norwood, NJ: Ablex.

Campbell, Anne. (1993). *Men, women, and aggression.* New York: Basic Books.

Campbell, Anne; Shirley, Louisa; & Caygill, Lisa. (2002). Sex-typed preferences in three domains: Do two-year-olds need cognitive variables? *British Journal of Psychology, 93,* 203–217.

Campbell, Constance R.; & Henry, John W. (1999). Gender differences in self-attributions: Relationships of gender to attributional consistency, style, and expectations for performance in a college course. *Sex Roles, 41,* 95–104.

Campbell, Rebecca; & Wasco, Sharon M. (2000). Feminist approaches to social science: Epistemological and methodological tenets. *American Journal of Community Psychology, 28,* 773–791.

Campenni, C. Estelle. (1999). Gender stereotyping of children's toys: A comparison of parents and non-parents. *Sex Roles, 40,* 121–138.

Cancian, Francesca M. (1986). The feminization of love. *Signs, 11,* 692–709.

Cancian, Francesca M. (1987). *Love in America: Gender and self-development.* Cambridge, England: Cambridge University Press.

Cancian, Francesca M.; & Oliker, Stacey J. (2000). *Caring and gender.* Thousand Oaks, CA: Pine Forge Press.

Cann, Arnie; & Vann, Elizabeth D. (1995). Implications of sex and gender differences for self: Perceived advantages and disadvantages of being the other gender. *Sex Roles, 33,* 531–541.

Cannon, Walter B. (1927). The James-Lange theory of emotions: A critical examination and an alternative theory. *American Journal of Psychology, 39,* 106–124.

Caplan, Paula J.; & Caplan, Jeremy B. (1994). *Thinking critically about research on sex and gender.* New York: HarperCollins.

Caplan, Paula J.; MacPherson, Gael M.; & Tobin, Patricia. (1985). Do sex-related differences in spatial abilities exist? A multilevel critique with new data. *American Psychologist, 40,* 786–799.

Capraro, Rocco L. (2000). Why college men drink: Alcohol, adventure, and the paradox of masculinity. *Journal of American College Health, 48,* 307–315.

Carlbring, Per; Gustafsson, Henrik; Ekselius, Lisa; & Andersson, Gerhard. (2002). 12-month prevalence of panic disorder with or without agoraphobia in the Swedish general population. *Social Psychiatry and Psychiatric Epidemiology, 37,* 207–211.

Carli, Linda L.; & Eagly, Alice H. (2001). Gender, hierarchy, and leadership: An introduction. *Journal of Social Issues, 57,* 629–636.

Carlo, Gustavo; Raffaelli, Marcela; Laible, Deborah J.; & Meyer, Kathryn A. (1999). Why are girls less physically aggressive than boys? Personality and parenting mediators of physical aggression. *Sex Roles, 40,* 711–730.

Carr, Judith G.; Gilroy, Faith D.; & Sherman, Martin F. (1996). Silencing the self and depression among women: The moderating role of race. *Psychology of Women Quarterly, 20,* 375–392.

Carrier, Joseph. (1997). Miguel: Sexual life history of a gay Mexican American. In Maxine Baca Zinn, Pierrette Hondagneu-Sotelo, & Michael A. Messner (Eds.), *Through the prism of difference: Readings on sex and gender* (pp. 210–220). Boston: Allyn and Bacon.

Carter, Stephen L. (1991). *Reflections of an affirmative action baby.* New York: Basic Books.

Casas, J. Manuel; Turner, Joseph A.; & Ruiz de Esparza, Christopher A. (2001). Machismo revisited in a time of crisis: Implications for understanding and counseling Hispanic men. In Gary R. Brooks & Glen E. Good (Eds.), *The new handbook of psychotherapy and counseling with men: A comprehensive guide to settings, problems, and treatment approaches* (pp. 754–779). San Francisco, CA: Jossey-Bass.

Casey, Kathryn. (2000, March). Who has the most stress? *Ladies Home Journal, 117,* 152–154.

Casper, Regina C.; Belanoff, Joseph; & Offer, Daniel. (1996). Gender differences, but no racial group differences, in self-reported psychiatric symptoms in adolescents. *Journal of the American Academy of Child and Adolescent Psychiatry, 35,* 500–508.

Catalyst. (1996). *Women in corporate leadership: Progress and prospects.* New York: Author.

Central Intelligence Agency. (2000). *World factbook.* Washington, DC: Government Printing Office.

Chaiken, Shelly; & Pliner, Patricia. (1987). Women, but not men, are what they eat: The effect of meal size and gender on perceived femininity and masculinity. *Personality and Social Psychology Bulletin, 13,* 166–176.

Chambless, Dianne L.; & Ollendick, Thomas H. (2001). Empirically supported psychological interventions: Controversies and evidence. *Annual Review of Psychology, 52,* 685–716.

Chandler, Daniel; & Griffiths, Merris. (2000). Gender-differentiated production features in toy commercials. *Journal of Broadcasting & Electronic Media, 44,* 503–520.

Chernin, Kim. (1978). *The obsession: Reflections on the tyranny of slenderness.* New York: Harper & Row.

Cherry, Frances; & Deaux, Kay. (1978). Fear of success versus fear of gender-inappropriate behavior. *Sex Roles, 4,* 97–101.

Chesler, Phyllis. (1972). *Women and madness.* New York: Avon.

Chess, Stella; & Thomas, Alexander. (1982). Infant bonding: Mystique and reality. *American Journal of Orthopsychiatry, 52,* 213–222.

Chia, Rosina C.; Moore, Jamie L.; Lam, Ka Nei; Chuang, C. J.; & Cheng, B. S. (1994). Cultural differences in gender role attitudes between Chinese and American students. *Sex Roles, 31,* 23–30.

Children Now. (1997). *New studies on media, girls, and gender roles: Media reinforces some gender stereotypes, breaks others.* Retrieved June 28, 2003, from www.childrennow.org/newsroom/news-97/pr-97-4-30.html.

Chodorow, Nancy. (1978). *The reproduction of mothering: Psychoanalysis and the sociology of gender.* Berkeley, CA: University of California Press.

Chodorow, Nancy. (1979). Feminism and difference: Gender, relation, and difference in psychoanalytic perspective. *Socialist Review, 46,* 42–64. Also in Mary Roth Walsh (Ed.) (1987), *The psychology of women: Ongoing debates* (pp. 249–264). New Haven, CT: Yale University Press.

Chodorow, Nancy J. (1994). *Femininities, masculinities, sexualities: Freud and beyond.* Lexington, KY: University Press of Kentucky.

Chrisler, Joan C. (2001). Gendered bodies and physical health. In Rhoda K. Unger (Ed.), *Handbook of psychology of women and gender* (pp. 289–302). New York: Wiley.

Christensen, Andrew; & Jacobson, Neil S. (1994). Who (or what) can do psychotherapy: The status and challenge of nonprofessional therapies. *Psychological Science, 5,* 8–14.

Christensen, Larry B. (2004). *Experimental methodology* (9th ed.). Boston: Allyn and Bacon.

Christian, Harry. (1994). *The making of anti-sexist men.* London: Routledge.

Christopher, F. Scott; & Sprecher, Susan. (2000). Sexuality in marriage, dating, and other relationships: A decade review. *Journal of Marriage and Family, 62,* 999–1017.

Cleary, David J.; Ray, Glen E.; LoBello, Steven G.; & Zachar, Peter. (2002). Children's perceptions of close peer relationships: Quality, congruence and meta-perceptions. *Child Study Journal, 32,* 179–192.

Cleary, Paul D. (1987). Gender differences in stress-related disorders. In Rosalind C. Barnett, Lois Biener, & Grace K. Baruch (Eds.), *Gender and stress* (pp. 39–72). New York: Free Press.

Cohen, Deborah. (1992). Why there are so few male teachers in early grades. *Education Digest, 57* (6), 11–13.

Cohen, Jacob. (1969). *Statistical power analysis for the behavioral sciences.* New York: Academic Press.

Cohen, Kenneth M. (2002). Relationships among childhood sex-atypical behavior, spatial ability, handedness, and sexual orientation in men. *Archives of Sexual Behavior, 31,* 129–143.

Cohen, Laurie L.; & Shotland, R. Lance. (1996). Timing of first sexual intercourse in a relationship: Expectations, experiences, and perceptions of others. *Journal of Sex Research, 33,* 291–299.

Cohen, Philip. (2001, May 12). Boy meets girl. *New Scientist, 170,* 29+.

Cohen, Philip N.; & Huffman, Matt L. (2003). Occupational segregation and the devaluation of women's work across U.S. labor markets. *Social Forces, 81,* 881–908.

Cohen-Kettenis, Peggy T.; Owen, Allison; Kaijser, Vanessa G.; Bradley Susan J.; & Zucker, Kenneth J. (2003). Demographic characteristics, social competence, and behavior problems in children with gender identity disorder: A cross-national, cross-clinic comparative analysis. *Journal of Abnormal Child Psychology, 31,* 41–53.

Cohen-Kettenis, Peggy T.; & van Goozen, Stephanie H. M. (1997). Sex reassignment of adolescent transsexuals: A follow-up study. *Journal of the American Academy of Child and Adolescent Psychiatry, 36,* 263–271.

Colapinto, John. (2000). *As nature made him.* New York: HarperCollins.

Cole, Johnnetta Betsch; & Guy-Sheftall, Beverly. (2003). *Gender talk: The struggle for women's equality in African American communities.* New York: Ballantine.

Coley, Richard. (2001). *Differences in the gender gap: Comparisons across racial/ethnic groups in education and work.* Princeton, NJ: Educational Testing Service.

Colley, Ann; Ball, Jane; Kirby, Nicola; Harvey, Rebecca; & Vingelen, Ingrid. (2001). Gender-linked differences in everyday memory performance: Effort makes the difference. *Sex Roles, 47,* 577–582.

Collins, Nancy L.; & Miller, Lynn Carol. (1994). Self-disclosure and liking: A meta-analytic review. *Psychological Bulletin, 116,* 457–475.

Coltrane, Scott. (2000). Research on household labor: Modeling and measuring the social embeddedness of routine family work. *Journal of Marriage and the Family, 62,* 1208–1233

Coltrane, Scott; & Messineo, Melinda. (2000). The perpetuation of subtle prejudice: Race and gender imagery in 1990s television advertising. *Sex Roles, 42,* 363–389.

Coltrane, Scott; & Valdez, Elsa O. (1993). Reluctant compliance: Work–family role allocation in dual-earner Chicano families. In Jane C. Hood (Ed.), *Men, work, and family* (pp. 151–175). Newbury Park, CA: Sage.

Colwell, John; & Payne, Jo. (2000). Negative correlates of computer game play in adolescents. *British Journal of Psychology, 91,* 295–310.

Comas-Díaz, Lillian; & Greene, Beverly. (1994). Overview: An ethnocultural mosaic. In Lillian Comas-Díaz & Beverly Greene (Eds.), *Women of color: Integrating ethnic and gender identities in psychotherapy* (pp. 3–9). New York: Guilford Press.

Condravy, Jace; Skirboll, Esther; & Taylor, Rhoda. (1998). Faculty perceptions of classroom gender dynamics. *Women and Language, 21,* 18–27.

Connell, R. W. (1987). *Gender and power: Society, the person and sexual politics.* Cambridge: Polity Press.

Connell, R. W. (1992). Masculinity, violence, and war. In Michael S. Kimmel & Michael A. Messner (Eds.), *Men's lives* (2nd ed. pp. 176–183). New York: Macmillan.

Connell, R. W. (1995). *Masculinities.* Berkeley, CA: University of California Press.

Connell, R. W. (1996). Teaching the boys: New research on masculinity, the gender strategies for schools. *Teachers College Record, 98,* 206–235.

Connell, R. W. (2001, Winter). Studying men and masculinity. *Resources for Feminist Research,* 43–56.

Constantino, John N.; Grosz, Daniel; Saenger, Paul; Chandler, Donald W.; Nandi, Reena; & Earls, Felton J. (1993). Testosterone and aggression in children. *Journal of the American Academy of Child and Adolescent Psychiatry, 32,* 1217–1222.

Constantinople, Anne. (1973). Masculinity–femininity: An exception to a famous dictum. *Psychological Bulletin, 80,* 389–407.

Cook, Ellen Piel; Warnke, Melanie; & Dupuy, Paula. (1993). Gender bias and the DSM-III-R. *Counselor Education and Supervision, 32,* 311–322.

Cooper, Alvin; Scherer, Coralie R.; Boies, Sylvain C.; & Gordon, Barry L. (1999). Sexuality on the Internet: From sexual exploration to pathological expression. *Professional Psychology: Research and Practice, 30,* 154–164.

Cooperstock, Ruth. (1970). A review of women's psychotropic drug use. *Canadian Journal of Psychiatry, 24,* 29–34.

Corliss, Richard. (2002, April 22). Girls just wanna have guns: Thrillers with female stars are hot. *Time, 159,* 58+.

Correll, Shelley J. (2001). Gender and career choice process: The role of biased self-assessments. *American Journal of Sociology, 106,* 1691–1730.

Courtenay, Will H. (2000a). Behavioral factors associated with disease, injury, and death among men: Evidence and implications for prevention. *Journal of Men's Studies, 9,* 81–142.

Courtenay, Will H. (2000b). Teaming up for the new men's health movement. *Journal of Men's Studies, 8,* 387–392.

Crain, Caleb. (2001). *American sympathy: Men, friendship, and literature in the new nation.* New Haven, CT: Yale University Press.

Crain, Rance. (2001). Husbands are boys and wives their mothers in the land of ads. *Advertising Age, 72,* 22+

Cramer, Duncan. (2002). Relationship satisfaction and conflict over minor and major issues in romantic relationships. *Journal of Psychology, 136,* 75–81.

Cramer, Kenneth M.; & Thoms, Norm. (2003). Factor structure of the Silencing the Self Scale in women and men. *Personality and Individual Differences, 35,* 525–535.

Crandall, Christian S.; Tsang, Jo-Ann; Goldman, Susan; & Pennington, John T. (1999). Newsworthy moral dilemmas: Justice, caring, and gender. *Sex Roles, 40,* 187–210.

Crawford, June; Kippax, Susan; Onxy, Jenny; Gault, Una; & Benton, Pam. (1992). *Emotion and gender: Constructing meaning from memory.* London: Sage.

Crawford, Mary. (1989). Agreeing to differ: Feminist epistemologies and women's ways of knowing. In Mary Crawford & Margaret Gentry (Eds.), *Gender and thought: Psychological perspectives* (pp. 128–145). New York: Springer-Verlag.

Crawford, Mary; & Kimmel, Ellen. (1999). Promoting methodological diversity in feminist research. *Psychology of Women Quarterly, 23,* 1–6.

Crawford, Mary; & Marecek, Jeanne. (1989). Psychology reconstructs the female: 1968–1988. *Psychology of Women Quarterly, 13,* 147–165.

Crichton, Michael. (1999). Ritual abuse, hot air, and missed opportunities. *Science, 283,* 1461–1463.

Crick, Nicki R.; Werner, Nicole E.; Casas, Juan F.; O'Brien, Kathryn M.; Nelson, David A.; Grotpeter, Jennifer K.; & Markon, Kristian. (1999). Childhood aggression and gender: A new look at an old problem. In Dan Bernstein (Ed.), *Nebraska Symposium on Motivation, 1999: Gender and motivation* (pp. 75–141). Lincoln, NE: University of Nebraska Press.

Crouter, Ann C.; Manke, Beth A.; & McHale, Susan M. (1995). The family context of gender intensification in early adolescence. *Child Development, 66,* 317–329.

Cuffe, Steven P.; Addy, Cheryl L.; Garrison, Carol Z.; Waller, Jennifer L.; Jackson, Kirby L.; McKeown, Robert E.; & Chilappagari, Shailaja. (1998). Prevalence of PTSD in a community sample of older adolescents. *Journal of the American Academy of Child and Adolescent Psychiatry, 37,* 147–154.

Culbertson, Frances M. (1997). Depression and gender: An international review. *American Psychologist, 52,* 25–31.

Cummings, Anne L. (2000). Teaching feminist counselor responses to novice female counselors. *Counselor Education and Supervision, 40,* 47–57.

Cummings, Jonathon N.; Sproull, Lee; & Kiesler, Sara B. (2002). Beyond hearing: Where the real-world and online support meet. *Group Dynamics, 6,* 78–88.

Cutler, Susan E.; & Nolen-Hoeksema, Susan. (1991). Accounting for sex differences in depression through female victimization: Childhood sexual abuse. *Sex Roles, 24,* 425–438.

Cyranowski, Jill M.; Frank, Ellen; Young, Elizabeth; & Shear, M. Katherine. (2000). Adolescent onset of the gender difference in lifetime rates of major depression. *Archives of General Psychiatry, 57,* 21–56.

Dabbs, James M., Jr. (1992). Testosterone and occupational achievement. *Social Forces, 70,* 813–824.

Dabbs, James M. (with Dabbs, Mary Godwin). (2000). *Heroes, rogues, and lovers: Testosterone and behavior.* New York: McGraw-Hill.

Dabbs, James M., Jr.; Carr, Timothy S.; Frady, Robert L.; & Riad, Jasmin K. (1995). Testosterone, crime, and misbehavior among 692 male prison inmates. *Personality and Individual Differences, 18,* 627–633.

Dabbs, James M., Jr.; de la Rue, Denise; & Williams, Paula M. (1990). Testosterone and occupational choice: Actors, ministers, and other men. *Journal of Personality and Social Psychology, 59,* 1261–1265.

Dabbs, James M., Jr.; Hargrove, Marian F.; & Heusel, Colleen. (1996). Testosterone differences among college fraternities: Well-behaved vs. rambunctious. *Personality and Individual Differences, 20,* 157–161.

Dabbs, James M., Jr.; Hopper, Charles H.; & Jurkovic, Gregory J. (1990). Testosterone and personality among college students and military veterans. *Personality and Individual Differences, 11,* 1263–1269.

Dabbs, James M., Jr.; & Morris, Robin. (1990). Testosterone, social class, and antisocial behavior in a sample of 4,462 men. *Psychological Science, 1,* 209–211.

Dabbs, James M., Jr.; Ruback, R. Barry; Frady, Robert L.; Hopper, Charles H.; & Sgoutas, Demetrios S. (1988). Saliva testosterone and criminal violence among women. *Personality and Individual Differences, 9,* 269–275.

Dana, Richard H. (2001). Clinical diagnosis of multicultural populations in the United States. In Lisa A. Suzuki, Joseph G. Ponterotto, & Paul J. Meller

(Eds.), *Handbook of multicultural assessment: Clinical, psychological, and educational applications* (2nd ed., pp. 101–131). San Francisco, CA: Jossey-Bass.

Darwin, Charles. (1872). *The expression of emotions in man and animals.* New York: Philosophical Library.

Daugherty, Cynthia; & Lees, Marty. (1988). Feminist psychodynamic therapies. In Mary Ann Dutton Douglas & Lenore E. A. Walker (Eds.), *Feminist psychotherapies: Integration of therapeutic and feminist systems* (pp. 68–90). Norwood, NJ: Ablex.

Davies, Paul G.; Spencer, Steven J.; Quinn, Diane M.; & Gerhardstein, Rebecca. (2002). Consuming images: How television commercials that elicit stereotype threat can restrain women academically and professionally. *Personality and Social Psychology Bulletin, 28,* 1615–1628.

Davis, Jody L.; & Rusbult, Caryl E. (2001). Attitude alignment in close relationships. *Journal of Personality and Social Psychology, 81,* 65–84.

Davis-Kean, Pamela; Eccles, Jacquelynne; & Linver, Miriam. (2002, April). *Influences of gender on academic achievement.* Paper presented at the biennial meeting of the Society for Research on Adolescence, New Orleans, LA.

Davison, Kathryn P.; Pennebaker, James W.; & Dickerson, Sally S. (2000). Who talks? The social psychology of illness support groups. *American Psychologist, 55,* 205–217.

Daw, Jennifer. (2002, October). Is PMDD real? *Monitor on Psychology, 33* (9), 58–60.

Day, Arla L.; & Livingstone, Holly A. (2003). Gender differences in perceptions of stressors and utilization of social support among university students. *Canadian Journal of Behavioural Science, 35,* 73–83.

Day, Dwayne. (2003). *Star Trek as a cultural phenomenon.* Retrieved July 9, 2003, from www.centennialofflight.gov/essay/Social/star_trek/SH7.htm.

Deal, Jennifer J.; & Stevenson, Maura A. (1998). Perceptions of female and male managers in the 1990s: Plu ca change. . . . *Sex Roles, 38,* 287–300.

Deaux, Kay. (1984). From individual differences to social categories: Analysis of a decade's research on gender. *American Psychologist, 39,* 105–116.

Deaux, Kay. (1993). Commentary: Sorry, wrong number: A reply to Gentile's call. *Psychological Science, 4,* 125–126.

Deaux, Kay; & Lewis, Laurie. (1984). The structure of gender stereotypes: Interrelations among components and gender label. *Journal of Personality and Social Psychology, 46,* 991–1004.

Degler, Carl N. (1974). What ought to be and what was: Women's sexuality in the nineteenth century. *American Historical Review, 79,* 1467–1490.

DeLamater, John; & Friedrich, William N. (2002). Human sexual development. *Journal of Sex Research, 39,* 10–14.

De Lisi, Richard; & Wolford, Jennifer L. (2002). Improving children's mental rotation accuracy with computer game playing. *Journal of Genetic Psychology, 163,* 272–282.

Del Parigi, Angelo; Chen, Kewei; Gautier, Jean-Francois; Salbe, Arline D.; Pratley, Richard E.; Ravussin, Eric; Reiman, Eric; & Tataranni, Antonio. (2002). Sex differences in the human brain's response to hunger and satiation. *American Journal of Clinical Nutrition, 75,* 1017–1022.

DeLucia-Waack, Janice L.; Gerrity, Deborah A.; Taub, Deborah J.; & Baldo, Tracy D. (2001). Gender, gender role identity, and type of relationship as predictors of relationship behavior and beliefs in college students. *Journal of College Counseling, 4,* 32–48.

Desjarlais, Robert; Eisenberg, Leon; Good, Byron; & Kleinman, Arthur. (1995). *World mental health: Problems and priorities in low-income countries.* New York: Oxford University Press.

DeSouza, Eros; & Fansler, Gigi. (2003). Contrapower sexual harassment: A survey of students and faculty members. *Sex Roles, 48,* 529–542.

Deuster, Patricia A.; Adera, Tilahun; & South-Paul, Jeannette. (1999). Biological, social, and behavioral factors associated with premenstrual syndrome. *Archives of Family Medicine, 8,* 122–128.

Deutsch, Francine M.; Roksa, Josipa; & Meeske, Cynthia. (2003). How gender counts when couples count their money. *Sex Roles, 48,* 291–304.

de Vaus, David. (2002, Winter). Marriage and mental health: Does marriage improve the mental health of men at the expense of women? *Family Matters,* pp. 26–32.

Deveny, Kathleen; Peterson, Holly; Wingert, Pat; Springen, Karen; Scelfo, Julie; Brewster, Melissa; Weingarten, Tara; & Raymond, Joan. (2003, June 30). We're not in the mood. *Newsweek, 141* (26), 40–46.

Diamond, Lisa M. (2003a). Was it a phase? Young women's relinquishment of lesbian/bisexual identities over a 5-year period. *Journal of Personality and Social Psychology, 84,* 352–364.

Diamond, Lisa M. (2003b). What does sexual orientation orient? A biobehavioral model distinguishing romantic love and sexual desire. *Psychological Review, 110,* 173–192.

Di Caccavo, Antonietta; & Reid, Fraser. (1998). The influence of attitudes toward male and female patients on treatment decisions in general practice. *Sex Roles, 38,* 613–629.

Dickerson, Lori M.; Mazyck, Pamela J.; & Hunter, Melissa H. (2003). Premenstrual syndrome. *American Family Physician, 67,* 1743–1752.

Diclementi, Deborah. (2001, April 1). Pressure to be perfect. *Teen People, 4* (3), 200+

Diefenbach, Donald L. (1997). The portrayal of mental illness on prime-time television. *Journal of Community Psychology, 25,* 289–302.

Diekman, Amanda B.; & Eagly, Alice H. (2000). Stereotypes as dynamic constructs: Women and men of the past, present, and future. *Personality and Social Psychology Bulletin, 26,* 1171–1187.

Dietz, Tracy L. (1998). An examination of violence and gender role portrayals in video games: Implications for gender socialization and aggressive behavior. *Sex Roles, 38,* 425–442.

Dijkstra, Arie; & De Vries, Hein. (2001). Do self-help interventions in health education lead to cognitive changes, and do cognitive changes lead to behavioural change? *British Journal of Health Psychology, 6,* 121–134.

Dingell, John D.; & Maloney, Carolyn B. (2002). *A new look through the glass ceiling: Where are the women?* Retrieved August 5, 2003, from www.equality2020.org.

Dinnerstein, Dorothy. (1976). *The mermaid and the minotaur: Sexual arrangements and the human malaise.* New York: Harper & Row.

Docter, Richard F.; & Prince, Virginia. (1997). Transvestism: A survey of 1032 cross-dressers. *Archives of Sexual Behavior, 26,* 589–605.

Dolado, J. J.; Felgueroso, F.; & Jimeno, J. F. (2001). Female employment and occupational changes in the 1990s: How is the EU performing relative to the US? *European Economic Review, 45,* 875–889.

Doll, Richard; & Peto, Richard. (1981). *The causes of cancer.* New York: Oxford University Press.

Dollard, John; Doob, Leonard; Miller, Neal; Mowrer, O. Hobart; & Sears, Robert. (1939). *Frustration and aggression.* New Haven, CT: Yale University Press.

Donaghue, Ngaire; & Fallon, Barry J. (2003). Gender-role self-stereotyping and the relationship between equity and satisfaction in close relationships. *Sex Roles, 48,* 217–230.

Donnelly, Denise; Burgess, Elisabeth; Anderson, Sally; Davis, Regina; & Dillard, Joy. (2001). Involuntary celibacy: A life course analysis. *Journal of Sex Research, 38,* 159–169.

Donovan, Roxanne; & Williams, Michelle. (2002). Living at the intersection: The effects of racism and sexism on Black rape survivors. *Women & Therapy, 25,* 95–105.

Dowd, Maureen. (2000, June 11). Freud was way wrong. *New York Times,* Section 4, p. 17.

Dreher, George F.; & Cox, Taylor H., Jr. (1996). Race, gender, and opportunity: A study of compensation attainment and the establishment of mentoring relationships. *Journal of Applied Psychology, 81,* 297–308.

Dreyfus, Colleen K. (1994, August). *Stigmatizing attitudes toward male victims.* Paper presented at the 102nd annual convention of the American Psychological Association, Los Angeles, CA.

Duarte, Linda M.; & Thompson, Janice M. (1999). Sex differences in self-silencing. *Psychological Reports, 85,* 145–161.

Dubbert, Patricia M. (1992). Exercise in behavioral medicine. *Journal of Consulting and Clinical Psychology, 60,* 613–618.

DuBois, Cathy L. Z.; Knapp, Deborah E.; Faley, Robert H.; & Kustis, Gary A. (1998). An empirical examination of same- and other-gender sexual harassment in the workplace. *Sex Roles, 39,* 731–750.

DuBois, David L.; & Hirsch, Barton J. (1990). School and neighborhood friendship patterns of Blacks and Whites in early adolescence. *Child Development, 61,* 524–536.

Dubow, Eric F.; Huesmann, L. Rowell; & Boxer, Paul. (2003). Theoretical and methodological considerations in cross-generational research on parenting and child aggressive behavior. *Journal of Abnormal Child Psychology, 31,* 185–192.

Duindam, Vincent; & Spruijt, Ed. (1997). Caring fathers in the Netherlands. *Sex Roles, 36,* 149–160.

DuLong, Jessica. (2002, November 26). Echoes of Brandon Teena. *The Advocate (The national gay & lesbian newsmagazine),* p. 14.

Duncan, Lauren E.; & Williams, Linda M. (1998). Gender role socialization and male-on-male vs. female-on-male child sexual abuse. *Sex Roles, 39,* 765–786.

Durkin, Kevin; & Nugent, Bradley. (1998). Kindergarten children's gender-role expectations for television actors. *Sex Roles, 38,* 387–402.

Durston, Sarah; Hulshoff Pol, Hilleke E.; Casey, B. J.; Giedd, Jay N.; Buitelaar, Jan K.; & van Engeland, Herman. (2001). Anatomical MRI of the developing human brain: What have we learned? *Journal of the American Academy of Child and Adolescent Psychiatry, 40,* 1012–1020.

Dutton, Mary Ann; Haywood, Yolanda; & El-Bayoumi, Gigi. (1997). Impact of violence on women's health.

In Sheryle J. Gallant, Gwendolyn Puryear Keita, & Reneé Royak-Schaler (Eds.), *Health care for women: Psychological, social, and behavioral influences* (pp. 41–56). Washington, DC: American Psychological Association.

Eagly, Alice H. (1987a). Reporting sex differences. *American Psychologist, 42,* 756–757.

Eagly, Alice H. (1987b). *Sex differences in social behavior: A social-role interpretation.* Hillsdale, NJ: Erlbaum.

Eagly, Alice H. (1997). Comparing women and men: Methods, findings, and politics. In Mary Roth Walsh (Ed.), *Women, men, and gender: Ongoing debates* (pp. 24–31). New Haven, CT: Yale University Press.

Eagly, Alice H.; & Johannesen-Schmidt, Mary C. (2001). The leadership styles of women and men. *Journal of Social Issues, 57,* 781–797.

Eagly, Alice H.; Johannesen-Schmidt, Mary C.; & van Engen, Marloes L. (2003). Transformational, transactional, and laissez-faire leadership styles: A meta-analysis comparing women and men. *Psychological Bulletin, 129,* 569–581.

Eagly, Alice H.; & Johnson, Blair T. (1990). Gender and leadership style: A meta-analysis. *Psychological Bulletin, 108,* 233–256.

Eagly, Alice H; & Karau, Steven J. (2002). Role congruity theory of prejudice toward female leaders. *Psychological Review, 109,* 573–597.

Eagly, Alice H.; Karau, Steven J.; & Makhijani, Mona G. (1995). Gender and the effectiveness of leaders: A meta-analysis. *Psychological Bulletin, 117,* 125–145.

Eagly, Alice H.; Mladinic, Antonio; & Otto, Stacey. (1991). Are women evaluated more favorably than men? An analysis of attitudes, beliefs, and emotions. *Psychology of Women Quarterly, 15,* 203–216.

Eagly, Alice H.; & Steffen, Valerie J. (1986). Gender and aggressive behavior: A meta-analytic review of the social psychological literature. *Psychological Bulletin, 100,* 309–330.

Eagly, Alice H.; & Wood, Wendy. (1999). The origins of sex differences in human behavior. *American Psychologist, 54,* 408–423.

Early, Frances H. (2001). Staking her claim: Buffy the Vampire Slayer as transgressive woman warrior. *Journal of Popular Culture, 35,* 11–27.

Easterbrook, Gregg. (1996). It's unreal: How phony realism in film and literature is corrupting and confusing the American mind. *Washington Monthly, 28* (10), 41–43.

Eccles, Jacquelynne S. (1987). Gender roles and achievement patterns: An expectancy value perspective. In

June Machover Reinisch, Leonard A. Rosenblum, & Stephanie A. Sanders (Eds.), *Masculinity/femininity: Basic perspectives* (pp. 240–280). New York: Oxford University Press.

Eccles, Jacquelynne S. (1989). Bringing young women to math and science. In Mary Crawford & Margaret Gentry (Eds.), *Gender and thought: Psychological perspectives* (pp. 36–58). New York: Springer-Verlag.

Eccles, Jacquelynne; & Bryan, James. (1994). Adolescence: Critical crossroad in the path of gender-role development. In Michael R. Stevenson (Ed.), *Gender roles through the life span: A multidisciplinary perspective* (pp. 111–147). Muncie, IN: Ball State University.

Eckes, Thomas. (2002). Paternalistic and envious gender stereotypes: Testing predictions from the stereotype content model. *Sex Roles, 47,* 99–114.

Edmonds, Ed M.; & Cahoon, Delwin D. (1993). The "new" sexism: Females' negativism toward males. *Journal of Social Behavior and Personality, 8,* 481–487.

Egan, Susan K.; & Perry, David G. (2001). Gender identity: A multidimensional analysis with implications for psychosocial adjustment. *Developmental Psychology, 37,* 451–463.

Ehrenreich, Barbara; & English, Deirdre. (1973). *Witches, midwives, and nurses: A history of women healers.* New York: Feminist Press.

Eichenbaum, Luise; & Orbach, Susie. (1983). *What do women want: Exploding the myth of dependency.* New York: Coward-McCann.

Eid, Michael; & Diener, Ed. (2001). Norms for experiencing emotions in different cultures: Inter- and intranational differences. *Journal of Personality and Social Psychology, 81,* 869–885.

Eisenberg, Nancy; & Lennon, Randy. (1983). Sex differences in empathy and related capacities. *Psychological Bulletin, 94,* 100–131.

Eisikovits, Zvi; Winstok, Zeev; & Gelles, Richard. (2002). Structure and dynamics of escalation from the victim's perspective. *Families in Society: The Journal of Contemporary Human Services, 83,* 142–152.

Ekman, Paul. (1984). Expression and the nature of emotion. In Klaus R. Scherer & Paul Ekman (Eds.), *Approaches to emotion* (pp. 319–343). Hillsdale, NJ: Erlbaum.

Ekman, Paul. (1992). Are there basic emotions? *Psychological Review, 99,* 550–553.

Ekman, Paul. (1994). Strong evidence for universals in facial expression: A reply to Russell's mistaken critique. *Psychological Bulletin, 115,* 268–287.

Ekman, Paul; Levenson, Robert W.; & Friesen, Wallace V. (1983). Autonomic nervous activity distinguishes among emotions. *Science, 221,* 1208–1210.

Elasmar, Michael; Hasegawa, Kazumi; & Brain, Mary. (1999). The portrayal of women in U.S. prime time television. *Journal of Broadcasting & Electronic Media, 43,* 20–42.

Elfenbein, Hillary Anger; & Ambady, Nalini. (2002). On the universality and cultural specificity of emotion recognition: A meta-analysis. *Psychological Bulletin, 128,* 203–235.

Ellestad, Myrvin H. (1996). *Stress testing* (4th ed.). Philadelphia: Davis.

Ellis, Albert. (1962). *Reason and emotion in psychotherapy.* New York: Stuart.

Emeagwali, Gloria. (1989/2003). *Eurocentricism and the history of science and technology.* Retrieved April 28, 2003, from http://members.aol.com/Sekglo/racism.htm. (Updated version of an article published in 1989, *Science and Public Policy, Journal of the International Science Policy Foundation, 16* [3].)

Enns, Carolyn Zerbe. (1992). Self-esteem groups: A synthesis of consciousness-raising and assertiveness training. *Journal of Counseling and Development, 71,* 7–13.

Enns, Carolyn Zerbe. (1997). *Feminist theories and feminist psychotherapies: Origins, themes, and variations.* New York: Harrington Park Press.

Enns, Carolyn Z.; & Hackett, Gail. (1990). Comparison of feminist and nonfeminist women's reactions to variants of nonsexist and feminist counseling. *Journal of Counseling Psychology, 37,* 33–40.

Epstein, Cynthia Fuchs. (1988). *Deceptive distinctions: Sex, gender and the social order.* New Haven, CT: Yale University Press.

Equal Employment Opportunity Commission. (2003). *Trends in harassment charges filed with the EEOC during the 1980s and 1990s.* Retrieved August 8, 2003, from www.eeoc.gov/stats.harassment.html.

Eron, Leonard D. (1987). The development of aggressive behavior from the perspective of a developing behaviorism. *American Psychologist, 42,* 435–442.

Eron, Leonard D.; Huesmann, L. Rowell; Brice, Patrick; Fischer, Paulette; & Mermelstein, Rebecca. (1983). Age trends in the development of aggression, sex typing, and related television habits. *Developmental Psychology, 19,* 71–77.

Estrich, Susan. (2001, December 9). The gender trap. *Mercury News* (San Jose), p. 1D+.

Evans, Lorraine; & Davies, Kimberly. (2000). No sissy boys here: A content analysis of the representation of masculinity in elementary school reading textbooks. *Sex Roles, 42,* 255–270.

Evans, Peggy Chin. (2003). "If only I were thin like her, maybe I could be happy like her": The self-implications of associating a thin female ideal with life success. *Psychology of Women Quarterly, 27,* 209–214.

Evans, William. (1996). Science and reason in film and television. *Skeptical Inquirer, 20,* 45–48.

Eyer, Diane E. (1992). *Mother–infant bonding: A scientific fiction.* New Haven, CT: Yale University Press.

Fagot, Beverly I.; & Hagan, Richard. (1991). Observations of parent reactions to sex-stereotyped behaviors: Age and sex effects. *Child Development, 62,* 617–628.

Fagot, Beverly I.; & Leinbach, Mary D. (1989). The young child's gender schema: Environmental input, internal organization. *Child Development, 60,* 663–672.

Fagot, Beverly I.; & Leinbach, Mary D. (1993). Gender-role development in young children: From discrimination to labeling. *Developmental Review, 13,* 205–224.

Fagot, Beverly I.; & Leinbach, Mary D. (1994). Gender-role development in young children. In Michael R. Stevenson (Ed.), *Gender roles through the life span: A multidisciplinary perspective* (pp. 3–24). Muncie, IN: Ball State University.

Fagot, Beverly I.; & Leinbach, Mary D. (1995). Gender knowledge in egalitarian and traditional families. *Sex Roles, 32,* 513–526.

Fallon, April E.; & Rozin, Paul. (1985). Sex differences in perceptions of desirable body shape. *Journal of Abnormal Psychology, 94,* 102–105.

Faludi, Susan. (1991). *Backlash: The undeclared war against American women.* New York: Crown.

Faludi, Susan. (1999). *Stiffed: The betrayal of the American man.* New York: Morrow.

Fang, Di; Moy, Ernest; Colburn, Lois; & Hurley, Jeanne. (2000). Racial and ethnic disparities in faculty promotion in academic medicine. *Journal of the American Medical Association, 284,* 1085–1092.

Farmer, Helen S.; & Sidney, Joan Seliger. (1985). Sex equity in career and vocational education. In Susan S. Klein (Ed.), *Handbook for achieving sex equity through education* (pp. 338–359). Baltimore, MD: Johns Hopkins University Press.

Fausto-Sterling, Anne. (1992). *Myths of gender: Biological theories about women and men* (2nd ed.). New York: Basic Books.

Fausto-Sterling, Anne. (2000). *Sexing the body: Gender politics and the construction of sexuality.* New York: Basic Books.

Faye, Jefferson. (2001). Subverting the captor's language: Teaching native science to students of Western science. *American Indian Quarterly, 25,* 270–274.

Federal Bureau of Investigation. (2002). *Uniform crime report, 2001.* Retrieved December 6, 2003, from www.fbi.gov/ucr/01cius.htm.

Fee, Dwight. (2000). "One of the guys": Instrumentality and intimacy in gay men's friendships with straight men. In Peter Nardi (Ed.), *Gay masculinities* (pp. 44–65). Thousand Oaks, CA: Sage.

Fee, Elizabeth. (1986). Critiques of modern science: The relationship of feminism to other radical epistemologies. In Ruth Bleier (Ed.), *Feminist approaches to science* (pp. 42–56). New York: Pergamon Press.

Fehr, Beverley. (2000). The life cycle of friendship. In Clyde Hendrick & Susan S. Hendrick (Eds.), *Close relationships: A sourcebook* (pp. 71–82). Thousand Oaks, CA: Sage.

Feingold, Alan. (1988). Cognitive gender differences are disappearing. *American Psychologist, 43,* 95–103.

Feingold, Alan. (1994). Gender differences in variability in intellectual abilities: A cross-cultural perspective. *Sex Roles, 30,* 81–92.

Feingold, Alan. (1998). Gender stereotyping for sociability, dominance, character, and mental health: A meta-analysis of findings from the bogus stranger paradigm. *Genetic, Social, and General Psychology Monographs, 124,* 253–270.

Feist, Jess; & Feist, Gregory J. (2002). *Theories of personality* (5th ed.). Boston: McGraw-Hill.

Feist-Price, Sonja; & Khanna, Neena. (2003, January/February). Employment inequality for women with disabilities. *off our backs,* pp. 10–12.

Feld, Scott L.; & Straus, Murray A. (1989). Escalation and desistance of wife assault in marriage. *Criminology, 27,* 141–161.

Felmlee, Diane H. (1994). Who's on top? Power in romantic relationships. *Sex Roles, 31,* 275–295.

Fennema, Elizabeth. (1980). Sex-related differences in mathematics achievement: Where and why. In Lynn H. Fox, Linda Brody, & Dianne Tobin (Eds.), *Women and the mathematical mystique* (pp. 76–93). Baltimore, MD: Johns Hopkins University Press.

Fetto, John. (2003, June 1). First comes love. *American Demographics, 25* (5), 5.

Field, Alison, E.; Camargo, Carlos A., Jr.; Taylor, C. Barr; Berkey, Catherine S.; Roberts, Susan B.; & Colditz, Graham A. (2001). Peer, parent, and media influences on the development of weight concerns and frequent dieting among preadolescent and adolescent girls and boys. *Pediatrics, 107,* 54–60.

Fields, Judith; & Wolff, Edward N. (1991). The decline of sex segregation and the wage gap, 1970–80. *Journal of Human Resources, 26,* 608–622.

Fiese, Barbara H.; & Skillman, Gemma. (2000). Gender differences in family stories: Moderating influence of parent gender role and child gender. *Sex Roles, 43,* 267–283.

Fine, Michelle. (1988). Sexuality, schooling, and adolescent females: The missing discourse of desire. *Harvard Educational Review, 58,* 29–53.

Fineran, Susan. (2002). Sexual harassment between same-sex peers: Intersection of mental health, homophobia, and sexual violence in schools. *Social Work, 47,* 65–74.

Finkelhor, David. (1980). Sex among siblings: A survey on prevalence, variety, and effects. *Archives of Sexual Behavior, 9,* 171–193.

Finkelhor, David. (1984). *Child sexual abuse: New theory and research.* New York: Free Press.

Finkelhor, David. (1990). Early and long-term effects of child sexual abuse: An update. *Professional Psychology Research and Practice, 21,* 325–330.

Finn, Jerry. (1999). An exploration of helping processes in an online self-help group focusing on issues of disability. *Health and Social Work, 24,* 220–227.

Fireman, Bruce; Koran, Lorrin M.; Leventhal, Jeanne L.; & Jacobson, Alice. (2001). The prevalence of clinically recognized obsessive-compulsive disorder in a large health maintenance organization. *American Journal of Psychiatry, 158,* 1904–1910.

Fischer, Agneta H. (1993). Sex differences in emotionality: Fact or stereotype? *Feminism & Psychology, 3,* 303–318.

Fischer, Ann R.; & Good, Glenn E. (1994). Gender, self, and others: Perceptions of the campus environment. *Journal of Counseling Psychology, 41,* 343–355.

Fisher, Michele. (2003, February). Just another walking stereotype. *Curve, 13,* 40–41.

Fiske, Susan T.; Bersoff, Donald N.; Borgida, Eugene; Deaux, Kay; & Heilman, Madeline E. (1991). Social science research on trial: Use of sex stereotyping research in *Price Waterhouse v. Hopkins. American Psychologist, 46,* 1049–1060.

Fiske, Susan T.; Cuddy, Amy J. C.; Glick, Peter; & Xu, Jun. (2002). A model of (often mixed) stereotype content: Competence and warmth respectively follow from perceived status and competition. *Journal of Personality and Social Psychology, 82,* 878–902.

Fitzgerald, Louise F. (1994, August). *Sexual harassment— A feminist perspective on the prevention of violence against women in the workplace.* Paper presented at the 102nd annual convention of the American Psychological Association, Los Angeles, CA.

Fitzgerald, Louise F.; Swan, Suzanne; & Magley, Vicki J. (1997). But was it really sexual harassment? Legal, behavioral, and psychological definitions of the workplace victimization of women. In William O'-Donohue (Ed.), *Sexual harassment: Theory, research, and treatment* (pp. 5–28). Boston: Allyn and Bacon.

Fitzgerald, Nancy. (2002). TV's big lie: They're some of your favorite television stars, but these actresses' bodies are sending teens the wrong message about how young women are supposed to look. *Scholastic Choices, 17* (7), 6–10.

Flaskerud, Jacquelyn H.; & Hu, Li-tze. (1992). Relationship of ethnicity to psychiatric diagnosis. *Journal of Nervous and Mental Disease, 180,* 296–303.

Flora, Stephen Ray; & Sellers, Melissa. (2003, May/June). "Premenstrual dysphoric disorder" and "premenstrual syndrome" myths. *Skeptical Inquirer, 27* (3), 37–42.

Floyd, Kory. (1995). Gender and closeness among friends and siblings. *Journal of Psychology, 129,* 193–202.

Fodor, Iris Goldstein. (1988). Cognitive behavior therapy: Evaluation of theory and practice for addressing women's issues. In Mary Ann Dutton Douglas & Lenore E. A. Walker (Eds.), *Feminist psychotherapies: Integration of therapeutic and feminist systems* (pp. 91–117). Norwood, NJ: Ablex.

Folkman, Susan; & Lazarus, Richard S. (1980). An analysis of coping in middle-aged community sample. *Journal of Health and Social Behavior, 21,* 219–239.

Fontenot, Kathleen; & Brannon, Linda. (1991, August). *Gender differences in coping with workplace stress.* Paper presented at the 99th annual convention of the American Psychological Association, San Francisco, CA.

Forbes, Gordon B.; Adams-Curtis, Leah E.; White, Kay B.; & Holmgren, Katie M. (2003). The role of hostile and benevolent sexism in women's and men's perceptions of the menstruating woman. *Psychology of Women Quarterly, 27,* 58–63.

Ford, Clellan S.; & Beach, Frank A. (1951). *Patterns of sexual behavior.* New York: Harper.

Foschi, Martha. (2000). Double standards for competence: Theory and research. *Annual Review of Sociology, 26,* 21–42.

Foster, Lesley Ann. (2002). South African experiences in fighting domestic violence. *Sexual Health Exchange, 2002* (3), 3–4.

Fouts, Gregory; & Vaughan, Kimberly. (2002). Television situation comedies: Male weight, negative references, and audience reactions. *Sex Roles, 46,* 439–442.

Fowers, Blaine J.; Applegate, Brooks; Tredinnick, Michael; & Slusher, Jason. (1996). His and her individualisms? Sex bias and individualism in psychologists' responses to case vignettes. *The Journal of Psychology, 130,* 159–174.

Fox, Ronald C. (1996). Bisexuality in perspective: A review of theory and research. In Beth A. Firestein (Ed.), *Bisexuality: The psychology and politics of an invisible minority* (pp. 3–50). Thousand Oaks, CA: Sage.

Franks, Peter; & Bertakis, Klea D. (2003). Physician gender, patient gender, and primary care. *Journal of Women's Health, 12,* 73–80.

Freedman, Estelle B. (2002). *No turning back: The history of feminism and the future of women.* New York: Ballantine.

Freud, Sigmund. (1959). An autobiographical study. In James Strachey (Ed. and Trans.), *The standard edition of the complete psychological works of Sigmund Freud* (Vol. 20). London: Hogarth Press. (Original work published in 1925)

Freud, Sigmund. (1989). Some psychical consequences of the anatomical distinction between the sexes. In Peter Gay (Ed.), *The Freud reader* (pp. 670–678). New York: Norton. (Original work published in 1925)

Freud, Sigmund. (1964). Femininity. In James Strachey (Ed. and Trans.), *New introductory lectures on psychoanalysis* (p. 112–135). New York: Norton. (Original work published 1933)

Fried, Linda P.; Kronmal, Richard A.; Newman, Anne B.; Bild, Diane E.; Mittelmark, Maurice B.; Polak, Joseph F.; Robbins, John A.; & Gardin, Julius M. (1998). Risk factors for 5-year mortality in older adults: The Cardiovascular Health Study. *Journal of the American Medical Association, 279,* 585–592.

Frieze, Irene Hanson. (2000). Violence in close relationships—Development of a research area: Comment on Archer (2000). *Psychological Bulletin, 126,* 681–684.

Frieze, Irene Hanson; Ferligoj, Anuška; Kogovešek, Tina; Rener, Tanja; Horvat, Jasna; & Šarlija, Nataša. (2003). Gender-role attitudes in university students in the United States, Slovenia, and Croatia. *Psychology of Women Quarterly, 27,* 256–261.

Frodi, Ann M.; Macaulay, Jacqueline; & Thome, Pauline R. (1977). Are women always less aggressive than men? A review of the experimental literature. *Psychological Bulletin, 84,* 634–660.

Frye, Marilyn. (1997). Lesbian "sex." In Maxine Baca Zinn, Pierrette Hondagneu-Sotelo, & Michael A. Messner (Eds.), *Through the prism of difference: Readings on sex and gender* (pp. 205–209). Boston: Allyn and Bacon.

Fulcher, Megan; Sutfin, Erin; & Patterson, Charlotte J. (2001, April). *Parental sexual orientation, division of labor, and sex-role stereotyping in children's occupational choices.* Poster session presented at the biennial meeting of the Society for Research in Child Development, Minneapolis, MN.

Funtowicz, Mirian N.; & Widiger, Thomas A. (1999). Sex bias in the diagnosis of personality disorders: An evaluation of the DSM-IV criteria. *Journal of Abnormal Psychology, 108,* 195–201.

Furman, Wyndol; Simon, Valerie A.; Shaffer, Laura; & Bouchey, Heather A. (2002). Adolescents' working models and styles for relationships with parents, friends, and romantic partners. *Child Development, 73,* 241–255.

Furnham, Adrian. (1999). Sex differences in self-estimates of lay dimensions of intelligence. *Psychological Reports, 85,* 349–350.

Furnham, Adrian; Dias, Melanie; & McClelland, Alastair. (1998). The role of body weight, waist-to-hip ratio, and breast size in judgments of female attractiveness. *Sex Roles, 39,* 311–326.

Furnham, Adrian; & Gasson, Lucinda. (1998). Sex differences in parental estimates of their children's intelligence. *Sex Roles, 38,* 151–162.

Furnham, Adrian; & Mak, Twiggy. (1999). Sex-role stereotyping in television commercials: A review and comparison of fourteen studies done on five continents over 25 years. *Sex Roles, 41,* 413–438.

Furnham, Adrian; Reeves, Emma; & Budhani, Salima. (2002). Parents think their sons are brighter than their daughters: Sex differences in parental self-estimations and estimations of their children's multiple intelligences. *Journal of Genetic Psychology, 163,* 24–39.

Gabbard, Glen O.; & Gabbard, Krin. (1999). *Psychiatry and the cinema* (2nd ed.). Washington, DC: American Psychiatric Press.

Gabbard, Krin. (2000, February 11). Therapy's "talking cure" still works—in Hollywood. *Chronicle of Higher Education,* p. B9.

Galegher, Jolene; Sproull, Lee; & Kiesler, Sara. (1998). Legitimacy, authority, and community in electronic support groups. *Written Communications, 15,* 493.

Gardiner, Maria; & Tiggemann, Marika. (1999). Gender differences in leadership style, job stress and mental health in male- and female-dominated industries. *Journal of Occupational and Organizational Psychology, 72,* 301–315.

Gardyn, Rebecca. (2003). Got game? *American Demographics, 25* (8), 18.

Garner, David M.; & Garfinkel, Paul E. (1980). Sociocultural factors in the development of anorexia nervosa. *Psychological Medicine, 10,* 647–656.

Garner, David M.; Garfinkel, Paul E.; Schwartz, Donald M.; & Thompson, Michael G. (1980). Cultural expectations of thinness in women. *Psychological Reports, 47,* 483–491.

Garnets, Linda D.; & Peplau, Letitia Anne. (2000). Understanding women's sexualities and sexual orientations: An introduction. *Journal of Social Issues, 56,* 181–192.

Garrahy, Deborah A. (2001). Three third-grade teachers' gender-related beliefs and behavior. *Elementary School Journal, 102,* 81–94.

Gartner, Audrey; & Riessman, Frank. (1998). Self-help. *Social Policy, 28* (3), 83–86.

Gay, Peter. (1988). *Freud: A life for our time.* New York: Norton.

Geary, David C.; & Flinn, Mark V. (2002). Sex differences in behavioral and hormonal response to social threat: Commentary on Taylor et al. (2000). *Psychological Review, 109,* 745–750.

Gentile, Douglas A. (1993). Just what are sex and gender, anyway? A call for a new terminological standard. *Psychological Science, 4,* 120–122.

Gerbner, George; Gross, Larry; Morgan, Michael; & Signorielli, Nancy. (1994). Growing up with television: The cultivation perspective. In J. Bryant & D. Zillman (Eds.), *Media effects: Advances in theory and research* (pp. 17–41). Hillsdale, NJ: Erlbaum.

Gergen, Kenneth J. (1985). The social constructionist movement in modern psychology. *American Psychologist, 40,* 266–275.

Gerhart, Barry. (1990). Gender differences in current and starting salaries: The role of performance, college major, and job title. *Industrial and Labor Relations Review, 43,* 418–433.

Geschwind, Norman; & Galaburda, Albert S. (1987). *Cerebral lateralization.* Cambridge, MA: MIT Press.

Gianakos, Irene. (2002). Predictors of coping with work stress: The influences of sex, gender role, social desirability, and locus of control. *Sex Roles, 46,* 149–158.

Gibbons, Deborah; & Olk, Paul. (2003). Individual and structural origins of friendship and social position among professionals. *Journal of Personality and Social Psychology, 84,* 340–351.

Gibbons, Judith L.; Hamby, Beverly A.; & Dennis, Wanda D. (1997). Researching gender-role ideologies internationally and cross-culturally. *Psychology of Women Quarterly, 21,* 151–170.

Gilbert, Lucia A. (1980). Feminist therapy. In Annette M. Brodsky & Rachel Hare-Mustin (Eds.), *Women and psychotherapy* (pp. 245–265). New York: Guilford Press.

Gilgun, Jane F. (1995). We shared something special: The moral discourse of incest perpetrators. *Journal of Marriage and the Family, 57,* 265–281.

Gilligan, Carol. (1982). *In a different voice: Psychological theory and women's development.* Cambridge, MA: Harvard University Press.

Ginsburg, Herbert; & Opper, Sylvia. (1969). *Piaget's theory of intellectual development: An introduction.* Englewood Cliffs, NJ: Prentice-Hall.

Giuliano, Traci A.; Popp, Kathryn E.; & Knight, Jennifer L. (2000). Footballs versus Barbies: Childhood play activities as predictors of sport participation by women. *Sex Roles, 42,* 159–182.

Glascock, Jack. (2001). Gender roles on prime-time network television: Demographics and behaviors. *Journal of Broadcasting & Electronic Media, 45,* 656–669.

Glick, Peter; & Fiske, Susan T. (1999). The Ambivalence toward Men Inventory: Differentiating hostile and benevolent beliefs about men. *Psychology of Women Quarterly, 23,* 519–536.

Glick, Peter; & Fiske, Susan T. (2001). An ambivalent alliance: Hostile and benevolent sexism as complementary justification for gender inequality. *American Psychologist, 56,* 109–118.

Glick, Peter; Fiske, Susan T.; Mladinic, Antonio; Saiz, José L.; Abrams, Dominic; Masser, Barbara; et al. (2000). Beyond prejudice as simple antipathy: Hostile and benevolent sexism across cultures. *Journal of Personality and Social Psychology, 79,* 763–775.

Golding, Jacqueline M. (1999). Intimate partner violence as a risk factor for mental disorders: A meta-analysis. *Journal of Family Violence, 14,* 99–101.

Goldsmith, Ronald E.; & Matherly, Timothy A. (1988). Creativity and self-esteem: A multiple operationalization validity study. *Journal of Psychology, 122,* 47–56.

Gonzales, Patricia M.; Blanton, Hart; & Williams, Kevin J. (2002). The effects of stereotype threat and double-minority status on the test performance of Latino women. *Personality and Social Psychology Bulletin, 28,* 659–670.

Gonzalez, Judith Teresa. (1988). Dilemmas of the high-achieving Chicana: The double-bind factor in male/female relationships. *Sex Roles, 18,* 367–380.

Good, Glenn E.; Gilbert, Lucia A.; & Scher, Murray. (1990). Gender aware therapy: A synthesis of feminist therapy and knowledge about gender. *Journal of Counseling & Development, 68,* 376–380.

Good, Glenn E.; & Sherrod, Nancy B. (2001). The psychology of men and masculinity: Research status and future directions. In Rhoda Unger (Ed.), *Handbook of the psychology of women and gender* (pp. 201–214). New York: Wiley.

Goodale, Gloria. (1999, September 24). His & hers TV: TV channels, video games, and Internet sites zero in on girls and boys. *Christian Science Monitor,* p. 13.

Gooden, Angela M.; & Gooden, Mark A. (2001). Gender representation in notable children's picture books: 1995–1997. *Sex Roles, 45,* 89–101.

Goodman, Lisa A.; Koss, Mary P.; Fitzgerald, Louise F.; Russo, Nancy Felipe; & Keita, Gwendolyn Puryear. (1993). Male violence against women: Current research and future directions. *American Psychologist, 48,* 1054–1058.

Goodwin, Stephanie A.; & Fiske, Susan T. (2001). Power and gender: The double-edged sword of ambivalence. In Rhoda K. Unger (Ed.), *Handbook of the psychology of women and gender* (pp. 358–366). New York: Wiley.

Gorski, Roger A. (1987). Sex differences in the rodent brain: Their nature and origin. In June M. Reinisch, Leonard A. Rosenblum, & Stephanie A. Sanders (Eds.), *Masculinity/femininity: Basic perspectives* (pp. 37–67). New York: Oxford University Press.

Gottman, John M. (1991). Predicting the longitudinal course of marriages. *Journal of Marriage and Family Therapy, 17,* 3–7.

Gottman, John M. (1998). Psychology and the study of marital processes. *Annual Review of Psychology, 49,* 169–187.

Gottman, John M.; & Notarius, Clifford I. (2000). Decade review: Observing marital interaction. *Journal of Marriage and Family, 62,* 927–947.

Gottman, John. (with Silver, Nan). (1994). *Why marriages succeed or fail.* New York: Simon and Schuster.

Gould, Ketayun H. (2000). Beyond *Jones v. Clinton:* Sexual harassment law and social work. *Social Work, 45,* 237–250.

Gould, Stephen Jay. (1996). *The mismeasure of man* (Rev. ed.). New York: Norton.

Gove, Walter R. (1984). Gender differences in mental and physical illness: The effects of fixed roles and nurturant roles. *Social Science and Medicine, 19* (2), 77–84.

Graham, Kathryn; & Wells, Samantha. (2001). The two worlds of aggression for men and women. *Sex Roles, 45,* 595–622.

Granello, Darcy Haag; & Pauley, Pamela S. (2000). Television viewing habits and their relationship to tolerance toward people with mental illness. *Journal of Mental Health Counseling, 22,* 162–175.

Granrose, Cherlyn Skromme; & Kaplan, Eileen E. (1996). *Work–family role choices for women in their 20s and 30s.* Westport, CT: Praeger.

Gratch, Linda Vanden; Bassett, Margaret E.; & Attra, Sharon L. (1995). The relationship of gender and ethnicity to self-silencing and depression among college students. *Psychology of Women Quarterly, 19,* 509–515.

Gray, John. (1992). *Men are from Mars, women are from Venus.* New York: HarperCollins.

Green, Richard. (1987). *The "sissy boy syndrome" and the development of homosexuality.* New Haven, CT: Yale University Press.

Greenberg, Harvey Roy. (1992). Psychotherapy at the simplex: Le plus ca shrink. *Journal of Popular Film and Television, 20,* 9–15.

Greenberger, Ellen; & O'Neil, Robin. (1993). Spouse, parent, worker: Role commitments and role-related experiences in the construction of adults' well-being. *Developmental Psychology, 29,* 181–197.

Greene, Beverly. (1994). African American women. In Lillian Comas-Díaz & Beverly Greene (Eds.), *Women of color: Integrating ethnic and gender identities in psychotherapy* (pp. 10–29). New York: Guilford Press.

Greenfield, Lawrence A. (1996). *Child victimizers: Violent offenders and their victims.* Washington, DC: U.S. Department of Justice.

Greenstein, Theodore N. (1996). Husbands' participation in domestic labor: Interactive effect of wives' and husbands' gender ideologies. *Journal of Marriage and the Family, 58,* 585–595.

Greenwald, Anthony G. (1975). Consequences of prejudice against the null hypothesis. *Psychological Bulletin, 82,* 1–20.

Gregory, Robert J. (1987). *Adult intellectual assessment.* Boston: Allyn and Bacon.

Greven, David. (2002). Dude, where's my gender? Contemporary teen comedies and new forms of American masculinity. *Cineaste, 27* (3), 14–22.

Grogan, Sarah; & Richards, Helen. (2002). Body image: Focus groups with boys and men. *Men & Masculinities, 4,* 219–232.

Groshen, Erica L. (1991). The structure of the female/male wage differential: Is it who you are, what you do, or where you work? *Journal of Human Resources, 26,* 457–472.

Gross, Bruce. (2003). A touchy subject: Sexual intimacies between therapists and clients. *Annals of the American Psychotherapy Association, 6,* 51.

Grunbaum, Jo Anne; Kann, Laura; Kinchen, Steven A.; Williams, Barbara; Ross, James G.; Lowry, Richard; & Kolbe, Lloyd. (2002). Youth Risk Behavior Surveillance—United States, 2001. *Morbidity and Mortality Weekly Report, 51,* (SS-4).

Guanipa, Carmen; & Woolley, Scott R. (2000). Gender biases and therapists' conceptualization of couple difficulties. *American Journal of Family Therapy, 28,* 181–192.

Gupta, Nabanita Datta. (1993). Probabilities of job choice and employer selection and male–female occupational differences. *American Economic Review, 83* (2), 57–62.

Gur, Ruben C.; Alsop, David; Glahn, David; Petty, Richard; Swanson, Charlie L.; Maldjian, Joseph A.; Turetsky, Bruce I.; Detre, John A.; Gee, James; & Gur, Raquel E. (2000). An fMRI study of sex differences in regional activation to a verbal and a spatial task. *Brain and Language, 74,* 157–170.

Gur, Ruben C.; Mozley, Lyn Harper; Mozley, P. David; Resnick, Susan M.; Kapr, Joel S.; Alavi, Abass; Arnold, Steven E.; & Gur, Raquel E. (1995). Sex differences in regional glucose metabolism during a resting state. *Science, 267,* 528–531.

Gutek, Barbara A. (1985). *Sex and the workplace.* San Francisco, CA: Jossey-Bass.

Gutek, Barbara. (2001). Women and paid work. *Psychology of Women Quarterly, 25,* 379–393.

Gutek, Barbara; & Done, Robert S. (2001). Sexual harassment. In Rhoda K. Unger (Ed.), *Handbook of the psychology of women and gender* (pp. 367–387). New York: Wiley

Guttman, Cynthia. (2001). When girls go missing from the classroom. *UNESCO Courier, 54* (5), 13–14.

Hackett, Gail; Enns, Carolyn Z.; & Zetzer, Heidi A. (1992). Reactions of women to nonsexist and feminist counseling: Effects of counselor orientation and mode of information delivery. *Journal of Counseling Psychology, 39,* 321–330.

Haddock, Shelley A.; MacPhee, David; & Zimmerman, Toni Schindler. (2001). AAMFT master series tapes: An analysis of the inclusion of feminist principles into family therapy practice. *Journal of Marital and Family Therapy, 27,* 487–500.

Hall, Judith A.; & Carter, Jason D. (1999). Gender-stereotype accuracy as an individual difference. *Journal of Personality and Social Psychology, 77,* 350–359.

Hall, Judith A.; & Halberstadt, Amy G. (1997). Subordination and nonverbal sensitivity: A hypothesis in search of support. In Mary Roth Walsh (Ed.), *Women, men, and gender: Ongoing debates* (pp. 120–133). New Haven, CT: Yale University Press.

Hall, Lynn S.; & Love, Craig T. (2003). Finger-length ratios in female monozygotic twins discordant for sexual orientation. *Archives of Sexual Behavior, 32,* 23–28.

Hall, Margery J.; & Tidwell, Wendell C. (2003). Internet recovery for substance abuse and alcoholism: An exploratory study of service users. *Journal of Substance Abuse Treatment, 24,* 161–167.

Hall, Ruth L.; & Greene, Beverly. (2003). Contemporary African American families. In Louise B. Silverstein & Thelma Jean Goodrich (Eds.), *Feminist family therapy: Empowerment in social context* (pp. 107–120). Washington, DC: American Psychological Association.

Halpern, Diane F. (1994). Stereotypes, science, censorship, and the study of sex differences. *Feminism & Psychology, 4,* 523–530.

Halpern, Diane F. (1997). Sex differences in intelligence: Implications for education. *American Psychologist, 52,* 1091–1102.

Halpern, Diane F. (2000). *Sex differences in cognitive abilities* (3rd ed.). Mahwah, NJ: Erlbaum.

Hantover, Jeffrey P. (1992). The Boy Scouts and the validation of masculinity. In Michael S. Kimmel & Michael A. Messner (Eds.), *Men's lives* (2nd ed., pp. 123–131). New York: Macmillan.

Hardie, Elizabeth A. (1997). Prevalence and predictors of cyclic and noncyclic affective change. *Psychology of Women Quarterly, 21,* 299–314.

Harding, Sandra. (1986). *The science question in feminism.* Ithaca, NY: Cornell University Press.

Harding, Sandra. (2001). Comment on Walby's "Against epistemological chasms: The science question in feminism revisited": Can democratic values and interests ever play a rationally justifiable role in the evaluation of scientific work? *Signs, 26,* 511–525.

Hare-Mustin, Rachel T. (1983). An appraisal of the relationship between women and psychotherapy: 80 years after the case of Dora. *American Psychologist, 38,* 593–601.

Hare-Mustin, Rachel T.; & Marecek, Jeanne. (1988). The meaning of difference: Gender theory, postmodernism, and psychology. *American Psychologist, 43,* 455–464.

Harlow, Harry F. (1959). Love in infant monkeys. *Scientific American, 200* (6), 68–74.

Harlow, Harry F. (1971). *Learning to love.* San Francisco: Albion.

Harlow, Harry F.; & Harlow, Margaret Kuenne. (1962). Social deprivation in monkeys. *Scientific American, 207,* 136–146.

Harmon, Robert J.; Bender, Bruce G.; Linden, Mary G.; & Robinson, Arthur. (1998). Transition from adolescence to early adulthood: Adaptation and psychiatric status of women with 47,XXX. *Journal of the American Academy of Child and Adolescent Psychiatry, 37,* 286–291.

Harris, Allen C. (1994). Ethnicity as a determinant of sex role identity: A replication study of item selection for the Bem Sex Role Inventory. *Sex Roles, 31,* 241–273.

Harris, Judith Rich. (1998). *The nurture assumption: Why children turn out the way they do.* New York: Free Press.

Harrison, Kristen. (2003). Television viewers' ideal body proportions: The case of the curvaceously thin woman. *Sex Roles, 48,* 255–264.

Hartup, Willard W., & Stevens, Nan. (1999). Friendships and adaptation across the life span. *Current Directions in Psychological Science, 8,* 76–79.

Harwood, Jake; & Anderson, Karen. (2002). The presence and portrayal of social groups of prime-time television. *Communication Reports, 15,* 81–98.

Hassler, Marianne; Nieschlag, Eberhard; & de la Motte, Diether. (1990). Creative musical talent, cognitive functioning, and gender: Psychobiological aspects. *Music Perception, 8,* 35–48.

Hatfield, Elaine; & Rapson, Richard L. (1996). *Love and sex: Cross-cultural perspectives.* Boston: Allyn and Bacon.

Hausenblas, Heather A.; & Symons Downs, Danielle. (2002). Exercise dependence: A systematic review. *Psychology of Sport and Exercise, 3,* 89–123.

Hawkins, Darren; & Humes, Melissa. (2002). Human rights and domestic violence. *Political Science Quarterly, 117,* 231–257.

Hawley, Patricia H.; & Vaughn, Brian E. (2003). Aggression and adaptive functioning: The bright side to bad behavior. *Merrill-Palmer Quarterly, 49,* 239–242.

Hawtin, Sarah; & Moore, Judy. (1998). Empowerment or collusion? The social context of person-centred therapy. In Brian Throne & Elke Lambers (Eds.), *Person-centred therapy: A European perspective* (pp. 91–105). London: Sage.

Hecker, Daniel E. (1998). Earnings of college graduates: Women compared with men. *Monthly Labor Review, 121* (3), 62–71.

Heckert, Teresa M.; Droste, Heather E.; Adams, Patrick J.; Griffin, Christopher M.; Roberts, Lisa L.; Mueller, Michael A.; & Wallis, Hope A. (2002). Gender differences in anticipated salary: Role of salary estimates for others, job characteristics, career paths, and job inputs. *Sex Roles, 47,* 139–151.

Hedrick, Hannah L. (1995). The self-help sourcebook: Finding and forming mutual aid self-help groups (5th ed.) (Book review). *Journal of the American Medical Association, 274,* 847–849.

Heesacker, Martin; Wester, Stephen R.; Vogel, David L.; Wentzel, Jeffrey T.; Mejia-Millan, Cristina M.; & Goodholm, Carl Robert, Jr. (1999). Gender-based emotional stereotyping. *Journal of Counseling Psychology, 46,* 483–495.

Heilman, Madeline E.; Black, Caryn J.; Martell, Richard F.; & Simon, Michael C. (1989). Has anything changed? Current characterizations of men, women, and managers. *Journal of Applied Psychology, 74,* 935–942.

Heise, Lori; Ellsberg, Mary; & Gottemoeller, Megan. (1999). Ending violence against women. *Population Reports,* Series L, No. 11. Baltimore, MD: Johns Hopkins University School of Public Health, Population Information Program.

Helgeson, Vicki S. (1990). The role of masculinity in a prognostic predictor of heart attack severity. *Sex Roles, 22,* 755–776.

Helgeson, Vicki S. (1994). Relation of agency and communion to well-being: Evidence and potential explanations. *Psychological Bulletin, 116,* 412–428.

Helson, Ravenna; & Picano, James. (1990). Is the traditional role bad for women? *Journal of Personality and Social Psychology, 59,* 311–320.

Helwig, Andrew A. (1998). Gender-role stereotyping: Testing theory with a longitudinal sample. *Sex Roles, 38,* 403–423.

Hendrick, Susan S.; & Hendrick, Clyde. (1992). *Liking, loving, and relating* (2nd ed.). Pacific Grove, CA: Brooks/Cole.

Hendrick, Susan S.; Hendrick, Clyde; & Adler, Nancy L. (1988). Romantic relationships: Love, satisfaction, and staying together. *Journal of Personality and Social Psychology, 54,* 980–988.

Hendryx, Michael S.; & Ahern, Melissa M. (1997). Mental health functioning and community problems. *Journal of Community Psychology, 25,* 147–157.

Henshaw, Stanley K. (2001). *U.S. teenage pregnancy statistics.* New York: Alan Guttmacher Institute.

Herdt, Gilbert H. (1981). *Guardians of the flutes: Idioms of masculinity.* New York: McGraw-Hill.

Herdt, Gilbert H. (1990). Mistaken gender: 5-alpha-reductase hermaphroditism and biological reductionism in sexual identity reconsidered. *American Anthropologist, 92,* 433–446.

Herdt, Gilbert; & Boxer, Andrew. (1995). Bisexuality: Toward a comparative theory of identities and culture. In Richard G. Parker & John H. Gagnon (Eds.), *Concerning sexuality: Approaches to sex research in a postmodern world* (pp. 69 83). New York: Routledge.

Herek, Gregory M. (2002). Heterosexuals' attitudes toward bisexual men and women in the United States. *Journal of Sex Research, 39,* 264–274.

Herrmann, Douglas J.; Crawford, Mary; & Holdsworth, Michelle. (1992). Gender-linked differences in everyday memory performance. *British Journal of Psychology, 83,* 221–231.

Hetherington, E. Mavis; & Kelly, John. (2002). *For better or worse: Divorce reconsidered.* New York: Norton.

Heusel, Colleen; & Dabbs, James M., Jr. (1996, August). *Testosterone predicts engineer employment status in an oilfield service company.* Paper presented at the 104th annual convention of the American Psychological Association, Toronto, Canada.

Higgins, Louise T.; Zheng, Mo; Liu, Yali; & Sun, Chun Hui. (2002). Attitudes to marriage and sexual behaviors: A survey of gender and culture differences in China and United Kingdom. *Sex Roles, 46,* 75–89.

Hilgard, Ernest R. (1987). *Psychology in America: A historical survey.* San Diego: Harcourt Brace Jovanovich.

Hill, John P.; & Lynch, Mary Ellen. (1983). The intensification of gender-related role expectations during early adolescence. In Jeanne Brooks-Gunn & Anne C. Petersen (Eds.), *Girls at puberty: Biological and psychosocial perspectives.* New York: Plenum Press.

Hill, Marcia; & Ballou, Mary. (1998). Making therapy feminist: A practice survey. *Women & Therapy, 21,* 1–16.

Hill, Melanie S.; & Fischer, Ann R. (2001). Does entitlement mediate the link between masculinity and rape-related variables? *Journal of Counseling Psychology, 48,* 39–50.

Hill, Shirley A. (2002). Teaching and doing gender in African American families. *Sex Roles, 47,* 493–506.

Hines, Melissa; Ahmed, S. Faisal; & Hughes, Ieuan A. (2003). Psychological outcomes and gender-related development in complete androgen insensitivity syndrome. *Archives of Sexual Behavior, 32,* 93–101.

Hines, Melissa; Golombok, Susan; Rust, John; Johnston, Katie J.; & Golding, Jean. (2002). Testosterone during pregnancy and gender role behavior of preschool children: A longitudinal, population study. *Child Development, 73,* 1678–1689.

Hines, Melissa; & Kaufman, Francine R. (1994). Androgen and the development of human sex-typical behavior: Rough-and-tumble play and sex of preferred playmates in children with congenital adrenal hyperplasia (CAH). *Child Development, 65,* 1042–1053.

Hippisley-Cox, Julia; Pringle, Mike; Crown, Nicola; Meal, Andy; & Wynn, Alison. (2001). Sex inequalities in ischaemic heart disease in general practice: Cross sectional survey. *British Medical Journal, 322,* 832–834.

Hiscock, Merrill; Inch, Roxanne; Jacek, Carolyn; Hiscock-Kalil, Cheryl, & Kalil, Kathleen M. (1994). Is there a sex difference in human laterality? I. An exhaustive survey of auditory laterality studies from six neuropsychology journals. *Journal of Clinical and Experimental Neuropsychology, 16,* 423–435.

Hiscock, Merrill; Israelian, Marlyne; Inch, Roxanne; Jacek, Carolyn; & Hiscock-Kalil, Cheryl. (1995). Is there a sex difference in human laterality? II. An exhaustive survey of visual laterality studies from six neuropsychology journals. *Journal of Clinical and Experimental Neuropsychology, 17,* 590–610.

Hochschild, Arlie. (1997). *The time bind.* New York: Metropolitan Books.

Hochschild, Arlie. (with Machung, Anne). (1989). *The second shift: Working parents and the revolution at home.* New York: Viking.

Hochwarter, Wayne A.; Perrewe, Pamela L.; & Dawkins, Mark C. (1995). Gender differences in perceptions of stress-related variables: Do the people make the place or does the place make the people? *Journal of Managerial Issues, 7,* 62–74.

Hoffman, Lorrie. (1982). Empirical findings concerning sexism in our schools. *Corrective and Social Psychiatry and Journal of Behavior Technology, Methods and Therapy, 28,* 100–108.

Hoffmann, Melissa L.; & Powlishta, Kimberly K. (2001). Gender segregation in childhood: A test of the interaction style theory. *Journal of Genetic Psychology, 162,* 298–313.

Hoffman, Saul D.; & Duncan, Greg J. (1988). What are the economic consequences of divorce? *Demography, 25,* 641–645.

Hoffner, Cynthia. (1996). Children's wishful identification and parasocial interaction with favorite television characters. *Journal of Broadcasting & Electronic Media, 40,* 389–402.

Hogan, Dennis P.; Sun, Rongjun; & Cornwell, Gretchen T. (2000). Sexual and fertility behaviors of American females aged 15–19 years: 1985, 1990, and 1995. *American Journal of Public Health, 90,* 1421–1425.

Hogshead-Makar, Nancy. (2003, July). The ongoing battle over Title IX. *USA Today Magazine, 132,* 64–66.

Holahan, Charles J.; Moos, Rudolf H.; Holahan, Carole K.; Cronkite, Ruth C.; & Randall, Patrick K. (2001). Drinking to cope, emotional distress and alcohol use and abuse: A ten-year model. *Journal of Studies on Alcohol, 62,* 190–198.

Holahan, Charles J.; Moos, Rudolf H.; Holahan, Carole K.; Cronkite, Ruth C.; & Randall, Patrick K. (2003). Drinking to cope and alcohol use and abuse in unipolar depression: A 10-year model. *Journal of Abnormal Psychology, 112,* 159–165.

Holroyd, Jean Corey; & Brodsky, Annette M. (1977). Psychologists' attitudes and practices regarding erotic and nonerotic physical contact with patients. *American Psychologist, 32,* 843–849.

Hong, Zuway-R.; Veach, Patricia McCarthy; & Lawrenz, Frances. (2003). An investigation of the gender stereotyped thinking of Taiwanese secondary school boys and girls. *Sex Roles, 48,* 495–504.

Horner, Martina. (1969, November). Fail: Bright women. *Psychology Today,* pp. 36–38, 62.

Horney, Karen. (1967). The dread of women: Observations on a specific difference in the dread felt by men and by women respectively for the opposite sex. In Harold Kelman (Ed.), *Feminine psychology* (pp. 133–146). New York: Norton. (Original work published 1932)

Horney, Karen. (1939). *New ways in psychoanalysis.* New York: Norton.

Hort, Barbara E.; Fagot, Beverly, I.; & Leinbach, Mary D. (1990). Are people's notions of maleness more stereotypically framed than their notions of femaleness? *Sex Roles, 23,* 197–212.

Hort, Barbara E.; Leinbach, Mary D.; & Fagot, Beverly I. (1991). Is there coherence among the cognitive components of gender acquisition? *Sex Roles, 24,* 195–207.

Horvath, Michael; & Ryan, Ann Marie. (2003). Antecedents and potential moderators of the relationship between attitudes and hiring discrimination on the basis of sexual orientation. *Sex Roles, 48,* 115–130.

Hotelling, Kathy. (1991). Sexual harassment: A problem shielded by silence. *Journal of Counseling & Development, 69,* 497–501.

House, James S. (1984). Barriers to work stress: I. Social support. In W. Doyle Gentry, Herbert Benson, & Charles deWolff (Eds.), *Behavioral medicine: Work, stress, and health.* The Hague, Netherlands: Nijhoff.

Houston, Thomas K.; Cooper, Lisa A.; & Ford, Daniel E. (2002). Internet support groups for depression: A 1-year prospective cohort. *American Journal of Psychiatry, 159,* 2062–2068.

Howard, Judith A.; Blumstein, Philip; & Schwartz, Pepper. (1987). Social or evolutionary theories? Some observations on preferences in human mate selection. *Journal of Personality and Social Psychology, 53,* 194–200.

Hrdy, Sarah Blaffer. (1981). *The woman that never evolved.* Cambridge, MA: Harvard University Press.

Hrdy, Sarah Blaffer. (1986). Empathy, polyandry, and the myth of the coy female. In Ruth Bleier (Ed.), *Feminist approaches to science* (pp. 119–146). New York: Pergamon Press.

Hrdy, Sarah Blaffer. (1999). *Mother nature: A history of mothers, infants, and natural selection.* New York: Pantheon Books.

Hsu, L. K. George. (1990). *Eating disorders.* New York: Guilford Press.

Hsuing, Robert C. (2000). The best of both worlds: An online self-help group hosted by a mental health professional. *CyberPsychology & Behavior, 3,* 935–950.

Hubbard, Julie A.; Smithmyer, Catherine M.; Ramsden, Sally R.; Parker, Elizabeth H.; Flanagan, Kelly D.; Dearing, Karen F.; Relyea, Nicole; & Simons, Robert F. (2002). Observational, physiological, and self-report measures of children's anger: Relations to reactive versus proactive aggression. *Child Development, 73,* 1101–1118.

Hubbard, Ruth. (1990). *The politics of women's biology.* New Brunswick, NJ: Rutgers University Press.

Hubbard, Ruth; & Wald, Elijah. (1993). *Exploding the gene myth.* Boston: Beacon Press.

Hudak, Mary A. (1993). Gender schema theory revisited: Men's stereotypes of American women. *Sex Roles, 28,* 279–293.

Huesmann, L. Rowell; Eron, Leonard D.; Lefkowitz, Monroe M.; & Walder, Leopold O. (1984). Stability of aggression over time and generations. *Developmental Psychology, 20,* 1120–1134.

Huesmann, L. Rowell; Moise-Titus, Jessica; Podolski, Cheryl-Lynn; & Eron, Leonard D. (2003). Longitudinal relations between children's exposure to TV violence and their aggressive and violent behavior in young adulthood: 1977–1992. *Developmental Psychology, 39,* 201–221.

Hughes, Diane L.; & Galinsky, Ellen. (1994). Gender, job and family conditions, and psychological symptoms. *Psychology of Women Quarterly, 18,* 251–270.

Hummer, Robert A.; Rogers, Richard G.; Amir, Sarit H.; Forbes, Douglas; & Frisbie, W. Parker. (2000). Adult mortality differentials among Hispanic subgroups and non-Hispanic Whites. *Social Science Quarterly, 81,* 459–476.

Hunt, Morton. (1974). *Sexual behavior in the 1970s.* Chicago: Playboy Press.

Hutson-Comeaux, Sarah L.; & Kelly, Janice R. (2002). Gender stereotypes of emotional reactions: How we judge an emotion as valid. *Sex Roles, 47,* 1–10.

Hyde, Janet Shibley. (1981). How large are cognitive gender differences? A meta-analysis using ω^2 and *d*. *American Psychologist, 36,* 892–901.

Hyde, Janet Shibley. (1984). How large are gender differences in aggression? A developmental meta-analysis. *Developmental Psychology, 20,* 722–736.

Hyde, Janet Shibley. (1986). Introduction: Meta-analysis and the psychology of gender. In Janet Shibley Hyde & Marcia C. Linn (Eds.), *The psychology of gender: Advances through meta-analysis* (pp. 1–13). Baltimore, MD: Johns Hopkins University Press.

Hyde, Janet Shibley. (1994). Can meta-analysis make feminist transformations in psychology? *Psychology of Women Quarterly, 18,* 451–462.

Hyde, Janet Shibley. (1996). Where are the gender differences? Where are the gender similarities? In David M. Buss & Neil M. Malamuth (Eds.), *Sex, power, conflict: Evolutionary and feminist perspectives* (pp. 107–118). New York: Oxford University Press.

Hyde, Janet Shibley; & Durik, Amanda M. (2000). Gender differences in erotic plasticity—Evolutionary of sociocultural forces? *Psychological Bulletin, 126,* 375–379.

Hyde, Janet Shibley, & Durik, Amanada M. (2001). Psychology of women and gender in the 21st century. In Jane S. Halonen & Stephen F. Davis (Eds.), *The many faces of psychological research in the 21st century.* Retrieved December 12, 2001, from http://teachpsych.lemoyne.edu/teachpsych/faces/facesindex.html.

Hyde, Janet Shibley; Fennema, Elizabeth; & Lamon, Susan J. (1990). Gender differences in mathematics performance: A meta-analysis. *Psychological Bulletin, 107,* 139–155.

Hyde, Janet Shibley; Fennema, Elizabeth; Ryan, Marilyn; Frost, Laurie A.; & Hopp, Carolyn. (1990). Gender comparisons of mathematics attitudes and affect: A meta-analysis. *Psychology of Women Quarterly, 14,* 299–324.

Hyde, Janet Shibley; & Jaffee, Sara R. (2000). Becoming a heterosexual adult: The experiences of young women. *Journal of Social Issues, 56,* 283–296.

Hyde, Janet Shibley; & Kling, Kristin C. (2001). Women, motivation, and achievement. *Psychology of Women Quarterly, 25,* 364–378.

Hyde, Janet Shibley; & Linn, Marcia C. (1988). Gender differences in verbal ability: A meta-analysis. *Psychological Bulletin, 104,* 53–69.

Imperato-McGinley, Julianne; Guerrero, Luis; Gautier, Teofilo; & Peterson, Ralph E. (1974). Steroid 5-α-reductase deficiency in man: An inherited form of male pseudohermaphroditism. *Science, 186,* 1213–1215.

Ireland, Doug. (1999, June 14). Gay ed for kids. *The Nation, 268* (22), 8.

Jack, Dana Crowley. (1991). *Silencing the self: Women and depression.* Cambridge, MA: Harvard University Press.

Jack, Dana Crowley. (1999). Silencing the self: Inner dialogues and outer realities. In Thomas Joiner and James C. Coyne (Eds.), *The interactional nature of depression: Advances in interpersonal approaches* (pp. 221–246). Washington, DC: American Psychological Association.

Jacklin, Carol Nagy; & Maccoby, Eleanor E. (1978). Social behavior at thirty-three months in same-sex and mixed-sex dyads. *Child Development, 49,* 557–569.

Jackson, Dorothy W.; & Tein, Jenn-Yunn. (1998). Adolescents' conceptualization of adult roles: Relationships with age, gender, work goal, and maternal employment. *Sex Roles, 38,* 987–1008.

Jackson, Helene; & Nuttall, Ronald L. (2001). A relationship between childhood sexual abuse and professional sexual misconduct. *Professional Psychology: Research and Practice, 32,* 200–204.

Jacobs, Janis E.; & Eccles, Jacquelynne S. (1992). The impact of mothers' gender-role stereotypic beliefs on mothers' and children's ability perceptions. *Journal of Personality and Social Psychology, 63,* 932–944.

Jacobs, Janis E.; Lanza, Stephanie; Osgood, D. Wayne; Eccles, Jacquelynne S.; & Wigfield, Allan. (2002). Changes in children's self-competence and values: Gender and domain differences across grades one though twelve. *Child Development, 73,* 509–527.

Jacobs, Jerry A. (1989). Long-term trends in occupational segregation by sex. *American Journal of Sociology, 95,* 160–173.

Jacobs, Jerry A. (1996). Gender inequality in higher education. *Annual Review of Sociology, 22,* 153–182.

Jacobs, Marion K.; & Goodman, Gerald. (1989). Psychology and self-help groups: Predictions on a partnership. *American Psychologist, 44,* 536–545.

Jacobs, Michael. (1992). *Sigmund Freud.* London: Sage.

James, William. (1890). *Principles of psychology* (Vols. 1 and 2). New York: Holt.

Janoff-Bulman, Ronnie; & Frieze, Irene H. (1987). The role of gender in reactions to criminal victimization. In Rosalind C. Barnett, Lois Biener, & Grace K. Baruch (Eds.), *Gender and stress* (pp. 159–184). New York: Free Press.

Janus, Samuel S.; & Janus, Cynthia L. (1993). *The Janus report on sexual behavior.* New York: Wiley.

Jet. (1997, September 22). Walt Whitman Community School, nation's first private school for gays opens in Dallas. *Author, 92* (18), 12–13.

Jewkes, Rachel. (2002). Intimate partner violence: Causes and prevention. *Lancet, 359,* 1423–1429.

Ji, Li-Jun; Peng, Kaiping; & Nisbett, Richard E. (2000). Culture, control, and perception of relationships in the environment. *Journal of Personality and Social Psychology, 78,* 943–955.

Johnson, D. Kay. (1988). Adolescents' solutions to dilemmas in fables: Two moral orientations—Two problem solving strategies. In Carol Gilligan, Janie Victoria Ward, & Jill McLean Taylor. (with Bardiger, Betty). (Eds.), *Mapping the moral domain: A contribution of women's thinking to psychological theory and education* (pp. 49–71). Cambridge, MA: Harvard University Press.

Johnson, Fern L.; & Young, Karen. (2002). Gendered voices in children's television advertising. *Critical Studies in Media Communication, 19,* 461–480.

Johnson, Maria; & Helgeson, Vicki S. (2002). Sex differences in response to evaluative feedback: A field study. *Psychology of Women Quarterly, 26,* 242–251.

Johnson, Michael P. (1995). Patriarchal terrorism and common couple violence: Two forms of violence against women. *Journal of Marriage and the Family, 57,* 283–294.

Johnson, Norine G. (2001). Women helping men: Strengths of and barriers to women therapists working with men clients. In Gary R. Brooks & Glenn E. Good (Eds.), *The new handbook of psychotherapy and counseling with men: A comprehensive guide to settings, problems, and treatment approaches* (pp. 696–718). San Francisco, CA: Jossey-Bass.

Jon, Deborah; & Lasser, Tharinger. (2003). Visibility management in school and beyond: A qualitative study of gay, lesbian, bisexual youth. *Journal of Adolescence, 26,* 233–244.

Jones, Diane Carlson. (2001). Social comparison and body image: Attractiveness comparisons to models and peers among adolescent girls and boys. *Sex Roles, 45,* 645–664.

Jones, Ernest. (1955). *The life and work of Sigmund Freud* (Vol. 2). New York: Basic Books.

Jones, James H. (1998). *Alfred C. Kinsey: A public/private life.* New York: Norton.

Jones, Kelly; Evans, Cay; Byrd, Ronald; & Campbell, Kathleen. (2000). Gender equity training and teacher behavior. *Journal of Instructional Psychology, 27,* 173–177.

Jones, Lisa; & Finkelhor, David. (2001, January). The decline in child sex abuse cases. *Juvenile Justice Bulletin,* Office of Juvenile Justice and Delinquency Prevention. Washington, DC: U.S. Government Printing Office.

Jordan, Kirsten; Wuestenberg, Torsten; Heinze, Hans Jochen; Peters, Michael; & Jaencke, Lutz. (2002). Women and men exhibit different cortical activation patterns during mental rotation tasks. *Neuropsychologia, 40,* 2397–2408.

Joyner, Kara; & Kao, Grace. (2000). School racial composition and adolescent racial homophily. *Social Science Quarterly, 81,* 810–825.

Jussim, Lee J.; McCauley, Clark R.; & Lee, Yueh-Ting. (1995). Why study stereotype accuracy and inaccuracy? In Yueh-Ting Lee, Lee J. Jussim, & Clark R. McCauley (Eds.), *Stereotype accuracy: Toward appreciating group differences* (pp. 3–27). Washington, DC: American Psychological Association.

Kahn, Robert S.; Wise, Paul H.; Kennedy, Bruce P.; & Kawachi, Ichiro. (2000). State income inequality, household income, and maternal mental and physical health: Cross-sectional national survey. *British Medical Journal, 321,* 1311–1315.

Kalish, Nancy. (2001, April 1). My son doesn't act like a boy: What it's like to have a child who challenges gender stereotypes. *Family Life,* p. 60+.

Kalisz, Aneta; & Cechnicki, Andrzej. (2002). Gender-related prognostic factors in first admission DSM-III schizophrenic patients. *Archives of Psychiatry and Psychotherapy, 4* (3), 25–36.

Kaminer, Wendy. (1993, October). Feminism's identity crisis. *Atlantic Monthly,* pp. 51–53, 56, 58–59, 62, 64, 66–68.

Kane, Penny. (1991). *Women's health: From womb to tomb.* New York: St. Martin's Press.

Kanter, Rosabeth Moss. (1975). Women and the structure of organizations: Explorations in theory and behavior. In Marcia Millman & Rosabeth M. Kanter (Eds.), *Another voice* (pp. 34–74). Garden City, NY: Anchor/Doubleday.

Kanter, Rosabeth Moss. (1977). *Men and women of the corporation.* New York: Basic Books.

Kantrowitz, Barbara; & Wingert, Pat. (1999, April 19). The science of a good marriage. *Newsweek, 133* (16), 52–57.

Kantrowitz, Ricki E.; & Ballou, Mary. (1992). A feminist critique of cognitive-behavioral therapy. In Laura S. Brown & Mary Ballou (Eds.), *Personality and psychopathology: Feminist reappraisals* (pp. 70–87). New York: Guilford Press.

Kaplan, Alexandra G. (1980). Human sex-hormone abnormalities viewed from an androgynous perspective: A reconsideration of the work of John Money. In Jacquelynne E. Parsons (Ed.), *The psychobiology of sex differences and sex roles* (pp. 81–91). Washington, DC: Hemisphere.

Kaplan, Alexandra G.; & Yasinski, Lorraine. (1980). Psychodynamic perspectives. In Annette M. Brodsky & Rachel Hare-Mustin (Eds.), *Women and psychotherapy* (pp. 191–216). New York: Guilford Press.

Kaplan, Marcie. (1983a). The issue of sex bias in DSM-III: Comments on the articles by Spitzer, Williams, and Kass. *American Psychologist, 38,* 802–803.

Kaplan, Marcie. (1983b). A woman's view of the DSM-III. *American Psychologist, 38,* 786–792.

Kaplan, Robert M.; Anderson, John P.; & Wingard, Deborah L. (1991). Gender differences in health-related quality of life. *Health Psychology, 10,* 86–93.

Karabenick, Stuart A.; Sweeney, Catherine; & Penrose, Gary. (1983). Preferences for skill versus change-determined activities: The influence of gender and task sex-typing. *Journal of Research in Personality, 17,* 125–142.

Kaschak, Ellyn. (1992). *Engendered lives.* New York: Basic Books.

Kaschak, Ellyn; & Tiefer, Lenore. (Eds.). (2001). *A new view of women's sexual problems.* New York: Haworth Press.

Katz, Alfred H. (1993). *Self-help in America: A social movement perspective.* New York: Twayne.

Katz, Jennifer; Joiner, Thomas E., Jr.; & Kwon, Paul. (2002). Membership in a devalued social group and emotional well-being: Developing a model of personal self-esteem, collective self-esteem, and group socialization. *Sex Roles, 47,* 419–431.

Katz, Phyllis A.; & Ksansnak, Keith R. (1994). Developmental aspects of gender role flexibility and traditionality in middle childhood and adolescence. *Developmental Psychology, 30,* 272–282.

Keen, Sam. (1991). *A fire in the belly: On being a man.* New York: Bantam.

Keller, Evelyn Fox. (1985). *Reflections on gender and science.* New Haven, CT: Yale University Press.

Keller, Teresa. (1999). Lessons in equality: What television teaches us about women. In Carie Forden, Anne E. Hunter, & Beverly Birns (Eds.), *Readings in the psychology of women: Dimensions of the female experience* (pp. 27–35). Boston: Allyn and Bacon.

Kelly, Jacqueline; & Bazzini, Doris G. (2001). Gender, sexual experience, and the sexual double standard: Evaluations of female contraceptive behavior. *Sex Roles, 45,* 785–799.

Kelly, Janice R.; & Hutson-Comeaux, Sarah L. (1999). Gender-emotion stereotypes are context specific. *Sex Roles, 40,* 107–120.

Keltikangas-Jarvinen, Liisa. (2002). Aggressive problem-solving strategies, aggressive behavior, and social acceptance in early and late adolescence. *Journal of Youth and Adolescence, 31,* 279–287.

Kennedy, Helen L.; & Parks, Joe. (2000). Society cannot continue to exclude women from the fields of science and mathematics. *Education, 120,* 529–537.

Kessler, Ronald C. (2003). Epidemiology of women and depression. *Journal of Affective Disorders, 74,* 5–13.

Kessler, Ronald C.; Brown, Roger L.; & Broman, Clifford L. (1981). Sex differences in psychiatric help-seeking: Evidence from four large-scale surveys. *Journal of Health and Social Behavior, 22,* 49–64.

Kessler, Ronald C.; Mickelson, Kristin D.; & Williams, David R. (1999). The prevalence, distribution, and mental health correlates of perceived discrimination in the United States. *Journal of Health and Social Behavior, 40,* 208–230.

Kidder, Louise. (1994, August). *All pores open.* Paper presented at the 102nd annual convention of the American Psychological Association, Los Angeles, CA.

Kiecolt-Glaser, J. K., & Newton, T. L. (2001). Marriage and health: His and hers. *Psychological Bulletin, 127,* 472–503.

Kiernan, Michaela; Rodin, Judith; Brownell, Kelly D.; Wilmore, Jack H.; & Crandall, Christian. (1992). Relation of level of exercise, age, and weight-cycling history to weight and eating concerns in male and female runners. *Health Psychology, 11,* 418–421.

Kimball, Meredith M. (1995). *Feminist visions of gender similarities and differences.* New York: Haworth Press.

Kimmel, Michael. (2000). A war against boys? *Tikkun, 15* (6), 57–60.

Kimmel, Michael S.; & Messner, Michael A. (1992). Introduction. In Michael S. Kimmel & Michael A. Messner (Eds.), *Men's lives* (2nd ed., pp. 1–11). New York: Macmillan.

Kimura, Doreen. (1999). *Sex and cognition.* Cambridge, MA: MIT Press.

Kimura, Doreen; & Clarke, Paul G. (2002). Women's advantage on verbal memory is not restricted to concrete words. *Psychological Reports, 91,* 1137–1142.

King, Patricia A. (1999, June 21). Science for girls only. *Newsweek, 133,* 64–65.

Kinsey, Alfred C.; Pomeroy, Wardell B.; & Martin, Clyde E. (1948). *Sexual behavior in the human male.* Philadelphia: Saunders.

Kinsey, Alfred C.; Pomeroy, Wardell B.; Martin, Clyde E.; & Gebhard, Paul H. (1953). *Sexual behavior in the human female.* Philadelphia: Saunders.

Kirschstein, Ruth L. (1991). Research on women's health. *American Journal of Public Health, 81,* 291–293.

Kissling, Elizabeth Arveda. (2002). On the rag on screen: Menarche in film and television. *Sex Roles, 46,* 5–12.

Kite, Mary E. (2001). Changing times, changing gender roles: Who do we want women and men to be? In Rhoda Unger (Ed.), *Handbook of the psychology of women and gender* (pp. 215–227). New York: Wiley.

Kite, Mary E.; & Whitley, Bernard E., Jr. (1996). Sex differences in attitudes toward homosexual persons, behaviors, and civil rights: A meta-analysis. *Personality and Social Psychology Bulletin, 22,* 336–353.

Klaus, Marshall H.; & Kennell, John H. (1976). *Maternal infant bonding.* St. Louis: Mosby.

Kling, Kristen C.; Hyde, Janet Shibley; Showers, Caroline J.; & Buswell, Brenda N. (1999). Gender differences in self-esteem: A meta-analysis. *Psychological Bulletin, 125,* 470–500.

Klinkenberg, Dean; & Rose, Suzanna. (1994). Dating scripts of gay men and lesbians. *Journal of Homosexuality, 26* (4), 23–35.

Klonoff, Elizabeth A.; & Landrine, Hope. (1997). *Preventing misdiagnosis of women.* Thousand Oaks, CA: Sage.

Klonoff, Elizabeth A.; Landrine, Hope; & Campbell, Robin. (2000). Sexist discrimination may account for well-known gender differences in psychiatric symptoms. *Psychology of Women Quarterly, 24,* 93–99.

Knight, George P.; Guthrie, Ivanna K.; Page, Melanie C.; & Fabes, Richard A. (2002). Emotional arousal and gender differences in aggression: A meta-analysis. *Aggressive Behavior, 28,* 366–393.

Knox, Sarah S.; & Czajkowski, Susan. (1997). The influence of behavioral and psychosocial factors on cardiovascular health in women. In Sheryle J. Gallant, Gwendolyn Puryear Keita, & Reneé Royak-Schaler (Eds.), *Health care for women: Psychological, social, and behavioral influences* (pp. 257–272). Washington, DC: American Psychological Association.

Koehler, Mary Schatz. (1990). Classrooms, teachers, and gender differences in mathematics. In Elizabeth Fennema & Gilah C. Leder (Eds.), *Mathematics and gender* (pp. 128–148). New York: Teachers College Press.

Koeske, Randi K.; & Koeske, Gary F. (1975). An attributional approach to moods and the menstrual cycle. *Journal of Personality and Social Psychology, 31,* 473–478.

Koff, Elissa; & Rierdan, Jill. (1995). Preparing girls for menstruation: Recommendations from adolescent girls. *Adolescence, 30,* 795–811.

Kohlberg, Lawrence. (1966). A cognitive-developmental analysis of children's sex-role concepts and attitudes. In Eleanor E. Maccoby (Ed.), *The development of sex differences* (pp. 52–173). Stanford, CA: Stanford University Press.

Komarovsky, Mirra. (1982). Female freshmen view their future: Career salience and its correlates. *Sex Roles, 8,* 299–313.

Konrad, Alison M. (2003). Family demands and job attribute preferences: A 4-year longitudinal study of women and men. *Sex Roles, 49,* 35–46

Konrad, Alison M.; & Harris, Claudia. (2002). Desirability of the Bem Sex-Role Inventory items for women and men: A comparison between African Americans and European Americans. *Sex Roles, 47,* 259–271.

Kopper, Beverly A.; & Epperson, Douglas L. (1991). Women and anger: Sex and sex-role comparisons in the expression of anger. *Psychology of Women Quarterly, 15,* 7–14.

Kopper, Beverly A.; & Epperson, Douglas L. (1996). The experience and expression of anger: Relationships with gender, gender role socialization, depression, and mental health functioning. *Journal of Counseling Psychology, 43,* 158–165.

Koss, Mary P. (1990). The women's mental health research agenda: Violence against women. *American Psychologist, 45,* 374–380.

Koss, Mary P.; Bailey, Jennifer A.; Yuan, Nicole P.; Herrera, Veronica M.; & Lichter, Erika L. (2003). Depression and PTSD in survivors of male violence: Research and training initiatives to facilitate recovery. *Psychology of Women Quarterly, 27,* 130–142.

Koss, Mary P.; Gidycz, Christine A.; & Wisniewski, Nadine. (1987). The scope of rape: Incidence and prevalence of sexual aggression and victimization in a national sample of higher education students. *Journal of Consulting and Clinical Psychology, 55,* 162–170.

Krahe, Barbara; Scheinberger-Olwig, Renate; & Bieneck, Steffen. (2003). Men's reports of nonconsensual sexual interactions with women: Prevalence and impact. *Archives of Sexual Behavior, 32,* 165–175.

Kramarae, Cheris; & Treichler, Paula A. (1990). Power relationships in the classroom. In Susan L. Gabriel & Isaiah Smithson (Eds.), *Gender in the classroom: Power and pedagogy* (pp. 41–59). Urbana, IL: University of Illinois Press.

Kravetz, Diane. (1978). Consciousness-raising groups of the 1970s. *Psychology of Women Quarterly, 3,* 168–186.

Kreeger, Karen Young. (2002, May 13). Sex-based longevity: Societal and lifestyle issues—not biology—appear to have the greatest influences on whether men or women live longer. *Scientist, 16* (10), 34–35.

Krishnan, Ahalya; & Sweeney, Christopher J. (1998). Gender differences in fear of success imagery and other achievement-related background variables among medical students. *Sex Roles, 39,* 299–310.

Kuehnen, Ulrich; Hannover, Bettina; Roeder, Ute; Shah, Ashiq Ali; Schubert, Benjamin; Upmeyer, Arnold; & Zakaria, Saliza. (2001). Cross-cultural variations in identifying embedded figures: Comparisons from the United States, Germany, Russia, and Malaysia. *Journal of Cross-Cultural Psychology, 32,* 365–371.

Kuhn, Deanna; Nash, Sharon C.; & Brucken, Laura. (1978). Sex role concepts of two- and three-year olds. *Child Development, 49,* 445–451.

Kulik, Liat. (2002). Like-sex versus opposite-sex effects in transmission of gender role ideology from parents to adolescents in Israel. *Journal of Youth and Adolescence, 31,* 451–457.

Kurdek, Lawrence A. (1993). The allocation of household labor in gay, lesbian, and heterosexual married couples. *Journal of Social Issues, 49* (3), 127–139.

Kurdek, Lawrence A. (1998). Relationship outcomes and their predictors: Longitudinal evidence from heterosexual married, gay cohabiting, and lesbian cohabiting couples. *Journal of Marriage and Family, 60,* 553–568.

Kurzweil, Edith. (1995). *Freudians and feminists.* Boulder, CO: Westview Press.

Kutchins, Herb; & Kirk, Stuart A. (1997). *Making us crazy. DSM: The psychiatric bible and the creation of mental disorders.* New York: Free Press.

Laband, David N.; & Lentz, Bernard F. (1998). The effects of sexual harassment on job satisfaction, earnings, and turnover among female lawyers. *Industrial and Labor Relations Review, 51,* 594–607.

Laflamme, Darquise; Pomerleau, Andree; & Malcuit, Gerard. (2002). A comparison of fathers' and mothers' involvement in childcare and stimulation behaviors during free-play with their infants at 9 and 15 months. *Sex Roles, 47,* 507–518.

LaFrance, Marianne; & Hecht, Marvin A. (1999). Option or obligation to smile: The effects of power and gender on facial expression. In Pierre Philippot, Robert S. Feldman, & Erik J. Coats (Eds.), *The social context of nonverbal behavior. Studies in emotion and social interaction.* (pp. 45–70). Cambridge, England: Cambridge University Press.

LaFrance, Marianne; & Henley, Nancy M. (1997). On oppressing hypotheses: Or, differences in nonverbal sensitivity revisited. In Mary Roth Walsh (Ed.), *Women, men, and gender: Ongoing debates* (pp. 104–119). New Haven, CT: Yale University Press.

LaFromboise, Teresa D.; Berman, Joan Saks; & Sohi, Balvindar K. (1994). American Indian women. In Lillian Comas-Díaz & Beverly Greene (Eds.), *Women of color: Integrating ethnic and gender identities in psychotherapy* (pp. 30–71). New York: Guilford Press.

Lahey, Benjamin B.; Goodman, Sherryl H.; Canino, Glorisa; Bird, Hector; Schwab-Stone, Mary; Waldman, Irwin D.; Rathouz, Paul J.; Miller, Terri L.; Dennis, Kimberly D.; & Jensen, Peter S. (2000). Age and gender differences in oppositional behavior and conduct problems: Cross-sectional household study of middle childhood and adolescence. *Journal of Abnormal Psychology, 109,* 488–503.

Lakkis, Jacqueline; Ricciardelli, Lina A.; & Williams, Robert J. (1999). Role of sexual orientation and gender-related traits in disordered eating. *Sex Roles, 41,* 1–16.

Lakoff, Robin. (1975). *Language and woman's place.* New York: Harper & Row.

Lalumiere, Martin L.; Blanchard, Ray; & Zucker, Kenneth J. (2000). Sexual orientation and handedness in men and women: A meta-analysis. *Psychological Bulletin, 126,* 575–592.

Landrine, Hope. (1987). On the politics of madness: A preliminary analysis of the relationship between social roles and psychopathology. *Psychology Monographs, 113,* 341–406.

Landrine, Hope. (1989). The politics of personality disorder. *Psychology of Women Quarterly, 13,* 325–339.

Landrine, Hope; Bardwell, Stephen; & Dean, Tina. (1988). Gender expectations for alcohol use: A study of the significance of the masculine role. *Sex Roles, 19,* 703–712.

Landrine, Hope; & Klonoff, Elizabeth A. (1996). The Schedule of Racist Events: A measure of racial discrimination and a study of its negative physical and mental health consequences. *Journal of Black Psychology, 22,* 144–168.

Landrine, Hope; Klonoff, Elizabeth A.; & Brown-Collins, Alice. (1992). Cultural diversity and methodology in feminist psychology: Critique, proposal, empirical example. *Psychology of Women Quarterly, 16,* 145–163.

Landrine, Hope; Klonoff, Elizabeth A.; Gibbs, Jeannine; Manning, Vickie; & Lund, Marlene. (1995). Physical and psychiatric correlates of gender discrimination: An application of the Schedule of Sexist Events. *Psychology of Women Quarterly, 19,* 473–492.

Laner, Mary Riege; & Ventrone, Nicole A. (2000). Dating scripts revisited. *Journal of Family Issues, 21,* 488–500.

Larson, Mary Strom. (2001). Interactions, activities and gender in children's television commercials: A content analysis. *Journal of Broadcasting & Electronic Media, 45,* 41–56.

Larson, Mary Strom. (2003). Gender, race, and aggression in television commercials that feature children. *Sex Roles, 48,* 67–75

Larson, Reed; & Pleck, Joseph. (1999). Hidden feelings: Emotionality in boys and men. In Dan Bernstein (Ed.), *Nebraska Symposium on Motivation, 1999: Gender and motivation* (pp. 25–74). Lincoln, NE: University of Nebraska Press.

Larson, Reed; & Richards, Maryse H. (1994). *Divergent realities: The emotional lives of mothers, fathers, and adolescents.* New York: Basic Books.

Larsson, IngBeth; & Svedin, Carl-Goran. (2002). Sexual experiences in childhood: Young adults' recollections. *Archives of Sexual Behavior, 31,* 263–273.

Larwood, Laurie; & Gutek, Barbara A. (1989). Working toward a theory of women's career development. In Barbara A. Gutek & Laurie Larwood (Eds.), *Women's career development* (pp. 170–183). Newbury Park, CA: Sage.

Laumann, Edward O.; Gagnon, John H.; Michael, Robert T.; & Michaels, Stuart. (1994). *The social organization of sexuality.* Chicago: University of Chicago Press.

Lauzen, Martha M.; & Dozier, David M. (2002). You look mahvelous: An examination of gender and appearance comments in the 1999–2000 prime-time season. *Sex Roles, 46,* 429–437.

Lavallee, Marguerite; & Pelletier, Rene. (1992). Ecological value of Bem's gender schema theory explored through females' traditional and nontraditional occupational contexts. *Psychological Reports, 70,* 79–82.

Law, David J.; Pellegrino, James W.; & Hunt, Earl B. (1993). Comparing the tortoise and the hare: Gender differences and experience in dynamic spatial reasoning tasks. *Psychological Science, 4,* 35–40.

Lazarus, Arnold A. (2003). Boundary crossings vs. boundary violations. *Annals of the American Psychotherapy Association, 6,* 24–27.

Lazarus, Richard S. (1984). On the primacy of cognition. *American Psychologist, 39,* 124–129.

Lazarus, Richard S.; & Folkman, Susan. (1984). *Stress, appraisal, and coping.* New York: Springer.

Leaper, Campbell; Anderson, Kristin J.; & Sanders, Paul. (1998). Moderators of gender effects on parents' talk to their children; A meta-analysis. *Developmental Psychology, 34,* 3–27.

Leaper, Campbell; Breed, Lisa; Hoffman, Laurie; & Perlman, Carly Ann. (2002). Variations in the gender-stereotyped content of children's television cartoons across genres. *Journal of Applied Social Psychology, 32,* 1653–1662.

Lee, Camille. (2002). The impact of belonging to a high school gay/straight alliance. *High School Journal, 85* (3), 13–26.

Lee, Christina; & Owens, R. Glynn. (2002). *The psychology of men's health.* Buckingham, England: Open University Press.

Lee, Rita. (2000). Health care problems of lesbian, gay, bisexual, and transgender patients. *Western Journal of Medicine, 172,* 403–408.

Lee, Shirley. (2002). Health and sickness: The meaning of menstruation and premenstrual syndrome in women's lives. *Sex Roles, 46,* 25–35.

Lee, Valerie E.; & Burkam, David T. (1996). Gender differences in middle grade science achievement: Subject domain, ability level, and course emphasis. *Science Education, 80,* 613–650.

Lefkowitz, Monroe M.; Eron, Leonard D.; Walder, Leopold O.; & Huesmann, L. Rowell. (1977). *Growing up to be violent: A longitudinal study of the development of aggression.* New York: Pergamon Press.

Leinbach, Mary D.; & Fagot, Beverly I. (1993). Categorical habituation to male and female faces: Gender schematic processing in infancy. *Infant Behavior and Development, 16,* 317–332.

Leitenberg, Harold; & Saltzman, Heidi. (2000). A statewide survey of age at first intercourse for adolescent females and age of their male partners: Relation to other risk behavior and statutory rape implications. *Archives of Sexual Behavior, 29,* 203–216.

Lengua, Liliana J.; & Stormshak, Elizabeth A. (2000). Gender, gender roles, and personality: Gender differences in the prediction of coping and psychological symptoms. *Sex Roles, 44,* 787–820.

Lepowsky, Maria. (1994). Women, men, and aggression in an egalitarian society. *Sex Roles, 30,* 199–211.

Lerman, Hannah. (1992). The limits of phenomenology: A feminist critique of the humanistic personality theories. In Laura S. Brown & Mary Ballou (Eds.), *Personality and psychopathology: Feminist reappraisals* (pp. 8–19). New York: Guilford Press.

Lerman, Hannah. (1996). *Pigeonholing women's misery: A history and critical analysis of the psychodiagnosis of women in the twentieth century.* New York: Basic Books.

Lerner, Alan Jay; & Loewe, Frederick. (1956). *My fair lady: A musical play in two acts. Based on Pygmalion by Bernard Shaw.* New York: Coward-McCann.

Levant, Ronald F. (1990). Psychological services designed for men: A psychoeducational approach. *Psychotherapy, 27,* 309–315.

Levant, Ronald F. (1996). The new psychology of men. *Professional Psychology, Research and Practice, 27,* 259–265.

LeVay, Simon. (1991). A difference in hypothalamic structure between heterosexual and homosexual men. *Science, 253,* 1034–1037.

Levenson, Robert W.; Carstensen, Laura L.; & Gottman, John M. (1994). The influence of age and gender on affect, physiology, and their interrelations: A study of long-term marriages. *Journal of Personality and Social Psychology, 67,* 56–68.

Levy, Gary D. (1989). Relations among aspects of children's social environments, gender schematization, gender role knowledge, and flexibility. *Sex Roles, 21,* 803–823.

Levy, Gary D. (1999). Gender-typed and non-gender-typed category awareness in toddlers. *Sex Roles, 41,* 851–874.

Levy, Gary D.; Barth, Joan M.; & Zimmerman, Barbara J. (1998). Associations among cognitive and behavioral aspects of preschoolers' gender role development. *Journal of Genetic Psychology, 159,* 121–126.

Levy, Gary D.; & Boston, Martha B. (1994). Preschoolers' recall of own-sex and other-sex gender scripts. *Journal of Genetic Psychology, 155,* 369–371.

Levy, Gary D.; & Fivush, Robyn. (1993). Scripts and gender: A new approach for examining gender-role development. *Developmental Review, 13,* 126–146.

Levy, Gary D.; Sadovsky, Adrienne L.; & Troseth, Georgene L. (2000). Aspects of young children's perceptions of gender-typed occupations. *Sex Roles, 42,* 993–1006.

Levy, Jerre. (1969). Possible basis for the evolution of lateral specialization of the human brain. *Nature, 224,* 614–625.

Levy, Sandra M. (1985). *Behavior and cancer: Life-style and psychosocial factors in the initiation and progression of cancer.* San Francisco, CA: Jossey-Bass.

Lewin, C.; Wolgers, G.; & Herlitz, A. (2001). Sex differences favouring women in verbal but not in visuospatial episodic memory. *Neuropsychology, 15,* 165–173.

Lewin, Miriam. (1984a). "Rather worse than folly?" Psychology measures femininity and masculinity: 1. From Terman and Miles to the Guilfords. In Miriam Lewin (Ed.), *In the shadow of the past: Psychology portrays the sexes* (pp. 155–178). New York: Columbia University Press.

Lewin, Miriam. (1984b). Psychology measures femininity and masculinity: 2. From "13 gay men" to the instrumental–expressive distinction. In Miriam Lewin (Ed.), *In the shadow of the past: Psychology portrays the sexes* (pp. 179–204). New York: Columbia University Press.

Lewin, Miriam. (1984c). The Victorians, the psychologists, and psychic birth control. In Miriam Lewin (Ed.), *In the shadow of the past: Psychology portrays the sexes* (pp. 39–76). New York: Columbia University Press.

Lewis, Andrea E.; & Fagenson-Eland, Ellen A. (1998). The influence of gender and organization level on perceptions of leadership behaviors: A self and supervisor comparison. *Sex Roles, 39,* 479–502.

Lewis, Carol D.; & Houtz, John C. (1986). Sex-role stereotyping and young children's divergent thinking. *Psychological Reports, 59,* 1027–1033.

Liben, Lynn S.; & Golbeck, Susan L. (1984). Performance on Piagetian horizontality and verticality tasks: Sex-related differences in knowledge of relevant physical phenomena. *Developmental Psychology, 20,* 595–606.

Lindberg, Laura Duberstein; Sonenstein, Freya L.; Ku, Leighton; & Martinez, Gladys. (1997). Age differences between minors who give birth and their adult partners. *Family Planning Perspectives, 29,* 61–66.

Linden, Mary G.; Bender, Bruce G.; & Robinson, Arthur. (1995). Sex chromosome tetrasomy and pentasomy. *Pediatrics, 96,* 672–682.

Lindsey, Eric W. (2002). Preschool children's friendship and peer acceptance: Links to social competence. *Child Study Journal, 32,* 145–156.

Linn, Marcia C.; & Petersen, Anne C. (1986). A meta-analysis of gender differences in spatial ability: Implications for mathematics and science achievement. In Janet Shibley Hyde & Marcia C. Linn (Eds.), *The psychology of gender: Advances through meta-analysis* (pp. 67–101). Baltimore, MD: Johns Hopkins University Press.

Lips, Hilary M. (1989). Gender-role socialization: Lessons in femininity. In Jo Freeman (Ed.), *Women: A feminist perspective* (4th ed., pp. 197–216). Mountain View, CA: Mayfield.

Livingston, Martha. (1999). How to think about women's health. In Carie Forden, Anne E. Hunter, & Beverly Birns (Eds.), *Readings in the psychology of women: Dimensions of the female experience* (pp. 244–253). Boston: Allyn and Bacon.

Livingston, Nancy. (1994, March 11). St. Paul, Minn., schools plan full-time coordinator for gay and lesbian students. *Knight-Ridder/Tribune News Service,* p. 0311 K2183.

Lobel, Thalma E.; Bar-David, Eva; Gruber, Reut; Lau, Sing; & Bar-Tal, Yoram. (2000). Gender schema and social judgments: A developmental study of children. *Sex Roles, 43,* 19–42.

Lock, James; & Steiner, Hans. (1999). Gay, lesbian, and bisexual youth risks for emotional, physical, and social problems: Results from a community-based survey. *Journal of the American Academy of Child and Adolescent Psychiatry, 38,* 297–304.

Lombardo, William K.; Cretser, Gary A.; & Roesch, Scott C. (2001). For crying out loud—The differences persist into the '90s. *Sex Roles, 45,* 529–547.

Long, J. Scott; & Fox, Mary Frank. (1995). Scientific careers: Universalism and particularism. *Annual Review of Sociology, 21,* 45–71.

Lont, Cynthia M. (Ed.). (1995). *Women and media: Content, careers, and criticism.* Belmont, CA: Wadsworth.

Loo, Robert; & Thorpe, Karran. (1998). Attitudes toward women's roles in society: A replication after 20 years. *Sex Roles, 39,* 903–912.

López, Steven Regeser. (1989). Patient variable biases in clinical judgment: Conceptual overview and methodological considerations. *Psychological Bulletin, 106,* 184–203.

Lorber, Judith. (1975). Women and medical sociology: Invisible professionals and ubiquitous patients. In Marcia Millman & Rosabeth M. Kanter (Eds.), *Another voice* (pp. 75–105). Garden City, NY: Anchor/Doubleday.

Lorber, Judith. (1989). Trust, loyalty, and the place for women in the informal organization of work. In Jo Freeman (Ed.), *Women: A feminist perspective* (4th ed., pp. 347–355). Mountain View, CA: Mayfield.

Lorber, Judith. (1997). Believing is seeing: Biology as ideology. In Maxine Baca Zinn, Pierrette Hondagneu-Sotelo, & Michael A. Messner (Eds.), *Through the prism of difference: Readings on sex and gender* (pp. 13–22). Boston: Allyn and Bacon.

Lott, Bernice. (1997). Cataloging gender differences: Science or politics? In Mary Roth Walsh (Ed.), *Women, men, and gender: Ongoing debates* (pp. 19–23). New Haven, CT: Yale University Press.

Loury, Linda Datcher. (1997). The gender earnings gap among college-educated workers. *Industrial and Labor Relations Review, 50,* 580–593.

Lowes, Jacinta; & Tiggemann, Marika. (2003). Body dissatisfaction, dieting awareness and the impact of parental influence in young children. *British Journal of Health Psychology, 8,* 135–147.

Luepker, Ellen T. (1999). Effects of practitioners' sexual misconduct: A follow-up study. *Journal of the American Academy of Psychiatry and the Law, 27,* 51–63.

Lueptow, Lloyd B.; Garovich-Szabo, Lori; & Lueptow, Margaret B. (2001). Social change and the persistence of sex typing. *Social Forces, 80,* 1–36.

Lye, Diane N. (1996). Adult child–parent relationships. *Annual Review of Sociology, 22,* 79–102.

Lyons, Nona Plessner. (1988). Two perspectives: On self, relationships, and morality. In Carol Gilligan, Janie Victoria Ward, & Jill McLean Taylor. (with Bardiger, Betty) (Eds.), *Mapping the moral domain: A contribution of women's thinking to psychological theory and education* (pp. 21–48). Cambridge, MA: Harvard University Press.

Maccoby, Eleanor E. (1988). Gender as a social category. *Developmental Psychology, 24,* 755–765.

Maccoby, Eleanor E. (1998). *The two sexes: Growing up apart, coming together.* Cambridge, MA: Belknap Press.

Maccoby, Eleanor Emmons; & Jacklin, Carol Nagy. (1974). *The psychology of sex differences.* Stanford, CA: Stanford University Press.

MacCoun, Robert J. (1998). Biases in the interpretation and use of research results. *Annual Review of Psychology, 49,* 259–287.

Mackey, Richard A.; Diemer, Matthew A.; & O'Brien, Bernard A. (2000). Psychological intimacy in the lasting relationships of heterosexual and same-gender couples. *Sex Roles, 43,* 201–227.

Macrae, C. Neil; & Bodenhausen, Galen V. (2000). Social cognition: Thinking categorically about others. *Annual Review of Psychology, 51,* 93–120.

Madson, Laura. (2000). Inferences regarding the personality traits and sexual orientation of physically androgynous people. *Psychology of Women Quarterly, 24,* 148–160.

Mahaffy, Kimberly A.; & Ward, Sally K. (2002). The gendering of adolescents' childbearing and educational plans: Reciprocal effects and the influence of social context. *Sex Roles, 46,* 403–417.

Mahalik, James R.; Good, Glenn E.; & Englar-Carlson, Matt. (2003). Masculinity scripts, presenting concerns, and help seeking: Implications for practice and training. *Professional Psychology: Research and Practice, 34,* 123–131.

Mahalik, James R.; Locke, Benjamin D.; Theodore, Harry; Cournoyer, Robert J.; & Lloyd, Brendan F. (2001). A cross-national and cross-sectional comparison of men's gender role conflict and its relationship to social intimacy and self-esteem. *Sex Roles, 45,* 1–14.

Maimer, Pamela J.; Bergeron, David; Bosetti, Heather; & Teed, Kenneth. (2003, March). Title IX at thirty: Equity in Athletics Disclosure Act (EADA) proportionality, revenue, expense, and opportunity for women and men. *Research Quarterly for Exercise and Sport, 74* (1), A88.

Maisey, D. S.; Vale, E. L. E.; Cornelissen, P. L.; & Tovee, M. J. (1999). Characteristics of male attractiveness for women. *Lancet, 353,* 1500.

Majors, Richard G.; & Billson, J. M. (1992). *Cool pose: The dilemmas of black manhood in America.* New York: Lexington.

Majors, Richard G.; Tyler, Richard; Peden, Blaine; & Hall, Ron. (1994). Cool pose: A symbolic mechanism for masculine role enactment and coping by black males. In Richard G. Majors & Jacob U. Gordon (Eds.), *The American black male: His present status and his future* (pp. 245–259). Chicago: Nelson-Hall.

Malamuth, Neil M. (1996). The confluence model of sexual aggression: Feminist and evolutionary perspectives. In David M. Buss & Neil M. Malamuth (Eds.), *Sex, power, conflict: Evolutionary and feminist perspectives* (pp. 269–295). New York: Oxford University Press.

Malinowski, Jon C. (2001). Mental rotation and real-world wayfinding. *Perceptual and Motor Skills, 92,* 19–30.

Malkin, Amy R.; Wornian, Kimberlie; & Chrisler, Joan C. (1999). Women and weight: Gendered messages on magazine covers. *Sex Roles, 40,* 647–656.

Mancus, Dianne Sirna. (1992). Influence of male teachers on elementary school children's stereotyping of teacher competence. *Sex Roles, 26,* 109–128.

Manger, Terje; & Eikeland, Ole-Johan. (1998). The effects of spatial visualization and students' sex on mathematical achievement. *British Journal of Psychology, 89,* 17–25.

Marecek, Jeanne. (2001). Disorderly constructs: Feminist frameworks for clinical psychology. In Rhoda K. Unger (Ed.), *Handbook of the psychology of women and gender* (pp. 303–316). New York: Wiley.

Marecek, Jeanne; & Kravetz, Diane. (1998). Putting politics into practice: Feminist therapy as feminist praxis. *Women & Therapy, 21,* 17–36.

Marecek, Jeanne; Kravetz, Diane; & Finn, Stephen. (1979). Comparison of women who enter feminist therapy and women who enter traditional therapy. *Journal of Consulting and Clinical Psychology, 47,* 734–742.

Mark, Daniel B. (2000). Sex bias in cardiovascular care: Should women be treated more like men? *Journal of the American Medical Association, 283,* 659–665.

Marketing to Women. (2002, June). Women in advertisements are getting younger, thinner, and more racially diverse. *Marketing to Women, 15* (6), 1–3.

Martell, Richard F.; Lane, David, M.; & Emrich, Cynthia. (1996). Male-female differences: A computer simulation. *American Psychologist, 51,* 157–158.

Martin, Carol Lynn. (1987). A ratio measure of sex stereotyping. *Journal of Personality and Social Psychology, 52,* 489–499.

Martin, Carol Lynn. (1995). Stereotypes about children with traditional and nontraditional gender roles. *Sex Roles, 33,* 727–751.

Martin, Carol Lynn; & Fabes, Richard A. (2001). The stability and consequences of young children's same-sex peer interactions. *Developmental Psychology, 37,* 431–446.

Martin, Carol Lynn; & Halverson, Charles F., Jr. (1981). A schematic processing model of sex-typing and stereotyping in children. *Child Development, 52,* 1119–1134.

Martin, Carol Lynn; & Little, Jane K. (1990). The relation of gender understanding to children's sex-typed preferences and gender stereotypes. *Child Development, 61,* 1427–1439.

Martin, Carol Lynn; Ruble, Diane N.; & Szkrybalo, Joel. (2002). Cognitive theories of early gender development. *Psychological Bulletin, 128,* 903–933.

Martin, Carol Lynn; Wood, Carolyn H.; & Little, Jane K. (1990). The development of gender stereotype components. *Child Development, 61,* 1891–1904.

Martin, Judith N.; Bradford, Lisa J.; Drzewiecka, Jolanta A.; & Chitgopekar, Anu S. (2003). Intercultural dating patterns among young White U.S. Americans: Have they changed in the past 20 years? *Howard Journal of Communication, 14,* 53–73.

Martinko, Mark L.; & Gardner, William L. (1983). A methodological review of sex-related access discrimination problems. *Sex Roles, 9,* 825–839.

Marván, María Luisa; & Cortés-Iniestra, Sandra. (2001). Women's beliefs about the prevalence of premenstrual syndrome and biases in recall of premenstrual changes. *Health Psychology, 20,* 276–280.

Marván, María Luisa; & Escobedo, Claudia. (1999). Premenstrual symptomatology: Role of prior knowledge about premenstrual syndrome. *Psychosomatic Medicine, 61,* 163–167.

Masters, William H.; & Johnson, Virginia E. (1966). *Human sexual response.* Boston: Little, Brown.

Matthews, Karen A.; Shumaker, Sally A.; Bowen, Deborah J.; Langer, Robert D.; Hunt, Julie R.; Kaplan, Robert M.; Klesges, Robert C.; & Ritenbaugh, Cheryl. (1997). Women's health initiative: Why now? What is it? What's new? *American Psychologist, 52,* 101–116.

Mays, Vickie M.; & Comas-Díaz, Lillian. (1988). Feminist therapy with ethnic minority populations: A closer look at Blacks and Hispanics. In Mary Ann Dutton Douglas & Lenore E. A. Walker (Eds.), *Feminist psychotherapies: Integration of therapeutic and feminist systems* (pp. 228–251). Norwood, NJ: Ablex.

Mazur, Allan. (1985). A biosocial model of status in face-to-face primate groups. *Social Forces, 64,* 377–402.

Mazur, Allan; & Booth, Alan. (1998). Testosterone and dominance in men. *Behavioral and Brain Sciences, 21,* 353–363.

Mazza, James J.; & Reynolds, William M. (1999). Exposure to violence in young inner-city adolescents: Relationships with suicidal ideation, depression, and PTSD symptomatology. *Journal of Abnormal Child Psychology, 27,* 203–214.

McCabe, Marita P.; & Cummins, Robert A. (1998). Sexuality and quality of life among young people. *Adolescence, 33,* 761–774.

McClelland, David C.; Atkinson, J. W.; Clark, R. W.; & Lowell, E. L. (1953). *The achievement motive.* New York: Appleton.

McCombs, Barbara L. (2000, July). Reducing the achievement gap. *Society, 37,* 29–35.

McCormick, Naomi B. (1994). *Sexual salvation: Affirming women's sexual rights and pleasures.* Westport, CT: Praeger.

McCreary, Donald R.; & Sasse, Doris K. (2000). An exploration of the drive for muscularity in adolescent boys and girls. *Journal of American College Health, 48,* 297–304.

McDougall, William. (1923). *Outline of psychology.* New York: Scribners.

McFarlane, Jessica; Martin, Carol Lynn; & Williams, Tannis MacBeth. (1988). Mood fluctuations: Women versus men and menstrual versus other cycles. *Psychology of Women Quarterly, 12,* 201–223.

McFarlane, Jessica Motherwell; & Williams, Tannis MacBeth. (1994). Placing premenstrual syndrome in perspective. *Psychology of Women Quarterly, 18,* 339–373.

McGinnis, Sandra L. (2003). Cohabiting, dating, and perceived costs of marriage: A model of marriage entry. *Journal of Marriage and Family, 65,* 105–116.

McHale, Susan M.; Crouter, Ann C.; & Tucker, Corinna J. (1999). Family context and gender role socialization in middle childhood: Comparing girls to boys. *Child Development, 70,* 990–1004.

McHale, Susan M.; Updegraff, Kimberly A.; Helms-Erikson, Heather; & Crouter, Ann C. (2001). Sibling influences on gender development in middle childhood and early adolescence: A longitudinal study. *Developmental Psychology, 37,* 115–125.

McHugh, Maureen C.; Koeske, Randi D.; & Frieze, Irene H. (1986). Issues to consider in conducting nonsexist psychological research: A guide for researchers. *American Psychologist, 41,* 879–890.

McKeever, Matthew; & Wolfinger, Nicholas H. (2001). Reexamining the economic costs of marital disruption for women. *Social Science Quarterly, 82,* 202–217.

McKeever, Walter F. (1995). Hormone and hemisphericity hypotheses regarding cognitive sex differences: Possible future explanatory power, but current empirical chaos. *Learning and Individual Differences, 7,* 323–340.

McKown, Clark; & Weinstein, Rhona S. (2003). The development and consequences of stereotype consciousness in middle childhood. *Child Development, 74,* 498–515.

McLain, Susan June; & Perkins, Carol O. (1990). Disabled women: At the bottom of the work heap. *Vocational Educational Journal, 65* (2), 54–63.

McManus, I. C.; & Bryden, M. P. (1991). Geschwind's theory of cerebral lateralization: Developing a formal, causal model. *Psychological Bulletin, 110,* 237–253.

McWhirter, Ellen Hawley. (1994, August). *Perceived barriers to education and career: Ethnic and gender differences.* Paper presented at the 102nd annual convention of the American Psychological Association, Los Angeles, CA.

Meehan, Anita M.; & Janik, Leann M. (1990). Illusory correlation and the maintenance of sex role stereotypes in children. *Sex Roles, 22,* 83–95.

Melson, Gail F. (2001). *Why the wild things are: Animals in the lives of children.* Cambridge, MA: Harvard University Press.

Melson, Gail F.; & Fogel, Alan. (1988). The development of nurturance in young children. *Young Children, 43,* 57–65.

Menaster, Michael. (2002, October 1). Controversies in eating disorders among men. *Psychiatric Times,* p. 83.

Mendonca, Berenice B.; Inacio, Marlene; Costa, Elaine M. F.; Arnhold, Ivo J. P.; Silva, Frederico A. Q.; Nicolau, Wilian; Bloise, Walter; Russell, David W.; & Wilson, Jean D. (1996). Male pseudohermaphroditism due to steroid 5-alpha-reductase 2 deficiency: Diagnosis, psychological evaluation, and management. *Medicine, 75* (2), 64–76.

Mesquita, Batja; & Frijda, Nico H. (1992). Cultural variations in emotions: A review. *Psychological Bulletin, 112,* 179–204.

Messner, Michael A. (1997). *Politics of masculinities: Men in movements.* Thousand Oaks, CA: Sage.

Meyer-Bahlburg, Heino F. L. (1980). Sexuality in early adolescence. In Benjamin B. Wolman & John Money (Eds.), *Handbook of human sexuality* (pp. 61–82). Englewood Cliffs, NJ: Prentice-Hall.

Michael, Robert T.; Gagnon, John H.; Laumann, Edward O.; & Kolata, Gina. (1994). *Sex in America.* Boston: Little, Brown.

Middaugh, Anne. (1994, August). *Clinical psychology interns' attitudes and information about women.* Paper presented at the 102nd annual convention of the American Psychological Association, Los Angeles, CA.

Miller, Katherine J.; Gleaves, David H.; Hirsch, Tera G.; Green, Bradley A.; Snow, Alicia C.; & Corbett, Chanda C. (2000). Comparisons of body image dimensions by race/ethnicity and gender in a university population. *International Journal of Eating Disorders, 27,* 310–316.

Miller, Laura J. (2002, June 1). Premenstrual dysphoric disorder. *Psychiatric Times, 19* (6), 54+

Miller, Merry N.; & Miller, Barney E. (2001). Premenstrual exacerbations of mood disorders. *Psychopharmacology Bulletin, 35,* 135–149.

Miller, Randi L.; & Gordon, Michael. (1986). The decline in formal dating: A study in six Connecticut high schools. *Marriage and Family Review, 10,* 139–156.

Mirowsky, John; & Ross, Catherine E. (1987). Belief in innate sex roles: Sex stratification versus interpersonal influence in marriage. *Journal of Marriage and the Family, 49,* 527–540.

Mischel, Walter. (1966). A social-learning view of sex differences in behavior. In Eleanor E. Maccoby (Ed.), *The development of sex differences* (pp. 56–81). Stanford, CA: Stanford University Press.

Mischel, Walter. (1993). *Introduction to personality* (5th ed.). Fort Worth, TX: Harcourt Brace Jovanovich.

Money, John. (1986). *Venuses penuses: Sexology, sexosophy, and exigency theory.* Buffalo, NY: Prometheus Books.

Monsour, Michael; Harris, Bridgid; Kurzweil, Nancy; & Beard, Chris. (1994). Challenges confronting cross-sex friendships: "Much ado about nothing?" *Sex Roles, 31,* 55–77.

Montecinos, Carmen; & Nielsen, Lynn E. (1997). Gender and cohort differences in university students' decisions to become elementary teacher education majors. *Journal of Teacher Education, 48,* 47–54.

Montello, Daniel R.; Lovelace, Kristin L.; Golledge, Reginald G.; & Self, Carole M. (1999). Sex-related differences and similarities in geographic and environmental spatial abilities. *Annals of the Association of American Geographers, 89,* 515–534.

Montemurro, Beth. (2003). Not a laughing matter: Sexual harassment as "material" on workplace-based situation comedies. *Sex Roles, 48,* 433–445.

Moore, Kathleen A.; McCabe, Marita P.; & Brink, Roger B. (2001). Are married couples happier in their relationships than cohabiting couples? Intimacy and relationship factors. *Sexual and Relationship Therapy, 16,* 35–46.

Moos, Rudolf; Schaefer, Jeanne; Andrassy, Jill; & Moos, Bernice. (2001). Outpatient mental health care, self-help groups, and patients' one-year treatment outcomes. *Journal of Clinical Psychology, 57,* 273–287.

Morawski, Jill. (1997). The science behind feminist research methods. *Journal of Social Issues, 53,* 667–681.

Morgan, Betsy Levonian. (1998). A three generational study of tomboy behavior. *Sex Roles, 39,* 787–800.

Morgan, Carolyn; Isaac, James D.; & Sansone, Carol. (2001). The role of interest in understanding the career choices of female and male college students. *Sex Roles, 44,* 295–320.

Morgan, Robin. (1970). Introduction: The women's revolution. In Robin Morgan (Ed.), *Sisterhood is powerful: An anthology of writings from the women's liberation movement* (pp. xv–xvii). New York: Vintage Books.

Mori, DeAnna; Chaiken, Shelly; & Pliner, Patricia. (1987). "Eating lightly" and the self-presentation of femininity. *Journal of Personality and Social Psychology, 53,* 693–702.

Mori, Lisa; Selle, Lynn L.; Zarate, Mylene G.; & Bernat, Jeffrey. (1994, August). *Asian American and Caucasian college students' attitudes towards rape.* Paper presented at the 102nd annual convention of the American Psychological Association, Los Angeles, CA.

Morin, Richard; & Rosenfeld, Megan. (1998, March 22). With more equity, more sweat. *Washington Post,* p. A1.

Morman, Mark T.; & Floyd, Kory. (1998). "I love you, man": Overt expression of affection in male–male interaction. *Sex Roles, 38,* 871–881.

Morris, Gary. (2000). *Hell in the heartland.* Retrieved June 30, 2003, from www.brightlightsfilm.com/27/boysdontcry.html.

Morrison, Todd G.; Morrison, Melanie A.; & Hopkins, Christine. (2003). Striving for bodily perfection? An exploration of the drive for muscularity in Canadian men. *Psychology of Men & Masculinity, 4,* 111–120.

Morrow, Susan L.; & Hawxhurst, Donna M. (1998). Feminist therapy: Integrating political analysis in counseling and psychotherapy. *Women & Therapy, 21,* 37–50.

Muehlenhard, Charlene L.; Friedman, Debra E.; & Thomas, Celeste M. (1985). Is date rape justifiable? The effects of dating activity, who initiated, who paid, and men's attitudes toward women. *Psychology of Women Quarterly, 9,* 297–309.

Mulrine, Anna. (2001, July 30). Are boys the weaker sex? *U.S. News & World Report, 131* (4), 40–47.

Mumenthaler, Martin S.; & Taylor, Joy L. (1999). Gender differences in moderate drinking effects. *Alcohol Research and Health, 23* (1), 55–61.

Murnen, Sarah K.; Wright, Carrie; & Kaluzny, Gretchen. (2002). If "boys will be boys," then girls will be victims? A meta-analytic review of the research that relates masculine ideology to sexual aggression. *Sex Roles, 46,* 359–375.

Murphy, Elaine M. (2003). Being born female is dangerous for your health. *American Psychologist, 58,* 205–210.

Murphy, Sheila T. (1998). The impact of factual versus fictional media portrayals on cultural stereotypes. *The Annals of the American Academy of Political and Social Science, 560,* 165–178.

Murray, Christopher J. L.; & Lopez, Alan D. (1997). Alternative projections of mortality and disability by cause 1990–2020: Global Burden of Disease Study (part 4). *Lancet, 349,* 1498–1504.

Murrell, Audrey J.; & James, Erika Hayes. (2001). Gender and diversity in organizations: Past, present, and future directions. *Sex Roles, 45,* 243–257.

Muska, Susan (Director & Producer), & Olafsdittir, Greta (Director). (1998). *The Brandon Teena story.* Zeitgesit Films.

Nanda, Serena. (2000). *Gender diversity: A cross-cultural perspective.* Prospect Heights, IL: Waveland Press.

Nannini, Dawn K.; & Meyers, Lawrence S. (2000). Jealousy in sexual and emotional infidelity: An alternative to the evolutionary explanation. *Journal of Sex Research, 37,* 117–122.

Nardi, Peter M. (1992a). "Seamless souls": An introduction to men's friendships. In Peter M. Nardi (Ed.), *Men's friendships* (pp. 1–14). Newbury Park, CA: Sage.

Nardi, Peter M. (1992b). Sex, friendship, and gender roles among gay men. In Peter M. Nardi (Ed.), *Men's friendships* (pp. 173–185). Newbury Park, CA: Sage.

National Center for Health Statistics. (1995, May 22). *National Economic, Social, and Environmental Data Bank* (electronic database). Hyattsville, MD: Author.

National Center for Health Statistics (NCHS). (2002). *Health, United States, 2002.* Hyattsville, MD: U.S. Government Printing Office.

Naversen, Laurel. (2001, September). Mood for thought: Is the new drug Sarafem a miracle treatment for severe PMS or just Prozac in disguise? *Harper's Bazaar,* pp. 252–253.

Neff, Kristin D.; & Harter, Susan. (2002). The authenticity of conflict resolutions among adult couples: Does women's other-oriented behavior reflect their true selves? *Sex Roles, 47,* 403–417.

Neil, Monty. (1999, August 31). *Press release: Females cheated again by SAT bias; SAT gender gap grows while narrowing on PSAT, ACT; test-maker "accountability" needed to stop illegal discrimination.* Retrieved June 7, 2003, from www.fairtest.org.

Nelson, Katherine. (1981). Social cognition in a script framework. In John H. Flavell & Lee Ross (Eds.), *Social cognitive development: Frontiers and possible futures* (pp. 97–118). Cambridge, England: Cambridge University Press.

Nelson, Wendy L.; Hughes, Honore M.; Katz, Barry; & Searight, H. Russell. (1999). Anorexic eating attitudes and behaviors of male and female college students. *Adolescence, 34,* 621–634.

Netting, Nancy S. (1992). Sexuality in youth culture: Identity and change. *Adolescence, 27,* 961–976.

Newman, Leonard S.; Cooper, Joel; & Ruble, Diane N. (1995). The interactive effects of knowledge and constancy on gender-stereotyped attitudes. (Gender and Computers, part 2). *Sex Roles, 33,* 325–351.

Nicholas, Donald R. (2000). Men, masculinity, and cancer: Risk-factor behaviors, early detection, and psychosocial adaptation. *Journal of American College Health, 49,* 27–33.

Nielsen, Laura Beth. (2002). Subtle, pervasive, harmful: Racist and sexist remarks in public as hate speech. *Journal of Social Issues, 58,* 265–280.

Nieva, Veronica F.; & Gutek, Barbara A. (1981). *Women and work: A psychological perspective.* New York: Praeger.

Nikiforov, Sergey V.; & Mamaev, Valery B. (1998). The development of sex differences in cardiovascular disease mortality: A historical perspective. *American Journal of Public Health, 88,* 1345–1353.

Nisbett, Richard E. (2003). *The geography of thought.* New York: Free Press.

Noddings, Nel. (1991/1992, December/January). The gender issue. *Educational Leadership, 49* (4), 65–70.

Nolan, Justin M.; & Ryan, Gery W. (2000). Fear and loathing at the cineplex: Gender differences in descriptions and perceptions of slasher films. *Sex Roles, 42,* 39–56.

Nolen-Hoeksema, Susan. (1987). Sex differences in unipolar depression: Evidence and theory. *Psychological Bulletin, 101,* 259–282.

Nolen-Hoeksema, Susan. (2001). Gender differences in depression. *Current Directions in Psychological Science, 10,* 173–176.

Nolen-Hoeksema, Susan; & Jackson, Benita. (2001). Mediators of the gender difference in rumination. *Psychology of Women Quarterly, 25,* 37–47.

Nolen-Hoeksema, Susan; Larson, Judith; & Grayson, Carla. (1999). Explaining the gender difference in depressive symptoms. *Journal of Personality and Social Psychology, 77,* 1061–1072.

Nosek, Brian A.; Banaji, Mahzarin R.; & Greenwald, Anthony G. (2002). Math = male, me = female, therefore math ≠ me. *Journal of Personality and Social Psychology, 83,* 44–59.

O'Brien, Edward J.; Jeffreys, Dorothy; Leitzel, Jeff; O'Brien, Jean P.; Mensky, Larissa; & Marchese, Marc. (1996, August). *Gender differences in the self-esteem of adolescents: A meta-analysis.* Paper presented at the 104th annual convention of the American Psychological Association, Toronto, Canada.

O'Brien, Marion; Peyton, Vicki; Mistry, Rashmita; Hruda, Ludmila; Jacobs, Anne; Caldera, Yvonne; Huston, Aletha; & Roy, Carolyn. (2000). Gender-role cognition in three-year-old boys and girls. *Sex Roles, 42,* 1007–1025.

O'Donnell, Meaghan L.; Creamer, Mark; Bryant, Richard A.; Schnyder, Ulrich; & Shalev, Arik. (2003). Posttraumatic disorders following injury: An empirical and methodological review. *Clinical Psychology Review, 23,* 587–603.

Ogletree, Shirley Matile; & Ginsburg, Harvey J. (2000). Kept under the hood: Neglect of the clitoris in common vernacular. *Sex Roles, 43,* 917–941.

Oguma, Y.; Sesso, Howard D.; Paffenbarger Ralph S., Jr.; & Lee, I-Min. (2002). Physical activity and all cause mortality in women: A review of the evidence. *British Journal of Sports Medicine, 36,* 162–172.

Okagaki, Lynn; & Frensch, Peter A. (1994). Effects of video game playing on measures of spatial performance: Gender effects in late adolescence. *Journal of Applied Developmental Psychology, 15,* 33–58.

Okazaki, Sumie. (2002). Influences of culture on Asian Americans' sexuality. *Journal of Sex Research, 39,* 34–41.

Olivardia, Roberto; Pope, Harrison G.; & Phillips, Katharine A. (2000). *The Adonis complex: The secret crisis of male body obsession.* New York: Free Press.

Oliver, Mary Beth; & Hyde, Janet Shibley. (1993). Gender differences in sexuality: A meta-analysis. *Psychological Bulletin, 114,* 29–51.

Oliver, Mary Beth; Sargent, Stephanie Lee; & Weaver, James B., III. (1998). The impact of sex and gender role self-perception on affective reactions to different types of film. *Sex Roles, 38,* 45–62.

Olson, Cheryl B. (1994, August). *Hostile environment: Gender, self-esteem and perception of sexual harassment.* Paper presented at the 102nd annual convention of the American Psychological Association, Los Angeles, CA.

O'Neil, James M. (1981). Patterns of gender role conflict and strain: Sexism and fear of femininity in men's

lives. *Personnel and Guidance Journal, 60,* 203–210.

Owens, Sherry Lynn; Smothers, Bobbie C.; & Love, Fannye E. (2003). Are girls victims of gender bias in our nation's schools? *Journal of Instructional Psychology, 30,* 131–136.

Page, Jessica R.; Stevens, Heather B.; & Galvin, Shelley L. (1996). Relationships between depression, self-esteem, and self-silencing behavior. *Journal of Social and Clinical Psychology, 15,* 381–396.

Pages from the history of the Indian sub-continent: Realism, skepticism, rational thinking, scientific progress and social ethics. (1989). Retrieved April 28, 2003, from http://members.tripod.com/~INDIA_RESOURCE/scienceh.htm.

Pain, Rachel. (2001, May 1). Gender, race, age and fear in the city. *Urban Studies,* pp. 899–914.

Palladino Green, Sharin; & Pritchard, Mary E. (2003). Predictors of body image dissatisfaction in adult men and women. *Social Behavior and Personality, 31,* 215–222.

Paludi, Michele A. (1984). Psychometric properties and underlying assumptions of four objective measures of fear of success. *Sex Roles, 10,* 765–781.

Paludi, Michele. (1997). Sexual harassment in schools. In William O'Donohoue (Ed.), *Sexual harassment: Theory, research, and treatment* (pp. 225–240). Boston: Allyn and Bacon.

Paolucci, Elizabeth Oddone; Genuis, Mark L.; & Violato, Claudio. (2001). A meta-analysis of the published research on the effects of child sexual abuse. *Journal of Psychology, 135,* 17–36.

Parker, Louise. (1997). Causes of testicular cancer. *Lancet, 350,* 827–828.

Parlee, Mary Brown. (1973). The premenstrual syndrome. *Psychological Bulletin, 83,* 454–465.

Patterson, Charlotte J.; & Chan, Raymond W. (1997). Gay fathers. In Michael E. Lamb (Ed.), *The role of the father in child development* (3rd ed., pp. 245–260). New York: Wiley.

Pedersen, William C.; Miller, Lynn Carol; Putcha-Bhagavatula, Anila D.; & Yang, Yijing. (2002). Evolved sex differences in the number of partners desired: The long and the short of it. *Psychological Science, 13,* 157–161.

Peirce, Kimberly (Director); & Kolodner, Eva (Producer). (1999). *Boys don't cry.* Searchlight Productions.

Pennebaker, James W. (1982). *The psychology of physical symptoms.* New York: Springer-Verlag.

Pennebaker, James W.; & Roberts, Tomi-Ann. (1992). Toward a his and hers theory of emotion: Gender differences in visceral perception. *Journal of Social and Clinical Psychology, 11,* 199–212.

People. (2002, February 11). Talking with Kim Cattrall. *People, 57* (5), 44.

People. (2003, February 24). State of the date 2003. *People, 59* (7), 82+.

Peplau, Letitia Anne. (2003). Human sexuality: How do men and women differ? *Current Directions in Psychological Science, 12,* 37–40.

Peplau, Letitia Anne; & Campbell, Susan Miller. (1989). The balance of power in dating and marriage. In Jo Freeman (Ed.), *Women: A feminist perspective* (4th ed., pp. 121–137). Mountain View, CA: Mayfield.

Peplau, Letitia Anne; & Conrad, Eva. (1989). Beyond nonsexist research: The perils of feminist methods in psychology. *Psychology of Women Quarterly, 13,* 379–400.

Peplau, Letitia Anne; & Spalding, Leah R. (2000). The close relationships of lesbians, gay men, and bisexuals. In Clyde Hendrick & Susan S. Hendrick (Eds.), *Close relationships: A sourcebook* (pp. 110–123). Thousand Oaks, CA: Sage.

Perls, Frederick S. (1969). *Gestalt therapy verbatim.* Lafayette, CA: Real People Press.

Perry, David G.; Perry, Louise C.; & Weiss, Robert J. (1989). Sex differences in the consequences that children anticipate for aggression. *Developmental Psychology, 25,* 312–319.

Peters, John F. (1994). Gender socialization of adolescents in the home: Research and discussion. *Adolescence, 29,* 913–934.

Petersen, Trond; Saporta, Ishak; & Seidel, Marc-David L. (2000). Offering a job: Meritocracy and social networks. *American Journal of Sociology, 106,* 763–816.

Peterson, Carole; & Biggs, Marleen. (2001). "I was really, really, really mad!" Children's use of evaluative devices in narratives about emotional events. *Sex Roles, 45,* 801–825.

Philadelphia, Desa. (2001, May 7). Tough guys in therapy. *Time, 157* (18), 6.

Phillips, Roger D.; & Gilroy, Faith D. (1985). Sex-role stereotypes and clinical judgments of mental health: The Brovermans' findings reexamined. *Sex Roles, 12,* 179–193.

Phillips, Susan D.; & Imhoff, Anne R. (1997). Women and career development: A decade of research. *Annual Review of Psychology, 48,* 31–59.

Piirto, Jane. (1991). Why are there so few? (Creative women: Visual artists, mathematicians, musicians). *Roeper Review, 13,* 142–147.

Piko, Bettina. (2001). Gender differences and similarities in adolescents' ways of coping. *Psychological Record, 51,* 223–235.

Pimlott-Kubiak, Sheryl; & Cortina, Lilia M. (2003). Gender, victimization, and outcomes: Reconceptualizing risk. *Journal of Consulting and Clinical Psychology, 71,* 528–539.

Pinel, John P. J. (2003). *Biopsychology* (5th ed.). Boston: Allyn and Bacon.

Pino, Nathan W.; & Meier, Robert F. (1999). Gender differences in rape reporting. *Sex Roles, 40,* 979–990.

Pittman, Frank. (1992, January/February). Why the men's movement isn't so funny. *Psychology Today,* p. 84.

Plant, E. Ashby; Hyde, Janet Shibley; Keltner, Dacher; & Devine, Patricia G. (2000). The gender stereotyping of emotions. *Psychology of Women Quarterly, 24,* 81–92.

Pleck, Elizabeth H.; & Pleck, Joseph H. (1997). Fatherhood ideals in the United States: Historical dimensions. In Michael E. Lamb (Ed.), *The role of the father in child development* (3rd ed., pp. 33–48). New York: Wiley.

Pleck, Joseph H. (1981). *The myth of masculinity.* Cambridge, MA: MIT Press.

Pleck, Joseph H. (1984). The theory of male sex role identity: Its rise and fall, 1936 to the present. In Miriam Lewin (Ed.), *In the shadow of the past: Psychology portrays the sexes* (pp. 205–225). New York: Columbia University Press.

Pleck, Joseph H. (1995). The Gender Role Strain paradigm: An update. In Ronald F. Levant & William S. Pollack (Eds.), *A new psychology of men* (pp. 11–32). New York: Basic Books.

Pleck, Joseph H. (1997). Parental involvement: Levels, sources, and consequences. In Michael E. Lamb (Ed.), *The role of the father in child development* (3rd ed., pp. 66–103). New York: Wiley.

Pliner, Patricia; & Chaiken, Shelly. (1990). Eating, social motives, and self-presentation in women and men. *Journal of Experimental Social Psychology, 26,* 240–254.

Polivy, Janet; & Herman, C. Peter. (1983). *Breaking the diet habit: The natural weight alternative.* New York: Basic Books.

Polivy, Janet; & Herman, C. Peter. (2002). Causes of eating disorders. *Annual Review of Psychology, 53,* 187–214.

Pollack, Andrew. (1998, December 1). Scientists seek a new movie role: Hero, not villain. *New York Times,* Section F, p. 1.

Pollack, William. (1998). *Real boys.* New York: Holt.

Pollitt, Katha. (1992, December 28). Are women morally superior to men? *Nation,* pp. 799–807.

Pomerantz, Eva M.; Altermatt, Ellen Rydell; & Saxon, Jill L. (2002). Making the grade but feeling distressed: Gender differences in academic performance and internal distress. *Journal of Educational Psychology, 94,* 396–404.

Pontius, Anneliese A. (1995). In similarity judgments hunter-gatherers prefer shapes over spatial relations in contrast to literate groups. *Perceptual and Motor Skills, 81,* 1027–1041.

Pontius, Anneliese A. (1997a). Lack of sex differences among east Ecuadorian school children on geometric figure rotation and face drawings. *Perceptual and Motor Skills, 85,* 72–74.

Pontius, Anneliese A. (1997b). No gender difference in spatial representation by schoolchildren in northwest Pakistan. *Journal of Cross-Cultural Psychology, 28,* 779–786.

Pope, Harrison G.; Kouri, Elena M.; & Hudson, James I. (2000). Effects of supraphysiologic doses of testosterone on mood and aggression in normal men. *Archives of General Psychiatry, 57,* 133–140.

Pope, Kenneth S. (1988). How clients are harmed by sexual contact with mental health professionals: The syndrome and its prevalence. *Journal of Counseling and Development, 67,* 222–226.

Pope, Kenneth S. (2000). Therapists' sexual feelings and behaviors: Research, trends, and quandaries. In Lenore T. Szuchman & Frank Muscarella (Eds.), *Psychological perspectives on human sexuality* (pp. 603–658). New York: Wiley.

Popp, Danielle; Donovan, Roxanne A.; Crawford, Mary; Marsh, Kerry L.; & Peele, Melanie. (2003). Gender, race, and speech style stereotypes. *Sex Roles, 48,* 317–325.

Population Reports. (2001). Can we avoid catastrophe? *Population Reports, 29* (3), 1–38.

Porter, Laura S.; Marco, Christine A.; Schwartz, Joseph E.; Neale, John M.; Shiffman, Saul; & Stone, Arthur A. (2000). Gender differences in coping: A comparison of trait and momentary assessments. *Journal of Social and Clinical Psychology, 19,* 480–498.

Portman, Tarrell Awe Agahe. (2001). Sex role attributions of American-Indian women. *Journal of Mental Health Counseling, 23,* 72+.

Postmes, Tom; & Spears, Russell. (2002). Behavior online: Does anonymous computer communication reduce gender inequality? *Personality and Social Psychology Bulletin, 28,* 1073–1083.

Poulin-Dubois, Diane; Serbin, Lisa A.; Eichstedt, Julie A.; Sen, Maya G.; & Beissel, Clara F. (2002). Men don't put on make-up: Toddlers' knowledge of the gender stereotyping of household activities. *Social Development, 11,* 166–181.

Powlishta, Kimberly K. (1995). Gender bias in children's perceptions of personality traits. *Sex Roles, 32,* 17–28.

Powlishta, Kimberly K. (2000). The effect of target age on the activation of gender stereotypes. *Sex Roles, 42,* 271–282.

Powlishta, Kimberly K.; Serbin, Lisa A.; & Moller, Lora C. (1993). The stability of individual differences in gender typing: Implications for understanding gender segregation. *Sex Roles, 29,* 723–744.

Pratto, Felicia; & Espinoza, Penelope. (2001). Gender, ethnicity, and power. *Journal of Social Issues, 57,* 763–780.

Prentice, Deborah A.; & Carranza, Erica. (2002). What women and men should be, shouldn't be, are allowed to be, and don't have to be: The contents of prescriptive gender stereotypes. *Psychology of Women Quarterly, 26,* 269–281.

President's Council on Physical Fitness and Sports. (1997). *Physical activity and sport in the lives of girls.* Minneapolis, MN: Center for Research on Girls and Women in Sport, University of Minnesota.

Pryor, John B.; & Whalen, Nora J. (1997). A typology of sexual harassment: Characteristics of harassers and the social circumstances under which sexual harassment occurs. In William O'Donohue (Ed.), *Sexual harassment: Theory, research, and treatment* (pp. 129–151). Boston: Allyn and Bacon.

Ptacek, J. T.; Smith, Ronald E.; & Zanas, John. (1992). Gender, appraisal, and coping: A longitudinal analysis. *Journal of Personality, 60,* 747–770.

Quatman, Teri; Sampson, Kindra; Robinson, Cindi; & Watson, Cary M. (2001). Academic, motivational, and emotional correlates of adolescent dating. *Genetic, Social, and General Psychology Monographs, 127,* 211–234.

Quinn, Susan. (1987). *A mind of her own: The life of Karen Horney.* New York: Summit Books.

Raag, Tarja; & Rackliff, Christine L. (1998). Preschoolers' awareness of social expectations of gender: Relationships to toy choices. *Sex Roles, 38,* 685–700.

Raety, Hannu; Vaenskae, Johanna; Kasanen, Kati; & Kaerkkaeinen, Riitta. (2002). Parents' explanations of their child's performance in mathematics and reading: A replication and extension of Yee and Eccles. *Sex Roles, 46,* 121–128.

Ragaza, Angelo. (1999, February 8). I don't count as "diversity." *Newsweek, 133* (6), 13.

Ragland, J. Daniel; Coleman, A. Rand; Gur, Ruben C.; Glahn, David C.; & Gur, Raquel E. (2000). Sex differences in brain–behavior relationships between verbal episodic memory and resting regional cerebral blood flow. *Neuropsychologia, 38,* 451–461.

Raichle, Marcus E. (1994, April). Visualizing the mind. *Scientific American, 270,* 58–64.

Raja, Sheela. (1998). Culturally sensitive therapy for women of color. *Women & Therapy, 21,* 67.

Ramsland, Katherine. (2003). *Teena or Brandon?* Retrieved June 30, 2003, from www.crimelibrary.com/notorious_murders/not_guilty/brandon/1.html.

Ranke, Michael B.; & Saenger, Paul. (2001). Turner's syndrome. *Lancet, 358,* 309–314.

Ratcliff, Kathryn Strother. (2002). *Women and health: Power, technology, inequality, and conflict in a gendered world.* Boston: Allyn and Bacon.

Raudenbush, Bryan; & Zellner, Debra A. (1997). Nobody's satisfied: Effects of abnormal eating behaviors and actual and perceived weight status on body image satisfaction in males and females. *Journal of Social and Clinical Psychology, 16,* 95–110.

Rawlings, Edna I. (1993). Reflections on "Twenty years of feminist counseling and therapy." *Counseling Psychologist, 21,* 88–91.

Reddy, Gayatri. (2003). "Men" who would be kings: Celibacy, emasculation, and the reproduction of hijras in contemporary Indian politics. *Social Research, 70,* 163–181.

Redman, Selina; Webb, Gloria R.; Hennrikus, Deborah J.; Gordon, Jill J.; & Sanson-Fisher, Robert W. (1991). The effects of gender upon diagnosis of psychological disturbance. *Journal of Behavioral Medicine, 14,* 527–540.

Regier, Darrel A.; Narrow, William E.; & Rae, Donald S. (1990). The epidemiology of anxiety disorders: The Epidemiologic Catchment Area (ECA) experience. *Journal of Psychiatric Research, 24* (Suppl. 2), 3–14.

Rehman, Jamil; Lazer, Simcha; Benet, Alexandru E.; Schaefer, Leah C.; & Melman, Arnold. (1999). The reported sex and surgery satisfactions of 28 postoperative male-to-female transsexual patients. *Archives of Sexual Behavior, 28,* 71–90.

Reid, Pamela Trotman. (1993). Poor women in psychology research: Shut up and shut out. *Psychology of Women Quarterly, 17,* 133–150.

Rejskind, F. Gillian; Rapagna, Socrates O.; & Gold, Dolores. (1992). Gender differences in children's divergent thinking. *Creativity Research Journal, 5,* 165–174.

Renk, Kimberly; Roberts, Rex; Roddenberry, Angela; Luick, Mary; Hillhouse, Sarah; Meehan, Cricket; Oliveros, Arazais; & Phares, Vicky. (2003). Mothers, fathers, gender role, and time parents spend with their children. *Sex Roles, 48,* 305–315.

Rennison, Callie Marie. (2003). *Intimate partner violence, 1993–2001. Bureau of Justice Statistics Crime Data Briefs.* Washington, DC: Bureau of Justice Statistics.

Renzetti, Claire M.; & Curran, Daniel J. (1992). *Women, men, and society* (2nd ed.). Boston: Allyn and Bacon.

Resnick, Heidi S.; Kilpatrick, Dean G.; Best, Connie L.; & Kramer, Teresa L. (1992). Vulnerability–stress factors in development of posttraumatic stress disorder. *Journal of Nervous and Mental Disease, 180,* 424–430.

Resnick, Heidi S.; Kilpatrick, Dean G.; Dansky, Bonnie S.; Saunders, Benjamin E.; & Best, Connie L. (1993). Prevalence of victim trauma and posttraumatic stress disorder in a representative national sample of women. *Journal of Consulting and Clinical Psychology, 61,* 984–991.

Ribalow, M. Z. (1998). Script doctors. *The Sciences, 38* (6), 26–31.

Ricciardelli, Lina A.; & Williams, Robert J. (1995). Desirable and undesirable gender traits in three behavioral domains. *Sex Roles, 33,* 637–655.

Rickert, Vaughn I.; Vaughan, Roger D.; & Wiemann, Constance M. (2003). Violence against young women: Implications for clinicians. *Contemporary OB/GYN, 48* (2), 30–45.

Riessman, Catherine Kohler. (1990). *Divorce talk: Women and men make sense of personal relationships.* New Brunswick: Rutgers University Press.

Riger, Stephanie. (1992). Epistemological debates, feminist voices: Science, social values, and the study of women. *American Psychologist, 47,* 730–740.

Riggs, Janet Morgan. (1997). Mandates for mothers and fathers: Perceptions of breadwinners and care givers. *Sex Roles, 37,* 565–580.

Risman, Barbara J. (1989). Can men "mother"? Life as a single father. In Barbara J. Risman & Pepper Schwartz (Eds.), *Gender in intimate relationships: A microstructural approach* (pp. 155–164). Belmont, CA: Wadsworth.

Riter, Robert N. (1997). I have breast cancer. *Newsweek, 130* (2), 14.

Roberts, Jonathan E.; & Bell, Martha Ann. (2000). Sex differences on a computerized mental rotation task disappear with computer familiarization. *Perceptual and Motor Skills, 91,* 1027–1034.

Roberts, Tomi-Ann. (1991). Gender and the influence of evaluations on self-assessments in achievement settings. *Psychological Bulletin, 109,* 297–308.

Roberts, Tomi-Ann; Goldenberg, Jamie L.; Power, Cathleen; & Pyszczynski, Tom. (2002). "Feminine protection": The effects of menstruation on attitudes toward women. *Psychology of Women Quarterly, 26,* 131–139.

Roberts, Tomi-Ann; & Nolen-Hoeksema, Susan. (1994). Gender comparisons in responsiveness to others' evaluations in achievement settings. *Psychology of Women Quarterly, 18,* 221–240.

Robertson, John; & Fitzgerald, Louise F. (1990). The (mis)treatment of men: Effects of client gender role and life-style on diagnosis and attribution of pathology. *Journal of Counseling Psychology, 37,* 3–9.

Robertson, John; & Fitzgerald, Louise F. (1992). Overcoming the masculine mystique: Preferences for alternative form of assistance among men who avoid counseling. *Journal of Counseling Psychology, 39,* 240–246.

Robertson, John M.; Johnson, Ann L.; Benton, Stephen L.; Janey, Bradley A.; Cabral, Jennifer; & Woodford, Joyce A. (2002). What's in a picture? Comparing gender constructs of younger and older adults. *Journal of Men's Studies, 11,* 1–27.

Robine, Jean-Marie; & Ritchie, Karen. (1991). Healthy life expectancy: Evaluation of global indicator of change in population health. *British Medical Journal, 302,* 457–460.

Robinson, David. (1979). *Talking out of alcoholism: The self-help process of Alcoholics Anonymous.* Baltimore, MD: University Park Press.

Robinson, S. J., & Manning, John T. (2000). The ratio of 2nd to 4th digit length and male homosexuality. *Evolution and Human Behavior, 21,* 333–345.

Rochlen, Aaron B.; Blazina, Christopher; & Raghunathan, Rajagopal. (2002). Gender role conflict, attitudes toward career counseling, career decision-making, and perceptions of career counseling advertising brochures. *Psychology of Men & Masculinity, 3,* 127–137.

Rodin, Judith; & Ickovics, Jeannette R. (1990). Women's health: Review and research agenda as we approach the 21st century. *American Psychologist, 45,* 1018–1034.

Rogers, Carl R. (1951). *Client-centered therapy: Its current practice, implications, and theory.* Boston: Houghton Mifflin.

Rogers, Carl R. (1961). *On becoming a person: A therapist's view of psychotherapy.* Boston: Houghton Mifflin.

Rogers, Carl R. (1980). *A way of being.* Boston: Houghton Mifflin.

Rogers, Stacy J.; & Amato, Paul R. (2000). Have changes in gender relations affected marital quality? *Social Forces, 79,* 731–753.

Rohlinger, Deana A. (2002). Eroticizing men: Cultural influences on advertising and male objectification. *Sex Roles, 46,* 61–74.

Rolls, Barbara J.; Fedoroff, Ingrid C.; & Guthrie, Joanne F. (1991). Gender differences in eating behavior and body weight regulation. *Health Psychology, 10,* 133–142.

Ronan, Colin A. (1982). *Science: Its history and development among the world's cultures.* New York: Facts On File Publications.

Roscoe, Will. (1993). How to become a berdache: Toward a unified analysis of gender diversity. In Gilbert Herdt (Ed.), *Third sex, third gender: Beyond sexual dimorphism in culture and history* (pp. 329–372). New York: Zone Books.

Rose, Amanda J.; & Asher, Steven R. (2000). Children's friendships. In Clyde Hendrick & Susan S. Hendrick (Eds.), *Close relationships: A sourcebook* (pp. 47–57). Thousand Oaks, CA: Sage.

Rose, Suzanna; & Frieze, Irene Hanson. (1993). Young singles' contemporary dating scripts. *Sex Roles, 28,* 499–509.

Rosenfeld, Megan. (1998, March 26). Little boys blue: Reexamining the plight of young males. *Washington Post,* p. A1.

Rosenfield, David; & Stephan, Walter G. (1978). Sex differences in attributions for sex-typed tasks. *Journal of Personality, 46,* 244–259.

Rosenfield, Sarah. (1982). Sex roles and societal reactions to mental illness: The labeling of "deviant deviance." *Journal of Health and Social Behavior, 23,* 18–24.

Rosenkrantz, Paul; Vogel, Susan; Bee, Helen; Broverman, Inge; & Broverman, Donald M. (1968). Sex-role stereotypes and self-concepts in college students. *Journal of Consulting and Clinical Psychology, 32,* 287–295.

Rosenthal, Patrice. (1996). Gender and managers' causal attributions for subordinate performance: A field story. *Sex Roles, 34,* 1–14.

Rothstein, Donna S. (1995). Do female faculty influence female students' educational and labor market attainments? *Industrial and Labor Relations Review, 48,* 515–530.

Rotundo, Maria; Nguyen, Dung-Hanh; & Sackett, Paul R. (2001). A meta-analytic review of gender differences in perceptions of sexual harassment. *Journal of Applied Psychology, 86,* 914–922.

Roy, Rosanne; Benenson, Joyce F.; & Lilly, Frank. (2000). Beyond intimacy: Conceptualizing sex differences in same-sex friendships. *Journal of Psychology, 134,* 93–102.

Royal, Cindy. (2003, August). *Narrative structure in Sex and the City: "I couldn't help but wonder. . . ."* Paper presented at the Association for Education in Journalism and Mass Communication Conference, Kansas City, MO. Retrieved July 28, 2003, from www.cindyroyal.com/royal_sex_paper.pdf.

Rozin, Paul. (1999). Food is fundamental, fun, frightening, and far-reaching. *Social Research, 66,* 9–30.

Rozin, Paul; Bauer, Rebecca; & Catanese, Dana. (2003). Food and life, pleasure and worry, among American college students: Gender differences and regional similarities. *Journal of Personality and Social Psychology, 85,* 132–141.

Rozin, Paul; Fischler, C.; Imada, Sumio; Sarubin, A.; & Wrzesniewski, Amy. (1999). Attitudes to food and the role of food in life in the U.S.A., Japan, Flemish Belgium and France: Possible implications for the diet–health debate. *Appetite, 33,* 163–180.

Rubin, Robert T.; Reinisch, June M.; & Haskett, Roger F. (1981). Postnatal gonadal steroid effects on human behavior. *Science, 211,* 1318–1324.

Ruble, Diane N.; & Martin, Carol Lynn. (1998). Gender development. In Nancy Eisenberg (Ed.), *Handbook of child psychology, Vol. 3: Social, emotional, and personality development* (5th ed., pp. 933–1016). New York: Wiley.

Ruby, Jennie. (2000). Man bites dog! Portrayal of women in mass media. *Off our backs, 30* (11), 12–13.

Rudin, Margaret M.; Zalewski, Christine; & Bodmer-Turner, Jeffrey. (1995). Characteristics of child sexual abuse victims according to perpetrator gender. *Child Abuse and Neglect, 19,* 963–973.

Russell, Denise. (1995). *Women, madness and medicine.* Cambridge, England: Polity Press.

Russell, Diana E. H. (1986). *The secret trauma: Incest in the lives of girls and women.* New York: Basic Books.

Russo, Nancy Felipe. (1990). Overview: Forging research priorities for women's mental health. *American Psychologist, 45,* 368–373.

Russo, Nancy Felipe. (1998). Editorial: Teaching about gender and ethnicity: Goals and challenges. *Psychology of Women Quarterly, 22,* i–vi.

Rust, Paula C. Rodriguez. (2000). Bisexuality: A contemporary paradox for women. *Journal of Social Issues, 56,* 205–222.

Sabo, Don. (2000). Men's health studies: Origins and trends. *Journal of American College Health, 49,* 133–142.

Sachs-Ericsson, Natalie; & Ciarlo, James A. (2000). Gender, social roles, and mental health: An epidemiological perspective. *Sex Roles, 43,* 605–628.

Sadker, David; & Sadker, Myra. (1985). The treatment of sex equity in teacher education. In Susan S. Klein (Ed.), *Handbook for achieving sex equity through education* (pp. 145–161). Baltimore, MD: Johns Hopkins University Press.

Sadker, Myra P.; & Sadker, David M. (1980). Sexism in teacher-education texts. *Harvard Educational Review, 50,* 36–46.

Salzman, Philip C. (1999). Is inequality universal? *Current Anthropology, 40,* 31–61.

Samuel, Steven E.; & Gorton, Gregg E. (1998). National survey of psychology internship directors regarding education for prevention of psychologist–patient sexual exploitation. *Professional Psychology: Research and Practice, 29,* 86–90.

Sanders, Geoff; Sjodin, Marie; & de Chastelaine, Marianne. (2002). On the elusive nature of sex differences in cognition: Hormonal influences contributing to within-sex variation. *Archives of Sexual Behavior, 31,* 145–152.

Sanderson, Susan; & Sanders Thompson, Vetta L. (2002). Factors associated with perceived paternal involvement in childrearing. *Sex Roles, 46,* 99–111.

Sandfort, Theodorus G. M.; de Graaf, Ron; & Bijl, Rob V. (2003). Same-sex sexuality and quality of life: Findings from the Netherlands Mental Health Survey and Incidence study. *Archives of Sexual Behavior, 32,* 15–22.

Sandnabba, N. Kenneth; & Ahlberg, Christian. (1999). Parents' attitudes and expectations about children's cross-gender behavior. *Sex Roles, 40,* 249–264.

Sapolsky, Robert. (1997, March). Testosterone rules: It takes more than just a hormone to make a fellow's trigger finger itch. *Discover, 18,* 44–48.

Saragovi, Carina; Koestner, Richard; Di Dio, Lina; & Aubé, Jennifer. (1997). Agency, communion, and well-being: Extending Helgeson's (1994) model. *Journal of Personality and Social Psychology, 73,* 593–609.

Sarason, Irwin G.; & Sarason, Barbara R. (2001). *Abnormal psychology: The problem of maladaptive behavior* (10th ed.). Englewood Cliffs, NJ: Prentice Hall.

Satpathy, R.; & Mishra, Saroj K. (2000). The alarming "gender gap." *Bulletin of the World Health Organization, 78,* 1373.

Saucier, Deborah M.; Green, Sheryl M.; Leason, Jennifer; MacFadden, Alastair; Bell, Scott; & Elias, Lorin, J. (2002). Are sex differences in navigation caused by sexually dimorphic strategies or by differences in the ability to use the strategies? *Behavioral Neuroscience, 116,* 403–410.

Savin-Williams, Ritch C. (1995). Lesbian, gay male, and bisexual adolescents. In Anthony R. D'Augelli & Charlotte J. Patterson (Eds.), *Lesbian, gay, and bisexual identities over the lifespan: Psychological perspectives* (pp. 165–189). New York: Oxford University Press.

Savin-Williams, Ritch C.; & Diamond, Lisa M. (2000). Sexual identity trajectories among sexual-minority youths: Gender comparisons. *Archives of Sexual Behavior, 29,* 607–627.

Scali, Robyn M.; Brownlow, Sheila; & Hicks, Jennifer L. (2000). Gender differences in spatial task performance as a function of speed or accuracy orientation. *Sex Roles, 43,* 359–376.

Schachter, Stanley; & Singer, Jerome E. (1962). Cognitive, social, and psychological determinants of emotional state. *Psychological Review, 69,* 379–399.

Scharrer, Erica. (2001). Tough guys: The portrayal of hypermasculinity and aggression in televised police dramas. *Journal of Broadcasting & Electronic Media, 45,* 615–634.

Scher, Murray. (1981). Men in hiding: A challenge for the counselor. *Personnel and Guidance Journal, 60,* 199–202.

Scherer, Klaus R.; Wallbott, Harald G.; & Summerfield, Angela B. (Eds.) (1986). *Experiencing emotion: A cross-cultural study.* Cambridge, England: Cambridge University Press.

Schiebinger, Londa. (1999). *Has feminism changed science?* Cambridge, MA: Harvard University Press.

Schmitz, Sigrid. (1999). Gender differences in acquisition of environmental knowledge related to wayfinding ability, spatial anxiety and self-estimated environmental competencies. *Sex Roles, 41,* 71–94.

Schneer, Joy A.; & Reitman, Freida. (1990). Effects of employment gaps on the careers of M.B.A.'s: More damaging for men than for women? *Academy of Management Journal, 33,* 391–406.

Schneider, Irving. (1987). The theory and practice of movie psychiatry. *American Journal of Psychiatry, 144,* 996–1002.

Schofield, Toni; Connell, R. W.; Walker, Linley; Wood, Julian F.; & Butland, Dianne L. (2000). Understanding men's health and illness: A gender-relations approach to policy, research, and practice. *Journal of American College Health, 48,* 247–256.

School Law News. (2002, June 21). Women's group charges gender bias in voc ed class. *School Law News, 30* (13), 1, 3.

Schroeder, Debra S.; & Mynatt, Clifford R. (1999). Graduate students' relationship with their male and female major professors. *Sex Roles, 40,* 393–420.

Schultz, Duane P.; & Schultz, Sidney Ellen. (2004). *A history of modern psychology* (8th ed.). Belmont, CA: Wadsworth.

Schutte, Nicola; Malouff, John; Curtis, Donna; Lowry, Manya; & Luis, Cheryl. (1996, August). *Women's acceptance of traditional roles and their career choice.* Paper presented at the 104th annual convention of the American Psychological Association, Toronto, Canada.

Schwartz, Pepper. (1994). *Peer marriage: How love between equals really works.* New York: Free Press.

Scott, Jacqueline. (1998). Changing attitudes to sexual morality: A cross-national comparison. *Sociology, 32,* 815–818.

Scully, Diana. (1990). *Understanding sexual violence: A study of convicted rapists.* London: HarperCollins Academic.

Seale, Clive. (2000). Changing patterns of death and dying. *Social Science and Medicine, 51,* 917–930.

Seeman, Mary V. (2003). Gender differences in schizophrenia across the life span. In Carl I. Cohen (Ed.), *Schizophrenia into later life: Treatment, research, and policy* (pp. 141–154). Washington, DC: American Psychiatric Publishing.

Segal, Julius; & Segal, Zelda. (1993, May). What five-year-olds think about sex: And when and how to give them the answers that they need to hear. *Parents' Magazine,* pp. 130–132.

Seid, Roberta P. (1994). Too "close to the bone": The historical context of women's obsession with slenderness. In Patricia Fallon, Melanie A. Katzman, & Susan C. Wooley (Eds.), *Feminist perspectives on eating disorders* (pp. 3–16). New York: Guilford Press.

Seidman, Steven A. (1999). Revisiting sex-role stereotyping in MTV videos. *International Journal of Instructional Media, 26,* 11–22.

Seligmann, Jean. (with Rogers, Patrick; & Annin, Peter). (1994, May 2). The pressure to lose. *Newsweek, 123* (18), 60–61.

Sell, Randall L.; Wells, James A.; & Wypij, David. (1995). The prevalence of homosexual behavior and attraction in the United States, the United Kingdom and France: Results of national population-based samples. *Archives of Sexual Behavior, 24,* 235–248.

Sells, Lucy W. (1980). The mathematics filter and the education of women and minorities. In Lynn H. Fox, Linda Brody, & Dianne Tobin (Eds.), *Women and the mathematical mystique* (pp. 66–75). Baltimore, MD: Johns Hopkins University Press.

Serbin, Lisa A.; Poulin-Dubois, Diane; Colburne, Karen A.; Sen, Maya G.; & Eichstedt, Julie A. (2001). Gender stereotyping in infancy: Visual preferences for and knowledge of gender-stereotyped toys in the second year. *International Journal of Behavioral Development, 25,* 7–15.

Serbin, Lisa A.; Poulin-Dubois, Diane; & Eichstedt, Julie A. (2002). Infants' response to gender-inconsistent events. *Infancy, 3,* 531–542.

Serbin, Lisa A.; Zelkowitz, Phyllis; Doyle, Anna-Beth; Gold, Dolores; & Wheaton, Blair. (1990). The socialization of sex-differentiated skills and academic performance: A mediational model. *Sex Roles, 23,* 613–628.

Serdula, Mary K.; Collins, Elizabeth; Williamson, David F.; Anda, Robert F.; Pamuk, Elsie; & Byers, Tim E. (1993). Weight control practices of U.S. adolescents and adults. *Annals of Internal Medicine, 119,* 667–671.

Serdula, Mary K.; Mokdad, Ali H.; Williamson, David F.; Galuska, Deborah A.; Mendlein, James M.; & Heath, Gregory W. (1999). Prevalence of attempting weight loss and strategies for controlling weight. *Journal of the American Medical Association, 282,* 1353–1358.

Sharpe, Mark J.; Heppner, Paul; & Dixon, Wayne A. (1995). Gender role conflict, instrumentality, expressiveness, and well-being in adult men. *Sex Roles, 33,* 1–17.

Shaywitz, Bennett A.; Shaywitz, Sally E.; Pugh, Kenneth R.; Constable, R. Todd; Skudlarski, Pawel; Fulbright, Robert K.; Bronen, Richard A.; Fletcher, Jack M.; Shankweiler, Donald P.; Katz, Leonard; & Gore, John C. (1995). Sex differences in the functional organization of the brain for language. *Nature, 373,* 607–609.

Sheets, Virgil L.; & Wolfe, Marlow D. (2001). Sexual jealousy in heterosexuals, lesbians, and gays. *Sex Roles, 44,* 255–276.

Shepela, Sharon Toffey; & Levesque, Laurie L. (1998). Poisoned waters: Sexual harassment and the college climate. *Sex Roles, 38,* 589–611.

Sherif, Carolyn W. (1982). Needed concepts in the study of gender identity. *Psychology of Women Quarterly, 6,* 375–398.

Sherman, Julia. (1978). *Sex-related cognitive differences: An essay on theory and evidence.* Springfield, IL: Charles C. Thomas.

Shi, Jianong; Xu, Fan; Zhou, Lin; & Zha, Zixiu. (1999). Gender differences from the results of a cross-cultural study on technical creativity of children from China and Germany. *Acta Psychologica Sinica, 31,* 428–434. (Abstract only)

Shields, Stephanie A. (1975a). Functionalism, Darwinism, and the psychology of women: A study in social myth. *American Psychologist, 30,* 739–754.

Shields, Stephanie A. (1975b). Ms. Pilgrim's progress: The contributions of Leta Stetter Hollingworth to the psychology of women. *American Psychologist, 30,* 852–857.

Shields, Stephanie A. (2002). *Speaking from the heart: Gender and the social meaning of emotion.* Cambridge, England: Cambridge University Press.

Shirley, Donna. (1999). Women in engineering: Focus on success. *The Bridge, 29* (2). Retrieved July 9, 2003, from www.nae.edu/nae/naehome.nsf/weblinks/NAEW-4NHM97?opendocument.

Shulman, Shmuel; & Scharf, Miri. (2000). Adolescent romantic behaviors and perceptions: Age- and gender-related differences, and links with family and peer relationships. *Journal of Research on Adolescence, 10,* 99–118.

Shumaker, Sally A.; Legault, Claudine; Rapp, Stepphen R.; Thal, Leon; Wallace, Robert B.; Ockene, Judith K.; Hendrix, Susan L.; Jones, Beverly N., III; Assaf, Annlouise R.; Jackson, Rebecca D.; Kotchen, Jane Morley; Wassertheil-Smoller, Sylvia; & Wactawski-Wende, Jean. (2003). Estrogen plus progestin and the incidence of dementia and mild cognitive impairment in postmenopausal women: A randomized controlled trial. *Journal of the American Medical Association, 289,* 2651–2662.

Sidanius, Jim; & Pena, Yesilernis. (2003). The gendered nature of family structure and group-based anti-egalitarianism: A cross-national study. *Journal of Social Psychology, 143,* 243–251.

Sidanius, Jim; Pratto, Felicia; & Bobo, Lawrence. (1994). Social dominance orientation and the political psychology of gender: A case of invariance? *Journal of Personality and Social Psychology, 67,* 998–1011.

Sigel, Roberta S. (1996). *Ambition and accommodation: How women view gender relations.* Chicago: University of Chicago Press.

Signorella, Margaret L.; Bigler, Rebecca L.; & Liben, Lynn S. (1993). Developmental differences in children's gender schemata about others: A meta-analytic review. *Developmental Review, 13,* 147–183.

Signorella, Margaret L.; Frieze, Irene Hanson; & Hershey, Susanne W. (1996). Single-sex versus mixed-sex classes and gender schemata in children and adolescents: A longitudinal comparison. *Psychology of Women Quarterly, 20,* 599–607.

Signorielli, Nancy. (1998). *A content analysis: Reflections of girls in the media: Television and the perpetuation of gender-role stereotypes.* Retrieved June 28, 2003, from www.aap.org/advocacy/sign298.htm.

Signorielli, Nancy; & Bacue, Aaron. (1999). Recognition and respect: A content analysis of prime-time television characters across three decades. *Sex Roles, 40,* 527–544.

Signorielli, Nancy; & Kahlenberg, Susan. (2001). Television's world or work in the nineties. *Journal of Broadcasting & Electronic Media, 45,* 4–22.

Silverman, Jay G.; Raj, Anita; Mucci, Lorelei A.; & Hathaway, Jeanne E. (2001). Dating violence against adolescent girls and associated substance use, unhealthy weight control, sexual risk behavior, pregnancy, and suicidality. *Journal of the American Medical Association, 286,* 572–579.

Silverstein, Louise B. (1993). Primate research, family politics, and social policy: Transforming "cads" into "dads." *Journal of Family Psychology, 7,* 267–282.

Silverstein, Louise B. (1996). Fathering is a feminist issue. *Psychology of Women Quarterly, 20,* 3–37.

Silverstein, Louise B.; & Auerbach, Carl F. (1999). Deconstructing the essential father. *American Psychologist, 54,* 397–407.

Silverstein, Louise B.; Auerbach, Carl F.; Grieco, Loretta; & Dunk, Faith. (1999). Do Promise Keepers dream of feminist sheep? *Sex Roles, 40,* 665–688.

Silverstein, Louise B.; Auerbach, Carl F.; & Levant, Ronald F. (2002). Contemporary fathers reconstructing masculinity: Clinical implications of gender role strain. *Professional Psychology: Research and Practice, 33,* 361–369.

Simi, Nicole L.; & Mahalik, James R. (1997). Comparison of feminist versus psychoanalytic/dynamic and other therapists on self-disclosure. *Psychology of Women Quarterly, 21,* 465–483.

Simon, Rita J.; Scherer, Jennifer; & Rau, William. (1999). Sexual harassment in the heartland? Community opinion on the EEOC suit Mitsubishi Motor Manufacturing of America. *Social Science Journal, 36,* 485–496.

Simon, Robert I. (1999). Therapist–patient sex: From boundary violations to sexual misconduct. *Psychiatric Clinics of North America, 22,* 31–47.

Simon, William; & Gagnon, John H. (1986). Sexual scripts: Permanence and change. *Archives of Sexual Behavior, 15,* 97–119.

Simoni-Wastila, Linda. (2000). The use of abusable prescription drugs: The role of gender. *Journal of Women's Health and Gender-Based Medicine, 9,* 289–297.

Simpson, Joe Leigh. (2001, November). Androgen insensitivity. *Contemporary OB/GYN, 46* (11), 73+.

Slavkin, Michael; & Stright, Anne Dopkins. (2000). Gender role differences in college students from one- and two-parent families. *Sex Roles, 42,* 23–37.

Small, Kevonne. (2000). Female crime in the United States, 1963–1998. *Gender Issues, 18,* 75–90.

Smith, George W.; & Smith, Dorothy E. (1998). The ideology of "fag": The school experience of gay students. *Sociological Quarterly, 39,* 309–335.

Smith, Jessi L.; & White, Paul H. (2002). An examination of implicitly activated, explicitly activated, and nullified stereotypes on mathematical performance: It's not just a woman's issue. *Sex Roles, 47,* 179–191.

Smith, Page Hall; Smith, Jason R.; & Earp, Jo Anne L. (1999). Beyond the measurement trap: A reconstructed conceptualization and measurement of woman battering. *Psychology of Women Quarterly, 23,* 177–193.

Smith, Thomas Ewin. (1997). Adolescent gender differences in time alone and time devoted to conversation. *Adolescence, 32,* 483–496.

Smith, Yolanda L. S.; van Goozen, Stephanie H. M.; & Cohen-Kettenis, Peggy T. (2001). Adolescents with gender identity disorder who were accepted or rejected for sex reassignment surgery: A prospective follow-up study. *Journal of the American Academy of Child and Adolescent Psychiatry, 40,* 472–481.

Snodgrass, Sara E. (1985). Women's intuition: The effect of subordinate role on interpersonal sensitivity. *Journal of Personality and Social Psychology, 49,* 146–155.

Snodgrass, Sara E. (1992). Further effects of role versus gender on interpersonal sensitivity. *Journal of Personality and Social Psychology, 62,* 154–158.

Solnick, Sara J. (2001). Gender differences in the ultimatum game. *Economic Inquiry, 39,* 189–200.

Somer, Eli; & Saadon, Meir. (1999). Therapist–client sex: Clients' retrospective reports. *Professional Psychology: Research and Practice, 30,* 504–509.

Sommers, Christina Hoff. (2000, May). The war against boys. *Atlantic Monthly, 285,* 59–74.

Song, Eun Young; Pruitt, B. E.; McNamara, James; & Colwell, Brian. (2000). A meta-analysis examining effects of school sexuality education programs on adolescents' sexual knowledge, 1960–1997. *Journal of School Health, 70,* 413–416.

Spataro, Josie; Moss, Simon A.; & Wells, David L. (2001). Child sexual abuse: A reality for both sexes. *Australian Psychologist, 36,* 117–183.

Spence, Janet T. (1985). Gender identity and its implications for the concepts of masculinity and femininity. In Theo B. Sonderegger (Ed.), *Nebraska Symposium on Motivation, 1984: Psychology and gender* (Vol. 32, pp. 59–95). Lincoln, NE: University of Nebraska Press.

Spence, Janet T.; & Buckner, Camille E. (2000). Instrumental and expressive traits, trait stereotypes, and sexist attitudes: What do they signify? *Psychology of Women Quarterly, 24,* 44–62.

Spence, Janet T.; & Hahn, Eugene D. (1997). The Attitudes Toward Women Scale and attitude change in college students. *Psychology of Women Quarterly, 21,* 17–34.

Spence, Janet T.; & Helmreich, Robert. (1978). *Masculinity and femininity: The psychological dimensions, correlates, and antecedents.* Austin: University of Texas Press.

Spence, Janet T.; Helmreich, Robert; & Stapp, Joy. (1974). The Personal Attributes Questionnaire: A measure of sex-role stereotypes and masculinity–femininity. *JSAS Catalog of Selected Documents in Psychology, 4,* 43 (Ms. no. 617).

Spitzer, Brenda L.; Henderson, Katherine A.; & Zivian, Marilyn T. (1999). Gender differences in population versus media body sizes: A comparison over four decades. *Sex Roles, 40,* 545–566.

Sprecher, Susan. (2001). Equity and social exchange in dating couples: Associations with satisfaction, commitment, and stability. *Journal of Marriage and Family, 63,* 599–613.

Sprecher, Susan; & Felmlee, Diane. (1997). The balance of power in romantic heterosexual couples over time from "his" and "her" perspectives. *Sex Roles, 37,* 361–379.

Sprecher, Susan; & Regan, Pamela C. (2002). Liking some things (in some people) more than others: Partner preferences in romantic relationships and friendships. *Journal of Social and Personal Relationships, 19,* 463–481.

Sprecher, Susan; Regan, Pamela C.; & McKinney, Kathleen. (1998). Beliefs about the outcomes of extramarital sexual relationships as a function of the gender of the "cheating spouse." *Sex Roles, 38,* 301–311.

Sprecher, Susan; & Toro-Morn, Maura. (2002). A study of men and women from different sides of earth to determine if men are from Mars and women are from Venus in their beliefs about love and romantic relationships. *Sex Roles, 46,* 131–147.

Springer, Sally P.; & Deutsch, Georg. (1998). *Left brain, right brain* (5th ed.). New York: Freeman.

Stabiner, Karen. (2001, June). Lost in space. *Vogue, 191* (6), 142, 147–148.

Stangor, Charles; & Ruble, Diane N. (1987). Development of gender role knowledge and gender constancy. In Lynn S. Liben & Margaret L. Signorella (Eds.), *Children's gender schemata* (pp. 5–22). San Francisco, CA: Jossey-Bass.

Stark, Ellen. (1989, May). Teen sex: Not for love. *Psychology Today,* pp. 10–12.

Steele, Claude M. (1997). A threat in the air: How stereotypes shape intellectual identity and performance. *American Psychologist, 52,* 613–629.

Steele, Claude M.; & Aronson, Joshua. (1995). Stereotype threat and the intellectual test performance of African Americans. *Journal of Personality and Social Psychology, 69,* 797–811.

Steffensmeier, Darrel; & Allan, Emilie. (1996). Gender and crime: Toward a gendered theory of female offending. *Annual Review of Sociology, 22,* 459–477.

Steil, Janice M. (1995). Supermoms and second shifts: Marital inequality in the 1990s. In Jo Freeman (Ed.), *Women: A feminist perspective* (5th ed., pp. 149–181). Mountain View, CA: Mayfield.

Steil, Janice M. (2000). Contemporary marriage: Still an unequal partnership. In Clyde Hendrick & Susan S. Hendrick (Eds.), *Close relationships: A sourcebook* (pp. 124–136). Thousand Oaks, CA: Sage.

Stein, Murray B.; Walker, John R.; & Forde, David R. (2000). Gender differences in susceptibility to post-traumatic stress disorder. *Behavior Research and Therapy, 38,* 619–628.

Steinke, Jocelyn; & Long, M. (1996). A lab of her own?: Portrayals of female characters on children's educational science programs. *Science Communication, 18,* 91–115.

Steinpreis, Rhea E.; Ritzke, Dawn; & Anders, Katie A. (1999). The impact of gender on the review of the curricula vitae of job applicants and tenure candidates: A national empirical study. *Sex Roles, 41,* 509–528.

Stephan, Cookie White; Stephan, Walter C.; Demitrakis, Katherine M.; Yamada, Ann Marie; & Clason, Dennis L. (2000). Women's attitudes toward men: An integrated threat theory approach. *Psychology of Women Quarterly, 24,* 63–73.

Sternberg, Robert J. (1986). A triangular theory of love. *Psychological Review, 93,* 119–135.

Sternberg, Robert J. (1987). Liking versus loving: A comparative evaluation of theories. *Psychological Bulletin, 102,* 331–345.

Stipp, David. (1996, May 13). The gender gap in cancer research. *Fortune, 133* (9), 74–76.

St. John, Warren. (2002, May 12). With games of havoc, men will be boys. *New York Times,* p. ST1.

St. Lawrence, Janet S.; & McFarlane, Mary. (1999). Research methods in the study of sexual behavior. In Philip C. Kendall, James N. Butcher, & Grayson N. Holmbeck (Eds.), *Handbook of research methods in clinical psychology* (2nd ed., pp. 584–615). New York: Wiley.

Stohs, Joanne Hoven. (2000). Multicultural women's experience of household labor, conflicts, and equity. *Sex Roles, 42,* 339–362.

Straus, Murray A.; & Gelles, Richard J. (1986). Societal change and change in family violence from 1975 to 1985 as revealed by two national surveys. *Journal of Marriage and the Family, 48,* 465–479.

Straus, Murray A.; Gelles, Richard J.; & Steinmetz, Suzanne K. (1980). *Behind closed doors: Violence in the American family.* Garden City, NY: Anchor.

Strelan, Pater; Mehaffey, Sarah J.; & Tiggemann, Marika. (2003). Self-objectification and esteem in young women: The mediating role of reasons for exercise. *Sex Roles, 48,* 89–95.

Stremikis, Barbara A. (2002). The personal characteristics and environmental circumstances of successful women musicians. *Creativity Research Journal, 14,* 85–92.

Stroh, Linda K.; Brett, Jeanne M.; & Reilly, Anne H. (1992). All the right stuff: A comparison of female and male managers' career progression. *Journal of Applied Psychology, 77,* 251–260.

Strough, JoNell; Swenson, Lisa M.; & Cheng, Suling. (2001). Friendship, gender, and preadolescents' representations of peer collaboration. *Merrill-Palmer Quarterly, 47,* 475–499.

Struckman-Johnson, Cindy; & Struckman-Johnson, David. (1994). Men pressured and forced into sexual experience. *Archives of Sexual Behavior, 23,* 93–114.

Stumpf, Heinrich. (1993). Performance factors and gender-related differences in spatial ability: Another assessment. *Memory & Cognition, 21,* 828–836.

Subrahmanyam, Kaveri; & Greenfield, Patricia M. (1994). Effect of video game practice on spatial skills in girls and boys. *Journal of Applied Developmental Psychology, 15,* 13–32.

Substance Abuse and Mental Health Services Administration (SAMHSA). (2001). *Summary of findings from the 2000 National Household Survey on Drug Abuse.* (DHHS Publication No. 01–3549). Rockville, MD: U.S. Government Printing Office.

Substance Abuse and Mental Health Services Administration (SAMHSA). (2002). *The National Household Survey on Drug Abuse report.* Retrieved August 25, 2003, from www.drugabusestatistics.samhsa.gov.

Substance Abuse and Mental Health Services Administration (SAMHSA). (2003). *The NHSDA Report: Treatment among adults with serious mental illness.* Retrieved August 5, 2003, from http://www.samhsa.gov/oas/2k3/SMIadultTX/SMIadultTX.cfm.

Sue, David. (2001). Asian American masculinity and therapy: The concept of masculinity in Asian American males. In Gary R. Brooks & Glen E. Good (Eds.), *The new handbook of psychotherapy and counseling with men: A comprehensive guide to settings, problems, and treatment approaches* (pp. 780–795). San Francisco, CA: Jossey-Bass.

Suggs, Welch. (1999, May 21). More women participate in intercollegiate athletics. *Chronicle of Higher Education,* p. A44.

Sugihara, Yoko; & Katsurada, Emiko. (2002). Gender role development in Japanese culture: Diminishing gender role differences in a contemporary society. *Sex Roles, 47,* 443–452.

Sugihara, Yoko; & Warner, Judith A. (1999). Endorsements by Mexican-Americans of the Bem Sex-Role Inventory: Cross-ethnic comparison. *Psychological Reports, 85,* 201–211.

Suitor, J. Jill; & Carter, Rebecca S. (1999). Jocks, nerds, babes and thugs: A research note on regional differences in adolescent gender norms. *Gender Issues, 17,* 88–101.

Suitor, J. Jill; & Reavis, Rebel. (1995). Football, fast cars, and cheerleading: Adolescent gender norms. *Adolescence, 30,* 265–272.

Sullivan, Michele G. (2003, Februray 1). Revised guidelines address hypogonadism in men. *Family Practice, 33* (3), 34.

Susskind, Joshua E. (2003). Children's perception of gender-based illusory correlations: Enhancing pre-existing relationships between gender and behavior. *Sex Roles, 48,* 483–494.

Swaab, D. F.; & Fliers, E. (1985). A sexually dimorphic nucleus in the human brain. *Science, 228,* 1112–1115.

Swaab, D. F.; Gooren, L. J. G.; & Hofman, M. A. (1995). Brain research, gender, and sexual orientation. *Journal of Homosexuality, 28,* 283–301.

Swain, Scott O. (1992). Men's friendships with women: Intimacy, sexual boundaries, and the informant role. In Peter M. Nardi (Ed.), *Men's friendships* (pp. 153–171). Newbury Park, CA: Sage.

Swim, Janet K. (1994). Perceived versus meta-analytic effect sizes: An assessment of the accuracy of gender stereotypes. *Journal of Personality and Social Psychology, 66,* 21–36.

Szymanski, Dawn M.; Baird, M. Kathleen; & Kornman, Christopher L. (2002). The feminist male therapist: Attitudes and practices for the 21st century. *Psychology of Men & Masculinity, 3,* 22–27.

Tannen, Deborah. (1990). *You just don't understand: Women and men in conversation.* New York: William Morrow.

Tavris, Carol. (1992). *The mismeasure of woman.* New York: Simon and Schuster.

Tavris, Carol. (1994). Reply to Brown and Gilligan. *Feminism & Psychology, 4,* 350–352.

Tavris, Carol. (2002, July 5). Are girls really as mean as books say they are? *Chronicle of Higher Education,* p. 7+.

Tavris, Carol; & Wade, Carole. (1984). *The longest war: Sex differences in perspective* (2nd ed.). New York: Harcourt Brace Jovanovich.

Taylor, Shelley E.; Klein, Laura Cousino; Lewis, Brian P.; Gruenewald, Tara L.; Gurung, Regan A. R.; & Updegraff, John A. (2000). Biobehavioral responses to stress in females tend-and-befriend, not fight-or-flight. *Psychological Review, 107,* 411–429.

Tennenbaum, Harriet R.; & Leaper, Campbell. (2002). Are parents' gender schemas related to their children's gender-related cognitions? A meta-analysis. *Developmental Psychology, 38,* 615–630.

Terman, Lewis M.; & Merrill, Maud A. (1937). *Measuring intelligence.* Boston: Houghton Mifflin.

Thompson, Linda; & Walker, Alexis J. (1989). Gender in families: Women and men in marriage, work, and parenthood. *Journal of Marriage and the Family, 51,* 845–871.

Thompson, Sharon. (1999). Putting a big thing into a little hole: Teenage girls' accounts of sexual initiation. In Carie Forden, Anne E. Hunter, & Beverly Birns (Eds.), *Readings in the psychology of women: Dimensions of the female experience* (pp. 93–108). Boston: Allyn and Bacon.

Thompson, Teresa L.; & Zerbinos, Eugenia. (1995). Gender roles in animated cartoons: Has the picture changed in 20 years? *Sex Roles, 32,* 651–674.

Thompson, Teresa. L.; & Zerbinos, E. (1997). Television cartoons: Do children notice it's a boy's world? *Sex Roles, 37,* 415–432.

Thorne, Barrie. (1993). *Gender play: Girls and boys in school.* New Brunswick, NJ: Rutgers University Press.

Thunberg, Monika; & Dimberg, Ulf. (2000). Gender differences in facial reactions to fear-relevant stimuli. *Journal of Nonverbal Behavior, 24,* 45–51.

Tichenor, Veronica Jaris. (1999). Status and income as gendered resources: The case of marital power. *Journal of Marriage and the Family, 61,* 638–650.

Tiedemann, Joachim. (2000). Parents' gender stereotypes and teachers' beliefs as predictors of children's concept of their mathematical ability in elementary school. *Journal of Educational Psychology, 92,* 144–151.

Tiefer, Lenore. (1995). *Sex is not a natural act and other essays.* Boulder, CO: Westview Press.

Tiger, Lionel. (2000). The decline of males. *Society, 37* (2), 6–9.

Timmerman, Greetje. (2003). Sexual harassment of adolescents perpetrated by teachers and by peers: An exploration of the dynamics of power, culture, and gender in secondary schools. *Sex Roles, 48,* 231–244.

Tjaden, Patricia; & Thoennes, Nancy. (2000a). *Extent, nature and consequences of intimate partner violence: Findings from the National Violence Against Women Survey.* Washington, DC: U.S. Department of Justice.

Tjaden, Patricia; & Thoennes, Nancy. (2000b). *Full report of the prevalence, incidence, and consequences of violence against women: Findings from the National Violence Against Women Survey.* Washington, DC: U.S. Department of Justice.

Tolman, Deborah L. (2002). *Dilemmas of desire: Teenage girls talk about sexuality.* Cambridge, MA: Harvard University Press.

Tomasson, Kristinn; Kent, D.; & Coryell, W. (1991). Somatization and conversion disorders: Comorbidity and demographics at presentation. *Acta Psychiatrica Scandinavica, 84,* 288–293.

Tomkiewicz, Joe; & Bass, Kenneth. (1999). Changes in women's fear of success and fear of appearing incompetent in business. *Psychological Reports, 85,* 1003–1010.

Travis, Cheryl Brown; & Compton, Jill D. (2001). Feminism and health in the decade of behavior. *Psychology of Women Quarterly, 25,* 312–323.

Trentham, Susan; & Larwood, Laurie. (1998). Gender discrimination and the workplace: An examination of rational bias theory. *Sex Roles, 38,* 1–28.

Trexler, Richard C. (2002). Making the American berdache: Choice or constraint? *Journal of Social History, 35,* 613–637.

Trierweiler, Steven J.; Neighbors, Harold W.; Munday, Cheryl; Thompson, Estina E.; Binion, Victoria J.; & Gomez, John P. (2000). Clinician attributions associated with the diagnosis of schizophrenia in African American and non–African American patients. *Journal of Consulting and Clinical Psychology, 68,* 171–175.

Turner-Bowker, Diane M. (1996). Gender stereotyped descriptors in children's picture books: Does "Curious Jane" exist in the literature? *Sex Roles, 35,* 461–488.

Twenge, Jean M. (1997). Attitudes toward women, 1970–1995. *Psychology of Women Quarterly, 21,* 35–51.

Twenge, Jean M.; & Nolen-Hoeksema, Susan. (2002). Age, gender, race, socioeconomic status, and birth cohort differences on the Children's Depression Inventory: A meta-analysis. *Journal of Abnormal Psychology, 111,* 578–588.

Tyre, Peg; McGinn, Daniel; Springen, Karen; Wingert, Pat; Pierce, Ellise; Joseph, Nadine Juarez; Dorfman, Vanessa; Scelfo, Daniel I.; Weingarten, Tara; & Schenfeld, Hilary. (2003, May 12). She works, he doesn't. *Newsweek, 141* (19), 45+.

Ülkü-Steiner, Beril; Kurtz-Costes, Beth; & Kinlaw, C. Ryan. (2000). Doctoral student experiences in gender-balanced and male-dominated graduate programs. *Journal of Educational Psychology, 92,* 296–307.

Unger, Rhoda K. (1979). Toward a redefinition of sex and gender. *American Psychologist, 34,* 1085–1094.

Unger, Rhoda K. (1995). Conclusion: Cultural diversity and the future of feminist psychology. In Hope Landrine (Ed.), *Bringing cultural diversity to feminist psychology* (pp. 413–431). Washington, DC: American Psychological Association.

Unger, Rhoda K.; & Crawford, Mary. (1993). Commentary: Sex and gender—The troubled relationship between terms and concepts. *Psychological Science, 4,* 122–124.

Upchurch, Dawn M.; Levy-Storms, Lene; Sucoff, Clea A.; & Aneshensel, Carol S. (1998). Gender and ethnic differences in the timing of first sexual intercourse. *Family Planning Perspectives, 30,* 121–127.

Urberg, Katheryn A. (1979). Sex role conceptualizations in adolescents and adults. *Developmental Psychology, 15,* 90–92.

Usall, J.; Araya, S.; Ochoa, S.; Busquets, E.; Gost, A.; & Marquez, M. (2001). Gender differences in a sample of schizophrenic outpatients. *Comprehensive Psychiatry, 42,* 301–305.

U.S. Bureau of the Census. (1975). *Historical statistics of the United States, colonial times to 1970.* Washington, DC: U.S. Government Printing Office.

U.S. Bureau of the Census. (2002). *Statistical abstract of the United States, 2002* (122nd ed.). Washington, DC: U.S. Government Printing Office.

U.S. Bureau of Labor Statistics. (2003). *Labor force statistics from the current population survey,* Table 8. Retrieved August 9, 2003, from www.bls.gov/cps.home.htm#data.

U.S. Department of Education, National Center for Education Statistics. (2000). *The condition of education 2000.* (NCES 2000-602). Washington, DC: U.S. Government Printing Office.

U.S. Department of Health and Human Services. (1990). *Alcohol and health: Seventh special report to the U.S. Congress.* (DHHS Publication No. ADM 90-1656). Washington, DC: U.S. Government Printing Office.

U.S. Department of Health and Human Services. (1997). *Child maltreatment 1995: Reports from the states to the National Child Abuse and Neglect data system.* Washington, DC: U.S. Government Printing Office.

U.S. Department of Health and Human Services (USDHHS). (1999). *Mental health: A report of the Surgeon General.* Washington, DC: U.S. Government Printing Office.

U.S. Department of Health and Human Services. (2000). *Healthy people 2010: Understanding and improving health* (2nd ed.). Washington, DC: U.S. Government Printing Office.

U.S. Department of Health and Human Services. (2001a). *Mental health: Culture, race, and ethnicity—A supplement to Mental health: A report of the Surgeon General.* Rockville, MD: U.S. Department of Health and Human Services.

U.S. Department of Health and Human Services. (2001b). *National strategy for suicide prevention: Goals and objectives for action.* Rockville, MD: U.S. Department of Health and Human Services.

U.S. Department of Health and Human Services, Administration on Children, Youth, and Families. (2003). *Child maltreatment 2001.* Washington, DC: U.S. Government Printing Office.

U.S. Department of Justice. (2003). *Criminal victimization in the United States, 2001: Statistical tables.* Washington, DC: U.S. Government Printing Office.

U.S. News & World Report. (2001, June 25). Boom (and busts) for plastic surgeons. *U.S. News & World Report, 130* (25), 10.

Vance, Carole S. (1984). Pleasure and danger: Toward a politics of sexuality. In Carole S. Vance (Ed.), *Pleasure and danger: Exploring female sexuality* (pp. 1–27). Boston: Routledge & Kegan Paul.

Vandervoort, Debra. (1999). Quality of social support in mental and physical health. *Current Psychology, 18,* 205–222.

Van Willigen, Marieke; & Drentea, Patricia. (2001). Benefits of equitable relationships: The impact of sense of fairness, household division of labor, and decision making power on perceived social support. *Sex Roles, 44,* 571–597.

Vasquez, Melba J. T. (1994). Latinas. In Lillian Comas-Díaz & Beverly Greene (Eds.), *Women of color: Integrating ethnic and gender identities in psychotherapy* (pp. 114–138). New York: Guilford Press.

Vasquez, Melba J. T.; & Kitchener, Karen Strohm. (1988). Introduction to special feature: Ethics in counseling: Sexual intimacy between counselor and client. *Journal of Counseling and Development, 67,* 214–217.

Vasta, Ross; Knott, Jill A.; & Gaze, Christine E. (1996). Can spatial training erase the gender differences on the water-level task? *Psychology of Women Quarterly, 20,* 549–567.

Verbrugge, Lois M. (1985). Gender and health: An update on hypotheses and evidence. *Journal of Health and Social Behavior, 26,* 156–182.

Vermeer, Harriet J.; Boekaerts, Monique; & Seegers, Gerard. (2000). Motivational and gender differences: Sixth-grade students' mathematical problem-solving behavior. *Journal of Educational Psychology, 92,* 308–315.

Visootsak, Jeannie; Aylstock, Melissa; & Graham, John M., Jr. (2001). Klinefelter syndrome and its variants: An update and review for the primary pediatrician. *Clinical Pediatrics, 40,* 639–651.

Voyer, Daniel; Nolan, Carla; & Voyer, Susan. (2000). The relation between experience and spatial performance in men and women. *Sex Roles, 43,* 891–915.

Voyer, Daniel; Voyer, Susan; & Bryden, M. Philip. (1995). Magnitude of sex differences in spatial abilities: A meta-analysis and consideration of critical variables. *Psychological Bulletin, 117,* 250–270.

de Waal, Frans B. M. (2000). Primates—A natural heritage of conflict resolution. *Science, 289,* 586–590.

Wade, Terrance J.; Cairney, John; & Pevalin, David J. (2002). Emergence of gender differences in depression during adolescence: National panel results from three countries. *Journal of the American Academy of Child and Adolescent Psychiatry, 41,* 190–198.

Waldo, Craig R. (1998). Out on campus: Sexual orientation and academic climate in a university context. *American Journal of Community Psychology, 26,* 745–774.

Walker, Betty A.; Reis, Sally M.; & Leonard, Janet S. (1992). A developmental investigation of the lives of gifted women. *Gifted Child Quarterly, 36,* 201–206.

Walker, Lenore E. (1989). Psychology and violence against women. *American Psychologist, 44,* 695–702.

Walker, Lenore E. A. (2001). A feminist perspective on men in emotional pain. In Gary R. Brooks & Glenn E. Good (Eds.), *The new handbook of psychotherapy and counseling with men: A comprehensive guide to settings, problems, and treatment approaches* (pp. 683–695). San Francisco, CA: Jossey-Bass.

Walker, William D.; Rowe, Robert C.; & Quinsey, Vernon L. (1993). Authoritarianism and sexual aggression. *Journal of Personality and Social Psychology, 65,* 1036–1045.

Wallace, Julia E. (1996). Gender differences in beliefs of why women live longer than men. *Psychological Reports, 79,* 587–591.

Wallston, Barbara Strudler. (1981). What are the questions in psychology of women? A feminist approach to research. *Psychology of Women Quarterly, 5,* 597–617.

Walsh, Mary Roth. (1985). Academic professional women organizing for change: The struggle in psychology. *Journal of Social Issues, 41* (4), 17–28.

Warin, Jo. (2000). The attainment of self-consistency through gender in young children. *Sex Roles, 42,* 209–232.

Watson, Cary M.; Quatman, Teri; & Edler, Erik. (2002). Career aspirations of adolescent girls: Effects of achievement level, grade, and single-sex school environment. *Sex Roles, 46,* 323–335.

Way, Niobe. (1997). Using feminist research methods to understand the friendships of adolescent boys. *Journal of Social Issues, 53* (4), 703–723.

Weber, Lynn. (1998). A conceptual framework for understanding race, class, gender, and sexuality. *Psychology of Women Quarterly, 22,* 13–32.

Wehmeyer, Michael L. (2001). Disproportionate representation of males in special education services: Biology, behavior, or bias? *Education and Treatment of Children, 24,* 28–45.

Weidner, Gerdi. (2000). Why do men get more heart disease than women? An international perspective. *Journal of American College Health, 48,* 291–294.

Weinberg, Nancy; Uken, Janet S.; Schmale, John; & Adamek, Margaret. (1995). Therapeutic factors: Their presence in a computer-mediated support group. *Social Work with Groups, 18* (4), 57–69.

Weinberg, William T. (2000). The role of sports as a determinant of popularity among high school students.

Research Quarterly for Exercise and Sport, 71 (1), A84.

Weinburgh, Molly. (1995). Gender differences in student attitudes toward science: A meta-analysis of the literature from 1970 to 1991. *Journal of Research in Science Teaching, 32,* 387–398.

Weisman, Claire V.; Gray, James J.; Mosimann, James E.; & Ahrens, Anthony H. (1992). Cultural expectations of thinness in women: An update. *International Journal of Eating Disorders, 11,* 85–89.

Weisner, Thomas S.; & Wilson-Mitchell, Jane E. (1990). Nonconventional family life-styles and sex typing in six-year-olds. *Child Development, 61,* 1915–1933.

Weiss, Maureen R.; & Barber, Heather. (1995). Socialization influences of collegiate male athletes: A tale of two decades. *Sex Roles, 33,* 129–140.

Weisstein, Naomi. (1970). "Kinde, küche, kirche" as scientific law: Psychology constructs the female. In Robin Morgan (Ed.), *Sisterhood is powerful: An anthology of writings from the women's liberation movement* (pp. 228–245). New York: Vintage Books.

Weisstein, Naomi. (1982, November). Tired of arguing about biological inferiority? *Ms.,* pp. 41–46, 85.

Weitz, Rose. (2001). *The sociology of health, illness, and health care: A critical approach* (2nd ed.). Belmont, CA: Wadsworth.

Welch-Ross, Melissa K.; & Schmidt, Constance R. (1996). Gender-schema development and children's constructive story memory: Evidence of a developmental model. *Child Development, 67,* 820–835.

Wellings, Kaye; Nanchahal, Kiran; Macdowall, Wendy; McManus, Sally; Erens, Bob; Mercer, Catherine H.; Johnson, Anne M.; Copas, Andrew J.; Korovessis, Christos; Fenton, Kevin A.; & Field, Julia. (2001). Sexual behaviour in Britain: Early heterosexual experiences. *Lancet, 358,* 1843–1850.

Welter, Barbara. (1978). The cult of true womanhood: 1820–1860. In Michael Gordon (Ed.), *The American family in social-historical perspective* (2nd ed., pp. 313–333). New York: St. Martin's Press.

Werking, Kathy. (1997). *We're just good friends.* New York: Guilford Press.

West, Candace; & Zimmerman, Don H. (1987). Doing gender. *Gender and Society, 1,* 125–151.

Westkott, Marcia C. (1997). On the new psychology of women: A cautionary view. In Mary Roth Walsh (Ed.), *Women, men, and gender: Ongoing debates* (pp. 362–372). New Haven, CT: Yale University Press.

Wharton, Amy S.; & Baron, James N. (1987). So happy together? The impact of gender segregation on men at work. *American Sociological Review, 52,* 574–587.

Wharton, Amy S.; & Baron, James N. (1991). Satisfaction? The psychological impact of gender segregation on women at work. *Sociological Quarterly, 32,* 365–387.

Whatley, Marianne H. (1990). Sex equity in sex education. *Education Digest, 55* (5), 46–49.

Whelan, Emma. (2001). Politics by other means: Feminism and mainstream science studies. *Canadian Journal of Sociology, 26,* 535–582.

Whisman, Mark A. (1999). Marital dissatisfaction and psychiatric disorders: Results from the national comorbidity survey. *Journal of Abnormal Psychology, 108,* 701–706.

Whitehead, Barbara Dafoe; & Popenoe, David. (2002). *The state of our unions: The social health of marriage in America.* Piscataway, NJ: National Marriage Project. Retrieved July 18, 2003, from http://marriage.rutgers.edu.

Whiting, Beatrice Blyth; & Edwards, Carolyn Pope. (1988). *Children of different worlds: The formation of social behavior.* Cambridge, MA: Harvard University Press.

Whitley, Bernard E., Jr. (2001). Gender-role variables and attitudes toward homosexuality. *Sex Roles, 45,* 691–721.

WHO International Consortium in Psychiatric Epidemiology. (2000). Cross-national comparisons of the prevalences and correlates of mental disorders. *Bulletin of the World Health Organization, 78,* 413–426.

Wieringa, Saskia E. (1994). The Zuni man-woman. *Archives of Sexual Behavior, 23,* 348–351.

Wiley, Mary Glenn; & Eskilson, Arlene. (1985). Speech style, gender stereotypes, and corporate success: What if women talk more like men? *Sex Roles, 12,* 993–1007.

Wilkinson, Richard G. (1996). *Unhealthy societies: The afflictions of inequity.* London: Routledge.

Wilkinson, Sue. (1999). Focus groups: A feminist method. *Psychology of Women Quarterly, 23,* 221–244.

Willemsen, Tineke M. (2002). Gender typing of the successful manager—A stereotype reconsidered. *Sex Roles, 46,* 385–391.

Willett, Walter C. (1999). Goals for nutrition in the year 2000. *Ca, 49,* 3–21.

Williams, Christine L. (1992). The glass escalator: Hidden advantages for men in the "female" professions. *Social Problems, 39,* 253–267.

Williams, Janet B. W.; & Spitzer, Robert L. (1983). The issue of sex bias in DSM-III: A critique of "A woman's view of DSM-III" by Marcie Kaplan. *American Psychologist, 38,* 793–801.

Williams, Joan. (2000). *Unbending gender: Why family and work conflict and what to do about it.* New York: Oxford University Press.

Williams, John E.; & Best, Deborah L. (1990). *Measuring sex stereotypes: A multination study* (Rev. ed.). Newbury Park, CA: Sage.

Williams, John E.; Satterwhite, Robert C.; & Best, Deborah L. (1999). Pancultural gender stereotypes revisited: The Five Factor Model. *Sex Roles, 40,* 513–526.

Willingham, Warren W.; & Cole, Nancy S. (1997). *Gender and fair assessment.* Mahwah, NJ: Erlbaum.

Willingham, Warren W.; Cole, Nancy S.; Lewis, Charles; & Leung, Susan Wilson. (1997). Test performance. In Warren W. Willingham & Nancy S. Cole, *Gender and fair assessment* (pp. 55–126). Mahwah, NJ: Erlbaum.

Wilson, Robert A. (1966). *Feminine forever.* New York: M. Evans.

WIN News. (1999, Winter). Educating girls: Gender gaps and gains—A chart. *Women in the News, 25* (1), 10.

Winstok, Zeev; Eisikovits, Zvi; & Gelles, Richard. (2002). Structure and dynamics of escalation from the batterer's perspective. *Families in Society: The Journal of Contemporary Human Services, 83,* 129–141.

Wise, Lauren A.; Zierler, Sally; Krieger, Nancy; & Harlow, Bernard L. (2001). Adult onset of major depressive disorder in relation to early life violent victimisation: A case-control study. *Lancet, 358,* 881–887.

Wiseman, Claire V.; Gray, James J.; Mosimann, James E.; & Ahrens, Anthony H. (1992). Cultural expectations of thinness in women: An update. *International Journal of Eating Disorders, 11,* 85–89.

Witkin, Herman A.; Mednick, Sarnoff A.; Schulsinger, Fini; Bakkestrøm, Eskild; Christiansen, Karlo O.; Goodenough, Donald R.; Hirschhorn, Kurt; Lundesteen, Claes; Owen, David R.; Philip, John; Rubin, Donald B.; & Stocking, Martha. (1976). Criminality in XYY and XXY men. *Science, 193,* 547–555.

Witt, Susan D. (1997). Parental influence on children's socialization to gender roles. *Adolescence, 32,* 253–259.

Witt, Susan D. (2000). The influence of television on children's gender role socialization. *Childhood Education, 76,* 322–324.

Wituk, Scott; Shepherd, Matthew D.; Slavich, Susan; Warren, Mary L.; & Meissen, Greg. (2000). A topography of self-help groups: An empirical analysis. *Social Work, 45,* 157–165.

Wolak, Janis; Mitchell, Kimberly J.; & Finkelhor, David. (2002). Close online relationships in a national sample of adolescents. *Adolescence, 37,* 441–455.

Women's International Network. (2000). Europe: Domestic violence—Some facts and figures. *WIN News, 26* (1), 47.

Wood, Eileen; Desmarais, Serge; & Gugula, Sara. (2002). The impact of parenting experience on gender stereotyped toy play of children. *Sex Roles, 47,* 39–49

Wood, James M.; Garb, Howard N.; Lilienfeld, Scott O.; & Nezworski, M. Teresa. (2002). Clinical assessment. *Annual Review of Psychology, 53,* 519–544.

Wood, Wendy; & Eagly, Alice H. (2002). A cross-cultural analysis of the behavior of women and men: Implications for the origins of sex differences. *Psychological Bulletin, 128,* 699–727.

Woodhill, Brenda Mae; & Samuels, Curtis A. (2003). Positive and negative androgyny and their relationship with psychological health and well-being. *Sex Roles, 48,* 555–565.

Woodside, D. Blake; Garfinkel, Paul E.; Lin, Elizabeth; Goering, Paula; Kaplan, Allan S.; Goldbloom, David S.; & Kennedy, Sidney H. (2001). Comparisons of men with full or partial eating disorders, men without eating disorders, and women with eating disorders in the community. *American Journal of Psychiatry, 158,* 570–574.

Wooley, O. Wayne. (1994). . . . And man created "woman": Representations of women's bodies in Western culture. In Patricia Fallon, Melanie A. Katzman, & Susan C. Wooley (Eds.), *Feminist perspectives on eating disorders* (pp. 17–52). New York: Guilford Press.

Worell, Judith. (1996). Opening doors to feminist research. *Psychology of Women Quarterly, 20,* 469–485.

Worell, Judith. (2001). Feminist interventions: Accountability beyond symptom reduction. *Psychology of Women Quarterly, 25,* 335–343.

Worell, Judith; & Etaugh, Claire. (1994). Transforming theory and research with women: Themes and variations. *Psychology of Women Quarterly, 18,* 443–450.

Worell, Judith; & Johnson, Dawn. (2001). Therapy with women: Feminist frameworks. In Rhoda K. Unger (Ed.), *Handbook of the psychology of women and gender* (pp. 317–329). New York: Wiley.

Worell, Judith; & Remer, Pam. (2003). *Feminist perspectives in therapy: Empowering diverse women* (2nd ed). New York: Wiley.

Writing Group for the Women's Health Initiative Investigators. (2002). Risks and benefits of estrogen plus progestin in healthy postmenopausal women: Principal results from the Women's Health Initiative randomized controlled trial. *Journal of the American Medical Association, 288,* 321–333.

Wyatt, Gail Elizabeth. (1994). The sociocultural relevance of sex research: Challenges for the 1990s and beyond. *American Psychologist, 49,* 748–754.

Xinhua News Agency. (2000, April 5). Local regulations issued to prevent domestic violence. Xinhua News Agency, p. 1008096h1161.

Yama, Mark F.; Tovey, Stephanie L.; & Fogas, Bruce S. (1993). Childhood family environment and sexual abuse as predictors of anxiety and depression in adult women. *American Journal of Orthopsychiatry, 63,* 136–141.

Yee, Doris K.; & Eccles, Jacquelynne S. (1988). Parent perceptions and attributions for children's math achievement. *Sex Roles, 19,* 317–333.

Yeoman, Barry. (1999, November). Bad girls. *Psychology Today, 32,* 54–57, 71.

Yoder, Janice D.; & Kahn, Arnold S. (1993). Working toward an inclusive psychology of women. *American Psychologist, 48,* 846–850.

Yoder, Janice D.; & Schleicher, Thomas L. (1996). Undergraduates regard deviation from occupational gender stereotypes as costly for women. *Sex Roles, 34,* 171–188.

Zajonc, R. C. (1984). On the primacy of affect. *American Psychologist, 39,* 117–123.

Zera, Deborah. (1992). Coming of age in a heterosexist world: The development of gay and lesbian adolescents. *Adolescence, 27,* 849–854.

Zhang, Jie; Norvilitis, Jill M.; & Jin, Shenghua. (2001). Measuring gender orientation with the Bem Sex-Role Inventory in Chinese culture. *Sex Roles, 44,* 237–251.

Zinik, Cary. (1985). Identity conflict or adaptive flexibility? Bisexuality reconsidered. *Journal of Homosexuality, 11,* 7–19.

Zittleman, Karen; & Sadker, David. (2002). Gender bias in teacher education texts: New (and old) lessons. *Journal of Teacher Education, 53,* 168–180.

Zucker, Kenneth J. (2001). Biological influences on psychosexual differentiation. In Rhoda K. Unger (Ed.), *Handbook of psychology of women and gender* (pp. 101–115). New York: Wiley.

Zucker, Kenneth J. (2002). A factual correction to Bartlett, Vasey, and Bukowski's (2000) "Is gender identity disorder in children a mental disorder?" *Sex Roles, 46,* 263–264.

Zucker, Kenneth J.; & Bradley, Susan J. (1995). *Gender identity disorder and psychosexual problems in children and adolescents.* New York: Guilford Press.

Zucker, Kenneth J.; Bradley, Susan J.; & Sanikhani, Mohammad. (1997). Sex differences in referral rates of children with gender identity disorder: Some hypotheses. *Journal of Abnormal Child Psychology, 25,* 217–227.

Zucker, Kenneth J.; Wilson-Smith, Debra N.; Kurita, Janice A.; & Stern, Anita. (1995). Children's appraisals of sex-typed behavior in their peers. *Sex Roles, 33,* 703–725.

Name Index

Aboud, Frances E., 219
Abrams, Dominic, 168
Abrams, Leslie R., 456
Adamek, Margaret, 445
Adami, Hans-Olov, 359
Adams, Patrick J., 330
Adams-Curtis, Leah E., 61
Addis, Michael E., 436
Addy, Cheryl L., 411–412
Adera, Tilahun, 69
Adler, Jerry, 337
Adler, Nancy L., 243
Ahern, Melissa M., 393
Ahlberg, Christian, 138
Ahmed, S. Faisal, 65
Ahrens, Anthony H., 380–381
Ajram, K., 44
Akiyama, Hiroko, 222
Alarid, Leanne Fiftal, 206
Alavi, Abass, 99
Alfieri, Thomas, 140
Allan, Emilie, 205
Allardyce, J., 417
Allen, Bem P., 166
Allen, Elizabeth Sandin, 248
Allmendinger, Jutta, 339
Allport, Gordon W., 167
Alsop, David, 99
Altermatt, Ellen Rydell, 316
Altman, Lawrence K., 353
Amato, Paul R., 236
Ambady, Nalini, 212, 213
Amir, Sarit H., 384
Amponsah, Benjamin, 92–93
Amsterdam, Jay D., 413
Anda, Robert F., 462
Anders, Katie A., 331
Anderson, Craig A., 197
Anderson, Elizabeth, 21, 41
Anderson, Ellen M., 245
Anderson, John P., 372
Anderson, Karen, 172, 173

Anderson, Kristin J., 145, 340
Anderson, Sally, 275–276
Andersson, Gerhard, 411
Andrassy, Jill, 445
Andronico, Michael P., 447
Aneshensel, Carol S., 273, 462
Angier, Natalie, 78
Antill, John K., 146, 228
Antonucci, Toni C., 222
Apodaca, Timothy R., 444–445
Applegate, Brooks, 432
Aranda, Maria P., 395
Araujo, Eddie, 157
Araujo, Gwen, 157
Araya, S., 412
Archer, John, 203, 241
Aries, Elizabeth, 340
Armesto, Jorge C., 195
Arnhold, Ivo J. P., 66
Arnold, Steven E., 99
Arnot, Madeline, 296
Aronson, Amy, 232
Aronson, Joshua, 100, 159
Asher, Steven R., 219
Ashton, Heather, 429, 431
Assaf, Annlouise R., 366–367, 371
Astin, Helen S., 324–325
Atkinson, J. W., 312–313
Attar, Beth K., 393
Attra, Sharon L., 407
Aubé, Jennifer, 436
Auerbach, Carl F., 13, 190, 193, 195, 215
Averill, James R., 187, 197, 198
Ayalon, Hanna, 302, 467
Aylstock, Melissa, 63

Babcock, D. R., 99
Bacue, Aaron, 148, 328, 329
Bae, Yupin, 85, 298, 302, 467
Baenninger, Maryann, 95

Bagley, Christopher, 268–269
Bailey, J. Michael, 138, 143, 283, 284
Bailey, Jennifer A., 392
Baird, M. Kathleen, 436
Bakan, David, 178
Bakkeström, Eskild, 63
Baldo, Tracy D., 223
Baldwin, Janice I., 272, 274
Baldwin, John D., 272, 274
Ball, Jane, 94
Ball, Richard, 233
Ballou, Mary, 430, 434
Banaji, Mahzarin R., 87, 300
Bancroft, John, 59
Bandura, Albert, 117–121, 128, 133, 325
Banks, Terry, 71
Bankston, Carl L., III, 315
Barak, Azy, 344
Barbaranelli, Claudio, 325
Barber, Heather, 308
Bar-David, Eva, 126
Bardwell, Stephen, 409
Barner, Mark R., 150
Barnett, Heather L., 375
Barnett, Rosalind Chait, 338, 372, 390, 455, 456, 471
Baron, James N., 339
Bar-Tal, Yoram, 126
Barth, Joan M., 126, 130
Bartkowski, John P., 13
Bartlett, Nancy H., 154–155
Basow, Susan A., 234
Bass, Hope, 100
Bass, Kenneth, 314
Bassett, Margaret E., 407
Baucom, Donald H., 248
Bauer, Rebecca, 372–374
Baumeister, Roy F., 16, 261
Baumli, Francis, 11–12
Baxter, L. C., 99

525

Subject Index

gender identity development and, 138–139, 143–144, 146–147

menarche and menstruation, 47–48, 60–61, 65, 66–70, 402

nervous system development and, 54–57

psychosexual stages (Freud) and, 108–109

reproductive organ development and, 51–54

separation from mothers, 113–114

sexual abuse of, 266, 269–270, 271

Glass ceiling, 331–332

Glass Ceiling Commission, 332

Glass escalator, 332

Global Assessment of Functioning Scale, 399

Gonads, 48–49

Gonorrhea, 370

Good Provider role (Bernard), 224

Good Will Hunting (film), 440

Graduate Record Examination (GRE), 85

Gross motor skills, 219, 300

Habituation, 135

Health and fitness, 353–386

cancer, 357–360

cardiovascular disease (CVD), 354–357, 366

diet and eating, 356–359, 372–379

diversity and, 381–384

exercise, 379–381

health care system and, 362–371

morbidity and, 353

mortality and, 353–362, 381–384

violent deaths, 360–362

Health care system, 362–371

ethnic bias of, 417–418

gender bias of, 13, 365–367, 401–405, 416, 429–432

gender roles and, 362–367

reproductive health and, 359–360, 367–371

Hegemonic masculinity, 164

Hermaphroditism, 65–66, 75

Heterosexuality, 271–281. *See also* Marriage and committed relationships

during adolescence, 272–275

during adulthood, 275–280

bisexuality and, 289–290

Hewlett-Packard, 323–324

High school years, 301–306, 319–320

academic achievement and, 301–303

sexual harassment and, 304–306

vocational education and, 303–304

Hispanic Americans

adolescent sexual activity, 273–274

body image and, 375

career expectations and, 326

diagnosis of mental disorders in, 417–418

discrimination in hiring, 331, 333, 347–349

division of household labor and, 236–237

educational attainment of, 307, 319–320

fear of success and, 315

gender stereotypes and, 166, 172, 180

mathematics performance of, 103

mortality and, 384

self-perceptions of, 34

social support and, 395–396

therapy and, 449

violence and, 360, 361

Historical perspective

on brain lateralization, 97–98

on college and professional school, 306–308

on emotion, 188–191, 196

on gender stereotypes, 160–164, 182–183

individual differences in, 4–5

on love relationships, 224–229, 230–232

men's studies in, 10–13, 15, 18, 447

psychoanalysis in, 5–6

on scientific approach, 21–22

on study of sex differences, 3–13

women's studies in, 7–10, 15, 18, 447

Histrionic personality disorder, 469

Homemaking, 324, 325–326, 459, 460, 467

Homicide, 360

Homophobia, 221, 223

Homosexuality, 154–155, 176, 281–289. *See also* Gay and lesbian relationships; Gays; Lesbians; Marriage and committed relationships

during adolescence, 285–286, 305

during adulthood, 286–289

bisexuality and, 289–290

coming out, 285–286, 287, 288

eating disorders and, 377

estimates of, 282

fear of, 221, 223

sex surveys and, 256, 259

as term, 256–257

therapy and, 449

Hong Kong, study of gender schema and, 126

Hormone replacement therapy, 366–367, 371

Hormones, 47–77. *See also* Androgens; Estrogens; Testosterone

abnormalities of prenatal, 64–66, 143–144, 283–284

behavior instability and, 47–48, 66–74, 402

changes during puberty and, 57–62

cultural differences in sexual development, 74–75

defined, 48

endocrine system and, 48–49

in menopause, 370–371

nurturing by mothers and, 193–196

sexual interest and, 59–62

stages of differences between sexes and, 50

steroid hormones, 48–49, 73

Panic attack, 411, 412
Paraphilias, 413–414, 416
Parents. *See also* Fathers; Mothers
    childhood sexuality and, 266–271
    differential treatment of boys and girls, 121
    in gender identity development, 144–146, 151
    as models in social learning theory, 119–120
    perceptions of mathematics performance of children, 102
    sex preferences of, 119, 383
Part-time employment, 324
Patriarchal terrorism, 115, 241
Patterns of Sexual Behavior (Ford and Beach), 254
Pearson product-moment correlation coefficient, 29–30
Pedophilia, 271
Peers. *See also* Friendships
    development of relationship styles in children, 218–220
    in gender identity development, 146–147
Penis envy, 106, 108–109, 111
Personal accounts of gender issues, xvi
Personal Attributes Questionnaire, 178
Personality. *See also* Theories of gender development
    Chodorow's theory of, 113–114
    Freud's theory of, 106–113
    Horney's theory of, 111–112
    Kaschak's theory of, 114–116
Personality disorders, 403–404, 469
Phallic stage, 107, 109–110
Phobias, 411, 412, 427, 469
Physiological development. *See also* Biological factors
    abnormalities in, 62–66, 75, 143–144, 283–284
    changes during puberty, 57–62
    of nervous system, 54–57
    of reproductive organs, 51–54
Pituitary gland, 48
Play. *See also* Toys
    development of relationship styles in children and, 218–220
Playboy Foundation, 258–259, 266
Positron emission tomography (PET) scans, 98–99
Posttraumatic stress disorder (PTSD), 411–412, 418
    diagnosis of, 399–401
    violence and, 392
Poverty
    discrimination and, 17, 418
    as source of stress, 393
Power
    aggression and, 115, 202, 249–250
    division of household labor and, 237, 390
    gender differences and, 96, 340–342
    in Kaschak's Antigone phase, 115
    in marriage and committed relationships, 216–217, 238–242

penis envy and, 106, 108–109, 111
    sexual harassment and, 304–306, 311–312, 346–347, 393–394
    in the workplace, 340–347, 393–394
Practical significance, 38–39
Pregnancy
    children's questions about, 266–268, 267
    fetus in, 51–54, 64–66, 143–144, 283–284, 368
    reproductive health and, 367–371
    teenage, 272, 275
Prejudice, defined, 167
Preliminary Scholastic Aptitude Test (PSAT), 85, 86
Premarital sex, 256, 260–261, 291
Premenstrual dysphoric disorder (PMDD), 47–48, 66–70, 402
Premenstrual syndrome (PMS), 47–48, 66–70, 402
Pre-Oedipal phase, 113–114
Price Waterhouse, 341–342
Privileged status, 12, 16–18
Progestins, 48–49
Promise Keepers, 13
Prostate cancer, 367, 371
Prostitution, 360
Psychoactive substances, 360–361, 409–410, 431, 441
Psychoanalysis, 5–6, 7, 10, 289
    defined, 423
    described, 423–424
    in feminist therapy, 434, 435
    gender bias in, 429–430, 431
    sexual exploitation in therapy and, 441
Psychodynamic approach, 106–116, 129
    assessing, 129
    Chodorow's theory of mothering, 113–114
    consequences of multiple roles and, 455, 456
    Freud's theory of personality, 106–113
    Horney's theory of personality, 111–112
    Kaschak's Antigone phase, 114–116
    psychoanalysis and, 5, 6, 7, 10, 289, 423–424, 429–431, 434, 435
Psychology of Sex Difference, The (Maccoby and Jacklin), 26
Psychology-of-women approach, xiv
Psychology of Women Quarterly (journal), 33
Psychosexual stages (Freud), 107–110
Puberty, 57–62
Punishment, 117–118, 119

Qualitative research, 30–33
    case studies, 31, 33
    compared with quantitative research, 34
    defined, 22
    ethnography, 32, 33
    focus groups in, 32, 33